D0966444

Modern Public Opinion

MODERN PUBLIC OPINION

William Albig

UNIVERSITY OF ILLINOIS

McGRAW-HILL BOOK COMPANY, INC.

New York   Toronto   London

1956

MODERN PUBLIC OPINION

Preface

Modern Public Opinion is a new book and not simply a revision of my *Public Opinion*, published years ago. Nonetheless, I have taken from that earlier work a great deal of the structure, and some readers may note that the organization and chapter headings are almost identical. Moreover, I have incorporated in the text of *Modern Public Opinion*, especially in the earlier chapters, a considerable number of pages directly taken from my *Public Opinion*. Though I have not counted the exact number of pages abstracted from the earlier work, let us say that they account for a fifth, or perhaps a fourth, of the total content of *Modern Public Opinion*. In the philosopher's story of the shoe, in which all the parts are successively replaced, the student is asked whether he is dealing with a new or an old shoe. Let us say in the case of these books that the solid heel and the shape of the uppers remain in the second book and all the rest has been replaced. Of no concern to the student reader, who was just beginning elementary school when *Public Opinion* was published, this statement is my accounting to those readers who were so generously responsive to the earlier book.

When I contemplate the materials with which I had to work fifteen years ago in constructing my *Public Opinion* of that day and then look at the contributions of the intervening years, I am amazed and encouraged by the energy and productivity of American scholarship, once attention is centered on an area of knowledge. There are the numerous bibliographies which have made unnecessary the fairly extended bibliographies of *Public Opinion*. During the past fifteen years several thousand articles dealing with public opinion, the mass media, and communication have been published. An industry devoted to polling, to the measurement of attitudes, and market research, has expanded to a research activity expending not less than $100 million a year. Propaganda has been practiced and studied *ad nauseam*. The study of mass communication content and effects has been conducted with enormous gusto. And, latterly, we are supposed to have learned a great deal about the theory of communication from the contributions of physical scientists to information theory. During the past decade I have come across thousands of interesting fragments. And yet, when I review what I have learned

v ·

of meaningful, theoretical significance about communication and about the theory of public opinion, I am not so encouraged. Gross generalization and theory have made little advance during these years. The bulk of research contributions has usually avoided generalizations, and skillful syntheses have been rare. The intellectual climate has been unfavorable to the emergence of logical theory, while the objectively accumulated data are far too fragmentary to provide the basis for much generalization or grand theory.

There are a number of tables of some size scattered through this volume. They present pertinent data related to the topics discussed. However, I have not accompanied each table with extensive listings of the meaningful relations of the items included and analysis of the meaning and significance of the contents of the tables. That is for the reader to winnow out of the facts, the reader who has time to study and ponder, to examine and reflect.

For the most part I have used simple, nontechnical terms in this discussion. But not in all cases. At the present time, no one can write on the field of public opinion in terms satisfactory to all his readers. If an author uses simple terms, satisfactory to the general reader, he ignores the pyramid of language hastily thrown up in recent years by the specialist in this field. These special terms are invented ostensibly to provide an exact definitive terminology of non-emotion-arousing words suitable for use among scientists. The absence of most of these terms would provide the basis for an indictment of the author as an outsider, an outlander, a stranger to the code of the jousts. As language is truly a bond of unity, he might be expelled into the outer darkness. On the other hand, if the author bandies about this esoteric jargon too freely, there is no doubt as to where the general reader would willingly consign him. Therefore, I have attempted to use certain of the special terms, developed in recent years, where such words seemed to make for clarity and objectivity. Elsewhere I have eschewed such terms and striven for relative simplicity.

There is one phrase that I would define briefly at this point. Throughout this book I have referred to the "common man." I mean the unintellectual man—unaware of intellectual traditions and the history of thought. As Harvey Fergusson has written, "By the common man I mean the man who is so absorbed in the immediate and personal ends of living that he cannot view his destiny with any intellectual detachment. Such a man is capable of receiving doctrines upon authority and accepting them, but he is typically not capable of making hypotheses on his own account." Or, as Carl Friedrich notes: "The common man is neither the mass-man nor the average man. He is the personal symbol, the embodiment and image of what all have in common when they personally participate in communal tasks and civic duties."

I have no apologies to offer for the various stories and anecdotes that are strewn through the pages of this book. I am well aware of the limitations of such material. Stories sometimes distort meanings, divert the attention or unstabilize the judgment by laughter. But they add interest for the reader and sometimes really illustrate. They are painfully objectionable only to the purists in any field.

This volume, as indeed all of my writings, is dedicated to Helen Humphrey Albig, collaborator and critic, faithful typist, friend and associate, woman of distinction—my wife.

WILLIAM ALBIG

Contents

PART SIX. THEORIES AND ISSUES

List of Tables

List of Figures

PART ONE

Public Opinion

CHAPTER 1

The Nature of Public Opinion

The discussion of human affairs, of personal relationships and of public issues and actions is persistent in all societies. Such discussion deals with all subjects about which there is information in the group. It is conducted in all groups, among the simple and the sophisticated, the ignorant and the learned, the common man and the expert. Discussion utilizes all the means of communication—speech, gesture, print and picture. The process of discussion is intensified by the appearance of unusual information or occurrences, by controversy and by conflict. It is said that "a happy people have no history." A people or group in essential agreement have little to discuss except the sporadic individual variations from the norm. In the simple folk societies such is normally the case. In such a situation, knowledge is limited by the common traditions of the folk, the happenings of the immediate area and the occasional infiltration of alien lore. Today, in the great society, the common man has access to a multitudinous and detailed bulk of information. He has that portion of the accumulated learning of his culture to which he is exposed and the news of the day which is purveyed by newspaper and gossip, by pictures and motion pictures, by radio, television and all other means of communication. During the past generation, this news has expanded enormously, as to both the size of the geographic areas from which it is drawn and the scope and variety of its subject matter. Discussion is greatly intensified.

Upon this mass of information, the common man projects those scales of value with which he has been equipped. Standards limit his discussion to some extent. Certain topics are not discussible in some groups, although in our day everything is discussible somewhere. Where popularly accepted standards can be applied to the various items of information, there need be no discussion, since there is only one value or principle involved. There is no debate, no controversy. Hence, there is no opinion. An opinion is some expression on a controversial point. Though attitudes, beliefs and other aspects of the mind-life are subjective, opinions are expressed statements. Opinions are expressed on topics which are controversial, or, at least, about which some diversity of views exists. Opinions deal with the controversial, rather than with materials which the group concerned considers to be proved, or which are generally believed to be true. Though opinions are usually expressed in words, they may be indicated by gesture or any other form of behavior which communicates. A reviewer, rebuked for having slept through the last act of a play on which he was to write an opinion, replied, "Sir, sleep is an opinion."

In a period of rapidly changing standards, the range of opinion topics rapidly widens as values are less absolute. In the United States in the mid-twentieth century, opinions are solicited and expressed on matters of religion, morals, education, the details of government, the choice of consumers' goods, the administration of justice in widely publicized cases and, in general, upon the widest variety of controversial topics ever presented simultaneously to the citizen. Advertisers of consumers' goods, special pleaders for political issues, representatives of interest-groups, and others clamor for his attention, his opinions and his decisions. Some confusion, frustration and flight from the responsibility of decision characterize the common man amidst this welter of demands and issues. On innumerable subjects, a person is asked to form opinions. Competitive appeals by various interest-groups assail, distract and confuse him. He is admonished, persuaded and cajoled. In the thinking of the common man there is much confusion. There is a glut of news and a lack of adequate standards from which to interpret the rush of news.

Villagers, with the codes that were the product of the village, are engulfed in cities, where complex indoctrination confuses those trained to the slow pace of decision in agrarian communities. In the primary group of the family and in intimate association, man has functioned on the basis of the rules, the traditions of the folk culture and also of procedures developed in his own experience of association.[1] He is accustomed to the development of opinion regarding variant behavior and thought in such an intimate scene. In many of his secondary-group relationships in modern life, however, neither the patterns of the traditional culture nor his own experience offer sharp, clear-cut ways of life. Yet, under democracy, he is called on to develop opinions and make decisions. His fumblings in this field, his economic and political ineptitudes, his lack of grasp of essentials, his following of personal phantoms when he should

---

[1] Ferdinand Tönnies noted that concord, custom and religion are characteristic of *Gemeinschaft* (community); and convention, legislation and public opinion of *Gesellschaft* (society). The *Gesellschaft* concept has had wide use and, indeed, exaggerated application in sociological literature. The first major critical foray against this overemphasis has been made by Richard T. LaPiere in his *A Theory of Social Control*, McGraw-Hill Book Company, Inc., New York, 1954, pp. 12 ff., and elsewhere in the volume. It is to be hoped that LaPiere's able analysis will stimulate a reexamination of some of the unwarrantedly broad generalizations recently made, especially by Erich Fromm, David Riesman and various followers.

be occupied with abstract realities, make the common man a creature for the satirical thrusts of the more informed observer. Modern authoritarian rulers also express distrust of his capacity. And the mounting disdain of the intellectual is increasingly in evidence. The common man exhibits a preference for the opinion process and decision relating to personal and private problems and issues. He would "win friends and influence people." He would survey the problems of personal relationships and values. This has always been the despair of the political reformer under democracy. As man in the mass has been thrust into situations in which opinions and decisions about economic issues were required of him, the despair of the theorists has frequently been abject. In the rising tide of popular decision many saw the "revolt of the masses." The people were projecting personal and individual values upon the larger scene. Yet that the common man, with guidance and adequate information, can be trained to function satisfactorily in the realm of public affairs is the premise of democracy. Later we shall consider the justifications for belief in the quality of the opinions expressed by large publics and the bases for skepticism of their worth.

THE MEANING OF PUBLIC OPINION

There has been little agreement among sociological theorists, political scientists and social psychologists on the exact meaning of "public opinion." The term has been loosely used, sometimes in reference to widespread beliefs, "climate of opinion," consensus, the mores and the more settled convictions of a group; at times, to the process of developing opinions, as distinguished from the product; elsewhere, to statements which are the result of a reasoned, logical process as contrasted with those which have been arrived at by illogical means; and the like. We shall not attempt a historical resumé of the various meanings that commentators of differing schools of thought and of different periods have ascribed to this term.[2] Let us consider merely a few of the more important recent distinctions and definitions.

[2] In spite of the widespread use of the term "public opinion" during the past two centuries, there is surprisingly little analytic writing concerning its meaning, its constituent elements and the opinion process. For outstanding discussions in different periods, see: W. Mackinnon, *On the Rise, Progress, and Present State of Public Opinion in Great Britain*, Saunders and Otley, London, 1828; W. Bagehot, *Physics and Politics*, 1872, chap. 5; G. C. Thompson, *Public Opinion and Lord Beaconsfield*, 1886, vol. 1, pp. 29–40; G. Tarde, *L'Opinion et la foule*, 1901; A. V. Dicey, *Law and Public Opinion in England*, 1905; J. Bryce, *The American Commonwealth*, 1889, vol. II, pp. 261–403; C. H. Cooley, *Social Organization*, chaps. 12, 13, 34, 1909, *Social Process*, chap. 31, 1918; A. L. Lowell, *Public Opinion and Popular Government*, 1913, *Public Opinion in War and Peace*, 1923; C. L. King, *Public Opinion as Viewed by Eminent Political Theorists*, University of Pennsylvania Lectures, 1916; W. Lippmann, *Public Opinion*, 1922; J. Dewey, *The Public and Its Problems*, 1927; L. J. Carr, in Cooley, Angell and Carr, *Introductory Sociology*, 1933, chaps. 22, 23, 24; Harris

Our position is that opinion is any expression on a controversial topic. Public opinion results from the interaction of persons upon one another in any type of group. The opinion process occurs in groups varying in size from two to the largest number ever responding to common stimuli on a controversial issue. Publics are simply large groups. At any time there may be a prevailing, or dominant, view existing in a group, but there are also any number of other opinions maintained by the members of that group. There may or may not be a majority expressing a common opinion. The opinion process is the interaction occurring within a group on a controversial issue. The group opinion is the product of that interaction, the resultant expression including all the positions maintained by members of the group. This group opinion is not static but is in flux as new elements are introduced into the discussion. The opinion process in the group may be a reasoned, logical analysis and procedure. In large groups it is more often involved in sentiment, emotion, casual impressions and various illogical elements. Let us amplify these statements.

Opinion is expressed through some of the means of communication. On the basis of the expressed opinion one may and does assume attitudes, mind-sets, beliefs and other subjective states, but the opinion is expression on a controversial issue. "There can be no such thing as opinion without stating the content of the opinion in language form. The response of individuals to this common stimulating situation may be either verbal or nonverbal. It may, for example, be a grimace, gesture or emotional expression. This reaction, however, must be capable of being readily translated into words, such, for example, as expressions of agreement or approval." [3] Opinion may achieve expression in any understandable and translatable act. Opinion expression is behavior. But this does not mean that opinions can be adequately described in behavioristic terms. By no means. Any fruitful examination of expression of opinion must relate the opinions to the subjective states out of which the opinions have emerged. "The extreme behaviorist assumes that there is only one way in which physical processes can be studied, namely through outward action. Now an object that is immediately presented may produce outward activity without either understanding or belief." [4] If ten people say that they do not like Italians, that is an expression of opinion. We may record that expression on any type of detailed test that has been created. But the reasons for that dislike may be so varied and diverse that in a changing situation one of those individuals may change his opinion statement

---

Foundation Lectures, *Public Opinion and World Politics*, University of Chicago Press, 1933; F. G. Wilson, *The Elements of Modern Politics*, 1936, chaps. 10, 11; W. Bauer, "Public Opinion," *Encyclopaedia of the Social Sciences*, 12: 669–674.

[3] F. H. Allport, "Toward a Science of Public Opinion," *Pub. Opin. Quar.*, 1: 1: 14.

[4] R. M. Eaton, *Symbolism and Truth*, Harvard University Press, Cambridge, Mass., 1925, p. 25.

within an hour, whereas another holds to his position for a lifetime. The record of opinion statements is a record of behavior, but that is simply a starting point for the description of the opinion process. To proclaim, as does the behaviorist, that he is concerned only with overt verbal behavior in this field is to depart very far from science, which is the description of reality.

An opinion is an expression about a controversial point. "An opinion may be defined as the acceptance of one among two or more inconsistent views which are capable of being accepted by a rational mind as true." [5] It may thus be distinguished from a demonstration or proof. There are certain relations, though fewer than commonly supposed, that are generally accepted as proved. A child may give a unique answer to the problem of three times three. But his answer is an error; it is not an opinion. It is variation from established truth. Now, of course, almost all our knowledge is relative, but that residue which is generally accepted at any given time is not the subject of opinion. In addition to the generally accepted demonstrations and proofs, there are those propositions which, within the limits of any group, are accepted as unquestionable. These, too, are not the subject of opinion within that group. Opinions emerge at controversial points, when the old, accepted patterns break down, when doubt has risen, when the tenets of any group are questioned. When there is an awareness of discrepancy, the situation is defined, solutions are presented and opinions are formed.

Opinion may be defined as contrasted to the noncontroversial, but what is a *public* opinion? This is a controversial concept. There are many opinions on public opinion. And real issues are involved. What constitutes a public? In sociological speculation, "public" is made synonymous with "group." In all groups there are some controversial issues. Therefore, the opinion process is operative to a greater or less extent in all groups, from a primary group engaged in gossip and discussion to an international organization. In a public involved in the opinion process, we have a group of people who are confronted by an issue, who are divided in their ideas as to how to meet the issue, and who engage in discussion over the issue. [6]

From the viewpoint of public as group, a public opinion is the expression of all those members of a group who are giving attention in any way to a given issue. The public opinion includes the expression of the majority (if there be a majority) and the minority or all the minorities at any given time. If the differences are so great and persistent that the minorities will not acquiesce to function with the majority, then there is

[5] A. L. Lowell, *Public Opinion in War and Peace,* Harvard University Press, Cambridge, Mass., 1923, p. 12.
[6] See Herbert Blumer in *Outline of the Principles of Sociology,* Barnes & Noble, Inc., New York, 1946, p. 189.

no public—there are several publics. Publics exist only when the constituent members will function together. In order to have public opinion,
"A majority is not enough, and unanimity is not required, but the opinion
must be such that while the minority may not share it, they feel bound,
by conviction, not by fear, to accept it; and if democracy is complete the
submission of the minority must be given ungrudgingly." [7] One might call
this the democratic definition of publics. In such publics, there is a process
of interaction, the maintenance of a plurality of positions, and the tolerance of minority views. In contemporary totalitarian states with monopolistic propaganda, such publics are intolerable. They must be churned
into masses conditioned to uniform expression.

There is another problem as to the nature of the public opinion, a
haunting and confusing subject for the social theorist. F. H. Allport has
referred to it as the personification of public opinion, the personification
of the public and the "group fallacy" of the public. "Public opinion, according to this fiction, is thought of as some kind of being which dwells
in or above the group, and then expresses its view, upon various issues as
they arise. The 'voice of public opinion,' or the 'public conscience,' are
metaphors of this sort. . . . A related fiction is one in which the notion
of a collective, superorganic being is applied not to the opinion process
itself, but to the public which holds it. . . . Somewhat less mystical, but
equally uncritical, is the usage of those who renounce the idea of a collective entity or group mind, holding that when they say 'the public' they
mean individuals; but who, nevertheless, go on employing such phrases
as 'the public wants so and so' or 'the country voted dry.'" [8] We have here
the old problem of the "individual" and "society" which has been recast
in myriad forms. Public opinion, it is maintained, is something more than
individual opinions. Obviously, the final expression of a public opinion is
more than the individual opinions with which the process starts. There
has been interaction. Though public opinion exists only in the minds of
individuals, it is the product of a collective mental life.

Will the resultant expressions of opinion, which appear after the opinion process in any group, be the average of individual opinions at the time
when the process started? Obviously not, for the opinion process has
introduced new elements; the convincing opinions of the better informed,
the prejudices and emotional responses aroused during the interaction,
the injection of personal prestige into the process, and the like. Will the
result be above or below the average, as measured by realistic judgment

[7] A. L. Lowell, *Public Opinion and Popular Government*, Longmans, Green & Co.,
Inc., New York, 1913, p. 15.

[8] Allport, *op. cit.*, pp. 7 and 8. For a critical discussion of this problem, see Allport's
article and also G. A. Lundberg, "Public Opinion from a Behavioristic Viewpoint,"
Am. Jour. Sociol., 36: 387–405.

and conclusions? In the absence of relatively exact, analytic interpretations of the opinion process in large publics, the answer will depend on the faith of the commentator in the capacity of the common man. A century ago, W. A. Mackinnon declared, "Public opinion may be said to be that sentiment on any given subject which is entertained by the best informed, most intelligent, and most moral persons in the community, which is gradually spread and adopted by nearly all persons of any education or proper feeling in a civilized state." [9] C. H. Cooley states, "There is a widespread, but as I believe a fallacious, idea that the public thought or action must in some way express the working of an average or commonplace mind, must be some kind of a mean between the higher and lower intelligences making up the group. . . . A little common-sense and observation will show that the expression of a group is nearly always superior, for the purpose in hand, to the average capacity of its members." [10] But another group of writers, in depreciation of the judgment and capacity of the common man, maintains that the opinions of the wiser members of a society are usually ignored and that the level of majority opinion and decision is very low indeed.

Great confusion in terms has occurred because "public opinion" has been used by one group of writers as a label for the content of group opinion (that is, the statements of all the members of the group at any given time), whereas another group of writers refers to public opinion as the process of opinion formation.[10a] C. H. Cooley wrote, "Public opinion, if we wish to see it as it is, should be regarded as an organic process, and not merely as a state of agreement about some question of the day." [10b] Certainly statements of opinion can be understood only in relation to the interaction that preceded the statement, but, as a matter of labels, we shall designate the formation of opinions as "opinion process." But on active issues, individual opinions may change rapidly. There is constant flux. A record of opinion at a given time may be true only momentarily. To make a record by means of opinion tests or polling simply freezes the process. However, the entire opinion process, as well as the reports on particular opinions from time to time, are all part of public opinion as we shall use the term.

[9] W. Mackinnon, *op. cit.*, p. 15.
[10] C. H. Cooley, *Social Organization*, Charles Scribner's Sons, New York, 1909, pp. 123, 124.
[10a] L. J. Carr has stated this issue clearly in "Public Opinion as a Dynamic Concept," *Sociol. Soc. Res.*, 13: 18–30.
[10b] C. H. Cooley, *Social Process*, Charles Scribner's Sons, New York, 1918, p. 378.

BELIEFS AND CONSENSUS

There are relatively stable beliefs which, at any given time, are not involved in the opinion process. A state of agreement following an opinion controversy is a consensus. It is a relatively quiescent period in the flux of social change. Every existing belief has been questioned at some time in the history of a culture. "Every consensus is a won agreement; to realize it as such requires a background of awareness of disagreements from which the harmony has emerged." [11] And, of course, large publics are not commonly aware of the history of their cherished beliefs and so regard them as universally true and self-evident.

A consensus may be achieved within groups widely differing as to size, maturity and the degrees of complexity of their psychological processes. Experts achieve consensus on theories. The history of ideas illustrates the starts and stops of the professional thinker. Publics reach consensus on ethical, political and economic issues. Even large publics may be in substantial agreement. There is then consensus of the type that Montesquieu designated as the *esprit général,* that Rousseau spoke of as the *volonté générale* and that the English theorists called "public will." The ethical consensus which W. G. Sumner labeled the "mores" are states of agreement and are outside the realm of opinion. Among the bulk of the inhabitants of Mississippi, a public opinion on intermarriage between whites and blacks cannot be said to exist. The subject is not discussible; it is part of the mores. Wilhelm Bauer speaks of organic opinion as meaning these relatively fixed views, and Ferdinand Tönnies notes three stages of fixity: *die Feste, die Flüssige* and *die Luftartige,* roughly translated as the solid, the fluid and the gaseous. In community, or *Gemeinschaft,* there are the popular beliefs, the *Volksstimmung* and *Volksgefühle,* which are to be sharply distinguished from the social judgments to be referred to as public opinion.[12] Public opinion, in the definition which we propose, deals with those topics which are controversial and discussible in the publics concerned, and not with those aspects of mind-life which are comparatively fixed. The political scientist usually has included the whole stream of community thought as part of public opinion, the values that have long been accepted in tradition, as well as the immediately controversial. I believe that the distinctions in terminology which I have proposed make for greater clarity in discussion.

The nineteenth-century social theorists quite generally included both the materials on which consensus existed and also the controversial items

[11] H. M. Kallen, "Consensus," *Ency. Soc. Sci.,* 4: 225.

[12] P. A. Palmer, "Ferdinand Tönnies and His Theory of Public Opinion," *Pub. Opin. Quar.,* 2: 4: 586 ff.

as part of the general content of public opinion. A. V. Dicey writes of public opinion as a body of convictions and beliefs and prejudices, as well as of what he calls crosscurrents due to controversy. But we may logically distinguish between consensus and opinion. Plato confined opinion to that which is subject to change. Opinions are developed about admittedly controversial topics, whereas, in belief or consensus, "an idea fills the mind to the exclusion of possible alternatives."

In modern life, awareness of other and conflicting beliefs has made for relativism. Certainty has been extensively undermined. The enlargement of communication first brought the variant beliefs, codes and standards to the attention of the professional thinker and then, to some extent, popularized such knowledge. The areas of certainty were narrowed. Thus, the field of opinion widens, and the sphere of consensus diminishes.

PUBLIC OPINION, REASON AND EMOTIONS

Confidence in the power of reason has waxed and waned throughout the history of thought. Rationalism "aims to regulate individual and social life in accordance with principles of reason and to eliminate as far as possible or to relegate to the background everything irrational." [13] P. A. Sorokin isolates the upward movements of rationalism as from 540 to 450 B.C.; the second half of the fifth and first half of the fourth century B.C. (Socrates, Plato, Aristotle); about 200 B.C.; about 80 B.C.; the twelfth, thirteenth and first half of the fourteenth centuries; the first half of the fifteenth century; the sixteenth and first half of the seventeenth centuries; and the end of the eighteenth and beginning of the nineteenth centuries. [14] Faith in the capacity of the common man to form his opinions on the basis of rational principles has fluctuated in like maner. During the last period of rationalism the great societies were emerging. Social and psychological thinking of the late eighteenth and early nineteenth centuries was dominated by the concept of reason and by the assumption that man is a rational animal. In politics there was the emergence of democracy and faith in the rational man. Economic assumptions posited rational choices, and philosophy assumed the calm deliberation of goods and ills. Rational capacity was believed to be inherent in the individual, to be cultivated by education and enlightenment. The optimism of the nineteenth century was based upon this faith. Knowledge could solve everything, and with industry it was yours.

Then another "flight from reason" began. Darwinian evolution linked the species, and there was no reason to believe that instinctive drives

---

[13] B. Groethuysen, "Rationalism," *Ency. Soc. Sci.*, 13: 113.
[14] P. A. Sorokin, *Social and Cultural Dynamics*, American Book Company, New York, 1937, vol. II, chap. 1.

might not dominate reason in man. Psychology was providing a description of man's thinking that made the doctrines of "rational man" appear to be speculative wishful thinking. It was increasingly assumed that the older breed of political and economic theorists had erred in regarding man as a purely rational being. In the twentieth century the flight from reason gathered momentum. In literature, an increasing number of influential writers rejected the primacy of the intellect and denied, as Aldous Huxley said, "that there is an intrinsic superiority in mental, conscious, voluntary life over physical, intuitive, instinctual life." The cult of D. H. Lawrence was built upon the assumptions about deep, instinctive drives, the voice of the blood, the final reality of deep-seated, primal, emotional urges. Considerations of orderly and logical analysis were supplanted by emphasis upon nerves, instinct, emotion, intuitive sensual memories and the like. Psychology disparaged the amount and thoroughness of rational and logical thinking. Emotional drives were emphasized, the instinct theories proliferated, behaviorism and conditioning were extensively described, emotional linkages with verbal and personal symbols were illustrated, the tricks of the mind in rationalizing and stereotyping were gleefully exhibited, the unconscious was uncovered and other psychological partial descriptions were paraded. The political theorist applied a portion of these doctrines to political functioning and public opinion. The first incisive analysis (1908) was Graham Wallas's *Human Nature in Politics*. His thesis was that "political thinking in the past has assumed a degree of intellectuality in mankind that mankind never really possessed. The human nature with which he is concerned is the pre-rational and non-rational behavior which complicates political processes everywhere." [15] Harold Laski declared that formal doctrine and popular opinion were rationalizations of deeper drives in men. These rationalizations were the orientations of each era to the new set of living conditions. There were many emulators of such writings.

Political practitioners provided antirationalistic and anti-intellectualistic ideologies in support of the new authoritarian states organized about Fascist, Nazi and Communist doctrines. There was a remarkable growth of bigotry and intolerance, of avowed faith in violence and of the consciously organized management of opinion through propagandas that promulgated conclusions and depreciated appeals to reason. There was a widespread decline in the prestige of reason.

During the past fifty years there has been a vast increase in organized special pleading. Reform groups were perfecting their techniques of popular appeal. Conflicting doctrines were seeking a hearing. Commercial advertising was creating markets for the distribution of the growing

[15] G. Wallas, *Human Nature in Politics,* Houghton Mifflin Company, Boston, 1909, p. 21.

number of consumers' goods. Newspapers and other media of communication fought for circulations. All of these showed by their practices that their directors had decreasing faith in the effectiveness of rational appeals. In commercial advertising, there is a score of attempts to influence buying by emotional appeals to one analysis of the quality of the product. Commenting on these trends, a philosopher states, "If, in the name of reason, you summon a man to alter his fundamental purposes—to pursue, say, the general happiness rather than his own power— you will fail, and you will deserve to fail, since reason alone cannot determine the end of life." [16] Those who maintain that the only proper way to influence a human being is to encourage him to think for himself and who have faith in his capacity to do so effectively are in combat with the pragmatic practitioners of power by any means.

PUBLICS AND THE SENTIMENTS

It it difficult to evaluate the relative importance of emotional responses and of other factors on major public issues.[17] Emotional elements usually bulk large, for as Professor Cooley has said, "the originality of the masses is to be found not so much in formulated idea as in sentiment. . . . The common people, as a rule, live more in the central current of human experience than men of wealth and distinction . . . some tendency to isolation and spiritual impoverishment is likely to go with any sort of distinction or privilege . . . the sentiment of people is most readily and successfully exercised in their judgment of persons." [18] Sentiment and emotional response are frequently related to the major stimulus, the symbol of the person, word, slogan, place, object, ceremony and the like. And the number and proportion of emotional appeals are multiplied as the publics increase in size. The popularization of a political program, economic doctrine or theological creed necessitates broad emotional appeals. Of American Methodism, an observer writes, "The advance of Methodism with its passionate propaganda, broadened and coarsened religious thought. The Methodists addressed themselves to the masses, and attempted to control their way of life. They may not have possessed the cultural traditions of New England, but they had the faculty of gripping the souls of the masses." [19] Excitement and emotional thrill, even of

[16] B. Russell, "Power over Opinion," *Sat. Rev.*, Aug. 13, 1938, p. 13.

[17] For an excellent, though popularized, statement of emotion in mass movements, see R. Fülöp-Miller, *Leaders, Dreamers and Rebels*, The Viking Press, Inc., New York, 1935; contrast this with a shallow and unscholarly treatment in J. H. Denison, *Emotional Currents in American History*, Charles Scribner's Sons, New York, 1932.

[18] C. H. Cooley, *Social Organization*, Charles Scribner's Sons, New York, 1909, pp. 135, 136, 138, 142. Quoted by permission.

[19] M. J. Bonn, *The American Adventure*, The John Day Company, Inc., New York, 1934, p. 249.

fear, if not too violent, is a pleasurable experience. Of course, popular emotional responses are of short duration, and successively stronger stimuli must be applied to retain the state. Hence, in wartime, in racial conflict or class struggles, increasingly crude and violent appeals usually appear as the struggle progresses.

Large publics cherish the emotions and sentiments and apply them to public issues. George Washington said, "The people must feel before they will see." Disraeli stated that we are not indebted to reason for the great achievements of man, for man is truly great only when he acts from the passions that appeal to his imagination. Emotion and sentiment are at once a basis of strength and of weakness in the opinions of large publics. Under political democracy, the sentiments of publics can mitigate the inhuman and frequently self-interested judgments of elites. But again, the sentiments frequently distort the judgment of masses. Elihu Root, as Secretary of State, wrote that when foreign affairs are handled by despots the danger lies in sinister purposes, but when policy on foreign affairs is largely dominated by the people, the danger lies in mistaken beliefs and emotions. Democracy holds to the principle that some men are rational and, on many issues, some are not, and that it is possible to bring popular judgments around to positions that are rationally defensible. To provide time for the emergence of such judgments, the system of democracy in the United States has incorporated many types of representation and of checks and balances upon the initial opinions of publics.

The personal and provincial interests, the sentiments and emotions of masses of people emerging in expressions of opinion, often place a salutary check on the excesses of special interests and elites. This was the strength of nineteenth-century democracy. But the sentiments may be confused in a complex culture with conflicting trends, and they may be corrupted, degenerated and exploited by leaders. This exploiting of the sentiments is one of the grimmer aspects of the twentieth century. It is a preoccupation of the Fascists and Communists converting publics into malleable masses, as well as a preoccupation of some private individuals and groups under political democracy.

THE IDEOLOGY

Popular opinions do not exist as separate, disjointed, unrelated items. Although the opinions of the common man are by no means totally consistent, there are underlying systems of thought. During the past century, general popular thought systems have been increasingly referred to as "ideologies." Confusion and glaring inconsistencies have become evident in popular thought and action as the common man has had access to conflicting ideologies in religion, politics and economics.

A consideration of the life of an individual, a people or an age must begin with an inventory of its systems of thought. There are always complexes of popular convictions and beliefs that are fundamental and decisive for the life of a time. Underlying such popular thought are the systems provided by the professional philosopher, theologian, political theorist and economist.[20] When both the professional thinker and the common man considered such beliefs as emanations from God, from nature or from underlying, immutable truth, they believed that the statements of their opponents or enemies were lies, errors, misinterpretations and misconceptions resulting from the activities of the devil or from the faulty perceptual or conceptual apparatus of misguided souls. There were absolutes, and the righteous and favored people received them. All others were in error and in some way personally responsible for their derelictions from the truth or for their failures to achieve it. On the other hand, ideology implies a system of ideas related to the life situations of its creators. As such it is changing, relative and nonabsolute. "The ideas expressed by the subject are thus regarded as functions of his existence. This means that opinions, statements, propositions and systems of ideas are not taken at their face value, but are interpreted in the light of the life situation of the one who expresses them. It signifies further that the specific character and life situation of the subject influence his opinions, perceptions and interpretations."[21] In the ideology, certain distorted and partially untrue conceptions of persons are regarded as legends, certain theories as myths, and postulates and assumptions as "guiding fictions."

Such a relative conception of human thought could not develop until very recently in the history of thought. The sociology of thought remains a startling view to many social theorists, and the concept has scarcely penetrated to the common man, except in the form of Marxian dialectics that brand opposing doctrines as class ideologies. Nor is it a comfortable or comforting doctrine to masses of mankind who still prefer to quest for the absolutes with self-styled infallible guides. Hitler, Mussolini, Lenin, Stalin and other dictators who have tinkered together certain dogmatic absolutes for the masses have proved once more that there is a persistent popular cry of "What shall I believe to be saved?" Hegel has cast a long shadow over large sectors of modern thought. As A. N. Whitehead has written, "Man has always sought the perfect, harmonious and orderly universe."[22] And John Dewey notes, "There is something deep within

[20] Professor Sorokin, *op. cit.*, vol. II, has provided a study, largely quantitative, of the fluctuations and trends in such systems.

[21] K. Mannheim, *Ideology and Utopia* (English trans.), Harcourt, Brace and Company, Inc., New York, 1936, p. 50. Quoted by permission.

[22] A. N. Whitehead, *Science and the Modern World*, New American Library of World Literature, Inc., New York, 1925, p. 230.

human nature itself which pulls toward settled relationships. Inertia and the tendency toward stability belong to emotions and desires as well as to masses and molecules." [23] But, in spite of the desire for absolutes and the "quest for certainty," the relative nature of thought systems and the relationships between thought and group interests become increasingly apparent in our diversified world.

The concept of ideology arose in western Europe when various popular thought systems were obviously in conflict as religious, political and finally economic controversies engaged the attention of the common man. Suspicion of the quality of the adversary's thinking found justification in branding that thinking as "ideological," that is, as partial, incomplete and limited by his time and place, his station and class. The seventeenth century had a phrase, "climate of opinion." It was beginning to be recognized that ideas had a setting, and that "whether arguments command assent or not depends less upon the logic that conveys them than upon the climate of opinion in which they are sustained." [24] Bacon wrote of the "idola," the idols, phantoms, preconceptions, the illusions, of the populace. Glimmerings of the concept of ideology were appearing in various writings. Montesquieu, in the narrow world of the eighteenth century and with scanty knowledge of civilizations other than the European and the Classical, tried to show the trends of civilization and to make people conscious of the fact that men's mentalities were conditioned by the systems in which they lived. Social organization was becoming more intricate; classes and interest groups were arising. Not only was the "thought of the palace one thing and that of the public square another," [25] as Machiavelli had noted, but there were also various groups with diverse ways of thinking. "The modern conception of ideology was born when Napoleon, finding that this group of philosophers was opposing his imperial ambitions, contemptuously labelled them 'ideologists.' Thereby the word took on a derogatory meaning which, like the word 'doctrinaire,' it has retained to the present day. . . . What is depreciated is the validity of the adversary's thought because it is regarded as unrealistic." [26] The derogatory connotations of ideology were furthered in the Marxian writings. Marx discussed religion, law and systems of thought as ideologies beneficial to the capitalists. Marxian thought placed emphasis upon class position and class interests in thought. A revolutionary movement must have an ideology. Just before fascism emerged in Italy, Mussolini

[23] J. Dewey, *The Public and Its Problems*, Henry Holt and Company, Inc., New York, 1927, p. 213.

[24] C. L. Becker, *The Heavenly City of the Eighteenth-century Philosophers*, Yale University Press, New Haven, Conn., 1935, p. 5.

[25] Mannheim, *op. cit.*, p. 55.

[26] *Ibid.*, p. 64. Quoted by permission of Harcourt, Brace and Company.

exhorted his followers to "utilize the coming months before our party convention to create a philosophy of Fascism."

But ideology was not only an intellectual weapon but also a valuable conceptual tool. Thought is conditioned by time and place and by group interests. Certainly this is not equally true of all kinds of thought. Scientific thought, theological thought and philosophy have their own histories and deep roots. But popular thought on political and economic issues is especially ideological. Values in a culture provide a frame of reference for thinking. In Spain, the Jesuits have left marks on the national character. Indirectness and cleverness are esteemed in conversation; frankness is considered unpardonable naïveté. It is difficult for an American or European, with his conceptions of sovereignty and of executive power, to grasp the psychological attitude of the Japanese people toward their emperor. There is no parallel, no Western analogy. The ideologies differ. The concept of ideology is a useful way of thinking about popular complexes and systems of ideas. As relativism in the description of thinking, it illumines many otherwise unintelligible differences between classes, interest-groups and entire cultures.

A popular ideology must be simple and must be adapted to simple mentalities. As a public creed it must be implemented with symbols of a readily comprehensible type. "Thus it is that most of man's behavior is symbolic of the various characters which he assumes. This is true not only of his behavior as a warrior or a priest, but extends even to such practical concerns as eating and drinking, with their little rituals of highly decorated tables and service. The words, ceremonies, theories, and principles and other symbols which man uses make him believe in the reality of his dreams and thus give purpose to his life." [27] So the ideology is couched in symbols to which the believer may respond. Mussolini wrote, "There must be music and banners to kindle enthusiasm. The mob is loose and dispersed as a shoal of fish until they're well disciplined and led. They don't need to know; but the faith that moves mountains must flash from the orator's soul into their own, like the radio that can excite the world with a mighty thought. Really the tendency of our modern folks to believe is . . . quite past belief." [28] The ideology is expressed in personal symbols, emblems and language forms. The uses of slogans, catchwords, cries and other popular verbal symbols are meaningful in their particular contexts. The associated emotional responses are usually ill understood by those of another time who may attempt to understand the potency of these phrases. Indeed, it is with great difficulty that we achieve any true appreciation of past symbols or of those of an opposing ideology.

[27] T. W. Arnold, *The Symbols of Government*, Yale University Press, New Haven, Conn., 1935, Preface. Quoted by permission.
[28] B. Mussolini, *Cur. Hist.*, 45: 4: 81.

In a religious, fear-ridden public of the seventeenth century, the cry of popery aroused emotional responses which today can be understood only by the meticulous historian.[29] When words are redefined and used as symbols of an ideology, confusion is compounded. The Marxian made "bourgeois" synonymous with "capitalist." But this term, originally meaning "city dweller," had come to mean "middle-class citizen," as opposed to nonurban elements, the aristocracy and the peasants, before Marxian jargon made an epithet of it. The puerilities, the vacuousness, the ambiguities and the absurd simplifications of popular ideological symbols alienate the intellectual analyst.

A political, religious or economic ideology is first inculcated by persuasion. In a broad sense, ideology is strategic and its changing propaganda is tactical. If its principal tenets fulfill needs that are widespread, the ideology wins adherents. The political theories accepted at any time and place are those which promise fulfillment of the hopes and utilitarian interests of some class or group. After a system becomes dominant, as did the recent and contemporary Fascist, Nazi and Communist doctrines, it is imposed by force. The viewpoints are crystallized into principles. Then violence, the venting of fierce partisan hatreds and the "liquidation" of those who espouse other principles ensue. Physical coercion may be used sincerely, ruthlessly, cruelly and without compunction. Afterward, a genuine belief may be engendered in the majority, making force less necessary.

The relative nature of ideologies does not mean that some systems of thought are not superior to others as adaptations to reality or that we can comfortably find rest in irrationality and skepticism as to all popular thought. The thinking of large publics is conditioned by their time and culture, but the awareness that such is the case may provide a bulwark against the more extreme illusions. Adversaries may be understood. Fervid adherence to a particular ideology cuts communication and isolates the convert. Awareness of ideologies may restore communication.

---

[29] A survey of twentieth-century ideologies may be found in Feliks Gross (ed.), *European Ideologies,* Philosophical Library, Inc., New York, 1950.

CHAPTER 2

Public Opinion and the Masses

THE DEVELOPMENT OF PUBLIC OPINION

As a member of large publics, modern man has a mass of information about many facts, systems of ideas, fragments of knowledge, ideologies and news. Most of this information is shallow, unrelated to any deep roots in integrated thought systems. It is predigested, simplified and served to him in catchwords and other simple symbols. A great deal of it is inaccurate. To a considerable extent it is a mental conglomerate, chaotic and transient. Much of his information is presented to him for a purpose, the furtherance of the interests of some organized group. There is great emphasis on publicity, some of it presumably in the public interest, such as publicity about government, income-tax returns, stock ownership, securities and the like (although the campaigns for such publicity are by no means disinterested from the viewpoint of their proponents). Other types of publicity, advertising and propaganda are obviously in the interest of the sources from which they emerge. But in all cases there is a vast to-do about informing the general public. Today the struggle for power is conducted by interest-groups implemented with the newer means of communication, the popular press, motion pictures, radio and television. Interest groups are more varied, better organized and very effective in winning large publics. They struggle with one another in a competitive attempt to inject their viewpoints into the various media of communication. Dictators meticulously organize propaganda bureaus, economic groups develop publicity organizations and individuals retain publicity agents to present their viewpoints and personalities to large publics. How has this scramble for publicity come about? Why does it seem imperative to so many groups that they should have a public hearing? What changes in social organization have accompanied the rise of contemporary public opinion?

The term "public opinion" was coined in the late eighteenth century. It appeared at that time because large publics were coming into existence owing to the rapidly increasing populations; their geographic concentration in cities where large mobs, crowds and assemblages made possible the speeding-up of the opinion process; the development of the means of communication, especially of printing, by which tracts, pamphlets and posters could be duplicated in larger numbers; the increase in literacy. At the same time the importance of the individual citizen's opinions and decisions was emphasized, owing to the rise of rationalism and of political democracy. The enlightenment of public opinion became a creed, a faith and an objective. Public opinion was not a new phenomenon, but the theorists' preoccupation with the opinion processes of the masses emerged during the eighteenth century when there was the maximum confidence in the judgment of the common man. Therefore, the developing emphasis on the role of public opinion must be viewed in terms of the culture history, the institutions and the values of the various national culture groups. In the popular ideology of democracy, there has developed a fundamental concern with human justice, personal freedom, representative or democratic political forms, the inclusiveness of the electorate and the widening of the areas of decision in which public opinion is dominant. In the general ideology of communism, there is no room for honest dissent, the recognition of the intrinsic worth of divergent interests, the conciliation of interests, or the enlightenment and cultivation of individual judgments which might develop opinions contrary to the official Communist ideology. Therefore, the significance and the role of public opinion are viewed quite differently under democracy and communism.

Older discussions of public opinion do not differ much from modern writings in estimating the influence that popular opinions exert upon the actions and daily life of men; they differ in assessing the influence popular opinions have or should have on the actions of statesmen and philosophers.[1] But three centuries ago, man in large publics was too uninformed about affairs beyond his provincial interests to develop significant opinions about the larger issues, certainly about international issues. Then the world and its people was for man a vague, mysterious, shadowy unknown. Untutored by mass media, man's interests were largely limited to the immediate area of the village where he was born, lived and died.

In earlier times and in primitive and folk societies, innovations are usually dealt with by the application of customary rules, rather than by discussion and the formation of opinions. The mores, the beliefs, the consensus and the customary procedures are invoked. There is little of the dynamic opinion process. "There exist many communities in which public opinion—if by that term be meant speculative views held by the mass of the people as to the alteration or improvement of their institutions—can hardly be said to have any existence. The members of such societies are

[1] For an extended discussion of this idea, see Hans Speier, "The Historical Development of Public Opinion," *Am. Jour. Sociol.*, 55: 4: 376–388.

influenced by habits rather than thoughts."[2] Of course, there are great variations among types of primitive societies and of folk communities. Contemporary scholars must be much more cautious about making facile generalizations about "primitive peoples" than were those of a generation ago. Since 1900 the ethnologists have described primitive peoples of great variety in social organization. Margaret Mead has illustrated three types of primitive communities on the basis of the individual's opportunities for expressing opinion.[3] In the first, illustrated by the Arapesh, the Andamanese, the Ojibway and the Eskimo, there is the maximum opportunity for the formation of individual opinion upon the issues of daily life. Personal opinion achieves expression in these groups, but Dr. Mead errs in identifying this type of personal opinion with the "public opinion" of the great societies. In these primitive groups there is no opinion process, no interaction with the resultant group opinion, comparable to the process in modern publics. In the second type, illustrated by the Iatmul people of New Guinea, there are clan, age and moiety groups within the tribe. Group attitudes are developed within these subdivisions, and these attitudes are applied to conflict situations. The attitudes which the individual acquires in one group may differ from those which are maintained by another group, and confusion ensues. But there is no public opinion in the sense of discussion on a controversial point. In the third type, illustrated by the Balinese, the rule of the general mores is relatively complete and all issues are decided by customary principles. There is no public opinion situation. There are distinctions as between various primitive peoples in the range of personal opinion expression. In whatever system exists, the individual is held within the limits of traditional expression. Among the Dionysiac Plains Indians, the individual could swagger, aggrandize his own accomplishments, tell unusual dream experiences and emphasize certain individual variations. Among the Apollonian cultures of the Southwest, the individual was expected to efface himself and proceed ceremoniously in most situations.[4] In any case, he was bound by the traditional values, and variation therefrom made him subject to the taunts, jeers and recriminations of his fellows. The deliberative judgment of groups, whether swayed by rational or irrational factors, but admitting new and alien values and arguments, is rare in the primitive and folk communities. They are swayed by custom and lack the comparative and relative habits of mind. These are static and tradition-bound cultures.

In the ancient civilizations, public opinion played some part, but the

[2] A. V. Dicey, *Law and Public Opinion in England,* Macmillan and Co., Ltd., London, 1905, p. 3.

[3] M. Mead, "Public Opinion Mechanisms among Primitive Peoples," *Pub. Opin. Quar.,* 1: 3: 5–16.

[4] R. Benedict, *Patterns of Culture,* Houghton Mifflin Company, Boston, 1934.

publics were limited in number and size, the mechanisms for expression of opinion were rudimentary and communication was limited. Among the early Hebrews, the institution of the prophets, who made direct appeals to crowds, canalized popular attitudes.[5] But there was little opportunity for popular discussion, and the role of the individual was that of a recipient of the supposedly revealed truth that the prophets trumpeted. However, among the Greeks, public opinion developed to an extent unequaled until modern times. By the sixth century B.C., "in their various struggles against aristocracy and tyranny as well as in their reaction against the mystical otherworldliness of such cults as Orphism the aggressive citizenry of the towns, particularly Athens, developed an atmosphere of individualism conducive to the unhampered competition of opinions and ideas." [6] Publicity was emphasized and there were popular appeals to the masses. Of course, the masses did not include all people, but were composed of all citizens. In the fourth century B.C., there were approximately 120,000 adults, of whom 40,000 were free citizens, 25,000 unenfranchised free foreigners and 55,000 slaves. In the communal assemblies of the city states, the citizenry deliberated and reached joint decisions. There were also public speeches and the theater. "A new sort of people, these people of leisure and independent means, were asking questions, exchanging knowledge and views, developing ideas. So beneath the march of armies and the policies of monarchs, and above the common lives of illiterate and incurious men, we note the beginnings of what is becoming at last nowadays a dominant power in human affairs, the free intelligence of mankind." [7] There were terms with which to refer to opinion and the opinion process. "The Greek concepts *ossa, pheme,* or *nomos* were familiar in Athens and were even accorded on occasion a niche in the Hellenic pantheon." [8] Argumentative conversation developed. Rules of the game emerged for intellectual conversation and debate, consisting of assertions and questions and the taking of contrary positions. The art of dialectics was codified. Political and philosophical argument became fashionable. Public opinion emerged on controversial issues. But the size of the publics was small, and there was no belief in general equality—only a democracy of the elite.

The urban culture of the later Roman Empire gave scope for the opinion process. And the Romans came to speak of the *vox populi.* The wide-ranging conquests of Rome provided information about many peoples with their values, religions, economic and political systems. The

[5] Read the fascinatingly vivid historical novel on Jeremiah, by F. Werfel, *Hearken unto the Voice,* The Viking Press, Inc., New York, 1938.

[6] W. Bauer, "Public Opinion," *Ency. Soc. Sci.,* 12: 671.

[7] M. Beard, *On Understanding Women,* Longmans, Green & Co., Inc., New York, 1931, p. 102.

[8] Bauer, *op. cit.,* p. 669.

size of the empire resulted in emphasis upon news. Hence the professional newsmongers, and in the later periods, the publications of the *Acta Diurna*. There was much to discuss, the culture was dynamic and the opinion process was stimulated.

Through the Middle Ages, with the diverse, scattered, small groups and agrarian communities and with cultures blanketed under a common religious ideology oriented toward revelation and the supernatural, there could be little of dynamic popular opinion. Rather, there were consensus and traditional mores. Ultimately, there was popular acquiescence in the forms of government and the religious hierarchy—not the support of popular opinion. Opinion emerges from the controversial. As Lord Bryce wrote, "In the earlier or simpler forms of political society public opinion is passive. It acquiesces in, rather than supports, the authority which exists, whatever its faults, because it knows of nothing better, because it sees no way of improvement, probably also because it is overawed by some kind of religious sanction." [9]

The opinion process was vivified when, in the fifteenth century, printing was invented in Europe, the Reformation questioned clerical authority and emphasized the individual, and arts, letters and science began to cast off the bonds of authoritarian revelation. Public opinion developed as larger groups became concerned with religious issues, political systems, relative values and with ideologies in general. And the new means of communication, printing, coupled with a slowly growing literacy, distributed the ideas. The opinion process began to ferment in the fifteenth century, although it was not until the eighteenth century that the term "public opinion" was created and the social theorists centered attention on the molding of this power for decision. The Enlightenment of the seventeenth and eighteenth centuries was the turning from the authority of divine revelation to the authority of reason and human understanding. When "natural reason" was posited, then individual opinions became important, and the theorists turned to an examination of the opinion process.

Public opinion elicited little regard from the elite until the close of the eighteenth century. Public opinion played little part in international affairs or the limited warfare before the revolutions. The professional soldiers recruited from the lower classes of society felt no need to know why they were fighting. Frederick the Great left to his historical apologists the justification of his conquests. In 1770 the new English Prime Minister, Lord North, declared: "The drunken ragamuffins of a vociferous mob are not exalted into equal importance with men of judgment, morals and property. I can never acquiesce in the absurd opinion that all men

[9] J. Bryce, *The American Commonwealth*, The Macmillan Company, New York, 1891, vol. II, p. 271.

are equal." Yet, in a few decades, a great change occurred. The revolutions idealized the common man's opinions. And, "After the Congress of Vienna, the utilization of public opinion in international affairs became, as it were, respectable also among statesmen who did not pursue any revolutionary cause. Once the importance of public opinion was discovered as a new factor in international relations, it became tempting on moral as well as on expediential grounds to utilize it." [10] By the middle of the nineteenth century, in 1859, John Stuart Mill could write, "In politics it is almost a triviality to say that public opinion now rules the world"; while Abraham Lincoln was stating that "With public sentiment on its side, everything succeeds, with public sentiment against it, nothing succeeds."

The rise of modern publics during the past four centuries is based upon certain material innovations and upon changes in social organization. The invention of printing, and later of the telegraph, telephone, photography, motion pictures, radio and television provided systems of communication whereby the great societies could be woven together. In this sense, the printing press of necessity preceded democracy, popular education and the diffusion and animation of communication. Communication is the fundamental human institution in that it sets the limits of community size and by its nature affects all types of human association. Speech confined association to the limits of human migration and the voice; writing and printing freed man for association in larger and more diverse societies. The increased organization of craft production and later of manufacturing, as well as of trading, brought about a growth of cities from the fifteenth century onward. As had been true in Greece and Rome, the animation of the opinion process followed the urban massing of populations. Membership in street crowds, mobs, audiences and other urban groupings provided more numerous opportunities for interchange of information and news. Varied discussion was physically possible. Impressions were multiplied, the city became a center of cultural diversity and mental flexibility was engendered. But, fundamentally, the city provided the arena and through the physical propinquity of large masses of people the stage was set for gossip, rumor, discussion, speechmaking, the reading of posters and, in general, the animation of the opinion process. The trading, manufacturing and commercial activities of the city changed the class structure of society also. And the emerging middle class was most influential in rejecting the ancient authoritarianism, in breaking down the medieval consensus and in providing a forum for the doctrines of the Enlightenment.

Of the nonmaterial factors that were most decisive in the beginnings

[10] Speier, *op. cit.*

of modern publics, the most important were the spread of literacy, the rise of a philosophy of rationalism and the assumption of man's natural reason, and the democratic ideal. That the individual can listen and understand may suffice in the folk community, but that he can read the newspapers, periodicals, captions, directions, posters, bulletins and the like, is requisite in the great society. Widespread literacy is a modern phenomenon. Protestantism, with its emphasis on the personal relationship between the individual and his God through Bible reading, gave the first great impetus to popular literacy. The doctrine of natural rights, as it was propounded in the eighteenth century, gave the second great impulse to the teaching of the common people. The nationalism of the nineteenth century, with the concomitant emphasis on welding together the culture of a nation, was the basis of the third great drive for mass literacy.[11]

The accumulation of the printed word opens to the reader the vicarious experience of the thoughts and deeds of man in all time. To unlock this treasure, man must be able to read and he must be permitted to read freely. Yet, today, of the two and a half billion people on the surface of this earth, more than half are illiterate. In the teeming populations of China and India, more than 90 per cent are illiterate. More than 75 per cent of the population are illiterate in Turkey, Morocco, Algeria, Ethiopia and throughout most of Africa. More than half of the people cannot read and write in Mexico, Guatemala, Brazil and Venezuela. Only in Western Europe, in Britain, France, the Scandinavian countries, and in the United States and Canada is illiteracy less than 5 per cent.[12] Millions of people have gone from a life based on personal experiences to the larger world of vicarious experience through reading.

THE SIGNIFICANCE OF THE COMMON MAN

Faith in the possibility of an enlightened popular opinion developed with eighteenth-century rationalism. Already in the seventeenth century, we find Descartes declaring that "good sense" is the most widespread thing in the world. Middle-class man had learned to exercise foresight and to organize life rationally, and he projected this capacity upon all men. Unrealistic theorizing about the rational man dominated the larger sector of eighteenth-century thought. The opinions of man in the mass were dignified and his capacity to achieve rational solutions cooperatively with his fellows became an article of faith. The opinion process, if freely

[11] DeW. C. Poole, *Princeton Alumni Lectures,* Princeton University Press, Princeton, N.J., 1936.
[12] Illiteracy figures for most of the countries of the world may be found in the second column of Table 4, chap. 4. In the United States, the Bureau of Census figures report illiteracy as: 1870—20.0 per cent; 1880—17.0; 1890—13.3; 1900—10.7; 1910—7.7; 1920—6.0; 1930—4.3. No data were collected in 1940 or 1950.

operative among masses of mankind, would produce truth and would arrive at rational decisions. During the past century, the psychological depreciation of the common man's capacity for rational decisions, the emphasis on the fact that man's thinking on public issues is not a formal intellectual game but is conditioned by his cultural values, his group allegiances and prejudices, and an increasing emphasis on the limitations of the data that the general public usually has as a basis for decision have undermined the rationalistic assumptions.

The importance of the opinion process in large publics was further emphasized in the tenets of liberal democracy. Freedom of opinion was made a preeminent value. The great proponents of democratic government did not declare that public opinion was always right, but they did place faith in the ultimate soundness of popular judgments. That the masses, under democracy, have cultivated values of a low order has been declared with increasing frequency of late years, not only by dictators but also by philosophers and psychologists.

A fundamental respect for the qualities or potential qualities of the individual person has been violated throughout almost all of human history. Autocracies, monarchies, oligarchies, dictatorships, all enslaved the body and failed to cultivate the mind of mass man. Democracy declared political equality of men, the right to freedom, and government through representation—all posited upon the belief in man's perfectibility. Attention was turned to the instruction of man. Popular education was requisite. Masses must have the necessary information to select representatives.

The political theory of democracy, then, requires that the electorate possess appropriate personality structures, that it be interested and participate in public affairs, that it be informed, that it be principled, that it correctly perceive political realities, that it engage in discussion, that it judge rationally, and that it consider the community interest.

Now this combination of requirements sets a high—an ideal—standard for the political process. And since this is a composite list, from a variety of sources, it is not necessarily a matter for disillusionment or even disappointment that the democratic electorate does not conform to every requirement in the full degree.[13]

It is true that the uninformed, the uneducated, the irresponsibles and the nonvoters are part of the larger publics in the United States. How influential are they amidst the total public? A new line of attack on the significance of popular opinion has been made of late years. It is that the common man, frustrated by complexities, has a growing feeling of in-

[13] B. Berelson, "Democratic Theory and Public Opinion," *Pub. Opin. Quar.*, 16: 3: 329.

significance and of lack of influence on great public issues. The "lonely crowds" are abdicating.[14] Two able young sociologists wrote, in 1949:

Present-day polling, in its main assumptions, exemplifies the 19th-century liberal's approach to the individual as a social atom. By a convenient fiction, polling tends to treat its subject as a "responsible citizen," one who considers the world in terms of issues. . . . To be sure, one can still find people like this—often people in the upper and upper middle classes, and many older persons of varying class position for whom opinion grows out of a feeling of responsibility, and out of a feeling of potency to affect political events which responsibility implies. Such people think that their opinion, and their vote, matter very much, and the mass media and the polling process encourage them in this belief. Maybe this is a good thing for society.

But it is evident that the authors would consider one who took this view as naïvely romantic.[15] Yet, withal, the sampling surveys of the past decades have provided much evidence of the remarkably high degree of common sense exhibited by their subjects. In the polls, a cross section of the public has evidenced an extremely high score of correct answers, answers logically defensible even when the public did not evidence the logic. It appears to me that the polls show very clearly that one should never overestimate the information and knowledge of large publics under democracy, nor underestimate their good sense and correct judgments. The pollers also believe this. Of all those engaged in the opinion indus- tries, the pollers state the greatest faith in the significance of public opinion. Perhaps the general public has not abdicated decision to the extent suspected by some intellectuals.[16]

Elmo Roper has tentatively classified the United States public into a half-dozen groups in terms of their members' comparative personal in- fluence and involvement with ideas and events.[16a] The most influential are the "great thinkers," possibly a dozen contemporaries and perhaps a few scores of others who have lived any time in the past two thousand years but are currently influential. The next small group is composed of the "great disciples," who are protagonists and explainers of the basic ideas of the great thinkers. The third group is the "great disseminators," possibly less than a thousand; the influential communicators who dis- seminate basic ideas among the elites, the intellectuals and the specialists. The "lesser disseminators" are the influential teachers, editors, labor

---

[14] I am referring here to the thesis of *The Lonely Crowd*, by David Riesman, Yale University Press, New Haven, Conn., 1950.

[15] D. Riesman and N. Glazer, "The Meaning of Opinion," *Pub. Opin. Quar.*, 13: 4: 635.

[16] The best extended discussion and defense of the significance of the common man may be found in Carl J. Friedrich, *The New Image of the Common Man*, The Beacon Press, Boston, 1950.

[16a] Elmo Roper, "Who Tells the Storytellers," *Sat. Rev.*, July 31, 1954, pp. 25 ff.

leaders and others who locally and popularly disseminate ideas and influence public opinion on public affairs. The fifth group is the "politically active," with the term "politically active" used in a broad sense to refer to persistent interest in public affairs, a group which Roper estimates as perhaps 10 million persons in the United States, and which others might estimate at a few million more or less. And finally, the 75 to 90 million adults who are the "politically inert" on public affairs most of the time, although large sections of the politically inert become intermittently active under the stimulation of self-interest, fear, envy, hatred and other emotions. It is this last classification which most of the time might be referred to as the "masses"; inactive, inattentive, manipulatable and generally uncritical. However, from time to time, on some topics, large sections of the politically inert masses become publics among whom some interaction occurs. This delineation by Elmo Roper would appear to be a fairly approximate description of the realities of the proportionate degrees of personal influence and differential involvement in public affairs and opinions by the various levels of the American public. Yet I would add that these intermittent involvements in public affairs by masses, who temporarily become publics, is a vital democratic check on the excesses of experts.

The reflective man, the philosophic man, the scholarly man, has nearly always castigated the mindlessness, the inattention to public affairs and the failure to achieve fine discrimination in the arts of the man of the masses and of large publics.

For a multitude of causes unknown to former times are now acting with a combined force to blunt the discriminating powers of the mind and unfitting it for all voluntary exertion, to reduce it to a state of almost savage torpor. The most effective of these causes are the great national events which are daily taking place, and the increasing accumulation of men in cities, where uniformity of their occupations produces a craving for extraordinary incident which the rapid communication of intelligence hourly gratifies.

This was not written by a contemporary commentator on the present glut of news and information, with the consequent superficiality and strain on the common man's attention, but by the poet Wordsworth in the year 1800.[17]

The critics of the worth of public opinion as a basis for decision on public issues have long dwelt upon the incompetence of the masses. There are several defenses. In the first place, while people may be ignorant of detailed fact, it is possible for them to choose wise representatives; second, the average person without the detailed knowledge necessary to construct governmental policies may, nevertheless, be competent to pass

[17] Preface, *Lyrical Ballads.*

judgments of right and wrong upon policies presented to him; third, people know their own interests and are best able to guard them; and, fourth, as we have noted earlier in this discussion, the masses preserve the sentiments which importantly bulwark decision in the public interest.

Ernest Griffith has pointed out: "Some great upsurge of popular opinion on international issues may be one of those waves of intuition which are not infrequently sounder guides than the supposedly more sophisticated reasonings of the 'experts.'" [18]

Yet it is true that public opinions are most effective on general issues which involve over-all policy and least trustworthy where self-interest is too directly involved. The opinions of large publics could not be expected to evidence the most balanced judgment on issues immediately personal, such as personal taxes, subsidies, how much pension one should receive, welfare grants and other detailed economic issues of immediate personal concern. On the other hand, have the various elites been impartial and striven primarily for the public good?

OPINIONS ON POPULAR OPINION

In our time, many types of leaders in the fields of politics, economics, and theology, and many theoreticians, ideologists and assorted intellectuals differ, as they have usually differed since the time of the great Greeks, concerning the general psychological capacity, the judgment and wisdom, and the significance of the opinions of the common man. Those whose fundamental attitudes are depreciative of the qualities of the mind-life of the common man are at best paternalistic, at worst crudely authoritarian, but in no case fundamentally democratic. The potentialities of the common man have been the subject of dispute throughout the history of mind-life in Western civilization. The intellectual leaders of America have reflected and amplified a controversy which has raged intermittently during the past two thousand years in political philosophy, theological interpretation, artistic evaluations, and theories of division and status in social life. In the United States, from Alexander Hamilton and Thomas Jefferson to Franklin Roosevelt, two streams of thought, two theories of human order, two views of the power, functions, and potentialities of the mind-life and opinions of masses of common men have been maintained and publicly, or at least privately, expressed. These two basic attitude complexes have traditional evolutions in politics, law, aesthetics, theology, ethics, literature and education. In politics and administration, doubts of the common man's opinions stream from Alexander Hamilton, John Adams and John Marshall to publicity men representing contemporary business

[18] Quoted by John F. Kennedy in "Foreign Policy Is the Nation's Business," *New York Times Mag.*, Aug. 8, 1954, p. 28.

leadership. On the other hand, more sanguine expectations find expression in the utterances of Jefferson, Jackson, Lincoln, Bryan, La Follette and Franklin Roosevelt.

At the end of the eighteenth century, Gouverneur Morris said, "The people never act from reason alone, but are the dupes of those who have more knowledge." And Alexander Hamilton spoke contemptuously of "the imprudence of democracy where the people seldom judge or determine right." These were sincere, honest and forthright conservatives. Contemporary psychological Tories have a long tradition to which they could appeal were they not muted by the present climate of opinion. Not so, the stalwart elites of an earlier age. A century and a half ago, a few years before he became the second president of the United States, John Adams said: "The people of all nations are naturally divided into two sorts, the gentlemen and the simple men." The simple men, the common men, could not be expected to harbor significant opinions. These were honest and intellectual reservations. They did not grow exclusively out of economic or political self-interest. That was a period in which popular democracy was viewed with suspicion by some of the better minds among the founding fathers.

Men by their constitution are naturally divided into two parties. 1. Those who fear and distrust the people and wish to draw all power from them into the higher classes. 2. Those who identify themselves with the people, have confidence in them and consider them as the most honest and most safe, although not the most wise, depository of the public interests. In every country these two parties exist—and they will declare themselves.

The fundamental issue of his day, as thus succinctly and clearly stated by Thomas Jefferson, remains a central and intensified issue today. In the twentieth century, authoritarian leaders, rabble-rousing demagogues and the propagandists of special-interest groups have attempted to propagandize the publics. In our time, consumer goods are distributed by publicity methods which evidence something less than a pristine belief in the rationality of the common man. It is more difficult to discern man's faith or disdain for the opinions of his fellows than in the days of the Jeffersonians and Hamiltonians. But, nonetheless, it remains an issue on which men sharply divide as to their fundamental attitudes, now as then. In our day, the attitudes are more often hidden. A fundamental faith in the efficacy of popular opinion may be partially concealed in an age when much has been done to make the common man appear irrational and even silly; and a disdain for popular opinion may be hidden in an age when there are goods to be sold, electorates to be wooed, publics to be cajoled, and personal legends to be built. In the United States, in the middle of the twentieth century, these attitudes must often be discerned through a cloud of protestation of faith in the opinions of large publics. The main-tenance of power today necessitates caution in making any public decla-ration of lack of faith in the mind-life of man in the mass. A screen of rhetoric of appreciation of the popular mind, of protestations of faith in majority rule, of declarations of faith in a truly free press may intervene between the true attitudes of numerous leaders in the opinion industries and their publics.

It is often with great difficulty that the professional philosopher and social scientist maintains his faith in the mental acumen of the man whose habitual reading is the comic strip and the Hearst press. It is even more difficult for the practitioners of the arts of advertising and propaganda to esteem the mind-life of their subjects. Such leaders have a keen sense of distinction between the "elites," that is, the effective rulers, and "the masses," who are manipulated by the rulers. Such managers in society may not be aware of Vilfredo Pareto's four-volume elaboration of the theme of elites and masses, but they cherish the characteristic attitudes of elites for masses. They could concur in Pareto's sneer at a liberal as one whose spinal column is utterly rotted from the bane of humani-tarianism. Believers in their own superior judgment, in moral relativism, and in the rights of the mentally alert, they are also increasingly con-cerned with the tools and methods of manipulation, as they are sur-rounded by ever increasing numbers of mass men needing guidance. Disdainful attitudes are the almost inevitable outcome of long experience in manipulating popular opinion. They are a distortion resulting from occupations which beget cynicism. A climate of opinion unfavorable to confidence in popular opinion frequently exists among men eminent in the fields of publicity, advertising, propaganda and professional special pleading of any kind. Becoming habituated to doubt, it is a not uncom-mon occurrence that they underestimate the significance of meaningful popular opinions which are developed intermittently, often at crises, and especially on subjects concerning general group welfare. Specialists and representatives of classes and special interests have often exhibited less than admirable acumen in understanding and in respect for the climate of popular opinion existing in their age.

PUBLICS AND MASSES

Today, the forces arrayed against the liberal assertion of the worth, dignity and significance of the opinions of the individual person are more formidable than at any time in the past two centuries. The extreme conservative and reactionary has always been doubtful of the worth of the common man. Now, the antiliberals, who have fervidly attacked the capitalistic economic philosophy of the conservative, have exhibited in

theory and in practice a marked disregard for the individual. Communists
disavow psychological as well as economic liberalism. Moreover, the first
object of attack of the Fascist political orders was individual personal
expression, as well as personal responsibility and freedom. Fascist tacticians must first pulverize diverse publics into amorphous masses. The
malleable masses are then propagandized, misinformed and degenerated
in mind-life. The evanescent impressions of such masses of people are
indeed worthy of disrespect. The product of such masses is characteristically the guided and stimulated outpourings of the basest emotional antipathies and hatreds, the envious debasement of the superior values, and
irresponsible demands for bread and circuses. In castigation of the contemporary politicians' degeneration of publics into masses, Pope Pius XII,
in the 1948 Christmas message, declared:

> The people lives and moves by its own life energy; the masses are inert of
> themselves and can only be moved from outside. The people lives by the fulness
> of life in the men that compose it, each of whom—at his proper place and in
> his own way—is a person conscious of his own responsibility and of his own
> views. The masses, on the contrary, wait for the impulse from outside, an easy
> plaything in the hands of anyone who exploits their instincts and impressions;
> ready to follow in turn, today this flag, tomorrow another.

But who creates contemporary masses? They are an inevitable concomitant of all forms of authoritarianism, political or ecclesiastical. Informed publics, not responsive and malleable masses, are the basis of
effective democracy. That common men, as members of large publics,
provided with adequate information, can be trained to function satisfactorily in the realm of public affairs is the premise and the faith of
political democracy. But authoritarians in any field distrust common men
and disseminate misinformation to mislead them.

Ancient tyrannies were personal, human, animal, physical relations;
men were degraded, treated as animals, which to some degree they are.
Modern tyrannies are largely organizational, inhuman, mechanistic, and
treat men as machines, which they are not. During the past fifty years, in
the great political democracies of the United States and Great Britain,
the general publics have been officially respected by their political representatives most of the time. But a stream of debasement of the mind-life
and the opinions of the common man may be found in the partial, distorted and interested information disseminated by the special pleading
of professional practitioners of publicity for economic and other private
groups. The types of appeal, gauged to low common denominators for
large publics, are limited only by the standards of intelligence, taste and
ethics of the largest publics. In their search for these lowest common
denominators and in the manipulation thereof, many publicity men in

press, radio, motion pictures and television in the United States become professionally cynical concerning the mental capacity and the basic value of the opinions of the members of their large publics. Political demagogues and the individuals and groups whom they represent also evidence little concern for the maintenance of rationality in the common man.

Men do not always strenuously resist the process of churning publics into masses. They may be tired and psychologically lonely, terrified and bedeviled, in quest of a leader and a cause, in quest of a belief and thereby ready to abdicate from a position of judgment, reason and responsibility. And so, as Gilbert Highet says, there is—

. . . a possibility that human thought will be deliberately and forcibly controlled and limited. This also has already happened a number of times in history; it is happening now. The aim of those who try to control thought is always the same, and they always work on the same principle. They find one single explanation of the world, one system of thought and action that will (they believe) cover everything; and then they try to impose that on all thinking people.

Critics discussing the imposition of belief usually write as though every normal man hated it, the currents of thought throughout history set against it, and only a minority of brutal and Machiavellian masters attempted to enforce it. This is wishful imagination rather than cool analysis. However absurd a system of belief may look from the outside, or in the perspectives of history, it can often be made acceptable to the average man by several powerful factors of attraction.[19]

At this point, publics become and are made into masses. And masses are intolerant, illiberal, brutal and mindless, and under the psychological necessity of defending their accepted ideology. They abominate liberalism, pluralism and tolerance. At this point, the harassed liberal wearily recalls the words of Alexis de Tocqueville, who was well aware of the threat of mass intolerance.

There is, and I cannot repeat it too often, there is here matter for profound reflection to those who look upon freedom of thought as a holy thing and who hate not only the despot, but despotism. For myself, when I feel the hand of power lie heavy on my brow, I care but little to know who oppresses me; and I am not the more disposed to pass beneath the yoke because it is held out to me by the arms of millions of men.[20]

It is evident that popular opinion has been considered increasingly important during the past century. All types of governments attempt to manipulate the opinions of their citizens and those of other countries. Economic groups depend upon the convincing of large publics as to the

---

[19] G. Highet, *Man's Unconquerable Mind*, Columbia University Press, New York, 1954, p. 57.

[20] A. de Tocqueville, *Democracy in America*, Alfred A. Knopf, Inc., New York, 1945, vol. II, pp. 11–12.

quality of the goods that are purveyed and upon the creation of good will. Many types of special-interest groups strive for a following. Through their hired publicity agents, societal leaders and notable personages attempt to create their legends or to explain their behavior, attitudes and purposes to those sectors of the great society which they consider important for their purposes. None of these leaders would publicly subscribe to the Marquis de Sade's cynical statement that "it is a danger to love men, a crime to enlighten them," but, in the pursuit of personal and group objectives, true popular enlightenment would be inconvenient. However, much of the confusion is unintended. As the late Charles Horton Cooley stated, "Most of the harm in society is done with the elbows, not with the fists."

The problem becomes one of values. Is the objective the unity of mass opinion for the furtherance of some societal institution, from the state on down to a minor interest-group? Or is the preeminent value the development of the individual's psychological experience through his having access to a rich and stimulating diversity of fare? Is it possible to achieve a sufficient unity for the successful organization of the economic and political activities of the modern great society without regimentation of popular opinion? Modern communication provides the means for either course.

CHAPTER 3

Communication

It is the nature of art to build languages, of which the verbal is but one. In sound, color, form and motion we beget evolving incarnations in which the human spirit can live and grow.

CHARLES HORTON COOLEY

We are in great haste to construct a magnetic telegraph from Maine to Texas; but Maine and Texas, it may be, have nothing important to communicate. Either is in such a predicament as the man who was earnest to be introduced to a distinguished deaf woman, but when he was presented, and one end of her ear trumpet was put into his hand, had nothing to say. As if the main object were to talk fast and not to talk sensibly.

HENRY THOREAU

Many shall run to and fro, and knowledge shall be increased.

DANIEL, 12: 4

Underlying all social process and all societal forms is the transfer of meaning between individuals. Social life can exist only when meaningful symbols are transferred from individual to individual. Group activities of any sort are impossible without a means of sharing experiences. In the terminology of the social studies, the process of transmitting meaningful symbols between individuals is designated "communication." [1] As Cooley has stated, "By communication is meant the mechanism through which human relations exist and develop—all the symbols of the mind, together with the means of conveying them through space and preserving them in time. It includes the expression of the face, attitude and gesture, the tones of the voice, words, writing, printing, railways, telegraphs, telephones and whatever else may be the latest achievement in the conquest of space and time." [2] Communication is the fundamental social process in that the way in which meanings are transmitted must inevitably affect all other social processes and the resultant forms, folkways, mores and institutions.

[1] M. M. Willey and S. A. Rice, *Communication Agencies and Social Life,* McGraw-Hill Book Company, Inc., New York, 1933, p. 6.

[2] C. H. Cooley, *Social Organization,* Charles Scribner's Sons, New York, 1909, p. 51. Quoted by permission.

Public opinion, among other social processes, is affected by the communication methods in many ways, but most fundamentally in the size of the
groups that may be involved and the distribution of these groups in space.
Because of their face-to-face speech and gesture methods of transmitting
symbols, the simpler primitive people can focus attention, discuss and
carry on other aspects of the opinion process only within small groups
and in limited geographic areas. Owing to the invention of new forms
of communication, the radio, telegraph, telephone and television, the
attention area [3] of a contemporary radio-listening urbanite may be practically world-wide and, at least for special interests, some of his discussion
groups may be international if not world-wide in area. The attention area
of the newspaper reader, at least for certain types of news such as the
particularly atrocious murder, an unusual incident in the romantic quest,
trade news or believe-it-or-not curiosities of behavior, is almost world-
wide in scope.

The methods of communication include all the ways whereby meaning
may be transferred from individual to individual. These range from the
most rudimentary of gestures, ill-defined and vague, to the most elaborate
deaf-mute codes; from the crudest pictograph to the most precise nota-
tions of mathematical symbolism; from the most spontaneous cry to which
meaning is attached to the most elaborately defined scientific terminology.
These meanings may be understood within groups of varying size from
the two schoolgirls whose special meanings for particular words give a
uniqueness to their association, to those versed in the universal codes of
mathematics, a special science or a world language. The methods of communication may be classified in terms of primary processes, those fundamental techniques which are universal, and secondary techniques, which
facilitate the process of communication.[4] Gesture and language are primary and universal in this sense. Writing facilitates the transfer of language and other symbol forms. The developing physical means whereby
symbols may be transported—messenger, domesticated animals, boats and
mechanical transportation—make it possible to disseminate the copies of
the writing or pictured symbols. Later, printing vastly multiplies the units
to be distributed. The telegraph, telephone and radio transmit code and
speech, and the motion picture preserves and disseminates pictured forms.
These methods of mediated communication have vastly increased the
swiftness of transfer and the diffusion of symbols.

Face-to-face communication is subject to many errors of meaning and
interpretation. One individual expresses by gesture or speech; other individuals interpret. Many psychological and cultural factors prevent a

---

[3] Term used by H. D. Lasswell, *World Politics and Personal Insecurity*, McGraw-
Hill Book Company, Inc., New York, 1935, p. 186.
[4] E. Sapir, "Communication," *Ency. Soc. Sci.*, 4: 78.

perfect transfer of meaning. Errors of perception, predispositions, the emotional state of the individuals and other factors distort the process of communication. However, in the direct contacts, when several sensory processes augment one another, the transfer of meaning may be less subject to error and distortion than in the mediated communication. The pictured representation of the cinema is not exactly that seen in face-to-face contact; the radio voice is not the voice of the public speaker or the conversationalist; writing notoriously formalizes speech and television distorts in various ways. The transmitters have somewhat modified the content while conveying it. This distortion results from the nature of the transmitting agencies, but it may also be augmented with conscious intent. When a speaker wrenches a phrase of his enemy from its context and ridicules it, when a photographer with a candid camera catches a political executive with cigarette smoke in his eyes making him look pained, they are consciously distorting in ways made possible by the media in which they operate.

All communication is based upon symbolic forms that are acquired from the cultures with which the individual has contact or are learned in personal experience. When a child learns a word and then experiences an idea, when it sees a gesture such as kneeling and learns its religious significance, when it sees symbolic pictured obscenity and learns to interpret, it is abstracting forms from the general culture. When the boys in a gang select a password and give it a special meaning, they are learning from personal experience. Both forms are transmissible. The symbols may be learned, and in this process man is clearly distinguishable from other species.

Individuals differ greatly in their ability to communicate and in their opportunities to do so. Differences in innate ability and in training and knowledge prevent the equal sharing of the culture of a period. Variations in skill of expression are also a differential. In gesture, for example, the trained actor is more superior to the average adult than the adult is to the small child. In speech forms there is a range from the vocabulary of the incoherent, loutish dolt to the skilled manipulations of language by a subtle poet. Expressiveness in writing varies from the average business letter to the nuances of a novel by Marcel Proust. Differences in ability to communicate may also be based upon structural variations from the normal. Sensory differences in sight, hearing and the like may partially isolate the individual, rendering him incapable of communication through the usual channels. Also, cultural differences between groups make communication difficult because of language differences, meanings, concepts, variable response to emotionally charged words and other symbols. Attention areas may be expanded without increase in the range of understanding of the diversity of culture. Thus, although the attention area of the urban newspaper reader of our time includes something of French politics, he usually has little understanding of the French political institution, the position of parties and their maneuverings. In the 1930's, a Japanese general in commenting on the Manchurian situation said, "The Japanese never retreat, but sometimes they advance in a rearward formation." Or so it was translated for the newspapers. Perhaps the general meant that psychologically they did not falter, although sometimes they were forced to give way a little in physical terms. Or perhaps not. But to the average newspaper reader, this was a play on words, nonsense, "legpulling" or just another instance of the bland chicanery and psychological duplicity of the Japanese military. There can be little understanding through such distorting media. Isolation may also be due to separation in space, which prevents communication. Individuals, long separated more than the average from their fellows, deteriorate in their capacities for communication. Prisoners, herders, long-exiled explorers, traders at isolated ports, illustrate this variation. It is an intriguing theme for the writer, and there are many literary descriptions of the result. There are some autobiographical sketches of psychological change in isolation.[5] However, under conditions of modern transportation and communication, isolation usually need not be prolonged except through choice. Even the hermits of Colorado formed a club. Partial isolation, either psychological or spatial, with the resultant variations in the communicative processes, limits the fields of discussion and the group memberships of those who are thus isolated. Isolation, quite obviously, modifies the opinion process.[6]

Of late years, the engineers, physicists, mathematicians and other scientists who have been concerned with the technical aspects of the communication process have developed a special vocabulary on communication, and have diagrammed the processes in rather exact fashion. Though their terminology might have some incidental usefulness to social scientists in assuring uniformly used symbols, most of the engineers' concepts and discussion are almost completely outside the areas of the cultural and psychological aspects of communication. If, as Claude Shannon notes, "The semantic aspects of communication are irrelevant to the engineering aspects," it is likewise true that the engineers' conceptualizations of mechanical processes have thus far added little to significant understanding of human communication. Claude Shannon and Warren Weaver diagram a communications system as follows: [7]

[5] A brilliant item is A. Kuncz, *Black Monastery*, Chatto & Windus, London, 1934.
[6] C. H. Cooley elaborated the relationship between communication and social life in his *Social Organization*, chaps. 6–10, 1909, thus drawing the attention of American sociologists to this fundamental process.
[7] C. Shannon and W. Weaver, *The Mathematical Theory of Communication*, University of Illinois Press, Urbana, Ill., 1949, p. 98.

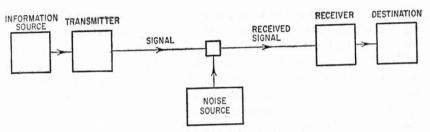

FIG. 1. A communications-system diagram.

The information source selects a desired message out of a mass of possible messages. The transmitter carries this message through a communication channel such as voice, signals over wire, pictures and the like. But in transmission, mechanical, semantic or psychological factors of noise are introduced. "If noise is introduced, then the received message contains certain distortions, certain errors, certain extraneous material that would certainly lead one to say that the received message exhibits, because of the effects of noise, an increased uncertainty." [8] "The receiver is a sort of inverse transmitter, changing the transmitted signal back into a message, and handing this message on to the destination. When I talk to you, my brain is the information source, yours the destination; my vocal system is the transmitter, and your ear and the associated eighth nerve is the receiver." [9] The activity of the transmitter is usually referred to as "encoding" and the activity of the receiver as "decoding." In the process there are various intervening distortions. Even the clearest message loses something in its journey, and these communication theorists refer to this loss as "entropy." In addition to the invention of a vocabulary, the scientists in communication study have attended increasingly of late years to the use of symbols in the processes of thinking and communicating, and to the construction of models for systematically describing the processes. "By a model is meant a structure of symbols and operating rules which is supposed to match a set of relevant points in an existing structure or process. Models of this kind are indispensable for the understanding of more complex processes. The only alternative to their use would be an attempt to grasp directly the structure or process to be understood; that is to say, to match it completely point for point." [10]

A great deal of communication about communication was effected before we had systematic models and much specialized vocabulary. In every area of knowledge in which experienced, skilled communicators are interacting it is exactly in the skill to "grasp directly" that efficient, rapid

[8] *Ibid.*, p. 109.
[9] *Ibid.*, p. 99.
[10] K. W. Deutsch, "On Communication Models in the Social Sciences," *Pub. Opin. Quar.*, 16: 3: 357.

communication is possible. If I am writing or speaking to matured, trained intellectuals and say that Woodrow Wilson once wrote of one of his contemporaries that "His mind is a great comfort to every man who has one"; or if I say that Schopenhauer wrote, "We understand our neighbor only to the extent to which we are like him," I expect to communicate without writing three paragraphs of explanation as to what was meant by Wilson or Schopenhauer. If it is necessary for me to do so, I have then a "communications problem" of popularization. It is to an understanding of the processes of communication downward that most communication theory is directed and this requires the development of "models."

Communication, as we are concerned with it in our study of public opinion, ranges from the simplest gesture of a responding, nodding member of an audience to a world-symbol gesture such as Churchill's V signal, from a two-person conversation to a televised speech seen by millions, from a letter or a rumor told in a tavern to the content of the mass media. In the main, we are concerned with mass communication in large publics. Even so, we shall seldom have occasion to use the new vocabulary of the communications experts. Has this paragraph been properly conceived at the information source, were the most effective language symbols selected, encoded and transmitted with the minimum intrusion of noise, then decoded and received by you, the reader, with little entropy? I hope so. Is it now clear that I do not believe that our significant understanding of the essence of the communication process in public opinion has been greatly aided by our new vocabulary constructs and models? You will seldom encounter these specialized terms in this volume.

GESTURE

All physical movements or postures to which meaning is ascribed comprise the form of communication known as "gesture." These forms of expression range from the interpretation of an involuntary movement in indicating attitude to the conscious use of an elaborate code of signals, as in the occupational codes of railwaymen, surveyors or structural workers, the wigwag of Boy Scouts, the deaf-mute sign language. Certain gestures, such as a small baby's smiles and grimaces, are unlearned, as are the involuntary movements of the eyes and hands of a witness. These are socially significant because they are interpreted, even though the fond mother or the juror may misinterpret. Most gestures have no such specialized and individual interpretation but are a part of the common culture groups where they are learned and used as an auxiliary and supplementary form of communication. Even the simplest of such gestures must be understood in terms of its associated meaning in the particular culture. Indicating, for example, is not invariably done by pointing arm or finger; some American Indian tribes indicate by pointing the lips in various directions while conversing. The play of features, the variety of facial expression must, with the exception of a few involuntary movements, be interpreted in terms of the conventional gestures. Likewise, many bodily movements convey meanings in accordance with a predetermined code. Symbolic gestures may have the same, varied or exactly opposite meanings in different cultures.

Gestures are related to the group opinion process in many ways. All transfer of meanings is of potential significance here. Especially, however, in television and in the face-to-face contacts of leaders and groups the significant role of gesture in indicating attitude may be noted. The orator or demagogue develops individually unique and meaningful movements. The confident toss of the head, the clenched and bared teeth, the wide, grimly closed mouth, the flailing arms, have characterized significant American leaders. During the most controversial periods in political opinion process, gestures may be significant symbols. The upraised arm, the Fascist salute, the threatening contortions of a war leader at a tribal dance when a primitive group is attempting to decide upon the desirability of a raid, the wildly gesturing leader demanding attention, the heroic pose of the dictator defying the world are phenomena of crisis conditions. Within group situations, crowds, mobs and audiences and other face-to-face groups, the membership is affected not only by the gestures of leaders, but by the physical poses, facial expressions and other gestures of their fellows. Such gestures may be profoundly indicative of attitude.

LANGUAGE

Language is superior to gesture because of its range, specific meanings, nuances and variety of expression and infinite capability for abstraction. At best, gestures are, in comparison, a rudimentary and auxiliary form of communication. However, unless they are written, language forms cannot be exactly preserved, as the changes in folk tale, the growth of verbal legends or the parlor game of "Gossip" illustrate.

Languages are a part of the culture of all peoples. The child, after its early experimental sounds and cries, begins to take over the language forms, as it acquires other elements of the culture. Thus the child is restricted to the limits of meaning and idea that exist within its language. Our language limits in a very real fashion the range of our thoughts. We acquire words and then learn meanings, ideas and concepts. As Cooley writes, "The word usually goes before, leading and kindling the idea—we should not have the latter if we did not have the word first. 'This way,' says the word, 'is an interesting thought: come and find it.' And so we are led to rediscover old knowledge. Such words, for instance, as good, right, truth, love, home, justice, beauty, freedom; are powerful makers of what they stand for." [11] The same process operates in various groups within a culture. Terminology may direct and limit the operation of thought. Within a Communist group, an oft-repeated Marxian terminology highlights certain economic processes but hides others in shadows. So does the language of every other particularistic philosophy. Words directing and limiting the individual's field of inquiry thus determine what the subjects of opinion may and may not be. The thought of the members of every group, national, occupational, class, religious or philosophical, is subtly guided by its language forms. Of this, the members are, for the most part, unaware.

Not only does language as communication limit the range of thought within which the opinion process may operate, but the content of language also in part directs the methods of controversy. The use of vague phrases and words, devoid of exact and absolute meaning, is a commonplace of controversial discussion. By the use of these catchwords and phrases, which are usually associated with general attitudes of emotional response, leaders in controversy attempt to build on existing attitudes in creating the new opinion. The pattern of controversy is also determined by the content of the existing language forms for name calling and epithet hurling at opponents. In this process, for the want of a differentiating language, opponents of quite divergent types may be categorized in common as "damn radicals," and the like. A solution of opinion controversy is sometimes achieved in the selection or coining of a popular phrase or word. In many a political and economic controversy, peace has been restored through the surrender of a word, phrase, title, party label, tax name or other significant language symbol. The way in which a thing is said may largely account for its controversial importance.

Not only is the individual limited in his thought and opinion problems by the range of language forms within particular interest groups, but he is also limited in the larger scene by the language or languages with which he is familiar. Amidst the growing extralingual contacts of the modern world there is a slowly growing demand for a type of communication that crosses the existing language boundaries. Simplification of existing languages, such as basic English, does not provide an adequate range of expression for international discourse. Various artificial languages such as Esperanto have been developed, but existing language loyalties are so powerful that these invented forms have not acquired many adherents. However, newly invented languages are tentatively put forward from time to time.[12]

[11] Cooley, *op. cit.*, p. 69.
[12] O. Jespersen, *An International Language*, George Allen & Unwin, Ltd., London, 1928.

Although the quantity and complexity of a language is not always an index of the complexity of a culture in other respects, these characteristics do, in general, indicate the possible range of thought. Languages have differentiated and grown at various rates, but all the languages of the Western world have grown rapidly during the past few centuries. One method of indicating that growth is by the number of citations in dictionaries. In English, for example, after the rapid growth through culture borrowings of the sixteenth century, there were listed about 16,000 terms in Thomas Blount's dictionary of 1656. In 1755 Samuel Johnson produced a two-volume dictionary in which were about 50,000 words. Noah Webster's two-volume dictionary of 1828 listed 70,000 words. *A New English Dictionary* published in ten volumes between 1884 and 1928 included 414,825 words. *Webster's New International* and the *New Standard Dictionary* have about 600,000 entries each. It is estimated by language scholars that there are probably from 1 million to 1¼ million English words.[13] The growth of language indicates the expansion of thought. It makes possible a wider range of opinion phenomena and in part illustrates opinion change in the past.

WRITING AND PRINTING

Writing gives permanence to communication, preserves the record and makes it accessible. Speech is transitory and distorted in remembrance. Oral tradition is faulty, perverted by human psychological factors and limited in amount by the capacity of memory. Without writing there can be little organization and permanence of knowledge. Religious, political and philosophical thought could develop complexity only after the accumulations of successive generations could be adequately recorded. Record sticks, cords, marks, tallies, pictorial representations of various kinds and on many media have been developed by many primitive peoples to give permanence to a part of their records. Obviously, these permitted but limited communication, however, and it was not until pictorial and phonetic writing developed that complete records of incidents, of history, folk wisdom and sayings, of legal forms, thought and opinion could be made. People were then freed from the immediate and the local. But these records were limited in number and accessible only to the elite. With printing came the diffusion of knowledge, but not immediately. At first, printing was viewed as a way of avoiding error, for even the most careful scribes made mistakes. Block printing was first developed in China in the sixth century, and movable type made of earthenware was invented in China between 1041 and 1049. The casting of tin type followed shortly, and by 1314 a typesetting machine using

[13] A. G. Kennedy, *Current English*, Ginn & Company, Boston, 1935, pp. 389 ff.

wooden type was employed.[14] Alphabetical type and the printing press were European inventions. In the second quarter of the fifteenth century, Gutenberg perfected the art of printing from movable type in Germany. Printing spread quickly, especially to Italy and France where scores of cities established presses and began to print the classics. The Renaissance was based in part upon printing.[15]

Printing could develop only in conjunction with satisfactory paper and inks. But these, too, had been invented by the Chinese in the early centuries of our era. Although the date A.D. 105, to which the invention of paper is ascribed in the Dynastic Records, may have been arbitrarily chosen, it is certain that by the third century the Chinese were using paper of rags, hemp and various plant fibers. Paper of various colors was used not only for writing but as wrapping paper, decoration and for other uses.[16] An oily ink, suitable for use with stencils, stamps, seals and type had likewise been developed by that time. Although type printing was independently invented in Germany in the fifteenth century, the arts of papermaking and of ink manufacture had, long before, been diffused from China throughout Europe.

The first significant use of printing to popularize knowledge, making appeals beyond the ranks of the elite, occurred when the leaders of the Reformation attempted to extend the influence of their doctrines and to arouse groups previously apathetic to the abuses of the church. They printed cheap books and pamphlets as propaganda. Indeed, proselyting zeal, especially for Christianity, has been responsible for the printing of scores of native languages since that time. In China, the earliest printed materials were Buddhist pictures and texts. Of religious influence in the development of printing, Carter states, "It can be said with equal truth that every advance into new territory made by printing has had its motive in expanding religion. In the whole long history of the advance of printing from its beginning in China down to the twentieth century, there is scarcely a language or a country where the first printing done has not been either from the sacred scriptures or from the sacred art of one of the world's three great missionary religions." [17] The disruptive effect upon existing institutions of the popularization of knowledge was recognized at once, and in 1501 Pope Alexander VI issued his edict against unlicensed printing. A decade before that, the German universities had established censorship boards. Printing made possible popular education and political democracy; it energized thought and stimulated agitation, enlarged publics and brought forth a new type of leadership.

[14] T. F. Carter, *The Invention of Printing in China,* Columbia University Press, New York, 1925, chap. 5.

[15] R. L. Duffus, "Printing," *Ency. Soc. Sci.,* 12: 480.

[16] See Carter, *op. cit.,* chap. 3.

[17] Carter, *op. cit.,* p. 17.

DIFFUSION OF COMMUNICATION

The factors contributing to the efficiency of communication have been characterized as "expressiveness, or the range of ideas and feelings it is competent to carry; permanence of record, or the overcoming of time; swiftness, or the overcoming of space; diffusion, or access to all classes of men." [18] Some gains have been made in expressiveness during the past century. The increased number of words, the rapid growth of which we have noted, has provided a more flexible language tool. Combinations of sensory stimuli in the talking picture or in television provide a somewhat different but not more expressive medium than actual face-to-face contacts. In the various art forms, experimental techniques of manipulation of line, color or words persistently attempt to make communication more expressive. Some increase in permanence of the record has been achieved through pictorial libraries (of still and moving and talking pictures), improved materials in books and papers (one New York newspaper prints a special rag edition for libraries) and the variety of sources from which information may be obtained, thus giving a better chance for survival. Yet much material from the far-distant past has been found in an adequate state of preservation. For example, in 1900, a mendicant Taoist priest discovered in a walled-up chamber in the Caves of the Thousand Buddhas in the province of Kansu, China, a collection of 1,130 bundles of manuscript written between the fifth and the tenth centuries. Most of the 15,000 books in the bundles were in as good condition as if recently written, so perfected was paper and ink manufacture among the Chinese by that time. Nonetheless, owing to climatic factors as well as to the quality of materials, most records have been lost. Preservation of records, thus ensuring cultural continuity through historical description, is now assured.

However, it is in swiftness and diffusion of the various media of communication that the great changes of the modern period have occurred. Before considering something of the social significance of this increased swiftness and diffusion, some quantitative materials, illustrative of the speed of transfer and of the distribution of books, newspapers, periodicals, motion pictures and radio, will be listed. The earliest known printed book, a Chinese block print, was discovered in China in 1900. It is a volume of six sheets of text about 2½ feet long by 1 foot wide. According to the preface it was printed on May 11, A.D. 868, by Wang Chieh for "free general distribution, in order in deep reverence to perpetuate the memory of his parents." A few thousand volumes had been printed by the Chinese before the improvement of the printing press by Gutenberg. By

[18] Cooley, *op. cit.*, p. 80.

the end of the fifteenth century there were, perhaps, 30,000 items in all Europe. After that they multiplied rapidly. The world's total book production to date has been estimated at 19 million volumes. The present annual output is about 283,000; while the total number published during the entire sixteenth, seventeenth, eighteenth and nineteenth centuries was, respectively, 520,000; 1¼ million; 2 million; and 8¼ million. The Library of Congress occupies first place among the libraries of the world, with its 8,956,993 volumes. The Bibliothèque Nationale of Paris is second, with 5 million volumes and 130,000 manuscripts. In the United States, in 1945, 6,026 libraries reported their holdings to be 124,675,283. The total number of volumes circulated in 1945 was 333,365,487. The number of copies of books and pamphlets issued in the United States by years was reported by the *Census of Manufactures*. In round numbers, there were 160 million in 1907, 470 million in 1927, 268 million in 1933, 889 million in 1947 and 766 million in 1952.

In 1952 the sale of books in various classifications, expressed in round numbers, was: book clubs, 48 million; inexpensive paper-bound books, 270 million; textbooks and workbooks, 142 million; Bibles and religious books, 78.6 million; technical and professional books, 23.7; subscriptions to encyclopedias, etc., 20 million; trade books, 184 million.

The development of various kinds of communication in the United States from 1900 to 1950, as compared to the growth of population, has been indicated in Fig. 2. The rate of increase is indicated therein.

In 1810 there were 359 periodicals and newspapers published in the United States; in 1953 there were 18,870. We have apparently become insatiable readers of monthly periodicals, for their circulation in 1947 was 195 million; whereas in 1899 there were but 37 million copies distributed. The household magazines, the farm journals, the pulps, the slicks and the weeklies have all gained enormously. The wide circulation of some of these journals may be indicated by the fact that of the household magazines, the *Ladies' Home Journal, Woman's Home Companion, Good Housekeeping* and *McCall's,* each has well over 3 million per month distribution. *The Saturday Evening Post* had a circulation in 1950 of over 4 million, *Life* over 5 million and the *Reader's Digest* circulated over 10 million copies per month. Diverse in content, policy and the reading publics to which they appeal, these monthly and weekly periodicals are potent factors in influencing popular opinion. The circulations of the monthly and quarterly periodicals, as compiled from the various issues of the *Census of Manufactures*, are presented in Table 1.

With the development of popular journalism in the 1890's, in the period of the "yellow" journalism of Hearst and Pulitzer, newspaper circulations began to mount rapidly as larger publics became newspaper readers. To the newspaper's essential function of reporting important news with com-

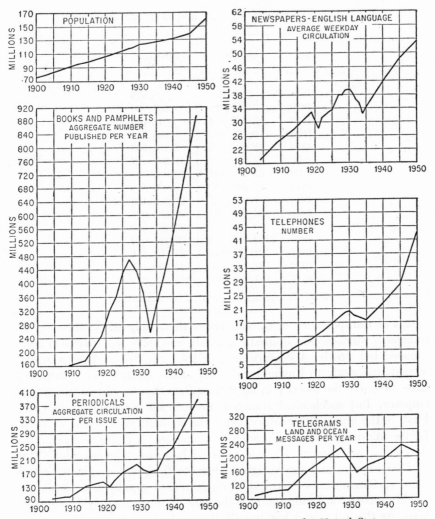

Fig. 2. Population growth and communication in the United States.

ments thereon, there were added the purveying of organized gossip, vicarious experience in the personal doings of great and of representative individuals, and numerous feature sections. The newspaper was circulated among new millions. Although accurate information on newspaper circulations, based upon publishers' sworn statements, exists for only the past few decades, what figures there are have been incorporated in Table 2.

Letters, pamphlets, periodicals, newspapers, books and the other media of communication could reach only those points to which there was some

Table 1. Circulation of Monthly and Quarterly Periodicals

Year	Monthly	Quarterly
1850	740,651	25,875
1860	3,411,959	101,000
1870	5,650,843	211,670
1880	8,139,881	1,964,049
1890	18,632,723	8,124,500
1900	37,869,897	11,067,422
1909	63,280,535	16,058,099
1919	91,681,807	18,920,544
1925	111,875,957	22,840,186
1929	133,048,488	20,605,002
1933	103,192,794	23,237,557
1935	102,193,740	23,277,089
1937	124,520,846	25,808,181
1939	134,766,467	26,238,181
1947	194,823,923	45,535,089

means of transportation and could arrive there only at the speed of the transport. Runners and domestic animals, rowboats and sailboats could proceed but slowly. A century ago, in 1834, Sir Robert Peel was summoned from Italy to England on secret affairs of state. Traveling post-haste he made the journey in no shorter time than would an old Roman emperor. But mechanical transportation means were being invented. First, in the nineteenth century, came the steamships, then the railroads. By the middle of the '80s Butler in England and Daimler in France had developed automobiles. Electric railways had also been invented. Then in 1905 Farman and the Wrights began to fly biplanes. The speeds of these various means of transportation increased rapidly after 1900. The world's record for a mile run is at the rate of approximately 15 miles per hour. At this rate, man has practically reached his limits. The running record for a horse is 38.5 miles per hour, which can be raised but very little by breeding and training. Locomotives in 1825 attained a speed of 15 miles per hour, in 1829 of 44, in 1848 of 68, and in 1901 of 120. Automobiles developed from 14.7 miles per hour in 1895 to 301 in 1935. Airplanes in 1905 had started with a speed of 33 miles per hour; in 1954 a practical speed of over 750 miles per hour was attained and a speed of 1,600 miles per hour was achieved in an experimental plane. The shrinkage of the world in terms of transportation speeds has often been commented upon. This may be illustrated by the record of the number of days required to circle the globe. The time was decreased from the 1,090

Table 2. Number of Books and the Circulations of Periodicals and Newspapers in the United States, 1904–1954

Year	Books and pamphlets, number of copies	Periodicals, aggregate circulation per issue	English language newspaper circulation, aggregate circulation per issue		
			Morning	Evening	Sunday
1904		96,312,570	19,632,602	(Morning and evening totaled)	12,022,341
1909	161,361,844	103,309,138	9,605,694	14,606,283	13,347,282
1914	175,166,698	135,453,780	11,692,368	17,085,086	16,479,943
1919	252,068,816	146,831,438	33,028,630	(Morning and evening totaled)	19,368,913
1921	325,950,602	134,795,803	10,144,000	18,279,000	19,041,000
1922			10,809,619	18,898,322	19,676,725
1923	359,391,018	150,819,366	11,457,071	19,978,632	21,463,289
1924			12,365,215	20,634,222	22,219,646
1925	433,211,253	176,314,991	12,440,387	21,298,982	23,354,622
1926			13,335,796	22,666,007	24,435,192
1927	470,374,947	187,003,338	14,145,823	23,820,933	25,469,037
1928			13,995,104	23,977,488	25,771,383
1929	430,199,433	202,021,595	14,448,878	24,976,737	26,879,536
1930			14,434,257	25,154,915	26,413,047
1931	370,515,790	183,527,411	14,342,790	24,418,397	25,701,798
1932			13,711,382	22,696,297	24,859,888
1933	254,277,392	174,759,493	12,521,533	21,968,533	24,040,630
1934			13,223,958	19,031,915	25,366,000
1935	335,261,371	178,620,672	13,447,719	20,852,911	25,969,106
1937	414,206,837	224,274,792	15,876,784	25,541,946	30,956,916
1938			15,107,981	24,463,858	30,480,922
1939	482,220,526	239,692,508	15,524,717	24,145,965	31,519,009
1940			16,114,118	25,017,593	32,371,092
1941			16,519,010	25,561,381	33,435,575
1942			17,110,611	26,264,239	35,293,543
1943			17,077,722	27,315,107	37,291,832
1944			18,059,252	27,895,586	38,612,705
1945			19,239,913	29,144,275	39,860,036
1946			20,545,908	30,381,597	43,665,364
1947	889,506,000	384,628,482	20,762,317	30,910,959	45,151,319
1948			21,081,905	31,203,392	46,308,081
1949			21,004,650	31,840,901	46,398,968
1950			21,266,126	32,562,946	46,582,348
1951			21,222,525	32,795,413	46,279,358
1952			21,159,527	32,791,088	46,210,136
1953			21,412,474	33,059,812	45,948,554
1954			21,705,436	33,367,044	46,176,450

Sources for Table 2

Year	Books and pamphlets	Year	Periodicals	Year	Newspapers
				1954 1951	Editor and Publisher International Year Book Numbers, 1955, 1954, 1953, 1952, p. 18.
				1950 1948	Editor and Publisher International Year Book Number, 1951, p. 20.
1947	Census of Manufactures: 1949, pamphlet, p. 13.	1947	Census of Manufactures: 1949, pamphlet, p. 12.	1947 1937	Editor and Publisher International Year Book Number, 1948, p. 19.
1939 1929	Census of Manufactures, 1939, Sixteenth Census of U.S., vol. II, Part I, Table 5, p. 708.	1939 1929	Census of Manufactures: 1939, Sixteenth Census of U.S., vol. II, Part I, Table 7, p. 702.	1935	Editor and Publisher International Year Book Number, 1936, p. 146.
1927	Census of Manufactures, 1929, Table 5, p. 386.	1927	Census of Manufactures, 1929, Table 22, p. 594.	1934	Editor and Publisher International Year Book Number, 1935, p. 133.
1925	Census of Manufactures, 1925, Table 6, p. 662.	1925 1923 1921	Census of Manufactures, 1925, Table 23, p. 676.	1933 1922	Editor and Publisher International Year Book Number, 1934, p. 109.
1923 1921	Census of Manufactures, 1923, Table 8, p. 607.	1919 1914	Census of Manufactures, 1921, Tables 530, p. 635; 535, p. 638; 536, 537, p. 639.	1919 1914 1909	Census of Manufactures, 1919, Table 109, p. 152.
1919 1914 1909	Census of Manufactures, 1919, Table 111, p. 154.	1909 1904	Census of Manufactures, 1914, Tables 51, p. 658; 57, 58, and 59, p. 661.	1914 1909	Morning and evening figures from Census of Manufactures, 1914, Table 41, p. 651.
				1904	Census of Manufactures, 1914, vol. II, Table 39, p. 649.

days needed by Magellan's crew in 1522 to the time of Henry Frederick, who made the trip in 1903 in 54 days; to that of Evans and Wells, who encircled the globe in 29 days in 1926; to that of the "Graf Zeppelin," whose record was 21 days in 1929; to that of Post and Gatty, who in 1931 flew around the world in 9 days; to that of Hughes and his associates, who circled the globe in 3 days, 19 hours, in 1938, and the current record of approximately 2 days. These are records; average transportation is, of course, much slower.

All means of transportation are used to carry the mails. From the time when Cyrus the Elder, 2,500 years ago, had conquered the Persian Empire and organized mail routes for political messages, until the coming of the railroads, there was no speedier method of transporting mail than the man on horseback.[19] In colonial America the mail service was a haphazard affair. After 1753 when Benjamin Franklin was made Deputy

[19] D. O. Woodbury, *Communication*, Dodd, Mead & Company, Inc., New York, 1931, p. 179.

Postmaster General for the Colonies, a more orderly system was developed, but it frequently was weeks before a letter posted in Philadelphia was delivered in Boston. Mail was first delivered by railroad in the 1830's. As the railroad mileage was extended, reaching 193,346 miles by 1900 and 225,149 in 1948, more and more towns received mail direct by rail without the use of auxiliary carriers. This trend has reversed and now more towns are receiving mail by auxiliary carriers. Transportation by water rapidly increased in speed through the nineteenth century, and the speediest vessels were used for mail delivery. In 1918, Congress made a first appropriation for an airmail system, the first route being from New York to Washington.[20] In the meantime, various means of intraurban mail transportation, such as the pneumatic-tube systems, were developed. The communication needs of our economic systems, the rise of special interest-groups with scattered memberships, the speedy development of printed forms and the mobility of populations, which created a larger need for correspondence, brought about a rapid increase in the quantity of mail. In the United States the pieces of mail carried were 4 billion in 1890, 8 billion in 1900, 14 billion in 1910, 25 billion in 1925, 28 billion in 1930, and 44 billion in 1949.

Other means of increasing the swiftness of communication likewise developed. Throughout human history, shouts, calls, signals, drum language and other means of transferring limited meanings have been used. With the invention of gunpowder, sound signals were used, especially in warfare or for special events. When the Erie Canal was opened, the inrush of waters was heralded in a few minutes by cannon fire from Erie to New York. Rapid communication of complete and elaborate messages, however, was possible only after the invention of electrical transmission in the nineteenth century. Mechanical extension of the range of the human voice had been slightly developed before that time. In 1670 Sir Samuel Moreland is said to have talked with the king by means of a *tuba stentorophonica* at a distance of 1½ miles.[21] The great step in the transmission of messages was made when Samuel Morse produced his first working model of a telegraph in 1837. Other telegraphic systems were in use in England and in France, but these were quickly superseded by Morse's simple device. With money appropriated by Congress he built a line from Washington to Baltimore and successfully transmitted messages in 1844. From then on, the growth of telegraph systems was rapid. In 1902 there were 237,990 miles of line, and in 1927 this had been increased to 256,809 miles.[22] But the capacity of these lines had increased many times, owing

[20] See the Rand McNally *Commercial Atlas* for the present network of railroads, motor roads and airlines over which mail is transported.
[21] Woodbury, *op. cit.*, p. 8.
[22] Willey and Rice, *op. cit.*, p. 123.

to inventions making possible the transmission of as many as eight messages simultaneously.[23] Transoceanic telegraphy by means of cables was accomplished in 1858 after numerous unsuccessful attempts. The cable functioned, but, owing to faults in insulation, it failed a few months afterward. It was not until 1866 that a successful North Atlantic cable was completed. By 1931 there were twenty-one North Atlantic cables. The Pacific had been spanned in 1903 and world service inaugurated. The number of messages transmitted by oceanic cables increased from 820 per day in 1902 to 13,987 in 1927. Land telegraphic messages during the same period increased from 90,835 to 215,595.[24] In 1949 transoceanic and land messages totaled 478,671 per day which is more than double the figure for 1927.

By the summer of 1876, after several years of experiment, Alexander Graham Bell not only had developed the central idea of telephonic communication but with the assistance of T. A. Watson had created a working model. At first viewed as a novelty exhibited at the Philadelphia Centennial and in Bell's lectures throughout the country, it was commercially established in 1877. Various lines were rapidly established, later for the most part joined together in the Bell System, a federation of independent units. The growth in the number of telephones in the United States is from 1,355,911 in 1900 to 43,003,832 in 1950. The per capita calls per year have increased from 64 in 1902 to 370 in 1950.

The theoretical background for the production of the radio had been developed before 1895 by the work of the physicists Faraday, Oersted, Maxwell and Heinrich Hertz, the discoverer of Hertzian waves. The inventor of wireless telegraphy, however, was not a professional scientist but an Italian boy, twenty years of age, Guglielmo Marconi. He obtained the first patent in 1896. Communication between ships at sea, between ships and land stations and from point to point without wire connections became possible. Remote areas were brought within the orbit of communication centers. This new agency was rapidly incorporated into the communication system so that by 1927 there were 3,777,538 messages transmitted.[24a] By 1906, wireless telephony had been achieved, but it was not until 1920 that popular programs were broadcast. In that year, the Westinghouse Electric and Manufacturing Company began to broadcast programs to nearby amateurs. Meeting with an enthusiastic popular response, radio spread rapidly. Within two years, there were 382 broadcasting stations scattered throughout the country, and by 1950 there

[23] Popular descriptions of the development of the telegraph may be found in W. Kaempffert, *Modern Wonder Workers*, Blue Ribbon Books, Inc., New York, 1931, pp. 289 ff. and D. O. Woodbury, *op. cit.*, chap. 5.

[24] Willey and Rice, *op. cit.*, Table 39, p. 126.

[24a] *Ibid.*, p. 130.

were over 3,100 in AM, FM and TV. In 1922 there were 190,000 receiving sets in use; the Bureau of the Census in 1930 enumerated 16,026,620 sets; in 1953 there were 120,500,000 sets used in the United States. In 1941 there were 5,000 television sets in the United States; in 1949 there were 1,720,786; and in 1955 there were approximately 39,000,000 sets in use. Television is the popular mass medium for news, education and entertainment.

The motion pictures, a most vivid pictorial portrayal, later augmented by sound, started in the United States in 1902. By 1930 there was an estimated weekly attendance of about 90 million. In 1948 the attendance was also 90 million, but, in 1953, when the population of the United States was over 160 million, the average weekly attendance was about 46 million. In 1954 this decreasing trend was reversed and an attendance of well over 50 million was achieved. Motion-picture attendance will probably continue to increase. The effects of the motion-picture presentation upon popular opinion, although obviously far-reaching, are not known in any exact fashion.

With the successive introductions of these various means of communication, there have been prophecies of the rapid decrease or disappearance of any widespread use of other forms. Thus the telephone was to oust the telegraph, the radio seriously to damage the newspaper, wireless telegraphy to eliminate the submarine cable, and television to rout radio. Naturally they have greatly affected one another, but, in a world of rapidly growing needs for communication, new uses and a secure place for each of them have been made. Preoccupied with the invention and development of all these forms and with the content of the materials communicated, our understanding of the social significance and of the effects upon the individual of this rapidly diversified world of contacts has not kept pace with the inventions themselves.

COMMUNICATION, SOCIAL RELATIONS AND PUBLIC OPINION

The organized communication systems in the United States are an enormous activity, larger in proportion to the national income than those of any other nation in the world. In the 1950's the people of the United States were expending some 15 billions of dollars a year to communicate information and entertainment. This was between 4 and 5 per cent of the total national income.[25] Since 1900 these mass communications of print, picture and the spoken word have diffused at an accelerating rate. And, indeed, the maintenance of the active social interaction within society is based upon these communications of all kinds. In the main, this rapid growth of the various media has not been consciously planned by any

[25] Estimate by Wilbur Schramm in an unpublished UNESCO report, 1954.

agency or group in our society. It has grown from mechanical invention and cultural needs.

After 1920 the widely diffused media of popular press, motion pictures, radio and television were increasingly referred to as the "mass media." When referring to the audiences of the mass media, one is speaking of heterogeneous audiences of millions of people. Mass communication, then, may be distinguished from other aspects of communication in that the communication by word or picture is transmitted from its source to very large numbers of people. But the communication is received by individuals or small groups. Except for motion-picture audiences, there is little group participation in reception. And of the 10 million or 50 million who ultimately see a motion picture, one experiences directly only a small audience from among that number. And these individual recipients of the mass media, in contrast to the situation of face-to-face communication, communicate back ("feedback") but very little to the publisher, producer, script writer, or television performer. In mass communication millions of recipients receive communications through the mass media from a very limited number of sources.

Most of the writing about the opinions of members of large publics has been done by the recently labelled communications experts, public-relations men, workers in the mass media, market researchers, journalists and a few social scientists. The mass media, diffused as they are among scores of millions of people, are profoundly influential in distributing information, standardizing human interest stories, regimenting humor, standardizing consumer purchases, and providing a considerable extension of vicarious experience. Yet the enormous impact of the mass media in some areas of opinion and information has resulted in an overestimation of their impact on other areas of opinion, notably those topics on which the interaction of primary groups is most important. Such interaction occurs in the intimate associations of contact-, status-, and peer-groups, in conversation among family members, and in the associations in recreational activities. Perhaps, above all, the tavern is a discussion center, for some estimates note that half the leisure time of industrial workers is spent in taverns.

It is an understandable occupational hazard of those in the communications and public opinion industries to overestimate the influence of the mass media. Hence their bewildered chagrin when a much developed political plea fails to convince (more than 50 per cent of the regular readers of large dailies often vote for the candidate opposed by their regular press), or when a "free enterprise" campaign, on which scores of millions of dollars are expended, notably fails to convince. The opinion industries are usually skillful, but the values inculcated in the primary group, the personal assessments of self-interest, and traditional cultural values may frustrate the skilled propagandist. There is no inconsistency in a public evidencing a high degree of malleability to the controls of commercial advertising (dealing, as much of it does, with materials and appeals not in conflict with group-inculcated values), along with obdurate resistance to many propaganda campaigns dealing with values on which the general public has deep-seated attitudes. Publics sense that advertising is frequently of little importance, as the choices between *A* and *B* are not vital, while the propaganda campaign deals with profoundly meaningful issues. Therefore, the mass media are significant in widening experience, stimulating, as well as dulling, the mind-life, but are not nearly so important in guiding and molding mental content on vital issues as is usually claimed.

Since 1920 a large professional class has developed to man the expanding activities of press, film, radio, and television. At the same time, commercial and academic analysts of the communication process have proliferated. To a marked extent these professionals discuss this vast communication activity in terms of process, techniques, stimuli, impact, effects and semantic analysis, but not in terms of the ethical and value problems of communications content and effect. Implicit in the works of contemporary communicators is the evidence of the intense excitement of professionals at the vision of the possibility of increased psychological control of their fellow man.

In contrast, Plato insists that the first question is always, "does the utterance correspond with the facts?" After this question has been answered in the affirmative, then rhetoric can move on to the secondary problem of techniques of effective communication. This is what Plato means when he says that the communicator must be a lover of wisdom, a philosopher in the broadest sense of the word, one who has some conception of what he believes to be truth. All of us in our time will do well to listen to him, for in the last analysis, on whatever level communication takes place, there is always the question of truth and validity. No concern for techniques will make it possible to avoid this question.[26]

However, the structure and objectives of the modern mass communication industries in the democracies do not permit many advertising copy writers, publicity men, editors and television producers to be Platonists in this sense. Often they cannot emulate Burke's admonition that "public duty demands and requires that what is right should not only be made known, but made prevalent." Beyond private, partial controls are the inclusive, comprehensive controls on communication exercised by authoritarian, totalitarian states. These, too, have mass communication agencies. There, the managers of press and radio can move only within the closed

[26] W. J. Oates, *The Communication of Ideas*, Harper & Brothers, New York, 1948, p. 36.

circles of a dogmatically asserted and imposed ideology. Today, "Societies, like individual selves, are open or closed in varying degrees and in various ways. We stand before the alternatives of a society more open than men have ever dreamed or a society more closed than men have ever endured." [27]

The effects upon social structures and processes, including the opinion process, of increased speed and diffusion of communication are discussed or implicit in the various sections of this volume. Later in this volume we shall essay generalizations on the influences on public opinion exerted by press, picture and radio-television. There is no attempt at this point to give a recapitulation of details. However, there are certain general effects that may profitably be summarized. Among these are the following: the creation of large political units; the expansion of interest-groups; effects upon individual and small-group uniqueness; the organization of the opinion processes; the spread of culture forms; the creation of new fields of vicarious experience; the bulk of communicated materials as compared with the individual's capacity to absorb them.

When Plato defined the limits of the size of a city as the number of people who could hear the voice of a single orator, he was illustrating the limits that communication places upon community. The integration of any social unit is dependent upon the capacity to transfer ideas, to transmit administrative orders and to prevent disintegration at outlying points. It is a truism that the size of political units is limited by the methods of communication and transportation. By means of horse travel, messengers and signals, the early empires governed sizable territories, but always with a precarious foothold in those areas far distant from the center of government. Effective coordination of even the then known world was impossible. It is often stated that the modern national and territorial states were brought into existence by the development of adequate means of communication. Indeed, "the central fact of history, from a psychological point of view, may be said to be the gradual enlargement of social consciousness and rational cooperation." [28] The organized sway of public opinion in the great society was possible only when opinion could be formed and expressed by large groups within relatively short time periods. Thus, the printing press preceded democracy, for large states could be based only upon common knowledge. In the maintenance of political integration the influence of the newspaper and periodical, the telegraph and telephone, and the recent influence of the radio and television is obvious.

The present means of communication have made possible an integration far beyond the present political boundaries. But even though physical

[27] C. Morris, *The Open Self*, Prentice-Hall, Inc., New York, 1948, p. 135.
[28] Cooley, *op. cit.*, p. 113.

space has been annihilated, the psychological differences among people of different countries remain. And these are often maintained or enhanced to ensure national unity in the struggle for some objective. Awareness of the opinions of other peoples is obscured by censorship, by iron and bamboo curtains, by a controlled press and by propaganda. Communication does not invariably bring either understanding or amity. On the contrary, clashes of interest are thereby frequently made more apparent not only to leaders but to whole peoples. Newspaper accounts, even when true, may inflame hatreds. Motion pictures, internationally distributed, may cause peoples to dislike each other rather than bring about mutual understanding. European colonial officers in Africa often bitterly complain that certain motion pictures, as interpreted by the natives, make the whites ridiculous. International propaganda battles by radio are a common practice.

Of late years, especially in England and the United States, the technique of solving international controversy by popular understanding of the issues has been enthusiastically endorsed by a host of international amity organizations. A method of round-table discussion of conflict situations on race, labor relations and economic problems, at times used successfully in face-to-face relations, is to be applied to larger groups. Place the cards on the table; frankly tell all the facts; explain attitudes; publicly verbalize the essential differences. Admirable and successful though this procedure often is in certain conflict situations, can it be doubted that with the present cultural diversity of national groups, a naïve application of this principle could disastrously antagonize the opposing peoples where real differences of interests are involved? Nonetheless, in spite of the intensified conflicts that sometimes ensue from widened popular communication, it is likewise true that understanding on an international scale has resulted at other points. There the numerous and growing international organizations have real scope, as, for example, on questions of slavery, child welfare, the relief of suffering resulting from catastrophe, and the like. Interchange of thought in universalizing certain principles made this possible. The methods of communication have so developed that any kind of international organization is possible in so far as the attitudes of divergent-culture peoples permit.

Interests and loyalties were once local, regional and based upon isolated units. The stranger, the outsider, the alien-culture element were viewed askance. Incorporation in the local group was a slow and tedious process. In a New England churchyard is a headstone put there by the neighbors of a dead man. On it is inscribed "He lived among us sixty years, and, though a stranger, we loved him well." Increased communication makes possible many types of association reaching beyond the local community. From the development of printing onward, man was partly released from the local and the immediate, for printing was not long monopolized by special classes. Innumerable organizations based upon a common interest were created, crossing local, regional and finally, national boundaries. These interest-groups vary from international organizations of a political, economic or class interest to an association of stamp collectors. Not only have special interests been organized, but attention areas of the newspaper reader, radio listener or television viewer are constantly widened. The materials he selects from these areas, however, are largely determined by interests and attitudes which to a considerable extent are still the product of community or local cultures. Hence, he may be primarily concerned with the incidental, ephemeral, anecdotal, personal and human interest items that these attitudes dictate. And in the newspaper, radio and newsreels the supply meets the demand.[29] And the very multiplicity of these contacts may weaken reflective thought. As Lewis Mumford has written:

> The lapse of time between expression and reception had something of the effect that the arrest of action produced in making thought itself possible . . . a series of inventions began to bridge the gap in time. . . . What will be the outcome? Obviously, a widened range of intercourse; more numerous contacts; more numerous demands on attention and time. But unfortunately, the possibility of this type of immediate intercourse on a worldwide basis does not necessarily mean a less trivial or less parochial personality. For over against the convenience of instantaneous communication is the fact that the great economical abstractions of writing, reading and drawing, the media of reflective thought and deliberate action, will be weakened.[30]

Interest-groups and attention areas have expanded beyond the local scene, but the interests and items attended to are still largely dominated by the values of the community. And the very plethora of such fare inhibits development of other attitudes in the individual.

It is frequently charged that local variations, not only in elements of material culture, but in ideas, attitudes and expressed opinion, have been greatly decreased by general communication. Implicit in this assertion is the idea that a dead level of mediocrity tends to supplant desirable local variations. It is apparent that standardization of elements of material culture, clothing, housing, food and the innumerable "gadgets," gewgaws and knickknacks of our civilization, has gone on apace. Elements of nonmaterial culture, language, anecdotes, legends and innumerable other elements are likewise more uniform over large areas. And what

[29] Lasswell, *op. cit.*, chap. 9.
F. S. Chapin, *Contemporary American Institutions,* Harper & Brothers, New York, 1935, chap. 1.
[30] L. Mumford, *Technics and Civilization,* Harcourt, Brace and Company, Inc., New York, 1934, pp. 239, 240. Quoted by permission.

of opinions? These, too, it is said, have rapidly become much more alike, molded by the mass agencies of communication, chains of newspapers, periodicals with circulation in the millions and national broadcasting networks. Variations based upon local isolation are being rapidly effaced.

Several points are frequently lost sight of in such discussions. These are: (1) the use of variations of opinion based upon membership in interest-groups transcending the local scene, which groups, as we have seen, have proliferated enormously; (2) the interaction in the larger scene, permitting the injection of more varied elements in the opinion process; (3) the question of how much real diversity in local opinion existed (for was it not largely based upon similar small community experience?); (4) the fact that opinion is affected, not only by the mass agencies of communication, but also by interests and attitudes based upon political, economic, and religious variations which often have a regional, if not local, variation. Variation remains, but it is based much more upon choice and interest than upon the chance of local position.

The growth of mass communication was accompanied by the rise of organized groups bent upon affecting the opinions of the larger publics. First, organized religion, threatened with growing dissent, censored and propagandized. Then states, whose governing groups felt endangered, increasingly controlled the newspapers and pamphleteering in the seventeenth and eighteenth centuries. Today, the press and other media of communication are absolutely controlled in Russia, China, the East European satellites and elsewhere. In the nineteenth century, economic groups developed advertising and sometimes acquired policy control of newspapers and periodicals. Then interest-groups, more and more dependent upon the support of large publics, entered publicity, advertising and propagandistic activities. Toward the close of the nineteenth century, various cliques, blocs, reform groups and special pleaders of many kinds began highly organized attempts to manipulate communication. Of course, interest-groups have always sought to influence the opinion of larger publics, but a truly revolutionary change has come in the development of organized methods.

In tribal society, the individual was limited to his personal experiences, the oral tradition and wisdom of his fellows and the local culture. With the development of pictorial forms, he could enter somewhat more vividly into certain experiences of his kind. Writing and printing provided the thought of men long dead, never seen or far distant in space. Limited at first to folk material and institutional pronouncement, printing rapidly became more diversified in content. Individual memoirs, introspective analysis, unusual experiences, were recounted. There were always limitations; the informal censorship of the mores was operative, when more formal restrictions did not exist. But a more varied collection of materials gradually developed. The individual, through vicarious experience, could now range far in time and in the varieties of human experience. Children shrill and squirm with emotional excitement at the action on motion-picture or television screens to an extent not usually accompanying reading. Vicarious experience has been popularized and made vivid. Where once the imaginative and highly literate were selectively affected, great masses of people now experience a buzzing confusion of newspaper, motion-picture, radio and television stimuli, which provide vicarious experience that sometimes satisfyingly titillates, thrills and emotionalizes but again frightens and makes uneasy.

The rapid transfer of culture forms, both material and nonmaterial, from one group or class to another and from one culture to another has been made possible by easy communication and transportation. Change was accelerated; fashion, style and fad increased their tempo. Static societies were in large part static because of the absence of easy mass communication. The individual attitudes and psychological factors encouraging rapid fashion change are themselves a product of the cultural situation that permits it. Communication is responsible for the enlargement of the area over which a fashion may spread and for the accelerated tempo of fashion change. Kroeber has quantitatively shown the increased speed of change in women's styles from 1844 to 1919.[31] The invention of new forms is likewise stimulated. Communication between inventors informs, accelerates, lessens duplication of effort and increases the probability of quickly bringing together the elements necessary for a new creation. Elements of nonmaterial culture, language forms, songs, literature, dances, games, as well as theories of all kinds, have likewise spread more rapidly over wider areas. Anthropologists have maintained that, in general, material elements are diffused more readily than nonmaterial elements. At many points of contact of modern cultures this would be a questionable thesis. Ideas, programs, types of organization and opinions now spread very rapidly indeed. Leaders more rapidly acquire popular prestige, symbols are more quickly learned, interaction is stimulated, the opinion process accelerated.

Owing to modern communication, as we have seen, the individual's attention areas have widened, his memberships in interest-groups involving certain opinions have increased, most elements of his culture change at a more rapid tempo and the blatant stimuli demanding his attention have enormously multiplied. To what extent can he intelligently deal with such multiplicity and complexity? In many discussions of this point, it is apparently assumed that there is a widespread popular attempt to arrange these thronging stimuli into neat and logically coherent patterns.

[31] A. L. Kroeber, "On the Principle of Order in Civilization as Exemplified by Change in Fashion," *Am. Anthro.*, 21: 235–263.

The intellectual demands such patterns and constantly projects his wishes. But man in the mass, although intermittently confused, baffled and frustrated, can usually project his own provincial attitudes upon this wider world of discourse and find no incongruity. Capacity to compartmentalize experience is apparently quite elastic. And a hurried, touch-and-go and incomplete contact with some fragment of information, some superficially experienced emotional response or some hasty action based upon rapidly changed symbols is not necessarily alien to the man on the street. His education and culture have trained him to respond thus to the flood of urgent suggestions. His experience and training have made him essentially anti-intellectualistic. He is not persistently harried by the need for consistency, logical patterns or rational relations.

CHAPTER 4

The Geographic Distribution of Communications
and Opinion

The record of man's beliefs and opinions, as well as his behavior, may be and has been developed from a number of different viewpoints and frames of reference. For example, historical studies have been written primarily in terms of personalities, of peoples and races, of cultures, of economic motivations, of political ideologies, of psychological and of geographic factors. Personal factors are the perennial preoccupation of the common man and, indeed, until very recently have been the center of attention for social philosophers and scientists. That innate racial characteristics are responsible for differences in behavior and belief has been the thesis of an enormous literature. The cultural divisions of mankind have been increasingly described and differentiated during the past century. Economic motivations have been especially emphasized since Karl Marx. Political ideologies have been a distinguishing classification since the rise of great states. And the spatial distribution of both material and nonmaterial culture elements has latterly proved a fruitful approach to the study of human life. Interrelations resulting from spatial positions have been explored in the literature of human ecology. We shall consider briefly the significance of position in space as this affects public opinion.

The influence of geographic factors in affecting man's beliefs, opinions and ideologies has been discussed ever since there has been an organized body of social theory. Hundreds of social theorists have dealt with such relationships. "There is scarcely any physical or psychical trait in man, any characteristic in the social organization of a group, any social process or historical event, which has not been accounted for through geographical factors by this or that partisan of this school." [1] That the thought life of man in both content and quantity has been considerably affected by either direct or indirect geographic influences is obvious. However, this

[1] P. A. Sorokin, *Contemporary Sociological Theories*, Harper & Brothers, New York, 1928, p. 100.

type of causal relationship has been carried to absurd extremes by many a geographic determinist.[2]

The influence of the natural environment has often been an important factor in the formation of beliefs and in the opinion process in changing those beliefs in the simpler primitive cultures and folk cultures. Hence, the relationship between physical environment and the content of myths, the conceptions of gods and their nature, the afterlife, the stories and folk tales, the language symbols and other items. Many figures of speech are taken from items common in the region. In the teachings of Christ the frequent references to vines, trees, sheep, the good shepherd and the like, illustrate this point. The proverbs of folk peoples also reflect their surroundings.[3] These elements have been colored by development in a given geographic area but have not been determined thereby, as is evidenced by the presence of similar elements elsewhere in the world and also by the existence of similar geographic areas in which no such culture elements have developed. The cultural anthropologists have been extremely critical of the excesses of geographic determinism; they have maintained that geographic factors are a limiting, but not a determining, factor. For example, climatic conditions may serve as a limiting factor in decreasing the quantity of mentation and the alertness of a people. The debilitating effect of the tropics on the mental life of the white man, the paucity of imaginative legendary elements in Eskimo cultures are extreme examples of such influences. However, although in the simpler cultures geographic influences place some limits upon the quantity and quality of man's thought, the possible range of the products of thought outside of these limits is almost infinite. And as one proceeds from the simpler to the more complex and mobile societies, the influence of geographic factors dwindles and other elements bulk larger.

During the past three decades the social sciences have increasingly considered spatial and territorial distribution of their phenomena. The concept "human ecology" refers to the way in which human beings and their institutions assume characteristic distribution in space. This is a significant frame of reference only in those cases where the spatial distribution assumes a meaningful pattern. Are there significant spatial distributions of opinion groups within communities, regions and areas? H. D. Lasswell states, "Attention groups, sentiment groups, crowds and publics have their geographical aspects. We may properly speak of attention areas, sentiment areas, crowd areas and public areas, and we may profitably explore their interrelationships."[4] In an extensive study of race atti-

[2] For a criticism of the most extreme examples, see *ibid.*, chaps. 3 and 7.

[3] W. Albig, "Proverbs and Social Control," *Sociol. Soc. Res.*, 15: 527–535.

[4] H. D. Lasswell, "The Measurement of Public Opinion," *Am. Pol. Sci. Rev.*, 25: 2: 316.

tudes, E. S. Bogardus noted the distribution of opinions within the community and concluded that "racial opinion occurs in high-pressure areas with low-pressure regions between. The first express either antipathy or friendliness. The antipathetic areas possess a higher emotional pressure than the friendliness-pressure areas. In between are the low-pressure or neutral districts in which high pressures are likely to be manifested at any time." [5] In this case a meaningful pattern may exist. The presence of such a pattern would have to be tested. As with other phenomena, significant relationship must be proved. In mapping opinions on race we must therefore have more than one map. Changing opinion must be shown to be associated with location, if spatial position is to be proved a significant factor. Sometimes spatial position is obviously the basic factor in determining opinions. This is the case when the immediate group is practically inescapable and is the sole source of information, as is usually true of the primitive community. In the folk society, also, the local community provides most of the data from which opinion decisions are made. The limited gossip and discussion areas of the individual are for the most part the limits of his world. As the great societies have emerged, increasingly equipped with new and more effective agencies of mass communication, the attention areas of the individual have widened. The impress of the local geographical community and of the neighborhood are of lesser importance for most opinions. Membership in interest-groups, contact with mass media of communication, and other factors may be much more important than place of residence. However, certain opinions are evidently a local product. Emile Durkheim made a distinction between physical and social density. Social density denoted the frequency of interaction and contacts between the members of populations. In the small, more intimate communities and neighborhoods of the past, social density was based on the personal contacts of primary-group association. Opinions were often formed locally. But in the modern cities of the Occident, there is characteristically great physical concentration of people with incidental contact and low social density. If opinions are found significantly distributed spatially in such cities, it is usually due to factors other than person-to-person association in the area.

The geographic distribution of communications may be readily noted. Certainly the availability of mass media to populations varies enormously between areas of a nation. The products of the press, the motion pictures, radio and television are very unevenly distributed even in the United States, the nation with maximum communications. Data on means of communication have usually been collected in terms of political rather

[5] E. S. Bogardus, *Immigration and Race Attitudes*, D. C. Heath and Company, Boston, 1928, p. 237; *The New Social Research*, J. R. Miller, Los Angeles, 1926, chap. 12.

than natural areas. For the United States, most such materials are summarized by states. The per capita distribution by states of forty-seven leading magazines, of newspaper circulation, of families owning radio sets, of library circulations and of families having telephones is presented in Table 3. The rankings of the states indicate a high correlation between items in the groups of states at the top and bottom of the list. There is a greater diversity and scattering among those in the middle of that list. Contact with the extracommunity world is least in the group of Southeastern and South Central states. Of course this is well known. These data support the generalization. A comparison of the rank of the states for various media discloses some interesting diversities. The literate but economically poor states of New Hampshire and Vermont, poorly supplied with newspapers and transportation, rank 7th and 8th in periodicals, 4th and 6th in circulation of library books, but 44th and 35th in newspaper circulation and 18th and 17th in radio ownership. Remote states, such as South Dakota, Montana, Idaho, Wyoming and Nevada, rank 4th, 2nd, 3rd, 5th and 1st in circulation of periodicals, but 37th, 30th, 43rd, 42nd and 13th in newspaper circulation. A score or more significant comparisons and contrasts may be studied from this Table 3.

However, the most enormous contrasts between areas in their communication facilities are to be found by comparison of national rates. Communications are said to have shortened physical and psychological distances, thus integrating peoples through increased understanding, but also making conflict tensions more acute. In this sense, it is today a commonplace to refer to the world as shrinking. This is all potentially true. But how limited today are the communications sources of far more than half of the world's populations! Examination of the figures in Table 4 will indicate the enormous range between those most liberally and least liberally provided with communications. It is hardly feasible to be a world citizen, engaging in democratic decision making, and be as ill-equipped with sources of information as are 2 billion of the 2½ billion of the world's population. (See Table 4.) Potentialities are not current realities.

One way in which significant spatial distribution of opinion is indicated is in the records of voting. Patterns may be noted by mapping the results of various elections. Voting records opinion at a given moment. Although often unsatisfactory for the purpose of predicting behavior, inasmuch as it forces the variety of attitudes into two opposing camps, voting does show the practical popular decision. There are hundreds of studies of voting records by states and other political units, but the most elaborate graphic portrayal of voting by states in American history is presented in the *Atlas of the Historical Geography*.[6] This monumental work is the prod-

[6] C. O. Paullin, *Atlas of the Historical Geography of the United States*, 1932.

Table 3. Distribution, by States, of Magazines, Newspapers, Library Books, Radio Sets and Telephones

State	Population, thousands 1930	Population, thousands 1950	47 leading magazines, circulation per 1,000 population 1935 Circulation[1]	1935 Rank[11]	1948 Circulation[2]	1948 Rank[11]	Newspaper circulation per 1,000 population 1932 Circulation[3]	1932 Rank	1952 Circulation[4]	1952 Rank	Circulation of library books per capita 1913 Circulation[5]	1913 Rank	1945 Circulation[6]	1945 Rank	Percentage of families owning radio sets 1930 Percentage[7]	1930 Rank[11]	1950 Percentage[8]	Percentage of families with telephones 1932 Percentage[9]	1932 Rank[11]	1950 Percentage[10]	1950 Rank[11]
New England and Middle Atlantic States																					
Maine	797	913	396	13	1,034	10	198	29	271	29	1.29	16	2.47	22	39.2	26	95	50.2	19	68	14
New Hampshire	465	533	418	9	1,090	7	140	39	206	44	2.31	5	4.43	4	44.4	18	97	53.1	15	70	12a
Vermont	359	377	429	8	1,087	8	168	31	240	35	1.68	9	4.16	6	44.6	17	96	52.1	17	67	15
Massachusetts	4,249	4,690	373	16	858	31	538	2	545	3	3.29	1	4.80	2	57.6	3	99	66.3	3	80	5a
Rhode Island	687	791	317	30	913	24	326	12	350	17	1.65	10	2.70	18	57.0	4	99	64.8	12	71	11
Connecticut	1,606	2,007	414	10	941	20	265	18	333	21	2.60	2	4.71	3	54.9	6	99	54.8	4	86	1
New York	12,588	14,830	345	23a	892	28	535	3	559	2	2.07	6	2.43	23	57.8	2	99	67.5	2	70	12b
New Jersey	4,041	4,835	315	31	883	30	196	30	244	34	1.95	7	3.06	14	63.3	1	97	53.5	14	73	9a
Pennsylvania	9,631	10,498	321	28	811	32	334	10	385	10	0.89	24	1.45	34	48.1	12	96	49.8	20	69	13
South Atlantic States																					
Delaware	238	318	346	22	1,028	11	219	26	276	28	1.22	18	2.69	19	45.8	16	95	44.3	26	72	10a
Maryland	1,631	2,343	255	35	734	36	331	11	297	26	0.65	26	2.09	28	42.9	21	96	44.4	25	65	16a
District of Columbia	486	802	626	1	928	23	957	1	1,033	1	2.39	4	3.74	9	53.9	7	97	104.6	1	85	2
Virginia	2,421	3,318	213	40	654	40	157	36	224	41	0.05	46	1.04	40	23.3	38	90	30.0	36	52	23a
West Virginia	1,729	2,005	238	37	772	33	138	40	252	33	0.147	41	0.41	49	11.2	34	92	18.6	37	47	25a
North Carolina	3,170	4,061	150	44a	559	41	105	45	229	40	0.07	45	1.63	33	7.6	43a	87	13.5	48	37	30a
South Carolina	1,738	2,117	120	48	536	43	79	48	193	45	0.04	47	1.66	32	9.9	48	83	19.5	43a	30	31a
Georgia	2,908	3,444	149	46	466	45	136	41	230	39	0.19	35	1.42	35		45	83	28.8	38	42	27
Florida	1,468	2,771	366	19	757	35	222	25	378	11	0.176	39	0.80	45	15.5	40	87			47	25b
East South Central States																					
Kentucky	2,614	2,944	174	42	521	44	141	38	231	38	0.42	32	0.70	47	18.3	37	89	26.4	40	41	28
Tennessee	2,616	3,291	184	41	541	42	239	21	292	27	0.186	37	1.08	39	14.3	41	87	27.0	39	52	23b
Alabama	2,646	3,061	132	47	426	48	116	43	184	47	0.11	43	0.85	43	9.5	46	83	14.1	47	37	30b
Mississippi	2,009	2,178	114	49	364	49	56	49	108	49	0.01	49	0.58	48	5.4	49	80	11.0	49	24	32
West South Central States																					
Arkansas	1,854	1,909	161	43	446	46	84	47	180	48	0.03	48	1.02	41	9.2	47	84	16.6	46	30	31b
Louisiana	2,101	2,683	150	44b	445	47	158	35	254	32	0.23	34	1.25	37	11.2	43b	84	22.4	42	47	25b
Oklahoma	2,396	2,223	247	36	706	38	225	24	310	24	0.13	42	1.19	38	21.6	35	90	35.6	33	58	19a
Texas	5,824	7,711	235	38	704	39	205	28	327	23	0.177	38	1.00	42	18.6	36	89	31.8	35	51	24

64

East North Central States

State	(1)	(2)	(3)	(4)	(5)	(6)	(7)	(8)	(9)	(10)	(11)	(12)	(13)	(14)	(15)	(16)	(17)	(18)	(19)	(20)	ref
Ohio	6,646	7,946	374	15	975	17	349	9	409	6	1.48	12	4.36	5	47.4	14	97	47.2	22	76	6
Indiana	3,238	3,934	343	26	1,000	14	307	13	388	9	0.98	21	4.11	7	41.6	23	97	44.0	27	73	9b
Illinois	7,630	8,712	345	23b	939	21	377	7	420	5	1.19	20	2.62	20	55.6	5	98	63.7	6	80	9c
Michigan	4,842	6,371	369	18	901	26a	263	19	354	15	1.20	19	2.73	16	50.6	10	98	41.7	28	80	5b
Wisconsin	2,939	3,434	310	32	901	26b	234	22	304	25	1.44	13	1.30	36	51.1	9	98	56.2	11	74	8a

West North Central States

State	(1)	(2)	(3)	(4)	(5)	(6)	(7)	(8)	(9)	(10)	(11)	(12)	(13)	(14)	(15)	(16)	(17)	(18)	(19)	(20)	ref
Minnesota	2,563	2,982	357	20	888	29	292	14	328	22	1.24	17	2.72	17	47.3	15	98	60.2	9	81	4
Iowa	2,470	2,621	370	17	989	15	276	15	353	16	0.94	22	3.40	13	48.6	11	97	64.3	5	82	3
Missouri	3,629	3,954	284	33	723	37	432	4	455	4	0.90	23	1.94	29	37.4	29	94	51.9	18	64	17
North Dakota	680	619	279	34	1,099	6	104	46	233	36	0.15	40	0.83	44	40.8	25	97	39.8	30	56	21a
South Dakota	692	652	320	29	1,182	4	131	42	232	37	0.188	36	2.14	27	44.2	19	96	46.2	23	70	12c
Nebraska	1,377	1,325	347	21	1,046	9	258	20	335	19	0.64	27	2.47	21	47.8	13	96	60.5	8	74	8b
Kansas	1,880	1,905	327	27	964	18	216	27	349	18	0.52	29	2.30	24	38.8	27	95	57.3	10	75	7

Mountain States

State	(1)	(2)	(3)	(4)	(5)	(6)	(7)	(8)	(9)	(10)	(11)	(12)	(13)	(14)	(15)	(16)	(17)	(18)	(19)	(20)	ref
Montana	537	591	451	7	1,395	2	163	33	262	30	1.39	14	2.19	25	32.0	31	97	32.6	34	59	18
Idaho	445	588	400	12	1,210	3	159	34	222	43	0.24	33	1.72	31	30.3	33	97	36.9	32	57	20
Wyoming	225	290	458	6	1,164	5	106	44	223	42	0.44	31	3.70	10	34.0	30	97	39.2	31	58	19b
Colorado	1,035	1,325	406	11	1,007	13	267	17	396	7	1.30	15	0.78	45	37.8	28	97	54.3	13	74	8c
New Mexico	423	681	227	39	911	25	145	37	188	46	0.09	44	1.89	30	11.5	42	91	19.5	43b	40	29
Arizona	435	749	377	14	948	19	166	32	260	31	0.45	30	3.50	11	18.1	39	94	26.3	41	45	26
Utah	507	688	344	25	758	34	226	23	334	20	0.66	25	2.15	11	41.1	24	99	44.8	24	72	10b
Nevada	91	160	492	5	1,497	1	272	16	370	13	0.57	28		26	30.6	32	96	41.0	29	55	22

Pacific States

State	(1)	(2)	(3)	(4)	(5)	(6)	(7)	(8)	(9)	(10)	(11)	(12)	(13)	(14)	(15)	(16)	(17)	(18)	(19)	(20)	ref
Washington	1,563	2,378	502	3	977	16	369	8	367	14	1.54	11	3.46	12	42.3	22	98	52.2	16	65	16b
Oregon	953	1,521	520	2	1,010	12	389	5	391	8	1.78	8	4.00	8	43.4	20	97	49.7	21	56	21b
California	5,677	10,586	497	4	935	22	382	6	375	12	2.45	3	5.02	1	51.9	8	98	60.6	7	72	10c

SOURCES:

1 Adapted from E. Allen, "Circulation Density," *Journalism Quarterly*, 12:2:122.

2 Compiled from circulation figures in *Standard Rate and Data Service*, vol. 31, no. 18, Part 1, Sept. 15, 1949.

3 Compiled from circulation figures for morning and evening papers in *Editor and Publisher*, 65:37:101, International Year Book Number, 1933.

4 Compiled from circulation figures for morning and evening papers in *Editor and Publisher*, 86:5:18, International Year Book Number, 1953.

5 Compiled from U.S. Bureau of Education, *Bulletin*, No. 25, 1915, p. 12.

6 Compiled from U.S. Office of Education, *Bulletin*, No. 12, 1947, p. 8.

7 Adapted from M. M. Willey and S. A. Rice, *Communication Agencies and Social Life*, Table 53, pp. 188-189.

8 Data taken from *Information Please Almanac*, 1951, p. 269.

9 Telephone statistics per 1,000 population taken from *Statistical Abstract of the United States*, 1948, Table No. 512, p. 478, then translated into terms of percentage of families with telephones.

10 Data taken from *Information Please Almanac*, 1951, p. 269.

11 a, b and c indicate a tie.

Table 4. Communication Facilities of the Nations

Country	(1) Estimate of total population in thousands midyear, 1952	(2) Per cent illiteracy	(3) Number of copies of daily newspapers per 1,000 inhabitants, 1952	(4) Number of receiving sets in thousands	(5) Number of receivers per thousand inhabitants	(6) Number of long- and medium-wave transmitters	(7) Number of short-wave transmitters	(8) Total number of transmitters	(9) Total power of transmitters (KW)	(10) Number of motion-picture theaters	(11) Motion-picture seats available per 1,000 inhabitants	(12) Motion-picture theater attendance, times per year, per capita	(13) Telephone conversations per capita, 1950
China	470,000	56	17	1,000	4	64	17	81	495.18	681 †	1	0.3 †	
India	367,000	80	8	667	2	16	12	28	358.85	2,060	4	0.6	66.6
United Kingdom	50,772	5	611	12,946	256	55	40	95	not given	4,595 †	84	26 †	
U.S.S.R.	207,000	19	161 †	13,000	64	70	30	100	not given	15,200 †	31 †	3	
United States	156,981	3	353	110,000	701	1,991	38	2,029	7,000 †	17,000 †	83	15 †	370.6
EUROPE													
Italy	46,865	22	107	4,261	91	30	3	33	793.54	9,502 †	82	16 †	45.4
France	42,600	3	239	7,926	186	54	6	60	1,717.18	5,385 †	64	8 †	36.7
Germany (Fed. Rep.)	48,478	5	263	10,830	223	23	4	27	998.0	4,853 †	35	12 †	42.8
Spain	28,306	23	196	605	22	39	11	50	333.6	3,583	62	11	50.2
Rumania	16,300	23	141	270	17	4	3	7	177.15	330	7	not given	
Bulgaria	7,390	31	113	225	31	4	1	5	129.0	291	14	not given	
Poland	25,230	23	258	1,747	70	13	1	14	637.5	574	10	4	
Yugoslavia	16,729	25	41	367	22	13	1	14	75.7	1,300 †	11	3 †	
Czechoslovakia	12,850	5	191	2,545	206	15	1	16	465.5	2,268	56	9	
Netherlands	10,377	5	249	1,728	167	7	6	13	333.0	512 †	26	6 †	70.7
Hungary	9,460	5	90	1,121	13	7	1	8	373.3	2,327 †	15	7 †	
Belgium	8,706	3	384	1,705	195	12	1	13	62.0	1,355 †	88	13 †	55.4
Greece	7,776	28	71	265	34	2	1	3	24.5	402	13	4	32.9
Austria	6,955	0-5 †	214	1,438	208	11	5	16	191.2	1,116 †	35	14 †	
Sweden	7,126	0	490	2,205	309	33	2	35	623.675	2,484 †	105	7	313.3
Switzerland	4,815	0-5 †	300	917	190	6	5	11	551.1	511 †	30	7 †	144.9
Denmark	4,334	0-5 †	381	1,285	296	2	1	3	140.0	453 †	32	13 †	259.6
Finland	4,091	16	269	855	209	11	4	15	351.0	525 †	34	8	131.2
Norway	3,327	0-5 †	396	819	246	22	8	30	542.5	526 †	38	10 †	156.7
Luxembourg	302	..	447	68	225	1	1	2	156.0	30	71	9	

	Col 1 (Population)	Col 2	Col 3	Col 4	Col 5	Col 6	Col 7	Col 8	Col 9	Col 10	Col 11	Col 12	Col 13
THE ORIENT													
Australia	8,649	4	416	1,504	219	138	12	150	not given	1,744†	182	16†	118.8
Japan	85,500	9	353	10,364	120	131	5	136	370.0	3,637†	15	8†	67.2
Pakistan	77,000	70†	2	80	1	4	4	8	137.8	228	1	0.4	
Turkey	21,983	39	32	412	19	4	2	6	540.0	275	9	1	4.0
Philippines	20,631		24	79	4	6	1	7	20.0	450	8†	1	8.5
Burma	18,859	60	8	11	1	1	4	5	15.7	150	10	0.6	
Federation of Malaya	5,506	62	50	72	13	8	4	12	53.9	100	18	not given	14.6
THE WESTERN HEMISPHERE													
Canada	14,430	4	248	2,314	162	140	12	152	858.0	1,808†	71	17	361.6
Brazil	54,477	52	106	781	15	211	12	223	717.6	2,411†	21	3	36.2
Mexico	26,922	54	48	1,220	46	196	18	214	1,284.0	1,726†	57	4	26.2
Argentina	18,056	14	100	1,500	90	53	10	63	200.63	1,750†	55	7	161.7
Peru	8,864	57	39	500	59	19	21	40	67.1	235	22	2†	20.0
Chile	5,932	26	76	550	96	65	13	78	340.0	300	46	5	79.7
Cuba	5,755	24	70	700	133	102	14	116	233.15	515	58	11	126.0
Venezuela	5,395	59	65	200	37	29	32	61	91.78	350	33	7	57.7
Bolivia	3,089	92†	23	150	50	26	14	40	19.39	60	8	0.3	
Haiti	3,200	90	3	4	1	2	6	8	6.6	24	1†		
Ecuador	3,399	44	49	50	16	35	33	68	30.95	177	23	2	116.5
Uruguay	2,446	15	225	362	151	45	10	55	190.91	77†	47	not given	
Dominican Republic	2,236	74	24	35	17	6	20	26	30.42	28	10†	2†	
Honduras	1,513	65	20	25	17	3	8	11	6.75	33	19	2†	11.5
Paraguay	1,464	36	12	35	25	6	4	10	18.7		9	0.7	
AFRICA													
Union of South Africa	12,912	72	57	583	46	15	7	22	79.2	470†	24	3	47.5
Egypt	21,425	78†	24	234	11	5	1	6	81.1	226	10	2	
Algeria	9,140	79†	28	235	26	11	4	15	175.85	200	14	2	
Morocco	8,052	50	23	221	25	3	3	6	64.5	138†	8	2	
Tunisia	3,600	83†	31	82	23	2	......	2	140.0	71†	8	1†	6.0

This table has been compiled for comparative purposes. It was not possible to secure data all of which had been taken at precisely the same time. Some figures are estimates. Precise variations in detail might be noted by reference to the original texts and tables. The author presents these columns only to give an over-all picture of the distribution of mass media facilities.

SOURCES:

Column 1   Population figures taken from: *Basic Facts and Figures*, UNESCO, 1954, Appendix, pp. 77 ff.

Column 2   Illiteracy figures taken from *ibid.*, Table 1, pp. 10 ff., except those marked †, obtained from Prof. Wilbert Moore of the Princeton University Office of Population Research, School of Public and International Affairs.

Column 3   Newspaper figures taken from: *The Daily Press: A Survey of the World Situation in 1952*, Clearing House, Dept. of Mass Communication, UNESCO, Table 1, pp. 4 ff., except that marked † from *World Communications*, UNESCO, May, 1950, pp. 18–19.

Columns 4 and 5   Radio information, taken from: *Basic Facts and Figures*, UNESCO, 1954, Table 17, pp. 71 ff. Figure for China taken from: *Geographic Distribution of Radio Sets and Characteristics of Radio Owners in Countries of the World*, U.S. Information Agency, Office of Research and Intelligence, Report no. IEV. B.A. 11, Sept. 1, 1954.

Columns 6, 7, 8 and 9   Information about radio transmitters taken from: *World Communications*, UNESCO, May, 1950, pp. 174–193. † This United States figure given in same source, p. 60, as approximate and is for domestic, medium-wave only.

Columns 10 and 12   Motion-picture data, taken from *World Communications*, UNESCO, May, 1950, pp. 37–137, except those marked †, from: *Basic Facts and Figures*, UNESCO, 1954, Table 16, pp. 68–69. United States figure excludes 4,501 drive-in theaters.

Column 11   *World's Motion Picture Theaters Show Marked Increase since 1947*,'' *Foreign Commerce Weekly*, June 6, 1949.
Young, ''World's Motion Picture Theaters Show Marked Increase since 1947,'' *Foreign Commerce Weekly*, June 6, 1949.

Column 13   Telephone figures given in N. D. Golden and E. H. ''Telephone Statistics of the World,'' American Telephone and Telegraph Company pamphlet, Jan. 1, 1951, p. 8.

uct of two decades of effort by a research staff. Selected and adapted maps from this source dealing with two major issues are given in Fig. 3. The political results of social reform conducted over many years are portrayed.

The boundaries of an area or a region are determined by the phenomena under consideration. If the data can be shown to be distributed in a number of significant geographic patterns, then we have regions. We have seen that such regions exist with regard to those stimuli which influence opinion, the newspapers, radio and other means of communication. What evidence is there of the existence of opinion regions? Such regional mapping is limited by the relatively few items of opinion that have been formally recorded by areas. Obviously the principal sources of data, therefore, must be voting records. Many years ago, S. A. Rice attempted to delimit some such regions.[7] Unfortunately the political scientists have been very slow in checking his conclusions or furthering this work. They have lagged in the application of experimental and quantitative techniques even in cases such as this where these methods were indicated. Rice instituted a remarkable series of studies. Certain changes in economic situation and in attitudes were correlated. Both the diffusion and social density of political attitudes, as indicated by votes for candidates, were traced in studies of voting in Wisconsin, Michigan and Philadelphia. The patterning of votes within states was tested. In Minnesota, "concentrations of the radical and conservative vote along geographical lines, with their correlated areas of crop specialization were noted." [8] In North Dakota the conservative eastern counties differed markedly from the radical western counties. Rural prosperity was greatest in the eastern part of the state. Regional groupings within the state associated with crop-producing areas appeared evident. In the Brookhart (Radical) and Cummins (Conservative) campaign in Iowa in 1920, cleavages of a regional nature rather than primarily on occupational or class lines appeared. In those counties in which the average farm values were highest, the largest vote for Cummins occurred. Similar evidence was collected from regions in Nebraska. If this is a true regional, rather than political, unit phenomenon, the similarities of vote should cross state lines. And Rice finds evidence to support this thesis. The Missouri River valley contains counties in Iowa, Nebraska and South Dakota. The Red River valley is in Minnesota and North Dakota. In each case there is a homogeneous geographical and economic area. Testing the hypothesis that the votes should show this economic uniformity, Rice concludes, "The hypothesis of culture areas of political attitudes has strong a priori support, and is consistent with the

[7] S. A. Rice, *Quantitative Methods in Politics,* Alfred A. Knopf, Inc., New York, 1928, especially chaps. 10 and 11.

[8] *Ibid.,* p. 126.

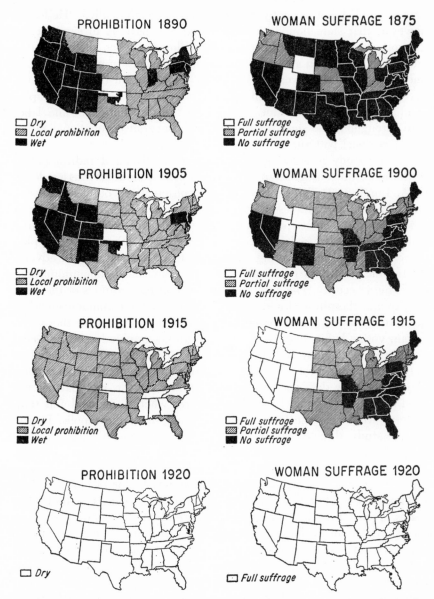

FIG. 3. The political results of two social reforms. (From C. O. Paullin, *Atlas of the Historical Geography of the United States*. Reproduced by permission of Carnegie Institution of Washington and the American Geographical Society of New York.)

data assembled, but has not yet been established empirically." [9] He found, however, that state boundaries interposed real barriers to similarity of the vote. These boundaries became less influential when shopping areas crossed state lines. In another study he finds changes in political opinion unevenly distributed over the state of Washington. In this case the underlying factors were economic conditions based, not upon geographic conditions (upon land value), but upon the distribution of the labor vote throughout the state. In this case we have an occupational rather than a regional pattern.

Another study attempting to relate conservative and radical voting to the more obvious geographic and economic conditions was made by G. A. Lundberg.[10] Ten radical and ten conservative voting counties in North Dakota and Minnesota were compared as to composition of population, improved acres per farm, average value of property per farm, value of crops, assessed valuation, mortgages and other economic phenomena. Radicalism in voting was found to be associated with adverse geographic conditions (western Dakota), undeveloped communities and economic insecurity. The author concludes that the attitudes of the community and the physical and social character of the community tend to be mutually selective and formative. These studies support the thesis that certain voting habits may be identified with geographic factors and economic regions. It may well be so. Of the numerous polls conducted in the United States, probably a thousand or more reported results contain regional or state data on the topics polled. As yet this material has not been analyzed. It would be well to discover whether regional and state patterns would emerge from a complex analysis of these polls. In one notable study, directed and reported by Samuel Stouffer, large regional differences, small town, rural and urban differences, were found in the tolerating of nonconformity on political beliefs and expressions and in the defense of civil liberties.[11] However, the distribution of most opinions will not be found to follow the patterns of economic regions of the United States, even when there is a spatial distribution. Economic class consciousness has not achieved so definite a distribution. On most public issues, the symbols and other stimuli in the formation of opinion are largely common to various economic classes. Business-class symbols are used by the industrial worker, and the symbols of rural aims and objectives may be mouthed by the farmer with a thousand fertile acres as well as by the scrabbling hillbilly.

[9] *Ibid.*

[10] G. A. Lundberg, "The Demographic and Economic Basis of Political Radicalism and Conservatism," *Am. Jour. Sociol.*, 32: 719–732.

[11] S. A. Stouffer, *Communism, Conformity, and Civil Liberties,* Doubleday & Company, Inc., New York, 1955, chap. 5.

In dealing with the record of past popular opinions, the mapping of opinion is of even more importance than for contemporary mass opinions. Owing to the limited means of communication, there was then a greater tendency for opinion to diffuse in concentric circles.[12] As has often been noted, the popular mass communication of the present century is destroying the neat patterns of diffusion of ideas and opinions that largely prevailed when opinion was based on face-to-face discussion.

The study of the spatial distribution of opinion in contemporary large publics is by no means futile. There often is a pattern. But probably more often this is not the significant frame of reference. In the United States there is greater diversity of beliefs and opinions than of the elements of material culture. There is an increasingly pervasive uniformity in most material things. Opinions and beliefs have been more resistant to regimentation. The local and regional cultural elements are inculcated in the family and primary group. But gradually in many fields locality and regional groups are superseded by interest-groups in providing stimuli for individual opinions.

[12] In his *Environment and Nation*, University of Chicago Press, Chicago, 1936, Griffith Taylor has published several hundred maps, many of which would illustrate this point. For example, there are those dealing with the spread of Christianity, language diffusion, the Renaissance, the spread of universities and architecture.

PART TWO

Psychological Processes

CHAPTER 5

Psychological Processes and Opinion

A great deal of the newer learning in the social sciences, especially of psychological knowledge as interpreted to large student groups, has tended to remove much of the dignity and significance of human life. The better social scientists have the dignity of the quest for knowledge. But the expositors and teachers of their findings, in providing popular guides to knowledge, have interpreted in such a way as constantly to lessen man's significance. The intellectual has revolted wildly from nine-teenth-century rationalism. Depreciation of our physical world in terms of a widening universe, the contrasting of nineteenth-century rationalism with man's persistent irrationality, the elevation of the instinctive life, the lauding of physical force and a flight from reason, and the purveying of a pseudoscientific psychological and psychoanalytic jargon are char-acteristic of our time. At the beginning of this century, psychological real-ity demanded the combating of the nineteenth-century intellectualistic assumption that human behavior resulted from a logical intellectual process. This clearing away of an intellectual myth was accomplished with a vigor that, by the third decade of the century, had become a questionably spirited attack and, apparently, in some cases evidenced an irresponsible intellectual abandon. The content of our discussion must inevitably emphasize many forms of irrational thinking. However, we should not gather the impression that all popular opinion is based upon illogical thinking.

The common man as a member of large publics may often be motivated by irrational impulses; he may respond to slogans and symbols; on public occasions he often experiences emotional "thrill" to his own betrayal; he persistently follows the personal leader while losing sight of the issue. As a member of a large public or group he may often be silly and absurd, but sometimes he desires not to be. To be sure, in the twentieth century, as in the nineteenth, the vast majority of men are unable or unwilling to be systematically rational in reflecting on the variety of public issues. But there is an enormous difference between recognition of the pervasive-ness of the irrational and the glorification of unreason, idealization of

73

emotions and enthusiasm for the unconscious. Intellectuals have usually been disillusioned and disgruntled by their interpretations of the mental processes of man in the mass. Since about 1920 there have been numerous trends of augmented disillusion.

Amidst these hectic times, for masses of harried mankind, a rational humanism apparently provides neither an adequate faith, a believable program nor an exciting vision. Those contemporary social scientists who have developed in the liberal tradition are now sadly and wearily defensive. They cannot be optimistically assured in the quest for the minds of men in competition with the dogmatic particularists of popularized communism or of impossible conservatism. The liberal is baffled by the pervasive emotional crusades. And so the kindly humanist, the man of good will, the tolerant liberal and the rational moderate is currently outmoded, outfought and outshouted.

Although generalizations about the processes of thought may be abstracted in psychological theory, thinking about thinking is usually most fruitful when the thought processes and the subject matter of thought are considered concomitantly. Much of the psychological process may not be generalized into universal verities. The materials of a particular culture determine the content of the mind and also, to some extent, the ways of the mind. The cultural anthropologist and the sociologist are peculiarly aware of this fact. The psychologist, in his preoccupation with the organism, has often been neglectful of the ways in which it is conditioned by culture. As yet there is no highly developed science of comparative psychology. Yet psychological study in divergent cultures has given insights on some relations between culture content and psychological processes. This has been most dramatically indicated in the ill-developed field of the psychology of primitive peoples.[1]

Perception is determined in part by what is to be perceived. There are characteristic directions of attention: an Apache of the original culture and a contemporary Chicago Y.M.C.A. dweller would attend to quite different elements in an Arizona landscape. Social factors modify the processes of memory as well as the materials remembered. This may be illustrated by primitive practices in remembering numbers, as compared with the memory practices of one equipped with the Arabic numeral system; by the memory of design as illustrated by interpretation of design sketches;[2] by the voluminous experimental psychology of memory in witnesses; and in many other fields. Ways of thinking have latterly been

[1] See M. Sherif, *The Psychology of Social Norms,* Harper & Brothers, New York, 1936; F. C. Bartlett, *Remembering,* The Macmillan Company, New York, 1933.

[2] A contemporary London dweller interprets a sketch of a hand pointing upward as an antiaircraft gun; Bartlett, *op. cit.,* p. 244.

ascribed somewhat more to cultural influences. For example, it has long been noted that primitive peoples usually think in terms of objects, situations and specific events rather than in terms of abstractions. The ability to recognize uniformities among apparent diversities is more characteristic of some groups of modern man. This difference was once ascribed to differences in quality of mentality. But in those areas of thought where abstract thinking prevails, modern man is guided, not only by the tradition of abstract thinking, but also by the accumulated abstractions of past generations. It now appears that the direction of attention and various aspects of the cultural life are primarily involved in determining thought processes.[3]

The ways in which individuals perceive, remember and think are determined in part by characteristics common to organisms, in part by individual differences and in part by cultural factors. Among the cultural factors are the traditional elements acquired in folk and group experience and those acquired from the professional thinker. Both types are involved in popular opinion. Let us illustrate. Thinking in American publics is in part conditioned by the background of American folk experience, as in the relation between man and nature in the conquest of the continent. Many of our dominant attitudes were developed in relation to this struggle. The pioneer, struggling with an adverse physical environment, must devote himself to the solution of his problems of adjustment to that environment. He cannot preoccupy himself with psychological nuances, introspective analyses, aesthetic values and the like. The frontiersman was not intellectual, not glibly skeptical, not a controversialist on aesthetic values. Characteristically, he was not flexible, he did not adjust well with human beings. In America today, as human action deals more with human beings and less with physical environment, we are undergoing a necessary modification of cultural values and individual attitudes. The individual's capacity for flexible adjustment has been increased.

If the differences between cultures condition the individual members and modify ways of thinking, class and group differences may partially isolate their members from one another. If the class or group has developed an ideology, its members may be partly insulated from representatives of other classes, not only by their interests, but also by their ways of thinking. Communication is made difficult. Their divergent use of words and other symbols, differences in emotional conditionings and the like make impossible the creation of a common opinion. They may

[3] Cf. W. I. Thomas, *Primitive Behavior,* McGraw-Hill Book Company, Inc., New York, 1937, pp. 772 ff.; and O. Klineberg, *Race Differences,* Harper & Brothers, New York, 1935; with L. Lévy-Bruhl, *Primitive Mentality,* The Macmillan Company, New York, 1923.

differ, not only in the use of symbols and in information and knowledge, but also, and more fundamentally, in ways of thinking.

We shall consider certain processes characteristic of the development of opinion in the larger groups and publics. The development of symbols, stereotyping, personification, the relations between emotions and opinions, rationalization, conditioning and memory, in the members of large publics, are the more important psychological processes relating to opinion formation in such groups. In a sense, it is much easier to isolate the principal psychological processes common to individuals as members of groups than it is to organize the more varied and diverse psychological processes of an individual in his total experience. Social psychology is making rapid strides in collecting data and generalizing.

SYMBOLS AND COLLECTIVE REPRESENTATIONS

To arrange the variety and complexity of human experience in intelligible terms, capable of classification and remembrance, the mind must create symbols. These symbols are a simplification and a concretion of a complex and sometimes abstract reality. Professor Whitehead has defined symbolism as follows: "The human mind is functioning symbolically when some components of its experience elicit consciousness, belief, emotions, and usages, respecting other components of its experience." [4] Language, figures, images and other concretions provide classificatory systems of referential symbols. Thinking in symbols is an inevitable basis for thought in common. When groups of phenomena are thus simplified into the symbol, we have artificially eliminated the variations in the world of experience. It is then possible to communicate readily as between individuals.

"Political symbols are representations of collective—that is, social—values which arouse common emotions. The abstract notion of freedom cannot be seen, heard, tasted, smelled or touched; it can only be simplified or typified in, say, an open trial before a court of law, the mace of the British House of Commons, or the legendary figure of Wilhelm Tell in the Swiss myth." [5] Such symbols arouse common emotions.

However, communication between individuals and between groups requires the common use of symbols on which there is mutually agreed meaning. Sigmund Freud said, "The polar bear and the tiger cannot fight." And so the Communist doctrinaire and the businessman free-

[4] A. N. Whitehead, *Symbolism*, The Macmillan Company, New York, 1927, p. 7.

[5] K. Lowenstein, "The Influence of Symbols on Politics," in R. V. Peel and J. Roucek (eds.), *Introduction to Politics*, Thomas Y. Crowell Company, New York, 1941, p. 66. Lowenstein has provided a historical sketch of symbols in politics in antiquity, the Middle Ages, the Renaissance, the Reformation and the French Revolution. He provides scores of illustrations of visual and sound symbols.

enterpriser often have great difficulty in communication, since many words and meanings are so differently used in their diverse ideologies.

There are major culture symbols, the symbols common to groups and associations within the culture and the person's individual symbols. The major culture symbols provide verbal or other labels for some complex of basic beliefs and sentiments. The thought and communication of a person may be culture-bound by his time and by culturally supplied ideas, so that these major symbols appear to him as inevitable categories of the human mind. Hence, the person does not view them in comparison to alternatives, but as universals. Most of the time he cannot criticize them, cannot get outside of the culturally determined patterns. These major symbol complexes have been labeled the "collective representations" by E. Durkheim, the "ruling myth" by Georges Sorel, the "dominant ideas" by Karl Marx, the basic "ideologies" by Karl Mannheim. These general popular ideas are partially represented by phrases, objects, persons and other symbols.

These symbols are venerated and emotionally defended. Flags, historic spots, shrines, phrases, songs, persons and other symbols must be generally respected or their prestige is lowered. Major cultural symbols, such as those of a religion or nation, may be purposely depreciated or defiled, as in the sacrilege of the Black Mass, the defilement of the flag or other national emblems. However, more often, significant symbols are cheapened by overuse or commercial exploitation. The cross is such a venerated symbol. Yet, recently, fashion has decreed the wearing by young women of "streamlined crosses." Crosses as religious symbols and crosses as simple designs for the adornment of young women have quite a different functional significance.

A British broadcaster, speaking to the people of nations conquered by the Nazis, employed a striking symbol, the opening four notes of Beethoven's Fifth Symphony, which in International Morse give V. To people who lived in darkness it meant hope, victory, liberation, restoration: many of them died for it. But presently news-reels were showing us baseball players making the V for Victory sign and candidates for the common council with upraised fingers on election day. . . . The fashion spread to 52nd Street, which engraved the symbol on cocktail glasses, and to Broadway, which set it in rhinestones over the navels of chorus girls. Whatever it meant to men and women in the Warsaw ghetto who risked death to listen for it at midnight, it signified nothing much in New York night clubs.[6]

Groups, associations, clubs, interest-groups, fraternal orders and play-groups have their significant symbols. In these groups, fashion change in symbols is characteristically, though not always, more rapid than among

[6] B. DeVoto, *The Literary Fallacy*, Little, Brown & Company, Boston, 1944, p. 7.

the general culture symbols. Also, the primary associations of family, peer-groups, the person-to-person associations of friendship, amatory relations and other intimate associations develop symbols uniquely cherished by the participants. A word, a phrase of music, an incident, a place, may be a symbol of shared intimacy.

Not all symbols are common to groups. All individuals develop some individually unique symbols. The psychoanalysts have constantly reiterated the importance of an understanding of the symbolic tendency of the mind. However, the problems of individual symbolism do not concern us in this discussion. We are concentrated on the symbols common to groups and cultures.

The stereotypes, personifications and other concretions of abstractions and of groups which we shall discuss are the symbols widely used in the popular opinion process. Key words, phrases, slogans, songs, images, pictures, statues, flags, become symbols common to large publics. All groups create and maintain a number of such symbols. In large groups, images are even more effective than words. "It is no doubt possible completely to supplant images as vehicles of thought by words or other conventional signs. Yet, when the major burden of significance is carried by symbols other than images, the latter usually arise in the process. In most minds significant imagery is never wholly absent."[7] The member of a large public or group usually understands but little of the theoretic and conceptual position of that group in social organization and process, but he can readily be conditioned to respond to its significant symbols. The symbolic objectification of abstractions in church and state are obvious. It is precisely at the points of greatest complexity and abstraction that the simplest and most concrete symbols are provided for popular consumption. These symbols provide a system of reference and condense the diffuse and complex. Since these symbols so neatly and simply organize the thinking of those who use them, it is inevitable that they should be emotionally defended. And such is usually the case. As Clemenceau wrote, "Nothing is so contagious as a symbol, and, moreover, no one ever adopts one without attaching to it something of the virtue of a talisman."[8] The symbols are related to favorable and unfavorable attitudes, and the manipulation of the symbols often evokes powerful emotional responses in large publics.

In the complex cultures there is a great difference in the quantity of symbols popularly used in various periods. "The slightest survey of different epochs of civilization discloses great differences in their attitude

[7] R. M. Eaton, *Symbolism and Truth*, Harvard University Press, Cambridge, Mass., 1925, p. 11.

[8] G. Clemenceau, *In the Evening of My Thought*, Houghton Mifflin Company, Boston, 1929, p. 321.

toward symbolism. For example, during the mediaeval period in Europe symbolism seemed to dominate men's imaginations. Architecture was symbolical, ceremony was symbolical, heraldry was symbolical. With the Reformation a reaction set in. Men tried to dispense with symbols as fond things vainly invented, and concentrated on their direct apprehension of the ultimate facts." [9] In the democratic and Protestant nations of the West, there has undoubtedly been a decrease in the number of popular symbols in religion and government during the past century. Symbols of respect for rank, ceremonials and the like have been simplified. The relation between the use of symbols and authoritarian control is clearly illustrated by the wealth of symbolism created by the Fascist, Nazi and Communist states.

We may note certain other relationships between the amount of symbolism and other aspects of the social process. (1) Symbolism flourishes in periods of well-integrated society, with an agreed underlying ideology.[10] (2) When the culture is complex, transitional and characterized by diverse definitions of the situation by various groups, symbolism develops in these groups, but the bulk of the symbols is not popularly diffused. (3) The development of symbolism, like other aspects of culture, arrives at a point where it proliferates and spreads over various human institutions.

There is a vast amount of conscious organization and manipulation of symbols in Western culture today. There is little of the veneration of persistent symbols, such as existed in the Middle Ages, but there is a vast to-do about conditioning the members of large publics to respond to symbols of various groups. Nazi political leaders consciously propagated a wealth of symbolism. We think at once of the swastika, the salute, forms of address, the flags, the seals, anthems, uniforms and the like. In Russia, and to a great extent in countries subject to it, people smoke cigarettes, but no cigars, wear caps and not hats. Neckties are under suspicion; Stalin never wore one of these symbols of the bourgeoisie. Other types of consciously propagated modern symbolism are to be found in advertising: its slogans, trade-marks, and pictorial symbols of various kinds; in consciously developed legends about living persons; in the conscious and organized manipulation of symbols by the leaders of clubs, lodges, luncheon clubs and a host of other groups. Leadership also cultivates the manipulation of a variety of pictorial symbols in the cartoon and poster and in motion pictures. With a wider knowledge of mass psy-

[9] Whitehead, *op. cit.*, p. 1. By permission of The Macmillan Company, publishers.
[10] On symbolism in medieval thought, see H. F. Dunbar, *Symbolism in Mediaeval Thought*, Yale University Press, New Haven, Conn., 1929; P. Sorokin, *Social and Cultural Dynamics*, American Book Company, New York, 1937, vol. 1, pp. 343 ff., 614 ff.; H. Silberer, *Problems of Mysticism and Its Symbolism*, Moffat, Yard and Company, New York, 1917.

chology, with new media of communication and with the size of publics increasing, modern leadership has become more conscious of the processes of symbol manipulation and better organized to create and distribute these symbols. Though modern leadership is so prolific in creating symbols and so active in promulgating them, most men in large publics develop no such allegiance to these transient symbols as did the crusader with his cross. The very plethora of modern symbols diffuses attention. A folk people evolve as many symbols as they need. A modern propagandist may become too enamored of his own handiwork. He may create too many symbols.

STEREOTYPES

There is a persistent tendency of the human mind to provide concrete illustrations of abstractions and to confer a greater reality than is warranted upon its own conceptions and perceptions. Although present in many types of thinking, it is especially characteristic of popular thought, that is, of the subject matter of thinking characteristic of individuals as members of large publics. This tendency has sometimes been called "reification." [11] Instances of reification common to the members of large publics often become so psychologically "real" as to be developed into rigid preconceptions or patterns of perception. Woodard has indicated four types of reification. (1) The conceptual is taken as the perceptual. "Examples of it are the reality and power given to names by primitive peoples and young children; conceptual realism in science; philosophic idealism; the failure to remember the fictional character of methodological fictions in science and philosophy." [12] (2) The relational is taken as if it had an existence. This may be illustrated by the conceptions of mana among primitives; by children's conceptions of relationships as absolutes; by the adult's acceptance of ethical statements of good and evil as absolutes, rather than as relative to cultural needs and situations. [13] (3) The quite nonexistent is given existence. "The hallucinations, emotionalized projections, and delusions of insanity, with relation to which the individual lacks insight"; [14] the personification of gods and demons; the per-

[11] From Plato onward this tendency has been known to philosophers. It has been given sociological orientation in J. W. Woodard, *Reification and Supernaturalism as Factors in Social Rigidity and Social Change*, The Sociological Press, Hanover, N.H., 1935.

[12] *Ibid.*, p. 9.

[13] *Ibid.*, p. 10. This tendency to make codes of morals rigid has caused many responses that are functionally destructive. Prof. G. Boas, *Our New Ways of Thinking*, Harper & Brothers, New York, 1930, p. 31, has written, "The only reason why the race has survived morality is, I imagine, that few have done more than attempt to make others practice it."

[14] *Ibid.*, p. 10.

sonification of abstractions and the like are illustrations of this tendency. (4) The subjective is taken as the objective. What is subjectively very real may be taken as if it were objectively real. Primitive magic is a case in point. Popular legends about living persons cause large publics to respond in this way. Although the individual develops his own reifications, we are here concerned with those which he acquires in the principal groups of his culture. Thus, in public opinion, the symbols of the flag, cross, altar, elephant and donkey, the projecting of corporations as personalities and hundreds of other concretions reify the fundamental institutions.

Another fundamental tendency of the thinking of the members of large publics is "simplification." Perhaps this is too common and well known to require illustration. On public issues the "pictures in our heads" are simplifications of reality. Indeed, it could not be otherwise. "For the attempt to see all things freshly and in detail, rather than as types and generalities, is exhausting, and among busy affairs practically out of the question." [15] Moreover, as the attention areas of modern man widen, he acquires more and more of these simplifications. These are the psychological basis of popular action. They may diverge very far from objective reality. In a society where the facts of interaction are comparatively uncomplicated, these simplifications may be essentially accurate. When the facts of human society were simple, it was possible to simplify them still further without disastrous consequences. Proverbs, simple images and folk wisdom were adequate guides to behavior. But in a society of increasing complexity in fundamental social relations, the gap between simple popular conceptions and objective reality widens. Yet the demand for simplicity persists as publics increase in size and the items attended to multiply. Large publics cherish the simple definition, the summarized conception, the simple melodrama of human relations, a phrase, a personified conception and the like.

The popular stereotype is based upon these two basic psychological tendencies to reification and simplification. "Stereotypes" are preconceptions acquired from the culture; those reifications and simplifications which are current in large groups.[16] This conception of classificatory thinking, though variously labeled, has been used since the beginnings of philosophical abstraction. Such thinking is an obvious mental necessity. As R. H. Thouless states, "The most finely developed mind reaches at some point the limit of complexity it can grasp. With the majority of men

---

[15] W. Lippmann, *Public Opinion*, The Macmillan Company, New York, 1922, p. 88.
[16] The term "stereotype" was brought into use among American writers by Walter Lippmann in his *Public Opinion*. This concept had long been common to philosophical thought. The English sometimes write of "tabloid thinking" (see R. H. Thouless, *Straight and Crooked Thinking*, Simon and Schuster, Inc., New York, 1932, chap. 7).

this limit is reached rather early. Long before it is reached a certain mental idleness steps in, making us tend to accept mental food well below the limits of our digestion." Among the increasing complexity and variety of symbols used by large modern publics there are the core symbols used in reference to groups, classes, the varied environments, the personality types, the nation and culture types, and the major social classifications when these are the subject of discussion on matters of opinion. These core symbols are the stereotypes. For example, Richard LaPiere states of personality stereotyping, "It is in an effort to avoid the time and errors involved in the working out of adjustments to strangers on the basis of trial and error that we stereotype them. This consists of putting a person into a simple personality type and treating him in terms of known type attributes, rather than attempting to treat him in terms of his actual, but unknown, personality." [17]

If the individual's reifications and simplifications often diverge widely from objective reality, those stereotypes which are bandied about in large publics may be even more erroneous. If sense perceptions are often so little determined by objective fact (as has been established by an extensive experimental psychological literature), the stereotypes acquired from the cultural definitions are often even greater distortions of objective reality. And, obviously, conscious distortion and manipulation of these channels are widely practiced today. Publicity, propaganda, advertising and all kinds of special pleading are sometimes avowed, often concealed.

The stereotypes are conventional labels. These labels consist of words, phrases and language forms, of images and pictorial symbols. They are acquired from the language itself and from all means of communication. As Lippmann has stated, "For the most part we do not first see, and then define, we define first and then see. . . . We are told about the world before we see it. We imagine most things before we experience them. And these preconceptions, unless education has made us acutely aware, govern deeply the whole process of perception." [18] But true statements about complicated issues, about groups of people or races or nationalities or about organizations and social classes cannot be summed up in a few words or a simple picture. The theory of relativity popularly expressed as "everything is relative"; the complicated ideology of evolution appearing as "the monkey theory"; and either verbal or pictorial stereotypes about capitalists, Nazis, Communists, Jews, labor, nationalities, the clergy and the gangster, distort the objective reality as it is preconceived in the mind. The stereotypes also motivate behavior toward the proponents of these

[17] R. T. LaPiere and P. Farnsworth, *Social Psychology*, McGraw-Hill Book Company, Inc., New York, 1949, p. 204.

[18] Lippmann, *op. cit.*, pp. 81, 90. By permission of The Macmillan Company, publishers.

theories and toward groups and classes. Stereotypes may be counterfeits of reality, but they are psychological realities.

A place may have a stereotyped label or a series of such labels, as in the phrases commonly used to refer to the continents, the regions, or to the great urban centers of the world, on down to Crystal City, Texas, which, as the "world's spinach capital," has erected a statue to Popeye. Even an imaginary place may be an important stereotype in popular thought, as Shangri-la labels a remote, alien, spiritual, healing place. And groups of people are characteristically stereotyped in popular thought. In H. L. Mencken's *Notes on Democracy,* he develops a picture of democratic man as "boob." It is a dismaying picture of a mindless, unintelligent, emotional nitwit; but in the 1920's Mencken's "boob" was a stereotype in intellectual circles. The popular referrent to the common man as Joe Doakes has implicit this denigrating evaluation, as John Doe or John Q. Public does not.

The stereotype may be no single label but rather a complex of label characterizations. In investigating the way members of any given nation perceive the members of another, a UNESCO study [19] asked the following question of a sample of eight nationalities: "From the list of words on this card, which seems to you to describe the American people best? Select as many as you wish and call off the letters and the words that go with them. If you have no particular feelings one way or the other, just say so." The words listed were Hardworking, Intelligent, Practical, Conceited, Generous, Cruel, Backward, Brave, Self-controlled, Domineering, Progressive, Peace-loving, Impossible to characterize. The procedure was repeated, replacing one by one the reference to the people of the United States with the Russian people, and then of six other nationalities. The results are reported in Table 5.

Of course, stereotyping is psychologically inevitable in thinking and in memory. The stereotypes provide the symbols of discourse. They are the postulates of popular discussion. And "the popular controversialist has indeed a serious complaint against those who do not accept the tabloids of thought ordinarily current, because these are the agreed postulates for popular discussion." [20] They provide consistent practical attitudes motivating action toward ideas, objects and people. Especially in times of popular emotional excitement, anyone who blurs the stereotypes is

[19] W. Buchanan and H. Cantril, *How Nations See Each Other,* University of Illinois Press, Urbana, Ill., 1953, pp. 46–47. The authors recognize the methodological limitations of this study, such as the procedure forcing the description of a people in a few words, and those a limited number of words selected by the investigators. For a study of stereotyping in TV programs, see D. Smythe, *Three Years of New York Television,* National Association of Educational Broadcasters, University of Illinois Press, Urbana, Ill., 1953, chaps. 8, 9, 10.

[20] Thouless, *op. cit.,* p. 131.

Table 5. How Nations See Each Other: National Stereotypes

Percentage of respondents in each country selecting each adjective

Country in which survey was made	Australia			Britain					Germany					United States			
People described	U.S.	Russ.	Self	U.S.	Russ.	Self	Fr.	China	U.S.	Russ.	Self	Brit.	Fr.	China	Russ.	Brit.	Self
Adjective																	
Hardworking	33	52	43	32	53	57	24	40	19	12	90	13	4	18	49	43	68
Intelligent	46	16	53	38	12	52	32	17	34	4	64	34	22	6	12	49	72
Practical	49	19	49	38	21	47	20	11	45	8	53	20	5	3	13	32	53
Conceited	42	14	17	52	13	11	29	2	15	3	15	23	20	.	28	38	22
Generous	40	4	63	52	3	48	14	7	46	2	11	14	5	1	3	13	76
Cruel	2	37	.	3	39	1	5	18	2	48	1	3	10	6	50	3	2
Backward	3	28	9	4	36	6	9	37	1	41	2	3	10	12	40	11	2
Brave	21	26	57	19	31	59	14	21	6	11	63	8	7	6	28	43	66
Self-controlled	18	15	26	10	9	44	3	15	11	3	12	24	5	5	14	35	37
Domineering	23	57	4	37	42	6	11	2	10	12	10	21	12	1	49	33	9
Progressive	77	25	39	58	21	31	14	8	58	2	39	17	7	1	15	25	70
Peace-loving	*42	7	71	39	6	77	21	22	23	5	37	15	12	5	7	42	82
Impossible to characterize	*	*	*	8	18	5	30	32	17	34	5	34	49	71	17	15	3
Average no. of																	
Positive Adj.	3.3	1.6	4.0	3.0	1.6	4.1	1.4	1.4	2.4	.5	3.7	1.4	.6	.4	1.4	2.8	5.2
Negative Adj.	.7	1.3	.3	0.0	1.3	.2	.5	.6	.3	1.0	.3	.5	.5	.2	1.7	.9	.4

Country in which survey was made	France			Italy			Netherlands						Norway		
People described	U.S.	Russ.	Self	U.S.	Russ.	Self	U.S.	Russ.	Self	Brit.	Fr.	China	U.S.	Russ.	Self
Adjective															
Hardworking	37	51	46	39	22	67	49	36	62	23	6	12	56	36	43
Intelligent	37	15	79	34	13	80	33	8	49	22	8	7	31	6	32
Practical	81	11	17	59	5	24	61	6	36	24	5	3	54	9	22
Conceited	24	14	30	22	12	24	15	10	14	24	10	2	11	7	19
Generous	34	7	62	60	5	41	40	3	23	7	16	2	39	5	31
Cruel	4	41	:	3	55	3	2	53	:	3	2	12	1	19	1
Backward	2	56	4	2	58	7	1	43	1	2	8	20	1	25	7
Brave	26	42	56	18	22	45	25	21	37	20	20	9	16	20	42
Self-controlled	34	9	12	16	4	5	16	3	36	34	3	9	15	5	21
Domineering	46	49	4	11	45	8	16	50	5	21	5	2	10	51	3
Progressive	75	19	34	32	13	17	57	15	43	17	10	4	42	7	27
Peace-loving	26	10	69	29	6	27	40	6	68	26	15	9	35	7	69
Impossible to characterize	4	12	3	9	20	7	10	13	8	22	46	54	13	31	8
Average no. of															
Positive Adj.	3.5	1.6	3.7	2.9	.9	3.1	3.2	1.0	3.6	1.7	.8	.5	2.9	.9	2.9
Negative Adj.	.8	1.6	.4	.4	1.7	.4	.3	1.6	.2	.5	.3	.4	.2	.8	.3

* Not tabulated.

source: W. Buchanan and H. Cantril, *How Nations See Each Other*, University of Illinois Press, Urbana, Ill., 1953, pp. 46–47. Prepared under the auspices of UNESCO.

suspect. The enemy must be simply defined; and the stereotypes of the cause, party, class or group may be emotionally defended. It is difficult to grasp even the essentials of a complex situation, and members of large publics have not the psychological equipment with which to do so. In addition, there is widespread lack of the mental vigor and activity required to deal with a multifarious reality. Further, these simplifications may be easily remembered and transmitted. The individual acquires thousands of stereotypes from many sources in his culture. Some of these constantly motivate, others are definitions infrequently called upon. If he discards one set of stereotypes, he acquires another.

PERSONIFICATION

There may be some innate basis for sociability, association and psychological preoccupation with persons. Whether this is true or not, it is obvious that the individual experiences people from the earliest days of life. That the human mind, therefore, should come to think persistently in personal terms, whenever it is not trained to think abstractly, is not surprising. Very early in life we evidence this personification in thought. The common experience of "imaginary conversation" in the psychological process of early childhood indicates the need to think in dialogue.[21] This early tendency of thought is later modified by the acquiring of other ways of thinking, but a large residue of personifications exists in every human mind. Of course, "people differ much in the vividness of their imaginative sociability. The more simple, concrete, dramatic, their habit of mind is, the more their thinking is carried on in terms of actual conversation with a visible and audible interlocutor." [22] The common man of large publics, either lacking in adequate data on which to form opinions or intellectually incapable of doing so, nonetheless develops opinions on these issues. These opinions are often based upon his personifications of the issues, his assumption of the personal symbols. It is precisely on some of the most complex issues of human association, issues puzzling to the abstract thinker of every age, that the common man provides the greatest wealth of personifications. These he dogmatically and stubbornly defends.

As large publics have successively turned their attention to a consideration of religious, political and economic phenomena, simplifications and personifications have proliferated in those fields. Personifications of the supernatural appeared in the conceptions of anthropomorphic gods and devils. The history of the devil is an interesting study of the successive personifications of evil. Ethical concepts have been presented in

[21] For an incisive discussion of this tendency see C. H. Cooley, *Human Nature and the Social Order*, Charles Scribner's Sons, New York, 1902, chap. 3.
[22] *Ibid.*, p. 95.

legendary figures, allegories, morality plays, and the like. Nature was early personified. Justice, liberty, law and a hundred abstractions are personified in folk art. Political power has been notoriously personified. Extreme personification is exemplified in Emerson's phrase, "There is no history, it is all biography." The economic process is largely translated into personified terms by the common man, with his beliefs as to what Morgan, Rockefeller, Ford, John L. Lewis and others "could do" to solve the economic problems. Groups are also personified. As Professor Cooley noted, "The sentiment by which one's family, club, college, state or country is realized in his mind is stimulated by vague images, largely personal . . . the impulse which we feel to personify country, or anything else which awakens strong emotion in us, shows our imaginations to be so profoundly personal that deep feeling almost inevitably connects itself with a personal image." [23] In personification, publics name and provide personal symbols for abstractions, concepts and sentiments.[24] The orator, popular artist, cartoonist and other special pleaders become experts in manipulating these personified symbols. Of course, general publics do objectify and depersonalize certain sectors of the subject matter to which they attend, but the resultant objectifications and abstractions never arouse the same group loyalties and warm emotional responses that accompany the personified symbol. Auguste Comte advised his disciples to create a visual image of Humanity in the form of the remembered figure of some known or loved woman. Personification is psychologically inevitable. It provides concrete, direct and simple mental content.

RATIONALIZATION

Human reason and logical thinking are constantly diverted into non-logical mental processes. "One recalls the argument of the German who insisted that stupid children make invincible soldiers, inasmuch as the gods themselves fight in vain against stupidity—*Gegen die Dummheit, streben die Götter selbst umsonst.* Human reason Luther compared to a drunken man on horseback: 'set it up on one side and it bumbles over on the other.' " [25] One of the ways in which individuals and groups frequently stray from logical thinking is by providing socially acceptable rather than real reasons for behavior. "Rationalization" is an ideal reconstruction of past behavior or thought. A belief or action is justified rather than explained. We search for the ostensibly good reason, a socially acceptable one. Providing the socially acceptable rather than the real

[23] *Ibid.*, pp. 113, 114. Quoted by permission of Charles Scribner's Sons.
[24] V. Pareto, *The Mind and Society* (English trans.), Harcourt, Brace and Company, Inc., New York, 1935, vol. II, pp. 636 ff.
[25] W. D. Wallis, "Some Phases of the Psychology of Prejudice," *Jour. Abn. Soc. Psychol.*, 24: 4: 424.

reasons may be observed even in very young children. A young neighborhood friend, a little girl aged five, watching gardening activities in our yard, was asked to carry a pair of wet, muddy, dirty gardener's gloves to our garage. She had an evident dislike of touching the soggy, muddy gloves. But what she said, was: "They're too dirty. My mother might not like it. If I did that and got my hands dirty, my mother wouldn't think you were taking very good care of me." This was an obvious rationalization instantly stated in resistance to an unwelcome task. And thus, too, in the public opinion process, where the present age is especially prolific in the spawning of good reasons for doing or thinking that which is considered morally bad. And this is especially true of egoistic, selfish, self-centered behaviors which conflict with the professed values of altruism in American culture.

As rationalization is an unconscious process, it is difficult conclusively to designate rationalizations, as such, either by introspective analysis of one's own thinking or by assumptions with regard to the reasons provided by others. The term "rationalization" was applied to this kind of thinking by Dr. E. Jones, who, in 1908, defined it as "unconsciously fictitious justification for behavior." [26] A considerable proportion of discussion consists of explaining actions and intentions. And many of the explanations are rationalizations. "The result is that most of our so-called reasoning consists in finding arguments for going on believing as we already do." [27] We have "good" reasons and "real" reasons.

The process of rationalization is by no means limited to those capable of only the elementary forms of thought. Great thinkers have propounded rationalizations which were afterward established and standardized in popular thought. The philosopher's defense of slavery among the Greeks was a rationalization. Interest on capital as a reward for abstinence is a rationalization when applied to interest on 100 million dollars. In male-dominated cultures, the incapacities of the female and her psychological inferiorities are proclaimed by the best minds. The Bohemian has used Freudian psychology as a rationalization for relatively unbridled licentiousness. "Freud says inhibitions are dangerous; let us be very careful to get rid of our inhibitions." Pareto says that professional thinkers long underestimated the amount of nonlogical conduct in society, for if that were admitted it would be much more difficult for them to construct systematic theories of social interaction.[28] The Russian judge does not say that Soviet justice is social expediency. He says that it is real justice as distinguished from the false justice of the *bourgeoisie*. Indeed, quite gen-

[26] W. S. Taylor, "Rationalization and Its Social Significance," *Jour. Abn. Soc. Psychol.*, 17: 410.
[27] J. H. Robinson, *Mind in the Making*, Harper & Brothers, New York, 1921, p. 41.
[28] Pareto, *op. cit.*, vol. I, p. 178.

erally, legal thinking includes numerous rationalizations. "It becomes more plain why the practice of law is often referred to as an 'art,' an art which cannot be taught rationally but must be grasped intuitively. Indeed the practice of law as now practiced is one of the major arts of rationalization." [29] It is clear that rationalization is pervasive in the thinking of the expert and professional thinker as well as in that of the common man.

The real motives of large groups are frequently disguised. The bulk of man's rationalizations of the social scene are acquired in the general culture. His opinions about other national groups, his foods, racial prejudices and class prejudices are enveloped in rationalizations. His extravagance becomes generosity, his party membership becomes loyalty, his lack of skepticisms becomes firm and noble conviction. One of the functions of successful leadership in large publics is the providing of many good, acceptable, and plausible rationalizations for the behavior of followers who are primarily motivated by other "reasons." Hitler provided a wealth of rationalizations for middle-class followers who had strong racial prejudices, in part based upon envious and avid self-seeking. Strong self-feeling, associated with beliefs and rationalizations, defends the self. "Passion and self interest may be our chief motives but we hate to admit the fact even to ourselves. We are not happy unless our acts of passion can be made to look as though they were dictated by reason, unless self-interest be explained and embellished so as to seem to be idealistic." [30]

The process is inevitable, persistent, and at many points rationalization is psychologically useful. It provides a defense against the exposure of socially undesirable motives and therefore maintains individual and group morale. Persistently to see oneself in the worst possible light is disintegrating. Groups, stripped of certain rationalizations, often look yearningly at the masquerades of their past. The reformer who would strip a society of some cherished rationalization should have something to offer in its stead.

EMOTION AND PUBLIC OPINION

For a half century, the simple, clear-cut dichotomies of mind and matter and of reason and emotion have no longer been satisfactory to the psychologist. The mind is viewed as part and parcel of the body, and bodily changes are considered as they affect mental processes. The ways of thinking characterized as reason and emotion are not distinct entities motivating particular instances of behavior, but exist in varying proportions in the different situations. Man is never exclusively, and usually not

[29] J. Frank, *Law and the Modern Mind*, Coward-McCann, Inc., New York, 1930, p. 31.

[30] A. Huxley, *The Olive Tree*, Harper & Brothers, New York, 1937, p. 16.

even essentially, a reasoning being. Feelings and emotions, likes and dislikes, in varying degrees are component parts of every human situation. It is only for descriptive purposes that one may use the terms "reason" and "emotion." Indeed, emotion is really a popular layman's term for the feeling states, especially the commonly recognized physical phenomena accompanying fear, love, rage and other emotional complexes.

Emotions have been quite variously defined and catalogued. Some groups of psychologists have described emotions primarily in terms of changes within the organism. Emotions are sometimes described in behavioristic terms of stimulus-response. The extended arguments of this dispute are not of concern here.[31] Watson distinguished fear, rage and love as the essential emotions. These are elsewhere amplified as anger, rage, fear, terror, sexual love, maternal love, laughter emotions, grief, disgust, jealousy, delight, agony and many others. However designated, it is evident that visceral disturbances relating to each caption have not been isolated. They are not entities. Latterly, the innate character of these complex states has been less assuredly declared than in Watson's day. Certainly the patterning of emotional expression is essentially learned, as are the principal stimuli inducing emotions. A considerable experimental literature on the recognition of the emotions has been developed by psychologists since 1920.[32]

Emotions, however they may be described and designated, are enormously significant in relation to the opinion process, in the fields of economics, politics, religion, education and the like. Appeals, primarily to arouse emotional response, are made by the demagogue, public speaker, preacher, advertising man, and, indeed, by all those who reach large publics. People fear want, isolation, disease, death, unpopularity; and to the dread of these, as to many other fears, the public pleader frequently addresses himself. Theoretically the educator has faith in logic and avoids the emotional appeal. The propagandist, advertising man or demagogue has no such qualms.

The stimulus to emotional response may be language, action, gesture or, indeed, any form of communication. A philosopher has recently differentiated between the permissible and (to him) not permissible use of communication to achieve such response. Poetry, romantic prose and emotional oratory are legitimate fields for emotional appeal; political or economic speeches should avoid emotionally tinged terms. He illustrates emotional appeal in poetry.

[31] For summary discussions see P. T. Young, *Motivation of Behavior*, John Wiley & Sons, Inc., New York, 1936, chap. 9; K. Young, *Social Psychology*, Alfred A. Knopf, Inc., New York, 1930, chap. 8.

[32] See especially J. S. Bruner and Renato Tagiuri, "The Perception of People," in *Handbook of Social Psychology*, Addison-Wesley Publishing Company, Cambridge, Mass., 1954, chap. 17.

The use of emotionally toned words is not, of course, always to be condemned. They are always harmful when we are trying to think clearly on a disputable point of fact. In poetry, on the other hand, they have a perfectly proper place, because in poetry (as in some kinds of prose) the arousing of suitable emotions is an important part of the purpose for which the words are used.

In the Eve of St. Agnes, Keats has written:

> "Full on this casement shone the wintry moon,
> And threw warm gules on Madeline's fair breast."

These are beautiful lines. Let us notice how much of their beauty follows from the proper choice of emotionally colored words and how completely it is lost if these words are replaced by neutral ones. The words with strikingly emotional meanings are *casement, gules, Madeline, fair,* and *breast. Casement* means simply a kind of window with emotional and romantic associations. *Gules* is the heraldic name for red, with the suggestion of romance which accompanies all heraldry. *Madeline* is simply a girl's name, but one calling out favorable emotions absent from a relatively plain and straight-forward name. *Fair* simply means, in objective fact, that her skin was white or uncolored—a necessary condition for the colors of the window to show—but also *fair* implies warm emotional preference for an uncolored skin rather than one which is yellow, purple, black or any of the other colors which skin might be. *Breast* has also similar emotional meanings, and the aim of scientific description might have been equally well attained if it had been replaced by such a neutral word as chest.

Let us now try the experiment of keeping these two lines in a metrical form, but replacing all the emotionally colored words by neutral ones, while making as few other changes as possible. We may write:

> "Full on this window shone the wintry moon,
> Making red marks on Jane's uncolored chest." [33]

Regardless of what, in the abstract values of the philosopher, may be considered permissible, emotional appeals have played the major role in popular thought and opinion. Nor can the relation of emotion to mass opinion be adequately described by considering original tendencies, even if these could be adequately isolated. Regardless of the innate character of emotional responses in the young child, the attitudes of adults with their emotional components have been conditioned by a variety of human experiences. When large American publics harbor attitudes and express opinions indicative of desire for security, love of money, resentment at class privileges, pacifist sentiment, race prejudice, or a yearning for isolation, the cultural history provides the more adequate description of the development of their opinions.

Various emotional feeling tones operate in the isolated individual stimulated by his own mental processes. Indeed, "the emotion following an

[33] Thouless, *op. cit.*, pp. 16–18. Quoted by permission of Simon and Schuster, Inc.

ideational process may possibly be far more turbulent than one preceded by a perceptual activity." [34] However, emotional responses are extraordinarily contagious and are much in evidence in group situations. Individuals, as members of crowds and large publics, are notoriously susceptible to emotional appeals. People are said to "lose their heads" in crowds. And as modern communication has increased the number and size of publics, the field of emotional appeals has widened.

We may illustrate this in the widening areas of appeals to fear. Fear has always been important in modifying and developing fundamental attitudes and opinions. In the simpler societies, fear is pervasive. "The great and primal dream, common to all the peoples of the earth, one which has troubled the mind of man since the dawn of his first beginnings, is an anxiety dream; for apprehension dominates the earliest and deepest strata of human thought and feeling; dread inspired by the vastness of the universe and by man's loneliness therein; dread of the mysterious, incalculable, capricious powers with which his imagination peoples the realms of space." [35] In Western societies the Christian religion made its lurid appeals to fear. Jonathan Edwards said, "The bow of God's wrath is bent, and the arrow made ready on the string, and justice bends the arrow at your heart, and strains the bow, and it is nothing but the mere pleasure of God, and that of an angry God, without any promise or obligation at all, that keeps the arrow one moment from being drunk with your blood." [36] However, fears of the supernatural abated with increasingly naturalistic descriptions of the universe. Through the late nineteenth century to the present, Western man, relieved somewhat of fear of the supernatural, has assumed a host of new and intensified fears, insecurities and apprehensions. Decreasing fear of the universe has been accompanied by increasing fear of other men, of social classes and groups, of insecurity of status and, indeed, of the functioning of one's own organism. And the conscious manipulation of these fears is very much in evidence. That the advertising man has increasingly used fear appeals since 1920 is not merely a fashion in advertising. He fishes in troubled waters. "Scare copy" manipulates opinion as to insurance of one's possessions or economic future, as to the choice of dentifrices, antiseptics, tobacco, the best talcum powder for baby, an adequate mausoleum for relatives, as to matters of social prestige and as to falling hair and a score of obscure and pseudoscientifically labeled ailments.

[34] J. R. Kantor, *Principles of Psychology*, Alfred A. Knopf, Inc., New York, 1924–1926, vol. II, p. 7.

[35] R. Fülöp-Miller, *Leaders, Dreamers and Rebels*, The Viking Press, Inc., New York, 1935, p. 8. Quoted by permission.

[36] Quoted by W. B. Graves (ed.), *Readings in Public Opinion*, Appleton-Century-Crofts, Inc., New York, 1928, p. 264.

In the 1950's, a ferment of fears existed and was cultivated in the United States. In the complexity of day-to-day life personal fears were widespread. Psychologists of the Illinois Institute of Technology, studying a representative cross section of American businessmen, found 80 per cent had fears of financial troubles, 74 per cent of job security, 69 per cent of real or imaginary health problems, 59 per cent because of their personal appearance, 44 per cent were worried by marital difficulties, 37 per cent were worried by religious problems, 34 per cent about their sexual morality, 56 per cent had apprehensions and anxieties about politics, and 33 per cent had anxieties about relatives.[37] In the midst of these personal and immediate fears, it is hardly surprising that large urban populations have not responded with extensive hysteria to ideas of complete destruction by hydrogen bombs with cobalt coatings. There is a point at which, for reasonably normal human beings, resignation and stoicism abate immediate fright; at least until catastrophe becomes an immediate issue.

In the modern age, beyond specific fears there is dread—vague, nameless, abysmal, diffused dread. As communication has brought to modern Western man some of the story of extermination camps, slave camps, psychological pressures and brainwashing, and the potential disasters as well as benefits of modern science, he is overcome at times with unfathomable dread. In modern authoritarian states, those groups who would impose their will through fear have experimented with fear without limit. The systematic organization of fear has been viewed in the Soviet terror as social prophylaxis.[38] "It is terror that has most sharply set off our time from its immediate predecessors and has caused us to doubt as never before the excellence of man and his capacity for progress. In terror we have glimpsed the triumph of a new barbarism." [39]

We have the wide variety of personal fears in modern culture; we have fear induced by the terror; there are the fears aroused by a fear-provoking environment in an atomic age; and then there are the numerous consciously applied fears aroused by politicians, advertising men, propagandists and various demagogic leaders. To be sure, fear-arousing appeals are not always immediately successful, nor do they invariably induce permanent attitude changes. Indeed, there is some fragmentary evidence to the contrary, though the experimental examination of this question is still very limited.[40]

[37] Reported in *This Week Mag.*, Oct. 9, 1954.
[38] J. G. Gliksman, "Social Prophylaxis as a Form of Soviet Terror," in C. J. Friedrich (ed.), *Totalitarianism*, Harvard University Press, Cambridge, Mass., 1954, pp. 60–84.
[39] H. S. Hughes, *An Essay for Our Times*, Alfred A. Knopf, Inc., New York, 1950, p. 109.
[40] See I. L. Janis and S. Feshbach, "Effects of Fear Arousing Communications," *Jour. Abn. Soc. Psychol.*, 1953, vol. 48, pp. 78–92; and C. I. Hovland, *Communication and Persuasion*, Yale University Press, New Haven, Conn., 1953, pp. 46–98.

In the political sphere, one of the dangers of overemphasizing fear is that fear is the greatest corrosive of reason. To maintain reasonable balance and personal as well as group poise and urbanity, fear must be minimized. Fear-obsessed men do not like freedom. Objectivity is lost in periods of mass fear and rationality may be hated if it interferes with the drive toward supposed security by submission and allegiance to leaders and causes.

In the preceding discussions we would appear to have been preoccupied with the essentially nonlogical forms of mental functioning. That is true. The inconsistencies and illogicalities of thinking in large publics are evident on every hand. "Neither the existence nor the positive value of the irrational in man is to be glossed over. All the instincts, impulses and emotions which push man into action outside the treadmill of use and wont are irrational. The depths, the mysteries of nature are nonrational." [41] Obedience is a necessary quality in a soldier. Yet, a German saying declares that any totally reasonable army would run away. However, the nonlogical and nonrational processes of large publics do not always result in irrational behavior. Indeed, William James said that "The recesses of feeling, the darker, blinder strata of character are the only places in the world in which we catch real fact in the making." Large publics often do the right things—those which may be supported by logical analysis—for the wrong reasons. Socially desirable causes are supported more often than not because of the personal characteristics of their leaders, the rationalizations that the leaders supply, the emotional responses that they stimulate and so forth. Large publics have persistently survived, and often quite happily, a vast amount of bumbling, emotional, personalized, simplified mentation. But the simplification has not been all on their side. When the logician would remedy such a situation with large doses of logical thinking among the masses, he shows a limited understanding of recent psychology. How could large opposing groups be trained to think logically about a specific issue, when they have been conditioned differently, respond to various symbols and perhaps embrace quite divergent ideologies?

However, the results of nonrational psychological processes among masses of people have not always been socially desirable, and in the immediate future they may be very unhappy indeed. For there is a terrifyingly intentional and deliberate cultivation of the irrational in modern life. The rise of a wide variety of interest-groups has been accompanied by the conscious cultivation of popular irrationality, for the

[41] J. Dewey, *Characters and Events*, Henry Holt and Company, Inc., New York, 1929, vol. II, p. 587.

achievement of the purposes of these political and economic groups. We cannot hope to achieve quickly, "a really educated democracy, distrustful of emotional phraseology and all the rest of the stock-in-trade of the exploiters of crooked thinking, devoid of reverence for ancient institutions and ancient ways of thinking, which could take conscious control of our social development." [42] The majority of men cannot now rapidly be trained to heroic doses of logical thinking. Fortunately, they do not need to be so trained. The rise of a skillful and socially well-intentioned leadership, with realistic definitions, logically achieved, may yet control and direct toward objectives that will make possible the good life for the common man. He may support these with his sentiments. It is to be hoped that this may be achieved within a politically democratic framework.

[42] Thouless, *op. cit.*, p. 226.

CHAPTER 6

Language and Public Opinion

It is difficult to see adequately the functions of language because it is so deeply rooted in the whole of human behavior that it may be suspected that there is little in the functional side of our conscious behavior in which language does not play a part.[1]

E. SAPIR

Most students of linguistics are preoccupied with a series of problems that do not concern the sociologist or social psychologist. The descriptions of the structures, roots and meanings of particular words and phrases; the historical development, tracing origins and growth of language; the comparative study of language forms and their diffusion; the grammatical classifications on the basis of etymology; are of but limited interest to the social psychologist. Few linguists have dealt in a more than incidental fashion with the relations of language to the social processes or with the relations of thought and language.[2]

The problem of the use of language for persuasion and control over opinions has intrigued the mind of the scholar from classical times to the latest effusions of semanticists. In Greece, rules for successful oratory and persuasion were formulated; in Rome, the effects of political oratory were studied in a somewhat orderly fashion; and in the Middle Ages, dominated by religion, the impact of the language was pondered. But it is in the modern age that attempted control through language manipulation has become of paramount importance to publicity men, politicians and publicists. Partial sciences of language analysis have developed since 1900. The psychological barriers to communication through language have been crudely explored, and the relations of thought and behavior to language have been partially analyzed.[3]

---

[1] E. Sapir, *Ency. Soc. Sci.*, 9: 159.

[2] There are exceptions. See, notably, O. Jespersen, *Language*, G. Allen & Unwin, Ltd., London, 1921; L. Bloomfield, *Language*, Henry Holt and Company, Inc., New York, 1933; E. Sapir, *Language*, Harcourt, Brace and Company, Inc., New York, 1921.

[3] A few of the recent books most likely to be useful to the student of opinion process are: Paul Kecskemeti, *Meaning, Communication and Value*, University of Chicago

96

A language is the product of a particular culture. It is composed of those words and expressions which label the material objects, relationships, ideas, concepts and values with which that culture is or has been concerned. The individual, in learning that portion of his language which he acquires, is guided in his thought to a considerable extent by the labels which he learns. In a very basic way, language largely determines the content of thought. This is quite obvious either to an ethnologist attempting to explain the concept of romantic love to an individual in a primitive culture or to a missionary struggling with the communication of the idea of the Trinity. Moreover, within a language group, the individual knows but a portion of the existing words. His vocabulary is a measure of his participation in his culture. Various estimates of the language of the contemporary common man have indicated a vocabulary of a few thousand terms.[4] Such limited language tools do not permit of a wide range of knowledge and of thinking. Further, one's thinking is canalized by the language used in the groups from which the individual has obtained his fundamental ideologies. The language forms of an ideology are made up of preconceived ideas. These thwart thought. Opinion process, as other mental processes, is carried on within a particular language, of which the individual has learned only a part. Moreover, he is limited by his ideological preconceptions.

A generation ago it was maintained that languages differed in their grammar and content of words because peoples thought differently. Contemporary social psychology would be more likely to maintain that peoples think differently because their language forms differ. The individual speaks the language of his culture group and thinks as that group thinks or has thought. In ethnological studies, since Wundt, language has been extensively analyzed as reflecting the social processes, values and standards of primitive life. Modes of behavior and life ways, the cultural framework and social processes, are reflected in language forms. Hundreds of such processes and relationships, strange to modern Western

---

Press, Chicago, 1952; Stuart Chase, *Power of Words*, Harcourt, Brace and Company, Inc., New York, 1954; Charles Morris, *Signs, Language and Behavior*, Prentice-Hall, Inc., New York, 1946; R. M. Estrich and Hans Sperber, *Three Keys to Language*, Rinehart & Company, Inc., New York, 1952; George A. Miller, *Language and Communication*, McGraw-Hill Book Company, Inc., New York, 1951; T. D. Weldon, *The Vocabulary of Politics*, Penguin Books, Inc., Baltimore, 1953; and a pamphlet issued by the U.S. Department of State in 1952, entitled, *Collected Papers on Metalinguistics*, by Benjamin Lee Whorf.

[4] These estimates have been thought to be too low by a few writers. J. M. Gillette devised a test whereby he found that he had a vocabulary of 127,800 words, and two of his students, 65,800 and 52,489. Admittedly these are highly selected subjects, however. J. M. Gillette, "Extent of Personal Vocabularies," *Sci. Mon.*, 29: 451–457.

I believe it is unquestionably true that the majority of the citizens of the United States have a usable vocabulary of less than 10,000 words.

thought, have been revealed by such studies. Degrees of relationship, often more complicated among primitives than in our society, are indicated by special words. Enumeration systems, sex classifications of objects, descriptive adjectives, the curiously involved tabooed language forms of various primitives, magic and words and many other topics can be studied, in part, in language forms.[5]

The values and preoccupations of a group are frequently expressed in the language terms most commonly used by its members. A young woman, born and reared in New York City, was visiting in the country for the first time. On the morning after her arrival in the rural scene, she rushed in from a walk to tell her host excitedly that she had seen the most beautiful "mink-colored" bird. Thus are judgments expressed in available language. More seriously and systematically, the special language of professional and vocational groups, the vocabulary of ideological groups, the identifying slang of adolescent groups and the like direct the attention and influence the opinions of their members. Legal talk, medical talk, educational jargon, the terms of economics, the language of science, all are partially special vocabularies differing from the language of general public discussion.[6]

The objectives of such special vocabularies are to depersonalize and to avoid emotion-arousing terms, as well as to provide the necessarily detailed descriptive and analytic terms. When an economist speaks of "personnel," he depersonalizes. Personnel, though in theory they are men and women, have only to be called personnel to lose their full status as human beings. In the 1930's, the talk among the bureaucrats of Washington was labeled "gobbledygook," a term which I believe Congressman Maverick coined. In the 1950's, *Time Magazine* reported:

> In Washington, the up-to-date word for gobbledygook is "bafflegab." A speech by an NPA official on materials allocations furnished a prime example: "We are peaking our program philosophically, but it is naive to assume the allotment program is an equity program unless the allotments are so abysmally low that they permit the agency to relax and allow market determination as a percentage of base period, sidetracking military return with adjustments."

This type of language grows and spreads to provide phrases for real or imagined special language needs among the groups concerned. Such language exercises some control over the thought and opinions of the members of groups. But, in general, such control is not planned nor intended by those inventing the words.

[5] See B. L. Whorf, "The Relation of Habitual Thought and Behavior to Language," in L. Spier, I. Hallowell and S. S. Newman (eds.), *Language, Culture and Personality*, Sapir Memorial Publication Fund, Menasha, Wis., 1941, pp. 75–93.

[6] For numerous examples of such language, consult Stuart Chase, *op. cit.*, pp. 107–293.

In modern political and economic life the more or less astute manipulation of language with intent to control opinions is commonplace procedure. "Political semantics examines key terms, slogans and doctrines from the point of view of how they are understood," writes Harold Lasswell. In politics, applied semantics is concerned with the effects and influences of words. Much of the growing interest in semantics during the 1930's and 1940's was based on preoccupation with the manipulation of language to effect social control. More and more groups and individuals concerned themselves with the problem of the manipulation of the thought and opinions of others.[7]

In the struggle for mastery of their own and other peoples, the leaders of Nazi Germany and of Communist Russia notably used the written and the spoken word as an instrument of struggle for power. Therefore, Communist definitions of words must be examined in terms of the effects which the words are intended to produce in the publics to which they are directed by Communist ideologists.[8] As one aspect of the tactic of confusion by redefinition, the Communists selected many words which were the captions of important ideological complexes in Britain and the United States and used these same words, but gave to them quite different meanings.

In a recent novel, describing the far from Utopian life in 1984 on Airstrip I, which earlier historians knew as England, the author notes that in the creation of Newspeak, a kind of simplified English, the managers of Society proposed to limit discussion and deviant thinking by limiting words for popular use to those which were ideologically pure. "The purpose of Newspeak was not only to provide a medium of expression for the world-view and mental habits proper to the devotees of Ingso (English Socialism) but to make all other modes of thought impossible." An heretical thought would be unthinkable for lack of word tools for such thinking. Political and intellectual freedom did not exist as concepts and were nameless.[9]

However, one need not await psychological totalitarianism to find examples of language manipulation in the interests of attempted control of publics. The advertising man of today is an applied semanticist in his coinage and popularization of language favorable to the products he seeks

[7] Detailed research study on semantics is now widespread in the universities, as well as in the research divisions of advertising agencies and other publicity organizations. At the University of Illinois, brilliant work has been carried on by the psychologist Charles Osgood, with his "semantic differential," and by Grant Fairbanks of the Speech Department.

[8] For numerous examples of definitions developed to incorporate the values of Communist ideology, see Harry Hodgkinson, *The Language of Communism*, Pitman Publishing Company, New York, 1955.

[9] George Orwell, *1984*, Harcourt, Brace and Company, Inc., New York, 1949, p. 303.

to sell, and the political special pleader spreads his particularistic panacea in a specially created jargon. The basic difference is that these special pleaders do not have monopolistic control of communications and hence cannot exercise totalitarian control. But in neither case are the controllers' attitudes favorable to the cultivation of critical, rational and logical thinking by the members of large publics.

As we have noted when considering psychological processes and opinion, key words and phrases are the stereotyped symbols used in public discussion. Of these, we shall discuss briefly the proverbs and traditional phrases, the slogans, and the process of name calling, as well as the relation of emotions to these phrases and the process of change of reference terms in public discussion.

PROVERBS AND TRADITIONAL PHRASES

We have defined opinion as expression on a controversial point. In primitive society and in the relatively static folk cultures the range of opinion material is usually very narrow. There is more individually divergent behavior in primitive societies than the ethnologists of a generation ago recognized. The writings of Malinowski, Benedict, Mead, Radin and many other recent and contemporary anthropologists have described such divergence. However, in general, preliterate groups are relatively static, and the cultural definitions are incorporated in individual attitudes to an extent that precludes much range to the controversially discussible. The group beliefs and values are incorporated in myths and legends, stories and songs, sayings and proverbs. Personal relations and intergroup relationships are fairly simple and usually clearly defined. The language form that most clearly reflects primitive values is the proverb. Proverbs preserve practical wisdom and can be quoted to quell individual expressions of divergent opinion. Likewise, among folk peoples, the proverb is an important agent in controlling opinion and behavior.

The proverb is a language form that has largely passed out of use in contemporary American culture.[10] Current speech and literature provide but few quotations or allusions to the proverb. There are isolated areas and surviving cultures, notably first-generation foreign-language groups of peasant origin, where the proverb retains some of its former vigor as an educational and controlling agent. Every popular proverb has seemed good to a multitude of men, but, in a culture that has largely dispensed

---

[10] There is no absolute agreement as to the definition of a proverb, but the sense of the definitions appears to be that it is a sentence or short statement indicating some supposedly profound reflection on human or, at times, cosmic and supernatural relationships. Lord John Russell called it, "the wisdom of many and the wit of one"; Lord Bacon indicated that it was the "genius, wit and spirit of a nation"; Cervantes declared the proverb to be "a short sentence drawn from long experience."

with them, even a single proverb quotation may call forth the wondering ridicule directed toward a cultural variation. Many a contemporary audience considers a proverb as somehow vaguely humorous. The proverb is a social definition of a situation. When that situation appears to the literary and political leaders, who coin such phrases, less simple, less personal and less subject to dogmatic solution, the supply is cut off and the old forms fall into disuse. Other forms of stereotyped phrases take their place. The proverb is a cultural invention. It is not inevitable.

The proverb frequently has characteristics of structure that give it a high memory value. Its success, like that of the slogan, the motto, the rallying cry and other condensed language forms, is in part dependent upon just such details. Furthermore, in periods during which a high degree of unanimity in social judgments exists, the proverb appears to masses of people as the expression of profound wisdom, a sort of well-rounded, easily communicable truth. It may happen that "they interfere between husband and wife, parents and children, and teach all of them manners with unsparing frankness. They play with the children, counsel their parents, and dream dreams with the old." [11] The specific types of proverbs in daily use are indicative of the conflict tensions in the social process and of problems common to everyday life.

Various cultures have similar daily problems and issues and have invented parallel proverbs, as is illustrated in the collection on page 102.

The proverb does not appear to be characteristic of a complex culture under conditions of rapid change in beliefs dealing with social and supernatural relationships. The forms in existence fall into disuse, and the literary, political and economic leaders provide no new forms. More transient word forms provide the current phrases. The variety of conflicting social judgments assumes a different language form, no less dogmatic probably, but much less permanent. Sentences from popular songs, slang phrases, "wisecracks," items from the cinema, slogans of economic advertising, phrases from the radio and the like, become the coin current in the process of communication.[12]

These phrases have succeeded the somewhat less transient language forms of a past generation in the United States. The generation of 1900 communicated a whole set of beliefs about the significance of heredity and environment in saying, "Blood will tell," "Born to the purple," "Born with a silver spoon in his mouth," "It's easy to see he's to the manor born." Dale Warren, in reminiscing about his Great-Aunt Lizzie, writes:

[11] W. Elmslie, *Studies in Life from Jewish Proverbs*, James Clarke & Co., Ltd., London, 1917, p. 24.

[12] The preceding discussion is largely drawn from W. Albig, "Proverbs and Social Control," *Sociol. Soc. Res.*, 15: 527–535. See J. O. Hertzler, *Social Thought of the Ancient Civilizations*, McGraw-Hill Book Company, Inc., New York, 1936, pp. 373–388.

Many Tongues—One Thought [13]

More than one would suppose, the peoples of the world think alike on many vital subjects. Words and expressions may differ from country to country but the wisdom they convey is universal, witness the proverbs below.

The translations are the work of Charles Berlitz of the Berlitz School of Languages. Mr. Berlitz has collected these proverbs in his travels throughout the world. Few of them, if any, will be found in foreign language textbooks.

ENGLISH	FRENCH	SPANISH	JAPANESE	ARABIC	GERMAN	RUSSIAN
Little drops of water make the mighty ocean.	Little by little the bird makes his nest.	Little by little the cup is filled.	Dust may pile to form a hill.	A hair from here and there makes a beard.	Steady dripping hollows a stone.	A thread from all over the world makes a shirt for a man.
Everyone has a right to his own opinion.	Everyone to his own taste.	Everyone has his own way of killing fleas.	Ten men, ten colors.	Every person is free in his opinions.	Don't quarrel about tastes.	Every baron has his own fantasy.
Look before you leap.	Turn the tongue 7 times, then speak.	Think before speaking.	Have an umbrella before getting wet.	Before you drink the soup, blow on it.	First weigh, then dare.	If you don't know the ford don't cross the stream.
There is something rotten in Denmark.	There is an eel under the rock.	There is a cat shut up.	There is a worm in the lion's body.	There is a snake under the hay.	There is something foul in Denmark.	There is a needle in the bag.
Don't count your chickens before they're hatched.	Don't sell the bear skin before you kill him.	Don't saddle before bringing the horses.	Before you kill badgers don't count their skins.	Don't say "lima beans" before they are weighed.	Don't hang people before you have caught them.	Chickens are counted in Autumn.

[13] *United Nations World*, November, 1951, p. 59.

I can hear her saying: "The trouble with your uncle is that he simply has no git up and git," or "If you ask me Cousin Hattie is turning into a crashing bore" (obviously the result of her recent trip to England), or "What would you expect of old Farmer Brown? He's just plain ornery," or "I wouldn't trust him for a minute; he's only a fair-weather friend, a Good Time Charlie," or with sly innuendo, "Well, if you believe all you hear she's really no better than she should be." [14]

Such phrases define the situation, provide a feeling of security of judgment for the person using them and channel opinion.

SLOGANS

Words and brief, easily remembered phrases label and stereotype social objectives and definitions. Publics persistently become attached to certain language forms. Social reform movements flourish on rallying cries. One of the early popular reform movements in the economic field was led by John Ball in England in the fourteenth century. His mass meetings began and ended with the chant, "When Adam delved and Eve span, who was then the gentleman?" But long before that, popular movements had been symbolized by mottoes, catchwords and slogans. Gibbon recounts that in Alexandria one religious faction chanted, "Glory be to the Father, and to the Son, and to the Holy Ghost," to which the other replied, "Glory be to the Father, in the Son, and by the Holy Ghost." Thereby street crowds were led to a fury that ended in head cracking. Effective conditioning to phrases is an ancient art. The modern process is merely characterized by more organization, a more sophisticated psychological analysis of language and a more conscious use of language by societal leaders. In *Middletown in Transition,* the Lynds reported a marked tendency to define the major political and economic problems in terms of a few phrases and language forms, such as "harmony," "boost," "we will reduce taxes," "economy," "civic unity," "radicalism is un-American," and the like. These are bandied about by speakers, the newspapers and the men's civic clubs.

The effective slogan has a few well-known, simple characteristics of structure. An advertising man writes:

The slogan should be simple to understand, easy to remember, and pleasant to repeat. Since the success of a slogan depends largely on its repetition, the qualities of brevity, aptness, and original approach are imperative. Seven short words would seem the maximum to use in a slogan, six just few enough to be within the margin of safety, and less than that even more desirable.[15]

[14] Dale Warren, "Aunt Lizzie's Lexicon," *Sat. Rev.,* Dec. 5, 1953, p. 56.
[15] O. Kleppner, *Advertising Procedure,* Prentice-Hall, Inc., New York, 1934, p. 112.

"Back to Normalcy" was an almost perfect political slogan, since it appeared to mean almost all things to all men and was inherently meaningless. Lumley describes the most effective slogans as brief; rhythmical; alliterative; repetitive; affirmative; appealing to curiosity, the sentiments, class and authority; punning; appearing to summarize a profound idea.[16] Select your own illustrations of slogans that have some of these characteristics. There is certainly plenty of material in the language of contemporary politics and business. The effective slogan becomes a stimulus-situation to arouse known attitudes.

The political and religious fields are the ancient stamping ground of the slogans. Their use in advertising, by causes, movements and various organizations, is a recent development appearing during the last fifty years. In the political field, slogans have been especially associated with popular mass movements. Those related to the prevailing attitudes such as the famous "Liberty, Equality and Fraternity" are strong, effective and persistent. Those applied from above which do not tap such attitudes are transient and relatively ineffective. Certain slogans are officially adopted by nations, parties, groups and organizations. "In God We Trust" is printed on American money. During the Depression a waggish banker suggested that there should be stamped on the other side, "I hope that my Redeemer liveth." National objectives may be stated, as in "Make the World Safe for Democracy." Group declarations are incorporated in slogans, as in the case of the Japanese feminists who rallied around the phrase "The Sun Is Female." Crisis and conflict situations are the breeding ground of slogans. All the wars and group conflicts of recent centuries have called forth many phrases. Emotional campaigns necessitate catchwords.

Many slogans are associated with particular personalities. General Pershing is credited with "Lafayette, we are here," Marshal Pétain with "They shall not pass." The Kaiser was the object of the phrase "The War Lord." William Jennings Bryan was long known by "You shall not press down upon the brow of labor this crown of thorns; you shall not crucify mankind upon a cross of gold." Vanderbilt never outlived "The public be damned." Bernard Baruch has disclaimed credit for the phrase "the cold war," ascribing it to Herbert Bayard Swope. This phrase became one of the most widely used captions of the early 1950's.

There is a fashion element in the coining of phrases. In the early nineties a Kodak company and a hook-and-eye company advertised with "You Press a Button; We Do the Rest" and "See That Hump," respectively. These were given wide publicity and were paraphrased and parodied on

[16] F. E. Lumley, *Means of Social Control,* Appleton-Century-Crofts, Inc., New York, 1925, chap. 7.

the stage, in the newspaper and in conversation.[17] For the next decade, advertising largely consisted of slogan making. This word jugglery often was crude, inept and ineffective. But many advertising men of that day appeared to believe that if they could only discover the proper phrase success was assured. Today, hundreds of phrases are retained in the advertising of various products, but such slogans have become a relatively minor part of advertising technique. Popular contests in the coining of slogans are primarily used today to preoccupy thousands of people with the advertised product rather than for the discovery of a telling phrase. When the playing with words is popular, sheer verbal exuberance leads to crude excess. The groceterias, morticians, shellubrications, and the like, are characteristic of the more flamboyant phases of American business life. Slogan making by the publicity men spread from commercial advertising to the campaigns of athletic groups, education, religious organizations, communities, reform groups and civic clubs.[18]

The mind of modern man is stimulated by an increasing variety of impressions. Condensation of appeals is inevitable, as is evidenced by forms of stereotyping, newspaper headlines, and the like. Slogans are peculiarly adapted to this need. They may distort, but they satisfy. Social psychology is not adequately developed to provide very exact answers as to their effectiveness. If the phrase happens to be adapted to existing attitudes, it is successful. But the special pleader cannot manipulate at will. Advertising men are frequently too sanguine as to the effect of slogans. But catchwords are persistent and inevitable.

NAME CALLING

Among the simpler peoples, the relationships between language forms and the objects they designate are often mystically conceived. The name is thought of as an intrinsic part of that which it designates. Therefore, primitives' magical conceptions frequently lead them to the use or avoidance of names as a way of manipulating that which is named. You may kill or injure a person by the proper spells or incantations in which you incorporate his name. Likewise, you may influence the spirits or objects in nature by naming them. The language of magical reference and the tabooed language forms of various preliterates provide a baffling and intricate problem for the ethnologist. When primitive peoples indulge in derisive name calling and in opprobrious epithets in face-to-face ridicule,

[17] F. Presbrey, *The History and Development of Advertising*, Doubleday & Company, Inc., New York, 1929, p. 369.

[18] The most extended discussion of the slogans of advertising may be found in *The Slogan in Modern Advertising*, written by Emanuel Faltz and published by the Association of National Advertisers in 1949.

there is an especially potent invasion of personality. One is not only socially depreciated but also magically attacked. Hence, many primitive
peoples find name calling and ridicule an effective method of social control. Formal name-calling ceremonies were a widespread method of conflict among North American Indians and Eskimos.[19]

Children's language, the verbalizations of the mentally aberrant and the
naming by opprobrious epithets indulged in by large publics, evidence
something of the same tendencies. Honorific and humilific terms exist in
every language. There are more of the latter. Both types are widely used
in social conflict, not only to designate those referred to, but also to
laud or depreciate them. When conflict develops between large popular
groups, the process is inevitable. Of course, there may be more or less
of it. Like other elements in a changing culture, there are fashions in name
calling. The practice waxes and wanes, depending upon the rise and
imitation of expert name callers and upon changes in the social structure
that present new tensions and conflict groups. A Theodore Roosevelt
greatly increases name calling for a political generation. Protestantism
provided ever new sects to hurl opprobrious epithets at one another,
since they had diverse interpretations of the ways of the gentle Christ.

As increasingly divergent definitions of religious, economic and political phenomena have developed during the past four centuries; as special-
interest groups of many kinds have arisen; as populations have become
more mobile and have come in contact with more diverse types of people;
as the attention areas of modern man have widened, providing him with
more things to be prejudiced against, the practice of name calling has
increased. Name calling is rife wherever there are major divisions in
society between which conflict intermittently occurs. Names are hurled
back and forth between political groups, between churches, economic
groups in conflict, town and country, between the sexes, at the physically
different, at foreigners and, indeed, wherever conflict is occurring between the standards and ideas of two or more groups. Political functioning in American democracy has persistently been conducted amidst more
or less name calling, taunts and crude buffoonery. J. G. Blaine's railroad
deals were referred to when crowds chanted, "Blaine, Blaine, J. G. Blaine,
The continental liar from the state of Maine. Burn this letter." Cleveland's
supposed illegitimate son gave rise to the campaign jingle, "Ma, Ma,
where's my pa? Gone to the White House. Ha, ha, ha!" In Chicago's
brawling primaries of the Thompson period, the candidates outdid one
another in hurling back and forth such names as "chimpanzee," "nut,"
"baboon," "looney" and the like. In the 1930's, Senator Huey Long and

---

[19] W. I. Thomas, *Primitive Behavior,* McGraw-Hill Book Company, Inc., New York,
1937, pp. 544 ff.

Father Coughlin were experts, and General Johnson was an astute manipulator of lurid epithets. The late Harold Ickes was perhaps the most notable name caller of the Franklin D. Roosevelt period. In 1940, he announced scathingly that Tom Dewey had just "thrown his diapers in the ring," and he characterized Wendell Willkie as "a simple, barefoot Wall Street lawyer." These were great word caricatures.

As the tensions of internal and international politics have increased, the art of smearing by name calling has reached new dimensions. Names are spawned from irrational fears and hatreds. Name calling increases with the popularization of issues. As issues are emotionally tinged in large publics, name calling increases. In the early 1950's, such terms as do-gooder, interventionist, collectivist, Red, pollyanna, huckster, aggressor, appeaser, internationalist, warmonger and many others were current. A political reporter during the campaign of 1952 found a new word to label the intellectual—the egghead. The reporter was presumably inspired by Adlai Stevenson's egg-shaped forehead as highlighted by the television camera. To be more explicit, Senator Ferguson said: "There's no difference in an egghead and a radical egghead. A radical egghead is just an egghead." But, as Seneca wrote, "To be able to endure odium is the first art to be learned by those who aspire to power."

In the struggles between Protestant denominations during the last half of the nineteenth century, a choice variety of names were created and mutually exchanged. These names are not so much in evidence now, which is perhaps an indication that the rank and file of their memberships are not now so much interested in the fine points of doctrinal difference. The conflict has shifted to religionists versus nonreligionists. The late Billy Sunday convulsed large audiences with his vivid name calling. He once said, "Our country is filled with a socialistic, I.W.W., Communistic, radical, lawless anti-American, antichurch, anti-God, antimarriage gang, and they are laying the eggs of rebellion and unrest in labor and capital and home; and we have some of them in our universities. I could take you through the universities and pick out a lot of black-hearted, Communistic fellows who are teaching that to the boys and sending them out to undermine America." [20]

Changing relationships increase or decrease name calling. One does not hear or read of the variety of names directed at the "city slicker" by the country folk or toward the "rube," "hayseed" or any of the other names thrown countryward by the city dweller of thirty years ago, probably because the more obvious and discernible differences of dress, speech and manners have diminished.

[20] Quoted by H. R. Huse, *Illiteracy of the Literate,* Appleton-Century-Crofts, Inc., New York, 1933, p. 175.

Professor Lumley has characterized the meaning of this name calling practice as a "protest against social change and thus as a means of social control." [21] It is a warning to innovators, but usually not a socially conscious process. Name calling may be most profitably described in terms of its influence on popular opinion in conflict situations. The Puritans were referred to by the Cavaliers as "Roundheads," because most of them had their hair cut short. Such names designate and depreciate the outsider and by implication elevate the name caller. In the community, groups call names at foreigners or at alien cultural or racial groups. "Bohunk," "wop," "dago," "chink," "greaser," "nigger" are all belittling names.[22] They denote the outsider, the stranger, the alien person who must be battered down. This name calling is a form of fighting; it is a protest against invasion and an attempt to assign an inferior position to the stranger. Other types of opprobrious epithets perform a similar function. The names usually apply to the most obvious differences, such things as personal appearance, manners, food preferences, variant religious exercises, speech and the like.

CHANGE IN REFERENCE TERMS

The meanings of words may be gradually changed by folk practice or through redefinitions by language experts. In English, "to haul" means to move by force and violence, but, in America, the meaning is "to transport"; "to heft" in English means "to lift up," but, in America, the meaning gradually came to be "to weigh by lifting." [23] In other cases the word is the same and its objective definition is the same, but popular responses to it have changed. Recently, a young woman of New York was being beautified by a French hairdresser who was a recent immigrant. He noticed a blue pin that she was wearing and inquired its meaning. "That," explained the young woman, "means that I am a Daughter of the American Revolution." "Oh, this is most terrible," said the Frenchman, throwing up his hands in horror. "I always thought Mademoiselle such a nice, sweet girl, and now you tell me you are a revolutionist." In still other cases, the word is changed to another, while the objective reality remains the same. Popular speech of the Victorian period changed "legs" into "limbs," a wine cooler into a "sarcophagus," "breast" into "bosom," and a young girl was informed that "only animals sweat, men perspire but young ladies merely glow." In many cases, changes in language forms

---

[21] Lumley, *op. cit.*, p. 300.

[22] For phrases indicating what the world's people have said of one another, see A. A. Roback, *A Dictionary of International Slurs*, Sci-Art Publishers, Cambridge, 1948.

[23] H. L. Mencken, *The American Language*, Alfred A. Knopf, Inc., New York, 1936, pp. 121–124.

reflect changing popular values and opinions. Many euphemistic terms result from popular aversion to certain words. Hence, the references to the "deceased" and the "departed" and to "misconduct" and girls "in trouble," the variety of terms for "drunken" and scores of other softened words.[24]

On the other hand, language changes may be brought about by individuals and groups who manipulate language in the interests of a cause, a viewpoint or some other special bias. John L. Lewis once labeled one of his miners' strikes a "no-day work week." When the break in sterling took the English pound to its lowest level, newspaper readers were not told that sterling was down but that "gold leaps up again." Groups change language in their own interests. "The concrete realities of politics are individual human beings, living together in national groups. Politicians—and to some extent we are all politicians—substitute abstractions for these concrete realities, and having done this, proceed to invest each abstraction with an appearance of concreteness by personifying it." [25] When a military writer likes to speak of "sabers" and "rifles" instead of "cavalrymen" or "foot soldiers," he has abstracted in this fashion.

The astute political leader substitutes new words for those which have become unpopular. LeBon noted that "when crowds have come, as the result of political upheavals or changes of belief, to acquire a profound antipathy for the images evoked by certain words, the first duty of the true statesman is to change the words without, of course, laying hands on the things themselves." [26]

Confucius attempted to reorganize Chinese culture by the power of ideas and in this he noted the importance of modifying concepts and labels. This process he called the "rectification of names." Changing terms and captions is a commonplace for the modern politician. An excess-profits tax was relabeled "defense-profits" tax. In 1951 the publicity men of the OPS avoided reference to the "price control program" and referred to "stabilization" and the "price program." In 1953 the mounting problem of surpluses of many farm products had come sufficiently to public attention and concern to cause the administration to decide that "surplus" was an evil word. It was decided to call surpluses "excess reserves." On the theory that it has less of a speculative ring to it, the word "shareholder" is preferred to "stockholder" by many financial people—including speculators. In 1954 it was decided that any new German army would be labeled *Streitkräfte* (military forces) in place of *Wehrmacht* (popularly translated "war machine"), since the latter term has accumulated evil

[24] Huse, *op. cit.*, pp. 32 ff., for further illustrations of euphemistic terms.
[25] A. Huxley, *The Olive Tree*, Harper & Brothers, New York, 1937, p. 96.
[26] G. LeBon, *The Crowd*, T. F. Unwin, London, 1896, p. 121.

associations. In the early 1950's, when most of the business community was desperately afraid of "depression," the economic decline was relabeled recession, readjustment, rolling readjustment, deflation or disinflation.

The manipulation of language by the advertising man is obvious. Corsets and underwear are far too unromantic and harshly descriptive for an advertising vocabulary which has been enriched by the following: Youthlastic, Chalkettes, Snugflex, Joylastiques, Sheathlynes, Lasteze, Scandalettes, Silkskin, Flexees and many others. It was said that "Van Raalte is unsurpassed in modifying the rear profile."

All of this is not mere legerdemain of the word, so to speak. Members of large publics do not understand words as mere labels. Ogden and Richards indicate that words become our masters because the nature of language fosters a belief in the independent reality of what are merely verbal contrivances. We are emotionally conditioned to certain words. That is why interest-groups manipulate language.

EMOTIONS, WORDS AND OPINIONS

That, as members of large publics, we are conditioned to respond with various emotions to certain words is an obvious fact. An American electorate, congregation, audience, reader of class periodicals or advertising public is, at times, the victim of a leadership manipulating emotionally tinged words. Emotional responses play a large part in the popular opinion process. Leaders and special pleaders, advertising men and publicity experts use various appeals to the emotions.

For example, the advertising researcher may find that certain words, such as leathery, sticky, matron, clingy and habit, are repulsive to women. Avoid them. There are good sales words that appeal to emotions and vanities, such as poise, charm, dainty, twinkle, bloom, crisp and the like. In the United States, the theme of countless advertisements has been "be lovely to come home to," but the scent makers seemed anxious to turn the waiting American housewife into the priestess of an altar to a frenzied Venus. The perfumes advertised included My Sin, Menace, Intoxication, Frenzy, Surrender, Tigress, Wild Harvest and Tabu. In France, the perfumers frankly stress the aphrodisiac qualities of the product. "Schiaparelli recently defined perfume for a French newspaper as the 'antennas of desire and memory.' She described her own marque 'Shocking' as 'the perfume that subjugates.'" [27] And yet the technicians of the perfume industries scoff at the idea that perfumes are specifically erotic. They state that perfumes are erotic by association with experience and also by the artificially generated whisper of the publicity agent.

[27] *New York Times Mag.*, Aug. 11, 1954, p. 12.

In the art of propaganda, the attempt is made to use catchwords that will arouse emotion and thwart reflection. However emotion may be described in psychological terms, the individual is aware of behavior during disturbed states of bodily and mental functions that differs from behavior in the absence of such disturbance. One of the uses of language is to stimulate such disturbances and the resulting behavior. Fear, anger, resentment, insecurity, avid self-seeking and many other emotional elements are related to certain words. Only the intellectually mature person, and he only under exceptionally favorable conditions of training and of the immediate situation, may partly escape from this bondage to words. His escape is only intermittent.

Appeals to traditional emotional attitudes may be made when the simplest logical analysis would indicate a quite different state of affairs. In the battle against votes for women, especially in England, women were appealed to as "ministering angels," "gentler natures" and "civilizing influences." In the name of "noble maternity," they were asked to abjure political functioning.

Escape from the emotive words is sometimes achieved by inventing new words or changing the designative terms. For example, certain human relationships and social processes have common names in popular parlance. A "science of society," however, develops an esoteric verbiage in sociology or ethnology or law. This is necessary in order not only to designate concepts and provide for the niceties of distinctions but also to create a certain popular respect and to avoid the connotations of the popularly used emotive words. A part of the Marxist appeal has been a complex language with the resultant appearance of objectivity. The two volumes on Middletown have achieved a large number of readers. These books are excellently written and, in comparison with the community surveys that preceded them, relatively thorough studies. However, one factor in their popularity among diverse reading publics has been that an ethnological terminology has largely concealed whatever bias their authors may harbor. When, in the middle of the last century, a few bold professors concluded that sex was neither an obscene mystery nor a dirty joke, they invented a polysyllabic Latin vocabulary with which to discuss it. Using terms that were devoid of popular emotional associations, they were able to discuss sexual functioning with the minimum of disturbance to large publics and to themselves.

Among masses of people, emotional attitudes are related to particular words by training, inculcation, formal and informal education. In earliest language experience there are words rich in emotional, rather than conceptual, connotation. "Bugaboo, hobgoblin, bugbear, hoo-doo, have no clear conceptual content, but they do stand for something to be feared. And in maturity we have a long list of terms whose real significance is as much emotional as it is conceptual. Such, for example, are the terms mother, home, country, traitor, and the like." [28] In the American community there are emotional responses to such words and phrases as "honesty," "kindness," "booster," "knocker," "success," "average man," "practical," "snob," "common sense," "steady," "progress," "radical," "conservative," "atheist," "community spirit," "the happy child," "red-blooded," "the American way," "expert" and scores of other terms.[29] Lists of words with obvious emotional connotations may be developed for different cultures, ages, groups and classes, and the like. Professor Friedrich notes a greater emotional response to the words and phrases of nation and country among rural dwellers than among urban proletarians.[30] The systematic study and use of accumulated information about emotionally tinged words is part of contemporary applied semantics. Modern leaders are not necessarily more astute than those of the past, but their knowledge of language use is more systematic and consciously applied.

The relations between language and communication, between symbol and meaning, between words and understanding, limit and also direct the opinion process, as well as other social processes.[31] But the study of these relations, being peculiarly baffling, has been relatively neglected in social psychology. What are the prevailing attitudes toward certain words and phrases in cultures, classes or groups? The words used in popular controversy and opinion have shifting, variable meanings. How widespread are such attitudes; who is involved; how were such attitudes developed; when and how were emotional conditionings accomplished; how may they be changed? To what extent are meanings involved? Is there a relatively clear-cut concept or understanding of the definitive limits of meaning within which the word may be used? Have certain words, contemporaneously used as catchalls or as vague and hazy reference terms, always been so vague when they have been used by large publics in the past? What is the history of their popular definition? For example, congregations contentedly sing popular hymns without the slightest understanding of many of the phrases therein. These phrases had meaning in the theological controversies of a century or two ago. In a sense, language makes possible the preservation of the emotions of bygone periods, because the anxiety dreams, the fears and the hopes of past ages may be

[28] H. H. Britan, "The Function of Emotions," *Psychol. Rev.*, 33: 37.

[29] R. Lynd and H. M. Lynd, *Middletown in Transition*, Harcourt, Brace and Company, Inc., New York, 1937, pp. 403–419.

[30] C. J. Friedrich, "The Agrarian Basis of Emotional Nationalism," *Pub. Opin. Quar.*, 1: 2: 50–61.

[31] For further discussion of language, thought and opinion, see T. W. Arnold, *The Folklore of Capitalism*, Yale University Press, New Haven, Conn., 1937, especially chaps. 5, 7, 8; S. Chase, *The Tyranny of Words*, Harcourt, Brace and Company, Inc., New York, 1938.

described. But if such emotional experiences of earlier publics are to be understood by contemporaries, they must be described in the language of contemporaries. Phrases, slogans and words about which were woven the warmest emotional loyalties or which aroused fear and antagonism a century ago may leave the modern reader undisturbed. To recapture in any adequate way the significance of any symbols of a people of a bygone age is always difficult. And language symbols are usually more difficult to understand adequately in retrospect than are concretizations in stone, design, pictures and images. How may sentiments be countered by other sentiments? What are the limits of language manipulation on any given topic? What is the record of the language of popular rationalizations in American experience? The members of a businessmen's luncheon club of the 1920's achieved an emotional glow over "service" and thereby often rationalized group acquisitiveness. When have publics learned formal definitions, but have not understood, or have misunderstood, the essence? These and many other questions about language, opinion and social behavior cannot be exactly answered. There is an art, but not a science, of these language forms.

CHAPTER 7

The Leader and Personal Symbolism

> How many turn back toward dreams and magic, how many children
> Run home to Mother Church, Father State,
> To find in their arms the delicious warmth and folding of souls.
> The age weakens and settles home toward old ways.
> An age of renascent faith: Christ said, Marx wrote, Hitler says,
> And though it seems absurd we believe.
> Sad children, yes. It is lonely to be an adult, you need a father.[1]
>
> ROBINSON JEFFERS

The problems of authority and individual freedom and of impersonal and personal authority are persistent. Such problems are also as old as the higher civilizations. Institutional authority of impersonal types is exhibited in the control exercised by laws, constitutions, creeds, symbols, and the like. For the past four centuries, the Western world has been the arena of intermittent revolts against the authority of church and state, and against standards in art and science and economic life.[2] Personal authority is exhibited in the activities of the leader as headman and symbol, as well as in his organizing, directorial, functional capacities. Such personal leadership may gain in authority in institutional crises. At such times, large publics exhibit their persistent fondness for the understandable personal symbol and follow the dramatic leader. The recent charismatic tendencies of Germans and Italians, of Russians and Chinese, illustrate the flight of harried masses to the personal leader.

The roles and functions of the leader, the characteristics of the leader and the techniques of leadership vary with the situation. Various groups, differing in size, the nature of their constituents and the group purposes and functions, require different types of leadership. The characteristics of the leader and the leadership process are obviously dissimilar in a

---

[1] Robinson Jeffers, *Such Counsels You Gave to Me,* Random House, Inc., New York, 1937, p. 105. Reprinted by courtesy of Random House.

[2] J. Dewey, "Authority and Social Change," in *Authority and the Individual,* Harvard Tercentenary Publications, Harvard University Press, Cambridge, Mass., 1937.

114

board meeting, a theater fire, and a Southern political gathering. More-over, types of leadership and of preferred personalities vary greatly in different cultures and at different periods of culture history.[3] There are no universal principles of leadership, but there are processes of leadership and patterns of relationship between leader and follower that are characteristic of types of groups.

It is an evidence of the crudity of the language of the social sciences that a single term "leadership" has been used to designate a process ranging from ascendency in a group of two persons to dominance in publics of hundreds of millions; from an individual as a symbol of an idea, a group or a group value to a functional military director ordering the lives of some millions of men; from the chief gossipmonger of a neighborhood to the headman of a world church or state. It would be better to abandon the word leadership and create a score of verbal symbols more properly designating entities. In this discussion, we shall not be so revolutionary as to create new terms, but will continue to use the word leadership in its present diffuse sense. However, our concern with leadership in relation to public opinion will center on the questions of (1) the leader as symbol, and (2) the characteristics of leadership in large publics.[4]

THE BASES OF AUTHORITY

The sociologist Georg Simmel declared that submission may be exhibited toward a person, a group or an impersonal principle. But in large groups, submission to personal authority is the kind most frequently and dramatically exhibited. The leader is the most vital authority to the common man. However, in special groups, also, thinking and discussion often depend on appeal to personal authority. Dostoevski has his Grand Inquisitor declare that mankind needed "miracle, mystery and authority," stating that "Man is tormented by no greater anxiety than to find someone quickly to whom he can hand over that gift of freedom with which the ill-fated creature is born."[5] Only some sections of modern democratic publics tend toward such extremes and, they, only under conditions of most acute anxiety, fear and frustration.

Large groups persistently ascribe social change, political innovation

[3] Prof. P. A. Sorokin has presented an ingenious analysis in his *Social and Cultural Dynamics,* American Book Company, New York, 1937, vol. III, chap. 15.

[4] An excellent systematic treatment of the literature on the leader process has been written by Cecil A. Gibb for *Handbook of Social Psychology,* Addison-Wesley Publishing Company, Cambridge, Mass., 1954, vol. 2, pp. 877–920. A. W. Gouldner has edited a well-organized book of readings entitled *Studies in Leadership,* Harper & Brothers, New York, 1950.

[5] F. M. Dostoevski, *The Brothers Karamozov,* Part II, book V.

and mechanical invention to personal leaders. Folk tales and legends reflect the doings of heroes, anthropomorphized gods and devils. The personal stereotype is pervasive. This tendency in the individual mental process we have described as a form of stereotyping. The popularization of abstractions and processes is achieved by personalization. The social philosopher has long understood this process. Milton stated, "Delineate so, by likening spiritual to corporal forms, as may express them best." Today, the terse slogan of *Time* magazine is "Names Make News." The names of significant personalities become tags for processes. The idea of mass production is referred to in Europe as "fordisme." The medieval churchman associated wanton destruction with the sack of Rome in 455 by the Vandals, hence "vandalism." Personal leaders provide many symbols of discourse. Members of large publics understand the functioning of personality and personal relationships better than they do the statement of abstractions, principles or ideologies. Concern with the personal characteristics of oneself and of others is a daily preoccupation.

Analysis of movements, parties and other large-group phenomena in the nonpersonal terms of general social process was achieving some increased popular understanding during the past century. The successive state and economic convulsions since 1914 made attractive once more the dramatic personal symbolism of the great man. Large publics have retrogressed to the values with which they were acquainted.

The quest for personal leadership is based in part upon fear and uncertainty. In projecting the father image onto the leaders of the great society, millions of followers seek for the security and personal response of an intimate primary group. There is more belief in authority than in fact and experimentation, because the members of large publics have more confidence in their ability to discern personal qualities than in their capacity to winnow out the pertinent facts.

The guide most favored by mankind has been the medicine man, or priest, reputed to have direct access to divine wisdom; and in his wake came along presently the philosopher who, sinking a shaft into his own mighty mind, and prospecting and introspecting through its darksome galleries, emerged with Absolutes infallible to the good life; Truth, Beauty, Duty, Faith, Loyalty. The philosopher has never seriously crowded his predecessor in popularity, because he could never tell people, in a few plain, loud words what to do. Besides, philosophers talked a mysterious jargon and each has contradicted the other. When the old-time priest rumbled out of his beard, "Thus saith the Lord: Fetch a goat!" that was something any clod could understand and carry in mind. He hurried off to get the goat.[6]

[6] A. G. Keller, *Man's Rough Road*, J. B. Lippincott Company (Stokes), Philadelphia, 1932, p. 4. Quoted by permission of Yale University Press and Frederick A. Stokes Company.

Today, the quest for certainty, the quest for simple, understandable, comprehensible plans in a world of complex social relationships, has intensified the quest for trustworthy personal authority. Authoritarian political leaders are not merely officials, directors, organizers and guides. They are spiritual chiefs. Reliance upon them may be misplaced confidence, but it is psychologically understandable.

But the demand for personal leadership in our time is, in a sense, a mystic quest. It is the search for a magic formula, as if someone had the big secrets and the problem of the masses were simply to find the right person. Fundamentally, however, the derangements of our social order are faults of balance, proportion, organization and the absence of a fundamental logic and philosophy of life. If there existed an adequate description of the flaws of our order—whereby masses of people are thwarted, frustrated and, hence, enraged—very ordinary leaders could explain it simply.

Personal leadership, as distinguished from other forms of authority, may be usefully differentiated into representative, or symbolic, and dynamic, or creative, leadership.[7] The representative leader serves as a symbol for a group without changing its direction or purposes. Dynamic or creative leadership exists when the personal leader directs or modifies the objectives of the group. Obviously, the same individual frequently functions in both capacities. Nevertheless, this is a useful theoretical dichotomy. It is also true that institutional authority and personal leadership are exhibited frequently by the same individual. The Popes of the Roman Catholic church have often been notable examples of this truth.

Although the authority of institutions is expressed in part through personal representatives, there is a vast difference between institutional authority and personal leadership. Institutional authority resides in the traditions, creeds, constitutions, laws and principles of a church, state, legal system, system of knowledge or traditional order. Although leaders of successful mass movements attempt to institutionalize their positions, so that they may be perpetuated, the power process is quite different in institutional administration from that of personal domination. Intermittent revolts against institutional authority are the dominant trend of the past four centuries, but there are some minor trends in the opposite direction. For example, one might cite the small but growing group of intellectuals, conscious of a need for order in the modern scene, who have joined the Roman Catholic church, thus reversing the intellectuals' centuries-old criticism of ecclesiastical authority.

[7] R. Schmidt, "Leadership," *Ency. Soc. Sci.*, 9: 282.

THE LEADER AS SYMBOL

A symbol is a representative simplicity substituted for some complexity. As we noted when discussing psychological processes and opinion, the process of symbolizing is inevitable. The leader not only organizes a wide variety of symbols for his followers, but in many cases he himself becomes a personal symbol of paramount importance. The dynamic or creative leader may intermittently serve as a symbol, but the representative of an institution is almost wholly a group symbol.

The principal reasons for personal representations are psychological. We discussed the need for personal imagery in commenting on the basis of stereotypes. These tags for groups and types are innumerable. There are popular symbols of the male and the female, the ignorant and the learned, the aristocrat and the boor, the rich man and the poor man, and so on, in the infinity of human classifications. Human variety is too complex for popular thinking. And so there are representative personal symbols. Many such figures are provided in the graphic arts. The cartoonist and the artist implement mass thinking by providing personal stereotypes. Distorted legendary figures provide many more. But living leaders also serve as representative figures. Washington, Lincoln, Lee, Hitler, Mussolini, Stalin, Gandhi and hundreds of others have been dynamic leaders who were likewise symbols. They caught the imagination of mankind. They were the representative figures. To such figures are related the warm emotional attachments and loyalties of masses of men. Questioning of the symbols is resented. But, if once they are questioned or generally discussed as symbols, they lose a part of their value. The popular discussion of the meaning of Britain's kingship during the crisis of 1937 may have done inestimable damage to the prestige of the British Crown.

The average man quests for the ideal personal figure. "The reason is that the function of the great and famous man is to be a symbol, and the real question in other minds is not so much, What are you? as, What can I believe you are? What can you help me to feel and be? How far can I use you as a symbol in the development of my instinctive tendency?" [8] Personal symbols are first obtained from the immediate environment, the father and mother, relatives and friends, but later the processes of communication provide a wealth of symbols from the general culture.

Which leaders become symbols will be determined by the paramount values of the culture. The heroes of the past have been representative personages who have achieved dominance through strength, war, sainthood, the championship of ideal values, dignified age, courageous explo-

[8] C. H. Cooley, *Human Nature and the Social Order,* Charles Scribner's Sons, New York, 1902, p. 341. Quoted by permission.

ration, learning, invention, industry, and the like. In primitive life the wise, the aged and the courageous; in the Middle Ages the knight, the scholar and the saint; in Chinese culture the formal scholar; in recent Western civilization the captains of industry have been representative men. The modern authoritarian state has reemphasized the leader principle, with its Führer and Duce, its Stalin and Mao. In the creation of contemporary symbols, modern publicity plays a dominant role. The process is speeded up. In the great society, ideas about leaders are acquired primarily from press, television and motion picture. The leader symbol of the past could not emerge so suddenly for large publics.

In addition to serving as symbols, modern leaders in large publics are actively engaged in manipulating the symbols which are most effective in influencing the opinions of large publics. "Because of their transcendent practical importance, no successful leader has ever been too busy to cultivate the symbols which organize his following. What privileges do within a hierarchy, symbols do for the rank and file. They conserve unity." [9]

THE HERO AS LEADER SYMBOL

The most effective leader symbols are the national, cultural and group heroes. These are personifications of values, causes and critical events. Their names, pictures and statues are a focus of the emotional loyalties of their publics. "The hero in history is the individual to whom we can justifiably attribute preponderant influence in determining an issue or event whose consequence would have been profoundly different if he had not acted as he did." [10] As Sidney Hook has characterized the hero, he is essentially an event-making man, "whose actions are a consequence of outstanding capacities of intelligence, will, and character rather than of accidents of position." The historical hero is a leader of unusual effectiveness in influencing his period who has also become an outstanding and distinguished symbol. As a symbol, he has become a legendary figure, usually obviously patterned to the desires, expectations and psychological needs of his mass admirers. The hero is a leader popularly assumed to be of unusually great competence who has become uniquely imbedded in the memory and consciousness of large publics.

Of all the presidents of the United States, Washington, Jefferson, Jackson, Lincoln and Theodore Roosevelt are leaders who are established as hero symbols in popular esteem. A series of the major military heroes from Washington to MacArthur and Eisenhower are known to every schoolboy. There are lesser-known heroes of reform movements, such as John Brown,

[9] W. Lippmann, *Public Opinion*, Harcourt, Brace and Company, Inc., New York, 1922, p. 177.

[10] S. Hook, *The Hero in History*, The John Day Company, Inc., New York, 1942.

Carrie Nation, Margaret Sanger, Anthony Comstock and Dr. Townsend. There are the more transient heroes of the world of entertainment, amusement and sports, the athletic heroes, the stars of motion pictures, television and popular music. Artists and writers are not esteemed as popular heroes in the United States, as they have frequently been in Europe. Perhaps Walt Whitman as a folk poet, chanting the virtues and vices of the common man, would come nearest to popular hero status as a writer. Scholars and scientists are not elevated to hero rank in the United States, although in a few instances those who have made applications of science which have resulted in extensions of the common welfare are idealized, as was Thomas Edison and, perhaps, Henry Ford.

THE CHARISMATIC LEADER

The leader symbol of greatest potency is the charismatic leader. A charismatic leader is a leader believed to be in some unusually intimate relation to supernatural power or to have some extraordinary qualities beyond the normally human. Charismatic authority is the leader's authority under conditions where the governed submit because of belief in the extraordinary quality of the leader.[11]

History abounds in illustrations of charisma in leaders, whether the power was assumed, alleged, believed or actual. Primitive priests, shamans and medicine men were essentially charismatic leaders, as were innumerable prophets and religious leaders. Julius Caesar, King Arthur, Charlemagne and hundreds of others have been major political charismatic leaders. Indeed, at crises this pattern has been the rule rather than the exception. Yet, in the twentieth century, we have been amazed at the recrudescence of charismatic power in the authoritarian rulers, Hitler, Lenin, Stalin and Mussolini. Not so firmly ensconced in practice or belief as were the charismatic leaders of the past, the modern examples have been the products of the crises of large publics; of insecurity, frustration, despair and fear.

Charisma must be potent, active, effective and successful or it withers rapidly. Perhaps the only exception is to be found in religion in the institutional headman, as, for example, the Tibetan Dalai and Panchen Lamas. To fail ruins the charismatic leader, as evidence of the departure of power. "If he wants to be a prophet, he must perform miracles; if he wants to be a war lord, he must perform heroic deeds. Above all, however, his divine mission must prove itself in that those who faithfully

---

[11] Max Weber emphasized the importance of the concept of charismatic leader, which he defined. The term refers to "the gift of grace." One may now refer to Weber in English translation in H. H. Gerth and C. W. Mills (trans.), *From Max Weber*, Oxford University Press, New York, 1946.

surrender to him must fare well. If they do not fare well, he is obviously not the master sent by the gods." [12] In any case, modern charismatic leadership would be of short duration in periods of crisis when short-lived mass emotions are intense.

THE AGITATOR

Leaders of diffuse economic, racial, religious and chauvinistic causes, the catalysts of the emotional discontents and frustrated envies of what has been called the "lunatic fringe" of the American public, are the "agitators." Unlike the reformer with a specific panacea, the agitator does not attempt to trace social dissatisfaction to a clearly discernible cause or to offer a specific solution. He is not a hero to large publics and does not arouse heroic, self-sacrificing emotions, but, characteristically, generates spite, venom and hate between races, classes, parties and nations. The host of political demagogues in the political history of the United States, inasmuch as they have functioned before the larger and more heterogeneous publics, have been somewhat more moderate than the more fugitive, commercialized purveyors of racial, economic and religious hatreds. However, they are all a product of real social malaise in which the grievances and fears of some sections of the population have been inadequately met by the more conservative leaders.

To many listeners who feel that in a confusing world they are the eternal dupes, conspired against by hostile individuals, forces and groups, the agitator offers a simple description of the nature of the menacing plutocrats, the Reds, the racial enemies or foreigners.

The listener does not directly participate in the major fields of social production and is therefore always fearful that, given the slightest social maladjustment, his insignificant job will vanish and with it will vanish his social status. He senses that in some way he cannot quite fathom life has cheated him. . . . And yet he wonders why his fate should have been so unhappy . . . Bound and circumscribed by a series of uncontrollable circumstances, he becomes increasingly aware of how futile and desperately aimless his life is. . . . He is on the bottom, on the outside, and he fears there is nothing he can do about it. . . . The listener would like to do something about it, something drastic and decisive that will do away with the whole mess. Imagine, strike one blow on the table and everything is changed.[13]

If even the less rational of the agitator's followers recognize that such simple, direct action is hardly feasible, they can at least hate and venom-

[12] Weber, *ibid.*, p. 249.

[13] L. Lowenthal and N. Guterman, *Prophets of Deceit*, Harper & Brothers, New York, 1949, p. 136. This excellent study of the American agitator is one of a series of reports entitled *Studies in Prejudice*.

ously envy or despise. And perhaps some day some more violent direct action can be possible. Actually, the agitator may lead to further frustration, but in the meantime the follower may achieve some psychological catharsis. The agitator influences opinion by profoundly agitating the emotions.

THE CHARACTERISTICS OF LEADERSHIP IN LARGE PUBLICS

The psychological discussion of the characteristics of personality, including leadership and subordination, has been carried on primarily in terms of "traits." Consideration of characteristic dispositions or traits as a "certain kind of response manifested in a particular kind of situation" and preoccupation with classifications of such traits for various human groupings have been hindered by the conflict between biologically minded psychologists and culturally minded sociologists. There are great individual differences, and there are great diversities of the social situation. To assume characteristic dispositions in particular situations means ignoring neither the basis of the disposition in the organism nor the diversity of expression of the disposition in various situations. Considered thus, the concept of trait is usable, just as the sociologist's concept of attitude is permissible. No single trait or any combination of traits determines behavior; the conditions of the moment are also decisive. Traits are discovered through inference from the individual functioning. But the psychologist must guard against any assumption of their existence as unvarying units. It is assumed, then, that there are characteristic dispositions or traits underlying the conduct of a person. The psychologist does not usually assume that the traits correspond exactly to the neuropsychic dispositions of individuals. Nor are traits assumed to be innate, although innate factors are related to some of them. In large measure, traits are acquired in the social experience of the individual, being determined by the prevailing values of the culture and its subgroups. And the many groups within a large public will view that public's leader quite differently and evaluate him on different scales of value. However, it may be that a few broad characteristics may be noted which are fairly general.

All dynamic or creative leadership influences the opinions of followers. Institutional authority may simply reflect the mores. But dynamic leadership also functions in guiding choices at levels below those at which opinions could be said to exist. Goldfish, placed in a bowl with a fish that has been successfully conditioned to a simple aquarium maze, learn at a faster rate than do those in a group without a leader.[14] In human groups, leaders provide many patterns of behavior which are copied by

[14] W. C. Allee, "Relatively Simple Animal Aggregations," in C. Murchison (ed.), *Handbook for Social Psychology*, 1935, p. 944.

followers who have not considered the alternatives. However, from the smallest to the largest groups the opinion process is influenced by leaders in varying degrees.

The characteristics of successful leaders and the processes of leadership in influencing opinion differ with the size and type of groups and with the situation or "field structure." There do not appear to be general characteristics of leadership that are everywhere effective in influencing the opinions of followers. The psychologist's quest for general leadership traits has been futile. The characteristics of leaders of small discussion groups—committees, gangs, families, clans, neighborhoods and other small groups—differ from leadership qualities in large publics consisting of thousands and hundreds of thousands of members. There is some experimental literature on leadership in small groups.[15] Certainly, opinions are influenced in all such groups, but we shall not discuss the studies of face-to-face relations. In the large groups and publics, there are diverse preferences for leadership qualities, depending upon the group's size, organization, purposes, relation to other groups, the prevailing attitudes and values and, in general, upon its field structure. The situation must always ultimately determine the preferred qualities. Leadership qualities vary under democracy, fascism, communism; in different ages, periods, cultures; under national ascendency or degradation; in an expanding or contracting economy.

Until recently, the psychologist rarely considered the situation in his search for leadership traits. But long before the social psychologist attempted his more detailed classifications, the social philosopher had much to say about the characteristics of leaders in large publics. Certain generalizations are essentially valid for whole groups of cultures and over long time periods. For example, the advantage of positive statements in comparison with negations has been realized in Western cultures for many centuries.

Regardless of the situation, large publics cherish the positive statement. Their own requirements may be vague, but the leader of opinion in any large public states a positive program most of the time, although his program may be an attack on the existing order. The individual thinker or small esoteric groups may maintain a negative or pessimistic viewpoint in philosophy, political ideas or economic doctrine. But not the large publics in the Western world of the last few centuries. Grim predestination never won the mass converts as did Methodism. And the village atheist of the last half of the nineteenth century trod his lonely way amidst the bounding folk life of America. The agnostic or atheistic attitude is disparaged. Political nihilism was never a mass doctrine. In such

[15] See especially the references in Gibb, *op. cit.*

a "climate of opinion," the confident leader with a positive statement is at an advantage. The Fascist leaders stated positive programs embellished as a great spiritual message. Mussolini mouthed grandiose generalities about the rebuilding of the glory that was Rome. A depressed and bewildered nation welcomed the positive and confident assertions of Roosevelt. Contemporary insecurities have intensified the quest for leaders with positive programs. In the democracies, this has made ever more true the old political maxim "You can't whip somebody with nobody."

Although leadership qualities cannot be considered abstractly but must be related to the type of situation and the specific situation, we may generalize somewhat about leadership qualities under nineteenth-century political democracy. Men were leaders in democracies without possessing all the qualities we shall note, but not without evidencing many of them. Viscount Bryce said that leaders in democracy must possess initiative, comprehension of the forces that affect the needs of the people, eloquence of voice and writing, self-confidence and the ability to inspire confidence, attract capable lieutenants and achieve personal publicity.[16] These he considered the minimum general requirements.

Political leaders must arouse faith in themselves. In the rapidly changing social order of the Western world, faith is accorded to the leaders who exhibit speed of decision. Decisiveness, especially at crises, injects something clear-cut into the vagueness and confusion of the situation. In a battery of tests given to a number of leaders, W. H. Cowley included three on speed of decision. The leaders made unquestionably high scores on these tests.[17] The most popular American presidents have all exhibited at least apparent speed of decision.

"The prime condition of ascendency is the presence of undirected energy in the person over whom it is to be exercised; it is not so much forced upon us from without as demanded from within."[18] Leaders survive and grow in power who reflect the vague feelings and general aspirations of large groups. Hitler hurled defiance at what many followers considered international persecution. President Roosevelt retained numerous followers who opposed almost every specific measure his administration had put forward. But they agreed with a general attitude that he seemed to express clearly and with obvious justice, portraying existing convictions in a vivid manner. It is in this sense that it has long been declared of leaders in democracy that they are "the common mind to an uncommon degree."

[16] J. Bryce, *Modern Democracies*, The Macmillan Company, New York, 1921, book II, chap. 76.
[17] W. H. Cowley, "The Traits of Face-to-face Leaders," *Jour. Abn. Soc. Psychol.*, 26: 304–313.
[18] C. H. Cooley, *Human Nature and the Social Order*, Charles Scribner's Sons, New York, 1902, p. 319.

The popular leader must have or build up some elements of personal uniqueness. The most popular American leaders have been colorful figures. Dramatic situations for exhibiting uniqueness must exist or be created. He is a character. A distinctive carriage and style of dress, unusual phrases, gestures and dramatic utterances have been his usual stock in trade. A political commentator has written, ". . . probably the most important single accomplishment for the politically ambitious, the most effective asset they can possibly acquire, is the fine art of seeming to say something without doing so." [19] The leader has uniqueness and magnetism.[20] If he does not have these qualities and attains high office, his publicity men ascribe them to him.

Breadth of sympathy is requisite for successful leadership. Contemporary insecurity increases the importance of friendliness in the leader. In crisis situations the great humane figure becomes legendary. Lincoln is our most notable example. Firm in public, he was kindly and sympathetic in personal relations. It is difficult to feign sympathy. Crude though the expressions of sympathy of the urban precinct leader may be, they are more often than not a product of genuine human interest, as well as of political tradition. Indeed, some of the most corrupt of political bosses have been men of genuine and strong sympathies. And constituents understand and appreciate such responses, though they may be vague as to the allocation of city funds. Smiles, greetings, participation in simple human incidents, kindliness, a measure of conviviality, are necessary to the politician who must come in contact with his public.

The leader appears as master of the situation. He is dominant and assured. In face-to-face situations he may be blatantly assured, as witness the techniques of the demagogue or revivalist. On coming upon the platform the demagogue commands, "Let's try that applause again," or, "I ought to get a better hand on that one," if one of his epigrams fails. Of Aimée Semple McPherson, it was said, "As a director she is incomparable. While others are performing, she never for an instant permits interest to flag; at the first sign of restlessness she steps forward. 'All join in with him now! Sail on!' If a young singer's voice proves weak and, therefore, uninspiring, Sister snatches her own tambourine and drives home the rhythm. Let a recitation be dull, she will advance beaming to inquire if it isn't grand." [21] However, browbeating is an unsubtle, though often an effective, form of command. Mastery and personal ascendency

[19] F. R. Kent, *Political Behavior,* William Morrow & Company, Inc., New York, 1928, p. 73.

[20] E. W. Bogardus, *Leaders and Leadership,* Appleton-Century-Crofts Company, Inc., New York, 1934, chap. 16.

[21] R. W. Nafe, "A Psychological Description of Leadership," *Jour. Soc. Psychol.,* 1: 250. Permission to quote granted.

depend upon a myriad of factors. Physical characteristics are important in the more visually dramatic types of situations. The oft-criticized studies of E. B. Gowin on the size and weight of executives indicated that the more important executives were heavier and taller than the less important.[22] Though part of the differences in weight may be explained in terms of age and sedentary life, the differences in height are not so readily explained. There are fashions in preferred physical types, but these characteristics cannot be considered in isolation.

A certain reserve and a modicum of mystery and inscrutability are characteristic of popular political leadership.[23] Mystery may be crudely presented, as in Hitler's assurance to mass audiences that he had the plans for the economic regeneration of the German Reich in the drawers of his desk in the Brown House in Munich. The imagination of followers is stimulated. Even the most frank and apparently confiding of leaders retains areas of reserve. The creation of mystery may be heightened by an inscrutable countenance, silence (von Moltke was said to be silent in seven languages), mysterious phrases, journeys, meetings and the like. The primitive leader and folk leaders made much of mystery. Doctors, lawyers and religious leaders are often titillatingly inscrutable. Certain professors and lecturers lead their audiences on and on by the method of the "big secrets." The modern political leader cannot forgo this effective technique of power.

The leader of large publics must be an organizer and also make astute use of existing organizations. Under the party system in democracies, the leader must have ability to function within party organizations. Indeed, Frank R. Kent insisted that nothing would compensate for the lack of ability to deal with party organization.[24] Leaders of mass movements must competently organize their contacts with lieutenants and must select subordinates who will organize the channels of communication and of administration out to the most distant followers. Of course, this is all carried on within the values of a particular culture. When Hitler spoke, the German people were told that there could be no excuse for not having listened to every word spoken by their beloved leader. But the American political leader, not only of groups in power but of those striving for power, must be capable of organizing or of selecting lieutenants to organize rituals, ceremonies, public relations, subgroups, committees, divisions, the efficient direction of energies of followers, the keeping of records and a host of other directorial duties. He organizes and integrates.

[22] E. B. Gowin, *The Executive and His Control of Men*, The Macmillan Company, New York, 1915.

[23] Cooley, *op. cit.* The chapter on leadership is the most brilliant essay in English on leadership and personal ascendency.

[24] Kent, *op. cit.*, pp. 68 ff.

In the United States, the leader must not appear to be primarily a theoretician, nor concerned with the maintenance of ideological consistency. Such preoccupation with idea systems is viewed askance. In our heterogeneous population, with a variety of cultural roots, there is the belief that the Constitution, the values emanating from the statements of the Founding Fathers and the American experience have provided an adequate philosophy for public life. Hence, it is generally thought that emphasis on ideologies could only be disruptive. As there is no general yearning for consistency or for a complete thought system, a popular leader must not be suspected of preoccupation with theoretical consistency.[25] A certain pragmatic calculation, adaptation and accommodation are considered the requisite characteristics of a popular leader. He is considered as more likely to be effective if he responds to opportunities without being overly concerned with consistency or theory.

We have not examined the question of the motivation of leaders of large publics. This issue is currently increasingly important as the disadvantages of major leadership are more evident. The pressures, strains, hard work and fatigue, the bitter public opprobrium, as well as adulation, are increasing. At the same time, the traditional rewards are less in evidence.

> In the bad old days it was not so bad:
>> The top of the ladder
> Was an amusing place to sit; success
>> Meant quite a lot—leisure
> And huge meals, more palaces filled with more
>> Objects, girls and horses
> Than one would ever get round to. . . .
>> Honours
> Are not so physical or jolly now,
>> For the sort of Powers
> We are used to are not like that. . . .
> The last word on how we may live or die
>> Rests today with quiet
> Men, working too hard in rooms that are too big,
>> Reducing to figures
> What is the matter, what is to be done.[26]

[25] On why a theory has seemed needless in the United States, consult the brilliant essay by D. J. Boorstin, *The Genius of American Politics*, University of Chicago Press, Chicago, 1953.

[26] Excerpt from "The Managers" from *Nones* by W. H. Auden, copyright, 1951, by W. H. Auden. Reprinted by permission of Random House, Inc.

CHAPTER 8

Legends and Myths

We may say that legends are modified accounts of the past events and of historic personages, whereas myths are imaginative accounts of the meaning of life. . . .

Myths and legends come down to us from the past as a part of our cultural heritage. . . .

The ordinary man today is as unaware of the myths and legends about him as myths and legends, as is the primitive person. . . .

The myth and legend are adult extensions of the infantile world of fantasy and make believe. . . .

The process is really inevitable. If we did not have our present legends to hand on, we would unconsciously create others. . . .

As we become more and more skilled in advertising and conscious propaganda, legend making has become more deliberate. . . .

Whether legends are deliberate or not, the fact remains that masses of mankind live in these images. . . .[1]

K. YOUNG

During the last half of the nineteenth century, various social theorists became increasingly preoccupied with the problem of myths and legends. Students of religious ideas and institutions, taking up the cudgels for rationalism, discussed the mythology of the various religious systems. The evolutionists studied myths and legends as an early development in culture history. Etymologists considered the development of myths as related to changes in language. Ethnologists found in the mythology of primitive peoples an inexhaustible source for the building up of theories about the past values and concepts of primitive peoples. Psychologists and psychoanalysts have examined mythology and found, to their satisfaction, evidence of persistent psychological drives. The historian pieced out the historic record with mythological evidence. And finally, by the close of the century and in the opening decades of this century, certain

[1] K. Young, *Social Psychology*, Appleton-Century-Crofts, Inc., New York, 1930, chap. 17. Quoted by permission.

modern beliefs were discussed in terms of mythology and legendry by Sorel, Pareto, Delaisi and others.[2]

A part of the beliefs and ideas of all peoples are the stories that of late years have been called "myths" and "legends." Among primitive peoples and in folk cultures the myths and legends are a part of the folklore of the people. These stories satisfy some psychological need and maintain cultural values. Today such stories are increasingly imposed by a self-conscious leadership which aims at the promulgation of some doctrine or the elevation of some individual. To be sure, leadership in the past had sometimes used myths and legends as an agency of control, but the leadership of the past did not have mass media and psychologically sophisticated publicity agencies at its command.

The aristocrats, who ruled feudal society (as was then believed) by divine appointment, buttressed their own dominion with an elaborate structure of myths concerning the nature of the physical universe. They looked with no tolerance whatever upon the early scientific discoveries. Bruno was burned and Galileo was threatened, not because they said true things about the world, but because the saying of true things about the world was incompatible with the lordship of the aristocrats. Physical science was one of the weapons which the middle class forged against the aristocracy; the aristocracy had therefore to do all in its power to prevent the weapon's being forged. For Galileo to assert that the earth is a sphere rotating upon an axis, when feudal myth held it to be stationary and flat, was subversive.[3]

The terms "myth" and "legend" are often used synonymously. However, myths are those stories which deal with the world of the supernatural. "Myths are tales of the supernatural world and share also, therefore, the characteristics of the religious complex."[4] Such tales have no factual origin. But the legend is a greatly exaggerated or untrue account, of some person or incident, that may have had some basis in fact but has been distorted in the telling. The legend recounts material about a person or incident; the myth relates to a general concept of supernatural relations or central folk value. All sacred books begin with myths of gods, demons, personalized animals and various animistic conceptions. There are the great social myths of God-ordained rulers, economic processes, utopias, and the like. In every society there is also a wealth of legendary ma-

[2] G. Sorel, *Reflections on Violence,* 1906. Authorized translation by T. E. Hulme, Peter Smith, New York, 1935.

V. Pareto, *The Mind and Society* (English trans.), Harcourt, Brace and Company, Inc., New York, 1935, vol. I, sections 650 ff.

F. Delaisi, *Political Myths and Economic Realities,* The Viking Press, Inc., New York, 1925.

[3] B. Dunham, *Man Against Myth,* Little, Brown & Company, Boston, 1947, p. 17.

[4] R. Benedict, *Ency. Soc. Sci.,* 11: 179.

terial about founders or early leaders; the legends of Roland, King Arthur, Robin Hood, Virgil, Washington and many others. There are also numerous legends of incidents in a people's history. Man evidences a persistent tendency toward what Henri Bergson called the "fabulatory function," that is, the creation and maintenance of exaggerated and fabulous legends. And these myths and legends obviously influence popular opinion when their subject matter deals with topics that have become controversial. The legends about other peoples are a basis for opinion formation in international crises; legends about economic processes influence boards of directors; legends about racial groups complicate race relations; legends about personality types affect everyday judgments; legends about national heroes and villains influence popular conceptions of history. Masses of people are not aware of such stories as legends, although the professional thinker has been aware of some of the popular stories as myths and legends since the time when Aristotle began the verificatory process.

THE PSYCHOLOGICAL AND CULTURAL BASES FOR MYTHS AND LEGENDS

Cultural values become incorporated in the psychological functioning of the individual. There are also drives, impulses and instincts which, although modified and conditioned by human social experience, are characteristic of the original structure of man. In describing the bases of cultural products it is common to contrast the cultural and the psychological bases. We thus set up a false dichotomy, for they are often inextricably intertwined. At the present moment we often belabor the obvious in discussing psychological and cultural factors. But it seems necessary for a contemporary writer to do so, inasmuch as individualistic psychology has been so diffused in popular thought. Social systems control the expressions of human drives, but human drives are also in part responsible for certain expressions in social systems.

The content of those accounts which we label myths and legends is primarily determined by the social situation and societal values, but it is also to some extent the product of the original nature of man. The individual has food hungers. When he is inadequately satisfied, he may create legends of bountiful fare. Paul Bunyan was a legendary figure created by American lumbermen. In the cycle of stories dealing with Bunyan's exploits, one whole group recounts in descriptive detail the types and amounts of food that he provided for his lumbermen. This "wishful thinking" of the raconteur is in sharp contrast to the actually scanty fare in American lumber camps in the last century.

The physical and psychological conditions of the upper-class Southerner "after the war" were wretched. It was in this period that legends of life "before the war" arose. Today, national stereotypes are still influenced by this picture—the white-columned houses, the boxwood hedges, the charming women, the gallant men, the numerous and contented slaves. A whole class, wounded in spirit, inflated the realities of Southern life into a legendary mélange. Sectional groups and the various families therein fostered the legends of their past importance.

After the Russian Revolution, a rationalistically minded leadership attempted to supplant the folk preoccupation with the supernatural by providing naturalistic explanations. The folk resisted with a flood of popular stores purporting to give accounts of supernatural intervention in the affairs of men. Later, the fabrication of legends of national heroes in the Communist state was almost on a propaganda assembly-line basis. When Marshal Rokossovski was assigned to Poland as commander of the Polish armed forces, his pictures were plastered all over Poland and a carefully fabricated and quite untrue biography was generally distributed.. Indeed, his Polish origin was brought to light only at that time. This official version was learned by rote by every Polish school child. But, according to fairly trustworthy information, the Marshal's mother was Russian, and he himself had never lived in Poland.

Legends develop about historic figures. Some of these legends are literary creations; others are folk products. Clusters of anecdotal stories are attached to the name of a folk hero. The stories are created or fall into disuse largely in terms of the prevailing values of any age. The "debunking" biographies of the 1920's primarily "debunked" those items in biographical accounts that were not then in good repute. Legends about historic figures have utility in supporting the prevailing social norms and as an agency of social control. The legendary figure becomes a type. He personifies useful values. The legendary stories are developed from experiences wrongly interpreted; from false inferences from actual occurrences; from incidents that might have happened to such a person; from incidents that actually happened, but not to the person to whom they are ascribed (Parson Weems, first biographer of Washington, told the cherry-tree story about Washington; this incident actually happened to Parson Weems, with the exception that he did tell a lie and did receive a whipping). Those things which augment his legend are ascribed to the legendary figure. For example, Virgil is a historical character, but there is also a Virgil legend. There were numerous legends of Virgil's birth, the most widespread of which is that when Virgil was born the whole city of Rome shook from end to end. (This satisfied the persistent folk belief that supernatural powers are especially concerned with superior persons. Similar legends of the cataclysms of nature accompanying their births have been created about practically all outstanding popular leaders. The Lincoln legend contains many such stories.) Virgil's amorous experiences became the basis of legend. The folk are persistently interested in this fundamental avocation. Virgil was credited with magical powers. The folk ascribe such power to most legendary personages. The Virgil of legend heroically defied the emperor of Rome. The more popular folk heroes usually illustrate the wishful thinking of the masses to defy constituted authority.[5]

Although folk values are preeminent in determining the content of myths and legends, the mental processes of the originators are also involved. The distortion of an incident, having some basis in fact, into the popular legendary account is due in part to individual psychological processes. K. Young lists the principal psychological factors as:

(1) The emotional state of the observers. This is usually increased at the time of observation, if the situation is dramatic.

(2) Errors of perception at the time of observation. If the event is spectacular or unfamiliar, it is more difficult to perceive it accurately. Attention will be limited to a few details.

(3) Errors in recall. These are especially evident when the event is later being described to others.

(4) Predispositions, the apperceptive mass of the observers. These predispositions are made of old stereotypes, prejudices and legends still persisting in the observers.

(5) False interpretations by the observers. As far as they imagine the characteristics of the observed individuals, the observers will err in interpreting their acts.

(6) The time elapsing between perception and recall. After a very brief interval, the event as recalled differs from the actual event. As the time elapsing between the event and its recall increases, observers begin to add or change or forget innumerable details.[6]

The content of a great many myths and legends is based upon desires and wishes of the narrators. These desires may have been culturally instilled or may be relatively innate, as in the case of hunger and sex drives. Among the psychologists, the psychoanalysts have been especially active in interpreting myths as symbolic expressions of suppressed wishes, or as frankly avowed expressions of conscious wishes of a general character. Desires for a glorious hereafter, for social achievement and prestige, for physical power and for other values are expressed in the mythology of various peoples. Such values are the product of cultures. But wish fulfillment in myths providing expression of the Oedipus complex, or of simple sexual adventure, or of the Madonna cult is more universal. Freud maintains that our psyche has the tendency to work over the world picture so that it corresponds to such wishes. Fairy tales, myths and legends

[5] Pareto, *op. cit.*, section 668.
[6] Young, *op. cit.*, p. 440. Quoted by permission.

are among the most popular expressions of such wish structures. For the psychoanalyst, myths represent the unconscious processes of whole groups and races. These stories have been adapted to the common needs of countless generations. The individually unique elements have been eliminated, and there remain the general themes that are common to all the individuals of the groups. Further, one may analyze myth content in terms of fundamental emotions. Obviously, many a story is related to fear. In many Southern towns there are few Roman Catholics. Yet the South is a breeding ground for legendary stories about the church leaders, especially the Pope.

The legends and myths which persist in a culture are those which fulfill some popular wish or maintain some generally accepted social value. Therefore, they can best be understood in terms of particular cultures. The legends of a people preoccupied with struggle, action and competition reflect that interest. The legendary figures who impassively contemplate life are primarily a product of Oriental cultures. Legendary figures among the Plains Indians had splendid "visions." The dominant values are reflected.

Legends and myths have a functional role in society. Opinions are influenced by the prevailing tales. The standards of primary groups, as well as those of the larger associations, are buttressed by such stories. Families, clubs, neighborhoods, gangs and numerous other primary groups create legends that are functionally useful in supporting dominant values. Most families develop legends that are used to influence the children and to maintain family pride and prestige in various ways. The role of such stories is obvious. The preciousness of the individual to the family and the importance of his position in the universe may be emphasized in family legend. Perhaps the most widespread type of family legends has to do with the superior wealth of an ancestor or with his clever economic dealings. This is inevitable in a society oriented, as is ours, to prestige from wealth. And there are the legends of lost opportunity for wealth, of social status of ancestors, of feats of arms and military prowess, of strength, courage and daring, of abilities in cooking and household duties, and, indeed, of whatever values are esteemed within the family. We are referring here to the legends that are created within a family group. And the dimmer these stories become with age, the more they can be varied in the telling. Increasing distortion makes possible their use for illustration of ever more varied values. In addition to the legends unique in a particular family, each family draws upon the varied store of popular folk legend.

MODERN LEGENDRY

The legends of primary groups relate to a relatively narrow range of values, whereas the scope of the subject matter of legends in the great society is much broader. New legends are created in connection with every social movement, and as the attention areas of modern man have widened the number of his legends has increased. The political legendry of primitive and folk peoples was relatively limited, dealing with a few folk heroes and leaders, past and present. Political legendry of man in the great society provides a galaxy of hundreds of legendary figures, taken from many national groups and from various historic periods.

These legends are now formally transmitted in textbooks, popular literature, political speeches and the motion pictures. In textbooks in use in the American public schools there are innumerable distortions at variance with the best contemporary scholarship concerning prominent American leaders. Washington, Franklin, Adams, Hamilton, Benedict Arnold, Andrew Jackson, Lincoln, Andrew Johnson and many others are still frequently presented in accounts that are more in accord with popular legendry than with historic fact. There is no need to tear down our national idols. But the present simplicity of presentation reflects the limited interests of the common man, rather than historic knowledge concerning these figures or our functional needs for more complex symbols.

Moreover, as societal leadership has become more skilled in manipulating popular impressions, legend making has become more deliberate. Every major political figure is concerned, as are numbers of his skilled lieutenants, with the development of his legend. Sometimes such legends are created in an incredibly short time, as, for example, the Calvin Coolidge legend. And not only in the political field has the manufacture of legends become a highly skilled and conscious art. Businessmen and financiers, society women and movie stars, religious leaders and reformers, and, indeed, all persons who achieve a high visibility are in quest of a legend. In the field of entertainment, Hollywood and TV have developed a whole industry devoted to legendry and gossip in the screen magazines and newspaper stories. The story of the stars follows the general pattern of the national fairy tale, of rise to fame, of material wealth and opulence, of sex and beauty. "The nation has turned to the worship of these picture gods, real and yet unreal, common as life and yet larger than life, known in minuter detail than the next door neighbor and yet shiningly remote, because they have come to represent certain national ideals reduced to the lowest common denominator." [7]

The particular structure of society and its pyramid of values has de-

[7] R. Suckow, "Hollywood Gods and Goddesses," *Harper's*, July, 1936.

termined the legendary figures of every age. Today the process of legend making is accelerated and the number of legends vastly increased. A folk people creates as many legends as it needs in the functional activities of its life and thought. But today, societal leadership provides a plethora of legendry, often more adapted and suited to the needs of the creators of the legends than to those of the masses who are asked to believe them.

The development of myths and legends, as used by groups and classes in the past, was seldom based on sheer invention by the mythmaker. They were usually picked up and elaborated from the great mass of all kinds of ideas accumulated through the centuries. However, the process of legend making today, as carried on by publicity men fabricating legends about persons and events, often presents untruths. But the ideas and stories must, in a general way, fit into the general climate of belief and opinion of masses of people. Thus a legend-making Hollywood agent must fit his fabrications about movie stars into the preferred values of American culture. Though he may ascribe virtues and behavior to his young woman star of which she is exceptionally innocent, these must be virtues and behavior that her "fans" cherish. In this free-enterprise legend making, competing groups clamor for attention and for acceptance of their product.

We shall briefly sketch four legends: the myth of the devil, which was primarily a folk product, although partly limned by the leaders of the church; the Lincoln legend, which contains many elements of folk invention and others produced by a self-conscious leadership; the legend of the fighting frontiersmen; and the legend of Calvin Coolidge, which is almost entirely the product of astute publicity men.

THE MYTH OF THE DEVIL

The mythologies of various peoples contain anthropomorphic devils. Personification of evil pervades folk thinking, and man has persistently imagined epic struggles between good and evil demons. Vritra, Ahriman, the Egyptian Set and the Christian devil, or Satan, are major evil spirits, but there is also a host of others. There is an evolution of the devil in Old Testament records. He was a fallen angel, the original tempter of man, the envious rival of Yahweh, and he was often conveniently identified with the enemy's gods.[8] Under early Christianity he assumed gigantic spiritual proportions, as all the greatness of the gods of the pagan world were centered in him. He was everything the Christian abhorred. But it was in the Middle Ages that the Satan mythology became most elaborate and specific. In that gloomy period Satan loomed increasingly large in the consciousness of the folk. Terror dominated the Middle Ages, and mass preoccupation with the devil became most evident in the frenzied

[8] M. Rudwin, "Diabolism," *Ency. Soc. Sci.*, 5: 119.

harassing of his earthly colleagues, the witch and the sorcerer. The theological concept of the devil changed rapidly through that period, but the folk interpreted in their own values those ideas of Satan which the professional churchmen gave to them. "In a very great number of popular beliefs and folk tales, we see before us a devil profoundly different from the Devil of the theologians and of the ascetic legends; a devil who has the form and nature of a man, has a house such as men have, and occupations and cares such as a farmer or an artisan might have; a devil who eats, drinks, and wears garments; who sometimes runs into debt, sometimes falls ill; and who retains nothing, or but very little of his diabolic character." [9] The folk spun rapidly changing descriptions of the devil's nature, works, ways, appearance.

Of the many phases of the devil's evolution and of the various aspects of his nature, we may choose a few illustrations to indicate the popular basis of this myth. The person of the devil changed with the changing antipathies of the mass. In the early Christian period his form was often that of pagan divinities, since the Christians' struggle was primarily with competing religions. The devil also appeared as various animals in accordance with the social reputation of those animals from age to age. The Trinitarian dispute is reflected in the three persons or three faces of the devil. In the Middle Ages, he is portrayed as a man of physical distinction and beauty, and later, as the masses came to despise the foppishness and dandyism of the upper classes, the devil becomes a dandy in the refinements of his dress, beard and behavior. In the sixteenth and seventeenth centuries the devout masses became ever more alienated from the frills, finery and fashion of their masters, and they ascribed these attributes to the devil.

The popular devil was a sexual adventurer. His inhuman sexual prowess was attested to by thousands of hysterical women who claimed intimate knowledge of his ways. The witches' Sabbath was in part a sexual orgy. The devil also made use of beautiful and seductive women to tempt the faithful. If the ascetic church leaders were bedeviled with such imaginings, masses of people also were not loath to concern themselves with these aspects of the devil's activity. And the variety of the mythological record rapidly increased.

The devil was a shrewd bargainer. The notion of compacts with the devil developed from the tenth century onward to the Faust motif. People thought in terms of simple, personal bargains. Various cults of devil worshipers made their formal bargains with Satan.

In the absence of naturalistic descriptions of physiological processes, it is understandable that the folk should ascribe much illness to the per-

[9] A. Graf, *The Story of the Devil* (English trans.), The Macmillan Company, New York, 1931, p. 231.

sonal activities of the devil. Through the Middle Ages, people attributed obscure diseases, indefinite pains, piercing sensations in the region of the heart, kidney pains, paralysis, impotence and many other disorders to the devil's invasion of their persons.[10] Unusual psychological experiences and various mental diseases were ascribed to demoniacal possession. The physical tribulations of the churchmen were often even greater than were those of the common man. One abbot declared that the devil, "afflicted him with bloating of the stomach and with diarrhoea, with nausea and giddiness; so benumbed his hands that he could no longer make the sign of the cross—made him cough, forced him to expectorate, hid in his bed and stopped his nostrils and mouth so that he could not breathe, compelled him to urinate, and bit him like a flea." [11]

As the conflicts of the religious ideology with rationalism increased, the devil was associated with reason, argument, dissension and questioning. "Satan was regarded as the incarnation of human reason in contrast to the Savior, who represented faith. To the dominion of the devil the church handed over all sciences and arts." [12] Folk suspicion of learning ascribed a splendid intellectuality to Satan.

Although church leaders used the myth of the personal devil as a potent means of social control, and although theologians in part guided the developing concept of the devil, the essential outlines of the devil myth through the Middle Ages were the simple ruminations of the folk. Later, the record of the devil's works, ways and person were essentially the product of the great writers, especially Dante and Milton.[13] But in the heyday of his earthly power, Satan was a folk myth.

THE LINCOLN OF POPULAR LEGEND

The Lincoln legends illustrate, not only the development of legends as a folk product, but also the increasingly conscious manipulation of legendary material by societal leaders, by churchmen, prohibitionists and politicians. The Lincoln who lives in the minds of masses of Americans is not the Lincoln of the biographers (eulogistic, realistic or debunking), but a legendary Lincoln of gossipy folk tale and of legendary stories promulgated by interested leaders.

There is a plethora of folk legend. The accounts of the poverty of the Lincoln family have been grossly exaggerated, because the folk required

[10] M. Garçon and J. Vinchon, *The Devil*, E. P. Dutton & Co., Inc., New York, 1930, p. 82.

[11] Graf, *op. cit.*, p. 98.

[12] Rudwin, *op. cit.*, p. 120.

[13] R. A. Tsanoff, *The Nature of Evil*, The Macmillan Company, New York, 1931, pp. 176–184.

a hero who had run the entire gamut from dire poverty to greatest eminence. He was born in a rude frontier community in a log cabin. But material wealth is relative, and in comparison with those round about Lincoln was not an underprivileged child.

Hero legends usually ascribe certain elements of mystery to the birth of the hero. The male progenitor is often assumed to be someone other and greater than the legal father. Such was the case in the Lincoln legend. "It was natural to wonder how so unpromising a backwoodsman as Thomas Lincoln could have begot so superhuman a son as Abraham. . . . Soon there was a feeling abroad that the hero must have had some author more plausible than 'Tom,' who was reputed to have been shiftless and dull. Inevitably there grew the myth that Lincoln's real father had been some greater man." [14] The willingness of masses of people to believe such stories made possible the organized "whispering campaigns" of the 1860 and 1864 elections. This was a natural folk legend, but it was spread about by political opponents. In an earlier age such a legend would have persisted, but with the means of communication in America of the nineteenth century the bastardy tale was finally scotched, but not until a half century after Lincoln's death.

Folk legend made of Lincoln a model boy, never late to school, cleanly, quiet, honest and kind to animals. But these stories were created after Lincoln was prominent, great and martyred. And so, the boy had to be great. Undoubtedly most of the later witnesses must have been unreliable. But true or false, these legends provided models for harassed mothers to hold before their sons.

Lincoln's gentleness and kindness were cherished by the folk. There are some true stories to illustrate these qualities, which the adult Lincoln undoubtedly possessed. But there are scores of untrue stories. If they were all true, Lincoln would have spent all his time interviewing distracted mothers, comforting the widows and orphans, solving the personal problems of soldiers and issuing pardons. Historians and biographers have proved most of the folk legends to be untrue. But the folk cherished the story of the kindly ruler and embroidered ever new accounts.

A heroic saga was created. The stalwart railsplitter, the adventurous bargeman, the heroic fighter in the Black Hawk War became legends long after the facts. The frontier provided a harsh life, and human endurance was tested. The popular record of frontier life required its hero symbols, and such a symbol was created from a man already great in political life. "What there is of the frontier hero in the great Lincoln of poetry and fiction, and the religious legend which they preserve, is spiritualized and

[14] L. Lewis, *Myths after Lincoln*, Blue Ribbon Books, Inc. (Garden City Books, Inc.), New York, 1929, pp. 368 ff.

hallowed by the simple process of omission, emphasis, and invention, which has so largely biased even the biographical accounts." [15]

The death of Abraham Lincoln inevitably gave rise to numerous legends of unusual, unnatural and supernatural occurrences. It was said in Illinois that the brown thrush was not heard singing for a year after Lincoln's death. There are many such stories.

Organized manipulation of Lincoln legends occurred in many fields. The most notable instance deals with the question of his religious faith. In the struggle between agnostics and churchmen in the closing years of the nineteenth century, each side collected and used stories that purported to align him with each. The Methodists, Quakers, and other sects claimed him. Their opponents gained solace from the stories told by Lincoln's law partner, Herndon. In the Prohibition struggle, Lincoln was claimed by both the wets and the drys. Lincoln was no friend of intoxicating drink, but there is considerable doubt as to his views on prohibition. The wets claimed that Lincoln had been a saloonkeeper in his storekeeping days.[16] Practically every social movement since Lincoln's day has attempted to link this magic name to its cause and in doing so has assiduously collected legends.

The human and historic greatness of Abraham Lincoln has been distorted by legends that highlighted those qualities which the common man or the special pleader has found it convenient to emphasize. Yet, with all its vagaries, distortions and emotional elements, the popular legend may be essentially true to the essence of its subject.

As time passes, Lincoln gathers more securely the significance of his period about him and becomes more and more a national mythos. The remarkable thing about the mythos is that if history and biography are to be trusted, Lincoln was a worthy man to be made into a symbol of justice, mercy, spiritual and intellectual strength, or a symbol of democracy and freedom. The biographers and historians may not be able to make every fact fit into this picture, even though the mass of facts fits naturally; but the mythos is undisturbed because it has seized upon the best of the Lincoln story as poetic truth.[17]

THE LEGEND OF THE FIGHTING FRONTIERSMAN

The fighting Westerner has been the subject of American legendry for over a hundred and fifty years. During the first decades of the nineteenth century, the popular exaggerations of the exploits of Daniel Boone and his ilk provided the legends about the Indian-fighting frontiersman of the

[15] R. P. Basler, *The Lincoln Legend*, Houghton Mifflin Company, Boston, 1935, p. 147.

[16] Basler, *op. cit.*, p. 296.

[17] P. Odegard, *Pressure Politics*, Columbia University Press, New York, 1928, p. 61.

"bloody ground" in the Middle West, east of the Mississippi. In the 1830's, 40's and 50's, the trapper of the plains and the mountain man of the Rockies were the then current folk heroes of the frontier. These folk legends were chiefly the product of word-of-mouth storytelling. The legendary figures personified values and virtues esteemed by those who talked about them. For they, too, had often experienced great danger and the usual fears of life on a harsh frontier menaced by Indians, animals and nature. The legendary figures exhibited the qualities for which others yearned and extraordinary skill in coping with the multitudinous dangers from hostile, savage man and merciless nature. To these legendary frontiersmen there was ascribed an almost superhuman accuracy with rifle and other weapons, an unbelievable skill in trailing and tracking, dauntless courage and physical prowess beyond normal humanity, and fighting tactics in which an individual outwitted or overwhelmed hordes of Indians.

The legends developed during the period before the 1870's and 1880's were chiefly folk legends spun out by generations of talkers and talemongers. Those exaggerations were well received by listeners who could esteem the superhumanly effective hero of Indian fights and of struggles with animals amidst a dangerous wilderness. The listeners could yearn for such abilities, thrill to the exaggerated skills of the legendary figure and feel more comfortable in a world that could produce such heroes in time of need. After 1880 the legends were increasingly diffused, not by word of mouth, but by the mass media; for several decades by popular literature, the dime novel, the newspaper account, the magazine, and then, after 1920, by motion picture, radio and now television. The legends of the plainsman, the scout, the Indian fighter, of the bad man and the sheriff, and, finally, of that equestrian knight, the fighting cowboy, were spun out in print and picture. Legends had become a marketable product. While the content of the legends still remained a subject matter welcomed by audiences of ever increasing size, the creators of the legends were no longer folk-tale bearers, but writers, script writers and serial producers. Moreover, the producers of the tales were less bound by firsthand, personal knowledge about the life described. Neither they nor their listeners had experienced that life, so the exaggerated legends could transcend reality to an even greater degree than in the legends created a century earlier.

However, the legends were no less esteemed and vigorously defended than those of an earlier age. The legends continued to provide a popular fare, satisfying real psychological needs of the audience. Though life was increasingly sedentary and the frontier had disappeared, the tale of the violent man of action with superhuman strength, wit and skill had a very great appeal to the vast majority of the people of the United States.

Your local newsstand stocks twenty pulp magazines devoted exclusively to cowboys wrecking barrooms, slugging sheriffs, shooting rustlers, and saving Lasca from the stampede. (They are President Eisenhower's favorite relaxation, as whodunits were President Wilson's.) Your neighborhood movie averages one horse opera a week, the television station at least a dozen, and every few minutes the local disc-jockey sets some variant of Gene Autry to wailing some variant of the tumblin' tumbleweed. Small fry in Hopalong Cassidy outfits chase others in Lone Ranger outfits down your block, and will presently be washed with Hopalong soap and tucked away in Hopalong beds.[18]

Anyone who endangers this stereotyped legendary picture of the fighting cowboy is endangering a cherished mass mental image and some large businesses. In the debunking during the age of the muckrakers (1900–1910), references to the cowboy as "the hired man on horseback" caused great pain and resentment. One of the best of the Western writers, Eugene Manlove Rhodes, restated the romanticized picture in a poem:

But the hired man on horseback is singing to the herd

.   .   .   .

The broker's in his office before the stroke of ten
He buys and smiles and he sells and smiles at the word of other men
But he gets his little commission flat, whether they buy or sell
So be it drouth or storm or flood, the broker's crops do well.

.   .   .   .

But the hired man on horseback is swimming with the herd

[There is a stampede and the cowboy is drowned and goes to an after life, whereupon—]

Cossack and Saracen
Shout their wild welcome then
Ragged, proud Conquistadores claim him kind and kin

Hat tip-tilted and his head held high
Brave spurs jingling as he passes by—
Gray hair tousled and his lips aquirk
To the Master of the Workmen, with the tally of his work.[19]

Writers of the mid-nineteenth century sometimes purveyed the exaggerated accounts and tall tales of the legendary folk heroes. David Crockett, frontier hero and Tennessee congressman, wrote three autobiographical books which built and spread a legend. (*Sketches of Col. David Crockett*, 1833, *Narrative of David Crockett*, 1834, *A Tour of North and Down East*, 1835.) This was before he became the typical Westerner

[18] B. DeVoto, "The Wild West," *Holiday*, July, 1954, p. 36.
[19] E. M. Rhodes, *The Best Novels and Stories of E. M. Rhodes*, Houghton Mifflin Company, Boston, 1949, p. 551.

and Texan, one of the country's most legendary figures, whose story was commercially exploited by various media in 1955. But never before Ned Buntline created the legend of Buffalo Bill in the 1870's was literary legend making a real commercial success. These legends of the cowboy, the frontiersman, scout-plainsman, badman, the gunfighter and the sheriff are an important part of the American daydream. They provide vicarious violence and action experience for millions of people. About 20 per cent of all feature motion pictures produced each year are Westerns, and TV devotes considerable time daily to this fare. We might illustrate the commercial development of such legends by two illustrations, the legend of the scout-plainsman as exemplified by Buffalo Bill and the development of the stereotyped legend of the cowboy.

In 1869, Ned Buntline was nationally known as the nation's principal writer of sea, adventure, and war stories published as dime novels and sold by the hundreds of thousands. He went West to gather materials for a series of Western stories about Indian fighting. The men whose exploits Buntline wished to celebrate in print proved physically and verbally disappointing, but he met a young scout, William Frederick Cody, who had the requisite handsome appearance and was a man of skill and daring in the use of horses and firearms. Cody had served without action in the Civil War, had then driven a scraper team for a railroad contractor and hunted for buffalo meat for the section crews. He had not performed major heroic deeds. The novelist found William Cody engaging and talkative and spent several weeks with him before returning to New York.

In December 1869, Street and Smith advertised a new serial by Ned Buntline in their *New York Weekly*, to be entitled *Buffalo Bill, The King of the Border Men*. The sobriquet "Buffalo Bill" did not originate with Buntline. For a dozen years the name had been popular on the frontier. Ned appropriated it for Cody just as he had copied titles and literary style from other writers all his life, but Ned Buntline, with the *New York Weekly*, introduced Buffalo Bill to the world.[20]

This was the first of scores of dime novels which ascribed to Buffalo Bill the numerous heroic exploits of the plains frontier. He had had no personal involvement in these various heroic deeds, but they became attached to William F. Cody as "Buffalo Bill," the legendary figure of the popular mind. Cody must have gasped when he first read accounts of himself as the greatest scout in the West. Shortly thereafter, James Gordon Bennett, owner of the New York *Herald*, made a trip West with a party of friends. Assigned to them as a scout was William Cody, now beginning to be celebrated as Buffalo Bill.

The hero of the *New York Weekly*, Buffalo Bill himself, rode over to their camp on a snow white horse, a gallant stepper. With a white buckskin suit he

[20] J. Monaghan, *The Great Rascal*, Little, Brown & Company, Boston, 1952, p. 7.

wore a crimson shirt, and a white sombrero crowned his flowing locks. James Gordon Bennett noticed that the hero was every bit as handsome as Buntline had pictured him and his guests were delighted when General Sheridan assigned him to them as guide.[21]

Soon in the New York papers the fame of Buffalo Bill grew apace. And Cody's quiet disposition soon gave way to the flamboyance of a master showman which he was to become for the next four decades in the Wild West shows and circuses that he ran and owned. He was launched on a public career of a living legend; an American, and finally a world figure, epitomizing the skills, the daring, the idealized appearance of the fighting plainsman until he was entombed in a public monument.

As a boy ten years of age, I remember this ostensibly heroic figure of a man galloping into a circus tent on several occasions. This handsome horseman was spirited, dramatic action incarnate. If he did not exist as a real historic hero, his age demanded that he be invented as legend. And it was so. He emerged at a moment when the time was ripe for a romantic symbol and he carried on through decades in which the recent frontier fighting was the subject of popular literary and pictorial sagas. Most of the deeds ascribed to Buffalo Bill were never done by Col. William F. Cody, but he was better than reality. He was a public daydream.

Immediately after the legends of the fighting plainsman came the figure of the cowboy. In less than a decade in the 1870's, the vast herds of buffalo had been killed, and in place of millions of bison munching the then abundant grass there were the domesticated cattle of the ranches and their attendant escorts called cowboys. They ranged a vast wild country from the Dakotas to Oregon and from Texas to Montana. It was the "world's greatest playground for young men." The cowboy was to become the most pervasive legend of all the frontier types and the most commercialized popular daydream as purveyed by press, motion picture and TV. At first he was a literary creation, but the rapidly developed popularity of the theme of the romantic fighting horseman led to exploitation by the motion pictures, the dude ranches, the Western communities with rodeos and frontier days, and finally the industries producing the paraphernalia of clothing, boots, hats and gadgets to objectify the dream for child and adult.

The cowboy legend was not projected from folk consciousness, but was first created by literature. It was then embraced by populations increasingly urban and sedentary but yearning nostalgically for at least vicarious experience of action, freedom, wide open spaces, mobility and uncomplicated choices among simple moral values. The cowboy was lifted from

[21] Monaghan, *op. cit.*, p. 11.

his mundane tasks at the rear of a trail herd to a pedestal of romanticized legendary heroism. The period of the authentic cowboy, the bronzed horseman, the trail drives, the cattle barons, the cow towns and the open range was the time between 1870 and about 1890. By then the range was closed, the farmers swarmed over the land and the cattle business was basically changed. But the legends began almost at once and have increased and crudely cheapened ever since.

As the frontier world and way of life ended, a public market for an exaggerated legendary portrayal of the Westerner was soon supplied by writers and artists and then by the motion-picture Westerns. Literary men from Owen Wister (*The Virginian*) and Andy Adams (*The Log of a Cowboy*) to romancers such as Zane Grey, William McLeod Raine, B. M. Bower, Eugene Manlove Rhodes and many others created the symbols of the cowboy legend which was soon a formula. Scores of writers for the dime novels and then the pulps fixed the picture indelibly. From about 1915 onward the motion pictures made the Western a part of the regular experience of the audiences in the United States and the occasional experience of foreign motion-picture audiences. The legend had great vitality and public interest is apparently persistent, unless television repetitiously bores even the ten-year olds. But for more than a half century the cowboy has been the master symbol of the West.

The legend of the cowboy emphasizes the quality of freedom. He was a free agent. As free action is circumscribed in the present, the idealized freedom of the past is cherished. He was not "fenced in," he had his life in invigorating climate amidst magnificent scenery—now reproduced every week in technicolor. He engaged in direct action and solved problems of justice directly. This is always an appealing theme to a populace ever more entangled in tortuous legal minutiae. His moral choices were of great simplicity, the good and the bad were obviously personified, and he was not called on to make "agonizing reappraisals" of complex political themes, the nightmares of contemporary man. As exhibited in the Western epic, sex is simple, not obtrusive, uncomplicated and relegated to a minor theme. This is appealing amidst the vagaries of the sexual history and ideas of modern man. The cowboy of legend did not plan to wear down his enemies by attrition. "The cowboy hero with steel-blue or slate-gray eyes, two-fisted and two-gunned, as fast on the draw with his left hand as with his right, fought his way through packs of enemies and never allowed the bruising he received en route to daunt his spirit or check his purpose." [22] How appealing is such direct action in a world in which realistic appraisal of one's international enemies necessitates planning for decades of "cold war." And the cowboy was innocent of a complex mind-

[22] L. Gurko, *Heroes, Highbrows and the Popular Mind*, The Bobbs-Merrill Company, Inc., Indianapolis, 1953, p. 180.

life, was not torn by warring political and economic ideologies or painful philosophic reflections. The cowboy was close to nature and to animal life. Amidst populations where cows and horses must be kept in the local zoos for the edification of urban children, the appeal of the cowboy-being-good-to-his-horse hero must be obvious.

In the film Western one is involved, without personal anxiety or responsibility or duty, in thrilling action. Comparable directly experienced adventure would involve anxiety and fear, but in the movie one can be carefree though excited. Thus they are the true folk entertainment of our times, the modern commercially prefabricated legendry. They are successful money-makers because they are not imaginative; they are simple action storytelling in which Western characters exhibit skill and energy and ability to come out on top. Obviously this cinematic and literary version did not coincide with reality, where evil must have triumphed in the usual proportions and the good sometimes proven physically inferior. But in the legendary figures and action one could rest assured without untoward anxiety.

The rugged individual engaged in successful psychological free enterprise has had many garbs, settings and postures throughout the history of popular heroes. But he has never appeared in purer form, more unaffected by vitiating reality than in the legend of the American cowboy.

THE LEGEND OF CALVIN COOLIDGE

The Coolidge legend was constructed very rapidly in the months immediately succeeding his elevation to the presidency. Organized publicity by the Republican National Committee and the less organized legend making of the Washington correspondents, soon limned the outlines of a silent, unintellectual, honest, cautious, shrewd, average man. The newspaper-reading public accepted and embellished the legend. It is now agreed that President Coolidge had the "best press" of any American president. Yet here was a man who, a few years earlier, had been considered by many party leaders as too weak and nondescript for the vice-presidential nomination. "Here is a sensible and normal man who until a few years ago was accustomed to taking political orders and being treated more or less indifferently, at times even contemptuously, by the party leaders in his state." [23] But shortly after Calvin Coolidge became president, an eminent newspaperman stated, "The indisputable fact is that Coolidge has to some degree been 'sold' to the nation, as the advertising men say, and by advertising men's methods." [24] There were more avenues of publicity than ever before: the radio was developing, the country was

[23] W. Sharp, "President and Press," *Atlantic*, 140: 239.
[24] B. Bliven, "The Great Coolidge Mystery," *Harper's*, 52: 45.

entering into a prosperous period, legend making by publicity was becoming more astute, the nation required a symbol of cautious conservatism, and the new President fitted, or could be made to fit, the need. And so, from that August morning in 1923 when the American people saw the lean face of their new President in the light of his father's kerosene lamp in a Vermont farmhouse, the legend grew.

From the beginning, the Washington correspondents praised and protected him. Why? F. R. Kent declares that reporters inflate important public figures, magnifying their good qualities and minimizing defects for two reasons. "The first is a more or less psychological one—a tendency, springing from the inferiority complex of the reporter and born of his poor pay and precarious position, to permit the public official to assume the superior or dominant attitude. . . . The second reason is a simple and practical one. The reporter's business is to get news. The more news he gets the more secure his job and the greater his value to the paper. The public official has what the reporter has to have, to wit, news." [25] He further states, "Not in the memory of anyone now living has there been a President who leaned so heavily on this newspaper tendency to praise and protect, who profited by it so much, who would shrivel so quickly if he lost it, as Calvin Coolidge." The newspapermen built the legend, but they built it for a receptive and acquiescent public.

What were the outlines of the legend? One of the principal strands in the tradition of this President was built of the innumerable stories of his silence. Historically, silence has often been noted in leaders and attributed to a sphinxlike wisdom. In personal relations President Coolidge was undoubtedly taciturn. Bruce Bliven says that this characteristic was magnified by newspapermen because it was in such startling contrast to their own volubility. "The trait is particularly puzzling to the newspaper men who come in closest contact with him and who write what the public reads about him, they being invariably expert and incessant conversationalists." [26] And certainly the President was not given to small talk. The American public hesitated for a moment in its chatter and was filled with wonder. A man must be profound to so control his speech. And then the flood of anecdotes began. It was said that when Coolidge was four years of age he was sitting quietly with his father and his grandfather. The grandfather spoke. "John," he said, "Cal don't say much." "No," said John, "Calvin, he ain't gabby." They smiled at each other. Neither were they. [27] Certainly in public life, Mr. Coolidge was not a silent man. He spoke for hours on end, he wrote lengthy addresses to Congress, he wrote

[25] F. R. Kent, "Mr. Coolidge," *Am. Mercury*, 2: 386.
[26] Bliven, *op. cit.*, p. 48.
[27] C. Rogers, *The Legend of Calvin Coolidge*, Doubleday & Company, Inc., New York, 1928, p. 11.

extensively. "We can begin with the fact that Mr. Coolidge not only talks in public frequently (265 times a year), but talks at length. His formal addresses are not snapped off short. They average something more than thirty-seven hundred words apiece." [28] But there was no glib loquaciousness in this man. And the bulk of the general public cherished the legend.

Another strand of the legend was the account of his lack of flexible intellectuality. This was well received by a public who were in general suspicious of flashing intellects and among whom a too high order of intelligence was suspect. Emphasis was placed on good intentions, conservative thinking, character and solidity.

Again, inaction was counted a virtue, and many stories were told to indicate that the President was not given to waste motion or a thrusting aggressiveness aimed at any new solution of economic and political problems. In a prosperous period the maintenance of the *status quo* was at a great premium. The President was portrayed as nursing prosperity by encouraging thrift and balancing the nation's books. Experimentalism was not considered a virtue in the 1920's. There was little popular demand for constructive solutions.

Much was made of the fact that the President was an "average man." Stories of his simple tastes in housing, food and daily living were spread abroad. His ethical standards and values were portrayed as simple and traditional. Here was no theorist ranting of the "new morality." "The average American saw in Coolidge just the virtues that were supposed to constitute the American ideal and supposed to have made America. Coolidge incarnated thrift, self-denial, plain and simple living, straightforward, hard-headed honesty. The average American had heard that his fathers had these virtues and had made a great nation by means of them." [29]

The President was portrayed as honest, cautious and shrewd. Honesty was especially stressed in comparison with the notorious scandals of the preceding administration. Stories were told of his meticulous and sometimes picayunish honesty. Cautiousness was prized in a period when there was a high level of national income. Shrewdness may be a limited virtue at best, but it is highly valued in a nation that developed this emphasis in the trading, haggling, small-bargaining, horse-trading, tricking days of nineteenth-century expansion.

The stage was set for the Coolidge legend. It was easy to star President Coolidge because he had to a considerable extent many of the characteristics ascribed to him. Lack of color helped rather than hindered the rapid growth of the legend. "In the absence of a national crisis and in a time of prosperity his lack of strength is an asset rather than a liability, pro-

[28] C. Mertz, "The Silent Mr. Coolidge," *New Republic*, 47: 51.
[29] G. Bradford, "The Genius of the Average," *Atlantic*, 145: 6.

vided he has sufficiently powerful press support and the approval of the great business interests—and no President of our time has had both to the same extent." [30] President Coolidge permitted the growth of his legend. The press agents and the correspondents painted a distorted picture of him, but, in fairness, it must be noted that he did not actively pretend to qualities he did not possess.

Since the days of relatively simple legend making in the Coolidge era, many a public figure in the United States has become legendary through his own efforts, the exaggerations spun by his friends, party and group members, and the professional distortions drawn by publicity agents. The emotional political, economic and military conflicts of the 30's and 40's were the setting for gross exaggerations of personal qualities. One thinks readily of a number of political and military leaders and a few spectacular business figures whose public images were consciously cultivated by themselves and others. Publicity tactics became more studied and astute. However, the record is not yet sufficiently complete, nor does time and perspective yet permit the limning of their legends.

Every age has myths and legends which are defended and propagated by the believers. Transmitted into simple myth and personal legendry these stories are symbols for masses of mankind. They are types of simplification. As such these popular stereotypes are constantly utilized in the opinion process. They are psychologically inevitable in the thinking of the common man about leaders and heroes, enemies and friends, and religious, political, philosophical and psychological ideas. They are a part of family, group and national traditions.

These myths and legends may or may not partly correspond to objective reality. In his *Political Myths and Economic Realities*, F. Delaisi contrasts the Christian myth, the feudal myth, the papal myth, the monarchical myth and the democratic myth with the economic realities. But systems of ideas have their own reality. In retrospect, the expert may discuss the utility that a system of ideas had for a particular culture. He may consider these as relative and transitory. But to an individual enmeshed in a particular ideology it has an absolute value and is considered immortal. A part of the ideology is the accompanying myths and legends. Sorel discussed the "myth" of the general strike, but he considered this idea to have a central function in the whole Socialist movement. The adherents of that movement did not discuss this idea as "myth."

Today, leaders promulgate myths and legends in a more conscious, organized and orderly fashion. New means of communication have aided the unification of large publics under common ideologies with their ac-

---

[30] F. R. Kent, "In Weakness There Is Strength," *Nation*, 124: 167.

companying myths and legends. A nation's communal values and attitudes, fears and wishes, dreams and rationalizations are reflected in the mass media which provide a reflecting mirror designed to show the desired distortions. An increasing proliferation of myths and legends may be anticipated. Many people vaguely sense the sterility for life processes of much of objective science. They are thrusting strongly for a more satisfying ideology as a basis for human social relations. Scientific leaders of the nineteenth century pursued objectivity with a vigorous enthusiasm that was in itself not objective but was humanly satisfying. They infected large publics with their faiths and hopes. But now there is a demand for a renewal of satisfying belief. And man begins once more the ancient task of spinning his subjective ideologies, more and more divorced from objective realities. Dramas become internal. Stereotyped heroes and legendary villains, personalized symbols of the perturbing, conflicting elements, are provided by interest groups for the general publics. The satisfactions that so many people cannot find in human relations are to be vicariously enjoyed in the world of imagination. The function of legends is not only to provide a basis for objective actions but also to satisfy psychological needs. And the tempo of changing needs and changing myths and legends is increasing.

PART THREE

Measurement

CHAPTER 9

The Measurement of Opinion and Attitude

I conclude, therefore, that the imaginations which people have of one another are the solid facts of society, and that to observe and interpret these must be the chief aim of sociology.[1]

CHARLES HORTON COOLEY

Yet social attitudes, once they are grasped in their full significance, become the counterpart, in individual equipment, of the richly varied customs of the peoples of the world—differing as customs differ from land to land, and changing as the mores change, from age to age. For the social attitudes of individuals are but the specific instances in individuals of the collective phenomena which the sociologists have labored for a century to bring to the consciousness of their colleagues in social science.[2]

E. FARIS

Preoccupation with the innate factors motivating behavior has existed among the experimental psychologists, since the early studies of Lange, Wundt, Külpe and others on the factors of preparation for action; among the theoretical psychologists, philosophers and theologians in the many varieties of instinct theory; and among the social psychologists and sociologists, since about 1920, in the study of attitudes. Of course, this organic basis of behavior is a fundamental problem of all those branches of learning concerned with the behavior of living forms, but our interest lies in those disciplines concerned with the psychological and social life of man.

In 1888 Lange propounded the theory that the process of perception was largely in consequence of muscular "set." Then, following Wundt and Külpe, the study of the preparation of the subject for action was experimentally described in the laboratory results of the Wurzburg school which appeared in the writings of N. Ach, A. Messer, K. Bühler and

[1] C. H. Cooley, *Human Nature and the Social Order,* Charles Scribner's Sons, New York, 1902, p. 121.
[2] E. Faris, *Social Attitudes* (K. Young, ed.), Henry Holt and Company, Inc., New York, 1931, p. 5. Quoted by permission.

others.[3] This experimental work was often very simple, consisting of introspective accounts of the process of judgment in differentiating weights, of tests with stimulus words and the subjects' responses and the like. States in the preparatory process were described. Although the German experimentalists of that period used a variety of words to express the set of the organism, the concept of "attitude," and later the term, came to be widely accepted by psychologists. These "tendencies to act" were not, however, always conceived of as irreducible elements.

The idea of an organic set for behavior likewise developed. It appeared in the most definite form in the concept of instincts. Although some conception of the innate drives called "instincts" appeared in the works of the Greek philosophers, in the theological literature of the Middle Ages and in the beliefs concerning innate sentiments, especially moral sentiments, during the seventeenth and eighteenth centuries, it was not until the middle of the nineteenth century that classifications of instincts were developed. By 1920 sociologists, intermittently attempting to relate tendencies to act to the action and behavior, found the instinct psychology, with its emphasis on the inheritance of specific innate behavior patterns, no longer tenable. They were too much aware of the variety of human behavior in various cultures. Some concept of tendency to act was required, a concept differing from instinct in that the tendency was, at least in part, acquired. The term "attitude" appeared, and became perhaps the most widely used and indispensable concept in social psychology and but little less widely used in sociology.

ATTITUDE

"Attitude" originally meant a position of the body suited to a certain action, a physical preparation by position for action. Its meaning was much broadened to cover all preparation and tendency to act, either overt or inner and psychic. The term has been quite variously defined in the sociological literature of the past years, but there is an underlying unanimity on general "set of the organism" and "tendency to act."

It is the set of the organism toward the object or situation to which an adjustment is called for. When the adjustment is made the attitude disappears, except in so far as it is retained in memory or in the habitual set of the organism.[4]

[3] See F. Fearing, "Experimental Study of Attitude," in S. Rice (ed.), *Methods in Social Science*, University of Chicago Press, Chicago, 1931, pp. 715–728; G. W. Allport, "Attitudes," in C. Murchison (ed.), *Handbook of Social Psychology*, Clark University Press, Worcester, Mass., 1935, pp. 798–844.

[4] L. L. Bernard, *Introduction to Social Psychology*, Henry Holt and Company, Inc., New York, 1926, p. 246.

By attitude we understand a process of individual consciousness which determines real or possible activity of the individual counterpart of the social value; activity, in whatever form, is the bond between them.[5]

An attitude is a tendency to act. The term designates a certain proclivity, or bent, a bias or predisposition, an aptitude or inclination to a certain type of activity.[6]

Attitude, whatever else it may be, denotes a functional state of readiness which determines the organism to react in a characteristic way to a certain stimulus or stimulus situation.[7]

An attitude is an enduring organization of motivational, emotional, perceptual and cognitive processes with respect to some aspect of the individual's world.[8]

An attitude is a mental and neural state of readiness, organized through experience, exerting a directive or dynamic influence upon the individual's response to all objects and situations with which it is related.[9]

W. I. Thomas first emphasized the concept of attitude as basic in social psychology.[10] Cooley, Faris and Dewey were also prominently associated with the early development of interpreting action ways in terms of the underlying attitudes.

"Attitude" as used in contemporary sociology and social psychology has a wide variety of meanings. These range from the temporary set of the organism, or *Aufgabe,* to relatively permanent and complex tendencies to act, such as one's attitude toward war. The term is used in reference to the preparation of the organism for overt physical behavior and to tendency to act in mental processes, such as the individual's response to the idea of adultery, patriotism or alma mater. Further, attitude is used for tendencies to act that are individually unique and also for those group attitudes, either cultural or collective, that the individual abstracts from culture or from group experiences.

Are attitudes specific in the sense of tendencies to respond in a definite way to a particular situation or may attitudes develop into general dis-

[5] W. I. Thomas and F. Znaniecki, *The Polish Peasant in Europe and America,* University of Chicago Press, Chicago, 1918, vol. I, p. 27.

[6] E. Faris, "Attitudes and Behavior," *Am. Jour. Sociol.,* 34: 2: 277, 1928.

[7] M. Sherif and H. Cantril, *The Psychology of Ego-Involvements,* John Wiley & Sons, Inc., New York, 1947, p. 17.

[8] D. Krech and R. S. Crutchfield, *Theory and Problems of Social Psychology,* McGraw-Hill Book Company, Inc., New York, 1948, p. 152.

[9] Allport, *op. cit.,* p. 810.

[10] The first section of *The Polish Peasant in Europe and America,* 1918, is devoted to an analysis of the concepts of value in society and attitude in the individual.

positions to respond to a whole class of phenomena? This question was much disputed in the 1920's. Cantril concluded in his study of general and specific attitudes that "general determining tendencies are more constant and enduring than specific content." [11] That there are general attitudes was the contention of almost all sociologists, although they had no experimental literature to present in evidence. However, they had long maintained the idea of general attitudes in discussions of race relations, of attitude toward nationalities and of the specific attitudinal base of stereotypes of groups, classes, types, associations and institutions. Apparently, both kinds of attitudes do exist. There are quite evidently specific attitudes developed by the individual toward particular objects, people and ideas. Attitudes as tendencies to act are developed in relation to material objects, animate beings and psychological processes. As a small boy, the author was given an air rifle. With it he happily prowled the hillsides for several summers, pursuing sparrows with more or less skill. Thirty-five years later, in an introspective moment, he realized that to this day sparrows are targets to him. When a sparrow is sighted, he frequently notes its position, the intervening obstacles, the best angle for a shot, and has a vague sense of the plump of the bullet as it would enter through the breast feathers. He has an attitude toward sparrows. However, this question of specific and general attitudes, a dichotomy which was principally based on the static trait theories of personality, is no longer considered valid. Obviously there are different levels and degrees of generalization.

The classification of all attitudes is clearly impossible. But lists of common attitudes are developed depending upon the author's purpose and viewpoints. Even these classifications are by no means satisfactory, because:

1. Attitudes are not units but complexes of other attitudes. As such they are general tendencies to modes of response, not to particular responses. And, as MacIver has stated, "When we attribute an attitude to a person, such as love or fear or pity, we do not completely express the state of consciousness so described. . . . the integral attitude is too complex for such summary description. All that we mean is that the attitude factor so named is dominant or at least recognizable in the subject. Our pity, for example, may contain love and fear as well." [12] Attitudes are not independent entities.

2. The existing language forms are totally inadequate to distinguish even common attitudes.

3. Attitudes shade into one another, and arbitrary classifications may distort reality.

[11] H. Cantril, "General and Specific Attitudes," *Psychol. Mon.*, no. 192, 1932.
[12] R. M. MacIver, *Society*, Rinehart & Company, Inc., New York, 1936, p. 44.

4. Even if idealized classifications are developed, the comparison of individuals *A* and *B*, who are said to have that common attitude, is only approximate, because the ingredients of the attitude in each may be in different proportions. However, fruitful results have been obtained by acting "as if" they were comparable.

ATTITUDE AND OPINION

When an overt expression on a controversial point appears, we have an opinion. Although usually expressed in language forms, it may be indicated by gestures, signs or symbols. "Thumbs down" decided a dramatically controversial point in the Roman amphitheatre; the nod of the judge, examining *in camera* during the political conflicts of the Middle Ages, might mean the prisoner's release or his extermination depending upon the system of signals. Any expression of opinion, therefore, involves attitudes. As a form of action it involves, first, a number of physical and muscular attitudes. Psychologists still use the term "attitude" to refer to motor preparedness. After behaviorism, there was a futile attempt to describe opinion in such terms. But "laryngeal behavior" has never proved helpful to those attempting to account for the opinions of the citizens of Kentucky on the United Nations. Then there are the various predispositions that have found expression in the stated opinion. And these may be many and varied; predispositions toward the questioner if the situation is face to face; toward his voice, tones, facial expression, and the like; toward his attitudes on the subject under discussion; toward the attitudes on that subject of the persons who are thought to be associated with the questioner; the attitude pattern of the person interviewed with regard to the problem itself; perhaps scores of other predispositions. Is it any wonder that the early naïve tests, questionnaires, interviews and other modes of attempting to bring the "real attitude" into overt opinion behavior, based as they were on so simple a concept of the nature of attitudes and their interaction, proved so discouraging? To be sure, opinions always express attitudes, but which attitudes? The attempts to distinguish attitudes and to isolate the ones related to an expressed opinion have been a special interest of the social scientists since 1920. The persistent interest in attitudes has developed, not only from the need to complete a theoretical schema, but also from the observed relationship between certain attitudes and successful life adjustment within our culture. Personnel workers, psychiatrists, educators, social workers and others have attempted to study, through various simple measurements and tests, certain social attitudes of the individual.

THE MEASUREMENT OF ATTITUDES

Since 1930 there have been hundreds of articles on the theory and methods of attitude measurement and thousands of applications in attitude studies. Comprehensive bibliographies of attitude studies have been compiled, so that the materials, though widely scattered, are now accessible. We shall discuss briefly only the simplest and most elementary methods and questions of attitude measurement. Detailed methodological description is properly the subject matter of entire university courses and necessitates an extended typological classification and illustration.[13] Let us trace briefly and in a very simple and elementary description the development of the methodology of attitude measurement since 1920.

YES-OR-NO, TRUE-OR-FALSE AND CROSS-OUT TESTS

Some years ago it was usual to seek solutions of educational and social problems by tabulating from questionnaires the responses of the subjects to statements of fact or of opinion on some controversial point. Indeed, the questionnaire, still widely used, has many legitimate functions, provided that it is used in accordance with the principles which have been established through extensive use. Questionnaires may be classified as: (1) those asking for facts which the reporter has observed; (2) those asking for facts to be found in records; (3) those asking for reactions of the individual, such as beliefs, preferences, likes and dislikes, wishes, judgments and choices. It is to the third type that attitude questionnaires belong. For some years, until about 1930, they were very extensively circulated, asking thousands of questions to be answered "yes" or "no" about the attitude of the individual members of many scores of groups. The attempt to collect opinions in this fashion developed, in part, from: (1) the wide gaps in information about prevalent social attitudes of which the social scientists were becoming acutely aware, (2) a lack of clear concepts of the nature of attitudes, (3) the growth of quantify-

---

[13] In my volume *Public Opinion*, published by McGraw-Hill Book Company, Inc., New York, in 1939, I found it desirable to include three lengthy chapters on attitudes and their measurement, since so little systematic summarization had been published up to that time. However, today there are a number of excellent summaries, surveys and descriptions of methodology. Refer especially to: Q. McNemar, "Opinion-Attitude Methodology," *Psychol. Bull.*, vol. 43, no. 4, 1946; L. Guttman and E. A. Suchman, *Studies in Social Psychology in World War II*, Princeton University Press, Princeton, N.J., 1950, vol. IV, chaps. 2–9; H. H. Remmers, *Introduction to Opinion and Attitude Measurement*, Harper & Brothers, New York, 1953; M. Riley, J. W. Riley and J. Toby, *Sociological Studies in Scale Analysis*, Rutgers University Press, New Brunswick, N.J., 1954; B. F. Green, "Attitude Measurement," *Handbook of Social Psychology*, Addison-Wesley Publishing Company, Cambridge, Mass., 1954, vol. I, chap. 9.

ing in other fields of social knowledge, (4) the ease with which these questionnaires could be constructed and answered, (5) a general belief that a majority is likely to be right, and (6) the ease with which the results could be compiled, a process of simple counting. Although the simple questionnaire serves a useful purpose, at times, in recording factual information, it is needless to emphasize that this method has been used with laborious futility when the questions have been direct requests to indicate an attitude "yes" or "no" by statements of opinion on controversial issues.

Sometimes instead of having the questions answered "yes" or "no," the wording was "true" or "false"; and in other studies the subject merely checked in one column or another, indicated plus or minus or crossed out one or the other of the terms used.

On the basis of our earlier discussion of the nature of attitudes, some of the limitations on the value of the use of such questionnaires are apparent.

1. An attitude is not an entity, but a complex of other attitudes in varying proportions. Moreover, an attitude of one individual may differ, in fine shadings, from that of another. In answers of "yes" or "no," these variations are ignored, quite different elements being thus forced into a single classification of opinion. This limited response provides a highly inaccurate opinion-representative of the essential attitudes. Ten persons may respond "yes" to a statement indicating dislike of the Japanese. However, the essential components of their attitudes may be very dissimilar, being based on personal experience with Japanese, on newspaper reading, on economic competition and on scores of other items. For most purposes, this limited opinion is worthless for any understanding of human attitudes.

2. The language difficulty leads to more serious error in the simple questionnaire than in any other form of measurement. In a response with a greater variety of possible positions, the words used may be misinterpreted, but that may cause a variation of one position on a scale of five or ten places, whereas in the "yes" or "no" categories there may be a complete change of position from positive to negative due to language misunderstanding. The language meanings to the individual are a partly uncontrolled variable, as every tester knows.

3. If, instead of simply counting the responses, there is an attempt to measure, that is, to indicate the relation of the answers to some standard, then the standard is constructed by the experimenter or by a limited group of judges. These judges, however, do not provide a valid scale for the group tested, since they themselves come from another group, often with varied attitudes. We shall consider this problem in greater detail in discussing the Thurstone test.

ESSAY TYPE OR CASE METHOD

Attitudes may be assumed from opinions expressed in written essays and in letters, case-history descriptions, autobiographies, diaries or oral or written interviews. The depth interview, unstructured and therefore usually long and rambling, may be analyzed for attitudes. All these permit an extensive range of expression, avoid the measurement limitations of the "yes-no" categories but offer methodological problems in any attempt to classify and quantitatively to manipulate the results.

In the brief essay type of response the judgment as to meaning and assortment of answers rests with the investigator; it is therefore unstandardized and subject to error. S. A. Stouffer attempted to overcome this difficulty by employing four judges.[14] His subjects, 238 students who had taken a Thurstone test on prohibition, wrote accounts of their opinions on prohibition. These essays were about 1,000 words in length. Four judges read the essays and rated the attitudes of their writers on a scale of favorable to unfavorable to prohibition. The judges had a remarkably high agreement: the intercorrelation of ratings of each judge with the ratings of each other judge was $+.87$, the range being from $+.83$ to $+.89$.

The oral interview, either following a definite outline or as apparently casual conversation, with the answers either transcribed at the time of the interview or written up later, presents special methodological problems in addition to those of the brief essay. Its superiority over written forms lies in the spontaneity of response; if the interview is made too formal, this advantage is lost. Further, the personal qualities of the questioner are introduced into the situation to a greater extent than in essay answers. Altogether, oral interviews are a much more difficult medium to arrange in any fashion permitting quantification. They are obviously useful for the collecting of informal, unstandardized accounts whereby some insight into the individual attitude process may be gained. Sometimes they have been transferred into simple quantitative terms by counting the answers common to a number of interviews.

This procedure was used years ago as a part of a study of opinions about Mexican immigrants in Flint, Michigan.[15] A number of ranking tests were constructed from statements made by junior college and high school students about the thousand Mexicans who had recently migrated

---

[14] S. A. Stouffer, *An Experimental Comparison of Statistical and Case History Methods of Attitude Research,* abstract of thesis, University of Chicago, Chicago, 1929–1930. Also reported by G. Murphy and L. B. Murphy, *Experimental Social Psychology,* Harper & Brothers, New York, 1931, p. 622.

[15] W. Albig, "Group Opinion and the Mexican," thesis, University of Michigan Library, Ann Arbor, Mich., 1929.

to that city. The tests were then given to 600 students throughout the city. In addition, the statements made during interviews with several hundred neighbors, businessmen, school children, teachers, police, social workers and professional men were recorded. In these interviews the author informally worked into the conversations a brief list of questions but strove to keep the discussion as spontaneous as possible. From these records it was possible to count similarities in statement, and the quantitative results were appended to each chapter dealing with the interviews with the various groups.

The desirability of the extended types of individual statement and of brief essays appears in the insight that may be gained into the individual attitude process, the origins and development of attitudes. However, they do not readily permit of quantitative analysis, because: (1) the providing of any formal outline of what to write about largely eliminates spontaneity and hence defeats the investigator's purpose; (2) the treatment of the results is dependent upon the judge or judges who read the essays or documents, and the standard or scale that he or they set up is a standard valid only for the judge or persons of similar attitudes (this applies both to the attitudes that they ascribe to the writers and also to their interpretation of language); (3) the essential problem still remains, the relation between this form of opinion and other types of behavior. Clearly preferable to simple tests, however, these sources have provided more understanding of the attitude process in the individual than has been obtained elsewhere by the social sciences. The methods of quantifying them should be experimented with extensively. They do not have quantitative validity.

MULTIPLE-CHOICE AND CROSS-OUT TESTS

As the range of response in the yes-or-no tests is too limited and as the essay, oral interview and other forms of extended response are so difficult to classify and score, some experimenters attempted a wider range of expression of opinion by providing a list of statements or words to be checked by the subjects. The situation might be presented in a paragraph or brief essay description, followed by a number of phrases or words, of which the subject was to check the one that most nearly agreed with his attitude.

A form of this type of test may be illustrated from the Allports' Ascendance-Submission Study.[16] A portion of their questions dealt with behavior, but some of them attempted to elicit statements of attitude. Of the forty-one items of the test, there were a number like the following:

[16] G. W. Allport and F. H. Allport, *A-S Reaction Study*, 1928.

Are you embarrassed if you have greeted a stranger whom you have mistaken for an acquaintance?

_____ very much
_____ somewhat
_____ not at all

Another variation is the word cross-out test. In an attempt to record fair-mindedness as an attitude, G. B. Watson used as the first part of the test fifty-one words such as bolshevist, mystic, Sunday blue laws, dancing, Unitarian, Holy Communion, and the like. The subject was instructed to cross out all those which he found annoying or distasteful. A tendency to cross out an unusually large number of words was taken as an indication of some sort of emotional set or conditioning.[17]

Although tests of these types may be indicative of some sort of emotional set, there are a number of difficulties involved in their use. The language difficulty is very apparent here. The terms are not mutually exclusive. They are not terms that have clear, definite meanings to the subjects. Nor are the categories scaled to clear-cut stages or steps of attitude difference. Just what is the line between "very much" and "somewhat"? Moreover, the descriptive words have been provided by the tester; perhaps the students tested would have developed a quite different list as significantly descriptive of that situation. The tester has, in part, projected his own attitudes by his selection of words. Moreover, the order and arrangement of the words may be significant factors. It has been pointed out that position may be so important in tests with alternate responses as to invalidate all the rest of the test. A response word when printed above its alternative was marked 33.8 per cent more often than when it was printed below its alternative. A response word when printed to the left of its alternative was marked 3.2 per cent more often than when printed at the right of its alternative. This source of perverting statements is likewise applicable to other types of tests. In spite of the limitations of the multiple-choice tests, we find some advance here as the range of response has been widened. But there is no adequate basis for measurement.

RATING

Another common form of attitude test is a rating device whereby a choice may be made of one of various degrees of opinion about a given question. In different tests the degrees of opinion have been presented in three, five, to as many as twenty-one categories. For example, a statement of opinion may be preceded by: "certainly right," "probably right," "doubtful," "probably wrong," "certainly wrong"; or by $+2$, $+1$, 0, -1,

[17] G. B. Watson, *The Measurement of Fair-mindedness*, Columbia University Press, New York, 1925.

—2; or by some other arrangement, one item of which is to be checked by the subject. Lund used a rating system in which there were twenty-one positions ranging from "belief allowing for no doubt" at +10 to "disbelief allowing for no doubt" at —10.[18] The difficulty of attempting introspectively to divide any attitude into twenty hypothetical divisions must have been a considerable strain upon the imaginations of those taking the test. How large a number of positions may be used in a rating device to deal with subjective phenomena? This can only be determined experimentally with specific material, but it is doubtful if more than five or seven positions could be successfully coped with by even a trained and serious student. Moreover, this is a rating device of abstract positions that are not objectified by indicating some concomitant behavior. In general, especially for tests to be widely administered, those rating tests are better which indicate a specific type of behavior as indicative of attitude. A more objective approach of this sort was made by Bogardus in his social-distance tests.[19] In these, the subject was asked to indicate his attitudes toward various nationality and racial groups by responses to questions as to his willingness to admit members of those groups to seven degrees of relationship. For example, the responses of 1,725 Americans to forty different races were recorded by percentages.

Table 6 shows the first four, the middle four, and the last four of the nationalities in the results of one of the Bogardus social-distance tests.[20] These tests represent a distinct advance over the preceding ones. Concrete potential behavior situations are substituted for abstract degrees of relationship. This makes for greater standardization in the understanding and response of the subjects to the steps. For example, the distinction between admitting to a club or to marriage is a difference in intimacy of relationships understood by the subject in a way that +5 and +3 on an abstract scale of attitudes is not differentiated. As the subjects' responses lie on a more common base, these tests have uses for comparative purposes. On the other hand, several points are apparent. (1) We do not have a scale in which the steps are of equal size, in that the intervals are similar. That is, we have no basis for judging the relative importance in decreasing intimacy between admission to kinship by marriage and to club membership and between admission to club membership and to the street as neighbor. Although there is apparently a general scale of stages of decreasing intimacy, it is not a measured scale. The steps are unknown. (2) The list of nationalities was chosen by the investigator. These are not necessarily nationalities on which even a majority of the subjects

[18] F. H. Lund, "The Psychology of Belief," *Jour. Abn. Soc. Psychol.*, 20: 63–81.
[19] E. S. Bogardus, *Immigration and Race Attitudes*, D. C. Heath and Company, Boston, 1928. Also numerous articles in *Sociol. Soc. Res.*
[20] Bogardus, *op. cit.*, p. 25.

Table 6. Reactions of 1,725 Americans to Different Races by Percentages

Regarding races	(1) To close kinship by marriage	(2) To my club as personal chums	(3) To my street as neighbors	(4) To employment in my occupation	(5) To citizenship in my country	(6) As visitors only to my country	(7) Would exclude from my country
English...........	93.7	96.7	97.3	95.4	95.9	1.7	0
Americans........	90.1	92.4	92.6	92.4	90.5	1.2	0
Canadians........	86.9	93.4	96.1	95.6	96.1	1.7	0.3
Scotch...........	78.1	89.1	91.3	92.3	93.3	1.7	0
Portuguese........	11	22	28.3	47.8	57.7	19	3.3
Poles............	11	11.6	28.3	44.3	58.3	19.7	4.7
Rumanians.......	8.8	19.3	23.8	38.3	51.6	22	4.6
Czechoslovaks.....	8.2	16.4	21.1	36	47.4	26	9.5
Chinese..........	1.1	11.8	15.9	27	27.3	45.2	22.4
Mulattoes........	1.1	9.6	10.6	32	47.4	22.7	16.8
Koreans..........	1.1	10.8	11.8	20.1	27.5	34.3	13.8
Hindus...........	1.1	6.8	13	21.4	23.7	47.1	19.1

have stereotypes and attitudes. (3) In such an extensive list of nationalities the subject may be unable to imagine the possibility of personal situations involving such choices with all of those on the list and yet be unwilling to acknowledge, even under the cloak of anonymity, lack of information or experience with regard to any one of the groups. (4) In this, as in other rating scales, the points on the scale are developed by the investigator on the basis of a logical arrangement, rather than from the attitudes of those tested. Related to this logical assumption of steps is the belief that the acceptance of each degree of intimacy implies a willingness to accept the succeeding ones. This is not necessarily true.

RANKING

The order-of-merit method is a simple type of measurement that the psychologist constantly uses. It has frequently been used in tests of judgment of weights, measures, sizes, colors, and the like. The materials of the test vary with the subject under consideration, but the principle is that of arrangement of units into scaled order by the person tested. This ranking of items does not make any assumptions with regard to the size of the intervals between the steps. That is, if there are eight objects to be placed in order of increasing weight, the differences in weight between that in the first position and that in the second position and between the second and third are not equal. One may be many times the other. Likewise, in the application of this method to the ranking of subjective states, there is no assumption of a scale with known steps. A study of statistical ethics, largely based upon this principle of ranking, was carried on for many years by A. P. Brogan.[21] After a series of questionnaires, in which students were asked to list the most reprehensible practices that they knew, he selected the sixteen that were most frequently mentioned. These were presented to class after class for ranking according to order of merit. This procedure illustrates one sound principle. The materials of which the test was constructed were taken from the same group as those later tested, or from a group similar to theirs. The students could therefore be expected to have attitudes toward the practices about which they were asked. The projecting of materials from the experimenter upon his group has been a serious shortcoming of all the tests we have so far considered. The ranking method, however, in addition to not being a measured scale, has one other basic limitation. How many items may be utilized in a ranking of attitudes? If the list is long, will there be an increase of inaccuracy toward the end of the list? For example, if a student is asked to list sixteen unethical practices or to enumerate twenty-five national groups in the order of their social distance from the subject, is there not the probability that the first named will be the most obnoxious practices or nationalities, that those toward the middle of the list will be the least obnoxious, and that the ones at the end will represent practices or nationalities which the student utilizes merely to fill in the requisite number? When the ranking of size or weight of units is used in a psychological test, the units are at least present to each subject. In the classification of opinions the units are not all necessarily of significance to each subject. The subject may have no attitude on which to base an opinion of a Korean, let us say, or of some unethical practice. He is asked, however, to rank in order of merit twenty-five nationalities or sixteen ethical practices. He has attitudes on fifteen and ten, respectively. Yet he must complete the requisite number. The test is not analogous to one in which twenty physical units are placed before the subject for discrimination. The number of items that may be used in a ranking of attitudes can be determined only in relation to the particular subject matter.

[21] A. P. Brogan, "Problems and Methods in Statistical Ethics," *Pub. Am. Sociol. Soc.*, 21: 174–177.

OPINION MEASUREMENT: THE ATTITUDE SCALES

An early study by Allport and Hartman had a considerable influence in stimulating later studies of attitude.[22] Thurstone, who worked extensively in this field, credited this study with arousing his interest. It was the first study that attempted to create a scale on which attitudes could be measured. The purposes of the study were (1) to develop a scale technique for measuring the distribution of opinion upon public questions and (2) to inquire into the psychological characteristics of those who adopt certain attitudes upon such questions. It is the first of these two objectives that interests us at this point. Seven issues of political interest, selected by the testers, were given to sixty upper-class students, who were asked to write their views on them. The resulting essays were read by six judges, who abstracted the principal statements of opinion from them and arranged these opinions in order from one logical extreme to the other. On each of the seven issues these statements were then mixed, so as not to be in order as arranged by the judges, and presented to 367 students. On each issue the student was to check one statement that most nearly expressed his opinion. For example, on the League of Nations question he could choose from twelve statements; on the qualifications of President Coolidge, from ten statements; on the distribution of wealth he could choose from five positions, and the like. The results were then arranged along the original scale as developed by the judges and the percentages of the persons taking the test who chose each statement as representing their opinions were distributed along this line. The results were graphed. For example, on the qualifications of Mr. Coolidge, the percentages of the students selecting each of the 10 statements as most important are:

14.9   Coolidge is perfectly fitted for the office of President of the U.S.
22.0   Coolidge is the best man we could find for the office today.
20.3   Although Coolidge has been a very good President, he cannot be compared to our strongest Presidents.
12.5   Coolidge is better than the men nominated by the other parties.
18.5   Coolidge may be the right man, but he has not yet had sufficient chance to prove it.
3.8   Coolidge is a little too conservative.
4.6   Mediocre is the word that sums up Coolidge's qualifications for President.
1.4   Coolidge favors the financial interests too much.
1.6   Coolidge is controlled by a band of corrupt politicians.
0   A man such as Coolidge is bound to bring with him a corrupt government.

[22] F. H. Allport and D. A. Hartman, "The Measurement and Motivation of Atypical Opinion in a Certain Group," *Am. Pol. Sci. Rev.*, 19: 735–760, 1925.

Charted, the results appear as indicated:

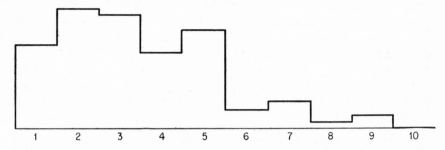

The steps are indicated along a base line, which has been developed from the decisions of the six judges as to the importance of the reasons. The vote of those taking the tests may then be figured in terms of percentages of those checking each of the statements. These results are then allocated to the proper division on the base line.

Certain advances in recording were scored by this test: (1) The statements were originally taken from students when students were to take the test. This eliminated positions suggested from outside the tested group. (2) A greater variety of possible positions was presented on each issue than in the simpler tests. (3) As a base line was developed from the decisions of the six judges and the results located on this line, we have actual measurement rather than merely counting.

The principal limitations of this test were that: (1) the statements were not mutually exclusive; (2) the determination of the base line was based upon the judgments of a group quite dissimilar in attitudes from those taking the test; (3) the points on this base line were not equidistant from one another; that is, in quantitative terms one statement might be many times as important as another. Hence, it would occupy many times the space on the base line. Therefore, we may not be dealing with steps that are even approximately equal. We are provided with no way of determining their relative size. It was to these problems that Thurstone turned his attention.

THE THURSTONE SCALE

L. L. Thurstone emphasized that the ranking of opinions may show the relative importance of one or the other opinion in the group tested but that ranking does not measure, in that it does not show the quantitative relationship between the opinion types as measured on some scale. He, more than any other, influenced opinion measurement from 1930 to 1940 and provided a score or more of attitude scales that have been widely utilized. Thurstone extended the psychophysical techniques to the measurement of attitudes that Cattell had first used for social phenomena. The development and application of Thurstone's methods have been extensively described in a monograph on measurement of attitude toward the church, in which study he collaborated with E. J. Chave. From that source we shall briefly describe his procedures.

Many individuals were asked to write their opinions about the church, and from these a list of statements was prepared. The list of 130 statements remained after the collection of statements had been edited, it having been kept in mind that:

(1) The statements should be as brief as possible so as not to fatigue the subjects who are asked to read the whole list; (2) The statements should be such that they can be indorsed or rejected in accordance with their agreement or disagreement with the attitude of the reader. Some statements in a random sample will be so phrased that the reader can express no definite indorsement or rejection of them; (3) Every statement should be such that acceptance or rejection of the statement does indicate something regarding the reader's attitude about the issue in question; (4) Double-barreled statements should be avoided except possibly as examples of neutrality when better neutral statements do not seem to be readily available. Double-barreled statements tend to have a high ambiguity; (5) One must insure that at least a fair majority of the statements really belong on the attitude variable that is to be measured. If a small number of irrelevant statements should be either intentionally or unintentionally left in the series, they will be automatically eliminated by an objective criterion, but the criterion will not be successful unless the majority of the statements are clearly a part of the stipulated variable.[23]

The collection of the materials of the test from opinions expressed by individuals of the same or a similar group satisfies the objection that we raised regarding the projection of attitudes of the experimenters upon those tested. The language difficulty still remains, as indeed it does to some extent in all tests, but the statements have been carefully culled to remove those containing words that would be likely to be misunderstood.

The next step was the sorting procedure, in which a group of judges were asked to sort into eleven piles the 130 statements, which had been mimeographed. At one end were to be placed those statements favoring the church, at the other those opposed, and in pile 6 the neutral statements. In the intervening spaces were to be placed those statements which the judges decided were less and less or more and more favorable to the church. The objective here was to develop a scale from the judgments of those who were to take the test or were similar in background and opinion statements to those who would take it. It was thought thus to eliminate the artificial scales developed when those of different back-

[23] L. L. Thurstone and E. J. Chave, *The Measurement of Attitude*, University of Chicago Press, Chicago, 1929. Quoted by permission.

ground do the judging, as in the Allport-Hartman test. Many judges supplanted few judges (there were 300 in this test); judges of similar opinions supplanted possibly alien judges. The results were then counted and worked out in a table of percentages in accumulative proportions.

Statement	A	B	C	D	E	F	G	H	I	J	K
1	0.00	0.00	0.00	0.00	0.00	0.08	0.17	0.23	0.33	0.52	1.00
2	0.02	0.13	0.35	0.72	0.93	0.97	0.98	0.99	1.00	1.00	1.00
3	0.00	0.00	0.01	0.01	0.01	0.09	0.33	0.60	0.84	0.98	1.00
39	0.16	0.57	0.85	0.95	0.99	0.99	0.99	1.00	1.00	1.00	1.00
40	0.00	0.00	0.00	0.01	0.05	0.08	0.21	0.43	0.71	0.93	1.00
100	0.40	0.85	0.95	0.98	1.00	1.00	1.00	1.00	1.00	1.00	1.00

We now have a table (the above is a sample of 6 statements out of the 130) in which the cumulative percentages of the judges' decisions on each of the 130 statements appear. That is, statement 39 was placed in classification A (most favorable to church) by 16 per cent of the judges, in classification B by 41 per cent, etc., but in this table the percentages are accumulative, that is, each classification includes all the preceding ones.

The next problem was the determination of the scale value (based upon the judges' decisions) of each statement. These scale values were determined graphically for each statement. The graphs were plotted from the accumulative proportions as shown in the above table. For example, statement 39 reads, "I believe the church is absolutely needed to overcome the tendency to individualism and selfishness. It practices the golden rule fairly well." In the judges' sorting, 16 per cent considered this statement as expressing highest appreciation of the value of the church; 57 per cent considered that it was either highest or next highest; etc. In Fig. 4 we have a graph showing the cumulative percentages.

On this graph the curve crosses the 50 per cent level at 1.8, and this is assigned as the scale value of this statement. Half of the judges classified this statement as more favorable toward the church than 1.8, half as less favorable.

The objective is to obtain a basis for selection of statements about which the judges have been in greatest agreement and of statements which are evenly distributed along a scale from 0 to 11, thus providing a test that covers the gamut of expressions of opinion from most to least favorable toward the church. The graphs for all the 130 statements will show curves of many shapes. In the case of statement 39, the quartile

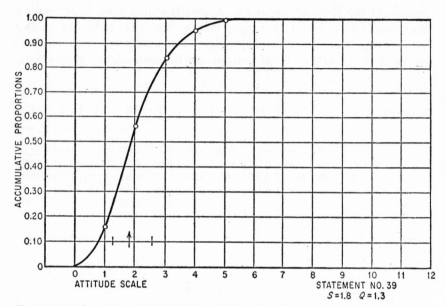

Fig. 4. Attitude scale graph. (From L. L. Thurstone and E. J. Chave, *The Measurement of Attitude*, p. 37. Reproduced by permission of the University of Chicago Press, Chicago.)

points for the curve are located at scale values 1.3 and 2.6 respectively. Thurstone labels the distance between these two points 1.3, the Q value, or the measure of ambiguity of the statement. If the Q value is low, there is a high degree of agreement among the judges; if the Q value is high, the statement is very ambiguous, the different readers having scattered their judgments. Such statements would be discarded.[24]

Ambiguous and irrelevant statements are discarded. Those remaining of the 130 statements are distributed at their scale-value points along the scale from 0 to 11. The selection of the questions for the test is now made by deciding approximately how many statements are desired and then selecting statements that are distributed by more or less uniform intervals along the scale. That is, if 22 statements are to be used, select, in so far as possible, statements whose scale values are separated from one another by one-half a point on the scale. Such an ideal distribution will not be possible, but it is to be approximated. In the Thurstone-Chave scale, 45 statements were retained.

The 45 statements are then shuffled and presented as a test, in which the subject is to check every statement that expresses his sentiment to-

[24] Thurstone determines the reliability of the scale values, develops an objective criterion of ambiguity and of irrelevance. These procedures are described on pp. 44–58 of the monograph cited.

ward the church. For scoring the results the procedure is as follows: The scale value of each of the 45 statements is known. Add the scale values of each of the statements endorsed by the subject, and calculate their arithmetic mean. The result is the subject's position on the scale. The authors felt justified in using this mean scale value of the opinions endorsed by the subject as his position on the scale, since there were approximately the same number of opinions available for him to check in each class interval. The reliability of scoring thus was tested. If a group of 100 subjects take such a test, the result will appear as 100 points on a scale line from 0 to 11. In conclusion, it may be noted that the selection of eleven divisions in sorting and on the scale was an arbitrary choice. This number might have been smaller; it probably could not profitably have been larger. The sorting judges would have been confused. However, this is a matter for experimental determination in each test.

The basic problem in this, as in the other tests, is whether attitudes, as expressed in opinions, are units that may profitably be handled quantitatively. Aside from this, there are certain technical objections to the construction of the tests; the source of materials; the range of those materials; the determination of a scale. The Thurstone test largely overcomes these problems. However, certain criticisms have been made. (1) The tendency of the judges to place a statement more frequently in the end piles than in the intermediate piles has been called the "end effect." This end effect tends to shorten the distances between the end statements and the adjacent statements so that in the final scale values the middle statements are further apart than the end statements, although the quantitative scale values may indicate an even distribution. It has been suggested that the division of all the statements into those "for" and "against" and then further sorting of each category would eliminate this skewing.[25] (2) Whether or not a scale developed by using one group of judges is applicable to quite different groups of subjects has been questioned. To what extent will the judges' attitudes affect the scale? [26] Some differences were found in calculating three independent sets of scale values for certain statements of opinion about the Negro: the first by Southern white subjects, the second by Northern subjects prejudiced in favor of the Negro, and the third by Negroes.[27] Although Thurstone and his students maintain that this factor is of little importance, it remains to be investigated. (3) The time and labor involved in the construction of

[25] D. D. Droba, "Methods for Measuring Attitudes," *Psychol. Bull.*, 29: 309–323. D. Katz and F. H. Allport, *Students' Attitudes*, p. 366, The Craftsmen Press, Inc., 1936.
[26] S. Rice, *Statistics in the Social Studies*, chap. 11 and commentary, University of Pennsylvania Press, Philadelphia, 1930.
[27] E. D. Hinkley, "The Influence of Individual Opinion on Construction of an Attitude Scale," *Jour. Soc. Psychol.*, 3: 284–292.

a Thurstone scale has been discouraging to many. The sorting procedure is especially laborious and time-consuming, so that none but selected judges have been effectively used. Instead of the sorting procedure, a method of rating on an eleven- or nine-point scale, printed in the left-hand margin of a mimeographed list of opinions, was suggested. It was maintained that a saving of more than 50 per cent in time is achieved.[28] (4) We have noted the superiority of the Bogardus test to some other simple nonscaled tests because Bogardus used concrete situations rather than abstract formulations. Katz and Allport suggested the development of a scale, using the Thurstone techniques, on which the scale continuum is one of behavior other than opinion.[29]

Rensis Likert refined the Thurstone technique further by a scoring procedure whereby a respondent was asked to indicate his agreement or disagreement with respect to each item, but in doing so also to indicate the intensity of his attitude on the item by rating. On each item he was asked to check his preferred position on a five-point scale from strong disagreement to strong agreement. Each point on the scale was given a numerical value, say from 1 to 5, and the individual taking the attitude test could then be scored, first as to his range on the scale and then by a numerical score obtained by adding his rating scores. This provided another dimension for the attitude scales.[30]

THE GUTTMAN SCALES AND SCALOGRAM

The Thurstone technique and the Likert refinement of scaling method assume that the items lie along a continuum and that the individual respondent's attitude range may be located on a sector of the continuum. Louis Guttman's procedures, in his early work, were aimed at the determination of whether the items to be used in a test were really scalable in the sense of lying along the attitude continuum or whether the items fell to one side or the other of the scale continuum.[31] Guttman devised a system of ascribing values to items in relation to the scale so as to obtain through total scores the best possible scoring of the individual and quantitative scale variable. However, this procedure did not exhibit a scale pattern and it was this problem of patterning of attitudes which

[28] R. Seashore and K. Hevner, "A Time-saving Device for the Construction of Attitude Scales," *Jour. Soc. Psychol.*, 3: 366–374. See also R. Likert, S. Roslow and G. Murphy, "A Simple and Reliable Method of Scoring the Thurstone Attitude Scales," *Jour. Soc. Psychol.*, 5: 228–238.

[29] Katz and Allport, *op. cit.*, pp. 368–371.

[30] R. Likert, "A Technique for the Measurement of Attitudes," *Arch. of Psychol.*, no. 140, 1932.

[31] With these Guttman tests, another basic line of development in attitude measurement was instituted. L. Guttman, "A Basis for Scaling Qualitative Data," *Am. Soc. Rev.*, 9: 139–150, 1944.

he later came to consider as of critical importance. Therefore, he abandoned the emphasis on category weights and values and turned to scalogram analysis.[32]

ATTITUDE, OPINION AND BEHAVIOR

Expressions of opinion, no matter how recorded, have frequently been objected to as indexes of attitude. It is urged that forms of behavior other than opinion will more reliably reveal attitudes. Considerable controversy has ensued from this division of opinion on verbalizations versus other forms of behavior as indicators of attitude. Like so many such controversies, it has arisen in part from a willful misinterpretation of the opponents' viewpoints and terms. Even the most enthusiastic investigator does not assume that all attitudes are amenable to measurement by language tests. That conventional answers, rather than opinion expressions of all attitudes involved, will usually be given to questions dealing with sex relations, miscegenation, religion or any other issue on which there have been strict mores is quite clear. The subject's rationalization, rather than conscious deception of the investigator, will usually be indicated. So basic is this tendency to give the conventional answer that even anonymity may not modify the subject's response. Most investigators have assumed that the individual's hidden attitude, rather than the conventional response given in such situations, is the real attitude. If by "real" is meant that which is more likely to result in action, it by no means follows that the individual's hidden attitude is more real than the conventional response. Although usually more willing to disclose the conventional attitude and thus avoid antagonistic responses, the individual may also be much more willing to *act* in accordance with that conventional attitude. Thus action as well as opinion is a fallible indication of all the attitudes involved in a situation. As Thurstone has maintained:

There comes to mind the uncertainty of using an opinion as an index of attitude. The man may be a liar. If he is not intentionally misrepresenting his

---

[32] The scope, variety and details of scalogram analysis are beyond the space or the function of this description. For detailed discussion, see L. Guttman, *Studies in Social Psychology in World War II*, Princeton University Press, Princeton, N.J., 1949–1950, vol. IV, pp. 60–171; Green, *op. cit.*; Remmers, *op. cit.*, pp. 106 ff.

A useful device for indicating the rank order of both the respondents and question categories so that the pattern may be graphically presented is the scalogram board. "In the work of the Research Branch, Information and Education Division, Army Service Forces, the standard technique was a scalogram board, constructed of movable rows and columns on which the responses of the individuals on each item could be indicated, and then these movable rows and columns manipulated in a manner to achieve, if possible, a pattern." Remmers, *op. cit.*, p. 106. The boards ordinarily consisted of 100 movable wooden strips, each strip containing 100 holes, so that the board was equipped to handle the responses of 100 individuals on as many as 100 responses.

real attitude on a disputed question, he may nevertheless modify the expression of it for reasons of courtesy, especially in those situations in which frank expression of attitude may not be well received. This has led to the suggestion that a man's action is a safer index of his attitude than what he says. But his actions may also be distortions of his attitude. A politician extends friendship and hospitality in overt action while hiding an attitude that he expresses more truthfully to an intimate friend. Neither his opinions nor his overt acts constitute in any sense an infallible guide to the subjective inclinations and preferences that constitute his attitude. Therefore we must remain content to use opinions or other forms of action merely as indices of attitude. It must be recognized that there is a discrepancy, some error of measurement, as it were, between the opinion or overt action that we use as an index and the attitude that we infer from such an index.[33]

In everyday life the individual's expressions of opinion are considered a significant part of his behavior. We use these, as well as other types of behavior, as indications of his attitudes. They are; although we may misinterpret the attitudes involved or have an incomplete understanding of them.

When I read in Mandeville's *Fable of the Bees* that "The poor have nothing to stir them up to be serviceable but their wants, which it is prudent to relieve, but folly to cure," I immediately assume a whole complex of attitudes in the author. When an individual says, or writes, the awkward but current phrase, "know-how," instead of skill, ability, knowledge, information or some descriptive combination of words, I assume in him an attitude of anti-intellectualism and of conformity to language fashion. When I read in *Life* magazine that "There are some real planners around—the old, hot-eyed New Deal types—who think they can remake society into some kind of Utopia," I am justified in assuming some attitudes among *Life's* editors. But I am also justified in assuming attitudes from nonverbal indicators. If I assume an attitude-complex from the flamboyant, assertive, attention-demanding necktie of a Middle Western businessman, I may be wrong about the individual, but not about the values of his group.

When expressions of opinion are made the subject of organized analysis in opinion testing, they are frequently significant indicators of attitude. And this would be admitted by those who favor stressing other forms of behavior in a research program on attitudes. In discussing racial attitudes, in 1938, LaPiere wrote:

For the conventional method of measuring social attitudes is to ask questions (usually in writing) which demand a verbal adjustment to an entirely symbolic situation. Because it is easy, cheap, and mechanical, the attitudinal question-

[33] Thurstone and Chave, *op. cit.*, p. 7. Quoted by permission of University of Chicago Press.

naire is rapidly becoming a major method of sociological and socio-psychological investigation. The technique is simple. Thus from a hundred or a thousand responses to the question "Would you get up to give an Armenian woman your seat in a street-car?" the investigator derives the "attitude" of non-Armenian males toward Armenian females. Now the question may be constructed with elaborate skill and hidden with consummate cunning in a maze of supplementary or even irrelevant questions, yet all that has been obtained is a symbolic response to a symbolic situation. The words "Armenian woman" do not constitute an Armenian woman of flesh and blood who might be tall or squat, fat or thin, old or young, well or poorly dressed—who might, in fact, be a goddess or just another old and dirty hag. And "yes" or "no" is but a verbal reaction, and this does not involve rising from the seat or stolidly avoiding the hurt eyes of the hypothetical woman and the derogatory stares of other streetcar occupants.[34]

Whenever possible, comparison and correlation of action and opinion as indicating attitudes are clearly desirable. Unfortunately, there are as yet few formal studies that attempt to show this relation.

[34] R. T. LaPiere, "Attitudes vs. Actions," *Soc. Forces,* 13: 230–237. Permission to quote granted. A recent discussion may be found in D. T. Campbell, "Indirect Assessment of Social Attitudes," *Psychol. Bull.,* January, 1950, pp. 15 ff., and in I. R. Weschler, "Indirect Methods of Attitude Measurement," *Int. Jour. Opin. and Att. Res.,* vol. 4, pp. 209–228, 1950.

CHAPTER 10

Straw Votes, Polls and Pollers

> Public opinion is no mere aggregate of separate individual judgments, but an organization, a cooperative product of communication and reciprocal influence.
>
> One who would understand public opinion should distinguish clearly between a true or mature opinion and a popular impression. The former requires earnest attention and discussion for a considerable time, and when reached is significant, even if mistaken. . . . A popular impression, on the other hand, is facile, shallow, transient, with that fickleness and fatuity that used to be ascribed to the popular mind in general. It is analogous to the unconsidered views and utterances of an individual, and the more one studies it the less seriously he will take it.
>
> CHARLES HORTON COOLEY

Although the attitudes of the members of large publics cannot be quantitatively measured in all their complexity, diversity and intensity, certain aspects of attitudes and some range of intensity may be assumed through the recording and measuring of opinions. Attitudes are also assumed from the observation of and recording of other than verbal behavior, but we are concerned here with the recording of opinions. No record of opinions is adequate which does not lead to accurate assumptions regarding the attitudes which underlie the opinions.

There have been two fundamental problems involved in the attempts at the measurement of public opinion. The one is the development of attitude tests sufficiently comprehensive to include at least the more typical attitude patterns of most of the individuals of a public. And significant publics today often number millions or scores of millions of individuals. The other basic problem is that of developing sampling methods adequate to the task of reporting on large publics by means of the smallest feasible representative sample. Often widely divergent attitudes motivating the same expression of opinion must be divulged by the attitude test, and at times publics numbering millions must be reduced to a sample of a few thousands.

There are many problems of attitude recording, not all of which are soluble, and there are also the problems of sampling, which will be solved eventually. The problem of adequate sampling is by far the simpler of the two. As yet, it has not been completely solved by the pollers, but the proper sampling of various publics on various questions is soluble. On the other hand, the problem of a comparable common denominator of opinions and underlying attitude complexes, a common denominator which adequately reflects the opinions and attitudes of the members of large publics, is less readily soluble and will never be recorded with complete accuracy. Attitudes are complex, variable and extensively diversified configurations in individual consciousness. Moreover, as publics increase in size and are less homogeneous in mind-life, the attitude scales are more difficult to formulate. However, there is no reason to desist from the attempt to record attitudes through measuring opinions, especially the opinions of samples of large publics on public issues. For it is on just those questions of general significance that attitude patterns, limited in number and discernibly similar, are to be found. It is, therefore, easier to record opinions concerning a political candidate or an issue of public policy than it is to find a reportable common denominator in a literary group about the literary merits of an author, in the opinions of painters about the worth of a fellow craftsman, or in the opinions of members of other highly individualistic groups. The attitudes are textured more similarly on public issues because the sources of information are discernibly channeled, especially through the mass communication media. Similar indoctrination, training and experience form common attitudes. Also most public issues involve eventual action and the number of alternatives in action are usually quite limited.

The pollers have become increasingly expert and have contributed much to the sampling of large publics (their errors in 1948 and in 1952 were not predominantly sampling errors), but the pollers have added little or nothing to significant attitude research. Academic research on attitude recording has, in general, provided instruments too cumbersome for commercial application or for the testing of large, general publics. But when the refined results of these two areas of research are fruitfully combined, we shall be near to at least a partial science of public opinion measurement. We may be quite hopeful concerning the speedy improvement of the sampling methods of pollers and other opinion measurers and we should be cautiously sanguine concerning improvement in attitude record-taking.

EARLY STRAW VOTES AND POLLS

Neither matured, significant public opinions nor numerous popular impressions are to be found extensively in stable, relatively static societies.

There, social customs, beliefs and convictions are inculcated by training, precept and example from earliest childhood. The controversial, at least on public issues, is at a minimum among masses of the simpler peoples. Such unity of mind-life has produced both the great popular ideologies of the past, usually logical and well-integrated thought systems perfected in their long evolution, and, also, some of the outstanding material objects symbolizing that mind-life, monuments to human integration, forethought and convictions. Early in this century, Henry Adams stood before one of Europe's great cathedrals with a friend. "He asked me," Adams wrote, "why it is we can no longer build such piles." I replied, "Men in those days had convictions. We moderns have opinions and it requires something more than an opinion to build a Gothic cathedral." Periods of limited opinion do not have need for the recorders of opinion, for the straw-vote takers and pollers, for the study of opinions as important phenomena.

However, in the United States of the mid-twentieth century, popular opinions and impressions have become more numerous than at any period in history. It is a time of maximum flux in cultural values, of opinions rather than convictions and beliefs. There is a complexity of social organization and process unimagined even a half century ago. The mass communication media are the arterial flow of the pulsing life of modern opinion. And, during the past two centuries in the Western world, a political and educational philosophy has emerged which has stressed the significance of popular opinion. The increasing animation, intensity and diversity of opinion has been viewed with concern by many groups. Publicists, politicians, the various types of publicity and public-relations representatives, the leaders of the numerous special-interest groups and many others increasingly have wanted to know the present state of public opinion on matters pertaining to their interests.

There were many opinions to be recorded, there were many groups wishing to ascertain them and, latterly, there were supposed to be social science methods for recording attitudes and opinions. And the theory of sampling large universes had developed to the point where its application to the large political and mass publics was considered feasible. The application of such sampling occurred in the mid-1930's when the commercial pollsters, or, as they later preferred to designate themselves, pollers, began reporting in private and, on some issues, in public about the state of popular opinion. But, before the pollers, there were the straw-vote takers and market surveyors and, before that there was the inquisitive, intelligent individual going about asking questions. For polls of public opinion have been taken in some fashion whenever leaders or anyone else wished to know the opinions of a public. The questioners might go about talking to individuals at random, but astute and knowledgeable questioners would begin to talk to representative individuals. In small publics this informal selection usually could be adequately representative without elaborate analysis of the composition of the public. On the basis of personal experience and observation the questioner could know who represented whom. For centuries leaders have been polling the opinions of their followers on the relatively few issues of their day. But usually such questioning was not very systematic as to the questions or the sampling of the publics, whereas the pollers, since 1935, have systematically made selective samples of publics, often of national scope, and of publics whose members were greatly diversified as to status, age, location, knowledge and other significant criteria. In reporting public opinion, the pollers have contributed representative sampling often of an amazingly accurate quality, but they have not always added anything to the significant questioning of individuals frequently achieved by their predecessors.

Thus, throughout the period during which public opinion has been considered significant, there have been those who sought to discover what that public opinion was and, also, to estimate how people would behave as a result of their opinions. Throughout the political history of the United States, political leadership has been estimating votes on the basis of straw votes and polls, while, during the past seventy-five years, the newspaperman has been testing his skill as a predictor on the basis of interviews with a sample of the general public.[1] A poll, originally meaning "head," hence, "a person," has come to refer to a listing, a counting, an enumerating or a registering of the persons of a public, or, again, an ascertaining of the sentiments or opinion of the members of a public. The representative sampling procedure in public opinion surveying is now called polling. Somewhat earlier, polls on persons, candidates and issues were frequently referred to as straw polls. "A straw vote is an unofficial canvass of an electorate to determine the division of popular sentiment on public issues or on candidates for public office."[2] This may be an inclusive canvass, but ordinarily it is conducted by some type of sampling. Thus "by testing a small sample, they have gained knowledge about a larger whole. The straw poll applies this principle to the measurement of political sentiment. In a preëlection poll, the voting intentions of a few citizens are ascertained in order that it may be known how the great mass of people are likely to vote."[3]

[1] See C. E. Robinson, *Straw Votes*, Columbia University Press, New York, 1932, chaps. 1 and 2. In the 1928 election, Robinson figures the 1928 average error for 16 state predictions as 7 per cent. The estimates of newspapermen on presidential elections showed average errors ranging from 9 to 22 per cent.

[2] *Ency. Soc. Sci.*, p. 417.

[3] Robinson, *op. cit.*, p. 46.

The detailed history of the straw polls of the nineteenth century remains to be written. Here and there one may note instances of early polls by newspapers or organizations, but polling does not yet have the status and dignity which stimulates historical research into every incidental detail of its nineteenth-century record. However, the lack of historical monographs is of no especial significance to those who are concerned with polling in terms of its significance in cultural history and not in terms of completeness in the compilation of historical trivia. For polls become significant, not in terms of sporadic instances which may be unearthed by exploration in the files of a few crumbling newspapers, but when the polls are really important to leadership and to mass publics. In the 1820's the straw polls were not thus significant; in the 1920's they had become so. "The straw poll began as an intermittent practice in U.S. journalism in 1824. In that year, the *Harrisburg Pennsylvanian* sent out reporters to inquire among the citizens of Wilmington, Delaware, whether they were going to vote for Henry Clay, Andrew Jackson, John Quincy Adams or William H. Crawford for president."[4] During the next seventy-five years, newspapers, for example, the Boston *Globe* and the New York *Herald*, conducted some straw polls. However, they were not representative sample surveys. In 1855 the president of the Maryland Agricultural Society "proposed a plan for making a poll of farmers as one means of obtaining more accurate information on crop conditions. Such information was needed, he believed, because dealers and speculators were reaping large profits through circulation of false rumors on the prospective size of crops and through producers' ignorance of crop values."[5] Although few returns were received in this particular instance, it was the first of several attempts made before the Department of Agriculture began its reports in 1866. Now information is collected for that Department, and polls of some opinions are taken from records of over 600,000 voluntary farm reporters and about 200,000 nonfarm reporters, such as merchants and millers. But, the straw-poll taking of the nineteenth century was incidental and ephemeral.

Claude E. Robinson has written the only extensive and significant monograph on the straw polls of the period 1900 to 1930, but discussion of the polls and pollers since 1935 has produced an extensive literature.[6]

---

[4] *Ency. Brit.*, "Public Opinion Surveys," p. 744.

[5] H. W. Henderson, "An Early Poll," *Pub. Opin. Quar.*, 6: 1: 450.

[6] Since January, 1937, the *Public Opinion Quarterly* alone has printed more than 100 articles on the polls. A bibliography based on all periodicals since 1937 would include, I believe, more than 3,000 items. During this period, there have also been published about a dozen books dealing exclusively with the polls or the results of polls, one of the most critical of polls and pollers being *The Pollsters*, by Lindsay Rogers, published by Alfred A. Knopf, Inc., New York, in 1949.

Straw votes employing the principle of sampling have been conducted in the United States since the early 1900's, chiefly by newspapers and periodicals. Among the outstanding sponsors have been the *Chicago Journal* (later the *Daily Times*), the *Chicago Tribune*, the *Cincinnati Enquirer*, the *Columbus Dispatch*, the Hearst newspapers, the *New York Herald*, the *New York Daily News*, the *Salt Lake Tribune*, the Scripps-Howard newspapers, and, among the magazines, the *Farm Journal*, the *Literary Digest* and the *Pathfinder*. The polls of the Hearst newspapers, the *New York Herald* and the *Literary Digest* have been national in scope.[7]

These early polls were concerned primarily with candidates, although a few of them, especially the *Literary Digest* polls, dealt, at times, with issues. The *Companion* poll, sponsored by the *Woman's Home Companion* since 1935, has conducted many polls and has had panels of 1,000 to 1,500 members who reported periodically on the topics polled. The newspapers conducted straw polls because the results were a kind of election news which interested readers and at times built circulations.

These early polls were conducted in several ways, by ballots, printed in the newspapers or magazines, which could be clipped and returned by the reader who chose to do so, by ballots left in stores, and by interviews. It was soon found that polls by clipped ballots could be and often were invalidated by ardent partisans who sent in large numbers of ballots in order to make a good showing for their candidate. The Rexall Drug Stores conducted a number of straw polls by placing ballot boxes in their stores throughout the country. Some of the newspapers used reporters to interview passers-by on the streets, in stores and elsewhere, or by going from house to house. The house-to-house method led to the first attempts to achieve a genuinely representative cross section of voters, for it was soon discovered that the results varied greatly from one section of a city to another. Using only a rough approximation of an accurate cross section, as it would be developed today, the Hearst newspapers conducted polls in 1924 and 1928 which forecast the results of the presidential elections in those years with a relatively small margin of error, an error amounting to about five percentage points in 1928.

All of these early polls involved and interested only a small proportion of the population and were not functionally important in the political process, as the polls since 1936 have become. Nor were they influential on the opinions of major publics on other issues. But various interests were developing which were to give the straw polls more influential

---

[7] C. E. Robinson, article on the "Straw Vote" in the *Encyclopaedia of the Social Sciences*, 1933. His monograph, *Straw Votes*, was published in 1932, and his article, "Recent Developments in the Straw Poll Field," in *Pub. Opin. Quar.*, 1: 3: 45–56, and 1: 4: 42–52, contains his discussion of the period preceding and just after the first commercial polls by George Gallup and Elmo Roper.

backers and an expanded audience. Newspapers, periodicals and other commercial interests, having become accustomed to the market survey, began to bombard people with straw ballots and increasingly to solicit opinion expressions on issues. The political utility of reasonably accurate straw polls seemed evident to many political leaders. It was possible that the poll results could be used for propaganda. The possibility of popular interest in polls aroused publicists. And commercial interests had many uses for poll results.

THE LITERARY DIGEST POLLS

The number of interviews or ballots in the early polls was small. At most, hundreds or thousands of people responded. Between 1916 and 1936, *The Literary Digest,* most famed poll of its period, mailed tens of millions of ballots to the people of the United States. On a single election, that of 1936, over 10 million ballots were sent out and 2,376,523 were returned. The sponsors gained in publicity, advertising, circulation and reader interest, until the debacle of 1936, when *The Literary Digest* prophesied a Landon victory with 370 electoral votes, whereas Roosevelt won 523 out of a possible 531 votes. On issues, the *Digest's* polls on the bonus and on prohibition were the most extensive and best publicized. Polls on opinions concerning prohibition were conducted in 1922, 1930 and 1932. In 1922, ballots were mailed to 8 million telephone owners, in 1930, to 20 million automobile and telephone owners (approximately 5 million returned the ballots), and, in 1932, to about the same number.

The mailing lists of *The Literary Digest* were compiled from telephone directories and automobile registration files. Its circulation list contained over 20 million names. In the polls on candidates for the years 1916, 1920, 1924 and 1928, *The Literary Digest* polls showed an average plurality error of 20, 21, 12 and 12 per cent.[8] These straw polls were unreliable because they did not obtain an accurate cross section of the voting population.

Many questioned the accuracy of the *Digest's* polls before 1936. It was noted that this poll depended neither on a random nor a weighted sample. The *Digest's* circulation of mailed ballots was based on considerations other than true sampling, in that the automobile and telephone lists were more suited to a commercial purpose of the *Digest,* that is, of sending out publicity material to potential subscribers to the *Digest* (which was often sent in the same envelope with the ballot), than for obtaining replies from a complete cross section of potential voters. Academic social scientists, market-research analysts, and the just-emerging commercial pollers all criticized *The Literary Digest's* procedures before

[8] Robinson, *Straw Votes,* p. 72.

the election of 1936. The reasons for its anticipated errors were explicitly stated. The mailing lists disproportionately represented the upper-income strata of the voting population and the lower-income strata would, under the conditions of 1936, disproportionately appear at the polls. Moreover, even of those who received the *Digest's* ballots, the returned ballots would come in larger proportions from those in the upper economic and educational levels of the lists used. And furthermore, under the conditions of 1936, as Archibald Crossley noted:

> The *Digest* with its millions of post cards offers an ideal medium for an expression of protest. In 1936 anti-Roosevelt feeling ran high in upper income classes. Those who have not made up their minds how to vote, those who have no strong feelings about the candidates, and those who are of minimum intelligence are less apt to read and return the *Digest* ballots than are those who possess an urgent desire to register their opinions.[9]

Aware of the nonrepresentative nature of the *Digest's* mailing lists, after a pretesting of the voting intentions of various income groups, George Gallup, just emerging as a commercial pollster, was able to predict within one percentage point [10] the *Digest's* probable error before the *Digest's* ballots were even mailed to their public. In 1935 Dr. Gallup had organized the American Institute of Public Opinion and assembled a staff to conduct polling on the basis of representative sampling. In 1936 the Institute's staff had grown aware that political sentiment was varying strikingly with different income levels. In the final election returns of 1936 President Roosevelt received 60.2 per cent of the popular vote, while *The Literary Digest* predicted 40.9 per cent for Roosevelt and 59.1 per cent for Landon. Moreover, the *Digest* predicted 161 electoral votes for Roosevelt and 370 for Landon. The Electoral College voted 523 for Roosevelt and 8 for Landon. After twenty years of popular interest and development of some faith in the "*Digest* polls," this fiasco in prediction was a very serious blow to a periodical already greatly weakened by *Time*. It soon ceased publication.

The *Digest* had not used a representative sample, a quota sample, an area sample, or even a random sample. Its unrepresentative but extensive mailing lists were inadequate to reflect the political alignments of 1936, when economic interests were more important than in any election after Bryan's campaign of 1896. Archibald Crossley, who in 1936 was already a market researcher and poller of long experience, shortly after the election summarized the qualities of the ideal poll as he then conceived it:

[9] A. M. Crossley, "Straw Polls in 1936," *Pub. Opin. Quar.*, 1: 1: 25.

[10] In this discussion of the polls I shall refer to percentage points of error. If a poller predicts that a candidate will receive 40 per cent of the vote and the election gives 48 per cent to the candidate, the poller's error is not 8 per cent. It is $\frac{8}{48}$ths or 16.6 per cent error.

First, it must be flexible. Its basis must not be an outdated mailing list. It must be so designed that it can be adjusted readily if new information such as registration figures becomes available during its course. As a part of its flexibility, it must reveal enough about the individual voters, and about individual cities and towns, economic groups, etc., to permit adjustment where needed. *Second,* a fairly small sample will work properly in all but close states. *Third,* the distribution of the sample is of paramount importance. *Fourth,* it should not be cumulative, but repeated in similar cross sections at intervals to show trends. On all these counts the *Literary Digest* method is outmoded.[11]

After 1936, the principle of sampling of a representative cross section was no longer disputed, but the battles over what constitutes a representative sample quite properly became central.

For two decades *The Literary Digest,* more than any other agency or publication in the United States, interested millions of readers in straw polls. Sometimes their predictive accuracy was high, as in the 1932 election when they made one of the best forecasts in the history of polling. Their blunderbuss methods could not always fail, but the method was obviously fallacious in many respects. However, the historian of polling must note that the *Digest* did arouse a widespread public interest which was inherited and quickly expanded by the new polling researchers working for the newspapers, periodicals, private interest-groups, distributive industries and governmental agencies. The *Digest* polls centered the attention of many statistical and other experts on the problems of polling. In the year preceding its debacle, the *Digest* was the indispensable target of many zealous critics, many of whom came to serve that uncomfortable role themselves in 1948. The *Digest* polls were a protracted stage in the development of straw polls. They were superseded by more exact, but by no means invariably accurate, sampling methods.

REPRESENTATIVE SAMPLE SURVEYS

Straw-vote taking by commercial concerns, politicians and periodicals was a limited and certainly an inconsequential activity as a commercial business. Market research, public opinion polls and associated research activities have become a large business, with an estimated current gross annual income for the industry as a whole of from 30 to 60 million dollars a year.[12] The results of only a small portion of this monumental research

[11] Crossley, *op. cit.,* p. 27.
[12] I cannot verify this figure and do not believe that anyone has a very exact estimate, but during 1949 the larger amount was mentioned in the discussions at the conclaves of the experts. The figure of 30 million is taken from the business columns of *Newsweek,* Nov. 15, 1948.

activity are made public. The great bulk of the studies and results have been prepared for private commercial enterprises and for governmental and other administrative agencies. Much of the governmental material has been marked for release at a later date, but most of the corporation market-research material is private property, unlikely to be released.

Only a very small portion of the total public opinion and attitude research deals with political and social issues, although these are the only studies of which the general reading public is informed as they peruse the news columns prepared by the American Institute of Public Opinion or read the results of a *Fortune* survey. In addition to this polling activity, the principal fields of commercial research are, as Albert Blankenship [12a] has noted: (1) advertising copy testing, (2) evaluation of advertising appeals, (3) motives for purchasing, (4) media measurement, that is, the relative effectiveness of advertising for a particular product in various types of media, (5) product research, which includes consumer opinion of the product, its uses, the way it is packaged, etc., (6) movement of branded goods and causes for shifts, (7) testing of sales methods and (8) public-relations studies. In this extensive and costly research field, there has developed a vested interest in the poller's public reputation for accuracy, notably on election predictions, and his reputation among his business corporation customers. In November, 1948, those reputations suffered, and some market-research men, notably Archibald Crossley, questioned the business wisdom of election predictions by those who were primarily market researchers. The various types of market research and other types of commercial polling remain the most extensive and by far the most profitable activity of the pollers.

Polling on political and social issues and on candidates for election developed rapidly after 1935. The pollers who succeeded the straw-vote takers used some purported representative sample, at first quite generally the quota sample, a proportional selection from all major groups in the population. After 1935, area sampling was used increasingly.

George Gallup began experimenting with nationwide canvasses on political and social issues in February, 1934, and in the following year organized the American Institute of Public Opinion. This reportorial agency has been conducting polls continuously since October, 1935, and through Publishers Syndicate, has released its results weekly throughout the country. The *Fortune* Quarterly Survey was developed early in 1935 by Paul T. Cherington and Elmo B. Roper, Jr. It has since appeared every third month as a leading feature of the magazine *Fortune*. The Crossley Poll was brought out by Archibald M. Crossley for the King Features Syndicate during the 1936 presidential campaign. Pri-

---

[12a] A. B. Blankenship, *Consumer and Opinion Research*, Harper & Brothers, New York, 1943, pp. 6 ff.

marily an election poll, the canvass was discontinued after the November balloting.[13]

But Crossley's research organization returned to election prediction and published predictions on the national elections of 1940, 1944, 1948 and 1952.

All of these pioneer pollers began polling on political, economic and other social issues after years of experience as market-research men. During the 1920's, market research expanded rapidly in many fields, but it was the development of sampling consumer, or potential consumer, publics that led to polling on public issues. These pollers, as market-research men, knew the principles of scientific sampling which had been used successfully in market research for a quarter of a century. But the sampling problems were more complex when the opinions were sought from larger and more diverse publics. In the first *Fortune* article on the polls which appeared in the July, 1935, issue (thus permitting *Fortune* to claim a few months' seniority on the other pollers whose first published materials appeared somewhat later), Paul T. Cherington and Elmo Roper state that:

The possibility of treating public opinion as the steel people treated the ore trains at Hibbing, sampling every tenth car, had simply never occurred to the popular mind. . . . No one—and least of all the journalists—seems to have remarked that what the advertisers had developed was a mechanism adapted not only to the selling of toothpaste but to the plumbing of the public mind.

However, the idea was a normal extension of their work and methods, and not a brilliant and original invention by Elmo Roper, George Gallup, Archibald Crossley or any of the less well-known figures among the pollers. George Gallup, after some years as a teacher of journalism, became Research Director of the publicity firm of Young and Rubicam in 1932. He organized his American Institute of Public Opinion in 1935, and in October of that year he released a public opinion survey to a group of Sunday newspapers. After a few years, he was releasing the results of the Institute's polls several times a week to over a hundred daily and Sunday newspapers. Gallup's polls became a new kind of journalism. Archibald Crossley, who in 1926 established Crossley, Incorporated, a commercial research organization which for years was best known for the Cooperative Analysis of Broadcasting, has remained through the years primarily a commercial research man who incidentally engaged in political polls. However, his market-research-developed skill has been evidenced by the fact that his forecast was closer to the actual result at times than any other forecast of an election. In the presidential election of 1944,

---

[13] C. E. Robinson, "Recent Developments in the Straw-Vote Field," *Pub. Opin. Quar.*, 1: 3: 46.

Crossley underestimated the Roosevelt electors by 78 and Gallup by 140, while Roper, though very accurate in forecasting the popular vote, made no prediction of the electoral vote. Crossley's results were published in the Heart newspapers and other subscribing papers.

In addition to the Roper, Gallup and Crossley organizations there are scores of organizations engaging in various kinds of polling and public opinion research. "It has been estimated that three hundred organizations in New York City alone are engaged in some type of public opinion measurement, if those phases of marketing research dealing with attitudes are included." Further, "Many industries have large research staffs of their own, a part of whose function is the sounding of public opinion." [14] Albert Blankenship has classified the principal types of organizations engaged in polling and public opinion research as: (1) public opinion survey agencies, such as the Gallup organization, (2) commercial research organizations of which there are a vast number doing many different kinds of work, (3) advertising agencies, (4) publishing firms, (5) manufacturers, such as the market-research department of Procter and Gamble, (6) public-relations firms, (7) trade associations, (8) the federal and state governments, (9) endowed organizations, such as the Office of Radio Research, until 1950 directed by Dr. Paul Lazarsfeld, or the National Opinion Research Center at the University of Chicago, and (10) colleges and universities, such as the Washington Public Opinion Laboratory. [15]

There are two organizations, both endowed, which for some years have been engaged in checking, criticism and review of the work of the commercial polling organizations, as well as in conducting polls themselves. They are the Office of Public Opinion Research, which was organized at Princeton University in 1940, and National Opinion Research Center, founded in 1941 by a grant from the Field Foundation. The NORC was located for five years in Denver and then was moved to the University of Chicago. The OPOR has engaged in extensive research, especially on the problems of the formation of public opinion and the problems involved in setting the issues in polling and in question wording. This organization has studied the issues involved in interviewing and the principles of sampling, especially size and representativeness of samples. In addition, the OPOR has conducted a number of polls. [16] Owing largely to the training and interests of director Hadley Cantril and his associates, this organization stressed the psychological aspects of opinion and its

14 E. C. Wilson, "The Measurement of Public Opinion," *Ann. of Am. Acad.*, 250: 121, March, 1947.

15 Blankenship, *op. cit.*, pp. 8 ff.

16 Hadley Cantril has reported on this work in *Gauging Public Opinion*, which he edited for the Princeton University Press, Princeton, N.J., in 1944.

polling. The NORC has engaged far more extensively in actual polling, and its directors, first Harry Field and, after 1946, Clyde Hart, were more concerned with political and sociological rather than the psychological aspects of opinions and polling.

The Department of Agriculture has carried on attitude surveying for a longer time and more extensively than any other governmental agency. Although the Department of Agriculture reports began in 1866, and from that time onward there were occasional sporadic reports on farmers' attitudes and opinions, it was not until 1939 that an organization was created for the more systematic measurement, reporting and study of rural public opinion. In that year, a new division, the Division of Program Surveys, was set up in the Bureau of Agricultural Economics. This Division, which in 1946 was reorganized as the Division of Special Surveys, during the 1940's studied attitudes and opinions of the rural population and reported to administrators on the responses of public opinion to the major agricultural programs of that period.

Sometimes it has helped action agencies plan the detailed operation of programs: occasionally, in this connection, it has worked with agencies to test new programs experimentally on a small scale before they were put into general operation in order to shake the costly "bugs" out of them. Sometimes it has tested popular knowledge levels with respect to a given fact such as wartime need for dairy production.[17]

The Division's studies have not only dealt with attitudes and opinions, but have also reported on the extent of information and ignorance about various topics and at times have reported on various kinds of behavior other than opinion expressions. Moreover, the Division has conducted studies for many federal agencies in addition to the Department of Agriculture, reporting at one time on "Public Response to the Seventh War Loan," at another on "Land Market Participation by Factory Workers in Detroit," and, again, on "Veterans' Readjustment to Civilian Life." There has been a large number of these interview surveys.

Attitude surveying in the Division of Program Surveys goes far beyond the simple determination of the approval or disapproval by a representative sample of people of some government program. The agencies interested are rarely satisfied with only the distributions of the frequencies with which various attitudes occur. The emphasis in Division work is on explanation of the attitude. . . . answers to "why" questions are especially important in cases where the public's reaction to a program has been un-cooperative or hostile. Many federal programs are based on the voluntary cooperation of the people whom they

[17] H. E. Skott, "Attitude Research in the Department of Agriculture," *Pub. Opin. Quar.*, 7: 2: 283.

affect; if this is not forthcoming, it is imperative that the officials responsible for the program should know why.[18]

It is this objective of the Division that was responsible for its most distinctive contribution to attitude research, the early use of the "depth interview," which uncovers attitude complexes to an extent achieved rarely and on few topics by the commercial pollers before 1952. The Division's "open question" method in the interview schedules provided a number of questions which the respondent could answer in his own words and at length. Thus, it was hoped, by nondirective probing, and without suggesting answers, that the interviewer would uncover significant attitude complexes. The difficulty and, at times, impossibility of complete quantification of the results is evident. However, the typical representative responses can be selected in general and reported with a richness of detail impossible with limited and channeled answers. In any case, it has been thought that the results were invaluable to some administrators, even if the replies could not be quantified in every detail. This Division has been perhaps the most fruitful, in imaginative pioneering, in experimentation and in conclusions and their interpretation, of the attitude-surveying agencies in the United States.

A number of federal governmental agencies have engaged extensively in surveying and polling, but have done so as inconspicuously and quietly as possible so as to avoid congressional and public criticism.

During the war, public opinion measurement played a little-known role in the development of both our domestic and overseas war efforts. The Bureau of Agricultural Economics, the Office of War Information, the Office of Civilian Requirements, the United States Strategic Bombing Survey, the Psychological Warfare Division of SHAEF, the Allied Military Government, as well as the Army and Navy themselves, maintained organizations for periodically surveying public opinion.[19]

Many other governmental organizations called on the opinion-study research groups of these agencies to conduct specific opinion studies. Indeed, the White House itself sometimes requested particular studies. Administrators have been less hostile than Congress toward opinion studies and polling; during World War II, under the necessity of assessing and influencing public opinion, many administrators sponsored and had a measure of confidence in such studies. "The principal work of serving war agencies on matters of attitude research was done by the Office of War Information and the Division of Program Surveys of the Department

[18] A. A. Campbell in *How to Conduct Consumer and Opinion Research* (A. B. Blankenship, ed.), Harper & Brothers, New York, 1946, p. 275.

[19] Wilson, *op. cit.*, p. 123. Extended discussion of polling in governmental organizations may be found in H. H. Remmers, *Introduction to Opinion and Attitude Measurement*, Harper & Brothers, New York, 1954, chap. 9.

of Agriculture." [20] The Bureau of Intelligence under the Office of Facts and Figures and, later, under the Office of War Information, engaged in research activities carried on by its Divisions of Surveys, Polls, Information Channels, Source Materials and Panels. Ambitious plans for public opinion research were soon reduced by the exigencies of a situation the pressure of which demanded limited and immediately utilitarian answers to specific questions. Somewhat later, congressional criticism reduced these polling activities. Under pressure, the Bureau of Intelligence was abolished in 1944. Some of its activities were carried on in The Surveys Division. "The Bureau of Intelligence, and later the Surveys Division, represented an attempt to apply the findings and techniques of social science to governmental information problems in a national crisis. It was an effort to unite public opinion research with operation in an important field of governmental activity." [21] This organization and the Agriculture Department's Division of Program Surveys made many studies of public morale, such as attitudes toward our Allies, confidence in victory and the areas of willingness for sacrifice, absenteeism in war plants, areas of racial tension and others.

Surveys abroad under the direction of various agencies were made on the effects on civilian morale of Allied bombings. After occupation numerous polls were conducted in Sicily, Italy, France and Germany. The responses of prisoners were studied extensively and intensively. Activities abroad were not subjected to the congressional criticism which was leveled at OWI's public opinion surveys. During the war period the numerous public opinion surveying activities acquainted many governmental administrators with these survey methods and their results, thus gaining for opinion research a considerable backing and even sometimes an unwarranted confidence. The results are to be found in expanded postwar activity in this field in governmental and in private agencies. Although no agency has the resources of the OWI, there are many new scattered activities. However, in reviewing the war experience with polling and attitude research, it is not evident to me that any significant advances in methodology were achieved. In the Bureau of Intelligence, a real opportunity for combining intensive reports on individual attitudes with adequate representative samples of large publics was not developed. However, this remains a step not made as yet in postwar polling, so the inadequacies of our partial science were no doubt involved as much as were failures in administration and imagination.

After the war, a considerable amount of public opinion study, surveying and polling was continued or started by governmental agencies. The

[20] H. F. Gosnell and M. C. David, "Public Opinion Research in Government," *Am. Pol. Sci. Rev.*, 43: 3: 565.

[21] *Ibid.*, p. 569.

Department of Agriculture, pioneer agency in attitude research, has continued research activities at a high level under the Division of Special Surveys, successor to the Division of Program Surveys. "Although the scope of survey research activities since 1945 has been further affected by pressures for reductions in government expenditures, the techniques continue to be used in various parts of the government. Within the Departments of State, Army, Navy, Agriculture, Commerce, and other agencies, there are public attitude research operations." [22] "Public opinion research has now well established itself as a tool of administration and a guide for the making of policy decisions. While the recognition of its uses by Congress has been slower than by administrative agencies, it has gained headway on the Hill also. It is not now as extensively used as during the early phases of the late war, but it is much more widely used than before the war." [23]

POLLS ABROAD

At the third international conference on public opinion research (held at Eagles Mere, Pennsylvania, September, 1948) of the World Association for Public Opinion Research, Jean Stoetzel, president of the association, announced that, "Public opinion research is now a truly international field of endeavor, and is being conducted in perhaps more than 20 countries as well as by international agencies, such as UNESCO." During 1948, opinion polling expanded to the point where an estimated one million people in about 20 countries answered questions on several thousands of topics.[24] In addition to the various polling organizations in the United States there are polls in Australia, Belgium, Brazil, Canada, Czechoslovakia (abolished), Denmark, England, Finland, Holland, France, Norway, Germany, Italy, Hungary (since repressed), Mexico, South Africa, Sweden and Switzerland. Additional organizations are being created every year. Poll-taking organizations in many countries have become affiliated with the American Institute of Public Opinion, the Gallup organization. Abroad, the polling process has been so identified with the name of George Gallup that Gallup and polling are practically synonymous.[25]

In 1946 Elmo Roper and Joshua Powers organized International Public Opinion Research, Inc., to conduct market research and polling in South America. The principal activity of this group has been market-research reports for corporate sponsors from the United States. Most of the polling

[22] *Ibid.*, p. 570.
[23] *Ibid.*, p. 572.
[24] *Ency. Brit. Yearbook*, 1949, p. 597.
[25] Paul Lazarsfeld returned from a European tour in late 1948 and reported Europeans speaking of the Danish Gallup, the Norwegian Gallup and the like.

organizations throughout the world have engaged in market research as well as opinion surveying. Some of the foreign polling organizations have been engaged in a somewhat systematic delineation of the basic attitude patterns and the structure of habitual social thinking in their national areas. Of course, this kind of surveying could gradually accumulate an invaluable fund of information about the mind-life of the common man throughout the world. This would be true if the polling methods were trustworthy and if the results were uncolored and not slanted by either the organizations or their governments. Such was far from the case in the first few years of polling abroad. Among a numerical majority of the world's people, at mid-century, private, institutional, commercial or any nongovernmental polling was forbidden and, where not forbidden, "Political restrictions in some countries made it impossible to ask certain types of questions, and difficulties existed in getting comparable samples, interviewers and interviewing situations from country to country." [26]

Despite the difficulties, in 1948 a survey was conducted for UNESCO by existing polling organizations in the various countries of the world where polling was then possible. Some fourteen questions were asked, among them: "Do you believe human nature can be changed?" "Which foreign people do you feel most friendly toward?" and "Which country in the world gives the best chance of leading the kind of life you would like to lead?" Studies of popular opinion throughout the world could obviously be of revealing character concerning national morale, but in many nations political forces stronger than the curiosity of the social scientist forbid such exploration. The mutual knowledge of the peoples' opinions, the comparisons of the attitudes, of the hopes, aspirations, beliefs, information, satisfactions and dissatisfactions of the peoples of the world is not viewed with equanimity by man's rulers in many nations.

Most of the foreign polling organizations were created after the end of the war. Engaged in polling and in conducting market research in their various countries, the pollers have become more aware than most that the peoples of the world have a great deal in common. The pollers believe that the public opinion survey could be an instrument for increasing understanding between peoples. And so it could, though the understanding would not in all cases decrease international friction. The widest publicity and mutual knowledge of the results of surveys of public opinion would sometimes increase animosity between the national peoples of the world, verifying their worst suspicions as to what their opponents were thinking. But, in many more instances, they would no doubt find a common denominator of human values, and understanding and tolerance would be increased. One may well believe that, in general, the

[26] *Ency. Brit. Yearbook*, 1949, p. 598.

understanding resulting from publicized results of surveys would far out-
weigh the intensified suspicions. Although, for obvious political reasons,
world public opinion surveying is not possible now, it is practicable to
broaden the scope of existing surveying on common questions. The affiliated Gallup organizations since 1947 have conducted joint polls once
a month on a question agreed on in advance. The results are published
quarterly in *Surveys of World Opinion,* issued by the American Institute.
After several yearly conferences on public opinion research, the pollers
of the world organized in 1948 as the World Association for Public Opinion Research, with representatives from 18 countries. The *International
Journal of Opinion and Attitude Research,* published in Mexico City (discontinued in 1952), was made the official journal of the organization.[27]

The political and technical difficulties of world surveying would be
enormous. Although polling on a world-wide scale is politically impossible now, the pollers hope to widen the area of their present activity.
There is evidently much scope for activity before arriving at the closed
gates of the dictatorships where the representatives of great blocs of
political power have no liking for impartial reporting. The technical difficulties are very great. In international opinion surveying there are always
the problems of question wording, of comparable understanding and information and of the meaning of words and concepts. Problems arise from
the different attitudes toward polls existing among various peoples. In
some cases where there is little of democratic traditions and thinking there
is doubt of the value of individual opinions and of their expression. Even
where there are democratic traditions, there are sometimes legitimate
fears of the possible consequences of opinions contrary to those of the
existing government. And there is a widely differential apathy toward
public affairs and issues among the peoples of the world. Very difficult
problems arise from suspicion of the poller and people's various ways of
deceiving him. For many countries, owing to inadequate statistics, quota
sampling is inadequate. And the classifications of one national survey
differ enormously from those of another. Laszlo Radvanyi notes that an
economic classification for Mexico has been used that was based on:
those who sleep (1) on the ground, (2) on straw matting, (3) in ham-
mocks, (4) on cots, (5) in beds. This is a little difficult to compare to
the economic classes of Kansas City. Further, there are differential problems of interviewing, and many others.[28] However, despite all difficulties,
the spread of attitude and opinion surveying to as many countries as

[27] See the *Proceedings* of this meeting, vol. 3, no. 2, pp. 310–346 of this *Journal.*
[28] See L. Radvanyi, "Problems of International Opinion Surveys," *Int. Jour. Opin.
and Att. Res.,* 1: 2: 3–23; S. C. Dodd, "Toward World Surveying," *Pub. Opin. Quar.,*
10: 4: 470–483; A. M. Lee, "Some Prerequisites to International Opinion Surveying,"
Int. Jour. Opin. and Att. Res., 2: 1: 54–62.

possible and the development of more international surveying should not only intrigue the imagination and arouse the inadequate activities of social scientists, but should increasingly engage the attention and gain the support of men of political affairs in the democratic nations of the world.

MASS OBSERVATION IN GREAT BRITAIN

In 1937 *Mass Observation* was founded in England by Tom Harrison, an anthropologist, and Charles Madge, newspaper reporter and poet. After taking part in several expeditions to Borneo and New Hebrides,[29] Harrison decided that he might more profitably remain at home and study the culture, especially the beliefs and habits, of Englishmen. Charles Madge had been working for London's tabloid daily, the *Mirror*, and had decided that a great gulf existed between the mind-life of England's leaders and that of the common man. He joined with Harrison in an exploration of the mind of the masses. Harrison and Madge wrote letters to the press explaining the idea of *Mass Observation*, since they wished to interest as many people as possible and to obtain their assistants from interested volunteers.[30]

On February 12, 1937, the first thirty observers made their reports on their experiences of that day. By Coronation Day, May 12, 1937, some hundreds of observers reported on what happened to them, what they thought and saw on that day. The quest for additional participant observers quickly achieved many volunteers. As Harrison and Madge believed that their first concern was to collect data, they thought that—

> The Observer will not need to have received scientific training in order to make his observations. He will make them in the course of his ordinary work, using to the full the environment in which he normally works. His function will be to describe fully, clearly, and in simple language all that he sees and hears in connection with the specific problem he is asked to work on. Everything will depend on the reliability of such an Observer compared with that of the trained scientist.[31]

It was the founders' theory that the trained social scientists who would summarize the data collected by the volunteer observers could come to know and allow for the biases of their untrained observers, whereas the

[29] See his *Borneo*, Victor Gollancz, Ltd., London, 1934, and *Savage Civilizations*, Gollancz, 1937.

[30] This information about *Mass Observation* is taken from C. Madge and T. Harrison, *Mass Observation*, Series Number One, Frederick Muller, Ltd., London, 1937; and H. D. Willcock, "Mass Observation," *Am. Jour. Soc.*, 48: 4: 445–456, 1943. The excellent article by Willcock is the only extensive description of *Mass Observation* in the social science publications in the United States. This is surprising, as contrasted to the literature on polling.

[31] *Mass Observation, op. cit.*, p. 31.

personal biases of scientists are more difficult to ascertain. "By the end of the year, there were some thousand voluntary observers on the lists, and special subjects for study were being sent out to them in monthly directives." [32]

In addition to the study of Coronation Day, the first year's work of *Mass Observation* was devoted to the study of the motives and fulfillments involved in smoking, pub-going and football. Six trained field workers were settled in a northern industrial town and these, in addition to their own observations and those of the volunteer observers, often used standard interviewing and opinion sampling methods.[33] However, *Mass Observation* has been interested persistently in what we call studies in depth, and in recording the variety of the forms of expression of opinions. In 1938, with war apparently approaching, *Mass Observation* turned largely to the study of the reactions of the British to the facts, news and rumors of that situation.[34] The origins and the popular response to the current dance craze, the Lambeth Walk, were studied that year, and a report on jazz, dancing and dance halls was prepared. At the outbreak of the war, *Mass Observation* had a panel of fifteen hundred volunteer observers scattered all over Britain. Throughout the war *Mass Observation* studied the people's worries, hopes, wishes, frustrations, fears and expectations. The first major publication, *War Begins at Home*, appeared in March, 1940, and reported on opinions and behavior resulting from the dislocation of personal lives in wartime England even during the period of the "phony war."

During the war, *Mass Observation* was continuously employed on the study of government propaganda. Many political, social, commercial and official bodies used this organization to make field studies and prepare reports. Some of these reports were published, while many more, for reasons of security and other reasons, have never been published. Six major wartime studies were made for the Advertising Service Guild, and were published by them. All of these studies dealt with change in the behavior and thought of the people of Great Britain under the impact of war. The first dealt with the subject of clothes rationing; the second was a report on home propaganda, that is, the propaganda directed by Britain at the inhabitants of Great Britain; the third reported on British war production, the people in production; number four was a survey of the people's expectations and wants for postwar housing; the fifth report dealt with the process of demobilization and what the people thought concerning it; the sixth report dealt with the reluctant stork, the birth

[32] Willcock, *op. cit.*, p. 448.
[33] *First Year's Work* (T. Harrison and C. Madge, eds.), L. Drummond, Ltd., London, 1938.
[34] *Britain*, Penguin Books, Ltd., London, 1938.

rate, and, therefore, with Britain's probable postwar population, all questions vital to commercial interests.[35] In these surveys the Advertising Service Guild, which paid for, sponsored and published the reports of *Mass Observation*, did not claim to be doing a disinterested public service, although actually these extensive reports on various facets of change in wartime were a very real public service. In the foreword to the final report, the Guild representative writes:

> If this work has been of any value we must modestly disclaim any credit for commercial disinterestedness. We have a vested interest in public opinion and attitudes. The man in the Forces, the mother in the home, the girl in the factory, are all interesting characters in the sociologist's history of the war. Today, part of the work of propaganda is to project them to themselves heroically. Tomorrow the same methods of propaganda will revert to its more prosaic task of regarding them as consumers again.

Regardless of the motives of the sponsors, these reports are revealing and colorful accounts, though certainly on many points they do not convince the pollers as to the representativeness of the sample of people interviewed, the respondents to questionnaires or the individuals whose behavior is observed. This is the crux of the American social scientists' criticism of the methods used in these fascinating studies.

In all of its reports *Mass Observation* states in the Prefaces that their directors are concerned with (1) ascertaining the facts as accurately as possible, (2) developing and improving the methods for ascertaining those facts, and (3) disseminating the ascertained facts as widely as possible. But what types of facts have been collected by *Mass Observation*, and what methods have been used in collecting and manipulating their data? H. D. Willcock, principal director of *Mass Observation*, reports:

> Since the war began, *Mass Observation* has devoted more and more attention to indirect methods of approach, to overheard conversations, to purely observa-

---

[35] The reports sponsored and published by the Advertising Service Guild are:
Change No. 1. Clothes Rationing. Bull. Ad. Serv. Guild, A Report Prepared by *Mass Observation,* London, 1941; *Change No. 2. Home Propaganda,* London, 1941; *Change No. 3. People in Production.* A Report on British War Production; *Change No. 4. People's Homes.* A Report on Postwar Housing; *Change No. 5. The Journey Home.* A Report on Demobilization; *Change No. 6. Britain and Her Birth Rate.* Published for the Advertising Service Guild by John Murray, London, 1945. In the years after the war, *Mass Observation* continued to conduct surveys of communities and organizations, and to report on various topics which interested their sponsors. A number of surveys were published in English periodicals. Among the longer reports, issued in book form are: *Puzzled People, A Study of Popular Attitudes to Religion, Ethics, Progress and Politics in a London Borough,* Victor Gollancz, Ltd., London, 1947; *Brown's and Chester, Portrait of a Shop, 1780–1946,* Lindsay Drummond, Ltd., 1947; *Peace and the Public,* 1947.

tional work among people. Technique for this qualitative study of behavior and opinion is at a more intimate level than that recorded by the doorstep interviewer. . . . It can be used in studying many questions where interviewing yields little result. For instance, the effects of war on religious faith, on feelings about death, on sex life. . . . In such cases either a more intimate approach than the doorstep interviewer or more time for thought than a verbal question allows is required.[36]

Mass Observation directors have been ingenious in collecting evidence and they have, in the main, interpreted that evidence with admirable judgment. They have carried on many kinds of interviews, have used numerous questionnaires, have analyzed letters and radio mail, have examined and gleaned data from the reports of meetings and discussion groups and have also observed such groups, they have had reports written by observers on many aspects of the behavior of their subjects and sometimes they have conducted a kind of poll. But I cannot discern a statistically accurate representative sample of subjects in any of the *Mass Observation* studies. In the main, the selection of subjects appears to be based on selections made by the directors of *Mass Observation* and their interviewers, who do not appear concerned with quotas or with area sampling. They carried on a good bit of random street sampling. In general, in the publications, we are not informed as to the basis for the selections from interviews or questionnaires which are printed. But the publications of *Mass Observation* are written with color, brilliance, cleverness and occasional wit. Nothing comparable, as interesting reading, is to be found in any of the reports of pollers or attitude researchers in the United States.

As an example of *Mass Observation*'s lack of preoccupation with quantitative exactitude, after stating in very general terms, in a preface, the sources of data for their long and substantial report on "Britain and Her Birth Rate," [37] the editor concludes, "At a rough estimate about 2500–3000 actual and potential mothers and fathers altogether are implicated in one way or another." Any social science report by attitude researchers in the United States would be expected to report on method and sources of data with an exactitude far beyond the general statement of "about 2500–3000 subjects." But the *Mass Observation* study has a qualitative richness that gives revealing insights into contemporary attitudes toward family size in the case of the subjects about whom they do report. No doubt the directors of *Mass Observation* have a greater concern with typicality than is revealed in their reports. They must have. In this report

[36] H. D. Willcock, "Mass Observation," *Am. Jour. Sociol.* (Copyright, 1943, University of Chicago), 48: 4: 456, 1943.
[37] "Britain and Her Birth Rate," *Mass Observation*, John Murray, London, 1945.

on the birth rate, they state that the main evidence on which the report is based is as follows:

1. About 1,000 interviews with married women between the ages of 20 and 45 in the streets and houses of London, in a factory, and in Gloucester. Of these, 787 are included in the tables of figures; the rest were made in five pilot-tests before finalising the questionnaire and give slightly different information. They were consulted as qualitative material but not included in the analysis.

2. The results of a series of questions relating to marriage, family planning, morality, attitudes to the decline in the birthrate, etc., asked of *Mass Observation's* National Panel of correspondents. These include detailed accounts by mothers and fathers—and some who refuse to be mothers or fathers—of the reasons behind their own decisions on how many children to have, and when to have them.

3. The postbag of the Radio Doctor, consisting of letters received as a result of talks in November 1943 and January 1944, on birthrate problems. These were mainly letters from women describing their own reasons for restricting their families; some letters from fathers; and some letters generalizing about the reasons for the birthrate decline from their own experience of others' problems.

4. A quantitative analysis of 400 letters to a birth-control clinic, made on lines suggested by *Mass Observation* by a member of the staff. These letters give the reasons women express for wanting to use contraceptives.

5. Several observational studies of households with children.

6. Reports of meetings, discussion groups, etc., where problems of marriage, birthrate, family-size, etc., were concerned.

7. Long, informal conversations with women on their reasons for having a small family.

From these sources, they present a long report which ends with a 163-point summary of generalizations and conclusions. Neither at the beginning nor at the conclusion do we know the representativeness of the data with any exactitude. Yet, for the authors—

The question is: which is more important, to know to within 3–5% the number of times women say they might want more children if they had more money; or to have a more approximate indication of the number of times they say this plus 787 examples of the way they say it? In our opinion the 787 examples of how they say it are of much more practical value than an exactly accurate indication of how many say it.[38]

The directors of *Mass Observation* state that their conclusions "have to be taken on trust as an honest attempt to get at the real meaning behind the words and to work out common factors and inter-relations which quantitative analyses cannot show." This is the essence of the *Mass Observation* methodology. It trusts that the insight gained by the social

[38] *Ibid.*, p. 11.

scientist in conducting the studies will provide the basis for the judgment which he exercises in selecting data, choosing subjects, making selections from the subjects' statements and then in formulating conclusions therefrom. It is essentially the art and not the science of social interpretation. But it is an art which has been skillfully plied by the practitioners of *Mass Observation*.

CHAPTER 11

Polling: How and Why

Even if the subjective element is capable of certain measurements and even if it is true that whatever exists exists in some quantity or number, nevertheless, it is obvious that where subjective elements play a large part, measurement becomes of less importance for accurate knowledge because it is confined to the superficial aspects of the total situation and fails to expose the nature of the process which is being investigated.[1]

C. A. ELLWOOD

The study and measurement of behavior, the outside of life, is a fruitful and promising method, but the idea of a human science consisting wholly of such study, without sympathetic observation of the mind, is, I think, only mystification.[2]

CHARLES HORTON COOLEY

The sciences of life, including the social, consist largely of description, the guaranty of which is the credibility of the observer.[3]

CHARLES HORTON COOLEY

Opinion recording through polling is a partial quantification of some aspects of what some people say their opinions are about certain questions about which they have been asked. These statements are recorded and counted, and the results are sometimes used to predict the opinions or other behavior, such as voting, of the individuals who have been polled, and also of the public of which they are considered representative. It is hardly surprising that the often very limited expressions of opinion by a sample of a sample of the public do not lead the poller to completely accurate predictions. It is astonishing that on election predictions the record of pollers in the United States is as good as it has been. But even when his predictions are almost accurate, the poller still is on very treacherous ground when he does not understand the nature of the process

[1] C. A. Ellwood, *Method in Sociology*, Duke University Press, Durham, N.C., 1933, p. 101.
[2] C. H. Cooley, *Life and the Student*, Alfred A. Knopf, Inc., New York, 1927, p. 151.
[3] *Ibid.*, p. 147.

which is being investigated, the complex of attitudes which underlie the expression of opinion, or the trends of changing attitude and opinion. The pollers have frequently failed in such discernment, though never before so publicly and so extensively as in the prediction of the 1948 elections.

Reputable though they have been in many respects, the pollers in the United States have been too extensively trained in commercial market research and in journalistic pursuits and values to limn adequately the popular mind on political, economic and ethical public issues. The relative exactitudes of commercial and market research are made possible by the public's habitual behavior and opinions on inconsequential and repeated issues. One who works with this apparently shallow-minded and predictable public may not be the best commentator on the more profound surges of public opinion for which there is no precedent. Publics, apparently gullible and habitually responsive to the wiles of commercial puffery, may prove singularly elusive and changeable on what are considered real issues of self-interest in political and ethical decisions. However, men of other than commercial training and bent have other biases. Effective polling still requires discerning and interpretive art in public understanding as well as some social science methods. As yet, no single group of pollers has all the requisite qualities.

Representative-sample polling is a new activity, surprisingly developed for its brief history. Polling has made the greatest advances in the selection of representative samples of publics. However, commercial polling has thus far been of little significance in developing methods of recording attitudes. Indeed, after the individual respondents have been selected, the problems of getting common denominators of complex and varied attitudes on public issues have not engaged the attention of pollers as has sampling. No significant advance has been made beyond the methods of the academic attitude recorders. But this is the crux of the problem of developing a science of public opinion measurement. Without an adequate record of the opinions and attitudes of the subjects, polling remains an activity of limited meaning and significance, no matter how skillfully the sampling is done. There is also the problem of the meaning of the responses of those interviewed. Similar statements may be made on the basis of quite different attitudes and therefore have quite different implications for future behavior and opinion. Therefore, the record is not in terms of quantitative units in any exact sense. When a critic of the polls, Lindsay Rogers, "considers the inability of the pollsters to tell us the loudness of the yeses and noes they say they hear," and concludes that the pollers are not engaging in exact measurement, he is correct, but belaboring the obvious. As we have seen in our earlier consideration of the problems of attitude measurement, the question of units is indeed crucial, but throughout the social sciences almost all quantification lacks the degree of exactitude of measurement to be found in the physical sciences.

Polling is a reputable, justifiable, socially useful, and, in the main, amazingly accurate sampling of public opinion. When the issues are reasonably clear and the opinions sufficiently matured to be somewhat stable, polling can have great significance in legislation and administration in a political democracy.

THE METHODS OF POLLING

Under conditions of general political coercion in the autocracies of the past, the polling of public opinion could have no significance, as the objectives of an autocratic regime were to keep the flow of information and the opinion process at a minimum. Such societies were hostile to such admission of the significance of the opinions of masses of people. In contrast, modern authoritarian societies with totalitarian ideologies encourage mass education and communications, but control the content of these channels by censorship and propaganda. The types of polling developed in the freer, open societies could not reveal the attitudes of the controlled, molded and fearful subjects. However, totalitarians demand a kind of all-inclusive polling in the regimented, enforced voting and other mass expressions which parrot the official statements but do not permit of alternative answers. Nonetheless, an enthusiastic participation and loyalty must be simulated, if not felt or believed. No one must be permitted the opinion of silence. Thus, there is a solemn counting of the "polls," but not polling.

It is only in the representative republican-democratic states that modern polling has developed significantly. In the democracies, public opinion analysis is vitally important, and, with all their limitations, the polls have created effective methods of recording opinions. The pollers' methods have improved astoundingly, yet an unknowing general public, accustomed to the precise marvels of physical science, querulously questions the limited failures of the pollers' election predictions. In this the general public is encouraged by the critics of the polls whose objections to the polls are not primarily based on the question of accuracy, but rather on the political and social implications of extensive polling.

There are many types of surveys and polls, and a widely diverse content of information, attitudes and opinions polled in the United States and abroad. There are commercial, educational, partly subsidized and governmental polling organizations. The output of published reports of these organizations is enormous. Yet the opinion polls conducted for private employers and never published are much more numerous than those publicly reported. I would calculate the number of polls listed in Hadley Cantril's useful compilation of published polls, entitled *Public Opinion, 1935–1946*, as at least 9,000, and would roughly estimate that at least 20,000 polls were conducted and published between 1935 and 1955.

Quite diverse methods of polling have been used, polling techniques have been experimentally tested rather extensively, and pollers' judgments in interpreting results have been attacked and defended. Although there has been considerable research on the details of selecting respondents, on question methodology, on interviewing and on interpreting the results, the essential methods of the commercial pollers had not changed much until 1952. The heart of modern polling procedure has been quota sampling, latterly trending toward area sampling. Area sampling was pioneered by the U.S. Bureau of the Census and extensively used by the Division of Program Surveys of the Bureau of Agricultural Economics before the commercial pollers made much use of this more expensive method. There are problems of method common to psychological measurement, market research, audience surveys and election polling. Indeed, an organization to study and report on problems and theories common to these areas has existed since 1947: The American Association of Public Opinion Research. Book-length analyses of the pollers' methodological problems are requisite for any detailed discussion of the numerous significant issues, and, indeed, well-organized volumes on the pollers' methods now exist.[4] Our brief discussion of method can note merely the crucial steps and issues in the conduct of polling, such as selection of questions, sampling, interviewing and interpretation of results.

It might be thought that asking a few questions of each of several thousand people would be a reasonably simple task. Actually, the planning and executing of a national poll is a complex process and requires a large and expensive organization.[5] In the early days of polling, it was difficult to obtain information on the commercial pollers' organizations and methods. These were trade secrets in a highly competitive field, but in the past few years the principal pollers' methods have become much better known.

The pollers' organizations may be briefly described as exemplified in the staffs of the American Institute of Public Opinion (Gallup) and the Fortune Survey (Roper). The Gallup organization, located in Princeton, New Jersey, conducts market and audience research, polls on social issues

[4] See especially Hadley Cantril, *Gauging Public Opinion*, Princeton University Press, Princeton, N.J., 1944; Mildred Parten, *Surveys, Polls and Samples*, Harper & Brothers, New York, 1950; H. H. Remmers, *Introduction to Opinion and Attitude Measurement*, Harper & Brothers, New York, 1954.

[5] Stuart C. Dodd, Director of the Washington Public Opinion Laboratory, lists fifty steps in conducting a poll. See "Dimensions of a Poll," *Int. Jour. Opin. and Att. Res.*, 3: 414–420 (1949).

and election polls. A field staff of about 1,200 part-time interviewers is located at carefully selected points throughout the United States. "All the interviewers are not used on any one assignment, but through a system of rotation, they are all brought into use. This system provides for greater geographical coverage. From 250 to 300 interviewers are used on any one Gallup Poll survey." [6] "In addition to election and social polls, Gallup and his associates conduct Audience Research Polls. A staff of 400 interviewers, of which 200 are usually on assignment, interview from 4,000 to 5,000 people a week in several hundred cities scattered over the nation. They ascertain public preferences for various types of movies, books, and radio programs, including plots, titles and stars." [7] Elmo Roper's Fortune Survey is located in New York City. This organization stresses the selection and quality of the field interviewing staff. The Fortune Poll conducts market research and, after 1947, reported at intervals a Consumer Outlook Study which had surveyed consumer anticipations. Roper also engages in opinion issue polls for the periodicals and does election surveys. A field staff of between 250 and 300 is used with a small, professional, broadly experienced field supervisory staff.[8] "The survey is conducted by personal interviews with a sample of the population distributed according to such factors as age, sex, section of the country, community and economic level. A very small sample is drawn. In 1948, Roper and a staff of 256 interviewers employed samples of several sizes. His presidential poll was about 5,000, his consumer polls covered 3,500, and his surveys of management and their opinions ran to 4,000 or more." [9]

Despite the large number of polls conducted, it may well be that the most significant questions are rarely asked. The most meaningful questions on public affairs may not be apparent to the poller and his sponsors, as both are enmeshed in the values and standards of their own cultural milieu and may lack perspective. Moreover, the selection of questions is determined largely by the sponsor, be he commercial or journalistic. The range of interests of the first is usually narrowly conceived and the interests of journalism are skewed in the direction of the current conflicts and flamboyant issues. Such distortions in question selection are inevitable in commercial polling. Subsidized polls could survey broader and less immediately significant issues, but would not inevitably do so. In any case, a large number of questions have been asked in the 20,000 polls taken between 1935 and 1955. The most important questions for the social scientist are those which either by repetition or by the variety of

[6] G. Gallup, *A Guide to Public Opinion Polls*, Princeton University Press, Princeton, N.J., 1948, p. 57.

[7] M. Parten, *Surveys, Polls and Samples*, Harper & Brothers, New York, 1950, p. 32.

[8] A detailed discussion of this organization may be found in D. Anderson, "Roper's Field Interviewing Organization," *Pub. Opin. Quar.*, 16: 2: 263–272.

[9] Parten, *op. cit.*, p. 27.

questions on one topic permit of assumptions regarding the process of attitude and opinion change.

Having questions to ask, the next step is the determination of the universe, that is, the public, a sample of which is to be questioned. Are the questions directed at a national, a regional or a local public, or at a level or type of population, a special interest-group, or any other subdivision? This being decided, what types of sampling shall be selected?

A sample, as the term is used in the social sciences, has the same connotation as in popular usage, that is, a sample is a selected part of a whole. One of the problems of statistics is the development of principles of sampling whereby the sample will be representative of the whole. Another question is the size of the sample in proportion to the whole which will be required to assure representativeness in terms of the attributes.

In public opinion measurement, the objective is the selection and polling of a representative sample of the group which constitutes "the public" under consideration. The public may be the people of a community, area, state or nation, or of some special group within the area public. The size of the sample in comparison to the size of the public will depend on the complexity of the issues and the degree of variety and complexity in the public to be tested. Sampling is possible because of the definitely limited variations to be found in publics on public issues. Hence, it is possible to sample and poll publics numbering scores of millions of people with samples of a few thousand. On national polls, Gallup, Roper and the others use samples of from 3,500 to 5,000.[10] As populations are heterogeneous, one must select individuals either on the basis of selected criteria (stratified-quota) or, systematically, on the basis of their distribution in space in sufficient numbers to give every population element an equal chance of being selected (area-random). However, the adequacy and representativeness of the sample remain a fundamental issue of polling. These are basic problems.

The theories of sampling originated with the handling of finite, discrete objects, which could be adequately defined and possessed relatively stable internal and external characteristics. The rules of sampling could, with some questionable manipulations, be used in population sampling when the purpose is merely to count bodies. However, when we move into the area of opinion,

---

[10] For the size of samples used by the various polling organizations in the world, consult the Introduction of H. L. Cantril, *Public Opinion, 1935–1946*, Princeton University Press, Princeton, N.J., 1951. The discussion of the calculations of sample size is beyond the scope of this volume. For a discussion of chance sampling errors (the standard error) and the methods of calculation of the per cent of standard error in relation to the numbers interviewed, see any standard book on statistics in the social sciences, or read the excellent, simple and summarized discussion of sampling in public opinion measurement in L. W. Doob, *Public Opinion and Propaganda*, Henry Holt and Company, New York, 1948, chaps. 6 and 7.

we have used several major assumptions which may or may not be true. First, are opinions or attitudes discrete, finite items? Are they continuous factors? Can they be adequately defined? Do they possess relative stability in expression or in subjective elements? This problem increases in importance when we leave opinion polling directed at dichotomous choices and attempt to sample infinite choices.[11]

The types of sampling in polling are essentially the variations of the stratified-quota and random-area procedures. Quota sampling consists of selecting certain factors (such as number of voters, sex, age, community size, economic position, party affiliation, etc., in election samples) in the population and attempting to represent these in correct proportion in the sample. On this basis, certain types and numbers of individuals are selected and interviewed by the field workers. The field worker approaches individuals until he finds the person who has the characteristics needed for his next interview and then questions this individual. The objective is to interview representative individuals with the selected characterstics and in sufficient numbers to warrant assumptions about the attitudes and opinions of the large universe, or public, which is being polled.

Area sampling is not based on assignment of quotas, thus eliminating interviewer judgment and possible bias. In area sampling, certain areas (block, section, ward divisions of city or town, section, township or other area of county, county or other division of state) are assigned to the interviewer. Within these areas he interviews every *nth* individual or member of a family located at an assigned position (the second house from the northeast corner of a block, etc.). The area units are selected randomly in various ways. Due to travel expenses, time consumption for the interviewer in proceeding from one interview to another remote interview, and other costs, area sampling is very much more expensive than quota sampling. Area sampling by pollers is a more recent and less tested procedure. The area sampling procedures of the Bureau of the Census in 1944 provided the first great impetus to the serious consideration and use of area sampling.[12] Area sampling was little used by the commercial pollers until 1952 when area sampling was used to supplement quota sampling in the election of that year.

There are advantages and disadvantages of both general methods of selecting a sample. Stratified sampling permits of tailoring the sample to those groups in the population which are expected to be more significantly involved both in opinion formation and other behavior on the

[11] J. E. Bachelder, "Problems in Public Opinion Polling," *Research Studies*, State College of Washington, Pullman, Wash., vol. XVI, p. 34.

[12] U.S. Department of Commerce, Bureau of the Census, Sampling Staff, *A Chapter in Population Sampling*, 1947.

issue with which the poll deals. This is a great advantage. If the strata are properly selected, there is great assurance of relatively complete coverage of all groups in the population. Moreover, stratified sampling can be carried on in smaller geographic areas than area sampling and is, therefore, much cheaper. The objective is to select persons from all significant major groups in the population in proportion to the numerical size of these groups. This involves judgments by the poller on the significance of strata, the quality of the data for the description of the strata, and the proportion of interviews to be taken in each stratum.

There are limitations and disadvantages of stratified sampling. The poller must be the final judge in the selection of strata and quite evidently the strata for one kind of issue will vary from the strata which should be used on other issues. Thus, to use the same strata in election polling and on public opinion in the United States concerning Southeast Asia would be fallacious, as significant opinion and other behavior on these two issues will be patterned quite differently in the population of the United States. But the judgment of the poller is the final arbiter for the selection of strata design and that judgment obviously can be in error, sometimes great error. Moreover, adequate data on the qualities of the strata, the numbers and distribution of the individuals who have the characteristics of the strata, do not always exist, and the existing information may be inadequate and fallacious. Even census data are not always adequate or up to date. The allocation of the numbers of individuals to be interviewed in each stratum involves further judgments by the poller as to the relative importance of the particular stratum in the design. Also, it is often difficult for the interviewer to locate the individual respondents fitting the requirements, and the interviewer's fallacious selections and biases have been the cause of various kinds of error. Fundamentally, the major question in stratified-quota sampling is whether the factors used in selecting the sample are the most important in the opinion-forming process.

Among the types of area sampling, that most favored by the commercial pollers is the pinpoint precinct sample. Areas are identified by analysis of election and census data and interviewers are assigned to interview certain individuals or household groups within that area.

The general characteristics of the system which we describe as "pinpoint" or "precinct" sampling are as follows: (1) The primary sampling units are election districts, (2) The sampling units are selected at random within regional and city-size strata, (3) Within the precinct interviews are obtained in every *nth* dwelling unit, and (4) Age and sex ratios are maintained by a rotation plan.[13]

[13] G. Gallup, "The Future Direction of Election Polling," *Pub. Opin. Quar.,* 17: 2: 203.

In 1952, the precinct sampling method was tested on a national basis for the first time by George Gallup as an auxiliary method to his quota sampling. He and many other pollers anticipate an increased use of this method of sampling, resulting in greater accuracy in polling. Why does the precinct sampling method work as well as it does?

(1) Interviewers are given no choice in the selection of neighborhood in which to interview and are required to follow a systematic plan in selecting households in which to interview and in selecting individuals within the household, (2) The vote in past elections in the precinct provides an excellent gauge of the political representativeness of the sample both by areas of the country and for the country as a whole, (3) The interviewer has every reason for following directions conscientiously because he knows that his survey results can be checked with election figures for the precinct after the election, (4) From the point of view of the researcher, precinct sampling has another outstanding advantage—namely, that each precinct election is, in essence, a miniature national election. Most of the factors present in a national election are reproduced in precinct elections.[14]

Gallup might well have added that perhaps the most important reason for the superiority of this area sampling, if after further testing it proves unquestionably superior, is the removal of the poller from the necessity of making judgments in which he, as well as his interviewers, has been in error frequently. However, area sampling does not separate potential voters from nonvoters, is not superior to quota sampling in revealing the probable behavior of those who have not made up their minds or refuse to reveal preference, nor is it superior in providing estimates of the probable total vote. In the case of other types of issues, area sampling is by no means always superior to quota sampling, for it is frequently preferable to poll some strata more intensively and selectively than other strata of the population.

Having determined the size, distribution and basis of selection of the sample in polling, the next step is the finding of the individuals to be interviewed. If some form of area sampling is used or random sampling from lists, directories or other compilations of names, as in telephone interviews, a proportion of the sample will not be at home. In radio-audience research this proportion is 20 to 30 per cent. If the sample is then changed, a degree of distortion may be introduced. If call-backs on the not-at-homes are made, a heavy expense is imposed on the pollers. No really satisfactory solution has been found for this problem.

The next major problems are those of constructing questions and conducting interviews. In the compilation and asking of questions there are many difficult issues. Question construction—

[14] *Ibid.,* p. 207.

. . . involves the whole area of semantics and a search for answers to our problems shows how little we have done about the sociology of language. In personal interviewing the semantic problem is increased by the addition of problems of phonetics and tonal symbolism. Moreover, the problem of meanings is complicated with the problem of emotional symbolism associated with words.[15]

The issues of question wording are so numerous and varied, the errors so general and the problems so subtle as to require discussion at book length.[16] No facile generalizations in a few sentences would suffice. Perhaps no aspect of polling, except sampling, has been so extensively studied as the effect of variations in question construction on interviewees' answers. Clarity of meaning and objectivity have been central aims of the poller who desires to eliminate emotionally toned words and prestige words. And yet—

. . . the social scientist who makes a fetish of objectivity, seeking neutral, objective phrasings of an issue, is to a considerable extent pursuing a will-of-the-wisp. Communication in terms of completely colorless and objective words can never be a reality. At most, affective loadings can be experimentally determined and allowed for.[17]

Having developed questions as skillfully as possible, how can one ask questions of people in such a manner as to be reasonably sure of finding out what they really think? Is it better to limit the answers to specific questions, to offer alternatives and ask for selection of statements made on some type of rating or attitude scale, or to use some open-end type of questioning which encourages the interviewee to express himself extensively and in his own words?[18] In answering specific questions or choosing among limited alternatives, the interviewee gives answers which are easily coded, counted and related to one another, but do we have a true, representative and adequate answer from him? On the other hand, though the open-end question is increasingly used in polling, the difficulty of recording and coding the answers has led interviewers to interpret in key phrases and short answers, thus perhaps losing the really significant variations of the extended answer. If the answer is recorded verbatim, then someone must interpret the answer, so as to classify and code before quantification. In large publics, perhaps the open-ended interview is most useful in pretesting, in order to assemble a wide variety

[15] Bachelder, *op. cit.*, p. 36.
[16] See Stanley L. Payne, *The Art of Asking Questions*, Princeton University Press, Princeton, N.J., 1951.
[17] H. H. Remmers, *op. cit.*, p. 143.
[18] Elmo Roper pioneered in the use of attitude scales in public opinion surveys, Rensis Likert in the development of "open-ended question" interviewing, and Paul Lazarsfeld in the panel technique.

of existing opinions as a basis for the construction of questions for the large sample.

The selection, training, and supervision of interviewers is from some points of view the key problem in polling. At least the interviewer errors are the ones over which we have least control and at the same time are almost impossible to predict statistically. . . . The great majority of interviewers are female, are extroverted, have at least a high school education, have spare time, and are able to use the small amount of money interviewing brings in. What makes a good interviewing approach? Can one class of personalities get similar information from diverse classes of personalities? To what extent are the respondent's answers shaped by the stereotype she sees in the interviewer? . . . Supervision of interviewers is a serious concern with no real solution. Under quota sampling there is no simple way of checking on interviewing. And if re-interviews are used under area sampling, interviewer morale is weakened. Spot re-interviewing is generally used but is not satisfactory. What is called "interviewer cheating" is a constant headache to pollsters. The best procedure to date is a bulletin to interviewers constantly reiterating the standards of polling and pointing out the errors made or suspected in the previous poll.[19]

At every stage of polling there are evident possibilities of error. Sample selection, question selection and formulation, the interview with its possible misunderstandings, the art of asking why and eliciting understandable answers, the coding and the interpretation of answers; all these require experienced, skillful and honest pollers to approximate the truth of existing opinion on any issue. Prophecy as to what those opinions will become and the trends of their potential changes is an art of a still higher order.

PREELECTION POLLING AND PREDICTION

Public opinion polls are best known to the newspaper-reading public through the election forecasts. In general, the popular reputation of the pollers is determined by their accuracy of prophecy as to the winners of elections, especially national elections. The election forecast record is viewed as dramatic validation of the pollers' methods or evidence of their fallaciousness. What is not commonly understood is that when a poller predicts the results of an election after ascertaining public opinion at the times of his polls, he is assessing many factors in addition to the existing public opinion of the electorate. In a volume derogatory to polling, *The Pollsters*, Lindsay Rogers ironically quotes one academic enthusiast for the polls as saying: "The polls may reflect the wishes of the electorate more faithfully than the elections themselves. Variables enter in to keep some people away from the voting booth. The weather, trans-

[19] Bachelder, *op. cit.*, p. 38.

portation difficulties, party activity, intimidation of various kinds may distort the final result but not affect poll results." But, as the poller's original purpose is the recording of public opinion, and, if in preelection polls he develops a skill which correctly reports that public opinion, then it is true that the polls may perhaps reflect the wishes of the electorate more accurately than the elections.

The election results do not prove or disprove the poller's exact accuracy as a poller of public opinion, but rather as a poller plus a prophetic assessor of many election factors which are not all based on public opinion. If he is to be a successful prognosticator, he must adjust his poll results on the basis of his estimates and judgments of these other political factors. He may be an efficient poller of public opinion, but an untrustworthy political seer.

Many opinion analysts contend that scientific surveys, more than elections themselves, are the most reliable expression of public opinion. They claim that surveys are not subject to political-machine manipulations in getting out a disproportionately large Republican or Democratic vote, to "short-pencil artists," to dead persons' voting, to gerrymandering, to the effect of the weather keeping the elderly and infirm from the polls, nor to the poll tax. Experts maintain that scientific surveys represent all types of persons in the degree to which they exist in the entire population, while the elections seldom do. It is common for less than half of the registered voters to go to the polls, not to mention the unregistered.[20]

The polling sample may accurately reflect the opinions of the population of the United States, but not of the population who actually vote on election day. Political behavior and opinion behavior may differ considerably, as the poller ruefully relearns from time to time.

Moreover, if the elections do not measure with complete accuracy the polling skill of the scientific surveyors in dealing with candidates, the election results can say little about the accuracy of the pollers' surveys of opinion on political and civic and social problems. The pollers' degree of accuracy or inaccuracy in predicting election results, a very special case of public opinion recording, in which the pollers have now had considerable experience, is not necessarily reflected in the case of polls on issues. A polling organization which had made very close predictions on many elections might be providing results of scores of other polls each year in which the error ranged from 1 per cent to 25 per cent on the various polls. Several hundred polls on issues are taken in the United States each year. Validation of the pollers' accuracy in such surveys would need to be established for each general type of survey and cannot be imputed

[20] H. H. Field and G. M. Connelly, "Testing Polls in Official Election Booths," *Pub. Opin. Quar.*, 6: 4: 610.

from the pollers' accuracy or inaccuracy in predicting elections. A newspaper-reading public which imputes such accuracy or inaccuracy is in error and does not understand the issues. And when George Gallup writes that "The problem of polling on issues is essentially the same as the problem of polling on candidates. The same polling procedures are used on both candidates and issues," [21] then he, too, is gliding over what should be a moot point for all pollers. For, on these varied issues on which the public is asked to express opinions, a quota sample would of necessity vary with each general type of issue, if stratified sampling were used. In any case, on these varied issues, the state of development and maturity of the opinion process and the possible relation between opinion behavior and other behaviors will vary enormously from that of a public just about to vote on candidates after several months of electioneering. Therefore, another basis for the development of significantly stratified sampling would be necessary if opinion, significant for later behavior, were to be polled.

The pollers' experience with preelection polling is now rather extensive. From 1935 through 1947, some 392 election forecasts were made by pollers; 197 by the American Institute of Public Opinion, 141 by other polling organizations in the United States, and 54 election predictions abroad. "Of these 392 elections, 71 were forecast with an error of 1 per cent or less, 118 with an error of 2 per cent or 3 per cent, or a total of 189 with an error of 3 per cent or less; 117 were between 3 per cent and 6 per cent; 64 were between 6 per cent and 10 per cent; and 22 were over 10 per cent." [22] Stated in terms of average errors for elections polled at various times, the results are:

Period	Number of elections	Mean average error for period
November 1936—October 1940......	136	5.6
November 1940—October 1944......	109	3.4
November 1944—December 1947....	147	2.9

The results in the United States of the presidential election of 1948 should not obscure the fact that polling accuracy definitely improved over a period of years.

By 1948 modern polling techniques had been employed to predict the

[21] Gallup, *A Guide to Public Opinion Polls,* p. 69.
[22] *Ibid.,* p. 68.

outcome of about 400 elections in 11 nations.[23] A year later, in March, 1949, at the Iowa Conference on Attitude and Opinion Research, Dr. Gallup could report that, up to that time, 512 election forecasts had been made by some twenty polling organizations operating in twelve democracies of the world, of which 446 forecasts had been made in the United States.

The average error in these forecasts—including those made in the presidential election of 1948—is approximately four percentage points. In short, poll predictions based upon the vote for all parties have on the average varied from absolute accuracy by this average degree in elections dealing not only with candidates but those dealing with issues as well, referenda issues. The winners have been predicted correctly in more than eight out of ten elections.[24]

Some quota sampling has resulted in very accurate predictions of the popular vote, not only in the United States but also in some foreign elections. Roy Morgan, a protégé of George Gallup, is Director of the Australian Public Opinion Polls. Morgan has an astonishing record of accuracy and is viewed as a political barometer in Australia. In 1946 he announced that the Labor party would win 54 per cent of the vote. It won 53.1 per cent. In 1949 he announced a Liberal party victory and came within 2 tenths of one per cent of the election results. In a 1951 forecast, on that year's forced general elections, he was only 1.5 percentage points off the actual outcome. He has refined some Gallup quota procedures in ways not applicable to the United States but thus far very effective in Australia. Of course, what also helps Morgan in his forecasting is Australia's system of compulsory voting, since this spares him from error in estimating turnout.[25] Despite the 1948 predictions, a debacle of prophecy shared by all other prognosticators as well as the pollers, the over-all record of accuracy in prediction of elections reflects a very creditable performance, indeed, by the pollers. In 1948 all made serious errors, but these were primarily mistakes in judgment as a basis for prophecy, rather than mistakes in sampling or other polling methods. The dominant pollers who have been election prophets are Gallup, Roper and Crossley. The most active of the subsidized research pollers who have worked on election polls have been the Princeton Office of Public Opinion Research, the National Opinion Research Center and, more recently, the Washington Public Opinion Poll. The percentages of the popular vote predicted for the various candidates in the last four presidential elections are summarized in Table 7.

[23] G. H. Smith in *Britannica Book of the Year*, 1949, p. 597.
[24] G. Gallup in (N. C. Meier and H. W. Saunders, eds.) *The Polls and Public Opinion*, Henry Holt and Company, New York, 1949, p. 177.
[25] From a report by Fred Hubbard in the Chicago *Daily News*, April 2, 1954.

Table 7. Polls and Elections

1936

Final election returns

Roosevelt 60.2% of total vote

	Prediction	Error
Fortune (Roper)...	61.7	+ 1.5
American Institute of Public Opinion (Gallup).................	53.8	− 6.4
Crossley Poll..	53.8	− 6.4
Literary Digest...	40.9	−19.3

1940

Final election returns

Roosevelt 54.7% of total vote

	Prediction	Error
Fortune (Roper)...	55.2	+0.5
American Institute of Public Opinion (Gallup).................	52.0	−2.7
Opinion Forecasts (Wall)....................................	52.0	−2.7
Crossley Poll..	52.9	−1.8

1944

Final election returns

Roosevelt 53.8% of two-party vote

	Prediction	Error
Fortune (Roper)...	53.6	−0.2
Princeton Office of Public Opinion Research...................	53.3	−0.5
Crossley Poll..	52.0	−1.8
National Opinion Research Center...........................	51.7	−2.1
American Institute of Public Opinion (Gallup).................	51.5	−2.3

1948

Percentage of total presidential vote

	Dewey	Truman	Thurmond	Wallace	Total *
National Vote.................	*45.1*	*49.5*	*2.4*	*2.4*	*99.4*
Crossley Poll.................	49.9	44.8	1.6	3.3	99.6
American Institute of Public Opinion (Gallup)...........	49.5	44.5	2.0	4.0	100.0
Fortune (Roper).............	52.2	37.1	5.2	4.3	98.8

1952

Final election returns

Eisenhower 55.1%, Stevenson 44.5%, others .4%

	Eisenhower	Stevenson	Others	Undecided
American Institute of Public Opinion (Gallup)..........................	47	40	..	13
Crossley Poll.......................	47.4	42.3	.4	9.9
Roper.............................	49	37	..	14
United States Poll (Fink).............	50.8	48.8	.4	....

* Exclusive of percentages for minor candidates. Gallup percentages calculated on total vote for four principal candidates.

FOUR PRESIDENTIAL ELECTIONS

Predicting elections is about as difficult or easy as predicting the course of business activity, employment, the stock market or the commodity markets. Regardless of the successful experience of others, I prefer to regard predictions in these fields as an art and not a science.[26]

L. H. BEAN

The prediction of elections by pollers is based on the results from a polled sampling in which a small quota or area sample represents large publics. The selection of individuals for this sample may be improperly made, questions may be inadequate or misleading, the interviewers may be variously inept, and the results of the interviews may fail to reveal significant attitudes relating to the central questions. But skills in these procedures have been developed which have made of polling a not-too-exact science. However, prediction also involves the art of selection, weighing and application of a large number of factors which are involved in voting behavior. Certainly this necessitates skillful choices and decisions by the poller, evidencing a high order of knowledge artistically blended from data of little exactitude. In this area, the pollers have not fared so well.

The Election of 1936—The Prophets Emerge. Straw votes of various kinds had been carried on intermittently for almost a century before the prognosticators of 1936 applied sampling. But, up to this time, the straw votes had been for the most part quite inaccurate. At times, the straw pollers were inadvertently near the mark because of chance factors or because the unquotaed sample served reasonably well on the particular election or issue which chanced to be reasonably accurately prophesied. However, the errors were usually large. In the polls on candidates for the years 1916, 1920, 1924 and 1928, *The Literary Digest* polls resulted in an average plurality error of 20, 21, 12 and 12 percentage points in the predictions. On the other hand, the *Digest's* extremely accurate prediction of 1932, when the magazine predicted the total popular vote on the two major presidential candidates within 1.4 percentage points, developed a high popular reputation for accuracy. Other straw polls had erred with percentage errors such as the 5 percentage points of average plurality error for states achieved by the Hearst newspapers in an exceptionally close prediction in 1928, to the more usual 17 percentage point error of the *Farm Journal* in the same election.

In the months before the election of 1936, *The Literary Digest,* widely known for its millions of ballots and the wide publicity given to its polls, proceeded with its last and most disastrous poll. The *Digest* mailed over

[26] L. H. Bean, *How to Predict Elections,* Alfred A. Knopf, Inc., New York, 1948, p. 138.

10 million ballots and 2,376,523 were returned, a high percentage of return for such a diverse group of recipients. When the election was held, the *Digest* poll and prediction had underestimated the Roosevelt vote by 19.3 percentage points, as the Democratic candidate's popular vote was 60.2 per cent of the total popular vote, while the *Digest's* prediction was 40.9 per cent. A new group of budding prophets, the representative quota samplers, Roper, Gallup and Crossley, had predicted the *Digest* errors months in advance of the election. Indeed, the most vociferous and publicized of the new pollers, Dr. George Gallup, predicted within one percentage point the results of the *Digest* poll two months before the ballots were mailed. This prediction was based upon an analysis of the probable returns on the basis of the *Digest's* incidental sample.[27] The *Digest* could not obtain a representative sample from its mailing lists which were compiled from telephone directories and automobile-registration files.

From the point of view of cross-sections this was a major error, because it limited the sample largely to the upper half of the voting population, as judged on an economic basis. Roughly 40 per cent of all homes in the United States had telephones and some 55 per cent of all families owned automobiles. These two groups, which largely overlap, constitute roughly the upper half or upper three fifths, economically, of the voting population.[28]

On any election, or on issues about which the voters divided sharply on economic lines, the *Digest* poll could be expected to be extensively in error. Moreover, this mailing list was biased toward male rather than female voters; the urban population was disproportionately represented over the rural; the upper educational groups were much overrepresented; and the middle- and upper-age group voters received too many cards. But, aside from the disproportionate representations among those who received the cards, it is evident that the returns would not come equally from all recipients. The American Institute of Public Opinion found that the largest response, about 40 per cent, came from people listed in *Who's Who*. Eighteen per cent of the people in telephone lists, 15 per cent of the registered voters in poor areas, and 11 per cent of people on relief returned ballots. Men are more likely to reply than women.[29] The returned ballots also reflected protest to a marked degree. In 1932 protest was sufficiently strong in all economic classes that the *Digest* poll somewhat overestimated the Roosevelt strength, but, nonetheless, prophesied

[27] So-called by Daniel Katz and Hadley Cantril in an article, "Public Opinion Polls," *Sociometry*, 1: 158. As early as 1932, Claude E. Robinson, in his *Straw Votes*, Columbia University Press, New York, pp. 58–59, had pointed to the nonrepresentative nature of the *Digest* ballots.

[28] Gallup, *A Guide to Public Opinion Polls*, p. 74.

[29] Katz and Cantril, *op. cit.*, p. 160.

with surprising accuracy. The class bias of the returns in 1936, with the strong anti-Roosevelt feeling among those who returned cards, multiplied the errors and greatly overestimated Landon. As the time of the ballot was two months and more before the election, the *Digest* prophets did not account adequately for opinion changes during that period, an error which was also extensively involved in the poor showing of the pollers in 1948. The *Digest* poll of 1936 was a fiasco, its methods were discredited and new types of polling were introduced.

The errors in prediction of the popular vote made by the competing pollers were not small, but, in comparison, their reputations soared. Gallup used a combination of mail ballots and personal interviews with subjects selected on the basis of the quota sampling methods already considered, and his prediction underestimated the Roosevelt vote by 6.4 percentage points. Crossley, using the more or less standardized field survey methods of market research, developed a quota sample survey, and likewise underestimated the Roosevelt vote by 6.4 percentage points. The *Fortune* poll, directed by Elmo Roper, used a weighted sample based on age, sex, geographical divisions, rural-urban districts, and economic class.

Fortune differed from the Gallup and Crossley polls in its conception of the nature of an adequate sample. Instead of attempting to secure a statistically reliable cross-section of the population, *Fortune* depended upon the selection of typical voters so characteristic of their groups that a single case was taken as representative of thousands of people. In the city of Chicago, for example, 75 people were interviewed. And for the whole nation only 4,500 people were polled—a sample of one-hundredth of one per cent of the actual voting electorate.[30]

In the *Fortune* poll there was also some attempt to record intensity of opinion about President Roosevelt, as well as voting intentions. The Roper poll predicted the popular vote very closely, overestimating the Roosevelt vote by only 1.5 percentage points. The prediction was accurate, but validity was yet to be proved.

The methods of representative sampling were now accredited. Great impetus was given to polling efforts. At the same time, criticism and denunciation of the polls began to swell in volume, and Senator McKellar threatened investigation. It was claimed that the polls were inaccurate and therefore misleading; that the revelation of majority position would create a "band-wagon effect"; and that extensive polling, if taken seriously by legislators and administrators, would corrupt the functioning of the representative democracy.

[30] Daniel Katz and Hadley Cantril, "Public Opinion Polls," *Sociometry* (published by Beacon House, Editor, J. L. Moreno), 1: 161.

The Election of 1940—The Burgeoning Prognosticators. After a hotly contested election campaign, in which Willkie vigorously challenged the leadership of President Roosevelt, the voters on November 5 cast 54.7 per cent of the total vote for Roosevelt. Since 1936 the pollers had been striving to improve their sampling methods and had predicted scores of local, state and national elections with errors seldom exceeding 6 percentage points. By 1940 the majority of the newspaper-reading public was aware of the polls and was vaguely informed about the pollers' methods. The pollers' predictions of the presidential election were followed with interest. Using small stratified samples, representing cross sections of the population proportionately represented as to age, sex, education, political record, community size and type, and economic position, the principal pollers, Roper, Gallup and Crossley, predicted the popular vote with surprising accuracy. In this election Crossley reported percentages only on the 17 states in which the vote was expected to be close. Roper overestimated the Roosevelt vote by one-half of one percentage point and Gallup underestimated the Democratic vote by 2.7 percentage points. The Crossley prediction underestimated the Roosevelt vote by 1.8 percentage points. However, these figures do not represent the relative merits and skill of these professional pollers, whose reputations were established, but at stake; as the apparently amazing accuracy of Elmo Roper must be modified by noting that, although many of his errors canceled one another, his prediction by sections of the nation was much less accurate than Gallup's sectional predictions or Crossley's predictions for the crucial states. "In no section of the country was Gallup off by more than 4 per cent, while Roper missed the Mountain states by 10 per cent and the East South Central by 12 per cent." [31] Even so, the record was one of impressive accuracy and the popular reputation of the pollers burgeoned.

Once more, as in 1936, the practice of interviewing quotas of small stratified samples of the electorate was proved to be superior to that of interviewing larger but unrepresentative samples. The preferability of interviews rather than mail ballots was also shown by the results. Emil Hurja, of the *Pathfinder* poll, although he claimed to be correcting the biases of the *Literary Digest* type of poll, especially by attempting to obtain more representative returns from lower-income groups, apparently failed to do so, for his prediction underestimated the Roosevelt vote by 6.3 percentage points. He had found no adequate way of obtaining mailing lists of lower-income groups or of correcting for the biases in returning mail ballots, because the upper-educational, the upper-income and

[31] D. Katz, "The Public Opinion Polls and the 1940 Election," *Pub. Opin. Quar.,* 50: 1: 57.

the disgruntled recipients returned their ballots in disproportionate numbers. The inferiority of the mailed ballot was clearly shown.

Political commentators, academic critics, and the professional pollers were not so easily satisfied with the results of the polls as was the general public when the pollers' methods and results were reviewed. Some political scientists were beginning to express doubts as to the significance of the numerous popular opinions being polled and of the impact of the results on legislators and administrators. Moreover, it was argued that the pollers were not accurate enough for close elections and that when the elections were not close the polls were unnecessary. It was claimed that even if the pollers became reasonably accurate in election predictions there would be no assurance that they would be equally accurate in their surveys on social and economic issues. Such surveys were being made in increasing numbers, and, contrary to the election-poll situation, the results were usually unchecked by the voting record or by any other public expression.

One attempt to check on comparative accuracy was made by the National Opinion Research Center. In Boulder, Colorado, a poll was taken on the preelection preferences of voters on the senatorial and gubernatorial contests of 1940 and on three issues formulated by the pollers: a national sales tax, old-age pensions, and a union of nations. The population was polled on the two candidates and the three issues. At the election, by state and local official collaboration with the pollers, every voter was handed a ballot on the issues and asked to vote on them, although they were not part of the regular election. The ballots were deposited in special ballot boxes. Approximately 5,000 of the 8,900 registered voters voted on the candidates, and a little over 3,700 voted on the issues. The actual errors of the pollers' predictions were 3 tenths of one percentage point on the senator, 2 tenths of one percentage point on the governor, 7.2 percentage points on the national sales tax, 1.1 percentage points on old-age pensions, and 3.2 percentage points on a union of nations. Those conducting the experiment noted a few shortcomings of the test. In this small city, adequate stratified sampling necessitated a large sample made up of 28 per cent of the voters. "Where a larger electorate could be sampled, as accurate a cross section could have been found in less than 1 per cent of the total voters." [32] And, fundamentally, the entire procedure was politically artificial in the use of poller-formulated issues. And, in any case, the fundamental question concerning accuracy and meaningfulness in polling on issues versus candidates lies in the adequate structuring of samples in the various cases and on the

[32] H. H. Field and G. M. Connelly, "Testing Polls in Official Election Booths," *Pub. Opin. Quar.*, 6: 4: 612.

maturity of popular opinions on issues versus those on candidates. This experiment does not deal with the basic questions involved in considering relative accuracy of polls on issues versus polls on candidates. To this day, no adequate evidence has been provided on this central issue of polling accuracy.

Understanding of the distinction between the polling results based on interviewing samples and the adjustments which the pollers must make in order to prophesy election returns was not widely diffused in 1940, nor do many newspaper readers of the pollers' predictions know about these problems today. Problems such as the pollers' estimate of probable turn-out of voters on election day, the allocation of the undecided vote, the estimates of differential appearance at the election booths of the members of various significant groups in the population, and other crucial judgments made by the pollers were not widely understood. But, on the basis of the rather high degree of accuracy of prediction by the pollers in 1940, the general public developed a considerable confidence in the polls after that election. The commercial pollers, though aware of their limitations, felt encouraged, largely vindicated as to their methods, and sanguine as to the possibility of still greater accuracy.

The Election of 1944—The Prophets Are Questioned. In the third national election in which the pollers made predictions, they had achieved a large audience and a considerable measure of public confidence. A large majority of the people of the United States knew of the existence of the polls and most of the nation were at least acquainted with the general results predicted. Over a hundred newspapers carried the syndicated columns of George Gallup, the King Features syndicate gave publicity to Archibald Crossley's predictions, and, in addition to the readers of *Fortune* magazine, many others knew the results of Elmo Roper's polls, for they were widely quoted.

The war was approaching a climax. The peoples of most of the world were watching the election campaign in the United States leading to November 7. Some of the more knowledgeable of these foreign observers had come to know something of polling in the United States by 1944. Indeed, a few small polling organizations had been started abroad. The pollers' audience was widening.

By 1944 the pollers believed that they knew with certainty that, "The first fact to get straight is that political behavior in this country is well solidified and that only a relatively small proportion of votes is affected by campaign arguments or the issues that bubble up from the ferment of events. If the issues of the campaign are to be seen in their proper perspective, it must be emphasized once more that issues, per se, account for only a small fraction of the total vote cast. At least nearly three-fourths of the voters seem to vote year after year for the party they call their own." [33] The pollers were not so certain as to these proportions after 1948.

In any case, the pollers dealt with a complex situation in 1944 in attempting to predict the political behavior of the 25 per cent of the still impressionable and undecided voters and of the servicemen whose experiences might make for unorthodox political choices. Moreover, the servicemen were too young to have fixed political habits and they were absent from the molding influences of normal community experience.

The campaign issues were unusually difficult for any poller to assess. In the war period, foreign policy and objectives were largely bipartisan, but it was found that President Roosevelt was credited by 81 per cent of the United States public with doing a good job in his handling of our military and foreign affairs abroad. "There can be no doubt that an overwhelming majority of voters believe the President and the present administration can get on better with the job of finishing the war quickly than Dewey and the Republicans can. Roosevelt advantage here is nearly two to one." [34] As 63 per cent of the public stated that after the war they would rather have President Roosevelt than Dewey to represent the United States at the peace conference, while 43 per cent stated that Dewey would do the best job of running affairs here in this country, in comparison to 46 per cent who thought that Roosevelt would do better, the popular judgment as to when the war might end was crucial. Of the many other issues involved in the voter's assessment of his choices, there were questions such as the President's health, the issue of the fourth term, the appeal of Thomas Dewey and the Republican platform, the relative importance of foreign and domestic issues, the question of the effectiveness of appeals for efficiency in government so stressed by Dewey, the willingness for economic risk-taking versus security and social welfare, and concern over the public debt and spending. And, due to war's dislocation of populations, the pollers' estimates of probable turnout on election day were unusually difficult to make in 1944.

Withal, the pollers' predictions of the popular vote in 1944 were surprisingly accurate. Again, the errors were in underestimation of the Democratic vote. Roper's prediction was only 2 tenths of one percentage point short of the 53.8 per cent of the two-party vote which President Roosevelt received; Gallup's national prediction was 2.3 percentage points short; the Crossley poll underestimated the Roosevelt vote by 1.8 percentage points; while two noncommercial pollers also made very accurate predictions, the Princeton Office of Public Opinion Research being one-half of one percentage point short, and the National Opinion Research

[33] H. Cantril, "The Issues—As Seen by the American People," *Pub. Opin. Quar.*, 8: 3: 331–347.
[34] Cantril, *op. cit.*, p. 332.

Center was 2.1 percentage points under the Roosevelt vote. This record of accurate polling of the popular vote was not equalled by accurate predictions of the electoral vote. Although Gallup correctly predicted the electoral winners in 41 states with 391 electoral votes, he wrongly predicted seven populous, important states with 140 electoral votes. Crossley's predictions were somewhat better, for he correctly predicted 43 states with 453 electoral votes and was in error on five states with 78 electoral votes. Some small errors in sampling, interviewing and recording, plus the adjustments which the poller must make for his estimates of the various factors, can easily provide an error of several percentage points, which in close elections can give the wrong answer on electoral votes. When the poller predicts elections, he becomes a more or less wise prophet and must go beyond the relative accuracies of social science recording.

The methods used in 1944 were of the same basic pattern as those used in 1940, that is, personal interviews with a sample considered representative through quota allocations according to the basic categories of significant characteristics of the population. The usual possibility of error through the interviewers' discretionary selection of respondents remained in the method. This potential error was, in practice, more evident where the interviewers were less skilled and more numerous. Gallup's staff of over a thousand part-time interviewers, predominantly women, contrasts to Roper's or Crossley's few score, mostly male, full-time professional interviewers. The samples interviewed cumulated to 20,000 to 30,000 people. Some limited concern with the composition of the attitudes involved in the voter's choices was emerging, as in Roper's use of a 6-point scale for his respondents, or in Crossley's questions to ascertain intensity of conviction, but these were simple, crude methods of attempting to record a complex reality. No elaborate attitude testing was used.[35]

The commmercial pollers were not conducting studies in depth, were not probing adequately the composition of voters' attitudes as a basis for determining probable allocation of undecided votes, were not assessing the proclaimed nonvoters' ideas, or the aspects of the mind-life of the minority of voters possibly responsive to campaign appeals. However, attention was turning to these central problems. In 1944, Paul Lazarsfeld reported on an intensive study of 600 residents of Erie County, Ohio, which had a population of 46,000. The study dealt with the election of 1940, but results had been developed during the intervening years and

[35] For more elaborate description and analysis of the 1944 polls, see D. Katz, "The Polls and the 1944 Election," *Pub. Opin. Quar.*, 8: 4: 468–487; E. Benson et al., "Polling Lessons from the 1944 Election," *Pub. Opin. Quar.*, 9: 4: 467–484; H. Field et al., "The Discussion Goes On," *Pub. Opin. Quar.*, 9: 4: 403–410; P. Lazarsfeld, "The Election Is Over," *Pub. Opin. Quar.*, 8: 3: 317–330.

were released during the 1944 campaign.[36] Erie County was half-indus-
trial, half-rural, and had been selected because it had been near the national average for many presidential elections. The representative sample
of 600 was interviewed each month for the 7 months before election day.
Over 250 questions were asked of each respondent. "About one-half the
voting sample made up its mind before May and did not change its vote-
intention; another 30 per cent made up their minds as soon as the candidates were nominated by the conventions; the other 20 per cent hesitated
long enough to be at least theoretically susceptible to propaganda influences." [37] This study analyzed the content and amount of radio programs, newspapers and magazines circulating in the county, the impact
of personal contacts upon voters, and something of the effects of these
various agencies of special pleading. They concluded that "The campaign propaganda does not reach the citizen in the proportion in which
it is offered. Social environment sifts propaganda; the undecided ones are
not easily reached by the propaganda of the party to which their group
is generally hostile." [38] A pioneer effort on analysis in depth, on recording
of opinion change, on relating mass-media content and influence on the
residue of the impressionable public, this study resulted in numerous
suggestive generalizations.

In 1944 some politicians were viewing the pollers' activity with a
jaundiced eye, especially Democratic representatives who questioned the
persistent and general underestimation of the Democratic vote by the
pollers in the preceding three presidential elections. A congressional investigation was held in which the principal testimony was given by Dr.
George Gallup.[39] All in all, considering the politically controversial nature
of the topic, the hearings were conducted with a minimum of recriminations and accusations. Although the congressmen of the committee were
not extensively critical of Dr. Gallup's American Institute of Public Opinion, the Advisory Technical Committee [40] was very critical of Gallup's
methods, noting that (1) the quota sampling methods were faulty, (2)
the pinpoint samples were faultily designed, (3) the samples were not
large enough in many states, (4) adjustments made on the basis of anticipated low turnout should be criticized, especially since, "The publication

[36] This study was directed by Paul Lazarsfeld, cosponsored by Elmo Roper, and
the field director was Elmo Wilson. It is reported chiefly in P. Lazarsfeld, B. Berelson
and H. Gaudet, *The People's Choice*, Duell, Sloan & Pearce–Little, Brown, New York,
1944.

[37] P. Lazarsfeld, "The Election Is Over," *Pub. Opin. Quar.*, 8: 3: 327.

[38] *Ibid.*, p. 321.

[39] House Resolution 551 of the second session of the 78th Congress provided for
hearings before the Committee to Investigate Campaign Expenditures. Part 12 of the
Hearings, pp. 1235–1299, dealt with the polls.

[40] Louis H. Bean, Bureau of the Budget; Philip M. Hauser and Morris Hansen,
U.S. Bureau of the Census; and Rensis Likert, U.S. Bureau of Agricultural Economics.

of the estimates without specific mention of the character and magnitude of the subtractions may be questioned," (5) the failure to explain adequately in his widely syndicated columns the nature of the various adjustments made after the poll results were summarized, stating: "It is possible to attempt a publication practice which, without unjustifiably undermining the confidence of the public in the poll nor burdening it with detail, would, at the same time, make clear the extent to which the published results are based, respectively, on scientific survey technique and on individual judgment." [41]

The Election of 1948—Debacle for Prophets. After the election of 1944, the polls and pollers had become much more widely known and had achieved an enhanced public confidence. The number of professional pollers was increasing and their services were utilized by interest-groups, publicity agencies and newspapers. In the years between 1944 and 1948 a mood of confidence in the validity of the pollers' methods and the accuracy of their reports and predictions increased in the clients, the general public and the pollers themselves. To be sure, the pollers and the ever more numerous peripheral observers and informed critics were becoming more critical and thoughtful concerning the political and social significance of polling. Confidence in predictive accuracy developed, especially on the basis of the pollers' accurate election predictions. By 1948 the pollers had made 512 election forecasts with an average error of approximately 4 percentage points and had correctly predicted the winner in eight out of ten elections. The public had gained the impression that the polls were dependably accurate. The pollers did little to reduce this belief.

The public's faith and the pollers' confidence in the polls' predictions were shaken by the results of the 1948 election. There was too much public confidence in the polls before the election and too little belief in polling for some time afterward, owing to a lack of public knowledge and understanding of polling methods and the nature of the errors to which polls are liable. In 1948 the errors were large and shocking. Truman received 49.5 per cent of the popular vote, though Gallup had predicted 44.5 per cent, Crossley 44.8 per cent and Roper 37.1 per cent; with errors, therefore, of 5.0, 4.7 and 12.4 percentage points. Dewey received 45.1 per cent of the popular vote, while Gallup predicted 49.5, Crossley, 49.9 and Roper, 52.2, thus being in error 4.4, 4.8 and 7.1 percentage points. The pollers' percentage errors vary for Truman and Dewey owing to their varying errors on Thurmond and Wallace, as can be noted in Table 7. These large errors should not be belittled. What happened to the pollers' methods and judgment?

[41] *Hearings, op. cit.*

The Social Science Research Council appointed a committee to analyze the polls immediately after the election.[42] At the beginning of their preliminary report, the Committee stated:

The pollsters over-reached the capabilities of the public opinion poll as a predicting device in attempting to pick, without qualification, the winner of the 1948 presidential election. They had been led by false assumptions into believing their methods were much more accurate than in fact they are. The election was close. Dewey could have won by carrying Ohio, California, and Illinois which he lost by less than 1 per cent of the vote. In such a close election, no polls, no advance information of any kind, could have predicted a Truman or Dewey victory with confidence. The failure of the polls was due to neglecting the possibility of a close election and the necessity of measuring preferences very accurately just before the election to determine whether a flat forecast could be made with confidence.

The pollers were overconfident. They could have forecast the possibilities of a close contest had they followed the trends more closely and up to the last week before the election, had they been suspicious of the possible disposition of the large undecided vote, and had they followed more closely the shifts in the labor and farm vote. This is readily seen after the fact, but at the time, all other prognosticators, newsmen, columnists and political pundits, were also betrayed into something less than a realistic assessment of voters' attitudes.[43]

After the election, the pollers and other social scientists reviewed the record of the polls and attempted assessment of the problems of sampling, of the sequence of events which betrayed the polls, and of the pollers' possible errors of judgment. The principal reasons for the pollers' gross underestimation of the Truman vote and failure properly to assess the popular vote for the other candidates are: (1) the unexpected shift to Truman in the last few weeks of the campaign which the polls failed to detect; (2) the failure to assess properly the intentions of the large numbers of undecided voters; and (3) the problems of who would vote. Among the less important sources of error were such factors as: (1) possible errors of sampling and interviewing; (2) the effect of the labor campaigns in the last month before the election; (3) the pollers' failure

---

[42] The report of this committee was published in the spring of 1949 in SSRC Bulletin 60, *The Pre-Election Polls of 1948.*

[43] A very extensive literature evaluating and criticizing the pollers' performance was published in 1949. See especially the SSRC Report, Bulletin 60; *The Polls and Public Opinion,* Henry Holt and Company, Inc., New York (Norman Meier and Harold Saunders, eds.); and the winter, spring and fall issues of the quarterly *International Journal of Opinion and Attitude Research.* The popular literature consists of scores of articles chiefly devoted to attacks on polls and pollers ranging from invective and unbridled criticism of the pollers as charlatans to more serious questioning of the meaning and social significance of election polling and prediction.

adequately to detect the late shifts in the farm vote; (4) the pollers' over-estimation of the numbers who would vote; and (5) the unexpected approximately 700,000 voters whose ballots did not contain a vote for president, although they voted for other candidates. For the most part, these errors of polling and of pollers' judgments were additive, did not cancel, and, therefore, compounded the pollers' errors in the election of 1948. All of these generalizations about the sources of error are too broad and oversimplified, but a detailed assessment of the reassessments of the pollers' errors in this election would be a report filling a volume.

The pollers had confidence, based on experience, that shifts in voting intentions and decisions concerning voting which might be made in the last few weeks before the election could be ignored. In this they would have been supported by political commentators of various kinds, for it was considered a well-known political fact that substantial shifts did not occur in this period. However, 1948 proved to be unique, for considerable changes in intentions in voting did occur during the last month. Elmo Roper, whose confidence had led him to cease polling in early September, was most seriously betrayed by these last-minute shifts, but all of the pollers had their error in prediction of the popular vote increased by at least 2 percentage points. For, as the Social Science Research Council's early report stated:

> Looking at the evidence available, the Committee tentatively concludes that in the last two weeks there was a net shift to Truman of 2 or 3 percentage points, probably varying quite a bit from state to state. The complexity of the problem of allowing for all the kinds of errors of interpretation is such that it is possible that the shift at the end of the campaign was even greater than these figures suggest.

The last month's shifts were especially based on the labor campaigns for Truman during that period, the farmers' shifts amidst a falling grain market, and the last-minute decisions of the undecideds. These late decisions were not caught by the pollers, whose record of prediction would have been relatively good otherwise. This is readily noted in retrospect, but for technical reasons, as well as the prevailing preelection judgments of the pollers, its detection was hardly feasible at the time.

It is an oversimplification to state that it was the practice of the pollers before 1948 to allocate the undecided voters in the same proportions as the decided, but this was approximately the practice and was essentially the decision of the pollers in the Dewey-Truman contest. This judgment had validity in preceding elections, but was quite wrong in 1948, thus providing another major polling error. Instead of a final distribution proportionate to that of the decided voters, postelection studies indicated that, "Truman received the votes of 4 out of 5 late deciders who said they were Democrats, the votes of 3 out of 4 with no party affiliation, and, according to respondents' reports, the votes of about 3 out of 5 Republican late deciders." [44] The pollers' error was increased still further at this point because in 1948 there was an unusually large proportion of undecided voters. At times, as many as 15 per cent were either "in conflict" or were evasive.

The problem of forecasting elections is always fundamentally complicated by the question of who and how many of the potential voters will actually vote. With 15 per cent of the respondents as nonvoters and undecideds, 85 per cent of the respondents state a preference or tell the interviewer how they are going to vote. But on election day on a national election, from 50 to 60 millions of votes will be cast in the United States, from a potential electorate of 80 to 85 million voters. In 1948 the pollers predicted about 51 million votes, but actually there were 49.4 million votes cast. The prediction by the poller of the composition of that 50 to 65 per cent of the potential electorate who actually do vote introduces a positively staggering possible margin of error in any election. But sometimes the problems are even more complicated than on other elections. For example, consider a single unpredicted complicating factor in 1948. The wives of organized labor had evidenced an apparently profound disinterest in the candidacies of both Truman and Dewey and had declared in larger than usual proportions their intention not to vote. Yet postelection investigations disclosed that they had voted in unprecedented numbers, apparently in response to the urgings of their union-member husbands during the last few weeks before the election. Another factor was the 1.4 per cent of voters who decided, for whatever reasons, not to vote for a presidential candidate, although they voted for candidates for other offices.

In general, the possible sampling errors were apparently not responsible for the major errors in this election. Earlier in this discussion we noted some of the issues involved in the controversy between the ardent proponents of probability, or area, sampling and the generally used quota samples. Probability sampling techniques, assuring greater randomness, might have reduced the error slightly but would have been of little or no value in detecting most of the sources of error noted in our discussion of this election.

It is evident that election forecasts from polls are hazardous, for the factors are numerous and complex. Even when a proper cross-sectional sample is approximately achieved, the exploration of the individual respondent's attitudes and intentions is something less than a science. In 1948 the pollers were somewhat careless and overconfident. Yet, in view

[44] SSRC Report, Bulletin 60, p. 254.

of the difficulties, and with the somewhat less than brilliant record of the pollers in 1948 before us, it still remains one of the astounding achievements of modern social science that the record of the polls is as good as it frequently has been.

The Election of 1952—Voters' Basic Conflicts Frustrate Pollers. The pollers were profoundly shocked and impressed by their errors in 1948. The results of their postelection studies reviewing their procedures, the recommendations of the Social Science Research Council Committee and others were pondered.[45] Criticisms were seriously examined by the pollers, but even the book-length review of the evidence by the SSRC, entitled *The Pre-Election Polls of 1948,* useful though it was in evaluating errors, offered little in the way of definite and verified or verifiable suggestions for improvement. Especially convincing was the evidence of their errors in judgment (though based on previous experience) in allocating the undecided voters and the failure to anticipate the changes in vote which apparently occurred in the last few weeks before the election. In any case, it seemed evident that more intensive and extended interviewing of subjects was necessary in order more carefully to reveal and assess the potential voters' and nonvoters' attitudes. Thus it should be possible to predict changes with greater accuracy. The methodological problems of recording, analyzing and interpreting these extended interviews in depth was "a puzzlement," to use the words of the musical-comedy King of Siam.

Gallup especially had been heartened by the results of the polls on the 1950 congressional election. He claimed to have achieved a phenomenal prediction accuracy of seven-tenths of one percentage point error under the actual Republican popular vote of 49.7, since he had predicted 49 per cent Republican. He claimed to have checked on last-minute shifts by polling until 3 days before the election, though in 1950 there probably were not many last-minute shifts. The intentions of the undecideds were scrutinized, for, should they become decideds and vote, the pollers needed a basis for allocation of their votes. However, this time, the undecideds, as had usually been the case, probably did not vote. Depth interviewing to attempt to determine who would vote was developed. In 1950 only 41 per cent of the potential voters did vote.[46] In any case, in 1950, without the intrusion of major unusual elements in the election, the pollers' record of prediction was very good.

By 1952, an unusual element had been added. That was the name of General, later President, Eisenhower, a candidate whose appeal rather

[45] See the report of the Iowa Conference on Attitude and Opinion Research, published as *The Polls and Public Opinion* (N. Meier and H. W. Saunders, eds.), Henry Holt and Company, Inc., New York, 1949.

[46] G. Gallup, "The Gallup Poll and the 1950 Election," *Pub. Opin. Quar.,* 15: 1: 16–22.

freely crossed party lines and group interests. The pollers approached the 1952 campaign using somewhat more varied methods than they previously had used. Gallup used quota samples, as usual, but added to these some probability samples, though I believe that he did not incorporate the results of the probability samples in his final figures. He investigated responses to issues more intensively than ever before. Crossley used small probability samples, but in the end this did not eliminate the major errors. Fink, of the United States poll, used street-corner polling, did not allow for the undecideds, but, even so, underestimated the Eisenhower strength by 4.3 percentage points. Roper used quota and probability samples of about 5,000, cumulating to 15,000 in several surveys, but his contribution in this election was to explore more thoroughly than any other poller, the composition of the voters' attitudes. This intensive exploration was to provide the basis for predicting voters' intentions, the certainty and consistency of intentions, and possible late changes of the undecideds. The trouble for the poller here proved to be that he found at least 30 per cent of the voters in basic confusion. How should a poller predict, when he found large numbers of respondents who would answer questions on issues and policies in a way which would logically indicate a Stevenson vote and then would state Eisenhower as their choice of candidate?

In 1952 the polls said that Dwight Eisenhower would win, but that the election would be very close. Actually, Eisenhower received 442 electoral votes and the greatest popular vote ever accorded a United States presidential candidate. It was a Republican victory, but a sweeping victory for President Eisenhower, who ran well ahead of his party ticket in most states. Angus Campbell, directing a nonpartisan postelection survey for the Survey Research Center, noted:

> After the election, there was a widespread attempt to attribute the cause of the Republican victory to some particular group of voters—new voters, women, defecting trade unionists, farmers. But the survey's data seem to indicate that it was not a shift in any one group, but a general shift pulling many different segments of the population—young voters, white collar people, people living in rural areas—into the Republican column that caused the outcome.

Apparently voters were motivated by profoundly felt sentiments for the man Eisenhower and by the belief that he would handle Korea and the cold war better than Stevenson and the Democratic party could do. The pollers underestimated the emotional force and the dimensions of this drive.

In their latest public reports in 1952 the pollers still found large numbers of undecided voters; Gallup, 13.0 per cent, Crossley, 9.9, and Roper, 14 per cent. It was later charged that these voters were not undecided in the polling booths and very probably were more noncommittal than undecided before the election. While it is true that some people refuse to reveal their political preferences, this group has not been sufficiently large to invalidate polling. In 1952 the professional commercial pollers were extremely cautious and noncommittal as to the eventual decisions of the undecideds. As well they might be, in view of the errors of 1948. Yet, had they allocated the undecided as they did in 1948 and earlier, the pollers would have produced a very accurate prediction of the popular vote in 1952. Joseph E. Bachelder, director of polling for the Republican party in 1952, wrote after the election:

In 1948 they had practically eliminated the undecided voter by allocating the Undecideds in proportion to the Decideds. They had been told, following 1948, that this was a great error and they should use some other system. It is interesting to see what the figures would have been if they had used their 1948 system of allocation in 1952 (data for the U.S. Poll are not given as it was not in operation in 1948):

	Eisenhower	Stevenson
Crossley	52.8	47.8
Gallup	54.0	46.0
Roper	56.9	43.1

It appears from these figures that the suggestions for allocating the Undecideds produced a worse estimate of the popular vote than the earlier systems.[47]

Indeed, as Eisenhower received 55.1 per cent and Stevenson 44.5 per cent of the popular vote, the predictions would then have been very accurate. But the pollers were frustrated by inconsistencies in the responses of those interviewed.

A person who was a member of a labor union, with an income under $4,000, who thought the Democrats were best for the working people, who could not find much to criticize about the last four years of the Truman administration, but who said he was going to vote for Eisenhower was the type which Roper called a person in basic conflict.[48]

There were many such in 1952. Postelection studies have indicated many splits of interest-groups. People of low incomes and labor-union members were much less Democratic than they had been in years, not as either low-income people or labor-union members, but as individuals, profoundly disturbed and fearful of world events.

Another error of the pollers in this national election was in their underestimate of the number of voters. Preelection estimates of 53 to 55 million

[47] J. E. Bachelder, "The Public Opinion Polls and the 1952 Election," *Ill. Bus. Rev.*, Dec., 1952, p. 8.
[48] Bachelder, *op. cit.*, p. 9.

voters proved far too low, in view of the unprecedented 61 million votes cast. Moreover, of these, some 12 million were new voters, a group always difficult to forecast.

The pollers, in 1952, did not assess properly an electorate, not primarily concerned with ideological consistency or immediate self-interest or group-interest, but powerfully drawn to a dramatic popular leader in whom they evidenced great confidence.[49] The enemies of polling were gleeful at this second instance of major error in a national election. But, in spite of these errors in prediction, there is no system of assessing public opinion that has a record of greater accuracy than the polls. Is it not phenomenal that with a sample of a few thousand the behavior of scores of millions of voters is forecast as accurately as has been the case? And the pollers' methods were greatly improved by the experience of the elections of 1948 and 1952, each of which had many special and unprecedented features.

SOCIAL AND POLITICAL IMPLICATIONS OF POLLING

Political theorists, congressional investigating committees, social scientists or romantically inclined academicians object to widespread use of public opinion polls for quite different reasons. They are variously concerned with objections to the emphasis on public opinion for pressure on executive and legislative decisions, with the implications for political parties of candidate and election-poll predictions, with the methodological techniques of the polls, or with the desire for vague, unfathomable public mind-life in preference to attempted exactitudes. The partial failures of the pollers on some election predictions have elated political theorists who really disapproved of the polls on grounds other than their accuracy,[50] aroused partisan politicians who were fearful of the polls' influence on votes,[51] given some social scientists an opportunity to criticize polling methods,[52] and delighted many aesthetes, comedians and competing prophets. And many vaguely resent the public opinion polls as another threat to privacy in an age in which privacy is already grievously assaulted. The polls are a controversial topic. However, viewed in so far as possible without violent partisanship, what are some of the social and political implications of polls and polling?

(1) What is and what should be the role of the opinions of members of large publics on public affairs? The pollers report on hundreds of

---

[49] See H. H. Hyman and P. B. Sheatsley, "The Political Appeal of President Eisenhower," *Pub. Opin. Quar.*, 17: 443–460.

[50] L. Rogers, *The Pollsters*, Alfred A. Knopf, Inc., New York, 1949.

[51] Committee to Investigate Campaign Expenditures, 1944, *op. cit.*

[52] R. Likert, "Why Opinion Polls Were So Wrong," *U.S. News*, Nov. 12, 1948, p. 25.

issues each year; on some of these fairly widespread matured opinions may exist, but on others there are but the most transient, popular impressions and sentiments. Is this public reporting of the very large number of polls in the public interest? (2) Do the polls perform a public service in displaying areas of public ignorance which they have so extensively exhibited? (3) Do the polls tend to distort and degenerate the quality of the decisions of legislative representatives and administrative leaders? (4) Has polling tended to check the otherwise largely unchecked and unquestioned claims of representatives of interest- and pressure-groups in the United States? (5) Do polls stimulate reflective thinking about public issues in the United States, or do they increase adherence to majority positions, that is, do they produce the band-wagon effect? (6) Do the commercial pollers properly warn their publics as to the quality, as well as the quantity, of the opinions of respondents? (7) Is there danger of corruption of the polling process and, therefore, the need to regulate polling by public regulation or by some kind of extralegal codes? These are among the crucial questions concerning the significance of this new type of news reporting.

It is often maintained that a natural occupational distortion of the pollers is the overestimation of the importance and significance of public opinion. It is true that Dr. George Gallup, especially, has been overly emphatic on the significance of the polls in implementing Lord Bryce's assertion of the importance in a democracy of ascertaining the will of the majority of the citizens at all times. The critics declare that the pollers have a fundamental misconception of the nature of democracy. It is said that though the United States is a republic with representative assemblies, the pollers appear to use the premise that we should have direct popular democracy on a national scale. Lindsay Rogers writes: "One reason, I suggest, is that they purposely misconceive the nature of the governmental arrangements under which we live. Dr. Gallup wishes his polls to enable the United States to become a mammoth town meeting in which yeses and noes will suffice. He assumes that this can happen and that it will be desirable. Fortunately both assumptions are wrong." [53] The critics of polling have fought a straw man in their attack on the pollers' political philosophy. Though the pollers have sometimes overestimated the importance of public opinion, I see no evidence of their revolutionary zeal to advocate extension of popular democracy. Gallup recognizes the limitations of the general public opinion in making sound decisions on methods and procedures of administration and legislation, though he properly asserts the usual soundness of public opinion in determining

[53] Rogers, *op. cit.*, p. 65. The thesis of Rogers' entire volume is the political naïveté of the pollers in their failure to recognize that popular democracy must be kept within strict limits.

the ends and objectives of political action. As to limitations, he states, "The public cannot be expected to render sound judgments on problems or issues about which they are ill informed. Nor, for the same reason, can they be expected to have intelligent views regarding matters of a wholly technical nature." [54] However, the pollers are guilty and should be severely castigated for overemphasizing the significance, without differentiation, of public opinion on hundreds of issues on which no really significant opinion exists. Polling as a form of journalism must maintain a steady flow of reports. Hence, the polls report on numerous issues on which the most limited, uninformed popular impressions exist at the time of the poll. The pollers largely fail to assess the quality, as well as the quantity, of public opinion.

The numerous polls of the larger public's knowledge of facts and information significant for decision on public issues have revealed astounding areas of ignorance. Elmo Roper notes that "We discovered, perhaps most usefully of all, the overwhelming importance of areas of ignorance that blanket a great section of the population. We learned to discover who has what misinformation and misconceptions concerning various aspects of public life." [55] Certainly, the more informed intellectual rears back in wide-eyed amazement when he learns from national polls that:

Only 55 per cent could correctly state how many Senators there are in Washington from each state.

Only 12 per cent had read a party platform.

Only 14 per cent could even approximately locate Singapore, 26 per cent Java, 36 per cent The Hague, etc., etc.

After the Atlantic Charter had been discussed for some time, only 40 per cent had ever heard of it and 95 per cent could not name a single one of its provisions.

A systematic examination of the compilations of the polls would multiply these instances of ignorance hundreds of times. The pollers regularly reiterate that we overestimate the knowledge and information of the average citizen. Educators, politicians and mass media creators might profitably scrutinize the polls to learn the areas of popular misinformation and ignorance as a basis for their educational programs, and also as a guide in evaluating the significance of majority popular opinions. Although frequently that majority, though uninformed, may state the correct conclusions on the larger issues. "Surprisingly few persons are completely informed on even a single issue and not until the millennium is reached will every voter be well informed on every matter of public importance. In a democracy such as ours the incontrovertible fact remains

[54] Gallup, *A Guide to Public Opinion Polls*, p. 7.
[55] E. Roper, *Fortune*, July, 1954, p. 263.

that the majority of citizens usually registers sound judgment on issues, even though a good many are ignorant and uninformed." [56] This is true because the voters in expressing the significant sentiments usually judge the essence of issues correctly, while experts, special groups and classes may be perverted more often by their special interests. In any case, the pollers' portrayal of popular ignorance on the details of public affairs has been extensive, though not systematic. This reporting is one of the most valuable results of the polls.

Those who deplore any trends toward an increase of direct democracy are fearful of the influence of polls on legislators and administrators. Fear is expressed that the polls tend to decrease independent leadership and courage. It is thought that representatives wishing to remain representatives after the next election will attend too closely to the reported popular opinions. This view appears to assume that administrators and representatives need to be lured into a high quality of statesmanship by being kept in ignorance of prevailing opinion. In the modern world of mass communications and of numerous analysts of the public mind, in addition to the pollers, one can hardly anticipate that the representative could be kept in pristine ignorance of the views of his constituency and of the larger public. The absence of polls would not keep a representative from attempting to assess public opinion. And, indeed, "Throughout history the most effective leaders have been those who have had a keen understanding of the public—leaders who have known the views and prejudices of their followers, their lack of knowledge and misinformation, their hopes and aspirations." [57] If the polls are more accurate than other sources of reporting on opinion, they should be required reading for men in public life. Great leaders will seek information about public opinion from all supposedly reliable sources and will then take calculated risks in their own political lives. At times, such leaders will attempt to change popular opinions which they consider erroneous. In the past, the less noble, routine politicians have seldom been made to function in the long-range public interest by failure to be informed about current public opinion. Indeed, both political types would behave more realistically with accurate information. To be sure, we do not know the present effects of the polls on legislative and administrative decisions, though I would assume considerable influence. [58] In any case, the poller is not the villain in this drama.

[56] Gallup, *A Guide to Public Opinion Polls*, p. 85.
[57] *Ibid.*, p. 8.
[58] G. F. Lewis, "The Congressmen Look at the Polls," *Pub. Opin. Quar.*, 4: 229–231; L. E. Gleeck, "96 Congressmen Make Up Their Minds," *Pub. Opin. Quar.*, 4: 3–24; M. Kriesberg, "What Congressmen and Administrators Think of the Polls," *Pub. Opin. Quar.*, 9: 333–337; W. Allard, "Congressional Attitudes Toward Public Opinion Polls," *Jour. Quar.*, 18: 1: 48–52.

The polls have given considerable insight into the variations in opinion in various groups and strata of the public, such as age categories, sex groups, area and regional groups, rural and urban publics, ethnic and political groups and a number of other classifications. Polls can find out quickly the views of a representative sample of any group in the population. In so doing, they have sometimes provided the legislator, or more often the administrator, with information to counter the claims of representatives of pressure groups. "Pressure groups have grown to their present powerful position in government because no organization or method existed to deflate their claims. When spokesmen talked about swinging millions of votes for or against a measure, the legislator had no effective way of countering these claims. . . . Polls can thus limit the claims of pressure groups to the facts, and thus prevent many insupportable demands for special privilege." [59] The polls could provide a desirable check on special-interest claims, though perhaps as yet they have not done so to the extent claimed by the oversanguine Dr. Gallup.

Often the polls greatly oversimplify complicated issues and provide gross alternatives to be selected. However, this oversimplification also characterizes the mind-life of by far the majority of those polled. Therefore, the polls do not bear any crucial responsibility for simplifying the thinking of the public. And, although the polls may guide the attention of some of their readers to the consideration of issues which are reported in polls, it is unlikely that profound reflective thought about issues is much increased. The reporting of the results of polls may influence opinions of readers at times, especially on topics on which the poll readers do not have deep-seated and well-crystallized attitudes.[60] That the polls are responsible for band-wagon effects on elections has been debated since the beginning of the widely publicized polls. The pollers have regularly disclaimed any discernible tendency for voters to swing to the winning side as reported by the polls. It has been maintained that the election of 1948 shattered any charges of band-wagon effect, but, of course, the failure in pollers' predictions does not disprove the possibility of such effect. I think it is probable that the band-wagon effect may be slight on elections, but could be responsible for considerable shift in opinion on some other types of issues, especially the issues on which the poll reader has little knowledge or emotional bias.

Are pollers reasonably competent and reasonably honest and ethical? The question of competence has been explored in our discussion of poll-

[59] Gallup, *A Guide to Public Opinion Polls,* p. 5.

[60] In 1945, some 81.2 per cent of social scientists and 72.5 per cent of journalists consulted stated that in their opinion public opinion polls had some influence on opinion. See L. Radvanyi, *Public Opinion Measurement,* Instituto científico de la opinión pública mexicana, Mexico, 1945, p. 13.

ing procedures. I believe that the principal commercial and academic pollers have been generally honest and ethical during the first twenty years of polling. But polling organizations are increasing rapidly and will be widely different in professional competence, as well as in ownership and control. The question of honesty in polling and in analysis and selection of results for public exhibition has been increasingly at issue.[61] It is difficult to provide adequate and effective social control of the opinion survey agencies by either voluntary trade association agreements or by legal regulation.

[61] This is a part of the larger issue of ethical standards for social science research in general. See R. B. Cattell, "Ethics and the Social Sciences," *Am. Psychol.*, 3: 193–198, 1948. Licensing of pollers was first proposed in 1945 by Edward Bernays. See "Attitude Polls—Servants or Masters," *Pub. Opin. Quar.*, 9: 264–268. The American Association for Public Opinion Research has not succeeded in establishing adequate standards, commonly agreed upon by the members and enforced by workable penalties. It has been proposed that a federal law be passed providing for the issuance of federal licenses to organizations engaging in interstate polling activities. See R. C. Myers, "Social Control of Opinion Survey Agencies," *Am. Psychol.*, 4: 18–20, and A. M. Lee, "Implementation of Opinion Survey Standards," *Pub. Opin. Quar.*, 13: 645–652.

PART FOUR

Opinion Change

CHAPTER 12

Censorship

Why should freedom of speech and freedom of the press be allowed?
Why should a government which is doing what it believes to be right allow
itself to be criticized? It would not allow opposition by lethal weapons.
Ideas are much more fatal things than guns. Why should any man be
allowed to buy a printing press and disseminate pernicious opinions calculated to embarrass the government?

NIKOLAI LENIN

The excesses of an unbridled intellect, which unfailingly end in the
oppression of the untutored multitude, are no less rightly controlled by the
authority of the law than the injuries inflicted violently upon the weak.

POPE LEO XIII

Though I disagree with every word you say I will defend with my life
your right to say it.

VOLTAIRE

I have sworn upon the altar of the living God eternal hostility against
every form of tyranny over the mind of man.

THOMAS JEFFERSON

Faith must be persuaded to men, and not imposed upon them.

ST. BERNARD

Yet it would be better that they were coerced by the sword of that
magistrate that beareth not the sword in vain than that they should be
suffered to bring many others into their own error.

ST. BERNARD

Not only the churchmen, the democrat and the Communist quoted above
but innumerable men of good will during the past several centuries have
found themselves torn between a liberal disposition and the urgency of
propagandizing a special cause. In the art of persuasion it is especially
difficult to realize that the end does not justify the sacrifice of an ab-

stractly liberal stand. Yet freedom from censorship has become increasingly important during the past two centuries as the agencies of mass communication have increased and diffused. The struggle for the control of these media assumed epic proportions. In heroic deeds and nobly liberal utterances, outstanding leaders of the eighteenth and nineteenth centuries defied authoritarian restriction. Twentieth-century pronouncements have been less heroic but have evidenced in greater degree an awareness of the complexity of the concept of freedom, the variety of types of restraint and censorship, and the difficulties of the defense of freedoms. Today a liberal, freedom-granting, democratic way of life stands in stark contrast to a now widely diffused authoritarian, censoring, propagandizing rule.

We cannot proceed to a discussion of the conflict between censorship and freedom of communication until we have briefly traced the rise of the ideas of liberty, freedom and liberalism in modern thought. One essential idea of that concept which, since the eighteenth century, has been designated as "liberalism" is the free play of intelligence out of which man may by rational consent subscribe to the organization and institutions of society. The idea had appeared in the ancient philosophies, but it was not until the excessive autocracies of the seventeenth century had awakened in many groups a popular demand for liberty that the social philosophy of liberalism emerged. Laski relates its appearance to the overthrow of the medieval papacy and the resulting widespread spirit of inquiry; to the development of a secular temper replacing spiritual with social values; to the widening of the physical world by geographic discovery and the accompanying enlarged data on primitive cultures; to the growth of scientific knowledge which challenged the accepted religious verities; to the accompanying philosophical systems which incorporated the experimental method.[1] In the field of political and economic power a large middle class was arising, increasingly cramped by the authoritarian concepts of church and state. Economic facts and theories, social relations, religious and political beliefs, were in rapid transition. Leaders of thought with new frameworks of definitions, philosophies and ideologies were awaited. The essential concepts came from England, where peaceful conditions and political history were more favorable to the development of liberal philosophy than in the war-torn and centralized states of the Continent. Locke (1632–1704) pronounced the basis of government to be in the consent of the people. Political organization existed for the individual good. Man has natural rights to life, liberty and property. The social contract of free men provides the area within which political institutions may operate. Moreover, theocratic government can

---

[1] H. J. Laski, "The Rise of Liberalism," *Ency. Soc. Sci.*, 1: 104–106.

claim no political validity. Reason was enthroned as innately characteristic of man. Locke's liberalism also defended the individual's right to property, safe from the confiscatory aggressions of the state.[2] His influence was enormous. The liberal temper of Locke's generation was canalized by his concepts. He became the "gospel of the Protestants," the progenitor of Rousseau and, in his insistence on the consent of the governed, was significant in the American and French revolutions.

This early liberalism, preoccupied essentially with political processes, was modified by the course of the economic history of the eighteenth century to relate primarily to freedom in production and exchange. Industrial and commercial expansion centered attention upon the role of the state in these fields. In England, Adam Smith (1723–1790) pronounced the economic activities of man an outgrowth of natural law, and state interference an invasion of individual liberty. In France, the Physiocrats, surveying an agrarian society, likewise protested governmental interference. The economists propounded a laissez-faire liberalism. Jeremy Bentham (1748–1832) denounced the existing legal restrictions upon industrial expansion as an unwarranted interference with individual happiness and the sum of happiness to be enjoyed by the greatest possible number. A growing and powerful class of industrial leaders espoused this economic liberalism which coincided with their interests. For these conservative liberals, liberty meant essentially the right of those who own property to control it.

In the nineteenth century, Kant stated the liberal ideal in that the individual emerged as the central subject of inquiry. Kant's central postulate was that the individual was unique and precious and should be free from the absolute authority of government. The philosophical core of liberalism became the doctrine of individualism. It was maintained that the individual should be free from interference of any kind in his religious life, in the expression of his opinions and in his economic activity. However, as applied in the economic field such liberalism led increasingly to widespread misery. The economic disadvantage of increasing numbers in the population became apparent. During the nineteenth century, the humanitarians, religionists and romanticists modified laissez-faire liberalism by advocating state interference through welfare legislation in the interest of the dispossessed, the exploited and the depressed workers. Liberalism was given a new definition. By the mid-twentieth century, a liberal could be defined as one who believed in "utilizing the full force of government for the advancement of social, political and economic justice at the municipal, state, national and international levels." Although modern liberals are in general committed to state interference in the

[2] J. Dewey, *Liberalism and Social Action*, G. P. Putnam's Sons, New York, 1935, pp. 6 ff.

interests of individual liberty, they rarely agree on the extent of state activity. Though the conceptions of liberalism had been completely reversed on the issue of economic controls, the various definitions of liberalism of the past two centuries have in common the vigorous promulgation of freedom elsewhere, especially freedom from restraints on the mind-life. An emphasis on freedom of opinion, necessitating the protection of civil liberties and freedom of the press and other communications, is a common core of liberal doctrines.

The development of various types of modern liberalism has given rise to the extended philosophic discussion of the nature of individual freedom and liberty and of authority and restraint. Under early Christianity the disinherited were appealed to in terms of the dignity of the individual personality and that person's right to religious freedom. But the development of the organized church provided for many centuries an institutional rather than an individual concept of liberty. Liberty was interpreted as freedom of the church institution from state control.[3] After the Reformation, from the sixteenth century onward, the various aspects of individual liberty became a preoccupation of the theorist. By the eighteenth century, freedom and liberty conceived as "natural rights" had become emotionally charged words to arouse masses of revolutionaries, and in the nineteenth century, they were applied to ever-increasing fields of human relationships. "Freedom is a new religion, the religion of our time," said Heine, and Byron wrote, "I desire men to be free as much from mobs as kings, from you as me."

The terms liberty and freedom may be used synonymously. It is apparent from the foregoing discussion that liberty and freedom have been variously conceived at different times during the past four centuries. Liberty in the abstract is of concern only to the metaphysician; but for liberty in the realm of politics, religion, the other institutional structures, and the media of communication, speech and the press, large groups of men have been willing to sacrifice and to fight. But the particular content of liberty will always be changing with the conditions of time and place. The sphere of action in which freedom is demanded will depend upon the area of behavior in which men feel momentarily most fettered. Cooley has noted, "Every person at every stage of his growth is free or unfree in proportion as he does or does not find himself in the midst of conditions conducive to full and harmonious personal development."[4] Negative freedom is the absence of external constraint or restraint; positive freedom is the presence of the necessary conditions for attaining the ends desired. Justice Holmes' remark that "the necessitous man is not free" is

---

[3] H. J. Laski, "Liberty," *Ency. Soc. Sci.*, 9: 444.

[4] C. H. Cooley, *Human Nature and the Social Order*, Charles Scribner's Sons, New York, 1902, p. 424.

often quoted. Thwarted at various points, masses of men have redefined freedom and partially achieved it, often by means of violence. The history of liberty is the record of changing objectives. Once achieved, a particular form of liberty may then be partly restricted by laws, by judicial procedure, by the encroachments of administrative authority and by popular apathy. It has often been noted that freedom degenerates unless it has to struggle in its own defense.

In the modern authoritarian states, political freedom has been sacrificed in part in the hope of enhanced economic security. It is said in defense of the Fascist state that the people are "enjoying the liberty of feeling themselves members, part and parcel, of a powerful, organic state, which is ruled for the welfare of everybody and not in the interests of a chosen few, a state which has social justice within and international prestige without its borders." [5] Alberto Martín Artajo, the Spanish foreign minister, has stated in a speech:

There are certain substantive freedoms derived from natural law—man's freedom to worship his God, to found a home, to educate his children, to work, and to act with self-respect and independence. These freedoms (in Spain) once succumbed to the action of license, as a result of the excess of other freedoms, like freedom of the press, of party, of trade unions, of strikes, which are not of the same nature and degree, because they are, so to speak, secondary freedoms, "adjective" freedoms, of a lower order. That is why the (Franco) regime has in some way repressed these other political freedoms, which, because they are secondary, must be the safeguard of the previous ones.

Likewise, Russian Communist ideologists maintain that governmental control of the press is freedom of the press. Such a conception is entirely alien to the tradition of political liberty as freedom of thought and expression, of education, of worship, of work, of association and assembly, and of the right to change the party in power by means of elections. Although freedom may have many aspects, showing first one facet and then another, such authoritarian organization violates its very essence.

Freedom is a conception which grants dignity and assumed maturity to the individual in society. The application of such a conception is possible only where men have common culture involving a strong sense of obligation to one another and to society based on common ethical beliefs. Burke wrote that the less discipline there is from within, the more need for coercion from without. Emphasis on freedom is the matured product of the culture which believes in and cultivates intellectual pursuits and inquiry and therefore tolerates diversity. When unsure and insecure, a man's worst difficulties may begin when he is able to do as he likes. During the first half of the twentieth century, in the Western nations,

[5] M. A. Pei, "Freedom under Fascism," *Ann. Am. Acad. Pol. Soc. Sci.*, 180: 13.

there occurred a considerable corrosion of the fundamental attitudes of masses of people which had bulwarked the defense of freedom and liberty. Many sought surcease from insecurity by willing surrender of liberties to authority, and others fearfully engaged in surveillance of thoughts alien to mass majority thought. Erich Fromm has emphasized that while the structure and functioning of modern society has made man more independent, critical and free from some of the restraints of the regulations of the in-group, it has also made him more isolated, alone and afraid.[6] Mass fears have often seriously decreased liberty and freedom. Today freedom is once again in jeopardy.

The achievement of liberty in any field is dependent upon freedom of thought and discussion. Freedom of assembly, speech, writing and all the forms of communication underlie individual liberty. Censorship is the restriction of the content of any means of communication. Such restriction defends some special interest usually incapable of defending itself under free discussion. Freedom of expression is never completely won. The beginnings of general public discussion in the Reformation were not immediately followed by the development of a principle of free discussion. The early Protestant church leaders eagerly censored their opponents when the opportunity to do so was presented. The passion for freedom of thought and discussion increased through the sixteenth and seventeenth centuries, being gradually extended among the theologians, philosophers, literary leaders, artists and scientists. With the coming of the eighteenth century, the principle of free discussion permeated the upper and middle classes, although it was by no means universally accepted. The French and American revolutions idealized freedom in general, freedom for all, especially in the realm of communications and speech. In the nineteenth century Hegel described history as "Nothing else than the progress of the consciousness of freedom." But along with this powerful current of advocacy of free thought and free expression there were and are many forms of censorship, both informal and formal. There are the projections of popular prejudices and mass standards, the informal censorship of those who control press, radio and motion pictures, and the organized censorship of church and state, legally imposed. The battle has been fought successively about each of the forms of communication from speech to the latest outbursts of popular censorship of motion pictures, comics and pocket books. To the nature of censorship, its forms, its history, its advocates and its applications we will now turn our attention.

Censorship is the process of restraint on freedom of thought and communication imposed by the minds of individuals, by climates of opinion

[6] E. Fromm, *Escape from Freedom*, Rinehart & Company, Inc., New York, 1941.

or by the process of deleting or limiting the content of any of the media of communication. Although the process has become more organized and consciously applied during the past four centuries, it has existed as an informal control in all societies. The term "censorship" comes from the Romans. In the fifth century B.C. the Roman Senate appointed two magistrates called "censors." Among the duties of the censors were the recording of a census of persons and the overseeing of their morals and manners, clothing, food and public and private behavior. The censors could, within limits, set standards in these fields and enforce their decrees by fines and other punishments. Modern censorship is preoccupied with the regulation of the transfer of ideas. This censorship policy arose with the popularization of the means of communication, especially the development of printing in the fifteenth century. Established power then faced new problems and sought protection by attempting to limit the spread of ideas. Authority, desiring unanimity of thought as well as of action within the province of its special interests, limits the "bad" ideas, apparently believing with Pope that—

> Vice is a monster of so frightful mien
> As to be hated needs but to be seen;
> Yet seen too oft, familiar with her face,
> We first endure, then pity, then embrace.

Unfettered authority perennially tends toward restriction on communication through censorship. In China—

In 1725 a special clause was added to the Code of the Manchu dynasty in which obscene fiction was again forbidden, very heavy penalties being incurred by those, whether author, publisher or bookseller, who infringed the clause. Officials were to be degraded, military men to receive a hundred lashes of the bastinado and be banished three thousand leagues. Booksellers were to receive a hundred lashes and be exiled for three years. People merely caught buying or reading such works were to receive a hundred lashes without exile.[7]

Two centuries later, Communist Russia, after a very brief period of freedom for literature, art and communications in general, turned quickly to a rigorous censorship. Lenin had maintained that the arts and communications should relieve, restore and relax the mind after the day's work. He ordered the state publishing houses to issue cheap editions of the classics and get them into the hands of as many people as possible. It was felt in those early years of the Soviet Union that literature and the arts needed no censorship. It was maintained that the climate of opinion would govern popular selections and communication habits. However,

[7] A. Waley in Introduction to *Chin P'ing Mei*, G. P. Putnam's Sons, New York, 1940, vol. I, p. xvii.

after Lenin's death this view was soon discarded. Literature, arts and sciences became part of the conflict of views between warring factions. Free production and communications were challenged by proponents of rigid party control and censorship of communications. The new young men became insistent that the content of all communications must follow the party line.[8] This view was quickly victorious and the effete liberties of communication of "decadent bourgeois culture" were largely eliminated. Latterly, even parts of the writings of Karl Marx are censored in Russia. During the 1940's and 1950's, the period of nationalist expansion, Soviet Russia did everything in its power to prevent Communists everywhere from obtaining copies of the writings of Karl Marx and Friedrich Engels on the Russian Menace to Europe. And so, from the first regulation of communications to the latest regulation by an authoritarian state, there are centuries of intermittent but often intensive censorship.

Authority assumes the correctness of its position. As John Fiske declared, "The persecuting spirit has its origin morally in the disposition of man to domineer over his fellow creatures, intellectually, in the assumption that one's own opinions are infallibly correct." The avowed objectives of censorship are the protection of incapable and incompetent groups from the harmful stimulus. The church members, the citizens, the newspaper readers, the females, the immature youth, the alien and other groups should, according to authority, be shielded from the sacrilegious, the seditious, the immoral or the unaesthetic. Authority propounds the political, the economic or the ethical equivalent of the theological notion of the weakness and depravity of man from which he must be saved by stern ordering and forbidding.

Assumptions of infallibility in the institutional definitions of church and state provided the defense of early censorship. In all institutional censorship it will be maintained at some point that the institution is in clear and present danger and that restrictions are necessary. "We are a Christian people," once declared our Supreme Court, "but we are also a nation with a duty to survive." Classic liberalism, in opposition to assumptions of infallibility, took its stand against censorship and defined freedom as "freedom from" these restrictions. The concept of "freedom for" individual and group development did not develop until the nineteenth century. Such freedom may require restriction in the individual or group interest. Defense of censorship on that basis has not yet been definitively stated by English and American scholars.

The classical defense of liberty and of freedom from censorship has had ardent and eloquent spokesmen during the past four centuries. John

[8] For an extended and incisive discussion, see H. M. Kallen, *Art and Freedom*, Duell, Sloan & Pearce–Little, Brown, New York, 1942, vols. I and II.

Milton in *Areopagitica* (1644) wrote: "Give me the liberty to know, to utter, and to argue freely according to conscience, above all liberties." Thomas Jefferson, in his first inaugural address, said, "If there be any among us who wish to dissolve this union, or change its republican form, let them stand undisturbed, as monuments of the safety with which error of opinion may be tolerated where reason is left free to combat it." And John Stuart Mill, in a spirited defense of the liberties of the individual, stated, "If all mankind minus one were of one opinion, and only one person were of the contrary opinion, mankind would be no more justified in silencing that one person than he, if he had the power, would be justified in silencing mankind." Yet withal, the corrosion of the ideal position that occurs when one has authority or has espoused a cause is logically astonishing. Perhaps no man of his generation was more devoted theoretically to the maintenance of the individual's freedom than the late Harold Laski. Yet after a lifetime of verbal and literary defense of freedom, in his latter days, as ideologist of the Labour party and enamored of the inevitability of the planned socialist society, he wrote, "The acceptance of a planned economy involved the necessity to think of freedom in terms of the assumption that the decision to plan is broadly respected. Freedom will not be maintained if there is room for doubt whether the decision to plan as an essential element of its life is likely to be reversed by some chance hazard of electoral fortunes." Apologists for ideologies are almost invariably drawn to the defense by censorship of the ideology's fundamental premises.

My conceptualization of the censorship process may be pictured best by the pyramidal chart labeled *Levels of Censorship in the United States*. The profound basic censorship process occurs in the individual mind-life. Censorship of communication and also of mental content is applied in the individual's mental processes. Of late years this has been described in psychologically sophisticated terms, especially by the psychoanalyst. Freud developed the idea of a censorship of thought whereby the dominant consciousness limited the admission of certain materials to conscious attention. In individual development, standards and values are learned from the general culture and also developed in ways that are individually unique. These standards, existing in the conscious mind, reject alien and dangerous subjects. This process may be so complete that the dominant conscious does not recognize the entrance of these alien words, impressions and ideas. But they exist in the preconscious or unconscious. In psychoanalytic literature, this material is assumed to lie in wait for a favorable opportunity to emerge, usually in symbolical form in slips of the tongue, puns, jokes, humor, mispronunciations, daydreams and dreams. The psychoanalyst sleuths through these symbols. He overemphasizes the frequency and amount of such materials. However, this limitation of the mental life may be verified by introspective analysis. It has never been adequately explained in neurological terms.

In everyday experience such censorship is important. The materials that are contrary to the individual's values may be labeled, whereupon refusal to attend to them is even more simply canalized.

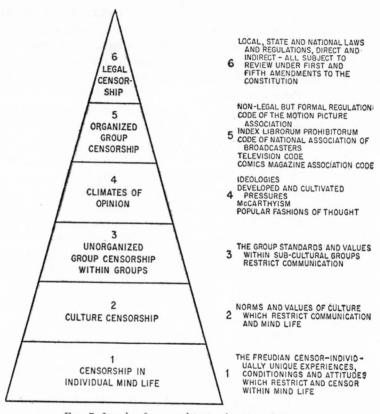

Fig. 5. Levels of censorship in the United States.

Labelling ideas, images and attitudes as evil, as immoral, as unpatriotic, is usually an effective method of stopping the development of such notions and attitudes. All forms of social taboos are designed to do just this. They furnish the individual with guide posts in his associative thinking which keep him within the boundaries set by the moral codes. The ideas, images or attitudes with which the new ideas conflict are sacred. They are right. They are proper. Therefore, persons having the same social and cultural heritage may develop a consensus of opinion that the divergent ideas or attitudes ought to be stopped.[9]

[9] K. Young, *Social Psychology*, Appleton-Century-Crofts, Inc., New York, 1930, p. 636. Quoted by permission.

Informal censorship is applied in the individual mental process, both in the case of restrictions of which he is not conscious and of limitations consciously applied.

The values, standards and ideas that are incorporated in the individual's attitudes are, for the most part, products of the culture in which he is involved. Shifting values determine the objects of censorship. When man's attention is turned to religion, heterodoxy and blasphemy are censored; the state represses treason; an ascendant industrial order attempts to restrict radical utterances; puritanical publics forbid verbalization of sexual processes; the Jones family does not mention the disgraced Uncle John. Folk values are imposed on discourse. V. Randolph writes of the Ozark hillman:

> Sex is rarely mentioned save in ribaldry and is therefore excluded from all polite conversation between men and women. . . . In general it may be said that the names of male animals must not be mentioned when women are present. . . . Such words as bull, boar, buck, ram, jack and stallion are absolutely taboo. . . . The Ozarkers usually say male cow-critter or cow-brute. . . . It was only a few years ago that two women in Scott County, Arkansas, raised a great clamor for the arrest of a man who mentioned a bull-calf in their presence. . . . A preacher recently told his flock that Pharaoh's daughter found the infant Moses in the flags, the poor man didn't like to say bull-rushes.[10]

This informal censorship in the interests of the folk values is pervasive and insidious. It is usually far more effective than the formal censorship of a ruler or hierarchy. Their tyranny is seldom crushingly effective or persistent. But the mores may restrict the area of discussion during long periods.

In addition to the censorship occurring in the individual mind-life and the censorship imposed by the cultural norms and values on communication and mind-life, which I would consider the most basic levels of censorship, there are middle levels of censorship in which unorganized group censorship and climates of opinion operate, and the upper levels of organized group censorship and legal censorship.

The standards, values and group ways of the innumerable groups within American culture restrict communication within these groups. In middle-class American society one does not ordinarily sympathetically discuss the theories of Karl Marx in the meeting of the local Chamber of Commerce, engage in excessive profanity and obscenity before one's grandmother and her associates, or address the Catholic Women's League on birth control. Moreover, it is this great diversity in group standards in American life, where one milieu permits speech, writing or fictional ma-

10 V. Randolph, *The Ozarks*, Vanguard Press, Inc., New York, 1931, p. 78. Quoted by permission.

terials which would be viewed as shocking, salacious or dangerous in another, which results in insoluble controversy over any attempt at over-all censorship standards such as motion-picture censorship.

Climates of opinion and the transient impressions and current ideas of mass majorities are an intermittent censorship threat. Though restricted at the level of formal communications by constitutional guarantees, such pressures are powerful censors of individual expression. Always a potential danger in political democracies, where there is the perennial problem of protecting minorities from majorities, such restrictions are most powerful in moments of fear and real or formulated crisis. In the history of the United States such moments are always exploited by demagogues and interest-groups. Those forces which accentuate the emotional, fearful, vindictive harrying of the deviant at such moments are guilty of the gravest sin against the integrity of political democracy. Thomas Jefferson's dictum that "Error of opinion may be tolerated where reason is left free to combat it" may be vitiated by political and other leaders exploiting the harried anxiety, insecurity and fears of the common man. In the United States in the middle of the twentieth century, the cowing of political and economic unorthodoxy appeared as a result and an objective in a cultivated climate of opinion.

Censorship is a conflict process. Any particular censorship is rapidly incorporated in the emotional responses of the individual combatants. Although ostensibly in the public interest, the actual objectives of the censor are all too often a punitive retribution upon stubborn minorities, and resistance to censorship becomes a holy cause. The tactics frequently become more and more extreme as the conflict progresses, for, as Heywood Broun said of Anthony Comstock, "A man who fights for the safety of his immortal soul can hardly be expected to live up to the best Queensberry traditions in the clinches." [11]

Organized group censorship is below the level of law but consists of the organized, often meticulously formulated, restrictions and regulations applied by organized groups. Illustrations of such censorship would be the four-century-old *Index Librorum Prohibitorum* of the Catholic church, the formulations and applications of the Production Code of the Motion Picture Association of America, or the Code of the National Association of Broadcasters.

THE CHURCH AND CENSORSHIP

Any institutional structure is erected upon certain fundamental premises which must be unquestionably accepted by most of its adherents. Other-

[11] H. Broun and M. Leech, *Anthony Comstock*, Gaer Associates, Inc. (Boni), New York, 1927, p. 265.

wise the institutional form, structure or very existence is threatened. This is obviously true of formal church organizations. Fundamental premises, if undiscussed and undiscussible, may thus be the more impregnably ensconced in an enveloping blanket of silence than behind a barricade of reasons, rationalizations and other argued defenses. In the authoritarian tradition this has usually been thought to be true. The High-churchman censors and is silent, the dictator does not permit comparative discussion, the autocratic boss pocket-vetoes the underling's suggestion without comment. Whereas the insurgent sect, the outsider, the rebel and the liberal desire discussion during the period of their insurgency, perhaps believing with Tertullian that "when a thing is hidden away with so much pains, merely to reveal it is to destroy it."

Many religious groups have attempted informal and formal censorship but the church of Rome in its long experience has instituted the most formal restrictive measures. The *Index Librorum Prohibitorum,* first issued a century after the invention of printing, is a list of books that communicants must not read. Exceptions are readily made in the case of scholars, theologians and other trained students who, in good faith, desire to examine the prohibited works. The local bishop may grant such exceptions.

Although there has been less formal organization of restriction of communication among other religious groups, the spirit of the censor is ever abroad. In America, the Christian Scientists have organized an extensive and sometimes effective censorship. Whenever Protestant groups have developed very extensive organization with central authority, the clamor for censorship has arisen intermittently. A century ago a Protestant writer in England, opposing the rising demand for censorship, declared, "Let Protestants be consistent, let them be Protestants indeed; let them revere in act as well as in word the sufficiency of the Holy Scripture; let there be no Protestant Index of prohibited books; let there be no shackles and cramps for the human mind." [12] Recently a Baptist leader drew loud cheers and applause from his audience by asserting that the Baptists have never persecuted those who differed with them or attempted to limit their freedom of expression. When the cheers had subsided, he drily added that they had never had a chance. Early Protestant churchmen zealously applied themselves to censorship and to the burning of books, although they lacked the system and organization of the Roman Catholic church. Savonarola enveloped Florence in a system of espionage. His child police visited homes, confiscating prohibited books and pictures, as well as personal adornments, which they carried off to the burnings. A few decades later Calvin, with even greater distrust of the capacities of man to resist the snares of the devil, organized in Geneva a rigid discipline by secular

[12] "Index Librorum Prohibitorum," *British Quar.,* 14: 133–156 (1851).

legislation. Catholic books of worship and song were confiscated and burned. Houses and shops were searched for all heretical books. In 1539, the magistrates decreed that all books must be examined and licensed before they could be printed. Considerable organization of censorship developed. Calvin's organization for suppression was carefully studied by representatives from England and Scotland, and similar restrictions were later applied in Great Britain. In the revulsion against Rome, art objects, images, pictures, monuments and books were burned and their production censored.[13] It is difficult today to appreciate the fear and horror of the Roman Catholic church that came to prevail in England and Scotland at that time.

The longest and most consistent record of censorship is that of the Roman Catholic church. "The first formal condemnation of a book, however, was at the Council of Nice in A.D. 325, which condemned Arius and his teachings as expressed in his book, *Thalia.* A decree issued by Gelasius in A.D. 496 and published at a council in Rome has been described as the first Roman Index of Forbidden Books. It is much more than this. Whereas a Roman Index is a list of banned books, the Gelasian Decree is a catalogue of recommended works as well." [14]

In the fifteenth century the invention of printing revolutionized the processes of communication. At first the rulers of the church welcomed printing as a valuable instrument for the spread of sound doctrine and supported a number of the early presses. The use of the presses in the pamphleteering activities of the leaders of the Reformation aroused the churchmen to the potential perils of printing to the authority of the church and the uncorrupted purity of the minds of communicants. If the incapables were to be protected against the new heresies, some system would have to be devised whereby the printing press could be supervised and controlled. Before the end of the fifteenth century, the University of Cologne was examining and censoring every book before printing.[15] Pope Sextus IV congratulated the university. In 1501 Alexander VI extended this practice by forbidding printers, under pain of excommunication, to print any book without permission of their bishops. A decree addressed to the entire world was issued by Leo X at the Fifth Lateran Council of 1515, the first general decree of censorship that was universally accepted. The first *Index Librorum Prohibitorum* was issued by Pius IV in 1559,

[13] C. R. Gillett, *Burned Books,* 2 vols., Columbia University Press, New York, 1932.

[14] Redmond A. Burke, *What Is the Index?,* The Bruce Publishing Company, Milwaukee, 1952, p. 5. This book is a good review and defense of the *Index* by the Director of Libraries of De Paul University.

[15] G. H. Putnam, *The Censorship of the Church of Rome,* 2 vols., G. P. Putnam's Sons, New York, 1906, is the most extensive and available work in English on church censorship; see also A. Bondinhon, "Index," *Ency. Religion and Ethics,* vol. XVII, pp. 207–209.

followed by the new *Index* of 1564, which was the work of the Council of Trent.[16] Its lists of condemned books were divided into three categories: (1) heretical works, (2) works on magic and immorality, (3) books generally unwholesome in doctrine, usually anonymous. In 1571 a Congregation of Cardinals and consultants was established to handle matters of censorship, condemn books and issue the *Index*. In 1917 this Congregation was merged with the Congregation of the Holy Office with the Pope as its chairman.

Preoccupation with the struggle with Protestantism determined the content of the early *Indexes*. Although the editions of the past century have increasingly stressed moral rather than theological problems, and thousands of the earlier prohibited items have been eliminated, it has been estimated that 90 per cent of the condemned works in the 1948 edition deal with theology, dogma, ritual or history of the church. The eleven classes of works on the *Index* are:

1. All books which propound or defend heresy or schism, or which of set purpose attack religion or morality, or endeavour to destroy the foundations of religion or morality.

2. Books which impugn or ridicule Catholic dogma or Catholic worship, the hierarchy, the clerical or religious state, or which tend to undermine ecclesiastical discipline, or which defend errors rejected by the Apostolic See.

3. Books which declare duelling, suicide, divorce lawful, or which represent Freemasonry and similar organizations as useful and not dangerous to the Church and to Civil society.

4. Books which teach or recommend superstition, fortune-telling, sorcery, spiritism, or other like practices (*e.g.*, Christian Science).

5. Books which professedly treat of, narrate, or teach, lewdness and obscenity.

6. Editions of the liturgical books of the Church which do not agree in all details with the authentic editions.

7. Books and booklets which publish new apparitions, revelations, visions, prophecies, miracles, etc., concerning which the canonical regulations have not been observed. (This practically means that such books and booklets are forbidden if they appear without the bishop's approbation. . . . Newspapers, weeklies, etc., are not prevented by this rule from relating uncommon happenings. They should, however, be careful not to make such events appear as undoubtedly supernatural, before the Church has taken a stand.)

8. All editions of the Bible or parts of it, as well as all biblical commentaries, in any language, which do not show the approbation of the bishop or some higher ecclesiastical authority.

9. Translations which retain the objectionable character of the forbidden original.

[16] Burke, *op. cit.*, p. 7.

10. Pictures of Our Lord, the Blessed Virgin, and angels and saints and other servants of God, which deviate from the customs and the directions of the church.

11. The term "books" includes also newspapers and periodicals which come under the foregoing classes, not, indeed, if they publish one or two articles contrary to faith and morals, but if their chief tendency and purpose is to impugn Catholic doctrine or defend unCatholic teachings and practices.[17]

The present *Index* prohibits a total of some 4,126 works. The modern *Index* forbids, in general, the reading of books prejudicial to the faith, and no attempt has been made to examine and list all books that might be condemned. "The *Index* was not intended to be a complete list of condemned books which would be an impossibility in our age of mass production of books. Rather it is an enumeration of all condemned books that have been referred to the Holy See for an official pronouncement. The *Index* also serves as a guide to indicate the types of literature that have been judged injurious enough for universal condemnation." [18] It is notable for its exceptions, as well as being an interesting historical document because of its selections. For example, no American literary writer is included. To judge by the *Index,* Ingersoll, Paine, Walt Whitman and scores of moderns never existed. Nor did Rabelais. A few examples of philosophers and reformers on the *Index* are: Comte, Diderot, Descartes, Grotius, Rousseau, Renan, Savonarola, Taine, Spinoza, Locke, Voltaire and John Stuart Mill. Names in literature, such as Addison, Steele, Goldsmith, D'Annunzio, Flaubert, France, Maeterlinck, Sand, Sue and Zola, are indexed.[19] The service of the *Index* in suppressing or discouraging books *contra bonos mores* has been characterized as unimportant.[20] The *Index* is not intended as a complete bibliography of prohibited books. It provides samples and notorious illustrations of types of condemned writings. The rate of additions to the *Index* is slowing. In the nineteenth century 1,354 books were condemned, but in the first half of the twentieth century only 255.

The *Index,* although variously applied, and with punishments of unequal severity at different times, has been one of the important instruments with which the church has attempted to guide and to restrict access of its members to the various means of communication. Sometimes it has merely advertised the prohibited writings; sometimes it has proved ineffectual in stemming a tide of communication, as in sex expression in literature; but the extent to which it has inhibited the expression of writers and lecturers can never be known. This is especially true

---

[17] Quoted in G. Seldes, *The Vatican,* Harper & Brothers, New York, 1934, p. 168.
[18] Burke, *op. cit.,* p. 38.
[19] See Appendix B in Burke, *op. cit.,* for lists of authors in *Index.*
[20] Putnam, *op. cit.,* p. 33.

of the sixteenth and seventeenth centuries. Today the variety of means of communication outside the authority of the church largely circumvents the effectiveness of an index. In its defense Cardinal Merry del Val wrote in the preface to the 1930 edition:

Hell is now stirring against the Church a more terrible battle than those of earlier centuries . . . for the evil press is a more perilous weapon than the sword. St. Paul, as we know, set the example for censorship, he caused evil books to be burned. St. Peter's successors have always followed the example; nor could they have done otherwise, for their Church, infallible mistress and sure guide of the faithful, is bound in conscience to keep the press pure . . . those who wish to feed the Holy Scriptures to people without any safeguards are also upholders of free thinking, than which there is nothing more absurd or harmful. . . . only those infected by that moral pestilence known as liberalism can see in a check placed on unlawful power and profligacy a wound inflicted on freedom.[21]

CENSORSHIP OF THE MOTION PICTURES

As the organized church, preoccupied with doctrine and faith, sought to censor the heretic, and a threatened state burned the treasonable books and repressed the traitor, so modern democracies turned to the restriction of what the good citizens considered their principal dangers. These were of a personal rather than an institutional character. In America, the confusion resulting from an allegiance to abstract liberty in the political sphere and a widespread desire to censor personal morality has become chronic. Books, plays, pictures, statuary and various art works have from time to time been subjected to the formal and legal, as well as informal, censorship by organized minorities supported by sizable publics. Minorities have frequently demanded increased legal censorship. The larger publics have fluctuated between dislike of the censorship process and an intermittent angry resentment at certain of the products of communication which have come to the local community from the extracommunity world of book publishers, playwrights, artists, radio and television script writers and motion-picture producers.

This confusion is most clearly illustrated in the history of the censorship of motion pictures in the United States. The motion pictures have appealed to the masses of people, children and adults, male and female, the ignorant and the learned. Although the occasional picture has been sophisticated, artistic or seriously propagandistic in the political and economic fields, the content of the vast majority have been largely dramatic action, individual conflict, the purveying of feminine nudity to the provinces, popular musical entertainment and the personal characteristics of

[21] Quoted by Seldes, *op. cit.*, p. 195. Reprinted by permission of Harper & Brothers.

stars. Such a content has from time to time provided a field day for organized censorship groups, recruited from reform organizations, worried parents and religious orders. Such censorship has been primarily concerned with sexual behavior, the nudity of females and certain types of criminal behavior. On these subjects, motion-picture content has been determined by a kind of tentative regulation, advancing and retreating before popular opinion. Every few years since the beginning of the motion picture there have been periods of cleansing induced by the organized attacks of censors. In this process, legal censorship has been of relatively little importance, but informal pressures have been enormously significant. Naturally the widespread motion-picture business has responded very quickly to any popular criticism.

A brief sketch of the periods of agitation for motion-picture censorship would begin with the incident in 1907 when, after the showing of a melodramatic film called "The Great Automobile Robbery" an actual automobile theft occurred which was associated with the picture. Numerous articles on the relation between the pictures and crime appeared, and discussion groups demanded state censorship. In 1908, the mayor closed the motion-picture theaters of New York City. A citizens' committee was formed to inspect films before they were released. This organization, the National Board of Censorship, was supported by the voluntary contributions of various organizations until 1914. It was then decided to accept fees from the motion-picture producers for reviewing the films, and the name was changed to the National Board of Review. It placed at the disposal of women's clubs and other organizations advance information about the pictures and evaluated and classified film content in a weekly bulletin.

In 1915, the way was cleared for legal censorship when the Supreme Court decided that the motion pictures differed from all other forms of communication. The films could be censored in advance of public showing, for they were viewed in this decision not as an art form communicating ideas but as an industry. The products of that industry, like foods or drugs or other products for general consumption, might therefore be inspected before being offered to the public, whereas means of communication such as the press, art forms and drama must, under constitutional amendment, be regulated only by prosecution after violation of the laws. In seven states, New York, Kansas, Maryland, Ohio, Pennsylvania, Virginia and Florida, censorship systems were established within a few years after this decision. But official state-censorship legislation has never been successfully advocated since that time. Although, by 1921, censorship bills had been presented in thirty-six additional states, none of them has ever passed. Strong and well-organized minorities have persistently agitated for municipal, state and national censorship, but majority opinion has apparently been reluctant to permit governmental regulation of this favorite form of commercial recreation. Municipal censorship boards have been created in more than fifty cities since 1915. For the most part these city boards have operated with inconsistent and ill-defined rules, untrained personnel and inadequate budgets. They have been relatively ineffective in achieving any results other than deleting incidental items of obscenity, profanity and nudity.

Agitation for national censorship legislation has welled up from time to time. Certain restrictions already exist under national laws, such as the prohibitions on the transportation of obscene or lascivious books or pictures in interstate commerce. These regulations have sometimes been applied. During the agitation by reformers in 1913 when prize-fight pictures were especially opposed, such films were forbidden interstate transportation. Congress has passed no general censorship legislation, although at three periods there has been extensive agitation for federal laws. From 1913 to 1915 there was a growing resentment among reform organizations, directed at the motion pictures featuring crime, violence and the prize-fight pictures. These groups sponsored the Hughes Bill of 1915, which provided for a federal motion-picture commission of five members who should direct the censoring and licensing of all films before they were admitted to interstate commerce. This bill was debated at some length but finally defeated.

The difficulty of determining satisfactory standards for censorship was rather generally admitted after a few years' experience with such laws. In January, 1925, the National Committee for Better Films stated, "It [censorship] has failed to recognize and dare not recognize, because it is based on the theory that there are final, unchanging, universal standards of good and evil and of good and evil influences, that fundamental in the whole question of the motion picture is a legitimate and inevitable difference of opinion between sections, communities, groups and individuals." Moreover, the limited field of censored topics is quite apparent when one examines the records of state censorship boards. The Division of Motion Pictures of the New York Department of Education (the censorship board in that state) examined 903 feature films and 1,394 shorts during the period Jan. 1, 1932, to Mar. 31, 1933. Of the feature films they passed 61.5 per cent, deleted something from 35.9 per cent and rejected 2.6 per cent. The rejections were almost all foreign films. Of the deletions the general categories were sex (44 per cent), crime (16 per cent), violence (29 per cent), government (5 per cent) and religion (3 per cent). No governmental censorship body in America ever achieved anything other than the deletion of a few items. It could not effectively censor the underlying theme. All such bodies were governed by laws, most sections of which were so general as to leave the standards of censorship in the hands of the board or commission which, in the long run, usually succeeded in pleasing no one.

From 1915 until 1952 the municipal and state censorship laws were upheld by the Supreme Court decision of 1915 which declared that motion-picture exhibition was a "business pure and simple." In early 1951 Catholic groups brought pressure on New York's State Board of Regents to ban Rossellini's "The Miracle" as a sacrilegious film. The ban was applied, and the courts of New York, finding the film "sacrilegious," upheld the censorship. In June, 1952, the Supreme Court reversed the judgment of the courts of New York and the Supreme Court decision of 1915. The Court ruled that the motion picture is entitled to the rights of free speech and free press and that New York could not legally ban "The Miracle" on the sole grounds that it is sacrilegious, and that no United States official is qualified to define what is sacred. Justice Clark, in the Court's unanimous decision wrote, "In seeking to apply the broad and all inclusive definition of sacrilegious given by the New York courts, the censor is set adrift upon a boundless sea amid a myriad of conflicting currents of religious views, with no charts but those provided by the most vocal and powerful orthodoxies. New York cannot vest such unlimited restraining control over motion pictures in a censor." However, Justice Clark drew a sharp distinction between the "sacrilege" ruling and the censorship of motion pictures done "under a clearly drawn statute designed and applied to prevent the showing of obscene films." Moreover, the Court's judgment must not be taken to mean that the First and Fourteenth Amendments sanctioned an "absolute freedom to exhibit every motion picture of every kind at all times and places."

In January, 1954, again by unanimous vote, the Supreme Court decided that the censors of New York had no right to ban the film "La Ronde" (on moral grounds) and the censors of Ohio had no right to ban "M" (as inciting crime). After this series of decisions the boards of censorship still have legal standing, but the Court would appear to be moving toward restraining, if not abolishing, them. Indeed, in the "La Ronde" case, Justice Douglas and Justice Black issued a separate opinion, holding all state film censorship contrary to the First Amendment. In any case, the word "Reversed" has been placed on the 1915 decision, and the motion pictures have moved from the legal status of a commodity to that of a significant agency of communication. The Court declared, "It cannot be doubted that motion pictures are a significant medium for the communication of ideas. They may affect public attitudes and behavior in a variety of ways, ranging from the direct espousal of a political and social doctrine to the subtle shaping of thought which characterizes all artistic expression."

Many types of interest-groups have exerted pressure, often very effective pressure, upon the producers and distributors of motion pictures in the United States. Religious groups, reform organizations, school and youth interest-groups and many others have been active. A few of the more powerful groups are joined together in the Film Estimate Board which classifies films for viewers of various age groups. These powerful groups are: American Association of University Women, American Jewish Committee, American Library Association, Children's Film Library Committee, General Federation of Women's Clubs, Girl Scouts of America, National Congress of Parents and Teachers, National Federation of Music Clubs, Daughters of the American Revolution, Protestant Motion Picture Council, Schools Motion Picture Committee, and the United Church Women. Films are classified as follows: A—Adults. Over 18 years. F—Family. All ages. YP—Young People. Over 12 years. MYP—Mature Young People. CPR—Children's Programs Recommended (8–12 years). CPA—Children's Programs Acceptable (8–12 years).

Widespread popular support has been given to reform and religious groups when, during four periods since 1912, these organizations have exercised a powerful informal censorship of movie themes by agitation and the threat of legislative action. Protests, agitation and discussion resulted in the voluntary deletion of the more objectionable themes by the producers. By 1921 the protests of reform groups, who were this time primarily objecting to the "vamp," had once more become vociferous. The larger motion-picture producers organized the Motion Picture Producers and Distributors of America and, in 1922, elected Mr. Will Hays as the much publicized "movie czar." A lull in hostilities ensued, especially owing to the fact that Mr. Hays appointed a committee composed of most of the prominent opponents of the movies to serve as an advisory board on motion-picture content. Most of these shortly withdrew in disgust at their futility, but in the meantime the producers had voluntarily eliminated most of the objectionable features. Then the reform groups, clamoring for national legislation, supported the Upshaw Bill which provided for a commission of seven members with broad powers to (1) preview and license films, (2) examine and censor scenarios, and (3) supervise production. In 1925 the idea of federal censorship was given the most thorough political and public discussion it has ever received. The bill was defeated. When, in 1934, the church-organized Legion of Decency, claiming 12 million members, was giving the worried producers the worst fright of their harried lives, there was less unanimity among the reformers as to the desirability of national censorship. Not only were most of the church and reform groups impressed with the ineffectiveness of state censorship as it had been applied during the preceding twenty years, but some of them, existing in the midst of the political and economic turmoil of that year, had glimpsed something of the political implications of a national censorship board. The chastened producers mended their ways, and the reform organizations, impressed with the effectiveness of informal censorship and boycott, subsided from their agitation.

On a number of occasions since 1934, economic boycotts organized by the Legion of Decency and at times by other groups, such as the American Legion on Charles Chaplin's film "Limelight," have frightened producers, intimidated exhibitors and organized boycott by patrons. There are many differences in degree in this type of pressure-group censorship. The American Civil Liberties Union, though recognizing as a legal right the use of such orderly and lawful means as peaceful and unobstructive picketing and the organization of a specific and primary boycott, even when they imply some degree of coercion, still condemns as excessive their use in the following ways: "(1) as pressure, or explicit threat thereof, at any time prior to the actual offering of a motion picture to the public; and (2) even after the actual offering to the public, in the form of a general or secondary boycott—designed, for example, to close a theatre entirely or to close other theatres whose proprietors ally themselves with the proprietor of the first theatre."

The principal and most effective type of censorship of the motion pictures has been the self-censorship by the producers under the administration of the Motion Picture Production Code. In 1922 Will H. Hays, Chairman of the Trade Association, organized a Committee on Public Relations in which were incorporated representatives of about thirty civic, religious and reform groups. This group advised with the industry on the content of pictures, and thus self-censorship began. The industry collected a list of items that had been condemned most often by censorship boards and censoring groups and made the avoidance of these the basis of voluntary trade practices. In 1930 the formal Motion Picture Production Code was instituted, the code whose general statements are substantially the same to this day. However, the standards of the code were flagrantly disobeyed until, after the Legion of Decency campaign in 1934, the industry developed an efficient method of enforcing the code, instituted detailed self-censorship before and during production of pictures, and established heavy fines for producing, distributing or exhibiting pictures without a certificate of approval. For twenty years thereafter the code authority provided detailed censorship of motion-picture content. The statement of the Production Code that has been the basic body of rules for so long a time is necessarily very general. The statement of principle with which it begins is: "(1) No picture shall be produced which will lower the moral standards of those who see it. Hence the sympathy of the audience shall never be thrown to the side of crime, wrongdoing, evil or sin; (2) Correct standards of life, subject only to the requirements of drama and entertainment, shall be presented, and; (3) Law, natural or human, shall not be ridiculed, nor shall sympathy be created for its violation." The sections of the code deal with (1) Crimes against the law, (2) Sex, (3) Vulgarity, (4) Obscenity, (5) Profanity, (6) Costume, (7) Dances, (8) Religion, (9) Locations, (10) National feelings, (11) Titles, (12) Repellent subjects.[22] The applications of the code in accordance with the prevailing rules and practices of any time are highly detailed; stop watches record the seconds of duration of a kiss, scenes of passion are scrutinized for nuances of expression, sections of exposed epidermis are carefully measured, violence is exactly rationed, the general theme analyzed for compensating moral values and the like.

As the motion-picture industry prefers self-regulation to censorship, the code has been its evolved answer to governmental censorship. Through the years the detailed applications of the code have been an attempted balance between the standards and demands of pressure groups, the tastes of the audience, the aims and objectives of producers and the zeal of producers and exhibitors for the last possible dollar at the box office. Granted that, in view of the undifferentiated mass appeal of the motion pictures, some regulation will be applied in our political democracy, the industry's self-regulation has been more effective in general and more sensibly applied than the city and state censorship laws.

In the desire of various groups to censor and limit the content of motion pictures several fundamental questions were seldom adequately considered. (1) To what extent does motion-picture content differ from the prevailing folkways and mores of our culture at the present time? (2) Wherein does motion-picture content differ from that of other media of communication and from objective life situations to which the individual ordinarily has access? (3) Are the fields of behavior to which objection is raised the most vital in contemporary life? May not the perversions of economic reality and, indeed, of the scales of values in general, as portrayed by the motion pictures, have as profound an effect as incidents of violence or sexual behavior? (4) Is it possible to define the meanings of immorality, indecency and obscenity in a way sufficiently objective to provide a legal basis for censorship? (5) To what extent do the patterns of behavior provided in the motion picture motivate similar behavior on the part of those who view them? It is quite obvious that these questions could be but partly answered by using whatever methods and techniques of investigation social psychology and the various sciences of behavior have developed. The censor has usually not even posed these questions. He has assumed the answers.

[22] Space does not permit the inclusion of the fourteen pages of statement of the code and its various special regulations. Copies may be obtained from The Motion Picture Association, or see Ruth Inglis, *Freedom of the Movies*, University of Chicago Press, Chicago, pp. 205 ff. A discussion of the operation of the Association for the first 25 years may be found in Raymond Moley's *The Hays Office*, a eulogistic, uncritical portrayal.

The regulation of the attendance of various age groups at motion-picture performances has frequently been urged. As the pictures are a major leisure-time activity of all age groups, the various parts of their diversified content are not equally suitable for all groups. Certain adults may be hardened to observation of sexual or violent behavior that would shock the adolescent, even if it did not lead to attempts at similar behavior. Such materials might provide a stimulating or compensatory vicarious experience for a large portion of the adult group and be a desirably integrating factor in their life experiences. The same materials might be distasteful to, or ignored or not understood by small children. In the case of the adolescent they might be an addition to the stress and strain of a period of sexual adjustment. Furthermore, an adult's impression is obtained from an understanding of the picture as a whole with its underlying theme, and a quite different impression is gained from the parts of the picture that the small child understands. A solution for this difference of response has been thought by many to lie in providing certain regular times each week for the showing of pictures suitable for small children, for family audiences of adults and children or for adults. Such regulation of attendance, if administered on the basis of a limited and narrowly prejudiced scale of values of what would be "good for" the child, might be more undesirable than subjecting him to unsuitable impressions. However, wisely administered in terms of the best social psychological knowledge of our time, such regulation of attendance could be in the public interest and it would permit the production of a much more varied motion-picture content for exhibition to adult audiences than has been possible in the past.

In the early 1950's the general public interest in and attention to television sharply reduced attendance at motion pictures, although the decline was halted and reversed in 1953. The remaining audiences varied somewhat in age composition, frequency of attendance and interests from the audiences of the preceding decades. Foreign films, unusual film content, and diversified themes of adult interest were drawing somewhat larger audiences. Basic change in the structure of motion-picture production and distribution appeared inevitable. Increasingly the motion-picture industry was producing films for television. However, the industry's quest for increased income would drive it into varied fields. Pictures of a much more diversified content than had characterized the Hollywood output in the past might be produced. The motion-picture industry had or could readily procure the skills for such production. Pictures might be produced economically for smaller audiences in smaller theaters. In that case, the industry might find that a more limited and less rigorous self-censorship code would suffice, legal censorship might be abolished, and the hue and cry of the censor would turn largely to the content of television.

CHAPTER 13

Authority and Censorship

I believe there are more instances of the abridgment of the freedom of the people by gradual and silent encroachments of those in power than by violent and sudden usurpations.[1]

JAMES MADISON

It is not the minds of heretics that are deteriorated most by the ban placed on all inquiry which does not end in the orthodox conclusions. The greatest harm done is to those who are not heretics, and whose whole mental development is cramped, and their reason cowed, by fear of heresy.[2]

JOHN STUART MILL

In the United States the most frequent restraints and prohibitions on free communication have resulted from the repressive effects of adverse climates of opinion, from majorities, from the pressures of interest-groups, from intimidation and from the self-censorship of those controlling the mass media. However, beyond all these indirect, informal and extralegal restraints there is, as in every body of law, the question of the legal status of censorship under various laws. The original draft of the United States Constitution contained no guarantee of religious and intellectual liberty with the exception that members of Congress were granted immunity for anything said in debates and religious test oaths were forbidden. But the citizens of many states were not satisfied, and state conventions in some instances condemned the absence of a guarantee of freedom of speech. Therefore, in the First Amendment to the Constitution, effective December 15, 1791, it was stated that: "Congress shall make no law respecting an establishment of religion, or prohibiting the free exercise thereof; or abridging the freedom of speech, or of the press; or the right of the people peaceably to assemble, and to petition the Government for a redress of grievances." The Fourteenth Amendment, which became effective in 1868, states in part: "No state shall make or enforce any law which shall abridge the privileges or immunities of citi-

[1] James Madison, Speech in the Virginia Convention, June 16, 1788.
[2] John Stuart Mill, *On Liberty.*

zens of the United States; nor shall any state deprive any person of life, liberty or property without due process of law; nor deny to any person within its jurisdiction the equal protection of the laws." It is under the various interpretations by the Supreme Court, in rulings on the meaning of these Amendments, that the restraints on censorship are maintained in the United States.

In peacetime legal censorship in advance of publication of printed materials, the prohibition of the exhibition of flags and pictures, and the distribution of other communications is in theory unconstitutional. Prosecutions under the laws and ordinances on obscenity or libel is another question. However, in practice, much control has been exercised by the Customs Service and the Post Office, by the censorship boards of cities and states, and in the various attempted restrictions on freedom of the press by indirect regulations. The history of this record is a long, complicated and refined, subtle legal labyrinth.[3]

FREEDOM OF SPEECH

The successive battles over freedom of speech have raged about freedom of assembly and public speech; the products of the press, newspapers, books, dramas and novels; pictures and pictorial art and, latterly, radio and television. The center of this conflict has shifted as authority has thought itself imperiled by one or the other medium of communication. Decrease of restriction and pressure in any field does not necessarily indicate an increased tolerance. It may mean that the form of expression is no longer thought to constitute a danger to authority, to social unity, and to traditional beliefs. A more conscious and intelligent leadership may permit soapbox oratory in the local scene, relatively unharried even by informal pressures, but may desire a considerable degree of control of motion picture, press, radio and television. Authority constantly encounters new problems in attempting to regulate communication.

Agitation may be carried on through gossip and discussion, but is usually most effectively achieved in assemblies and mass audiences. Such groups give publicity to the issues. Thus freedom of speech is balked if freedom of association is denied. Such freedom has never been universally admitted as a legal right. Even when, in recent times under democratic governments, freedom of assembly has been granted in principle, it has been hedged about by various restrictions. In Great Britain there is no direct legal barrier, but activity in many fields may bring one in conflict

[3] After forty years of preoccupation with this area of legal study and the publication of a number of notable books on civil liberties, Prof. Zechariah Chafee summarizes the issues and the law in *Government and Mass Communications*, University of Chicago Press, Chicago, 1947, vols. 1 and 2.

with the sedition laws. In the United States, most states have laws forbidding the promotion of syndicalist and Communist viewpoints, public discussion of birth control, a meeting assembled to plan crime (that is, violation of existing laws), the gathering of a group intending to commit a breach of the peace and a meeting assembled to use force or the threat of force (three or more persons creating a disturbance to terrify others constitute a riot). It is clear that no state charged with the maintenance of social order can admit unlimited right of association. In a democracy, bodies advocating the use of violence rather than persuasion to bring about social change threaten not only an existing government but the basic concept of majority rule. But at just what points should restrictions be applied and with regard to which issues? Which opinions should be prohibited? In which media of communication? Should one rule apply in normal times and another in crises? When will attempted interference with freedom of assembly simply exacerbate the temper of those interfered with and bring about a more vigorous opposition? These and many other questions of tactics must be answered by authority. And frequently they are not answered wisely from the point of view of self-interest of that authority. In the conflict situation the emotional responses of the representatives of authority are also a factor in the situation. H. J. Laski questioned whether restriction on association is ever effective in the long run. "It is difficult in the light of history to see that anything has been gained in the long run by multiplying prohibitions upon the right of association. Where men feel passionately upon some object they will combine to promote it; and any prohibition upon their effort to do so only serves to drive their activities into secret channels." [4]

The record of restrictions in the United States shows many inconsistencies in attempted regulation in the interest of religious, state and special interests, especially economic interests. Until well toward the middle of the nineteenth century there were prosecutions for blasphemy based on the old strict Colonial statutes. Expressions considered dangerous to morals are still restricted under the Comstock Act of 1873. National restrictions on speech in assembly range from the Sedition Act of 1798, in which the Federalists induced Congress to make seditious libel a crime, to the Sedition Act of 1917 passed under the conditions of world war. The provisions of this act prohibited: (1) conveying false reports with intent to interfere with military or naval forces; (2) attempting to cause disloyalty, insubordination or mutiny; (3) obstructing recruiting or enlistment; (4) obstructing the sale of United States bonds; (5) uttering abusive or disloyal language intended to cause contempt or disrepute as regards the form of government of the United States, the constitution,

[4] H. J. Laski, "Freedom of Association," *Ency. Soc. Sci.*, 6: 449.

the flag or the uniform of the Army or Navy, or any language intended to incite resistance to the United States; (6) urging any curtailment of production of any things necessary to war; (7) advocating, teaching, defending or suggesting doing any of these acts; (8) words supporting or favoring the cause of any country at war with us.[5]

In commenting on this Act, Zechariah Chafee wrote:

> Never in the history of our country, since the Alien and Sedition Laws of 1798, has the meaning of free speech been the subject of such sharp controversy as during the years since 1917. Over nineteen hundred prosecutions and other judicial proceedings during the war, involving speeches, newspaper articles, pamphlets, and books, were followed after the Armistice by a widespread legislative consideration of bills punishing the advocacy of extreme radicalism.

The states, likewise, have passed a great many laws dealing with the conditions of freedom of assembly and freedom of speech. As each major issue in American history has come to the fore, there have been frequent denials of the freedom of assembly and speech to minority groups. Whoever has power usually has freedom of assembly and speech. Such freedom has frequently been denied, in practice, to minorities in the United States. As an increasing number of public officials came to recognize the "safety-valve" function of such freedom, there was somewhat less tampering with assembly, talk and discussion. However, in crises, old restrictions are invoked.

In the early 1950's the courts were faced with the cases of prosecutions of Communists. New rulings were necessitated in an age of popular fear and anxiety with a frightened public less concerned in general with the preservation of freedom of speech and the maintenance of civil liberties than with the problem of security. Decades before, during World War I, Justice Holmes had laid down his famous "clear and present danger" principle, stating:

> The character of every act depends on the circumstances in which it is done. . . . the question in every case is whether the words used are used in such circumstances and are of such a nature as to create a clear and present danger that will bring about the substantive evils that Congress has a right to prevent. It is a question of proximity and degree.

And hence, in charging the jury in the Communist trials in New York, Judge Medina stated: •

> I charge you that if the defendants did no more than pursue peaceful studies and discussions or teaching and advocacy in the realm of ideas you must acquit

[5] An extended description of procedure under this act will be found in Z. Chafee, *Freedom of Speech,* Harcourt, Brace and Company, Inc., New York, 1920.

them. . . . Do not be led astray by talk about thought control, or putting books on trial. No such issues are before you here. You must be satisfied from the evidence, beyond a reasonable doubt, that the defendants had an intent to cause the overthrow or destruction of the Government of the United States by force and violence . . . as speedily as circumstances would permit it to be achieved. . . . I charge you that it is not the abstract doctrine of overthrowing or destroying organized government by unlawful means which is denounced by this law, but the teaching and advocacy of action for the accomplishment of that purpose, by language reasonably and ordinarily calculated to incite persons to such action.

Despite the maintenance of reasonable legal protections for the individual before the courts, the methods and atmosphere of the Congressional investigating committees of the early 1950's and the intimidating climates of opinion of these times grievously restricted discussion and impressed conformity. As the historian, H. S. Commager, noted:

There was, to be sure, nothing new about political intolerance in America—witness the Alien and Sedition laws—but before the first World War the incongruity of persecution with the First Amendment had been generally acknowledged. With the Sedition and Espionage Acts of that war, the "red hysteria" of the twenties, the Alien Registration Act of 1941, the loyalty tests and purges of the mid-forties, the establishment of un-American activities committees, intolerance received, as it were, the stamp of official approval. Loyalty was identified with conformity, and the American genius, which had been experimental and even rebellious, was required to conform to a pattern. Congressmen more and more displayed that never-ending audacity of elected persons which had been thought characteristic of the Old World and outlawed in the New. No less audacious and equally shabby was the attempt by corporate business to identify its own version of private enterprise with Americanism.[6]

The maintenance of proper legal protections of civil liberties is the responsibility not only of the political administrations and the courts, but also of a vigilant and informed public opinion. Therefore, there must be the perennial education of publics concerning the vital importance of civil rights, the eternal vigilance of groups devoted to protection of civil rights by providing aid to the accused, and the restatement and redefinition of civil rights by private and public groups, such as the Report of the President's Committee on Civil Rights in 1948, entitled, "To Secure These Rights."

CENSORSHIP OF THE PRESS

Throughout the world the power of governments over the sources of information has been growing during the period since World War I. This

[6] H. S. Commager, *The American Mind*, Yale University Press, New Haven, Conn., 1950, p. 113.

is due to the spread of Fascistic, Communistic and other autocracies, to the increased national fears, tensions and suspicions that have permitted governmental bureaucrats to extend controls in the name of public safety. However, in the United States there has been no important legal encroachment on freedom of the press. "The restrictive function of government does not now seriously interfere with freedom of communication in the United States. The present legal limitations arising out of the desire for national security and the requirements of decency, if properly applied, give writers wide liberty to say what they think." [7]

Freedom of the press is not and never can be absolute. Some regulation has always prevailed. From the beginning of printing the issue has been the degree and type of regulation.[8] The issues of regulation of the press have developed differentially for the newspaper, the periodical, the book and other printed forms.

During the seventeenth and eighteenth centuries the news periodicals and the developing newspapers were viewed with suspicion and harassed by governmental restrictions.

During the first century of the history of newspapers, there was not a government in the world which did not look upon them as a dangerous nuisance, to be abated if possible, and to be tolerated only under strict control. Roger L'Estrange, when he accepted his office as licenser of the English press in May, 1680, said: "A newspaper makes the multitude too familiar with the actions and Councils of their Superiors, and gives them not only an itch, but a kind of colourable Right and License to be meddling with the Government." [9]

But gradually the restrictions were removed or lessened under the pressure of a developing political democracy. The first constitution in the world to enunciate freedom as a right was that of the State of Pennsylvania in 1776, which stated in Article XII, "That the people have a right to freedom of speech, and of writing, and publishing their sentiments; therefore the freedom of the press ought not to be restrained." This principle was based on the developing view that truth would emerge from the clash of ideas on a free and open market, a principle succinctly stated by Jefferson as, "Error of opinion may be tolerated where reason is left free to combat it." However, this principle was far from general acceptance then as now. It has been estimated that, of the 2½ billions

[7] Z. Chafee, *Government and Mass Communications,* University of Chicago Press, 1947, vol. I, p. 4.

[8] An excellent historical and analytical record of the rise and decline of governmental controls of the press during the first three centuries of printing now exists in F. S. Siebert, *Freedom of the Press in England, 1476–1776,* University of Illinois Press, Urbana, Ill., 1952.

[9] F. L. Mott, *The News in America,* Harvard University Press, Cambridge, Mass., 1952, p. 176.

of people on the earth, some 300 million have enjoyed freedom of speech for as long as 30 years, unbroken except by war.

"Modern society will be destroyed by ink" is a saying attributed to Napoleon. At the beginning of the nineteenth century, authority was already well aware of the power of the newspaper. Napoleon is said to have feared a powerful German newspaper more than an army corps. The European press was at that time fettered by libel laws and systems of licensing, and the newspaper in the United States was just obtaining protection from political interference under the First Amendment to the Constitution. The legal restrictions, however, are meaningful only in terms of their administration. Nominal freedom may be accompanied by large numbers of prosecutions under those laws which do exist, whereas laws may be ignored elsewhere. Yet legal limitations are not the only restrictions on freedom of expression. An absolutely free press exists nowhere except in the theoretical suppositions of extreme libertarians. There is always the restraint of social conventions, the popular standards, prejudices and beliefs of the society in which publication occurs. There is always the restraint imposed by the policy and interests of the owners or managers of the press. Their commercial objectives place obvious limitations on its content.

The defense of formal censorship by authority is usually quite simple. The newspaper readers are to be protected from subversive minorities; from alien influences; from their own fears in wartime; from morally debasing accounts, and from such materials as are forbidden by the obscenity laws; from a too intrusive interest in the personal experiences of others; and, in general, from their own fallible thinking in whatever field authority decrees them to be peculiarly subject to error. Authority assumes a greater wisdom.

After World War I, under the authoritarian governments that arose, countries theretofore permitting some measure of freedom instituted repressive measures. The postwar dictatorships limited freedom of speech both in theory and practice. The newspaper and the radio, as the most potent channels of communication, were especially manipulated and controlled. The absolute right of the state to supervise the formation of public opinion was proclaimed. Censorship and propaganda were open and avowed. Walter Funk, of the Nazi Propaganda Ministry, stated the government's position that the German press was "no longer a barrel organ out of which everybody is permitted to squeeze whatever melodies he likes, but a highly sensitive and far-sounding instrument or orchestra on which and with which only those shall play who know how, and in whose hands the Führer himself has placed the conductor's baton." [10] In

[10] *New York Times Mag.*, July 14, 1935, p. 8.

pursuing this objective, the opposition press was abolished and there were left only the National Socialist papers, supported by the party and later part of the government, and the so-called "coordinated" press, which, although under private ownership, was subject to such rigid state control that its content on essential subjects was the same as that of the party papers. In either case both the editors and editorial writers were licensed by the state. A law passed in October 1933, provided, among other qualifications, that the men who served the press must be "morally mature and nationally minded." Their conduct outside as well as during working hours was subject to state supervision. "Not every one has the right to write for the public," Dr. Goebbels explained, "for that right has to be earned through moral and patriotic qualifications." [11] He stated further that freedom of thought and opinion must be curbed at the point where these conflict with the interests of the nation as a whole.

Though complete control and censorship of all means of communication was not implicit in Communist ideology, the practices of the Soviet Union and other Communist states soon provided the most complete control of the press the world has ever seen. Of course, with the typical semantic obfuscation of the Communist, it was declared that Russia had freedom of the press through governmental control of the press.

Freedom of the press for the newspaper is vigorously defended in the United States. This freedom is a product not only of our history, of the development and defense of the idea from the first Constitutional amendment onward, but also of our form of government. Under parliamentary governments, the heads of state have the greater reason to desire restriction of press comment since they are subject to recall, but our elected officials have time, within the limits of their terms in office, to justify and explain their positions. [12] Hence, in normal times the newspaper in the United States is restricted only by the laws of libel and obscenity and various associated legal limitations. The courts have consistently maintained this press freedom from legal censorship in the many cases of attempted invasion of that right. One attempt, that of Senator Long, in 1933, to tax the opposition papers of Louisiana into submission, was stopped by the Supreme Court, as was the Minnesota "Gag Law" in 1931. American press history contains many incidents of attempted restriction in the various states. The first case from which the struggle for press freedom in the United States is usually traced is the famous Zenger trial, which occurred in New York in 1733, two generations before the revolution. After the infamous restrictive episode of the Federalists' rule and the passage of the First Amendment, the principle of press freedom was

[11] *New York Times*, Oct. 8, 1933.
[12] A. Krock, "The Press and Government," *Ann. Am. Acad. Pol. Soc. Sci.*, 180: 163.

established. Thomas Jefferson, ardent champion of the newspaper, declared that "our liberty depends on the freedom of the press and that cannot be limited without being lost." Thus far, that freedom has been legally invaded only in time of war. Informally, however, such freedom has been denied to various groups on many occasions. In the period of agitation during the thirty years preceding the Civil War the printing establishments of Abolitionists were in many instances destroyed by mobs. In the later years of this period the Postmaster General was forbidding Abolitionists the use of the mails, although he had no legal basis on which to do so. During the Civil War, many printing establishments were destroyed by mobs, sometimes by soldiers. Over thirty newspapers were suspended under temporary legislation. During World War I, the restrictions were used to decimate the ranks of the foreign language and immigrant press.[13] Censorship of the press under special legislation was also instituted in the interests of the conduct of the war. Military censorship is usually justified on the basis that it prevents the transmission of important information to the enemy and that such press censorship prevents discouragement at home and at the front. Under the conditions of modern communication such assertions are of doubtful truth. In a brilliant discussion of the limitations of military censorship, L. M. Salmon [14] has noted the following points: (1) The lack of consistent policy as to standards of censorship caused the Allies to censor so variously that almost everything got through—accounts of defeats deleted by some were reported by others. (2) The means of communication are now so many and their content so enormous that the organization of censorship will be cumbersome and leaks will be inevitable. (3) An ordinarily free press will soon be at odds with the censors and will attempt in every way to circumvent them. (4) Censorship arouses suspicion among the troops and adversely affects the general morale at home. (5) Deceit, concealment and evasion have deleterious effects on the morale of the censors and administrative officers themselves. (6) Censorship is essentially negative and unproductive, and the deletions are in part supplanted by crops of wild rumors. News vendors grasp at straws. (7) Suppression of news prevents desirable criticism of official incompetency, inefficiency and stupidity. (8) Censorship will inevitably be prolonged after the end of hostilities. In France, censorship, in spite of numerous government promises, was continued until after the Peace Conference. (9) The ability in circumventing censorship that the press developed during World War I indicates the futility of such suppression in the modern world. (10) Censorship will inevitably

---

[13] See R. E. Park, *The Immigrant Press and Its Control*, Harper & Brothers, New York, 1922.

[14] L. M. Salmon, *The Newspaper and Authority*, Oxford University Press, New York, 1923. These statements are a summary of chap. 5.

be linked with propaganda which becomes more and more irresponsible as it is protected. (11) An intelligent public opinion cannot be created under such conditions. Censorship is ineffective in preventing the transmission of military information, its ostensible purpose, but it does permit political manipulation which is undesirable from the viewpoint of the general national interest. And although usually defended in general theory, military censorship in its application in the modern state inevitably arouses opposition because these discrepancies become obvious.

Denial of freedom of printing has been informally applied, by mobs destroying the output, wrecking the establishments and intimidating the editors of various papers and journals published by reform groups, racial groups, labor groups, suffragettes, municipal factions and others. Large publics do not display tolerance when they feel endangered or outraged. It requires a mature, liberal wisdom to understand that an obnoxious opinion is less dangerous to public welfare than its arbitrary suppression. The chief extralegal limitation on the newspaper has been the policy of its owners and advertisers. The general or specific interests of these have led to the most usual American types of suppression and distortion of news. The press in the United States is free, more free than any other, from governmental control. It has enjoyed liberties without parallel. Informally and extralegally, however, it has inevitably been censored many times in many ways.

CENSORSHIP OF BOOKS

An informal, extralegal censorship of books is always operative. As a rule the prevailing standards of a culture limit the expression of an author in so far as they are incorporated in his own standards, in his hopes for large sale and wide circulation and in the standards set up by his publisher. The publisher usually desires to avoid court action and knows the standards of his clientele. Through the nineteenth century the publisher was even more influential than he is today in determining the content of books. Not only were popular standards more integrated and uniform, but the publisher could, with especial clarity, discern the standards of the middle class which provided the bulk of readers. In England, the publishers, in conjunction with the managers of the great circulating libraries, were especially responsive to the public opinion of their readers. Inasmuch as most of the readers obtained their copies of books from the circulating libraries, the managers of these exercised an effective informal censorship for several generations. They lost their dominant position in this field during the first decade of this century.[15] In America, the public

---

[15] M. L. Ernst and W. Seagle, *To the Pure*, The Viking Press, Inc., New York, 1929, chap. 5.

libraries exercised a similar but much less effective censorship. The contemporary circulating libraries are likewise guided by the tastes of their readers, but, as tastes have become extremely varied, there is little informal censorship by these organizations. They are limited only by the applications of existing laws. And these have not been vigorously enforced during the past thirty years in the United States. Our authors have publicly explored the varieties of amorous experience and the deviations of sexual and psychological behavior. Their work has been purveyed in the crudest of cheap pulp magazines and in the most expensive privately printed erotica. With the exception of the inhabitants of limited geographic areas we are largely free from the legal censor's ban at the present time. However, the attempted informal consorship of pressure-groups demanding rejection of schoolbooks in terms of the groups' interests, or pressures on librarians to withdraw books from circulation, of the stamping of books "For Adults Only" in state libraries and other indirect restraints have never been more prevalent than in the 1950's.

After the development of printing and the pamphleteering activities of the Reformation, formal censorship was developed by the church which organized its list of prohibited books. The states of the Western world likewise condemned, burned and forbade the publication of books thought to be deleterious to their interests. Gradually through the eighteenth and nineteenth centuries greater freedom of expression was achieved, first on religious, then on political and finally on moral subjects. After World War I the authoritarian states, Communist, Fascist and Nazi, reversed the trend within their borders and rigorously censored political and ethical utterances. The Nazi state was especially assiduous in publicly burning books on communism, books favorable to or written by Jews and books, not only of erotic but also of scientific vintage, dealing with sexual behavior, as well as in controlling the projected publication of such books.

Censorship in the United States has been primarily concerned with moral questions. Formal censorship has been applied by local ordinances, state laws and some federal legislation. Boston has been most notorious in local regulation of bookselling. Most of the states have laws on obscenity and blasphemy which have been used from time to time in prosecuting book publishers and sellers. As the principle of freedom of the press is recognized in the federal Constitution, as well as in the constitutions of the various states, most censorship of books has been indirect. There was no legal basis for such censorship in the eighteenth and early nineteenth cenutry. The short-lived Alien and Sedition Act of 1798 passed by the Federalists, ostensibly to check French propaganda in the United States but actually to serve as a weapon against the Republicans, was used to censor a number of newspapers, periodicals and books. Jefferson, when he became president, pardoned all those punished or prosecuted under this law. The earliest statutes on obscene publication were passed in Vermont, 1821; Connecticut, 1834, and Massachusetts, 1835.[16] The Postmaster General may exercise a censorship by his power to exclude materials from the mails. For two decades before the Civil War it was customary to exclude Abolitionist propaganda from the mails to the South. During the Civil War, exclusion of various materials from the mails was justified as an emergency measure. Afterward, Congress granted authority for such censorship by a series of acts in 1865. Adequate legal basis for prosecution and the suppression of publications by the Post Office was finally provided by the so-called "Comstock Law" of 1873. It declared, in part, that "every obscene, lewd, or lascivious, and every filthy book, painting, picture, paper, letter, writing or print, or other publication of an indecent character . . . and every article or thing designed for . . . preventing conception or producing abortion . . . or the giving of information directly or indirectly, where or how or from whom or by what means any of these articles can be obtained, is a crime." [17] Under this law, Anthony Comstock, as a special officer of the Post Office department from 1873 to 1915, was instrumental in "bringing 3,648 prosecutions and he obtained 2,682 convictions. He secured the destruction of 50 tons of books, over 28,000 pounds of stereotype plates, almost 17,000 photographic negatives, and 3,984,063 photographs." [18] The Supreme Court declared this act to be, not an invasion of the principle of freedom of the press, but a necessary regulation in the interest of public morals. In interpreting this act, the lower courts have shown an amazing variety of definitions of the "obscene, lewd and lascivious." Of late years, the number of prosecutions has been very small.

The national censorship of books has also been accomplished through forbidding entrance and importation of books considered obscene. There has been some regulation since the Tariff Act of 1842. Customs agents have, until recently, acted as judges of the obscene, under standards set up by numerous court decisions. Under the Tariff Act of 1930, such literary censorship was taken away from the customs agents and put in the hands of the United States district courts. It was believed that this change would liberalize the administration of the law, since the Customs Division had built up a bibliography of almost 800 forbidden books. It was thought that customs officers would be somewhat more hesitant to censor if their rejections had to be defended in court.

Of late years, as even the more extreme reformers now realize, the

[16] H. D. Lasswell, "Censorship," *Ency. Soc. Sci.*, 3: 290–294.

[17] L. Whipple, *The Story of Civil Liberty in the United States*, Vanguard Press, Inc., New York, 1927, p. 285.

[18] P. Odegard, *The American Public Mind*, Columbia University Press, New York, 1930, p. 263.

principal result of attempted censorship of books has been widespread publicity and the calling of popular attention to the forbidden book. Hence, some decidedly third-rate books have been widely read. It is often maintained that censorship of books, however administered, is dangerous as an opening wedge for invasion of the general principle of free speech. Further, there are great differences of opinion as to the effects of reading even avowed pornography. Heywood Broun, maintaining that sheer nastiness is feeble stuff and that "indecency is a tiny kingdom and one tour covers it," declares that one road to purity lies in making the not particularly grand tour and being done with it.[19] Jimmy Walker, as state senator, in objecting to a proposed censorship law once asked his associates, "Did you ever know a woman who was ruined by a book?" The implication is, in the words of Herman Melville, that "those whom books will hurt will not be proof against events. Events, not books, should be forbid."

Nevertheless, censors, public and private, assume that they should determine what is good and what is bad for their fellow citizens. The atmosphere of censorship was so pervasive in the United States in 1953 that President Eisenhower, in an address at Dartmouth College, advised students:

> Don't join the book burners. Don't think you are going to conceal faults by concealing evidence that they ever existed. Don't be afraid to go in your library and read every book as long as any document does not offend your own ideas of decency. That should be the only censorship.

During the same year, the American Library Association and the American Book Publishers Council, gravely alarmed about the prevailing censorship attempts, affirmed a number of propositions, among which were:

1. It is in the public interest for publishers and librarians to make available the widest diversity of views and expressions, including those which are unorthodox or unpopular with the majority. . . .

2. The present laws dealing with obscenity should be vigorously enforced. Beyond that, there is no place in our society for extra-legal efforts to coerce the taste of others, to confine adults to the reading matter deemed suitable for adolescents, or to inhibit the efforts of writers to achieve artistic expression. . . .

3. It is not in the public interest to force a reader to accept with any book the prejudgment of a label characterizing the book or author as subversive or dangerous.

4. It is the responsibility of publishers and librarians, as guardians of the people's freedom to read, to contest encroachments upon that freedom by individuals or groups seeking to impose their own standards or tastes upon the community at large.

[19] H. Broun and M. Leech, *Anthony Comstock,* Gaer Associates, Inc. (Boni), New York, 1927, p. 269.

We have traced some of the essential elements in the authoritarian position and in that of the classic liberal and have noted fields in which the conflict between them was especially bitter. Classic liberalism, narrowly conceived in terms of "freedom from," inevitably rejected the principle of censorship, whereas authority embraced it, both for punitive and restrictive purposes. We have noted the pervasiveness of an informal censorship based upon individual psychological processes and the standards of the mores. We have sketched the formal applications of censorship in several fields. Both the censors and the opponents of censorship have frequently been motivated by deep convictions, stubbornly maintained and emotionally defended. However, social psychological knowledge as to the actual effects of the various media of communication upon individuals of various age, sex and knowledge groups is very imperfect. The same stimulus may have very different effects upon the mental life and behavior at different times and under various conditions. Censorship has been based upon folk beliefs rather than upon data provided by social science.

CHAPTER 14

Publicity and Propaganda

Slogans about the "menace of propaganda" contribute to the confusion
and intensify the insecurities which threaten democratic government. . . .
Propaganda against propaganda is just another propaganda.

H. D. LASSWELL

The propagandist is a man who canalizes an already existing stream.
In a land where there is no water, he digs in vain.

A. HUXLEY

While publicists, educators, and politicians realize the tremendous
power of suggestion and emotional propaganda but are reluctant to use
it for fear of paralyzing the power of judgment in the next generation, the
Fascist ruthlessly uses these methods in all human relations. He not only
replaces the methods of political discussion by organized propaganda, but
even transforms education and all important human relations into compart-
ments of propaganda.

KARL MANNHEIM

Popular opinion becomes increasingly important in the modern world.
Under diverse political systems—Fascistic, Communistic, Monarchical,
representative democratic and popular democratic—leadership is increasingly dependent upon popular approval. Under Protestantism, religious
ideas and practices were democratized. Today, ethical codes very often
reflect the folkways and are not developed into an integrated, consistent
and logical ethical order. Economic groups search for the popular desires
in consumers' goods. Large publics are increasingly consulted. Government, perhaps authoritarian rule most of all, must ascertain the wishes of
the governed. However, leadership in diverse fields does not merely reflect the popular values; it also attempts to mold them. Hence, there is
special pleading of many kinds. Governments develop varieties of propaganda bureaus, special-interest groups retain specialists in public relations
and individuals hire publicity agents. The public-relations counsel is a
significant product of twentieth-century social relations. In class relations, such interpreters create popular stereotypes of their employers.

The families dominant in economic status in America during the nineteenth century often did not think it necessary to placate popular opinion. By 1911 the late Mr. Rockefeller had retained a public-relations counsel. Today, personal reputations are molded or even created by publicity agents. The public reputation of a motion-picture or television star, a politician or a man of business may be largely the product of the imagination of an astute publicity man. The number of groups and individuals attempting to create a certain impression or to distribute interested information constantly increases.

Of late years, there is some popular understanding of the prevalence of special pleading.

> We live among more people than ever who are puzzled, uneasy, or vexed at the unknown cunning which seems to have duped and degraded them, . . . these people probe the mysteries of propaganda with that compound of admiration and chagrin with which the victims of a new gambling trick demand to have the thing explained.[1]

Exposés of governmental propaganda in World War I, of the publicity of utility companies and the like, stimulated an emotional quest for the villain in the piece. Like the barber of Dayton, Tennessee, who, during the evolution trial, bit the ear of a customer who expressed an opposing viewpoint, there are many who wish to snap at the elusive special pleader. However, students of human relations must eschew personal praise and blame, except in so far as these are functionally useful, cease haranguing on the propaganda menace and first attempt to understand special pleading in terms of the general social process. It is an inevitable concomitant of the growth and organization of society during the past century.

The attempt to disseminate interested information and to win adherents to special viewpoints is as old as human society. The maneuverings of the primitive chieftain and the circumlocutions of Mary Jones, in her attempt to persuade her brother to do her household chores, illustrate special pleading. Such personal relationships are persistent. There is always competition for control of behavior and opinion. But in recent times there is far more organization of the process, special pleading is more consciously attempted and more individuals and publics are engaged in the process. The competition for popular support has been intensified.

The phenomenal increase in special pleading is based upon a number of general factors. We have discussed at some length the development of communication. Technological changes produced printing, pictorial representations and finally radio and television. With increased means of communication came literacy and the ability to use these agencies. On

---

[1] H. D. Lasswell, *Propaganda Technique in the World War*, Alfred A. Knopf, Inc., New York, 1927, p. 2.

this was based the development of political democracy and popular suffrage. Popular education emerged and resulted in the diffusing of all sorts of information and viewpoints. Society rapidly became more complex. Diverse interests became apparent. And these interests led to a widespread proliferation of interest-groups. Representatives of these groups proselyted for their particular viewpoints. Competitive special pleading for the control of publics outside these groups has been constantly intensified. But with the emergence of diverse interests and viewpoints there was also a heightened popular awareness of the variety of possible positions. This has resulted in psychological insecurity. Insecurity begets a quest for definitive statements. New special pleaders emerge to meet this popular need. These special pleaders, in turn, have expanding needs for communication. Hence, the intensified struggles for the control of newspapers, cables, motion pictures and radio stations that have characterized the past fifty years. And, as the public enlarged, the methods of appeal and the various techniques of transmitting information reached lower common denominators. The power of modern publicity is that it is directed by individuals who have greater understanding of the effective manipulation of motives, impulses and attitudes. Hence, with all its limitations, the effectiveness of modern publicity is unprecedented in history. All these trends have been developing for many years. However, there has recently developed an increased popular awareness and suspicion of the process.

Fear of the Machiavellian propagandist and the astute publicity man is deeply felt by many.

A deep sense of apprehensiveness and futility arises from certainty of having been duped in the past; certainty that men in high places today are seeking to continue that dupery; and uncertainty as to what one's own goals would have been had the dupery not taken place. The specter of the omnipotent but amoral propagandist now haunts the educated and semi-educated strata of society—and worries even those strata who are but dimly informed of the propagandist activities of recent decades.[2]

Speculation as to the exercise of psychological controls of the minds of men has latterly intrigued the producers of popular literature and, presumably, their customers. The enslavement of man by groups, by states or by future governments, using various psychological processes and drugs in "brainwashing" and then creating new mental content, is the central topic of some books which vary widely in literary and imaginative skill.[3]

---

[2] B. L. Smith, H. D. Lasswell and R. D. Casey, *Propaganda, Communication and Public Opinion*, Princeton University Press, Princeton, N.J., 1946, p. 31.

[3] Some randomly chosen examples are: D. L. Teilhet, *The Happy Island;* Aldous Huxley, *Brave New World;* George Orwell, *1984;* Shepherd Mead, *The Big Ball of*

In a political democracy in which there is widespread dislike of propaganda, a certain advantage can be gained by the propagandists of that nation pointing to the propaganda efforts of the enemy, exposing particular instances of enemy propaganda, and thus arousing the animosity of the home population. The authoritarian propagandist does not have this advantage, dealing as he does with populations surfeited with propaganda and beyond moral indignation at propaganda as propaganda.

For modern special pleading, the labels publicity, advertising and propaganda are used. "Publicity is a technique for directing the interest or good will of the public toward some individual or organization." [4] Commercial advertising is avowed publicity for the sale of economic goods and services. Education endeavors to show people why they think and act as they do, to present a variety of positions showing many sides of the question, and to present all the available data. Propaganda attempts to disseminate conclusions, frequently from concealed sources or with concealed objectives. Indeed, avowed, admitted, acknowledged, special pleading is one process, while devious, hidden, circuitous, special pleading is another. But we shall return to this question of distinction and definition somewhat later in the discussion. Now let us consider the variety and development of interest-groups, the process of publicity and advertising, and, then, the proliferation of propagandas.

ASSOCIATIONS AND INTEREST-GROUPS

Since 1920 the emphasis on the mass media as the preeminent source of the individual's opinions has obscured the fundamental importance of primary associations and of interest-groups in molding the individual's opinions.[5]

In modern complex societies there is a large and growing number of organized associations and interest-groups. These groups are developed about a wide variety of special interests. In the simpler societies there are fewer associations, with each association performing a much wider range of functions. In the folk society there are the family, clan, age and sex groups, but not the variety of political, economic, vocational and avocational interest-groups. In the simpler organization of the folk societies a

---

Wax; Kurt Vonnegut, *Player Piano;* John F. Crossen, *Year of Consent;* Jerry Sohl, *The Altered Ego.* There is an extensive array of such themes in the paper-bound books.

[4] *Ency. Soc. Sci.,* vol. XII, p. 698.

[5] This underemphasis on the associations as the area of most effective social control and influence on the individual has been very ably stated by Richard LaPiere in his *A Theory of Social Control,* published by McGraw-Hill Book Company, Inc., New York, in 1954. It is to be hoped that LaPiere's volume will be influential in bringing about some reconsideration of the relative influence of various communication stimuli. I shall return to the discussion of this basic issue in the concluding chapter of this volume.

large proportion of the individual's interests, time and personal functioning was involved in each of the great associations. In the highly diversified interest-groups of contemporary society only a small proportion of
the individual's interests and time is involved in each of the numerous
groups of which he is a member.[6] Another fundamental distinction may
be made on the basis of the processes of association in the various groups.
In the associations of the simpler societies interaction occurs primarily
in face-to-face relations. Hence, opinion is formed on the basis of discussion, gossip, personal influences and the variety of stimuli provided in such
contact. Many of the activities of the interest-groups of the great society
are carried on through the indirect contacts of writing, publications, pictures, radio and the other methods of secondary communication. Publics
of various types emerge.

In a sense, all groups are interest-groups. But the interest may be transient and the association fleeting. In a narrower sense, interest-groups are
those organized round about some enduring interest. "When a number of
men unite for the defense, maintenance, or enhancement of any more or
less enduring position or advantage which they possess alike or in common, the term interest is applied both to the group so united and the
cause which unites them."[7] Thus, in the fundamental divisions of society
there are sex groups, age groups, political groups, economic groups, class
groups, race groups, and the like. These may be considered interest-
groups when they organize to provide some effective means for the attainment of aims held in common by their memberships. Interest-groups arise
when women organize associations, when the aged join a Townsend
movement, when a political party organizes, when employers or employees, bondholders or the unemployed form associations, when a class
organization appears with a more or less developed ideology or when a
racial group develops an organization to face its foes or advance its
status. Within such interest-groups there are habitual and similar modes
of behavior on the part of their individual members. They have their
organizations and means of communication.

As societies became larger, as their memberships were more widely
distributed in space and as their cultures became more complex, the
number of interest-groups increased. As the modern state has assumed
more functions in the lives of individuals, the number of organizations
of sectors of its citizenship has increased. In modern political theory
there is a persistent dispute over the extent to which the state should be

[6] Prof. F. H. Allport, in his volume *Institutional Behavior*, University of North
Carolina Press, Durham, N.C., 1933, has used the terms "total inclusion" groups and
"partial inclusion" groups, so as to distinguish the proportion of the personality involved in each.

[7] R. M. MacIver, "Interests," *Ency. Soc. Sci.*, 8: 144.

based on group interests or on general community interests. Meanwhile, the state has had to adjudicate conflicting interests. "With the increase in organization the conflict of interests takes new forms, and the problem of establishing harmony between them thrusts new tasks upon the state." [8] Since the emergence of Protestantism, ever new religious interest-groups have been formed. In the economic field, thousands of new interest-groups have been organized since the beginning of the nineteenth century. As divergent ideologies and values in the fields of ethics and in social relationships in general have been formulated, their proponents have organized many thousands of additional associations.

All such groups influence opinion outside their own memberships. But it is often difficult to determine the importance of an interest-group. Membership number is an inadequate criterion. Membership distribution, composition and intensity of interest are factors in ascribing weight. And all such groups have their spokesmen. In the welter of conflicting testimony today, it is often difficult to determine who really represents whom. The general publics are frequently baffled. They cannot always distinguish between spokesmen, each of whom claims to represent a million followers. The failure to stress adequately the weight and extensiveness of influence makes possible the quoting of all kinds of statements as expressions of public opinion. But—which publics?

Interest-groups and pressure-groups are sometimes distinguished. "A pressure group is defined by its techniques, an interest group by its objectives." [9] However, this distinction is not consistently maintained in the literature of political and social science, and, as interest-groups are also pressure-groups, we shall use the terms interchangeably. Among the interest-groups, the pressure-groups are those which are so organized as to exert pressure on administrative and legislative agencies of government at every level. These voluntary associations have existed in the past, with varying degrees of formal organization, but modern pressure-groups in the United States have proliferated since 1900. Individuals have always exerted pressure and do so today. Personal political intrigue characterizes politics today as yesterday. But powerful interest-groups exerting pressure are now usually more important than individuals. The profession of representation of interest-groups, whose functionaries range from a routine executive secretary to a powerful, skillful lobbyist, now enrolls thousands of ambitious men.

The lobbies, representatives of groups interested in furthering particular legislative objectives, have existed since the middle of the nineteenth century. But by the turn of the century the lobby, devoted directly to

[8] MacIver, *op. cit.*, p. 147.
[9] R. M. MacIver, "Social Pressures," *Ency. Soc. Sci.*, 12: 347.

the influencing of lawmakers, in many cases evolved into the broader social organization of the pressure-group, with more diffuse objectives. The self-interest of nineteenth-century lobbies became more or less hidden in the pressure-group's multiple activities, their concern with public relations, and their more or less skillful pressing of their claims as in the public interest, or, at least, the interest of a large section of the public. These voluntary associations multiplied rapidly. "An estimate of the United States Office of Domestic Commerce, in 1950, found 150 national labor groups and 40,000 to 50,000 local ones; and over 3,000 national business groups and some 2,000 local ones." [10] The estimated total number of pressure-groups in Washington has been compiled by Alfred DeGrazia from materials supplied by the Library of Congress Legislative Reference Service. During the 80th Congress, 1947–1948, there were the following estimated numbers of organizations with Washington offices and activities.

Agriculture	51	Real Estate	45
Business—General	78	Religious	42
Civic and Political	115	Tax groups	42
Economic	38	Textile and apparel	34
Education	34	Trade groups (misc.)	129
Financial	49	Transportation:	
Food and beverages	96	Air	17
Health	28	Highways	34
International	58	Rail	96
Labor	134	Water	30
Lumber	30	Veterans and Military	53
Official (governmental)	113	Welfare	28
Oil, Gas and Metal	107	Women's organizations	30
Power and Communication	41	Individual's representatives	107
Printing and Publishing	34	Total	1,810
Professional	117		

About 1,500 lobbying representatives of pressure-groups were actually registered by the second session of the 80th Congress; about three lobbyists to each Congressman.[11] "Each major type of lobby employs techniques of persuasion and influence appropriate to its particular kind of strength.

[10] A. DeGrazia, *The Elements of Political Science*, Alfred A. Knopf, Inc., New York, 1952, p. 227. A study of the influence of associations will be found in H. E. Freeman and M. Showell, "Differential Political Influence of Voluntary Associations," *Pub. Opin. Quar.*, 15: 703–714. A list of the national organizations with permanent representatives in Washington may be found in T.N.E.C., *Economic Power and Political Pressures*, Monograph no. 26, pp. 197–201.

[11] See W. B. Graves, "Administration of Lobby Registration," Government pamphlet, February, 1949.

Business groups, as has been indicated, do not typically operate in close-knit organizations. The peak cartels and the top trade associations may on critical occasions band together for a time, but they have always been a minority influence, even when popular myth regards them as ruling the government." [12]

No one can say how many interest-groups there are, nor do there exist exact data on their memberships. However, to attempt to catalogue all such groups would be a futile and pedantic exercise. Charles A. Beard classified the chief interest-groups as economic, reform, professional and religious organizations. [13] In the first group are the numerous industrial, trade, farm and labor associations. The reform groups are quite varied in their interests. There are patriotic societies, women's reform groups, governmental reform groups, prohibition organizations and the like. Scores of professional groups scan the horizons of political action and of popular opinion to discover and change actions and beliefs inimical to their interests. Most of the Protestant churches maintain national organizations, some of which are powerful, such as the Board of Temperance, Prohibition, and Public Morals, or the Federal Council of Churches of Christ in America. And also there is the National Catholic Welfare Council. In addition to activities aimed at the influencing of opinion in general publics, many of these groups maintain representatives at Washington to influence the opinions of and exert pressure upon governmental officials. Of these, some of the larger and more important organizations are the Chamber of Commerce of the United States, National Association of Manufacturers, National Education Association, National League of Women Voters, American Legion, and the larger trade associations.

The influence of pressure-groups upon public opinion is obviously dependent upon the opposing organizations or the general attitudes that are encountered. Some groups that encounter little opposition have a significant influence without exerting much effort. Their effectiveness is also dependent upon the quality of their leadership, the size, character and distribution of their memberships and upon their material and psychological resources.

The pervasiveness of voluntary associations in the United States is evident and formidable. The special-interest organizations designed to further the objectives of businesses, professions, unions and farmers are perhaps the most powerful, but the organizations whose object is reform are undoubtedly the most colorful. The urge to improve the world is persistent and especially endemic in the United States. It is based upon a dominant value in our culture, that of the possibility of progress. Under

[12] DeGrazia, *op. cit.*, p. 237.

[13] C. A. Beard, *The American Leviathan*, The Macmillan Company, New York, 1930, pp. 212 ff.

democracy, like-minded individuals gather together in reform organizations. There have been hundreds of such groups in American history, ranging from transient and sporadic organizations, advocating a position on an immediate issue, to powerful organizations that have continued their agitation for decades. Such groups are preoccupied with some aspect of what they consider the general welfare and, presumably, not with the furthering of self-interests. They would better the conditions of some group or class (the elimination of slavery, the obtaining of votes for women, the protection of child life, the prevention of cruelty to animals, etc.), prohibit or not prohibit alcoholic beverages, introduce more or less violence in international relations, or improve public administration and the like. There are several hundred such organizations of national scope at the present time. In addition, many of the other interest-groups become reform organizations from time to time. Representatives of reform groups often exhibit great self-confidence in their ability to order and arrange desirably the lives of others.

One of the most effective reform groups in American life was the Anti-Saloon League. Fifty years of temperance and prohibition agitation preceded the organization of the Anti-Saloon League in 1893. It developed a paid staff of professional workers and an extensive speakers' bureau, made use of a number of existing church organizations, created lobbies in each of the states and in Washington, exerted pressure on Congress and the assemblies and maintained an elaborate organization for publicity to influence public opinion and voting. The astute leadership of the league recognized the tactical value of emotional appeals, dramatized the saloon as the enemy of the child and corrupter of youth, personalized their inanimate enemy in cartoon and symbol, and related the saloon to vice, crime and evil in general.[14] They were early users of fear propaganda and drew vivid pictures of alcohol as the great destroyer and inciter to violence. In addition to their numerous speeches, the league tacticians broadcast their appeals and viewpoints in an enormous literature.

By 1912 its eight presses were printing more than forty tons of temperance literature each month, including thirty-one state editions of the American Issue, with an aggregate monthly circulation of more than 500,000. . . . By 1916 the Westerville plant was printing six different temperance journals, including four monthlies with an aggregate circulation of about 420,000, one weekly with a circulation of over 130,000 each week, and a daily with a circulation of approximately 15,000. . . . One might almost say that the liquor business was drowned in a flood of temperance literature. From October, 1909, to January, 1923, the American Issue Company turned out 157,314,642 copies of temperance papers.

[14] P. Odegard, *Pressure Politics*, Columbia University Press, New York, 1928.

The periodical literature so far discussed comprised only a part of the League propaganda. The record of the job department at Westerville follows. The figures cover the period from 1909 to 1923.

Books	1,925,463	Other cards, tickets, etc. ...	18,522,471
Pamphlets	5,271,715	Miscellaneous	21,553,032
Leaflets	104,675,431	General printing	80,512,132
Window cards	2,322,053		
		Total	234,782,297

SOURCE: Reprinted from Odegard, *op. cit.*, p. 74. By permission of Columbia University Press, New York.

The League worked extensively in the public schools. Talks, leaflets, poems, prose, motion pictures, essay contests and songs declared their message.[15]

The increase in the number of interest-groups results from the emergence of new interests and from the schisms within existing groups, which occur as the memberships disagree about interests and policies. This trend will no doubt continue for some time. And in so far as these groups represent real interests of their memberships and are really effective in molding the attitudes and opinions of their members, a certain isolation from the general public results. "Some tendency to isolation and spiritual impoverishment is likely to go with any sort of distinction or privilege. . . . These foster special tastes, and these in turn give rise to special ways of living and thinking which imperceptibly separate one from common sympathy and put him in a special class."[16] Moreover, as these groups become fixed and their organizations develop effectiveness in publicity and pressure, they put an ever-increasing strain upon political government. Compromise and adjudication become more difficult. At times they are effective aids to formal government, but the more powerful groups have often made serious inroads on genuinely democratic government.

What do they presage for popular opinion? In the United States, interest-groups have been permitted a maximum of freedom to compete for opinion control. They use all the means of communication and all the methods of publicity. There is relatively little official control of such groups. The result has been a clarification of some issues but a confusion of counsel on many others. Much of the information distributed by pressure-groups is distorted, incomplete and fragmentary, and sometimes untrue.

[15] B. L. Pierce, *Citizens' Organizations and the Civic Training of Youth*, Charles Scribner's Sons, New York, 1933, chap. 27.
[16] C. H. Cooley, *Social Organization*, Charles Scribner's Sons, New York, 1909, p. 138.

The development of these interest-groups and their use of publicity and propaganda are inevitable results of the growth of modern society. Several schools of thought now advocate divergent policies in dealing with existing groups. There are advocates of various plans based on some variation of the European practice of incorporating them into the governmental framework of the state. Others would achieve unity by increasing the activities of the Federal government in opinion leadership and the formulation of policy.[17] Others would increase the number of opinion groups, encourage the creation of groups to counter those now existing, give additional publicity to the activities of all of them and struggle for some regulation of their activities and statements by legal restrictions. This objective is logical in principle but difficult to achieve. The unhappy liberal realizes the difficulties of governmental and legal control to assure veracity of interest-group propaganda and fair competition between groups. However, in principle he espouses such objectives.

PUBLICITY

At the close of the nineteenth century and during the first decade of the twentieth, there was an age of the muckrakers. Writers for magazines, cartoonists and some newspapermen and many politicians were engaged in various attacks on business organizations. Many corporations needed to assuage public hostility. And so, as Edward L. Bernays notes in the chapter headings of his *Public Relations,* the public-be-damned period (1865 to 1900) was followed by the public-be-informed (1900-1919). The rise of a new profession, the public-relations counsel (1919-1929), developed as public relations came of age (1929-1941).[18]

The press agent of the earlier periods was often crude, blatant and direct in ballyhooing the qualities of his clients, as well as their wares. The public-relations counsel, a functionary distinct from the advertising man with his specific objectives, engaged in securing or avoiding publicity for his clients, usually by indirect means. "Public relations has three meanings: (1) information given to the public, (2) persuasion directed at the public to modify attitudes and actions, and (3) efforts to integrate attitudes and actions of an institution with its publics and of publics with that institution." [19] Publicity as a technique for directing the interest

[17] E. P. Herring, *Public Administration and the Public Interest,* McGraw-Hill Book Company, Inc., New York, 1936.

[18] E. L. Bernays, *Public Relations,* University of Oklahoma Press, Norman, Okla., 1952. Mr. Bernays is considered by many as the preeminent public-relations counsel of the United States.

[19] *Ibid.,* p. 3.

or good will of the public toward some individual or organization is, therefore, but one of the activities of the public-relations man. In his persuasive role, the public-relations counsel is fundamentally engaged in "the engineering of consent," a phrase frequently encountered in this profession. He is engaged in "opinion engineering in the big time."

Although the overwhelming bulk of advertising in the United States is designed to promote the sale of products and services, there is a substantial and growing publicity for ideas, causes and ideologies. The activity devoted to these campaigns was estimated in 1949 to cost 100 million dollars a year,[20] and by 1950 a single area of this activity, the great free-enterprise campaign, was accounting for 100 million dollars of industry's annual advertising expenditure. Most of such publicity campaigns are initiated by or stimulated by The Advertising Council. The Council is a private, nonprofit organization formed by the agencies to carry on certain public-service campaigns. It is supported by advertisers, agencies and various media groups. The War Advertising Council, formed in 1941, led to the later development of the Council to conduct peacetime campaigns. Illustrative of publicity campaigns to influence ideas have been the United States Bond Sales, the campaigns for the Community Chest, the Go-to-Church movement, the Register-and-Vote campaigns, the Public School Movement, the Blood Bank, CARE, Natural Resources Conservation (Smoky the Bear, etc.), and, above all, the free-enterprise campaigns, spread over several years. By many, the free-enterprise campaigns are viewed as the most notable failure in the history of publicity in the United States.[21]

In a crude type of content study in 1949, I developed a simple classification of the dominant appeals in all full-page institutional ads appearing in *Life, Fortune, Time, Newsweek* and *The Saturday Evening Post* for the year 1948. All classification was done by a single classifier, Emily Dunn Scott, so no question of differences of interpretation arose. The dominance of certain themes and types of appeal is indicated by the figures in Table 8, which shows the number of instances in which the dominant appeal, according to the classifier, was freedom, service, progress, etc. A great many of the full-page institutional ads in that year were already dealing with the free-enterprise theme, although the peak of the campaign came a little later.[22]

[20] "Admen's Giveaway," *Wall Street Jour.*, Nov. 17, 1949.

[21] The argument as to the fact and reasons for that failure is most cogently presented by William H. Whyte, Assistant Editor of *Fortune* magazine, in *Is Anybody Listening?* Simon & Schuster, Inc., New York, 1952.

[22] A good classification of the types of appeal in radio commercials appears in L. I. Pearlin and M. Rosenberg, "Propaganda Techniques in Institutional Advertising," *Pub. Opin. Quar.*, 16: 5–26, Spring, 1952.

Table 8. Frequency of Certain Appeals in Institutional Advertising in Selected Magazines in 1948

	Life	Fortune	Time	Newsweek	Saturday Evening Post	Total
Freedom.....	16	18	33	49	13	129
Service.......	17	23	18	58	68	184
Progress.....	22	56	66	57	49	250
Prosperity....	3	21	30	28	14	96
Equality.....			6		1	7
Protection....	14	7	14	25	33	93
Local Pride...	21	28	10	34	30	123
Tolerance....	20	3	15	32	29	99
Efficiency....	16	4	15	32	45	112
Inefficiency...	4	4	5	2	3	18
Superiority...	8	18	27	28	25	106
Inferiority....		2	2			4
Patriotism....	21	6	22	18	22	89

ADVERTISING AND PUBLIC OPINION

Advertising may be distinguished from propaganda in that the sources of the advertisement are stated and the motives of the advertiser may be readily assumed (when the sources are concealed, as in the case of a food-products company publicizing its claims over the name of a supposed scientific research organization, we have commercial propaganda). There is a perennial debate over the effectiveness of advertising as a creator of markets, but it is quite obvious that advertising has been enormously influential in causing people to buy particular products. At many points commercial advertising has been far more successful in swaying opinions than has propaganda for causes. Aldous Huxley has reasonably maintained that the commercial advertisers have modified opinions more extensively than the political or ethical propagandists, not because their techniques are superior but because advertising is concerned with matters of no importance. When the political propagandist begins a campaign, he does so because there exist some real differences of opinion among the members of a general public. He deals with issues. But when an advertiser urges one to buy one soap or another of equal merit or worthlessness, or one kind of cigarette among a number of cheap cigarettes, and the like, there is no real issue for the consumer.[23]

[23] A. Huxley, "Notes on Propaganda," *Harper's,* 174: 32.

As a means of spreading of information, rather than as high-pressure persuasion, advertising has existed from earliest times. Modern persuasive advertising is a product of modern methods of communication, of the historically recent orientation of industry toward the production of masses of consumers' goods and of the development of the advertising business itself which further stimulates its own activity. Advertising of the high-pressure, persuasive type has developed in the period since 1890. American publicity men have been the most effective high priests of commercial publicity.

Advertising itself is a business of very considerable size. The national expenditure on all kinds of advertising has been estimated for 1850 as 50 million dollars, for 1900 as 542 million, 1909 as 1,142 million, 1920 as 2,935 million, 1929 as 3,426 million, 1930 as 2,647 million, 1935 as 1,690 million, and 1940 as 2,087 million. Increasing from that year onward, and in the postwar period increasing rapidly, the volume of advertising in 1953 was 7,809 million dollars. Of course, these dollars must be translated into their proportion of the grand total of national income. Speaking thus broadly, we may say that since 1920 the advertising figure is from 2 to 3 per cent of the national income each year.[24] Of the total advertising expenditure in 1953 (a total of 7,809.2 millions), 2,644.8 was expended on newspaper advertising; 667.4 on magazines; 610.5 on TV; 649.5 on radio; 30.8 on farm publications; 1,099.1 on direct mail; 395.0 on business papers; 176.3 on outdoor advertising; 1,535.8, miscellaneous.

It is quite obvious that advertising has been very effective in swaying popular opinion as to the qualities of consumers' goods and in influencing the choice of those goods. It was primarily the advertising man who lifted the product of the cigarette manufacturers from its status of lowly "coffin nail" to that of a national necessity. Folkways with regard to gum chewing were created by publicity. The citizen's preoccupation with the cleanliness of his teeth and skin surfaces was developed largely from the information provided in the advertisements he read. The hunt for germs in the various orifices and on the surfaces of the body was stimulated by the manufacturers of germicides. Information and misinformation about food values have led to fashions in foods. Cereals used for the American breakfast have been pounded, exploded, inflated, sieved and woven as the "scientific" facts propounded by the advertising man have convinced consumers that their foods should be so treated. And so on. Opinions and behavior have been rapidly changed as the advertiser has presented his phantasmagoria of changing information.

The forces affecting the demand for different consumers' goods are evidently quite various. Indeed, a complex of factors is usually involved

[24] These figures are taken from a master table published in the Advertisers' Annual 1955 number of *Printers' Ink*, Oct. 29, 1954, p. 59.

so that market research often does not show a simple cause and effect relationship between advertising and demand. Advertising is but one force among many that are involved in determining consumers' attitudes. Sometimes advertising plays little part in the creating or stimulating of primary demands. The average per capita consumption of sugar in 1830 was about 12 pounds, while by 1930 the average per capita consumption had become 112 pounds. Yet direct advertising of sugar has been very limited. It is true that there has been a great deal of advertising of candies, soft drinks and other products using sugar.[25] On the other hand, the demand for spinach has been created almost entirely by advertising. Advertising of shoes is a very small item in comparison to the total sale price of shoes. And so with many primary items of consumption. "Among marketing and advertising executives of companies producing domestic sheeting there is general agreement that advertising probably had little if any effect on the total consumption of sheets and pillow cases."[26] In contrast, dentrifices are so dependent on advertising that the advertising expenditures are from 10 to 15 million dollars to develop retail sales of from 40 to 55 million dollars. And there are scores of products which would be unknown and unused had it not been for intensive advertising. The advertising man works within the context of consumers' attitudes, only a part of which are developed or stimulated by advertising appeals. However, he labors mightily and expensively for the stimulation of selective demand.

It is only since the 1920's that the advertising process has been extensively discussed and attacked. In the 1930's, a number of intellectuals, evidencing that they felt the appeals and wiles of the advertising man to be a personal insult, indicated their revulsion in no uncertain terms.[27] The principal types of discussion have been as follows.

First, the expenditures on advertising have been attacked as economically wasteful. Since 1910 advertising in the United States has cost from 1 billion to almost 8 billion dollars annually. The opponents of modern advertising maintain that the effort and materials utilized in advertising might have been expended on the creation of more goods. The defenders of the process declare that, inasmuch as advertising informs potential consumers of the existence of goods and stimulates purchase, advertising has been responsible for a part of the consumption of goods. They de-

---

[25] See Neil Borden, *The Economic Effects of Advertising*, Richard D. Irwin, Inc., Homewood, Ill., 1947, chap. X.

[26] *Ibid.*, p. 315.

[27] S. Chase, *The Tragedy of Waste*, The Macmillan Company, New York, 1925, chap. 7; and J. Rorty, *Our Master's Voice*, The John Day Company, Inc., New York, 1934. On a less grim note, see E. S. Turner, *The Shocking History of Advertising*, E. P. Dutton & Company, Inc., New York, 1953; and T. Whiteside, *The Relaxed Sell*, Oxford University Press, New York, 1954.

clare that national income, as measured in dollars, is, therefore, increased by much more than the billions of dollars spent on advertising. No reputable economist has essayed the difficult, if not impossible, task of calculating just what the advertising expenditure should be to achieve the maximum distribution of goods without waste in the advertising process itself. And, of course, the critics would not desist even if they were convinced that in terms of counters (dollars) the total national income had been increased. They would turn at once to the problem of the relative quality of goods, as—

Second, the critics of advertising say that the appeals of the advertising man have led to the consumption of inferior and ill-selected types of consumers' goods. Instances of adulteration, misrepresentation and quackery are stressed. The advertising man declares, "This, then, is the gist of the matter; somebody must determine what goods are to be produced. The decision must rest either with the government or with consumers. As society is now organized, consumers decide. The only way they can make their decisions effective is through exercising their freedom of choice in the ordinary course of marketing. This freedom of choice constitutes the chief risk of business and gives rise inevitably to profits and losses." [28] "Little by little it seems to be recognized that this demand factor is not a spineless effect but a restless and irresistible cause." [29] But the advertising man does not stress that the psychologically bound consumer—harried, frightened, cajoled, and misinformed— is not free. And it is to the methods of appeal that the critic most violently objects, stating that—

Third, only a small proportion of advertising is based on logical appeals or argumentative procedures (long-circuit appeals); the bulk of advertising is based upon appeals to the emotions, upon unworthy motives or upon direct suggestion (short-circuit appeals). Indeed, a large proportion of the textbooks and articles on the "psychology of advertising" are devoted to the analysis of the relative strength of various appeals in relation to particular types of products. D. Starch noted the basic desires as those for food, comfort, mating, power and approbation.[30] A. T. Poffenberger inventoried the fundamental desires as those for drink, food, sex experience, ease, escape from danger, dominance, conformity, parenthood, play, cleanliness, beauty and economy.[31] It is assumed, not

[28] P. T. Cherington, *The Consumer Looks at Advertising*, Harper & Brothers, New York, 1928, p. 63.

[29] *Ibid.*, p. 38.

[30] D. Starch, *Controlling Human Behavior*, The Macmillan Company, New York, 1936, p. 32.

[31] A. T. Poffenberger, *Psychology in Advertising*, McGraw-Hill Book Company, Inc. (Shaw), New York, 1925, chap. 3. For a criticism of the earlier desire inventories, see H. C. Link, *New Psychology of Selling and Advertising*, The Macmillan Company, New York, 1932.

that these desires are innate, but simply that they are dominant in our culture. There are scores of such classifications in psychological literature dealing with advertising. Certainly the advertising man knows that however limited the capacity of the common man for sustained logical analysis, his responsiveness to appeals to fundamental desires is almost limitless. The consumer responds to suggested short cuts ("learn French in ten lessons"); to the titillation of sex interests; to the prestige of individuals; to fear (the whole gamut of scare copy of the advertising of germicides, insurance and scores of products); to pseudo science; to numerous other widely distributed appeals. Certainly the advertiser has investigated desires in greater detail than has any other type of special pleader. And he persistently exploits the limited capacity of most of us for logical thinking. To his critics, the defender of persuasive advertising simply replies that he is not responsible for popular dispositions, nor is he the creator of psychological values. He is simply utilizing those which he discovers extant in the general public, so that he may distribute the maximum quantity of goods. And many of these goods—though, he sometimes admits, not all of them—add to the general standard of living. Moreover, the advertiser sometimes defiantly asks his critics to answer his contention that the advertising of many products creates values other than those of the immediate utility of the product. A girl buying a beauty product may not be made beautiful thereby, but the advertiser helps to kindle hope. The general issue is fairly clear. The advertising man is not responsible for societal values. But he does at times accentuate values that the moralist deplores. However, it is a waste of time to attack the advertisers personally. Certain of their more extreme activities, especially direct falsehoods, may be regulated in the public interest. Exaggeration, misleading implications, unfounded scientific claims, the use of questionable testimonials and the like may be somewhat more carefully regulated. That is all. Either that, or a dictatorship of consumption. But any interested minority may attempt to educate the general public in values in consumption.[32]

Fourth, the critic also accuses the advertising man of vulgarity, defacing the landscape, a low level of aesthetic appeals and a number of other misdemeanors of which some advertising is obviously guilty. But so are all the media of communication in a culture that stresses a low common denominator of popular appeal. The advertising man is likewise accused of furthering standardization of goods and abetting the creation of a dull uniformity of material things. This uniformity is peculiarly grueling to the aesthetically sensitive. But it is obviously an inevitable concomitant of mass production and distribution.

[32] In the ten years after 1945, the *Consumers Reports* of Consumers Union astonishingly increased their circulation from a few thousands to about a million per issue.

Those who have attacked advertising have generally left the impression of advertisers as low, unethical fellows involved in chicanery and deceit and having nefarious designs on the welfare of the general public. Obviously, this is sometimes an accurate description. There is much untrue, insincere and misinformative advertising. There is much more of advertising that disseminates false impressions indirectly. Advertising is special pleading, and a highly competitive special pleading at that, so that in many an advertising campaign each side stimulates the other to more and more extreme statements. If advertising is really effective, it leads consumers to make purchases they would not have made without having seen the advertisement. In the quest for these purchasers the advertising man has used every type of appeal that he found to be effective. He is limited only by the attitudes of the general public, by very fragmentary legal restrictions and by the rudimentary ethics of his profession. By experience and by knowledge of the general culture values he learns what will be believed. The attempt to place greater legal restrictions upon his claims has not yet been successful.[33] To some extent, business has regulated the content of advertising. Many of the more blatant untruths have been eliminated from some types of advertising, owing to the activities of business groups with a "Truth in Advertising" slogan. But, of course, distortions of the truth in the special pleading of contemporary advertising are a part of the very fabric of our modern competitive economy. As long as goods compete for markets, the art of "puffing" will play an important part. And granted the wide variety of economic goods for modern consumers, informative advertising would exist under any economy or any political system.

The critic of advertising stresses the more obvious and dramatically antisocial activities of the advertising man. Many of the large advertisers make and sell products of dubious or little value. But, of course, the bulk of advertising consists of special pleading for articles that have raised the standard of living of modern populations. If there is great waste in the competitive clamor about wares, it is also true that this clamor has been in part responsible for the swift acceleration of the production of consumers' goods. Certainly, advertising has influenced popular opinions about these goods. It has forced the national economy into the present mold. The selection of which goods shall be produced is in part determined by existing popular wants and, in part, by wants that are to some extent created by the advertiser. But in any case, either when the advertiser verbalizes existing wants or when he tells a public what it should want, the new importance of popular opinion is indicated by the

---

[33] The question of federal regulation versus voluntary controls is discussed in M. A. Geller, *Advertising at the Crossroads*, The Ronald Press Company, New York, 1952.

assiduous cultivation of large publics since the closing decades of the nineteenth century.

Indeed, in the United States, advertising has become a major institution, exercising diverse controls. It is a concomitant of opulence, of the plethora of consumers' goods. As we have seen, publicity and advertising are an inevitable development in our economy. The depth of the advertiser's penetration of American culture is seldom discussed and has never been incisively described, in spite of the hundreds of books devoted to the techniques of advertising. "One might read fairly widely in the literature which treats of public opinion, popular culture, and the mass media in the United States without ever learning that advertising now compares with such long-standing institutions as the school and the church in the magnitude of its social influence. It dominates the media, it has vast power in the shaping of popular standards, and it is really one of the very limited group of institutions which exercise social control." [34]

PROPAGANDA [35]

The definition of the term propaganda, as it has been used in the political democracies, especially in the United States, since World War 1, differs both from the historic meaning of the word and from the use of this term under authoritarian regimes. The disrepute into which the word propaganda has fallen in popular usage is reflected in the avoidance of the term propaganda by groups of special pleaders in the democracies. Offices of Information are established to counter the Propaganda Ministries of the enemy. In the democracies, the current popular condemnation of propaganda arises out of the ethical abhorrence for selected, partial information disseminated in the interests of the cause of the disseminator and often secretly and circuitously insinuated into the stream of communication without acknowledgment of the source. In authoritarian regimes, the dissemination of propaganda of the exclusively correct political ideology or the one true religion is not considered to require defense or ethical justification. Hence, in contemporary democracies, propaganda has become a derogatory epithet hurled accusingly at opposing views and groups, while elsewhere propaganda continues simply to refer to "any organized or consistent group effort to spread a particular doctrine or series of doctrines." Thus, in its simplest and most inclusive meaning, the propaganda process is an attempt to convince. There is a

[34] D. M. Potter, *People of Plenty*, University of Chicago Press, Chicago, 1954, p. 167.
[35] A number of paragraphs in the ensuing discussion are quoted from the article, "Propaganda," by William Albig in the *Encyclopaedia Americana*.

conscious, definite interest in the inculcation of a particular content in the attitudes and opinions of as yet unconvinced individuals and groups, rather than an attempt to convince through objectivity and discussion.

We may first delimit the field of our concept by noting that propaganda is developed within the processes of communication, in contrast to the control of opinion by violent coercion or other types of behavior. "Propaganda may be defined as a technique of social control, or as a species of social movement. As technique, it is the manipulation of collective attitudes by the use of significant symbols (words, pictures, tunes) rather than violence, bribery, boycott." [36] Propaganda is disseminated through all the channels of communication.

We may further delimit by noting that propaganda is material that is consciously disseminated. There is intent on the part of the propagandist. "Propaganda refers to the conscious attempt to manage the minds of other and usually more numerous publics." [37] Doob has written of unintentional as well as intentional propaganda, noting that many of the social consequences of the propagandist's activity are unforeseen and unintended.[38] This is true regarding particular items, but the propagandist may be assumed to have a general objective. In any field, classifications based on motives are difficult, as motives must be assumed from indirect evidence. And the objective of the propagandist may not be evident from one particular statement. However, from a mass of evidence one may usually glean some knowledge of his intent.

Further, propaganda is usually characterized by the selection of materials favorable to the interest of the propagandist and the suppression of unfavorable information. There is no attempt to present the facts objectively. There is deliberate distortion by selection. There are partial and deliberately misleading statements. The objective of the propagandist is to achieve public acceptance of conclusions, not to stimulate the logical analysis of the merits of the case. In this he differs from the avowed objective of the educator under democracy. Obviously, the educator does not consistently maintain an objective presentation, but such is his ideal. But "it is obvious that propaganda has little respect for human personality. Propaganda is not education, it strives for the closed mind rather than the open mind. It is not concerned about the development of mature individuals. Its aim is immediate action. The propagandist merely wishes you to think as he does. The educator is more modest; he

[36] H. D. Lasswell, "The Person: Subject and Object of Propaganda," *Ann. Am. Acad. Pol. Soc. Sci.*, 179: 89.

[37] H. L. Childs in *The American Political Scene* (E. B. Logan, ed.), Harper & Brothers, New York, 1936, p. 226.

[38] L. W. Doob, *Propaganda*, Henry Holt and Company, Inc., New York, 1935, pp. 76, 77.

is so delighted if you think at all that he is willing to let you do so in your own way." [39]

Further, not only does the propagandist distort by partial and misleading statements, but he usually, by preference, appeals to the emotions of his subjects rather than attempting to stimulate a logical and rational analysis of his material. "Propaganda, as I understand it, means the process whereby public opinion is formed and controlled by appeal to the irrational side of man's nature in such a way that it is usually favorable to the interests of those directing the propaganda." [40] With all this intentional distortion and selection of materials to be disseminated as conclusions by emotional appeals, it is little wonder that to the common man propaganda has come to mean deliberate lying.

Propaganda, in the sense of diffusion of conclusions while discouraging the subjects from examining the reasons for the positions which they are asked to accept, has existed throughout the history of human society. Leaders and institutional representatives are always desirous of furthering their objectives without argument. They wish to win converts and to reproduce (*propagare*) the conclusions, the essential statements and values of their ideology. As an organized group effort to spread a system of doctrines, specifically labeled as a propaganda effort, The College of Propaganda, a committee of Cardinals devoted to instruction in methods of propagation of the faith, was instituted by Pope Gregory XV in 1622. This organization was charged with the supervision of liturgical books, the reports of bishops and other officials abroad, instruction in methods of proselyting for the faith, and the carrying on of political, as well as religious, propaganda. This was one of the earliest uses of the term propaganda. Lay organizations became interested in disseminating political, and many other, points of view in the eighteenth century; in the nineteenth century the propaganda of economic views and the advertising of economic products developed; and the first half of the twentieth century saw the proliferation of hundreds of special-interest views by propaganda methods, the development of highly organized propaganda efforts of the democratic states, and of the monopolistic governmental propaganda in the authoritarian states.

Although astute societal leaders have used propagandistic special pleading at times throughout history, it was not until the twentieth century that highly organized dissemination of propaganda by various groups developed and professional practitioners of propaganda emerged. In general, the propagandas of the past were the work of chance enthusiasts,

[39] E. D. Martin, *The Conflict of the Individual and the Mass*, Henry Holt and Company, Inc., New York, 1932, p. 29.
[40] E. Beaglehole, "Some Aspects of Propaganda," *Australian Jour. Psychol. Phil.*, 6: 96.

were incidental and poorly organized, had access to but limited channels of communication and influenced relatively few people. However, some exceptional historic illustrations, in which the propaganda efforts were somewhat organized because of the skill of unusual leaders, could be presented. According to Bertrand Russell, Herodotus, the father of history, was a hired propagandist for the Athenian state. Indeed, propaganda has appeared whenever a skilled leadership has attempted to weld the opinions of a people. The simplicity of the language of Caesar's *Commentaries,* which has made it a favored introductory exercise for Latin scholars, has been ascribed to Caesar's political appeals to the Roman masses. Such appeal was necessarily couched in simple language. Octavian and Antony are reported to have engaged in every then-known trick of political propaganda, and Cicero is portrayed as an accomplished propagandist.

Sporadic appearances of propaganda are to be noted at various times in the Middle Ages, especially in connection with the Crusades. The atrocity stories at the time of the Crusades are remarkably similar to those distributed during World War I. At the time of the Armada, both Philip and Elizabeth indulged in energetic propaganda campaigns. Philip accused Elizabeth of every imaginable crime, while the friends of Elizabeth made all England shudder at the horrors of the Inquisition. Potemkin was an astute propagandist for Catherine the Great. In the political upheavals at the end of the eighteenth century, propaganda was used with some increased degree of organization.

In the American Revolution, Sam Adams engaged in pamphleteering and rumormongering with energy and skill. Benjamin Franklin exhibited great talent as a propagandist. He distributed rumors about the British, including atrocity stories such as his famous fabrication concerning the bales of colonists' scalps collected by the Indians for bounty and shipped to Great Britain. This rumor agitated many an Englishman who had relatives in America. Washington also spread rumors and urged his friends to give publicity to fabricated as well as real tales of British cruelty. He instructed his friends that such rumormongering should be done "seemingly with indifference, drop it at the table before the servants," and let the story filter out to the men. Three decades later, in Europe, Napoleon was developing propaganda activities which have been viewed by many as the forerunners of twentieth-century propaganda. He devoted considerable attention to creating a favorable public opinion, himself talking to his subjects frequently and directly, and using some of the machinery of government to spread propaganda which would aid morale at home and arouse hatred of the enemy. Napoleon's propaganda techniques were much more organized than those of earlier leaders, but, as the mass media of communication were not yet developed, intensive propaganda for the masses could not yet be created.

From the late nineteenth century onward, the basic factors in the rapid development of modern publicity and propaganda emerged. The media of mass communication were developed and spread. It was in the 1890's that the newspapers rapidly increased circulation and sought for new millions of readers; after 1915 the motion pictures increasingly influenced opinion; and the radio was important as a public medium from its birth in 1920. These mass media provided the channels through which publicity, advertising and propaganda could be carried on. Society was rapidly becoming more complex and splitting into interest-groups which engaged in competitive special pleading for the control of the larger publics, thus increasing the flow of publicity and propaganda. Moreover, special pleaders working through mass media could be devious, selective, and untruthful to a degree impossible in the more direct, primary face-to-face communication. Added to this were the psychological insights that a science of social psychology had placed in the hands of special pleaders. Partisan appeal by means of misinformation, emotional pleading and the short-circuiting of thought is no new thing. It has been the familiar accompaniment of special pleading. But the power of modern publicity is that it is directed by individuals who have greater understanding of the impulses and attitudes of masses of people, and who can influence large publics through the mass media. Hence, during the first half of the twentieth century, there was ever more communication, more organization, more groups, more special interests and causes, more competition for opinion control and more professional practitioners of publicity and propaganda.

In the United States the distinction between publicity, advertising and propaganda developed just after World War I. The advertising of economic goods and publicity for organizations and their special viewpoints, for individuals and their legends, for groups and institutions, had been extensively developed in the two decades preceding World War I. The techniques and methods of avowed and of devious, hidden publicity were somewhat developed. These tools had not been used as yet, at least in a highly organized way, by the national governments. In World War I, there was great diversity in the cultural backgrounds of the peoples engaged in the struggle. It was necessary for the Allies, and also for the Central Powers, to weld together the ideas and opinions of their peoples. This diversity also offered each side a fertile field for special pleading among the enemy who might be divided and their morale disrupted. The national governments were also concerned with the influencing of opinions of peoples not directly engaged in the war, so that neutrals might be convinced as to the essential justice of the conflict, and, perhaps, be induced to friendly action. Hence, the widespread use of propaganda in that war was inevitable. General public approval and the mobilization of civilians, as well as servicemen, was necessary in such general warfare. In World War I, German propaganda was not well organized and did not successfully conclude effective national campaigns among their people. The General Staff did not become convinced of the necessity or effectiveness of propaganda. Allied propaganda was much better organized and much more extensive. As the war progressed, the methods of the propagandists became more and more devious. Almost inevitably the propagandist became a liar. He not only distorted, he also fabricated falsehoods about opposing leaders, falsified statistics, created news stories, started rumors, and invented atrocity stories so numerous that they have not to this day been completely classified by the historians. Indeed, the propagandists falsified the processes of discussion and engaged in a degree of deviousness that had not been previously institutionalized and condoned by governments.

After the war many Allied propagandists, themselves products of the nineteenth-century rationalist tradition, were uneasy and conscience-stricken because of the methods into which they had been driven in these propaganda campaigns. A considerable number wrote autobiographical exposés of their part in the propaganda effort. Sir Arthur Ponsonby bitterly declared in a volume on *Falsehood in Wartime,* "When war is declared, Truth is the first casualty," and, "Falsehood is a recognized and extremely useful weapon in warfare, and every country uses it quite deliberately to deceive its own people, to attract neutrals, and to mislead the enemy." These British and American propagandists were often shocked by their own activities, for their intellectual tradition was that of the Kantian principle: that every man should be treated as an end, and that he should not be viewed as a tool or as a means to the ends of someone else. The confessional exposés of the propaganda leaders became widely known, and considerable popular discussion of the war propaganda process ensued. The general public was extensively disillusioned. It was at this time that the term propaganda became a derogatory epithet in popular usage. Propaganda was defined not as avowed, admitted, acknowledged special pleading, but as special pleading in which there was a marked degree of deviousness, irrationality and the hiding of sources. It became the "secret or clandestine dissemination of ideas, information, gossip, or the like, for the purpose of helping or injuring a person, an institution or cause." Propaganda was contrasted to education. In the United States, education was conceived as a process of rational enlightenment in which impartial information was imparted. With this information, a person was left to draw his own conclusions. Propaganda was distinguished from publicity and advertising. Publicity meant all public special pleading, while advertising referred to the publicity for the sale of economic goods. In advertising, the sources were stated and the objectives were implicit and made manifest. Propaganda was now defined as the dissemination of conclusions of questionable validity from concealed sources or with concealed objectives.

In the years between the world wars, propaganda was extensively used by private organizations and by governments. In the democracies, thousands of business, reform and other types of special-interest groups found propaganda a valuable adjunct to publicity, and the United States became notable as having the highest propaganda density in the world. However, governmental agencies were restricted in their use of propaganda in peacetime by custom, suspicion, by administrative and legislative surveillance and by law. Authoritarian governments of the world assumed monopolistic control of this powerful agency within their boundaries, and increasingly used propaganda as a weapon in international communication. Ethical considerations, which so dismayed some World War I propagandists, were increasingly outmoded for private special-interest groups and were considered invalid in authoritarian ideologies. The protection of the integrity of the individual mind-life for the achievement of as much rational mentation as its capabilities permitted, a keystone of democratic faith, was less rigorously defended. Publics became masses to be manipulated. The criterion of good propaganda was successful indoctrination. Qualms remained among leaders in democracies, especially concerning political propaganda, but the authoritarian leaders, Communistic, Fascistic, Nazi and of assorted ideologies, ruthlessly, though not always effectively, utilized propaganda for molding public opinion and exercising social control.

Preceding and during World War II political propaganda achieved an intensity and extensiveness which reflected the judgment of societal leaders as to its importance. In World War I German leadership had depreciated propaganda, but under the Nazis it was viewed as a prime strategic and tactical weapon. The Ministry of Propaganda was prepared, having gleaned from the world, especially from the advertising techniques used in the United States, from the social psychological literature of modern Western life, and from the history of political propaganda, a host of devices, generalizations and principles. These had been organized according to the German flair for system, formulation and theoretic tidiness, expanded and modified by the insights of the Nazi leadership, and simplified according to a rather rigid framework of a few general ideas. Correlated with the astonishingly rapid successes in the field of battle, the propaganda of the *Angstkrieg* achieved considerable success in the war of nerves. The Allied propagandists, after the early obstacles of mili-

tary failure and the skepticism of their own publics, who had been indoctrinated by twenty years of antipropaganda propaganda, achieved what
many viewed as notable successes in the latter part of the war, when
their own armies were winning. And yet, in retrospect, it is evident that
events, action in the field, dramatic defeats and victories, and other objective realities usually changed opinions of large publics to a degree that
was not matched nor prevented by propaganda campaigns. No great
nation in the modern world can neglect political propaganda, which
achieves many marginal successes, but none can achieve by propaganda
alone the results envisioned by enthusiasts for psychological manipulation.

It is instructive to examine some charts relating the state of civilian
morale and expectations of victory in World Wars I and II, as compared
to the objective realities of the military situation. Apparently the military
situation, in so far as the larger publics have the information accurately
to assess that situation, looms larger than the special pleaders' words in
determining public opinion.

In 1918 the Allies conducted an extensive propaganda campaign within
Germany by means of leaflets, books, newssheets and pamphlets which
were distributed by planes and balloons and in various ways smuggled

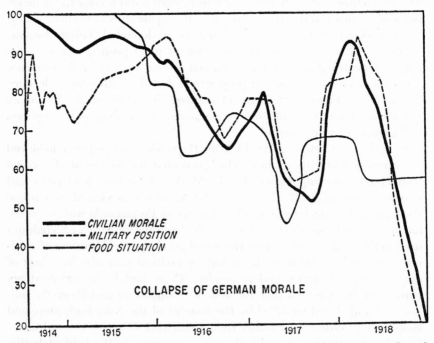

Fig. 6. German morale in World War I. (From G. G. Bruntz, "Allied Propaganda and
the Collapse of German Morale in 1918," *Public Opinion Quarterly,* January, 1938,
p. 64. Permission to reproduce granted.)

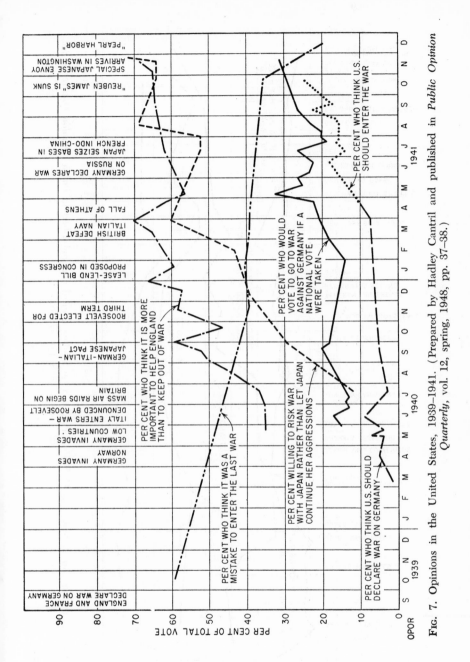

FIG. 7. Opinions in the United States, 1939–1941. (Prepared by Hadley Cantril and published in *Public Opinion Quarterly*, vol. 12, spring, 1948, pp. 37–38.)

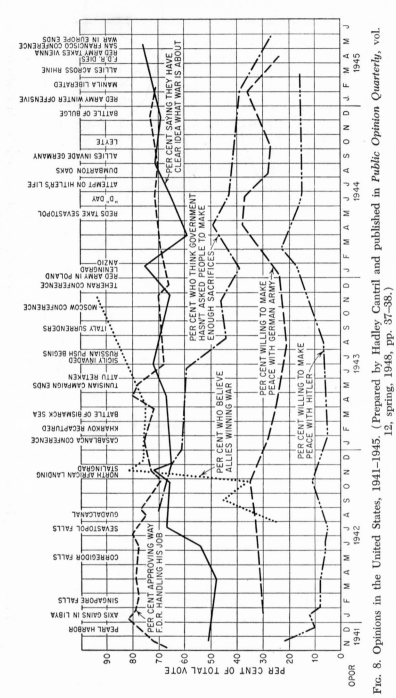

FIG. 8. Opinions in the United States, 1941–1945. (Prepared by Hadley Cantril and published in *Public Opinion Quarterly*, vol. 12, spring, 1948, pp. 37–38.)

300

into Germany. These aimed to shatter the faith of Germans in their own leaders and ideas and thus disrupt morale. Dr. Thimme credits the United States with providing the fundamental thesis of this drive through President Wilson's utterances for freedom and democracy against militarism and autocracy. Though it cannot be denied that Allied propaganda was an important factor in disrupting German morale in 1918, it is possible that its influence in bringing about the German downfall has been overestimated. Most of the Allied propagandists who have written about this campaign have perhaps overestimated the effectiveness of their own work, and German commentators, likewise, have had patriotic reasons to overestimate the results of this drive. Civilian morale appears to have followed closely the trends of German military position and success and failure. G. G. Bruntz, using the original charts of the United States War Department, has developed a simple chart indicating military position and the percentages of civilian morale (Fig. 6).

Figures 7 and 8 were prepared and published by Hadley Cantril of the Princeton Office of Public Opinion Research. The opinion materials included in those charts are based on polls gathered for Princeton by the AIPO until 1942, and by the Princeton group after that time. These charts evidence, in the main, a very close parallel between opinions and events.

CHAPTER 15

The Art of Propaganda

Education and true leisure enable men to exercise judgment; propaganda and mass entertainment persuade them to surrender it.

CHARLES MORGAN

Propaganda, used in the broadest sense, as social psychologists have sometimes defined it, simply means any attempt to influence minds and opinions, thus including almost all of communication, education and publicity. Thus used, the term has no specific meaning and is useless for discussion and analysis of the process. A somewhat narrower conception of propaganda is enunciated by those social scientists who "understand by propaganda all sets of symbols which influence opinion, belief, or action on issues regarded by the community as controversial." [1] Yet such a definition would include much of education, most of instruction in the social sciences and most advertising, whenever the public is persuaded that there is really an issue in the selection of x rather than y brand of a product. We have more narrowly defined propaganda as the dissemination of conclusions from concealed sources or with concealed objectives. This process short-cuts reflection and thought, utilizes selection and distortion, in place of more impartial education, and involves an element of deviousness. It is this delineation of the propagandist in terms of motives which alienates the social psychologist, who professionally avoids wherever possible the consideration of motives. Motives are difficult to designate and record, can be reported only indirectly, since they are subjective states, and the discussion of motives usually involves evaluation. Yet a motive of devious manipulation and of its evaluation is involved in what most social scientists and the common man have designated propaganda. F. Tönnies characterized propaganda as "the agitation of public opinion on a large scale for the purpose of spreading an idea without regard to its truth or accuracy." [2] To the common man, propa-

[1] R. K. Merton, *Social Theory and Social Structure*, Free Press, Glencoe, Ill., 1949, p. 265.
[2] F. Tönnies, *Kritik der Öffentlichen Meinung*, Berlin, 1922, p. 79.

ganda implies devious manipulation in which he is not left free to "draw his own conclusions" and is the object of systematic, deliberate manipulation. What are generally called the propaganda campaigns of special-interest groups and of governments characteristically include much general publicity as well as propaganda in this narrower sense.

The process of propaganda is inevitable in modern society. Indignant discussion of propaganda as a "social evil" or "menace" and the advocacy of programs to eliminate propaganda are futile. Propaganda is here to stay. That a great deal of propaganda has been directed toward ends that are harmful to the larger society or to special groups is obvious. Such propaganda cannot be entirely eliminated from the present order, except through a monopolistic control by governments of all the channels of communication. This substitutes official political propaganda for all other special pleadings, as has occurred in the authoritarian states. But under democracy the channels of communication must be kept open. However, there are many limitations upon the activity of contemporary propagandists under relatively free discussion.

The propagandist may be exposed, and a long-drawn-out and expensive campaign may prove a boomerang if a large public is incensed as a result of the exposure. The utilities campaigns and the free-enterprise campaign brought about such repercussions. Then, too, a propaganda campaign may create opposition and arouse a counterpropaganda movement. If the counterpropaganda movement taps widespread popular prejudices, the propagandist cannot be successful, even if he has access to large financial subsidies. The propagandist is also hampered by regulations set up within the various means of communication. Certain legal restrictions may be set up enforcing publicity of the sources of material disseminated in newspapers, motion pictures, radio and other channels of communication. Evasion would probably be easy, and the legal restrictions would need to be carefully worded to avoid interference with freedom of expression, but some regulation is possible. Further, as we have noted, the propagandist is always limited by the existing popular beliefs and prejudices. The best organized special pleading may shatter on a prejudice In addition, the propagandist may be thwarted by popular stupidity, lack of interest or apathy. Mental sluggishness may prove a defense against rapid modification of opinions at the behest of a special pleader. Again, the point is often made that the common man is at a disadvantage because propaganda costs money and special interests have the larger war chest. This is sometimes true, but it must not be forgotten that the general public has political defenders who delight in tilting a lance at special interests. The general public is not defenseless before an organized interest. And finally, the general public may be protected in part by an increased knowledge of the propaganda process. Many believe that if the common man can achieve enough insight into the propaganda process, he can thwart the special pleader who is advocating causes not in the general interest. General publics can also hamper the propagandists if they can select champions of the larger interests who will organize counterpropaganda. The propagandist is himself ruled and limited by his social milieu, and a part of that environment is the alertness, intelligence and critical ability of the publics with which he operates. Although propaganda is pervasive and will be persistent, it need not be fatal to intelligent popular decisions.

How may a public be educated to detect and resist propaganda? I believe that the answer lies in the cultivation of general awareness of the propaganda process, the development of intelligent suspicion as to sources of information, and not in the providing of specific methods for propaganda analysis.

If the methods and techniques of propaganda are not always new, as of course they cannot be, since the general principles are not infinitely variable, they must be at least innovations in application. In a complex culture, the essence of propaganda is attention-achieving variety. In the case of the simpler peoples, the Communists have found the repetition of simple ideas most effective. But this applies to untutored peoples, half-crazed by malnutrition, poverty, frustration and hate. In the propaganda of interest-groups in the United States, the means and methods are as varied as the ingenuity of complex practitioners of publicity arts can devise. In this situation, it is not possible, by formulating a few simple principles and rules, to implement the propagandee to resist the propagandist. In any case, propaganda is not a devilish process that can be exorcised by a magic formula. From 1936 to 1942, the Institute for Propaganda Analysis, whose publications were widely distributed in high schools, enunciated such a formula. The Institute taught that the knowledge and recognition of seven devices would enable the instructed student to detect and reject propaganda. They were:

1. Name calling—applying a label generally disliked.
2. Glittering generality—applying a term generally considered as "good."
3. Transfer—using symbols of generally revered authority.
4. Testimonial—using endorsements by people with prestige.
5. Plain folks—emphasizing that an individual shares group membership with the audience, is just a common man.
6. Card stacking—selecting facts and falsehoods to line up an argument that is completely convincing.
7. Band wagon—emphasizing the theme of universal endorsement.[3]

Armed with these labels, the informed student could detect the products of the astute propagandist, attach the labels to the appropriate phrases

[3] The descriptive phrases are taken from E. L. Hartley and Ruth E. Hartley, *Fundamentals of Social Psychology*, Alfred A. Knopf, Inc., New York, 1952, p. 85.

and then reject the entire appeal as effectless on one cultivated, educated student sleuth.[4]

The Institute's labeling procedure rigidly channels analysis and is much too limited a device to survey properly the vast terrain between the channels. Moreover, forms of appeal and the assessment of motives of the propagandist are not examined adequately. The Institute emphasizes the essentially emotional nature of propaganda appeals and castigates emotional appeals. But, as we have noted in our earlier discussions, emotional appeals in communication are inevitable and, indeed, frequently desirable. The question is which emotions, how used and to what ends.

The Institute's procedures are not all futile. To educate people to scrutinize closely the content of statements, to attempt to ascertain exact meaning, to search for ambiguities, to be suspicious of some types of emotional appeals, all these provide useful education. But the particular propaganda utterances should not be wrenched from their context, broken into small units, and then picked up in a large meshed bag from which most significant items escape.

RUSSIAN PROPAGANDA THEORY AND METHOD

Though the propagandas of private special-interest groups were most extensively discussed in the United States from 1920 to 1940, the propagandas of governments have engaged the popular attention since that time, especially the propagandas of Nazi Germany and Soviet Russia.

Since 1945 the most pervasive and complete governmental propaganda and censorship is to be found in Russia and its satellites. For governments, censorship is the concomitant of propaganda. In the democracies, even in wartime, extensive legal restrictions on censorship are retained. Indeed, censorship is ruefully viewed by most as a temporary expedient made necessary by the dangers of war. In authoritarian ideologies, censorship, as well as propaganda, is not an expedient to be discarded in time, but a permanent process of power for control of the masses by a political elite. The censor deletes, while the propagandist more than fills the gaps.

Russian censorship and propaganda, if it does not drop an iron curtain between itself and the remainder of the world, at least imposes extremely substantial obstacles which pervert and distort such communication as does occur. Thus, a book entitled *The Soviet Image of the United States*

---

[4] Perhaps the best exposition of the Institute's position could be found in A. M. Lee and E. B. Lee, *The Fine Art of Propaganda*, Harcourt, Brace and Company, New York, 1939. Professor Lee was Director of the Institute for a time. In my opinion, the student would be much better prepared to understand the propaganda process and detect specific propagandas, if he had read a general book on the subject, such as A. M. Lee, *How to Understand Propaganda*, Rinehart & Company, Inc., New York, 1952, than by studying all the reports that the Institute ever published.

is properly subtitled *A Study in Distortion.* The considerable outward flow of propaganda from Russia to the rest of the world is composed of opportunistically selected materials that are intended to confuse, disrupt and, ultimately, to disintegrate the enemy.[5]

Moreover, the great bulk of such propaganda is disseminated according to the "oral agitation" policy of Russia, by convinced Communists, of whatever nationality, who rumormonger as amateur and personal propaganda agents, in contrast to the institutional agents of the democracies, such as radio's Voice of America. Many populations of the world offer a more fertile field for the personal oral agitator than for the mass media.

From 1917 until after the purges of the mid-thirties, when the control of the Russian people by the Communist leaders became firm, the principal propaganda effort of Russia had been directed by the masters of the Kremlin at the Russian people themselves. After the mid-thirties, more secure at home, the Communist Party increasingly directed propaganda efforts abroad. Political propaganda properly begins at home and the bulk of Soviet propaganda is directed at Russian and satellite publics. The amount of Communist propaganda was estimated as $1,500,000,000 for the year 1951, of which $840,000,000 was expended by Russia.[6] When Lenin said that the Soviet regime must rest on a proper balance of coercion and persuasion, the gospel statement for the importance of persuasive propaganda had been enunciated. In the early period after the Russian revolution, a diverse people, unequipped with mass-media devices, had to be welded together by the oral agitator; and from this experience there emerged the organized techniques of person-to-person

---

[5] A social science literature about Soviet Russian organization, methods and psychology is developing in the 1950's. The voluminous writings from 1930 to 1950 were largely concerned with the Russian experiment, the revolutionary socialist state, the possible pattern of tomorrow, and the like. The more recent and realistic analysis is devoted to the dissection of the strategy and tactics of Russia, the monolithic fighting machine. Among these books are:

G. A. Almond, *The Appeals of Communism,* Princeton University Press, Princeton, N.J., 1954.

F. C. Barghoorn, *The Soviet Image of the United States,* Harcourt, Brace and Company, Inc., New York, 1950.

R. A. Bauer, *The New Man in Soviet Psychology,* Harvard University Press, Cambridge, Mass., 1952.

M. Fainsod, *How Russia Is Ruled,* Harvard University Press, Cambridge, Mass., 1953.

S. King-Hall, *The Communist Conspiracy,* Constable & Co. Ltd., London, 1953.

A. Inkeles, *Public Opinion in Soviet Russia,* Harvard University Press, Cambridge, Mass., 1950.

N. Leites, *The Operational Code of the Politburo,* McGraw-Hill Book Company, Inc., New York, 1951.

P. Selznick, *The Organizational Weapon,* McGraw-Hill Book Company, Inc., New York, 1952.

[6] A. Leviero, *New York Times,* Dec. 11, 1951.

persuasion so widely and, often, successfully used by Russia at home and abroad. The Cominform, or Communist Information Bureau, directs propaganda efforts outside Russia. In contrast, the Western nations have had neither the techniques, the field personnel, the opportunity nor the desperate drive to convince alien populations one person at a time. The big guns of radio, press and economic programs have spoken for the United States, but often have not been heard. Of course, Russia has controlled and used the mass media also, for propaganda purposes at home and abroad, but has done so on top of the vast substructure of oral propaganda. In Russia the administration of the molding and mobilizing of public opinion by propaganda, as well as other aspects of persuasion, is carried on by the Department of Propaganda and Agitation, the generally labeled *Agitprop* organization. The head of this department ranks high in importance in the Soviet hierarchy, administering an organization which has the central responsibility for manipulating public opinion. Having received the basic policy decisions of the Politburo, the department determines the general line and the specific tactics of opinion formulation. There is no area of intellectual activity, no communication which might influence public opinion, which is free from the scrutiny and control of this department.

The ultimate test of Soviet, as of other political propaganda, will be determined by the vicissitudes of the Russian Communist political system in winning and retaining popular favor by providing the essential wants of masses of people. These are not infinitely malleable by words. In the meantime, owing especially to the tactics of oral agitation and propaganda, Soviet Russian propaganda is far from ineffective among the propertyless, resentful, politically unenfranchised, frustrated, mentally undeveloped masses of mankind.

The cleverness and skill of the Soviet propagandist are vastly overrated by the common man of Britain or America. To a lesser degree, the effectiveness of Russian propaganda has been overstated, as many conquests have been too largely ascribed to propaganda and psychological warfare, when they are primarily the product of situation, of force and terror, of organization and the seizure of power. "If the communists have discovered anything new, it is not the power of the word, but the power of a dedicated, disciplined, ruthless combat party. We risk dangerous misunderstanding if we try to interpret this kind of operation in terms of our own most commonly held folklore about psychological warfare." [7] It is more likely the propagandist spawned by a Madison Avenue advertising agency who overstates the importance of word appeals alone. Nonetheless, the Russian propagandists have almost monopolized certain

[7] Wilbur Schramm, unpublished paper on "Soviet Psychological Warfare."

simple key words which label dominant values in human wants. For example, they have urgently promulgated the "peace" campaigns. The harried, worn, harassed masses of the world yearn for peace. So Communist propaganda has stressed the slogans and symbol of peace (the peace dove) during the 1950's. There has been an attempt to present Russia and its satellites as primarily concerned with peace. China has also taken up the theme. Volunteer peaceful armies of peace-loving peoples perpetrate peaceful annihilation on the surrounded warmongering French in Indo-China and arm huge armies against the non-peace-loving warmongering Americans! In early 1956, it was said, in the classic upside-down language of communism: "The Chinese people unanimously support the peace policy of their government. They are ready to stand together to fight for the return of Formosa to the motherland." [7a]

After conferences in Stockholm and Warsaw, completely stage-managed by Russia, a World Peace Council was set up and held its first congress in Berlin in February, 1951. An enormous propaganda in the ensuing years demanded international legislation against international propaganda. All peace-loving peoples should surrender all their ideological and physical weapons, desist from psychological or physical preparation for war, and, as an evidence of good will, should surrender to a force that had swept over a dozen nations in which untold numbers of human beings then found themselves looking into the end of a rifle barrel, just before an ardent, peace-loving man on the other end pulled the trigger. Absurd appeal? Not at all, in a world in which there is much pacifist sentiment and much more that can be cultivated.

The motivating policy of Communist Russia cannot be discerned by first examining the materials of the propaganda campaigns. Attempting to work back from these often apparently contradictory items, one would frequently conclude, in the words of Sir Winston Churchill, that one is dealing with "a riddle wrapped in a mystery inside an enigma." For the Party leadership is not concerned with consistency in its statements, especially in the exported propaganda claims. But the Russian Communist Party is vitally concerned with clear doctrine and ideological consistency. To Western minds, unimpressed with the cogency and consistency of that doctrinal pattern, the varying doctrinal interpretations may appear as tactics, whereupon the British or American newspaper reader attempts to interpret what is back of the propaganda statements. He is immediately confused, for you cannot understand Russian propaganda if it is merely examined to see whether it is consistent, truthful or sensible. To analyze thus is to work backwards. A propaganda output that ascribes a Republican victory to the diversionary tactics of Marilyn Monroe, that claims food packages from the United States to East Germany contained polio

7a *Time*, Jan. 9, 1956.

germs, that states that floods in Holland "testify to the criminal indifference of the Marshallized governments of Western Europe toward civil works of public utility," and that declares that a dog in New York inherited 75 million dollars, requires some unifying concepts. Such stories make sense only when they can be made to fit into an ideological pattern fairly consistently maintained among the Russian, Chinese and satellite populations. The stories are not clever nor complex, but work, to some degree, among uninformed indoctrinated masses who have been taught that there is no limit to the inhuman cruelty and chicanery of capitalist ruling classes.

Throughout the world of industrial society, there are perennial tensions between worker and industrialist or manager that can be exploited by emotional appeals. Where conditions are most favorable to the worker, as in the United States and Britain, this appeal has little success. In the rigid orders of Italy and France, it has been very successful. Among the agricultural workers of the Orient, the exploitation of hatred of landowners has been relatively easy. "Belly" Communist victories require little cleverness and little formal, consistent ideology. Simple emotional appeals will serve. The propaganda cannot be understood if it is merely examined to see whether it is consistent or truthful or sensible.

As was frequently true of Nazi propaganda, a flood of items, mutually inconsistent, may be poured on the world outside the Soviet orbit. The intent is not the conversion of the enemy, but the creation of confusion, a condition under which authoritarian administrations believe they can survive better than the democracies. "Their main purpose is to confuse the majority with contradictory stories that will be repeated here and there until people do not know where the truth is. They aim to start lies that will discourage those who hope for a free world, that will poison the trust between friendly nations, and stir up hatred between races and classes." [8] The aim is to sow discord and dissension, to induce argument and tension, while at the same time presenting the Soviet Union as monolithic and impregnable to ideas, as well as to force.

Along with a flood of peripheral items, there are the central themes, such as the peace campaigns, the germ warfare charges, and the "hate America" program. After the war, the Russians apparently hoped, for a time, that the United States would leave Europe and revert to isolationism. For some years, Great Britain was castigated as the chief enemy of communism and the Soviet Union. But with the Marshall Plan and NATO, it appeared that the United States would be the new leader of the Western world. From 1948 onward the United States has been attacked as the archenemy of Russia, and successive hate campaigns have been organized. However, the organization is not just that of a publicity

[8] *Confuse and Control*, U.S. Department of State Publication 4107, p. 5.

bureau sending out stories. Once the policy line was determined, the 6 million Communist Party members in Russia and the Communists elsewhere in the world took up the theme of "hate America" for persistent, insistent and perennial oral agitation. The basic strength of Communist propaganda exists in this organizational structure of the Party.

Communist theory in Russia demands that the control of the media of communication and of the propaganda and agitation must be concentrated in the Party. And so it is. The Central Committee created the Department of Propaganda and Agitation, the popularly designated *Agit-prop*. There is a Sector (Sektor) on Agitation which provides the few central appeals to the masses, and a Sector on Propaganda which is responsible for the indoctrination of Party members and the special groups of the intelligentsia who require more diversified appeals than the masses. The department takes the basic policy decisions of the Politburo and decides the course of action in all matters affecting Soviet public opinion at all levels. It is also the chief agency responsible for transmitting mass attitudes to the leaders, though the secret police also prepare reports on the state of mass thinking.

Despite the range of its responsibilities, however, the department is not primarily an operational agency. It does not do any major publishing; it does not operate the Soviet radio or make films. It is devoted to setting policy and to securing the execution of that policy by the party, government, and public organizations which actually operate the media of communication. Its function, of the broadest scope, is exercised at the national level, yet its impact is felt at the lowest reaches and in the smallest matters.[9]

A third unit, the Sector for Cultural Enlightenment, supervises the activities of village reading huts, libraries, museums and related institutions. There are subsections on the central press, on the regional press, another on the local press, on motion pictures, on radio, a science sector, a school sector, and a sector on art which guides writers, dramatists, musicians and other creative workers. Such is the organization control in Russia and its satellites.

Soviet propaganda is carried on throughout all communications. It is totalitarian, vigorous and ruthless. Russian authors were instructed in 1954 that the mortal sins of deviation from the ideological purity of socialist realism were naturalism, art for art's sake, objectivism, cosmopolitanism, nihilism, sociologism, primitivism, conflictlessness, idealessness, decadence, philistinism, formalism and bourgeois nationalism.[10] Whereupon

[9] Inkeles, *op. cit.*, p. 31. The information contained in the preceding paragraph is drawn from chap. 3.

[10] Reported by Tom Whitney from Moscow, Dec. 25, 1954, for Associated Press.

all literature and the popular arts reflect Communist ideology. Social science, cultivating objectivity as a basic value, does not exist. Name calling permeates supposedly serious communication, such as encyclopedias and philosophy. For example, the *Soviet Encyclopaedia* describes the American Federation of Labor as: "An American trade union organization, uniting primarily the trade union aristocracy and headed by a bought clique of reactionary leaders, the agents of imperialism in the labor movement in the United States." And, of abstract art, the *Encyclopaedia* notes, "One of the reflections of the reactionary ideology of the imperialist bourgeoisie, primarily the Americans, directed against realistic and democratic traditions in art." [11] Elsewhere, in the *Short Philosophical Dictionary,* semantic philosophy is defined as, "A fashionable subjective-idealist movement in bourgeois philosophy which has been particularly widely spread in the U.S.A. in recent years by reactionary ideologists. It is a characteristic form of decadent philosophy in the age of imperialism."

Outside the Soviet Union, after 1947, the Cominform organization of Russia and its satellites systematized and coordinated Communist radio and press propaganda. Using Russian propaganda and agitation techniques, and under predominant Russian control, this organization directed the political attack outside the Communist world.

But above all, at home and abroad, Russian propaganda must be understood, not as the clever emanations from a national publicity bureau, but as an integral part of a forceful combat organization. The propaganda materials are built upon basic policy and theory, aimed at specific objectives, and intended to achieve power victories over less integrated enemies.

Such propaganda is a struggle for the mind of man, from the Soviet point of view, only in the sense that it is a struggle for the material means by which the minds of the masses are believed to be molded. Hence the purpose of Russian propaganda is not peaceful persuasion of the majority of the people in a given country as a prelude to the taking of power. Rather, the task is conceived as that of a minority that must remain an ideological minority until it succeeds in accumulating the material means of obtaining consensus.[12]

The determination, the will and the power to organize, to persuade and impose systems other than communism upon those numerous governments and peoples wavering toward communism, is the best antidote. Anticommunism is inadequate. But which systems, how imposed? The existing political or economic order of the United States or Britain should not be posed as the single alternative to communism, for they are in-

[11] From *New York Times*, Aug. 5, 1951.
[12] H. D. Lasswell, "The Strategy of Soviet Propaganda," *Proceedings Acad. Pol. Sci.*, 24: 2: 77, January, 1951.

applicable in many crucial nations in ferment. A flexible pattern of diverse programs is the only practicable strategy of the noncommunist world.

PUBLICITY PROBLEMS OF THE UNITED STATES

In contrast to the central themes stemming from the ideological system of communism, the United States has experienced diversity in its culture, multiplicity in its ideas, considerable free enterprise in special pleading, and is, in essence, a pluralist society, an open rather than a closed society. This, too, is the culture-background experience of those who determine policy for the United States propaganda program. It is difficult for a person with no real training in a monopolistic ideological system to understand the Communist religion. Perhaps the propaganda agents of a rich, democratic nation were not the most efficient or realistic policy makers to determine the content of propaganda appeals to be made to hungry, jealous and venomous millions living near or below subsistence levels in the ten years after 1945.

Moreover, there are ardent and powerful interest-groups within the United States who would object, and have objected, to the use of realistic appeals (such as the promise of economic reforms and other changes) being made to the peoples of foreign areas in revolutionary mood. So it was difficult and often impossible for the American propagandist to be realistic in his appeals.

Ardent anticommunist agents to serve as agitators in the crucial areas were scarce. The role of emotion and hate as a basis for effective oral propaganda can hardly be overstated. Communism has had large numbers of enthusiasts, concentrated and intense. Soviet propaganda is an expression of ruthless will to defeat the opponents. How can the members of a rich culture, concerned with personal lives, expenditures, adventures, consumption, amours and the like, achieve such levels of intensity? Here is a problem. The peoples and leaders of the West are reluctant to believe and admit that they are engaged in a life-and-death struggle. There is always the reservation that perhaps the enemy will abate his ruthless drive, relax, and cultivate more diverse values. It may be thought that perhaps nothing should be done to make this hoped-for ultimate transformation of the Soviet regime less likely. Such thoughts do not bring the anticommunist propagandists to furious and unending battle. The forces of anticommunism in headlong effort, material and psychological, would be something quite different from the measured opposition of the decade after 1945.

The kaleidoscopic changes in the organization and the program of the United States information services during the decade after 1945 were due to a lack of consistent national policy in international affairs; the suspicion of psychological warriors, expressed frequently by Congress; the rapid organizational changes of agencies, caught in a crossfire between the attacks of their enemies at home and those abroad; and the propaganda failures which led to employment of new personnel and changed organization.

To some extent, the information services are engaged in psychological warfare, which is a more inclusive process than the special pleading of propaganda. "Psychological warfare comprises the use of propaganda against an enemy, together with such other operational measures of a military, economic, or political nature as may be required to supplement propaganda."[13] But, in a broader sense, psychological warfare includes all psychological attacks on the military or civilian ranks of the enemy. Included, in addition to propaganda, are all aspects of the war of nerves, the strategy of terror, and, indeed, any psychological devices expected to debilitate the enemy and provide advantage to the user. Propaganda, therefore, is but one aspect of the broader attack of psychological warfare.

Various agencies of the United States government engaged in propaganda activities in the decade after 1945, though none were devoted to unremitting, dedicated psychological attack on the national enemies.[14] The Office of International Information (OII), under the Assistant Secretary of State for Public Affairs, directed extensive propaganda activities for some years through its divisions on press, on motion pictures and on radio and television. In 1951 the International Information Administration (IIA) was organized within the State Department as a separate agency with a Director responsible to the Secretary of State. This organization had greater funds and facilities at its disposal than the OII. The IIA, having greater freedom of operation, enlarged and expanded the information program. The best-known division of the IIA is the Voice of America in the International Broadcasting Division. By 1952 the VOA was operating 38 short-wave transmitters in the United States and about 50 stations in Europe, Asia and South America. It was broadcasting 70 programs in 48 languages each day. These broadcasts of news, features and music were sent out by professionals, by the regular staff of VOA, and by thousands of citizens of the United States and foreign countries who broadcast in their native languages to their original home-

---

[13] P. M. Linebarger, *Psychological Warfare*, Combat Forces Press, Washington, D.C., 1948, p. 40.

[14] The Brookings Institution report by Charles A. Thomson, entitled *Overseas Information Service of the United States Government*, contains an excellent report on the problems and achievements of the postwar information agencies up to 1948. The Council on Foreign Relations reported on *Public Opinion and Foreign Policy* in 1949, and again, in 1950, Harper & Brothers, New York, published for this organization Frederick S. Dunn's *War and the Minds of Men*.

lands behind the iron curtain.[15] Congressional inquiries and criticism of VOA programs have resulted in a very checkered career for this basic propaganda agency. Except for straight news broadcasts, almost all other content of VOA programs involved this agency in chronic controversy with Congress, various administrative agencies and many private interest-groups. The export of several hundred films in thirty languages is another information activity of the State Department. The Press division sends out scores of thousands of news items and pictures, pamphlets and periodicals each year. Publicity was also involved in educational exchange programs, library and institute programs, the Marshall Plan program and other activities. The specific organizations need not be described here, since they have changed so rapidly and will probably be reorganized again and again amidst the conflicting policies of changing government. But in the decade after 1945, from a third to a half of the personnel of the Department of State were engaged in what might be called publicity and propaganda activities.

Outside the government, there were various private organizations engaging in international information programs, of which the Crusade for Freedom, with its Radio Free Europe and its propaganda balloons, received the most publicity. Moreover, peoples abroad learned much from the commercial nongovernmental distribution abroad of motion pictures, books, periodicals, press agency dispatches and other mass media. Of course, the partial impressions of American life and culture did not add up to a balanced and accurate representation of life in the United States.

In this postwar decade, the results of the governmental and the private propaganda efforts of the United States were generally disappointing. It was said that the United States was the home of high-powered advertising and that from long experience in skillful commercial advertising its propaganda efforts should flourish. Yet its salesmen were generally ineffective in countering Communist propaganda and winning popular allegiance in the world's critical centers of unrest. The failures should not have been surprising. Implacable psychological warfare could not be adequately countered by publicity techniques. A rampant ideology could not be canceled by somewhat opportunistically composed fragments of special pleading. A Communist propaganda, geared to a Russian national political administration and theory, could not be effectively frustrated by a propaganda which could not depend on consistently maintained policy. Due to a number of fallacies in propaganda strategy and to a

[15] In 1952 the VOA had been expanded a little. In 1951 the VOA was broadcasting 57 hours a week by short wave to Western Europe, the BBC 178 hours and USSR 180 hours; 15 hours to the Near and Middle East and South Asia, compared to 79 by the BBC and 92 by USSR; and 45 hours to the iron curtain countries, in comparison to the 57 hours by the BBC and 75 by the USSR. SOURCE: U.S. Department of State Report.

number of political and economic conditions in the critical areas of the world in which communism and the free world strove for victory, the achievements of the United States in international political propaganda were rather disappointing.

These generalizations applied, especially, to the propaganda approach to the undeveloped peoples of the world, the teeming masses of the Orient, of Asia and Indonesia, of parts of South America and Africa. In the cases of the satellite peoples, it was the Russian propagandists who were frequently disadvantaged, and among the propaganda weary and resistant West Europeans, both Russia and the United States were likely to be less well received than the more cautious British.

It was a fallacy to believe that commercial advertisers had adequate skill to develop the strategy of effective international propaganda. Indeed, their skills had been somewhat less than brilliantly effective in conducting campaigns to influence basic attitudes in the United States, as in the "free-enterprise" campaign. Techniques, at best, were of secondary importance. Propagandizing an idea was not the same as advertising a commodity. With the exception of a few statesmen of publicity to be found among the public-relations counselors, those skilled in commercial advertising should have been used as functionaries in the realm of tactics and then carefully supervised by the policy makers of strategy. The latter are more often to be found among social scientists of much broader training and knowledge in the analysis of cultural diversities than is characteristically found among advertisers. Such strategists would not attempt to "sell" phrases, but would strive to closely relate appeals to the cultural values of the recipients. Moreover, such strategists would have been more aware of the need to integrate propaganda with national policy. Of course, they, too, would have been largely frustrated when the administrative and legislative representatives of conflicting policies exerted pressure upon them.

The advertising approach to international propaganda is not conducive to the development of functionaries who are dedicated practitioners of the propaganda arts. Skills without conviction are inadequate. This is not to say that the propagandist should be evidently straining or desperately intense. And certainly it does not mean that he should present a single program, the United States way of life or the British, as the single alternative to communism. As these are evidently inapplicable to many areas of the world today, such intense propagandizing of a way of life would be self-defeating. I would say only that the propagandas of the West, whatever their contents, had better be promulgated with drive, vigor and energy comparable to that of communism's advocates.

In any case, the lack of consistent policy made impossible the development of a clear, affirmative line by the propagandists of the United States. Therefore, much effort was devoted to countering the Communist charges and vituperations. The radio, movies, books, libraries, speeches, the information and education programs, were engaged in campaigns of truth to counter the "big lies" of the Communists. The United States agencies denied that this country tolerated great racial injustices, engaged in germ warfare, and was inhabited by reactionaries, imperialists and warmongers. Countering enemy propaganda is important, but does not add up to a positive program. Moreover, much of the effort appeared to stem from some general desire for esteem, a wistful wish to be admired, to be the recipients of gratitude and to be emulated. Yet, no national culture could loom over the world, as that of the United States at this time, and be loved by the other peoples of the world. Historically, the dominant power had usually been hated, feared and envied, and the current discrepancy between the wealth and power of the United States and most of the rest of the world guaranteed the persistence of these unlovely emotions. At most, a dominant nation might salvage a degree of honor and respect, but these are rarely accomplished by special pleading.

Another fallacy of the United States effort during this period was an inadequate attention to the voices of others. Hundreds of millions of dollars were spent to communicate to the "free world." But adequate communication does not consist of shouting through a megaphone and listening for echoes. Robert Redfield correctly states that we have attended too little to the national character and personality, the cultural values, the mood, and the more transient feeling tones of other peoples.

I do think that our talking is insufficiently balanced by listening. I do not think that we listen enough to what other people are trying to say to us about themselves, and I do not think we listen enough to the sound of what we say in the ears of him to whom we say it. We are guided chiefly in deciding what to say by the conceptions we have of what those others ought to like about us if they were just like us. And they aren't. They are different in respects to which we are inattentive.[16]

As publicity in the United States is directed at large publics, the propaganda of our psychological warfare has likewise been disseminated among mass populations abroad. That the United States has too exclusively aimed its appeals at large foreign publics rather than at selected minorities therein has been noted as the democratic fallacy in mass propaganda.[17] Our democratic propagandists by inclination and training

[16] R. Redfield, "Does America Need a Hearing Aid?" *Sat. Rev.*, Sept. 16, 1953, p. 11.

[17] H. Speier, "Psychological Warfare Reconsidered," *The Policy Sciences*, Stanford University Press, Stanford, Calif., 1952, pp. 252–271.

think first of mass audiences. But mass audiences are not invariably a rewarding target in international propaganda. What is expected in response to the appeals? In Russia, the now long-taught official Communist ideology provides masses of population with a modicum of psychological security.

As the political elite blankets the area it controls with approved opinions fitting into the official ideology, it offers security, however costly, to the minds of all as it stabilizes the regime. In view of these considerations it is folly to expect that the dissemination of another ideology by foreign propagandists can convert the masses of a population living under despotic rule to become adherents to a new ideology.[18]

Therefore, the propagandist attempts to breech iron or bamboo curtains with believable descriptions of other ways of life and policy-determined news items. Or again, mass appeals may be directed at the exploitation of grievances, the agitation of emotions, and the augmenting of disillusions. As this is direct international psychological warfare, it must obviously be adjusted to over-all national policy; and in peacetime, the democracies are loath to conduct agitation. Among captive satellite populations, it is desirable to maintain a hope of change and augment resistance, but they should not be exploited to their own grave injury. In neither case can the populations overthrow modern despotic regimes without armed domestic and foreign support. The populations remaining outside Communist control offer the best possibilities for propaganda to mass audiences. In all cases, the organization of differentiated propaganda directed at various subgroups within nations was underdeveloped by the United States in the decade after 1945. Overconcerned with mass appeals, the propagandists did not concentrate on selected groups and individuals whose self-interests might be exploited into deviant political behavior.

After 1945 the crux of the propaganda strategy confusion in the United States consisted to a considerable extent in the failure to determine what constituted permissible appeals in the economic field. In impoverished countries, initiative could have little play and, at best, was restricted to a few people. There, masses of people could not be expected to become enthusiastic for a "free enterprise" which they could not envision nor realistically anticipate. Yet the directors of the United States policy, congressional, administrative and propagandistic, were so deeply and so emotionally involved in commitment to "free private enterprise," as the basic and sound economic pattern and as the cure for the economic problems elsewhere in the world, that they resisted the advocacy of and the promise of support for other systems. Alternative systems were

[18] *Ibid.*, p. 258.

inevitably in some degree state socialistic, in view of the economic state of vast areas of the undeveloped or underdeveloped areas of the world. Therefore, though the need for economic programs in the Orient was recognized, indecision was dominant. Nor was it surprising that in the European aid programs the expenditures had, at times, achieved something less than maximum popular response abroad.

However, this indecision frustrated not only the propaganda programs, but also the international economic action programs of the United States. The propagandists needed to show how a rather high degree of economic controls (necessary in the poor, overcrowded, underdeveloped areas of the world) could have been combined with individualism and freedom in other areas of life. They were not free to do so.

During these years, the Communists branded the United States as primarily materialistic. It is true that this American culture is pervaded by material, sensate values. But it also values individualism. A society which has at its center the importance of the individual is a society of spiritual, ethical and nonmaterial values. When the Communists declared our materialism and militarism as the heart of the American system, they were wrong, but their ideology so guided them. Neither they nor the Europeans recognized that the Americans have not simply sought technical innovation, but as a result of material techniques have sought and achieved a revolutionary and widely distributed abundance. Material abundance was to have made man freer, though it did not invariably do so.

Without a totally consistent ideology, the United States was nonetheless committed to certain basic values, and of these human freedom was the most important. We have been committed to human freedom for a long time. In a sense, therefore, we were irrevocably committed to a war of ideas, for freedom and against the police state. This idea is so appealing to masses of mankind, when they understand it, that the Communists dare not let down on propaganda warfare. There could be no compromise or coexistence on ideology and propaganda. Our society would not be readily invaded by the Communist values of control, the police state and restrictions of freedom. But, contrariwise, the Communists dared not permit the intrusion of the idea of greater freedom from regimentation and the increase of individualism to permeate their populations, or the "hard core" of Communist administrators would be in trouble—not only in China, not only in already restive satellites, but, also, in Russia itself. Therefore, they could make no propaganda truce with us—they must have a constant stream of attack so as to divert attention from this value. That the campaigns of the propagandists for the delineation of American freedom should be believable and effective, it was necessary that freedom must be maintained in attractive form in the

United States. It should not be nibbled away by governmental interests, business interests, or interest-groups impressing too much conformity. Unfortunately for the success of the United States propagandists in this decade, a number of congressional and other investigations cast doubt on the state of freedom in the United States. The peril to the individual's freedom was overstated by friends, as well as enemies, abroad, but, in any case, our propagandists' freedom programs were extensively blunted after 1950.

The failures and limited successes of United States propaganda were not primarily failures due to a lack of technical skill among our information officers. The basic fallacies that have been involved in the information programs of the United States were evidently implicit in the international situation and in American culture and politics. They were neither the product of planned obstructions by individuals or groups, nor were they to be overcome by simple panaceas. Within the restrictions and frustrations of the limitations that have been discussed, the programs were quite successful at times, especially when directed at the satellite peoples. They were less successful when received by peoples who had developed rather extensive propaganda fatigue, notably the French, and were least successful when directed at the simpler peoples of the world. The most skillful special pleading by propaganda and information programs could not always be successful in the world of today with its basic warring ideologies. There are some cultural differences which could not be explained, understood or tolerated. There are differences with which we must coexist. We have always done so; and were it not for the menace of spreading communism, cultural diversity and the cultivation of mutual tolerances would be a good greatly to be sought.

THE TECHNIQUES OF PROPAGANDA

A considerable body of information has been accumulated about the psychology of advertising economic goods. In a partial sense there is a science of advertising. There is much verifiable psychological knowledge in this field. Many problems of attention, as related to advertising, have been investigated; categories of appeals and the relative strength of human desires have been inventoried for advertising purposes; the psychologist can tell us much about problems relating to the magnitude, position, color, illustration, line and form, preferable type and the functioning of association in advertisements. Also, he knows something of the manipulation of language in advertising and selling. An expert in sales appeals advises his clients on preferred words and phrases in their advertisements and sales talks. On the basis of verifiable experiment, a great many generalizations have been developed by the psychologist in advertising. The propaganda process has not been so exactly described. There is no literature on the techniques of propaganda comparable with that on advertising. As yet there are very limited experimental data on the methods and the results of propaganda activity. Everyone is at times a propagandist in his daily life experience. And, although we understand a great deal about such person-to-person relationships, there is no compact handbook of generalizations about effective manipulative activities. Propaganda campaigns for groups and organizations are conducted by professional special pleaders, recruited principally from former newspaper and publicity men. Many of these have a vast experience in attempting to manipulate popular attitudes. But they have not been successful in providing generalizations about the process. The reason is quite apparent. The propagandist attempts to manipulate attitudes about political, economic and other controversial issues. The situation in which each issue occurs is individually unique. There are infinite nuances of situation and group attitudes, whereas a great deal of advertising deals with oft-repeated situations. Therefore, at least a portion of advertising may be conducted according to rules. But there is an art and not a science of propaganda. When the students and practitioners of propaganda attempt generalizations, the unsatisfactory nature of the results is evident. The generalizations are too general, the exceptions too apparent. Nevertheless, we shall essay some discussion about generalizations on propaganda techniques.

THE STRATEGY AND TACTICS OF PROPAGANDA

Some broad generalizations on the strategy of propaganda may be possible here, but the description of the very large variety of tactics of propaganda is beyond the scope of this volume. The strategy and tactics of propaganda are obviously quite variable. Are generalizations feasible about the propaganda process among the populations of one nation-culture, as compared to another; about the methods of propaganda for home populations in wartime, and the propagandas of a private interest group, such as Facts Forum; about the international propagandas of peacetime and those of psychological warfare? The following generalizations do not purport to be completely systematic or conclusive. They are simply commentary on some significant characteristics of the propaganda process today.

A. Perhaps a first generalization would be that one must never forget the limitations of propaganda. It cannot cancel basic objective realities, and propaganda is certainly no substitute for policy goals and decisions. The propaganda process may be enormously important, but of itself is rarely basically and finally decisive. If land reform is zealously, emotionally and indignantly demanded and yearned for by an agrarian population, they are not likely to be diverted by information about "free enterprise" in an advanced, industrial society. If great numbers of United States troops are stationed abroad, the foreign population's interpretations of their behavior will not rest on interpretive pamphlets alone. If the "terror," as a power process, is used in the attempted intimidation of a West Berlin stenographer by Communist agents informing her of the "wrath to come," she probably sensibly desires the assurance of continued, effective police protection, rather than a pamphlet on individual freedom under democracy. Yet it is easy for the propagandist to forget or minimize the frequent ineffectiveness of propaganda divorced from action. Moreover, if national policy does not implement the propagandist's promises of a brave new world, or if the facts of political alliances negate words favorable to the aspirations and demands of masses abroad, the propagandist must retreat to generalized political and moral platitudes and the promise at least of "truthful news," in contrast to his opponent's lies. Objective realities and his government's policies circumscribe the propagandist.

B. Amidst maturely experienced populations living under political democracy, the most effective setting for propaganda lies in the creation of an impression that one's own propaganda, both at home and abroad, is bungling, ineffective, inefficient, relatively straightforward and not too clever. In general this impression regarding the quality of propaganda emanating from the United States (the home of the most efficient advertising in the world) had been maintained in the United States during World War I and World War II. During the first postwar decade our population was thoroughly convinced that our international propaganda had been inept and ineffective. As we have seen, this was, in part, true, but there were notable propaganda victories. When national propaganda is avowedly efficient and effective, according to their propaganda ministries, as was the case in Nazi Germany and Fascist Italy, it is evident that such claims are made to impress the home populations, rather than the foreign targets. In this, our propagandists helped, gladly seizing upon these claims and elaborating them into the stereotyped picture of the diabolically effective, efficient and clever foreign propagandists, while our inept experts were bungling along. In a democracy, the astute propagandist does not break cover.

C. The reception of propaganda messages relates to the mood of the public. Mood is dependent upon the dominant personality characteristics of the recipients, their knowledge, situation and experience. In North Korea, the psychological warfare strategists faced a conglomerate enemy composed of North Korean Communists, Chinese Communists, conscripted Chinese Nationalists, and prisoners forced to fight. The enemy was 70 to 90 per cent illiterate. The moods of these groups were various elementary emotions and wants and, above all, were dominated by fear and, sometimes, hunger. Therefore, appeals could be made primarily by the simplest leaflets, containing photographs and illustrations and at most a few hundred language symbols. The appeals were largely unpolitical. At the same time, propaganda to Western Europe faced a fundamental complex of distrust of propaganda that had been growing for three decades.

> The world is more and more tired of propaganda. This is the fundamental, all-embracing fact which every propagandist must face, and the implications of which he must recognize, if he is even to have an entree into the minds of those who are not already emotionally on his side. The psychological resistances of a skeptical, propaganda-weary world must be respected and intelligently taken into account; they cannot be simply battered down.[19]

If propagandists for causes in industrial relations, social welfare and economic issues in America at times have made fundamentally erroneous assessments of the mood of people of their own culture, it is hardly surprising that egregious errors have not been infrequent in international propaganda.

D. In the confusion of contemporary ideas and amidst the prevailing mental insecurities, propagandas perform the dual functions of catharsis and readjustment.[20] Tensions may be partially relieved by mass preoccupation with the symbols that the propagandist provides. There may be little or no change in the objective reality, and yet a partial catharsis results from adherence to a particular propaganda. Thus, propaganda for many causes cannot reasonably be expected to result in the changes that are demanded, but the emotional zeal of the adherents may prove an end in itself. The Townsend movement could not have been expected to be economically practicable in the form in which it was presented, but it could and did result in release of tensions through "wishful thinking." And, incidentally, a leadership achieved prestige. On the other hand, propaganda may be directed toward definite and explicitly stated readjustment. The utilities propaganda has had such an aim, the minimizing of the demand for government ownership. The techniques of propaganda will vary, depending upon whether that propaganda may reasonably expect merely a psychological or an objective response. Unfortunately, we do not now possess a descriptive and analytical literature of specific propaganda campaigns that is extensive or detailed enough to permit of

---

[19] R. K. White, "The New Resistance to International Propaganda," *Pub. Opin. Quar.*, 16: 4: 539.

[20] This useful characterization was suggested by H. D. Lasswell, in *Propaganda and Dictatorship* (H. L. Childs, ed.), Princeton University Press, Princeton, N.J., 1936, p. 111.

logical classifications of types of propaganda and their respective techniques.

E. Another generalization is that propagandists persistently appeal to the emotions of their subjects. Argument and discussion openly carried on is one thing; veiled propaganda appealing to hate, fear, pride, selfishness, greed and the like, is a quite different process, short-circuiting discussion of the issue. Much mass propaganda relies on emotional appeals. The propagandist mobilizes hatred of the enemy, appeals to the fear that economic chaos would result from the opponent's plans, taps the popular allegiances to some loved symbol, and the like. The propagandist does not respect the human mind. He holds man's reason cheap, and he attempts to deprive man of the opportunity to display logical processes. He is not unique in this attempt. Various other types of special pleaders likewise predominantly use emotional appeals. An intelligent minority which recognizes propaganda as such can sometimes discount a part of the emotional appeals, attempt to obtain additional information, partially identify themselves with the opponents, read the literature of the other side and attempt to become intelligent partisans. If he has not hopelessly alienated this group, the propagandist must then prepare appeals calculated to persuade its members. For example, he may utilize the authority of economists, historians and other social theorists to distribute appealing rationalizations; he may prepare subtle, but partial, arguments; he may confuse with statistics, and so forth. But most of his subjects respond to direct emotional appeals, if these are linked with existing attitudes.

F. The propagandist may become a liar. He is often driven by the logic of events to more and more extreme falsehoods. He creates stories about the opposing leaders, falsifies statistics, creates news stories, starts rumors and in many ways falsifies the process of discussion. Such falsification is most effective if it cannot be contradicted because the means of communication are controlled. This is obviously true of much national propaganda in wartime. Of course, in the international propaganda battles, all sides vociferously declare that their opponents are liars. Goebbels, notable as the proponent of the tactic of the "big lie," labeled the BBC, "The Ministry of Lies." In general, the propaganda tactician usually pushes toward those techniques which appear likely to be immediately successful. Therefore, he will use lies, unless checked by the strategists' longer-range values. Implicit in the principles of the Psychological Warfare Division of SHAEF were—

several operating rules of technique, which were never explicitly formulated but were fairly scrupulously observed by the output sections of Sykewar. These rules may be distinguished as follows:

1. When there is no good reason to suppress or revise the facts, tell them.

2. Aside from considerations of "military security," the only good reasons for suppressing or revising the facts are that the audience will not believe them or will detect their inaccuracy.

3. Every time your audience catches you in a lie, of omission as well as commission, your power over it is seriously weakened.

4. For this reason, overt ("white") Sykewar output will *never* tell a lie in which it might be caught by the audience.[21]

However, truth telling for policy purposes is readily corruptible.

Sir Arthur Ponsonby collected a number of official and unofficial falsehoods of the English in World War I. Among these were the atrocity stories. They were circulated by word of mouth, leaflets, speeches and newspapers. Stories of assaults, torturings, rapes, attacks on children, and the like, were widely circulated. The German army as invaders were at a disadvantage in the dissemination of such stories. Their propagandists could not reply in kind. Of course, amidst the brutalities of war, such things do happen. But the majority of the atrocity stories were outright fabrications. Some of these stories were officially created; few were denied. Faked photographs, the doctoring of official papers, the falsehoods about the enemy's strength and morale, the ascribing of satanic motives, were commonplace techniques of the propaganda bureaus. The crop of propagandists' lies in wartime can be large because the means of communication are controlled, the general population has developed a maximum will to believe and no substantial opposition exists. Due to the later debunking of these frequently false World War I atrocity stories, publics were very skeptical of such stories at the beginning of World War II. Therefore, during most of the war, the actually horrible atrocities of Nazi Germany were little used by the British and American propagandists.

G. In deviations from the truth the success of fabrications depends on the credibility and plausibility of the stories to the recipients, the credulity of the audience and the improbability of effective refutation. In the Korean War, the United States dropped leaflets that contained photographs of their North Korean and Chinese prisoners eating well and playing games. Wishing to protect the men in the photographs from possible identification and later reprisals by the Communists, the photographs were retouched, placing a black band across the eyes (the type of procedure to be found in any United States magazine hiding the identity of a person in a photograph). These photographs were intended to bring about desertions of enemy troops, or at least to make them not fear capture. However, the Communists told and apparently persuaded

[21] D. Lerner, *Sykewar*, George W. Stewart, Publisher, Inc., New York, 1949, p. 195. See also, A. Koyre, "The Political Function of the Modern Lie," *Contemp. Jewish Record*, June, 1945, pp. 290 ff.

most of their own troops that the reason for the masked photographs was that the United States torturers had so mutilated the faces of the prisoners that they could not be shown. Finally, the United States had to stop dropping these masked photographs.

In February, 1952, the North Korean, Chinese and Russian Communists began their world-wide "germ warfare" accusations against the United States. This violent propaganda campaign was aimed primarily at the arousal of emotions in the Communist-dominated areas and among the less informed peoples of the world, although large Communist protest parades were organized in Italy, France, West Germany and elsewhere. The charge was that Korean and Chinese Communists had been made the target of bacteriological weapons. It was charged that flies, fleas (seldom disease carriers, and difficult to raise in laboratories), spiders, ants, crickets and various objects, leaves, crackers, goose feathers, and what not, were germ laden and dumped on the Communist armies and civilians. The usual cholera, plague, anthrax and other outbreaks that spring were ascribed to bacteriological warfare. The International Red Cross and the World Health Organization were refused permission to investigate and report, but a Russian Communist scientific organization "reluctantly concluded" that "the American imperialists have perpetrated a new crime, a bacterial attack." Evidence was forged, confessions were extorted from airmen (as was later presented in detailed report to the United Nations), and Chinese drives were organized for the extermination of rats and flies. The Communists' clean-up campaigns were furthered, emotions were aroused, and the United States accused of a dastardly form of warfare. The germ-warfare campaign was intended to appeal to millions of people who were already suspicious of and fearful of the power and scientific achievements of the United States. The campaign might not convince Jacob Malik's colleagues in the UN (indeed, the press reported that Sir Gladwyn Jebb, who sat on Malik's left, said that "my right ear has become seriously infected by the perpetual dissemination of verbal bacilli"), but it seems to have had plausibility to many millions of the credulous.

The United States "Campaigns of Truth," started in 1950, were propaganda of another order, less emotional, more rational, and sound propaganda strategy in the West, as were the Communists' "Peace Campaigns" of 1949.[22] Western Europe was as weary of propaganda prevarications as it was eager for peace. And, indeed, a strategy of truth is compatible with democratic theory and should be its practice. However, the practitioners of propaganda are perennially intrigued by the tricks, stunts and

---

[22] An account of the launching of the Truth programs may be read in E. W. Barrett, *Truth Is Our Weapon*, Funk & Wagnalls Company, New York, 1953. Mr. Barrett had charge of these programs at their inception.

clever gadgets of the profession. Unless held back by policies administratively applied to restrain them, most propagandists try to innovate clever tactics. The very process of propaganda tends toward increasing deviousness, unless sharply curbed.

H. Just as individuals in face-to-face conversation exaggerate the stories, rumors and information that they transmit so that they may gain effectiveness, the propagandist exaggerates in the interest of his cause. The publicity men of political parties exaggerate the derelictions of their opponents, the propagandists for grain manipulators exaggerate the news reports of crop shortages, the military propagandist exaggerates victories, the actress's publicity man exaggerates the value of her stolen jewels— indeed, all special pleaders exaggerate at times. In this activity they are aided by the popular tendency to embellish an account. In the copying of newspaper stories the account is sometimes garbled into an exaggerated form. This is often intentional. The processes of exaggeration are inevitable, but the propagandist consciously distorts in this way, thereby adding to existing confusions.

I. The propagandist further distorts by selection. He is not concerned with providing impartial data. He has a cause to plead. His problem consists principally in selecting such information and such social suggestions as are best calculated to evoke the desired responses. A propagandist for the Federation of Utility Investors (renamed American Federation of Investors) cannot be expected to disseminate impartial information about the TVA. Selection and particular emphasis become so much a commonplace in the propagandist's experience that after a time he is not consciously aware of his choices. Just as a veteran newspaper correspondent "slants" the news in the direction of his employer's or readers' attitudes, so the propagandist plays up materials favorable to his cause and underemphasizes the rest. The propagandist's selection of his comments upon any controversial issue will be determined by what he can successfully work into any medium of communication. In the total situation in which he operates there may be very little that he can inject into communication. When St. Thomas' Church in New York was built, a waggish young architect worked in a dollar sign over the bride's door and three moneybags initialed J. P. M. over the choir stalls. Anything more obvious would have been discovered even sooner than were these items. In extreme instances the propagandist may work painstakingly to introduce one item favorable to his cause. About 1920 the late Ivy Lee inspired the writing of an article about the Cathedral of St. John the Divine for the *New York Times Magazine,* so that he could incorporate therein a single phrase. This phrase declared that the metalwork of the cathedral was made of copper, "The Metal of the Ages." At that time, Mr. Lee was a propagandist for the copper producers. These are unusual illustrations. However, in his more normal activities, the propagandist persistently selects items, slants the news and omits data favorable to the opposition. He is the foe of even a relative degree of impartiality.

J. One of the oldest devices of the manipulator of public opinion is the distraction of attention by the use, among others, of the "red-herring" technique. The propagandist finds it invaluable. In face-to-face argument, a simple device for confuting an opponent is to lead him off the track of the principal issue into the discussion of some trivial point or to divert him into the discussion of something quite beside the point at issue. State other propositions, inject irrelevant objections and change the issues. Just so, in dealing with publics, the propagandist frequently attempts to distract attention from items dangerous to his cause. The methods of popular diversion are of infinite variety. Inject humor and satire, call names, divert attention to personalities, change the issue, center attention upon unimportant and harmless matters or distract the group's attention to points favorable to one's own position. The hard-pressed employer in labor disputes may divert attention to welfare activities; publics are distracted from political issues by "bread and circuses"; the opponents of woman suffrage turn attention upon the role of woman as mother and homemaker; the political boss diverts attention from political issues to his party's beneficences; the special pleader questions the honesty and motives of his opponents. Of course, not only the hidden propagandist, but all special pleaders, use this device at times.

K. The propagandist eternally repeats his assertions. The value of repetition has been experimentally tested by advertisers, as any volume on the psychology of advertising will attest. "If you have an idea to put over, keep presenting it incessantly. Keep talking (or printing) systematically and persistently." [23] In *Mein Kampf*, Hitler stated, "The intelligence of the masses is small, their forgetfulness is great. Effective propaganda must be confined to merely a few issues which can be easily assimilated. Since the masses are slow to comprehend, they must be told the same thing a thousand times." One need not be a cynical commentator on the mental limitations of the common man functioning in large groups to realize the psychological effectiveness of repetition.

L. It is a propagandist's rule to avoid argument. Dr. Goebbels, major propaganda chief of Germany, had this to say. "The ordinary man hates nothing more than two-sidedness, to be called upon to consider this as well as that. The masses think simply and primitively. They love to generalize complicated situations and from their generalizations

[23] Rule number one of propaganda, in K. Dunlap, *Social Psychology*, The Williams & Wilkins Company, New York, 1925, p. 256.

to draw clear and uncompromising conclusions." In this rule he has the blessing of the psychologist. Professor Dunlap writes, "Avoid argument as a general thing. Do not admit there is any 'other side' and in all statements scrupulously avoid arousing reflection or associated ideas, except those which are favorable. Reserve argument for the small class of people who depend on logical processes, or as a means of attracting the attention of those with whom you are arguing." [24]

M. The contemporary propagandist can and does tap all the accumulated lore and science regarding the most efficacious methods of attracting attention. The principles of attention are too many and varied for discussion at this point. Startling statements, sudden appeals, color, size and position of published items, novelty, appeals to interests, an infinite variety of direct sensory stimuli, the spectacular, the creation of conflicts, and the like, are standard methods of attracting attention.

N. However, such generalizations as we have been enunciating are of but limited usefulness to the propagandist or to those who would understand the propaganda process, because they must be applied with infinite variation to the particular situations. As Dr. Goebbels said, "Propaganda in itself has no fundamental method. It has only purpose— the conquest of the masses. Every means that serves this end is good." The propagandist must adapt his methods and the content of his appeals to the common social attitudes of his subjects. For example, when dealing with large publics in the United States, he ordinarily should not appeal to avowed self-interest on the part of his subjects. Such publics have long been nurtured in an atmosphere of professed unselfishness. Hence, the development of special pleading or of a program of action based upon consciously selfish interests, the pursuit of individual or group self-interest, is repugnant in a culture that, at least verbally, subscribes to the larger group interests. Therefore, any programs of self-interest must usually be camouflaged with a protective coating of rationalizations which interpret them in terms of the values of the prevailing mores. This is necessary, not only for the popular acceptance of the propagandist's statements, but also for the comfort of really self-interested minorities. For, incorporated in the attitudes of these, too, are the altruistic catchwords.

O. The propagandist must know the prevailing attitudes of his subjects. And he must, in every possible way, connect with their dominant attitudes the idea that he wishes to promulgate. Many a propaganda item has failed of acceptance because of the ineptitude of the propagandist who has failed to inform himself of some deep-seated prejudice. Class appeals have often been futile in the development of the American labor movement. Lasswell recounts the failure of German propaganda in

[24] *Ibid.*, p. 256.

World War I to arouse the desired response with its account of Belgian Roman Catholic priests' having urged their parishioners to bushwhack the invading German troops; the failure was due to the prejudice of Roman Catholics both abroad and in Germany against believing that priests would give such advice. The propagandist must use traditional prejudices to which he may relate his cause and be careful not to run afoul of deeply imbedded adverse prejudices. B. Russell maintains that successful propaganda essentially makes people hold more emotionally to their opinions and beliefs, rather than develop new opinions. For example, the propagandist knows, as does the advertising man, the value of relating his cause to popular figures having prestige. Attitudes favorable to these prominent personages already exist. And so, such personages are urged to say a few words, be four-minute speakers, endorse a cause, sign a proclamation, enunciate the desired rationalizations. We have referred to propaganda as an art and not a science, because there can be no hard-and-fast rules that may be experimentally verified about such procedures. The propagandist must study existing popular beliefs and opinions, so that he may know which ideas, words, symbols, persons and organizations the majorities of a population are for and against. Then he relates his cause to the favorable attitudes, usually stating the relationship in very general and nonspecific ways. Thus he hopes to stimulate decision and not debate.

P. As the technique of propaganda is the manipulation of symbols, the propagandist must have a thorough knowledge of the symbols whereby attitudes are expressed. Incomplete knowledge of some of the nuances of symbol meaning and popular emotional linkages to these symbols has led to fatal errors in appeal. This problem is especially acute when the propagandist is dealing with people of a culture alien to his own. He must then rely upon the advice of those intimately acquainted with the meanings of words (the dictionary is inadequate for popular meanings), with the popular responses to pictorial representation and with all other types of symbols.

Q. The propagandist must be simple, clear and precise. He may attempt to provide a spurious but convincing clarity to the workings of his program by giving opportunity for firsthand contacts with his program. Hence, the propaganda tours which were conducted through Soviet Russia, Nazi Germany, Fascist Italy or Communist China. He may simplify with exhibits, personalizations, simple statistics, oversimplified definitions, slogans, concretions of abstractions, catechisms of questions and answers, dramatizations, stories and illustrations, pictures, specific instances, demonstrations, familiar terms, and the like. Most of these procedures for simplification appear in any well-organized propaganda campaign. Quantifications are increasingly used, since general publics are even less competent in analyzing statistics than in winnowing out significant facts from verbal presentations. Yet there is a widespread faith that figures do not lie. Such simplifications are frequently fatal to impartial consideration but are usually useful in the dissemination of conclusions.

But, as we stated at the beginning of this discussion of propaganda techniques, we cannot satisfactorily generalize about the propaganda processes.[25] The propagandist exercises his ingenuity upon a particular situation, and, if he is a successful propagandist, his methods are infinitely adaptable to situations. He utilizes whatever he can of the techniques of publicity that, at the same time, permit him to remain concealed. He works through the various secondary means of communication, the press, printed forms in general, radio, pictures, inspired rumors and the like. As he must appeal to large groups, there is a premium upon simplicity, emotional appeals and direct suggestions. He seeks to exert social pressures but works indirectly. His aim is the widespread acceptance of his conclusions. But he is limited by his own inadequacies, by the existing "field structure," by existing ignorances, by popular prejudices, by the limitations upon his control of and his access to the various media of communication and by his opportunities to obtain a monopoly by the silencing of oppositions by censorship. Finally, the more successful propagandists usually are able to convince themselves. A part of the technique of propaganda consists of the ways in which the propagandist manipulates his own attitudes and values. If he cannot integrate his own position, he usually lacks zeal. Skillful propagandists may have doubts, but these doubts must not loom too large in their daily work.

[25] In this book I have not attempted to provide a general description of the various national propaganda organizations and their methods in World Wars I and II. Nor can such descriptions be found in any one source. A brief, working bibliography on the war propagandas includes: *World War I*—H. D. Lasswell, *Propaganda Technique in the World War*, Alfred A. Knopf, Inc., New York, 1927; H. Thimme, *Weltkrieg ohne Waffen*, Cotta, Berlin, 1932; G. G. Bruntz, *Allied Propaganda and the Collapse of the German Empire in 1918*, Stanford University Press, Stanford, Calif., 1938; J. R. Mock and C. Larson, *Words That Won the War*, Princeton University Press, Princeton, N.J., 1939. *World War II*—F. C. Bartlett, *Political Propaganda*, The University Press, Cambridge, England, 1940; H. Lavine and J. Wechsler, *War Propaganda and the United States*, Yale University Press, New Haven, Conn., 1940; H. L. Childs and J. B. Whitton (eds.), *Propaganda by Short Wave*, Princeton University Press, Princeton, N.J., 1942; C. J. Rolo, *Radio Goes to War*, G. P. Putnam's Sons, New York, 1942; D. Sington and A. Weidenfeld, *The Goebbels Experiment: A Study of the Nazi Propaganda Machine*, Yale University Press, New Haven, Conn., 1943; E. Kris and H. Speier, *German Radio Propaganda*, Oxford University Press, New York, 1944; R. K. Merton and others, *Mass Persuasion*, Harper & Brothers, New York, 1946; C. I. Hovland and others, *Experiments on Mass Communication*, Studies in Social Psychology in World War II, Princeton University Press, Princeton, N.J., 1949; D. Lerner, *Sykewar: Psychological Warfare Against Germany*, George W. Stewart, Publisher, Inc., New York, 1949.

The process of propaganda is inevitable in modern society and this form of special pleading is increasingly pervasive. Managerial technicians, private or political, might wish that the process had become more efficient, while those perturbed by the attempted molding of mind-life may over-rate the effectiveness of propaganda. The general public has defenses in addition to the resistances inherent in mental sluggishness, prejudices and relatively fixed habits of mind. The propagandas of private interest-groups are in part cancelled by the competition of other organizations, though by no means always or on all topics. Propaganda analysis par-tially arms some of the more literate sections of the population, as long as freedom of inquiry endures and the channels of communication are kept open. Also the propaganda of many a special-interest will be countered by political leaders who are self-appointed champions of large publics, and by the criticisms and analyses prepared by humanistically minded spokesmen from education, religion and, sometimes, from the legal profession. In political democracy, governmental propaganda is restrained, except under conditions of war, by regulations, the restric-tions of law, the watchfulness of parties and the balance of executive and legislative power. International propaganda is restricted or countered in various ways by the democratic and authoritarian states. Iron and bamboo curtains are not impenetrable, nor is the effective con-ditioning of publics against alien appeals invariably accomplished most successfully by totalitarians.

CHAPTER 16

Opinion Change

Individuals express opinion about controversial issues. In relatively static societies the number of such issues at any time is small; elsewhere the scope of the controversial widens. Change in any aspect of culture involves the opinion process in groups. Many issues involve large groups. In a sense, therefore, all culture change is a record of opinion change. Anything may become controversial, and, considering all human cultures, almost everything has at some time been the subject of conflict. In the simpler societies, at those periods which are highly static, any innovation is attended by vigorous disagreement. Changing forms evidence the momentarily victorious position. For example, simple art forms are dependent upon the structure of the human organism which permits of almost infinite variety, upon the qualities of the materials and upon the tribal patterns. Although changes may occur but intermittently, individuals do become innovators and for various reasons change the patterns. The earliest known drawings are those sketches of other species which appear on the walls of caves of what is now southern France. When innovations appeared in the methods of portraying these various animals, one can imagine the indignation of a tribal elder, ruefully viewing this sacrilege to his magical beliefs about the potency of an arrow placed here or there on the drawing, and the animated discussion that ensued.

There are certain basic processes developed out of the common human experience of the simpler primary groups that are less often questioned, but even these are controversial in some groups. There is also the residue of that which at any given time is not controversial. Especially in mathematics and the physical sciences there are certain materials, much fewer than is popularly supposed, which may be verified and established to the satisfaction of the expert group. This is scientific fact, and it is cumulative, serving as the basis for new developments. Yet all these fields have changed at times with amazing speed, so that, as a seventeenth-century man of learning said, "what was conjuring in the last age is Mathematiques in this." Opinion thereon is formed in the expert group. Popular opinion enters more immediately and more often into the statement of positions on the subject matter of the social studies. Large publics are always involved in some type of controversy in religion, economics and politics. The experts are less often in agreement, and their lack of agreement is more generally exposed. Because their propositions are less irrefutably proved, they more persistently turn to popular support for some hypothesis or cause. It is in the field of the social studies, therefore, that there has been the greatest eagerness to devise methods of discovering what opinions are held by the members of large publics. When large numbers of issues are popularly controversial, the need for such techniques for taking a record is more apparent. This, in large measure, accounts for the present preoccupation of psychology and the social sciences with the methods of opinion study.

It is evident that the purpose of opinion measurement is prediction and control. But even the most sophisticated of the present methods of measurement merely breaks down the statements of general position into a scale of statements running the gamut of possible positions in that group. But this is not adequate for prophecy, for the resulting statements to which an individual may accede may still be based upon quite · variable attitudes. It is apparent, therefore, that whatever merit these tests possess exists in their usefulness as instruments for discovering what lies behind the statements of opinion. This may best be done by attempting to use them to chart opinion change. Thus, it may be possible to infer the process.

There are several ways by which changes in opinion may be studied: (1) Observers may present generalizations about the process, based upon their experiences, upon participant observation or upon a nonquantitative examination of records, newspapers, documents, and the like. (2) Tests may be given at time intervals and quantitatively treated. (3) Tests may be given with partly controlled stimuli, such as a speech, movie or other item, intervening. (4) Quantitative studies of opinions other than those expressed in tests may be made, such as studies of voting records, changing content of various media of communications, buying habits and other behavior records. Without making any attempt to provide a critical summary of the literature, we may illustrate these procedures.

GENERALIZATIONS ABOUT OPINION CHANGE

In those sections of political and social philosophy in which the opinion processes of large publics are considered, thinkers have long pondered over the problem of opinion change. Numerous generalizations may be found in the writings from Plato to the latest treatise on political science. Let us sample a few, taken at random.

There are certain generalizations, based upon common experience and similar observations, which are repeated time and again. Robert Owens' famous tactic "Never argue, repeat your assertion" has been otherwise expressed many times. Recognition of the force of repetition existed among political leaders, tacticians and philosophers long before the advertiser, under the tutelage of the psychologist, made himself almost insufferable to the sensitive.

Thomas Jefferson had an intense dislike and a great distrust of personal arguments. He wrote, "No one will ever change his mind on account of a mere argument." He was fond of saying, "A man may change his mind as a result of his own reflections, of what he has read and slowly digested, but debates are a waste of time, as they will never persuade a person to accept a different point of view from that which he happens to hold." Santayana also noted that, "We do not nowadays refute our predecessors, we pleasantly bid them good-bye."

Another long recognized procedure for bringing about a change of popular opinion is the so-called "red-herring" technique, the diversion of public attention from one subject to another. In this connection Lecky remarked that "people do not disprove miracles, they outgrow them." In large publics, few opinions are changed by being disproved. Much more often, attention is simply diverted to something else. The effectiveness of positive statements in contrast to indirect or indecisive statements is likewise a generalization learned from experience and frequently stated. The effective political leader of large publics has a program, not a policy of negation. Change in opinion is brought about by specific positive appeals. Two hundred dollars a month to everyone above a certain age, share our wealth with ten thousand dollars' capital for every man, woman and child—such proposals are specific enough. The demagogue knows this. The positive religious program has a permanent popular advantage over agnosticism. The positive statement is appealing. William James once referred to Wilhelm Wundt as a perfect professor, because he had an opinion on every subject and, having an excellent memory, he seldom forgot what his opinions were. Recognition of this principle will be found scattered throughout the literature of group processes. These positive statements, moreover, should more often be hope-bringing and optimistic rather than pessimistic appeals, if they are effectively to modify mass opinion. Sorel said that there was a popular aversion to every pessimistic idea, while the song writer declares, "accentuate the positive." This is usually held to be true, except for short-time periods in crises. Or we may consider generalizations such as those of the economic determinists of the nineteenth century. They maintained that shifts in opinion were brought about, primarily, by modifications of the economic order, not by ideas. The politician who, following a sweeping defeat, said that "we couldn't expect to beat fifteen million unemployed" was momentarily of this school of thought. These and many other generalizations have been repeated so often that they are the principles assumed in most discussions of the process of opinion change.

It has long been noted, and but lately supported by descriptions of instances of opinion change, that the presentation of facts or the changes in the objective reality more readily change opinions than do arguments or abstract analyses. Such a generalization is based on observations, especially in the United States and Great Britain whose pragmatic populations do not respond readily to ideological appeals and who are latterly quite distrustful of special pleading. "The concrete incident, rich in circumstantial detail, serves as a prototype or model which helps orient people toward a part of the world in which they live." [1] However, one may assume that such a generalization is culture-bound, may relate only to certain types of materials and facts, and, as yet, is inadequately supported by evidence. On the basis of general observation, the generalization appears to be probably true of the population of the United States.

Opinions are developed, influenced and changed more readily on topics on which the individual does not have well-organized opinions and fixed attitudes. Moreover, opinions are more easily changed on peripheral rather than crucial issues. This has long been logically evident. In modern social science terminology it is stated, "Communication content is more effective in influencing public opinion on new or unstructured issues, i.e., those not particularly correlated with existing attitude clusters." [2] "Verbal statements and outlines of courses of action have maximum importance when opinion is unstructured." [3]

In October, 1945, the *Fortune* survey published a summary of its four-year findings on the influence of information on opinion. It demonstrated that well-informed people reach definite opinions more readily than do uninformed people, and that the opinions reached by the well-informed are more moderate in character. The uninformed tend to go to extremes.

Changes of opinion, according to Plato, are forced when they occur under the violence of some pain or grief. "The enchanted are those who change their minds either under the softer influence of pleasure or the sterner influence of fear." Cooley notes, "A group makes up its mind in very much the same manner that the individual makes up his. The latter must give time and attention to the question, search his conscious-

---

[1] R. K. Merton, *Social Theory and Social Structure*, Free Press, Glencoe, Ill., 1949. Pages 280–285 contain a discussion of the propaganda of facts.

[2] B. Berelson in *Communications in Modern Society* (W. Schramm, ed.), University of Illinois Press, Urbana, Ill., 1948, p. 176.

[3] H. L. Cantril, *Gauging Public Opinion*, Princeton University Press, Princeton, N.J., 1944, p. 226.

ness for pertinent ideas and sentiments, and work them together into a whole, before he knows what his real thought about it is. In the case of a nation the same thing must take place, only on a larger scale." Such a description of popular opinion process is based upon a faith in the rationality of the process and the ultimate triumph of logic. That the shifts in opinion are based upon sound judgment was also stated by Locke who, disparaging the demagogue, wrote, "Nor let anyone say that mischief can arise from hence as often as it shall please a busy head or turbulent spirit to desire the alteration of government. It is true, such men may stir whenever they please, but it will be only to their own just ruin and perdition." Distinguishing between two types of subjects on which opinions may be changed, some by reasonable arguments, others by emotional appeals, E. A. Ross noted, "In areas where, after all, feeling or instinct, not reason, decides, discussion can do little to accelerate the issue." Alexis de Tocqueville, commenting on changing public opinion in a democracy, notes an increase in the depreciation of the elite in proportion to the decrease in class differences, saying, "The hatred which men bear to privilege increases in proportion as privileges become fewer and less considerable, so that democratic passions would seem to burn most fiercely just when they have least fuel." The principal processes of opinion change, according to A. L. Lowell, are that "opinions change by making exceptions to general rules until the rule itself is broken down" and "opinions have this in common with intrenchments that they offer an obstinate resistance to a frontal attack, but not to a turning movement." Lord Bryce concluded that opinion changes were instigated in America by a limited group, principally politicians, a "set of men, who are to be counted by hundreds rather than by thousands; it is the chiefs of great parties who have the main share in starting opinion, the journalists in propagating it." In his *Public Opinion and Lord Beaconsfield* G. C. Thompson summarizes the changes in public opinion during a generation in England. One illustration of rapidly changing popular opinion occurred during the Turkish war when atrocity stories were circulated. Thompson thus describes the steps in the process: "At first there had been doubt, then astonishment, then a great emotion of pity and indignation, a desire that the persons who had suffered should be helped and the persons who had done wrong should be punished, then came the perception that things of this kind were not strange and unheard of exceptions, but only a capital example of the incidents of Turkish rule, and finally the conviction indelibly branded into the public mind that Turks were not fit to be trusted with sovereignty over Christian populations." We have here an instance of generalization based upon a specific situation.

In the preceding quotations we have only fragments, snatched from the writings of these eminent commentators. Let us summarize one other source in which there is a more complete discussion of the bases for sudden changes in group opinion.[4] According to E. H. Paget, sudden opinion change in large publics occurs under the following conditions: (1) A group opinion that is neither founded on a thorough comprehension of the points at issue nor supported by strong associations with some enduring prejudice may easily disintegrate. (2) Many expressions of opinion are but empty formalism. Changes in opinion may seem to occur suddenly, but actually the attitudes behind the opinion have been changing for a long time. (3) Group opinion may shift quickly because of unwise and overaggressive action of those who attempt to direct opinion. Leaders may become too confident of public backing and attempt to go too far. (4) There is a general willingness of members of large publics to respond positively (voting "yes") to propositions when they still retain doubts. Therefore, a majority may change very quickly. This has been experimentally verified. (5) As a rule, people oppose situations, not principles. Sudden shifts in opinion may occur if the situation is modified. (6) The introduction of a new personal force, vividly dramatizing an issue, may bring about a sudden change in opinion. Facts, reasons and evidence have rarely gained a secure hold on the minds of most men.

Politicians, reporters, publicity men and commentators on world affairs work out informal, usually nonquantitative devices for testing opinion change. Prognostication based thereon may be far from an exact science, but it is often amazingly accurate. Walter Lippmann stated:

Newspaper men develop devices of various sorts by which they test opinion. Many of them sound absurd when described in cold print. For example, a political writer once told me that he used to take the pulse of Woodrow Wilson's emotional attitude by watching how often the word "very" appeared in a speech of Mr. Wilson's. He had found that when Mr. Wilson was least sure of himself, he put a very in front of all his adjectives and generally doubled his adjectives as well; that, said my friend, was Mr. Wilson's way of whistling when he had to pass a cemetery at night. Another Washington observer used to look to see how long Mr. Hoover's sentences were and particularly how many dependent clauses were hanging onto their coat-tails. On days when Mr. Hoover was unusually complicated, this newspaper man would shake his head and say: "The President has certainly been worrying over that." My own particular method of guessing at the state of confidence among those who in the chief centers of population strike the key-notes of feeling among business men is a gadget that I am almost ashamed to acknowledge. It is the stock market average of industrial securities.[5]

[4] E. H. Paget, "Sudden Changes in Group Opinion," *Soc. Forces*, 7: 438–442.

[5] W. Lippmann, syndicated article in "Today and Tomorrow" column, May 5, 1935. Quoted by permission of New York Tribune, Inc.

We have strung together this rather chaotic list of quotations, which could readily be amplified, in order to indicate something of the variety of comment on opinion change. Such wise and experienced thinkers as Bryce, de Tocqueville, Thompson, Lowell and many others, on the basis of their observations and logical analysis of the mass opinion process, have formulated many valid generalizations. It is questionable whether contemporary social science can, at least for some time, improve upon the sympathetic insight of the political theorist and the social philosopher. However, a more exact science of social relations may provide certain information that they could not supply. For example, it might be very illuminating to analyze and note the frequency with which opinion changes appear to be induced by the "red-herring" technique, by reiteration, diversion, positive assertions and the like. Public information is canalized through well-known agencies. Examine their output. Surely a more exact science of society would provide information, not only on what the techniques were, but upon the frequency of their use by different agencies as well as exact descriptive accounts of the specific case.

Opinion change generalizations based upon a number of studies which provide data from which similar general statements may be drawn are very limited in social science literature as yet. Repeated or similar studies are not numerous. However, I have compiled in Table 9 [6] some generalizations, each supported by several studies, that appear in some recently published work by Berelson, Lazarsfeld and McPhee. We have here a sample of partially substantiated generalizations based on the evidence of at least several studies.

SOME EXPERIMENTAL STUDY OF ATTITUDE CHANGE

Attempts to change opinions may aim at the creating of new attitudes and opinions, or their deletion, or at conditioning against the development of some attitude-opinion complex. Those concerned with advertising, propaganda, the changing of race relations and other attitudes have engaged in innumerable tactics of change. However, much of their work does not permit rechecking or validation of their claims of directed opinion change. Experimental study of opinion change with control groups and attempts to equate variables and to control the extraneous

[6] I compiled this table by selecting 10 of the 35 generalizations about change in political opinion which Bernard Berelson, Paul Lazarsfeld and William McPhee present in their volume, *Voting*, University of Chicago Press, Chicago, 1954. The generalizations on change in political position are to be found among 209 generalizations made on the basis of a number of studies which have been published in 14 volumes, monographs or articles. A list of the studies appears on page 31 of *Voting*.

Table 9. Generalizations about Change in Political Position

	Erie County, Ohio, 1940	Nationwide study NORC, 1944	Nationwide study Survey Research Center, 1948	Greenwich, England, 1950	Bristol, England, 1951	Nationwide study Survey Research Center, 1952	Elmira, New York, 1948
1. From one election to the next, over three-fourths of the voters in both do not change party position............					x	x	x
2. From two-thirds to three-fourths of the voters settle on their final vote by the time the political conventions are over	x	x				x	x
3. From late October to election day there is from five to ten times more gross turnover than net change in party support, i.e., the shifts are compensatory..................	x	x	x		x	x	
4. Only a small proportion (under 10 per cent) of the changers during a campaign move from one party to the other.....	x				x		
5. The majority of voters who change their vote intention change it in the direction of the prevailing vote of their social group..	x	x	x			x	x
6. The people who do not expect to vote during the campaign but then actually do vote on election day tend to follow the predominant party pressure in their locale...........	x	x					
7. The less homogeneous the family in its political position, the more change among its members..................	x		x		x		x
8. The less interested the voter is in the election, the more likely he is to change his vote preference during the campaign, in any direction...............................	x	x			x	x	x
9. The more cross-pressures and inconsistencies the voter is subject to, the more change in his vote preference........	x	x					x
10. Voters who change from one party to the other support their initial candidate on the issues less strongly than the nonchangers..		x			x		

variables have, as yet, been quite limited.[7] Perhaps the work of Carl Hovland has been most notable.

The experimental study of opinion record and opinion change has just begun. Most of its fundamental problems are as yet unsolved.

[7] The discussion of opinion change provided in this chapter does not purport to provide a systematic bibliography of the subject, nor, indeed, has such a bibliography been compiled. Moreover, our discussion does not classify and summarize experimental or descriptive studies of opinion change. This has not been done in any single monograph. Among the best sources for summaries of studies and bibliographies are: Carl I. Hovland, Irving L. Janis and Harold H. Kelley, *Communication and Persuasion,* Yale University Press, New Haven, Conn., 1953; Gardner Lindzey (ed.), *Handbook of Social Psychology,* Addison-Wesley Publishing Company, Cambridge, Mass., 1954; the UNESCO report for 1948, which has a section on methods that have been developed in the social sciences for changing attitudes; and A. M. Rose, *Studies in Reduction of Prejudice,* American Council on Race Relations, 1947. This monograph lists about thirty studies on the attempted reduction of prejudice in race relations by changing attitudes.

To what extent may the results of present opinion tests be trusted? Under what conditions will the subject sincerely express his real opinion? How is it possible to differentiate between such opinions and conventional responses? On what subjects will conventional responses be most likely in various kinds of publics? Will there be a consistency between opinion expression and other forms of overt behavior? Has the subject had an opinion before the test, or was his response induced by the test? Has he been conscious of the attitudes underlying his opinions? Will the same opinion be expressed at another time under similar circumstances? May the processes of opinion change be considered with any measure of detachment as processes, or will the variation with different subject matter be so great as to prevent the development of social science in this field? There are many fundamental problems of method here.

Experimental literature has touched on but few points and has dealt with limited subject matter. Its reliability and validity are often questionable. The tests have frequently created wholly abnormal and unusual conditions. The subjects tested have been a limited group, most often those in educational institutions. Faulty though the procedures are, they must be refined and increasingly used in the future. The variety of human interactivity and of the opinion process has become too great for adequate synthesis and generalization otherwise. The results of experimental procedures must provide suggestions for the synthesizer and interpreter. From these studies of behavior he must assume human attitudes and be able to enter into sympathetic observation of individuals as members of groups. These processes cannot be disjointed. There is no choice. All of the process must be comprehended.

In 1955 Professor Samuel Stouffer, Director of the Laboratory of Social Relations at Harvard University, published a study of attitudes toward communism, conformity and civil liberties. This study is a model of careful, reliable formulation of a research program and of the conduct of field work. Some 6,000 men and women from all parts of the country and all types of occupations and vocations were interviewed by the field interviewers of two of the best polling agencies working independently. Rigorous safeguards in the interests of accuracy were employed. Their trustworthy results support generalizations about the essentially personal nature of the primary fears and worries of most people. In spite of the lowering and ominous climate of international conflict in 1954, including the possibility of atomic disaster, some 80 per cent of the men and women interviewed stated that their primary worries were solely personal and family problems. Many of the remainder added personal worries to some worries about public issues. Concern about world affairs was expressed by 8 per cent of the total sample. However, among the community leaders 22 per cent were worrying about world problems; 25 per cent about national or local problems (in comparison to 6 per cent of the entire cross section so worried); and 5 per cent of the leaders expressed some worries about civil liberties and the internal Communist threat. The older generation, less educated, was found to be less tolerant of nonconformists than the younger generation, and the Southern section of the United States much less tolerant than the West, while women tended, with small but consistent differences, to be less tolerant than men with respect to suspected nonconformists such as Socialists, atheists, or Communists.[8]

A few investigations have been made on the effect of majority and expert opinion upon attitudes. Though the evidence is very limited, there is evidence that when subjects know the positions of majorities and of experts there is a tendency to move toward the majority opinion and, in a somewhat lesser degree, toward the experts' opinions. Marple presented attitude tests on economics and education before and after information on majority and expert opinion was given to the subjects and found somewhat greater influence of majority than of expert opinion.[9] H. T. Moore, in an early experiment (1921), had his subjects evaluate statements on music and on morals with and without information as to the opinions of the majority who had marked the statements and, also, as to the opinions of experts. He found that the subjects moved toward the majority opinions and to a somewhat less degree toward the expert opinions.[10] In 1941 H. E. Burtt and D. R. Falkenburg, Jr., presented attitude scales on religious doctrines, observances, missions, preachers, pacifism and religion, and on social aspects of religion to 500 subjects and later informed them as to both the majority positions on the earlier test and of the position of experts (clergymen) on the statements on the scales.[11] The changes in the direction of majority and of expert opinion were significantly greater than the changes in corresponding controls. The results showed a move toward both majority and experts' opinions in about the same amount. But it is possible that the expert in the religious field carries comparatively more weight than the expert on politics or economics.

The study of attitude change in the context of at least a large section

[8] Crude generalizations, wrenched from their context and from the supporting data, are frequently misleading. The reader is advised to turn to the meticulously compiled data, the well-organized and tightly written conclusions reported in Samuel A. Stouffer, *Communism, Conformity and Civil Liberties,* Doubleday & Company, Inc., New York, 1955.

[9] C. Marple, "The Comparative Susceptibility of Three Age Levels to the Suggestion of Group Versus Expert Opinions," *Jour. Soc. Psychol.,* 4: 176–186.

[10] H. T. Moore, "The Comparative Influence of Majority and Expert Opinion," *Am. Jour. Psychol.,* 32: 16–20.

[11] H. E. Burtt and D. R. Falkenburg, Jr., "The Influence of Majority and Expert Opinion on Religious Attitudes," *Jour. Soc. Psychol.,* 14: 269–278.

of the subject's life situation is illustrated in Leon Festinger's studies of community process. In his studies of the Regent Hill Project,[12] Festinger reports on the attitude changes brought about by a program to change social attitudes in Regent Hill, and on changes of attitudes and behavior within the project which were not stimulated from without. This type of study at least relates attitude change to social group experience in broad context, an aspect of attitude change that is just beginning to be studied. Nor has the relation of specific attitude changes to broader aspects of mind-life been systematically studied. In a pioneering study, Patricia Kendall has reported on mood shifts and attitude change, conflicts between ideology and personal attitudes and other related matters. This approach is very promising.[13] The most fruitful study of attitudes and their change will ultimately study attitudes in process, which will mean as related to social environment and individual mind-life in all pertinent relations so that attitudes will not be dealt with as discrete entities.

THE POLLS RECORD CHANGES OF OPINION

Organized and accredited polling has now existed for many years. As we have noted in discussing the validity of the polls, successive polls make comparable errors, if they are in error, and the comparison of the results of polls on the same topics made by the same organizations should be very accurate. Indeed, for the student of the opinion process, one of the principal uses of the polls (as is true, also, of content studies) is to establish trends. If you ask the question: "Do you think schoolteachers should be allowed to spank disobedient children at school?" and on March, 1938, the response is 53 per cent yes, no 44 per cent, no opinion 3 per cent, while in August, 1946, your respondents say, yes 35 per cent, no 61 per cent, no opinion 4 per cent, it is evident that considerable opinion change on a basic bottom problem has occurred in a relatively short time. From the data which now exist in the published polls, it is possible to establish hundreds of trends. We have compiled scores of such trends from a scrutiny of Hadley Cantril's *Public Opinion, 1935–1946*. As examples, three items from this source are exhibited in Table 10.[14]

From the study of opinion changes as reflected in successive polls, with assumptions as to the intervening events, communication and other variables, one may essay prediction as to future trends in opinion change.

---

[12] L. Festinger, *Changing Attitudes through Social Contact*, Institute for Social Research, University of Michigan, Ann Arbor, Mich., September, 1951.

[13] P. Kendall, *Conflict and Mood*, Free Press, Glencoe, Ill., 1954.

[14] Item 4 is taken from a study entitled *An International Police Force and Public Opinion*, Princeton University Press, Princeton, N.J., 1954, p. 15.

Table 10. Trends in Opinion Change

Item 1

Question: Do you think it was a mistake for the United States to enter the last war (World War I)?

	Jan. 1937	Feb. 1939	Oct. 1939	Nov. 1940	Jan. 1941	Mar. 1941	Apr. 1941	Oct. 1941	Dec. 1941
Yes........	62%	48%	59%	39%	40%	39%	39%	35%	21%
No.........	30	37	28	42	44	43	48	47	61
No opinion..	8	15	13	19	16	18	13	18	18

Item 2

Question: What do you consider is the ideal size of family—a husband, wife, and how many children?

	No child	1	2	3	4	5	6 or more
1936	..	2%	32%	32%	22%	7%	5%
1941	..	1	31	27	27	6	8
1945	..	1	22	28	31	9	9

Item 3

Question: Do you prefer public ownership or private ownership of the electric power industry?

	Jan. 25, 1937	Jan. 18, 1938	July 31, 1940	June 12, 1945	Sept. 6, 1945	Dec. 31, 1946
Government ownership..	67%	54%	31%	29%	27%	28%
Private ownership.......	33	34	49	50	61	64
Don't know.............	..	12	20	21	12	8

Item 4

Question 1 (Peacetime): Would you like to see the United States join in a movement to establish an international police force to maintain world peace?

	August 1939 (AIPO)	April 1947 (NORC)	July 1953 (AIPO)
Yes...........................	46%	75%	56%
No............................	39	17	30
No opinion....................	15	8	14

Question 2 (Wartime): Should the countries fighting the Axis set up an international police force after the war is over to try to keep peace throughout the world?

	July 1942 (AIPO)	March 1943 (OPOR)	April 1943 (AIPO)	October 1943 (OPOR)	April 1944 (OPOR)
Yes...........	73%	80%	74%	79%	77%
No...........	16	12	14	11	13
No opinion.....	11	8	12	10	10

In the present state of social science methods, this is very hazardous prophecy. However, T. W. Anderson has attempted the construction of probability models for analyzing time change in attitudes by using the polled results of seven successive interviews of 600 people in the voter studies in Erie County, Ohio, during 1940. He has pioneered in attempting to develop such formulae.[15]

Content studies may be used as indirect evidence of opinion change. The investigator may show changes in proportions of content of a similar kind in successive studies, or changing relations between parts of the content of periodicals, newspapers, television programs, and the like. His assumption, not always valid, is that the mass media essentially reflect reader and audience tastes and values. Content studies may also be used to indicate changes in the opinions of the communicators, as in the analysis of the papers and publications of totalitarian states.[16]

A number of quantitative studies of opinion change as reflected in statements of opinion in periodicals, in citizens' voting records, in the voting records of legislative bodies, in changing buying habits and in other behavior records have been made. These sources have long been used as indicators of opinion, but only recently has there been any quantitative treatment. For some purposes such indirect evidence is superior to testing; but, as we have previously shown, forms of behavior other than that recorded on tests are by no means invariably superior indexes of attitude. Further, it must be very certain that the samples are adequate if they are to be used as a basis for generalization. This is very difficult to determine in any exact fashion. For example, Hornell Hart counted the titles of the *Readers' Guide to Periodical Literature* from 1905 to 1932. The titles were classified by subjects, and the increase and decrease of discussion were thus noted. This was a most ingenious utilization of sources. But if, on this basis, one presumes to report on the changing social attitudes and interests for America during those years, one may well be questioned on the adequacy of the sample, as the author himself recognizes.[17] In addition, to what extent does magazine opinion express general social attitudes? What sections of the population are not thus represented? What geographic areas produce and read few periodicals? Printed opinion is but one kind of expression of opinion; others will be found in movies, books, speeches, radio and other media. Do articles express the attitudes of readers? Even after

[15] T. W. Anderson, "Probability Models for Analyzing Time Changes in Attitudes," in P. Lazarsfeld (ed.), *Mathematical Thinking in the Social Sciences,* Free Press, Glencoe, Ill., 1954, pp. 17–66.

[16] See the *Hoover Institute Studies on Symbols and Elites,* of which about a score of pamphlets have been published.

[17] H. Hart, "Changing Social Attitudes and Interests," in W. F. Ogburn (ed.), *Recent Social Trends,* McGraw-Hill Book Company, Inc., New York, 1933, chap. 8.

classifying periodicals according to general circulation, does a mere counting of titles of articles therein provide an adequate sample? Do titles adequately reflect subject matter? Does the amount of discussion in periodical literature necessarily introduce or even herald change? Would not the proportion of articles pro and con be indicative of probable change in mass opinion? There is often a great deal of discussion about some spectacular issue which is not seriously defended by many people and upon which there is little likelihood of popular opinion change. Is it adequate to consider only the number of articles, when one article, because of the prestige of its author, the way it is written, and the like, may have ten times the readers and a hundred times the effectiveness of another article with the same title? These and other questions evidence the caution that must be exercised in generalizing from these results. The amount of discussion on the twoscore of topics classified in this study was expressed in terms of articles per thousand indexed by years. If we agree with the author's premise that discussion is most intense at two periods in the life of a social institution, when it is under construction and when it is being remodeled or demolished, we have here a rough sort of measure of opinion change from indirect evidence.

Some elaboration of this procedure appears in a later contribution of Professor Hart.[18] In this study of opinion change about business prosperity, there was not only a mere counting of the number of articles dealing with this and allied topics, but also some qualitative analysis of statements made in the articles and of types of words used. For example, in support of the proposition "Economic conditions are good or sound," there were found in the huge-circulation magazines during 1929, 283 affirmative attitude indicators and only 63 negative, whereas during the first three months of 1932 there were 89 affirmative and 266 negative statements. This is not exact measurement, but it is counting, which gives a rough approximation of trends. There was also some counting of the optimistic and pessimistic words used in titles and headlines. Another comparison was made in contrasting the magazines of large circulation with the *Survey, New Republic, Nation* and *Christian Century* in the number of articles dealing with the "buy now," "antihoarding" and similar campaigns. There were fifteen times as many articles in the journals of mass circulation. The entire study covered the years 1929 through 1932, and, in addition to the mere counting of titles in the *Readers' Guide,* some analysis of content was attempted by the counting of statements made in the articles on some twenty-five propositions and topics.

[18] H. Hart, "Changing Opinions about Business Prosperity," *Am. Jour. Sociol.,* 38: 665–687.

Throughout there is a comparison of journals of mass circulation (a million or more) with the *Survey, Nation, New Republic* and *Christian Century.* The problems of size, of sample, the definition of units and the question of the extent to which the media of communication express the opinions of their readers must be carefully considered in studies of this type. However, with all the limitations, some gains result from supplanting impressionistic accounts with quantitative data. In many fields, quantitative analysis of certain aspects of the changing content of various media might be profitably attempted. For example, the journals, papers and other records of reform movements might be studied in this way; the changing content of certain sections of the newspaper might profitably be quantified; the output of various special-interest groups might be dealt with in a more detailed and significant fashion with a closer definition of units than was possible with these journals of huge circulation.

OPINION CHANGE WITH CONTROLLED STIMULI

During the past years there have been a number of attempts to record the effects of certain oral, printed and pictorial materials upon the opinions of those subjected to them. It has been demonstrated that shifts of opinion may occur after but very limited contact with spoken, written or pictorial stimuli. More and more detailed analysis of the process of changing attitudes is being attempted, although the experimental methods are necessarily very crude and the stimuli but partly controlled. From the limited body of experimental literature that has been produced we may select a few items for brief discussion. Most of the studies thus far have used students as subjects since they were an available and a fairly homogeneous group. The shortcomings of many of the experimental techniques are fairly obvious and must be criticized, but at the same time the difficulties of this pioneering research should be well understood.

Certainly the most systematic, careful and ingenious experimental study of opinion change has been done at Yale University by Carl I. Hovland, Irving Janis, Harold Kelley and their associates.[19] These studies, much too extensive for review here, report on opinion changes resultant from fear-arousing appeals, the organization of persuasive arguments, the relations of group membership to opinion malleability, the relation of personality to susceptibility to persuasion and some studies on the retention of opinion change.

W. H. Wilke conducted an interesting comparison of the relative

---

[19] See *Communication and Persuasion*, Yale University Press, New Haven, Conn., 1953; and H. H. Kelley and E. H. Volkart, "The Resistance to Change of Group-Anchored Attitudes," *Am. Soc. Rev.*, 17: 453–465.

effects of speech, radio and printed page, by giving speeches on war, on the distribution of wealth, on birth control and on the existence of God, to classes in New York University.[20] These speeches were transmitted by microphone to other classes and were given in printed form to a third group. There were 341 subjects in all. Opinion scales were given two weeks before and after the speech, radio or reading, dealing with the subjects discussed therein. These attitude tests were the rating-scale type containing five steps, of which position 3 was neutral, position 1 in agreement with the speaker and position 5 in greatest disagreement. Of all the neutral or undecided scores on the original test, that is, those checking position 3 on the scale, the greatest number were brought nearer to agreement with the special pleading by the speaker, the loud-speaker being next most effective and the printed material least effective. Attitudes that in the first test were opposed to the views expressed by the propaganda material were more likely to change to a position of agreement than to swing merely to a neutral position. Further, those who in the original test espoused the more extreme positions tended to retain these positions much more than any other group. The average of all changes on all topics brought about by the speaker was 9.5 per cent of the total possible changes; by the loud-speaker, 7.9 per cent; by the printed materials, 6.3 per cent. These differences, though not large, are significant. Obviously, such fragmentary data, collected from a limited number of subjects on a few topics by means of an inadequate testing method, do not provide a basis for generalization about the effectiveness of different stimuli. But this is the type of study, with the stimuli at least partially controlled, which may in time provide an accretion of materials from which such generalizations may be adduced.

W. K. Chen studied the influence of oral propaganda material on student attitudes.[21] An opinion test of forty-five statements selected from speeches, articles and interviews on the Manchurian problem was developed and made up as a five-point rating scale. These statements favored both the Chinese and the Japanese viewpoints. They were presented to nine university classes in various schools from Stanford to Columbia, to be checked on the "absolutely true" (A.T.), "partly true" (P.T.), undecided (U), "partly false" (P.F.) and "absolutely false" (A.F.) scale. If a statement favoring the Chinese viewpoint is endorsed A.T. it is in position 1, and if A.F., in position 5, undecided being 3. The positions of the students before hearing propaganda material were recorded. Then two articles, one favoring the Chinese position and another the Japanese

---

[20] W. H. Wilke, "An Experimental Comparison of the Speech, the Radio and the Printed Page as Propaganda Devices," *Arch. Psychol.*, No. 169, 1934.

[21] W. K. Chen, "The Influence of Oral Propaganda Material upon Students' Attitudes," *Arch. Psychol.*, No. 150, 1933.

position, were developed, and a neutral article was taken from a publication of the Foreign Policy Association. These were given to instructors
of classes, who, after memorizing the arguments in them, gave talks to
their classes on one or the other position. The students were tested once
more a few days thereafter. Each group was found to shift its position
in the direction toward which the particular propaganda to which it had
been subjected impels. Apparently a few minutes of oral propaganda
produces large and measurable results. In each case more than half of
the members of the class shifted from the original undecided position to
one of the others. When, instead of propaganda for the Chinese or
Japanese positions, neutral material was presented, a tendency to reduce
the originally more popular opinion was noted. The author further concludes that propaganda material does not need to cover a large number
of issues to bring about a shift in general attitude. It does need to create
a vivid general impression. And, moreover, the author suggests that
information did not play a determining role in shaping attitudes toward
the Manchurian problem. A definite attitude was possible in the absence
of any specific information. Although the materials are too limited
for such generalizations, the author has here posed some basic problems
of opinion change. The stimuli were quite variable in this test and the
conditions not carefully controlled (it was given during a period of widespread popular discussion of this problem so that the effectiveness of the
single class speech could hardly be isolated). Among the greatest variables are the personal characteristics of the speakers, including methods
of presentation. These are not equated in this study. With all its
limitations, this experiment nonetheless poses some basic questions on the
effectiveness of speech forms in changing opinions.

Tests of opinion change, however, have appeared only recently, and
as yet there are only a few of them. A. D. Annis and N. C. Meier
studied the influence of editorial material on students at the University
of Iowa.[22] Using the regular daily editions of the newspaper, they
"planted" thirty editorials, fifteen of them favorable and fifteen unfavorable to a Mr. Hughes, Prime Minister of Australia from 1915 to 1923.
Previous to the tests they ascertained that none of their 203 subjects
knew anything about Mr. Hughes. The editorials were from 150 to
300 words in length and resembled the usual editorials in style. They
purported to give information and opinions about Mr. Hughes who was
supposed to be traveling on a lecture tour through the Middle West.
One group read the editorials favoring Mr. Hughes, the other, those
opposed to him. This reading was done during the regular psychology

[22] A. D. Annis and N. C. Meier, "The Induction of Opinion through Suggestion
by Means of Planted Content," *Jour. Soc. Psychol.*, 5: 65–81.

laboratory meetings, two a week, over a period of two months. The objective was to attempt to record the influence upon opinion of such limited contacts with editorial writing about an individual. This problem of editorial influence has long been disputed in conferences on journalism and social psychology. Of course, this test varied from the usual conditions of editorial reading, as the moot point usually is whether the editorials are or are not read, whereas here the reading was assured. At the conclusion of the two-month period tests were given. Ninety-eight per cent of the subjects reading the favorable editorials became favorably biased toward Mr. Hughes, and 86 per cent of those reading the unfavorable editorials became adversely biased. Moreover, the attitude toward Mr. Hughes was recalled four months later when another test disclosed approximately the same expressions of opinion as were made immediately after reading. Further, seven editorials were found to be as effective as fifteen in developing the opinions one way or the other. The authors conclude that by means of a very few editorials, presenting but little factual information and largely through indirect suggestion, it is possible to build up definite attitudes toward individuals. Limited though the materials of this study may be, the authors have made a definite contribution to method in using a medium to which the subject is accustomed, and modifying but one section of it. The conditions are thus more nearly normal. One of the most difficult problems in opinion testing is the need of duplicating, in so far as possible, actual life situations. Indeed, this is a problem of all psychological experimentation. Theoretical abstractions may go far astray from the humanly possible. It is reported of Catherine the Great that when her friend and teacher Diderot urged upon her the voluntary renunciation of autocracy, saying that despotism was criminal even if benevolent, the Czarina replied with amiable sarcasm, "These fine-sounding principles of yours may be all very well in the world of books, but they do not suit the world of affairs. You do your work on patient paper. I, who am only an empress, have to work on human skins, and they are ticklish." [23] In opinion testing, the closer the approximation to life situations, the better the test.

READING MAKETH A CHANGED MAN?

The problem of the influence of the literary, pictorial or musical artist upon popular opinion and beliefs is discussed perennially. Since the commentaries upon the artist by Plato and Aristotle, the philosophers of every age have dealt with the problem of the artist's influence. In periods of fervid social controversy, the political leaders and the artists

[23] Quoted by R. Fülöp-Miller, *Leaders, Dreamers and Rebels*, The Viking Press, Inc., New York, 1935, p. 130.

themselves analyze the artist's products and his influence from the sociological point of view. The selection of literature for popular consumption in the interests of propaganda for a special viewpoint is advocated by Plato, who declares that there must be "a censorship of the writers of fiction, and let the censors receive any tale of fiction which is good and reject the bad." [24] The poets tell lies, says Plato. Although the intentional lie might be politically expedient, Plato would regulate the literary lies that were not expedient. Further, he objected to the poets because they made popular instruction by the philosophers more difficult and aroused human passions. Plato enunciated the propaganda role of literature and declared censorship necessary, so as to restrict all but the state propagandist poet. "Aristotle limits the political control of the arts to the regulation of them in the education of young children. He says no more, however, than that their governors and preceptors 'should take care of what tales and stories it may be proper for them to hear.' " [25] Aristotle states that fiction and literature may be viewed from the political and moral points of view but that they may also be considered psychologically in their uses for purgation and diversion in popular thinking. Stressing as he does the function of literature in providing amusement, relaxation, and recreation, he would permit freedom to the literary artist to an extent not permitted by Plato. The discussion of the function of the artist, including the literary man, has in large part stemmed from the Platonic and Aristotelian positions. With the victory of Christianity, literature was increasingly valued in proportion as it was thought to inculcate moral values. "Art for art's sake" appeared in neither the Platonic nor the Christian traditions. With the development of printing, mass literacy begins and popular literature burgeons. By the eighteenth century literatures of classes, groups and various subdivisions of society were emerging. Literature then portrayed the characteristics of subgroups within particular cultures, as well as of universal types. For example, there was a growing literature of the middle classes. In England and France, the portrayal of middle-class life, with the accompanying values of diligence, frugality and honesty, appeared in the writings of Defoe and Molière, John Bunyan and Jonathan Swift, Fielding and Richardson. In the nineteenth century Macaulay, Thackeray, Eliot, Dickens and a host of others carried on the representations of the middle classes.[26] Likewise, other societal groups were portrayed. Increasingly during the past three centuries the

[24] *Republic,* 377C.

[25] M. J. Adler, *Art and Prudence,* Longmans, Green & Co., Inc., New York, 1937, p. 42.

[26] F. C. Palm, *The Middle Classes,* The Macmillan Company, New York, 1936, chaps. 9, 18, 19.

varieties of types, classes and groups in Western society have been portrayed in popular literature.

National and group literatures provide symbols for their adherents and opponents. "We may say of the great passages in a people's literature that they form, as it were, a national liturgy. There are passages in the Authorized Version, speeches and lyrics and single lines in Shakespeare, stanzas of Gray's 'Elegy in a Country Churchyard,' and verses in some of our hymns, which exercise a dominion over the mind." [27] Such symbols evolve in the experience of a people. Now the propagandist is a manipulator of symbols, and the modern propagandist attempts the management of literary forms. Propagandist literature is that which is used by some special group to plead a cause. The author may or may not have intended that his product be used as propaganda. The author of "The Face on the Bar-room Floor" never intended that a generation of Anti-Saloon Leaguers should quote his poem. On the other hand, when a Herr Julius Streicher had a literary lieutenant turn out an anti-Semitic *Mother Goose* for German children we had direct literary manufacture.

In the nineteenth century a growing number of reform groups selected or manufactured a literature to further their causes. One thinks at once of Charles Dickens' *Nicholas Nickleby* and the abuses of the private schools of England; of *Uncle Tom's Cabin* and the antislavery movement in the United States; of *Black Beauty* and the campaign against cruelty to animals; of the Socialist movement in America and the novels of Upton Sinclair, Frank Norris and Jack London; of the muckrakers and Lincoln Steffens' *Shame of the Cities;* of Upton Sinclair's *The Jungle* and the reform of the meat-packing industry through the Pure Food and Drug Act of 1906; of a host of second-rate novels, poems and essays and the Prohibition movement; of many other instances of privately organized reform movements and the literatures by which they plead their causes.

The problem of propaganda literature entered a new phase of both discussion and practice in the state-inspired propaganda literatures of Russia, Italy and Germany. "Until recently these varying conceptions of literatures, which may be traced from Plato to Cocteau, have proceeded on the whole undisturbed by authoritarian intrusion. The victory of the Bolsheviks over the White armies in 1920 and the subsequent consolidation of the U.S.S.R. have brought the question of literature out of the realm of theoretical abstraction and converted intellectual polemics into revolutionary partisan warfare." [28] The Bolsheviks attempted the

---

[27] E. Barker, *National Character*, Methuen & Co., Ltd., London, 1927, p. 222.
[28] M. Lerner and E. Mims, Jr., "Literature," *Ency. Soc. Sci.*, 9: 539.

organization of proletarian culture. The question of bourgeois literature was immediately to the fore. Although many of the earlier revolutionary leaders, especially Lenin, did not favor a too detailed control of literary output, the extremists soon won the day.[29] They clamored for a literary dictatorship. Literature was viewed as a handmaid of the state. "Only he is an artist," they claimed, "who at the present moment can instill in the minds of millions the conviction that a return to the past is impossible." Since 1925 policies on the control of literature have fluctuated somewhat, but, in the main, literary output has been rather closely controlled. The Communists have insisted that the arts have always been propaganda for the dominant ideology. Preoccupied with the class struggle, organizations of the Communist enthusiasts, such as the Artists International, have declared that art renounces individualism and is to be collectivized, systemized, organized, disciplined and molded as a weapon. Within Russia, the Communist leadership has extensively propagandized for a political viewpoint through the selection of what people should read. Vast government printing houses have produced an amazing flood of printed materials. Since the revolution, many billions of copies of books have been printed. There are about 45,000 new titles each year. There are over 1,800 Soviet periodicals. (Some of the selected writers are presented in enormous editions: 12 million copies of the works of Tolstoy, 32 million of Gorky's, and for his centennial a total of 8,150,000 copies of Pushkin's.[30]) Literature has been used in an organized way for the propaganda of cultural values. There has been systematic preparation of a children's literature. The old fairy tales and folk tales were considered harmful. In place of these a children's literature that reflects the values desired by the Communist leadership is being created.

As the authoritarian states appeared in Italy, Germany and elsewhere, the principle of state control of literature spread. There was an orgy of burning books and banishing authors. In the liberal democratic states, propaganda literature has been disseminated by special-interest groups, not by the state. America has a propaganda literature of the slavery movement, the Prohibition movement, the muckraking days and other crusades. There are only a few instances of state-sponsored literature. One illustration is that of the selection of reading material for the soldiery in World War I.[31]

But the most powerful special pleading is that which occurs without formal propaganda. There is always a selection of literary content in

[29] M. Eastman, *Artists in Uniform,* Alfred A. Knopf, Inc., New York, 1934.

[30] A. R. Williams, *The Soviets,* Harcourt, Brace and Company, Inc., New York, 1937, p. 377.

See also S. N. Harper, *Civic Training in Soviet Russia,* University of Chicago Press, Chicago, 1929, chap. 14.

[31] G S. Hall, *Morale,* Appleton-Century-Crofts, Inc., New York, 1929, pp. 83 ff.

terms of the dominant values. For example, the Communist and Fascist leaders have selected a propaganda literature to highlight certain aspects of the class struggle and economic groups. But from the early nineteenth century onward a growing part of all literature in the Western cultures has been concerned with the class struggle and economic groups. As Sorokin has written, "In brief, in the nineteenth- and twentieth-century economic problems, economic motives, economic behavior, economic ideology, the economic interpretation of almost all the actions of the heroes of literary works, became a mania, an obsession, a fashion, the sign of a supposedly deep insight into human nature." [32] If a certain set of values is dominant in literature, these values may be instilled all the more effectively because certain minority positions are also stated. The propagandist may be too thorough in his selections and exclusions. Credulity may be strained. In Germany in the 1930's the propaganda leadership remade the country's songs, literature and schoolbooks. In America five small books called the *McGuffey Readers* were printed between 1836 and 1840. During the last half of the nineteenth century these readers were the standard textbooks of the rural schools of the American Middle West. Political, economic, ethical and religious values as reflected in the *McGuffey Readers* were inculcated in untold millions of pupils.[33] These readers were not propaganda disseminated by a self-conscious leadership or special-interest group. They were selected on the basis of common beliefs and values that were widely diffused. They were read in a culture in which there were other and minority statements of position on these problems. They were contemporaries of Ingersoll. Yet it remains to be proved that state-inspired propaganda textbooks will be more effective in unifying values for school children than were the folk-selected *McGuffey Readers*. Propaganda literature may be effective if it fits into prejudices, beliefs, loyalties and self-interests that are already widely disseminated. Those who are already partially or entirely convinced of the truth of the material propagandized may be fortified in their beliefs. Others may remain unconvinced though forced to be quiescent. A folk-selected literature waxes in influence; an imposed literature does not have equal vitality.

WHEN SPEECH CHANGES OPINIONS

During World War II, the strategy and tactics of the enemy propagandists were described by various types of content analysis of their

[32] P. A. Sorokin, "Fluctuation of Forms of Art," in *Social and Cultural Dynamics*, American Book Company, New York, 1937, vol. I, p. 641.

[33] H. C. Minnich, *William Holmes McGuffey and His Readers*, American Book Company, New York, 1936.

radio programs. Monitors recorded the content of the programs, and analysts attempted to discern the basic patterns of enemy propaganda to mass audiences, as well as the gleaning of any military intelligence that might be assumed from the broadcasts. Of course, one of the enemy's objectives in broadcasts to large publics was to induce opinion change and depress morale. One pattern of the Nazi tactics during the first year of the war was described by Charles J. Rolo, who reported that the *Angstkrieg,* or war of nerves, fell into four distinct phases. In the first phase, the broadcaster aimed at acquiring an audience and gaining a measure of popularity. In the Nazi broadcasts to England, this was most effectively done by Lord Haw-Haw, that interesting English traitor, who, at his peak, was received over 14 million British radio sets. In the second phase, Lord Haw-Haw began to foment psychological civil war. Attacks were made on the fundamental British institutions and leadership, and then name calling and highly emotional appeals were used. "The third phase was that of sinister threats, superlative lies, incessant warnings of the wrath to come and almost frenzied injunction to get rid of corrupt leaders and appeal for peace." In the case of Poland, France and the smaller occupied countries, there was a fourth phase after the military armistice, in which the objective was to prolong the state of confusion and keep the populations subject to their new masters.[34]

However, this study reported by Rolo was based on limited monitoring privately done at Princeton before the United States monitoring system was established. A more definitive work on Nazi propaganda was being prepared by Ernst Kris, Hans Speier and others of the Graduate Faculty of the New School for Social Research. Published in 1944, *German Radio Propaganda* was a report on home broadcasts by the Nazis to the German people from 1939 through 1942. The materials analyzed were the regular-wave German broadcasts monitored by the British Broadcasting Corporation and later placed at the disposal of Kris and Speier. These authors were exceptionally competent in terms of knowledge of German culture and proficiency in psychological and social science methods; and they were endowed with unusually incisive analytical minds. Therefore, their report is a definitive content analysis and assessment of the significance of the content of radio broadcasting by the Germans during this three-year period. They evidenced the most skillful use of broadcast materials to assess the attitudes of the communicator, the probable opinions of the recipients, and the changes of opinions during the period among the communicators and among the German population.

The authors note that the Nazi propagandist "functioned as a celebrator

[34] C. J. Rolo, "The Strategy of War by Radio," *Harper's,* November, 1940, pp. 640–649; and *Radio Goes to War,* G. P. Putnam's Sons, New York, 1942.

of accomplishments and an eliminator of dissent." He was regularly engaged in the formation and changing of opinion, an activity which Dr. Goebbels characterized as *öffentliche Meinungsbildung,* that is "public formation of opinion." These leaders were concerned with the guidance and control of men. Let us refer to a single illustration of attempted opinion change.[35] After six years of Nazi military training and indoctrination, it was generally reported that the German troops went to war without cheering or enthusiasm. The beginning of the war was a shock to a people who had begun to become accustomed to victory without bloodshed. And there were depressing memories of the defeat in World War I. Therefore, "It was Goebbels' first task to destroy the analogy between the two wars, while Hitler tried to lead the German nation from peace to war as imperceptibly as possible." Intensive propaganda campaigns were instituted over the radio and other media insisting that the German armies had never been defeated in World War I and that, in any case, the second war was totally different from the first. At the same time, Hitler did not order a general mobilization and the Polish campaign was spoken of not as a war, but as a punitive expedition. After it became evident that a continuing war was going on, the propagandists stressed increasingly the differences between the two wars. This time they were prepared. A blockade would not be successful, as the farseeing Nazis had set up a rationing system and had stockpiled materials. This time the enemy would be blockaded. And Germany could count on vast food supplies from friendly Russia and the conquered enemies. World War I had been long drawn out, but the Nazis declared that their war would be pursued by a sequence of blitz victories which would speedily lead to peace. And, indeed, such was the case for the first two years. All of these and many other themes on this subject were winnowed out of the Nazi radio broadcasts by our analysts. And these Nazi propaganda campaigns were accompanied by a rising tide of hope and moderate exultation—for the first two years. Goebbels' propagandists fought with varied argumentation. But the opinion changes were basically the product of the Nazi blitz victories in the field. Propaganda was important for interpretation and the day-to-day maintenance of morale, but the basic attitude change came with victories in the field. But soon, once again there were defeats and doubts and specters which propaganda could not exorcise, though it did for a time blur their fearful shape and lessen their menace.

[35] The contents of this paragraph are the essence of chap. III of *German Radio Propaganda,* Oxford University Press, New York, 1944. Space does not permit of a more extended consideration of the various aspects of propaganda and opinion change reported in this voluminous work. For the serious student of psychological warfare, Kris and Speier's report is a work to be studied in great detail.

An instance of opinion change through mass persuasion was Kate Smith's war-bond campaign which resulted in 39 million dollars of bond pledges in the course of one day. On War Bond Day, September 21, 1943, this popular radio entertainer made sixty-five radio appeals in which she pleaded, demanded and cajoled her listeners to buy war bonds. Robert Merton studied this real-life example of the social psychology of a specific instance of special pleading. In contrast to laboratory studies of opinion change, we have here a real life situation, an index of influence on opinion (bond buying), profound ego involvement by participants in the matter under consideration, and a number of subjects who were not artificially assembled. One hundred detailed interviews, seventy-five with persons who had bought bonds and twenty-five with unpersuaded listeners, were conducted in New York City. Each interview lasted three or four hours. The result of this pioneer study is a very significant case report.[36]

The theme appeals made by Kate Smith were subjected to content analysis, and the percentage distribution of time to themes of sacrifice, participation, competition, family and personal appeals were noted. Using the materials of the one hundred interviews, the probable effectiveness of these themes was reported. The listeners' predispositions, general orientations and specific attitudes were gleaned from the interviews. The opinion changes that occurred in the social and cultural context of the particular subjects were reported. By the conclusion of his study of this instance of mass persuasion achieved through highly emotional appeals focused at the probable audiences at different times of the day, Professor Merton is led to ponder the essential problem of the moral dimensions of such appeals even in socially desirable causes. Democratically oriented social scientists must always come to this problem.

Thus far most study of opinion change has been much too simple to describe adequately the reality of this usually complex social process. A too immediate and exclusive stimulus-response, cause-and-effect relationship has been assumed as between mass media and their users or between the dominant leaders and their publics. Moreover, as a source of opinion change, the influence of interpersonal contacts in face-to-face associations has apparently been understated since the mass media became the center of attention in the 1920's. The beginnings of a more subtle analysis are now emerging. There is differentiation of various pat-

[36] Published in 1946, the volume, *Mass Persuasion*, by Robert K. Merton, Harper & Brothers, New York, is the type of monograph which furthers social science. If we had a score of other parallel and comparable studies, we could generalize about such campaigns.

terns and flow of influence, depending on the topics, the sources of influence and the varieties of recipients.[36a]

In contrast to an atomistic conception of masses of individuals responding directly to the content of the various mass media, it may be found that on many topics the mass-media content is significantly mediated and modified by influential persons in the community. In late 1955 Elihu Katz and Paul Lazarsfeld published a very significant pioneering study in a volume entitled *Personal Influence*.[36b] This study was concerned with the flow of influence from person to person and the delineation of the interpersonal networks of communications. A cross-sectional sample of 800 women in Decatur, Illinois (about 60,000 population), was interviewed during the summer of 1945. A very extended questionnaire schedule was used. The women were asked concerning their sources of information in four areas of everyday decisions: the daily household marketing decisions and opinions; fashion, as represented especially by dresses, cosmetics and various beauty treatments; the selection of motion pictures to attend; and the formation of opinions on local public affairs which happened to be under discussion at the time of the study. The respondents designated some 634 persons as influential sources of personal influence on their formation or change of opinion. In the case of marketing shifts in buying habits, personal contacts were directly effective or contributory in the shifts in brand choice in 27.9 per cent of the cases; in motion-picture selection, personal contacts were involved in 16.3 per cent of the choices; in fashion changes, some 19.6 per cent of the choices could be ascribed to personal contacts. In addition to these percentages of changes related to personal contacts, salespersons were involved in an additional 13.3 per cent of marketing shifts and 16.8 per cent of fashion changes. And what appear to be private opinions and attitudes were found to be often generated or reinforced by members of the family, by friends and co-workers, and by the influential persons among one's local contacts. Indeed, on everyday matters of opinion formation, the authors make a

---

[36a] A preliminary study of the patterns of interpersonal influence was reported by Robert K. Merton in 1949. (R. K. Merton, "Patterns of Influence," in *Communications Research, 1948–1949*, P. F. Lazarsfeld and F. N. Stanton (eds.), Harper & Brothers, New York, 1949, pp. 180–219.) This study was concerned with persons, apart from immediate family members, who were reported by 86 informants as most influential on the informants. Some 379 persons of the city of "Rovere" were referred to by the informants as "influentials." Of these influentials some were predominantly "locals" in their contacts and interests, and some were "cosmopolitans." Some were influential on a narrow range of topics and others were generally influential. This was a pioneer study, the details of which are not divulged in the brief, résumé report, but which would appear to be a potentially fruitful delineation of the influence patterns in community interpersonal relations.

[36b] E. Katz and P. F. Lazarsfeld, *Personal Influence*, Free Press, Glencoe, Ill., 1955.

strong case for the frequently more dominant influence being the horizontal communications among intimates, rather than the downward vertical force of influence from important national leaders or mass media.

When it comes to choosing a movie, young people influence older people. When it comes to buying small consumer goods the older housewife influences the younger. The actual vote of a person in a presidential campaign where major social allegiances are involved is established within a social stratum rather independently of the choices made by people considerably higher or lower on the social scale; but when it comes to making up one's mind on local affairs where party tradition doesn't matter and where more need is felt for specific information, then the wage earner is more likely to take advice from the better educated white collar person.[36c]

RUMORS AND OPINION CHANGE

Opinions are often changed or modified by rumors, and rumor sometimes calls into question that which had previously been considered knowledge or fact. A rumor is an account about a person, group or occurrence which is passed about usually by word of mouth and which is not adequately verified by any acceptable evidence. Rumors have defeated political candidates, perpetuated prejudices, sold merchandise and attacked the products of competitors. They have been very important in speculative markets and in psychological warfare. Rumors are ephemeral accounts of persons and events which may or may not be true but are statements that spread quickly through contact-groups, such as intimate communities, barracks, campuses, crowds and others. Though they originate in one or a few individual sources, they are usually spread by many individuals. The rumormongers may have diverse motivations for their activity in spreading the accounts, but the rumor itself must be an item which interests, intrigues, arouses and captivates the attention of usually diverse individuals. It is an account with common appeal.

It is characteristic of rumors that they are considerably changed in transmission. Like gossip, they arouse rivalry in embellishment of the original story. And rumors which spread primarily by word of mouth, as might logically be expected, are most changed and distorted in the telling. "The crystallization of the dramatic elements, including the addition of supplementary detail, and the acquisition of some authority are characteristic of all rumors. These elements constitute what might be called a 'mass invention' to which each of those who hear the story and then retell it in slightly different form makes a small contribution." [37]

[36c] *Ibid.*, p. 6.

[37] R. T. LaPiere and P. R. Farnsworth, *Social Psychology,* McGraw-Hill Book Company, Inc., New York, 1949, p. 412.

Usually a rumor-spreader seeks attention, but fundamentally, "Rumor is set in motion and continues to travel in a homogeneous social medium by virtue of the strong interests of the individuals involved in the transmission. The powerful influence of these interests requires the rumor to serve largely as a rationalizing agent: explaining, justifying, and providing meaning for the emotional interest at work." [38] Personal and group fear and insecurity are the almost inevitable precedent of active rumor-mongering. Wishful thinking spawns many a rumor. In the inactive period (September, 1939, to April, 1940) of World War II, the hopes of the French that there would never be an active war were responsible for many rumors to that effect.

Rumors proliferate especially at times of insecurity when there is lack of knowledge but when general curiosity is aroused. At crises of group life rumors abound. Anyone who has experienced life in the armed services is well aware of the number of such rumors and the speed of their circulation. They also disappear quickly. In a time of some confusion and crisis, such as the immediate post–Pearl Harbor months, rumors were widespread in the United States. Though some were no doubt planted by our enemies, many were the product of anti–Roosevelt-Administration groups in the United States, and most just welled up out of insecurity and lack of information about the extent of the losses in that debacle. Many individuals for a time distrusted the news that reached them.

In the comment and belief of expert observers rumors have long been thought to have a considerable effect on the stock and grain markets. Rumors are rife about possible political decisions of executive leaders and congressional intentions, as well as the beliefs of wealthy men who are supposed to have inside information. In a study attempting to observe the relation of rumor and stock-market prices, Arnold M. Rose concluded that rumor and seven other factors were involved in certain price shifts. By statistical analysis he linked three factors together, one of which was rumor, and concluded, "We know not only that rumor affects stock prices, but also that it is one of three factors which, individually or collectively, are affecting stock prices to the extent measured by the factor of stickiness." [39] As crisis is frequent in the exchanges and as there is much personal control, we have the conditions for rapid

[38] G. W. Allport and L. Postman, *The Psychology of Rumor,* Henry Holt and Company, Inc., New York, 1947, p. 43. This is the most extensive systematic treatment of the rumor process published in English. Some experimental evidence is also presented in this work. However, the bulk of all studies of rumor by psychologists and others thus far are descriptive and analytical rather than experimental. No doubt the present concern with interactive processes in groups will bring research to the rumor process in the near future.

[39] A. M. Rose, "Rumor in the Stock Market," *Pub. Opin. Quar.,* 15: 467–486.

spread of rumor, and, indeed, such spread occurs. Further, the rumors are often reported in the gossip columns of newspapers and trade journals. These journals are sometimes used by interested groups to circulate rumors to serve their own ends. In the early days of less exact crop and weather reporting, many a crop was killed for a few days on the grain markets of the United States.

Rumors have frequently been used in political conventions to support, as well as to attack, candidates for nominations. In postwar political campaigns rumormongering about rival candidates appears to be almost standard practice.

Ever since Lincoln's tomb was erected in Springfield, Illinois, custodians have been answering the questions of people who do not believe that Lincoln's mortal remains rest there, since widely diffused rumors since the 1880's have maintained that his corpse is missing. Wherever masses of people are emotionally involved about a topic and feel insecure about their sources of information, they will create rumors.

Atrocity rumors have been important in war situations to attack morale and to arouse anger. In 1940 the Nazi war of nerves made extensive use of rumors to undermine morale of French soldiers through whispers that their wives were unfaithful, their government corrupt and their families starving. The Nazis also spread rumors extensively among other national groups and at times among the German population. In the United States psychological warfare activities, rumor-spreading as a part of "black propaganda" was used far less extensively than by the Nazis and only in some instances toward the close of the war.

There are numberless commercial rumors. Of late years these have been more systematically promulgated. Rumors about rivals have long been a part of commercial warfare. The whispering-campaign industry is carried on by some less reputable publicity firms, who will provide individuals and teams to spread rumors on subways, buses and trains, on elevators and at public meetings. In the 1930's rumor campaigns became a widespread commercial practice.[40] We may note just a few typical but major instances of commercial rumormongering. In the early 1900's absinthe was rumored in France to be an antiaphrodisiac, and this rumor about the strongest of all alcoholic beverages has had circulation since

[40] For illustrations see: D. J. Jacobson, "The Rumor Racket," *Tomorrow*, October, 1948, pp. 10 ff.; and "How Speculators Increase Our Food Bill," *Reporter*, March 20, 1951, pp. 8 ff.; and D. J. Jacobson, *The Affairs of Dame Rumor*, Rinehart & Company, Inc., New York, 1948. Some hundreds of rumors of various types will be found reported in Jacobson's volume. The social scientist's objection to such collections would be that there are no data from which he can note frequency of each rumor, its change in transmission, the diffusion pattern, the proportion of those who hear the rumor who believe it, the temporal duration of the rumor, etc. The rumor process, recognized as widespread for centuries, has just recently aroused the attention of social psychologists who may be expected to provide systematic studies.

then. The rumor has been ascribed to an unscrupulous liquor salesman. In 1934 a whispering campaign broke out first on the Atlantic seaboard and then across the country that a leper had been found working in the Chesterfield cigarette factory in Richmond, Virginia. Reports by the Mayor and Board of Health were publicized by the tobacco company and many rewards were offered by Liggett and Myers for information as to who was spreading the rumor which appeared to be carefully planned. Such campaigns are illegal, but legal proof is difficult to accumulate. Some companies have been caught circulating rumors, but in this case no public charges were made. Somewhat later, the numerous rumors of the oleomargarine-butter competition were spread. There were rumors as to the foul, filthy coconut oils supposed to be used in making oleo, and many others. A cigarette company found itself staggered by the rumor that the T on the back of its package was supposed to be a secret "Popish" symbol. Such rumors obviously would spread most extensively and rapidly among the less intelligent portions of the general population. It has also been generalized that they spread more rapidly in small towns and the smaller cities rather than in the great metropolitan complexes.

During World War II there was systematic classification of rumors, of which some reports have been published, though most studies still repose in government files. An early study by Robert H. Knapp classified the rumors reported during September, 1942, of which there were 1,089 collected by his organization. Table 11 shows the percentages of the 1,089 rumors in each classification as found in various areas of the United States. This was the period at the beginning of the war during which rumors were especially numerous. Later the Office of War Information's strategic principle was that a rumor should be smothered with facts rather than attempting to disprove it, for the disproving process might undesirably advertise the rumor.

In 1945 after V–E day, a study of the rumors concerning the pretended or actual illness of Stalin showed that the thirty Paris newspapers examined reported or ignored these rumors in terms of the paper's editorial political attitudes. As the French papers at that time were limited to two or four pages, the inclusion of ephemeral stories could only relate to intentional slanting by editors.[41]

Rumor has unquestionably been an important agent of opinion change throughout human history. Especially in the past, before the present age of mass communications, rumored information must have been a vital source of opinion. And even the best-informed publics, well supplied

[41] E. H. Zerner, "Rumors in Paris Newspapers," *Pub. Opin. Quar.*, 10: 3: 382–391. The data analyzed were 129 articles containing 198 news items.

Table 11. Rumors Reported during September, 1942

	U.S.A.	New England	Atlantic Sea-board	South	Middle West	Far West
Wedge-Driving Rumors	65.9	63.2	62.0	61.6	72.5	67.8
Anti-Semitic	(9.3)	(13.6)	(13.5)	(5.2)	(7.7)	(8.0)
Draft evasion	3.6	7.2	6.6	.9	3.2	1.1
Others	5.7	6.4	7.0	4.2	4.6	6.9
Anti-British	7.3	9.6	9.4	5.2	7.0	5.8
Antiadministration	(21.4)	(13.6)	(10.9)	(20.2)	(28.4)	(22.3)
Roosevelt personal	3.1	2.4	2.0	3.3	6.3	
Salvage and rationing	6.1	4.0	3.5	8.9	6.7	6.9
War Bonds and savings unsafe	3.7	1.6	2.7	1.4	6.0	5.8
Selective service: grievances, abuses	2.2	2.4	.8	1.8	4.2	1.6
Graft, waste, inefficiency, accidents	4.4	3.2	2.0	4.7	5.3	6.9
Anti-Negro	3.1	.8	2.3	8.5	2.1	1.1
Anti-Army and -Navy	(19.6)	(17.6)	(20.7)	(21.2)	(20.3)	(20.7)
Government leaders incompetent	3.1	1.6	2.0	2.3	4.2	4.8
Abuses of soldiers and sailors	6.7	8.8	9.8	5.6	5.6	4.2
Drunkenness and immorality	2.6	1.6	2.7	2.8	1.8	4.2
Supplies, equipment: no good, lacking	6.0	4.0	4.1	7.5	7.0	5.3
Supplies, equipment: wasted, misused	2.1	2.4	1.2	2.8	1.8	3.2
Anti-Red Cross	2.2	4.8	2.3	.5	2.8	1.6
Antilabor	1.6	.8	.4	.5	1.8	4.8
Antibusiness	2.3	1.6	2.3	.5	2.5	4.8
Fear Rumors	25.4	28.2	26.9	33.8	20.3	19.6
In Armed Forces	(8.0)	(9.6)	(12.9)	(6.6)	(7.7)	(2.1)
Suicides	.6	....	1.2	....	1.1	
Insanity	1.0	....	.8	1.4	1.8	.5
Plagues and epidemics	1.2	....	2.0	2.3	.4	1.1
Excessive casualties	5.1	9.6	9.9	2.8	4.6	.5
Fifth-column Activities	(6.9)	(10.4)	(3.9)	(16.0)	(3.9)	(3.2)
Bread and submarine story	2.0	1.6	1.6	6.1	.4	.5
Supplying the enemy	.7	2.4	.4	1.4	....	.5
Spy activity, sabotage	4.2	6.4	2.0	8.5	3.5	2.1
Atrocities	(4.8)	(1.6)	(2.3)	(4.7)	(7.0)	(7.4)
Tongue and stamp story	3.7	....	1.6	3.8	6.0	5.8
Others	1.0	1.6	.8	.9	1.1	1.6
Unrevealed Enemy Action	(5.7)	(7.2)	(7.8)	(6.6)	(1.8)	(6.9)
Secret weapon or plans	1.2	.8	.8	1.4	1.4	1.6
Shipping losses	1.0	.8	1.2	2.8	....	1.1
Unrevealed enemy activities	3.3	5.6	5.9	2.3	.4	4.2
Pipe-Dream Rumors	2.0	2.4	3.9	1.4	.7	1.6
Peace rumors	.6	.8	2.0			
Corpse in car	.4	....	.8	....	.7	
Enemy sub washed up, destroyed	.6	.8	.4	.9	....	1.1
Victory rumors	.5	.8	.8	.5	....	.5
Miscellaneous Rumors	6.7	5.6	7.8	3.8	6.0	11.6

NOTE: Anti-Russian rumors constitute 0.6% of all rumors reported—a surprisingly low figure.
SOURCE: Robert H. Knapp, "A Psychology of Rumor," *Pub. Opin. Quar.*, 8: 25–26.

with mass media, may often preferably rely on rumor and distrust public or official sources. Today, when psychological attacks upon publics are more organized and far more general than ever before, the social sciences should be accumulating evidence about the rumor process, the kinds and classification of types of rumors, the channels and speed of rumor diffusion and additional information about the effects on the receiver of rumors.

THE IMAGES CHANGE THE ATTITUDES?

On the influence of motion pictures on attitude change we shall consider a few studies, from the pioneer work of L. L. Thurstone to the extensive army-sponsored studies of Carl Hovland. For several years after 1929, in connection with the Payne Fund Studies of Motion Pictures and Youth, Professor Thurstone gave attitude tests to high school students in Illinois communities and to children at the Mooseheart Home, before and after showing them selected motion pictures.[42] The problems of opinion change that were dealt with were the effects of single pictures, the cumulative effect of pictures and the persistence of effect. The tests used were attitude scales and paired-comparisons tests. The procedures and results follow:

1. An attitude scale on the Germans and on war was given to 133 high school children of Genoa, Illinois. Twelve days later the motion picture "Four Sons," a picture sympathetic to the personal problems of a German family, was shown. The following day the students were retested. On a scale of 11 points the average attitude of the group before seeing the picture was 5.66, afterward 5.28, a change of opinion favorable to Germans in the amount of the difference, which is not large. The tests on war indicated a change from an average attitude of 5.19 to 5.10, a small change toward disapproval of war.

2. A number of pictures on gambling and on prohibition shown in several communities brought about practically no change in opinion; in one case the average on the scale was 6.96 before and 6.97 after seeing the picture. Likewise a picture on capital punishment, "The Valiant," was shown without appreciable effect. A picture "The Criminal Code" shown to 276 students in Watseka and 246 in Galesburg brought about considerable change in attitude toward the punishment of criminals. Greater leniency was espoused with changes from 5.30 to 4.80 in Watseka, and from 5.13 to 4.64 in Galesburg.

[42] R. C. Peterson and L. L. Thurstone, *Motion Pictures and Social Attitudes of Children*, The Macmillan Company, New York, 1933; L. L. Thurstone, "The Measurement of Change in Social Attitude," *Jour. Soc. Psychol.*, 2: 230–241; "Influence of Motion Pictures on Children's Attitudes," *Jour. Soc. Psychol.*, 1: 291–304.

3. Marked changes in expressions of opinion about racial groups were brought about by the showing of pictures. Two pictures, "Son of the Gods," a romantic melodrama with a Chinese hero, and "Welcome Danger," a picture so alien to Chinese interests that the Chinese ambassador had lodged a complaint against it, were shown, the first in Geneva, the other in West Chicago, Illinois. The picture with the Chinese hero made the high school students more favorable toward the Chinese on the average of 6.72 on the scale to 5.50, a very great change. The other brought about a slight (5.71 to 5.88) increase in antipathy. Although it is probably true that in general there is a greater willingness to make favorable rather than unfavorable changes, these results could not be cited in proof of that contention, since the pictures are in no way equated.

The most pronounced change in opinion on the race question was brought about by the picture "The Birth of a Nation," which in its 1931 edition with sound accompaniment was exhibited to 434 high school students in Crystal Lake, Illinois. The change to attitudes unfavorable to Negroes was very pronounced, from an average on the scale of 7.41 to 5.93. The distribution of the results is indicated in Fig. 9.

4. The cumulative effect of pictures was tested at Mooseheart, where the pictorial experiences of the subjects could be controlled. About 750 children were divided into five groups, to which pictures were exhibited in various combinations. Some slight cumulative effect on opposition to war was noted when "All Quiet on the Western Front" and "Journey's End" were combined. These pictures differed greatly from one another in the potency of their appeal to children of these age groups, and the conclusions are not very satisfactory.

5. The persistence of effect was studied by retesting at intervals from 10 weeks to 19 months. The effects of the motion pictures were claimed to persist, although there was a general tendency to return part way to the position held before the picture was presented. The adequacy of this retesting might be questioned. Would not a number of other factors, including the subject's memory of how the previous test had been answered, be involved in a series of retests, in addition to the effect of the single picture?

How effective are films for the changing of attitudes when the conditions are those of normal commercial motion-picture attendance and when the films are shown to special audiences under experimental conditions? Such comparisons have not been reported. But we may describe briefly illustrations of each type of situation.

J. E. Hulett, Jr., reported on estimating the net effect of a commercial motion picture upon the trend of local public opinion by interviewing the members of a stratified sample of a Middle Western university com-

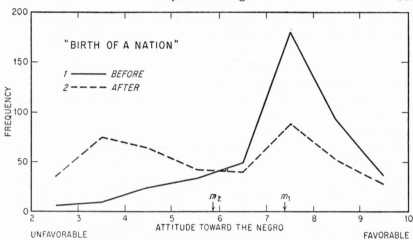

FIG. 9. An attitude graph. (From R. C. Peterson and L. L. Thurstone, *Motion Pictures and Social Attitudes of Children*, 1933, p. 37. Reproduced by permission of The Macmillan Company, publishers.)

munity before and after the local showing of the "Sister Kenny" movie.[43] The panel was stratified for socioeconomic, race, sex and age proportions of a public of approximately 30,000. A one per cent sample provided 298 individuals in the first sample, which was reduced to 207 by the second interview. Of the 207 interviewed, just 25 had seen the film, but 29 more had discussed the content of the film. These two groups were combined and these 54 individuals who had been exposed to the film or to discussion thereof were 26 per cent of the panel.

The film "Sister Kenny" was a romanticized account of Sister Kenny's life and a one-sided presentation of the efficacy of the Kenny method of mild therapy for infantile paralysis patients, a method about which there was much publicized controversy between Sister Kenny and orthodox M.D.'s for some years. Among the questions asked in the interviews was whether the patient had about the same chance of crippling with the Kenny treatment as with other treatments. A small net increase of 5 per cent favorable to the Kenny method appeared among the exposed group, presumably ascribable to the film. There was a slight increase among the exposed group in the opinion that doctors are slow to adopt new methods. There was a very slight increase among the exposed group in the belief that the patient has a difficult time in getting doctors to try out a new method. However, the changes in position are generally slight and the number of subjects who had seen the film precludes generaliza-

[43] J. E. Hulett, Jr., "Estimating the Net Effect of a Commercial Motion Picture upon the Trend of Local Public Opinion," *Am. Soc. Rev.*, 14: 263–275, 1949.

tions having statistical validity, so that the author was forced to con- clude that: "Results of the study were generally negative—that is, the film *Sister Kenny* was an unexpectedly ineffectual propaganda instru- ment—its arguments though dramatically and skillfully presented, in most cases apparently were not intrinsically convincing." [44] But Hulett's study was carefully organized, properly analyzed and well reported. Though all parts of his intended study could not be carried through, since the sample of those who actually saw the picture was disappointingly small, the author has provided the design for a careful study of motion-picture effects.

Although the influence of the motion pictures on opinions has been discussed in hundreds of articles and books,[45] the more exactly descrip- tive accounts, the test evidence and the experimental data are very limited indeed. The most substantial body of evidence since the Payne Fund Studies, to which we have already referred, was collected by the Experimental Section of the Research Branch of the Army's Information and Education Division. A number of these experimental studies are re- ported in one of the volumes of the *Studies in Social Psychology in World War II*.[46] The army made extensive use of films for informational, in- structional and indoctrinational purposes during the war. The Experimen- tal Section made numerous studies of the effectiveness of the film. The best social science methodology available for the recording of attitudes and their change was used by Carl Hovland and his associates. Detailed description of the methods and their results should be examined in their report. We can provide here only a few broad generalizations.

The army used a "Why We Fight" series of films designed for indoc- trination of the armed forces concerning the events leading up to Ameri- can participation in the war. "Before and after" tests were used on ex- tensive samples of servicemen and proper control groups were used. The authors conclude:

> The film was also quite effective in changing opinions in some areas—that is, the film altered the men's interpretations of the facts as well as giving them new facts. However, these changed opinions were nearly all closely related to the material specifically covered in the film. . . . While this film produced rela- tively large effects on material it specifically covered and while opinions were markedly changed about the performance of the British during the Battle of Britain, reliable effects were not obtained on questions of a general nature dealing with the war effort or the integrity of the British.[47]

[44] *Ibid.*, p. 275.
[45] See *The Film Index*, vol. I.
[46] C. I. Hovland, A. A. Lumsdaine and F. D. Sheffield, *Experiments on Mass Com- munication*, Princeton University Press, Princeton, N.J., 1949.
[47] *Ibid.*, p. 53.

In other words, the general implications of this entire series of studies of orientation films are that considerable change in specific opinions was not accompanied by changes in general attitudes.[48]

In another series of studies the authors find no reliable evidence as to the superiority of sound films over filmstrips in transmitting information, though they did find that a short verbal introduction and a short review of content considerably increased the effects of film presentation.

About the relative effectiveness of presenting one or both sides of an issue in the attempt to change opinions, it was concluded that giving both sides was more effective on men who were initially opposed to the point of view being presented and on those men who had better educations. Arguments on both sides were less effective on men already convinced and least effective on poorly educated men. Indeed, in general throughout these studies it was evident that on opinion materials differential procedures and arguments were necessary for those of different mental levels. One very interesting and unexpected finding from these extensive studies was that on "opinion change" indoctrination films, as contrasted to factual instructional films, the maximum result in changed opinions did not appear immediately after the showing of the film but in tests administered nine weeks later. Apparently when a change in direction of an opinion is induced that change tends to build up in the individual's mind. This is a very interesting result which should be extensively tested now with materials to induce opinion changes in civilian audiences. The significance of such a generalization on procedure in presenting political arguments and propaganda materials could be enormous.

[48] The use of the film to route specific messages to specific target groups and the difficulty of inducing generalized attitude changes is also substantiated in the results reported in "Analysis of the Film 'Don't Be a Sucker'; A Study in Communication," by Eunice Cooper and Helen Dinerman, *Pub. Opin. Quar.*, 15: 243–264.

PART FIVE

Mass Media

CHAPTER 17

The Newspaper

The modern newspaper is the most important medium of communication for the distribution of news and opinions to large publics. This is true despite the fact that the majority of the voting public in the last five out of six national elections in the United States has assumed a position contrary to the stand of over 80 per cent of the newspapers. But these elections were a special case and a special situation. Steadily, day after day, the press influences public opinion on various issues, on what types of goods one should buy, on the financial trends and economic ideology, on domestic and foreign politics, on spectacular public trials, on fashions and beauty standards, on cooking and food values, on popular science, and the like. The news is so various, the influence of the press so pervasive and the results of many types of news so controversial that one hesitates to attempt to discuss these problems within the limits of a chapter in this general volume on public opinion.[1]

THE DEVELOPMENT OF THE NEWSPAPER

The newspaper is a modern method for satisfying an old need—that of distributing news and informing publics as to the events of the day. Primitive and folk peoples, living in communities of a few hundreds or thousands, distributed information and news by word of mouth. In the early civilizations, Egyptian, Greek and Roman, there was the gossip of the public square, neighborhoods and baths, and placards were posted in public places. There were also formal newsmongers and newsletters. These same methods were used to distribute news through the Middle Ages. Printing was developed in the fifteenth century, but the regular newspaper did not appear until two centuries later. The early and effective use of pamphleteering by the Protestants during the Reformation

[1] See: A. M. Lee, *The Daily Newspaper in America*, The Macmillan Company, New York, 1937; R. W. Desmond, *The Press and World Affairs*, Appleton-Century-Crofts, Inc., 1937; E. Emery and H. L. Smith, *The Press and America*, Prentice-Hall, Inc., New York, 1954.

convinced those in authority of the disruptive possibilities of the printed page. "Thus when a *Weekly Newes* was launched in England in 1622 as the first contribution of the press in that country, it was restricted to the reporting of foreign news, presumably on the theory that news of developments far removed is relatively innocuous." [2] But the early English newspapers were relatively uninfluential in comparison with the gossip of the coffeehouses in London and the newsletters that were distributed to subscribers in the provinces. In France the *Gazette de France* was founded in 1631.[3] The news presented in these early papers was selected by those in governmental authority. In England the press did not become an independent political power for two centuries. " 'The development of the Press as an independent political power,' says Pebody, 'dates from the Reform Bill in 1831. Till then the newspapers had never thought of discussing the principles of Government in their broadest sense.' " [4] A few years later the press was a potent power in public decision. "It is therefore not surprising to find that Cobden's famous struggle against the tariff on grain (1838–1846) was already completely fought outside Parliament and through the press. . . . After 1860 the press entered upon its new career and commenced to rival Parliament as a platform of political discussion." [5]

During the seventeenth and eighteenth centuries newspapers were small, limited in content, personally edited and had few readers. It was a handicraft industry. The mass circulations that were achieved in the nineteenth century were based upon inventions that made rapid duplication of large numbers of copies possible, upon the developing literacy of the masses, upon the popularization of the content of the papers and upon the development of the newspaper as an advertising medium for the distribution of consumers' goods. In 1814, the London *Times* applied steam to its printing presses, thus speeding up the production. In the United States, the popularization of the press occurred under the aegis of a succession of dramatic personalities. Until 1833 no paper had as many as 5,000 subscribers. In 1833 Benjamin Day started a penny paper, the *Sun,* which achieved a circulation of 30,000 daily within four years of its founding. Day wrote for laborers and emphasized the formula of police news and crime.[6] In 1835 the elder James Gordon Bennett started to publish the New York *Herald.* By 1850 the New York *Herald* could

[2] D. M. Keezer, "Press," *Ency. Soc. Sci.,* 12: 346.

[3] L. M. Salmon, *The Newspaper and the Historian,* Oxford University Press, New York, 1923.

[4] *Ibid.,* p. 34.

[5] C. J. Friedrich, *Constitutional Government and Politics,* Harper & Brothers, New York, 1937, p. 427.

[6] Keezer, *op. cit.,* 12: 328.

claim to be the world's largest newspaper, with a circulation of 77,000. Editors were previously more concerned with molding opinion than with presenting news. Bennett went after news, human-interest stories, personal intimacies, fashion news, business deals, and the like. He demonstrated the popular appeal of such items, aiming his paper at the masses and caring little if he outraged fashionable folk. The mid-nineteenth century was a period of personal journalism, of strong personal editorial opinion. Horace Greeley, who founded the New York *Tribune* in 1841, was the dean of the personal journalists. He sought to improve society through his editorials. He achieved wide circulations by building up a personal following, as well as by presenting a diversity of news items. But Greeley avoided the sensationalism of the Bennetts. To the popularization of the newspaper, Charles A. Dana contributed "original, clever, concise writing, seeking to develop an American style in contrast to the heavier English news style, the imitation of which had persisted in American papers." [7] The next important stage in the development of popular journalism was the purchase of the New York *World* by Joseph Pulitzer in 1883. Pulitzer renewed the sensationalism of the Bennetts. He created news by starting crusades and reforms. He emphasized sensational news, political cartoons and illustrations and, after a few years, the comics, and spectacular headlines. Indeed, the term "yellow journalism" was coined in connection with a comic character colored yellow. This was in 1897. By that time, Pulitzer was engaged in a titanic struggle with William Randolph Hearst, who in 1896 had purchased the New York *Journal*. Hearst emphasized emotional appeals, and his papers have been unequaled in sensationalism in both news content and make-up. Circulations increased rapidly, and the urban daily newspaper became a great business enterprise. Yellow journalism was impudent, impertinent, inaccurate and emotion arousing. During the first decade of the twentieth century, the period of the muckrakers in the periodicals, the newspapers also engaged extensively as the people's champions in numerous crusades. This zeal for social reform soon decreased, and after World War I increased circulations and profit were sought. A new cycle of sensationalism in journalism, an age of jazz journalism, welled up in the 1920's. Yet lower depths were plumbed by the tabloids. In 1919 the Chicago *Tribune* started a tabloid paper in New York City called the *Daily News*. The tabloids are smaller papers, five columns wide instead of eight and with an unusually large number of illustrations. The *Daily News* reached a million circulation in a few years. The rival papers, the *Mirror* and the *Graphic*, had smaller circulations. The tabloids featured spectacular and dramatic stories, the public trials, the Hall-Mills and Snyder-Gray murder

[7] G. F. Mott (ed.), *An Outline Survey of Journalism,* Barnes & Noble, Inc., New York, 1937, p. 23.

cases, and the like, used flamboyant make-up, large headlines, numerous photographs (some faked) and sensational language. They cheapened the press in a period which was prosperous and politically conservative, a time when public issues were ignored and masses attended avidly to stories of sex, crime, gossip and entertainment. In general, the racy tabloids flourished best in New York City. When the tabloid format was adopted elsewhere, the content was generally less flamboyant. The tabloids disappeared or changed content in the serious, troubled times of the 1930's and 40's. Interpretive reporting of public affairs then became increasingly important, though the press generally retained the pursuit of the big human-interest story which had been at the center of the tabloid's appeal.

As the newspaper was popularized, it became "big business." Its organization and ownership changed. Chains were instituted or combined. The Scripps brothers started a chain in 1878. By 1900 the various chains or groups circulated from 12 to 15 per cent of the daily circulation. Group ownership increased rapidly thereafter. In 1910 thirteen groups operated 62 papers. In 1926 there were fifty-five group chains with 228 daily papers.[8] Following Raymond B. Nixon's definition, a chain or group consists of two or more newspapers in different cities with the same ownership or control.

On January 1, 1954 there were 95 corporations or individuals owning dailies in two or more U.S. cities, as compared with 76 in 1945. The number of group papers was 485 or 27.6 per cent of the total, as against 368 or 21.1 per cent in 1945. This growth is reminiscent of the expansion which took place in both local combinations and chains following World War I. . . . Circulation of all group dailies in 1953 was 45.3 per cent of total daily circulation, as compared with percentages of 42.0 in 1945, 41.6 in 1935 and 43.4 in 1930. The percentages of total Sunday circulation for the same years were 53.9, 53.8, 52.4 and 54.1, respectively.[9]

Since 1930 the percentages of group circulations to total circulations have changed very little. Based on his surveys of ownership and circulations in 1945 and 1954, Raymond Nixon concludes that we are about at an end of the long-time trend toward fewer papers nationally and that a period of stability impends.

The number of daily newspapers has decreased since 1915, although the total circulations for the United States have increased enormously. In 1881 there were 956 dailies, but by 1900 there were 2,209. In 1915 there were 2,502 daily newspapers, in 1935 this number had decreased to 2,084, and the 1955 report lists 1,760. Weekly newspapers increased

---

[8] Lee, *op. cit.*, p. 215.

[9] R. B. Nixon, "Trends in Daily Newspaper Ownership since 1945," *Jour. Quar.*, 31: 1: 13–14.

from 8,207 in 1881 to 16,323 in the peak year, 1915, and had, by 1952, decreased to 8,892. In round numbers, the total daily circulations of the daily newspapers were 27 million in 1920, 39 million in 1930, and 55 million in 1954. The circulation per 100 population which was 26 in 1920 had increased to 30 in 1954.

THE CONTENT OF NEWSPAPERS

The newspapers report the world only in part—they are selective in emphasis. This selection occurs on the basis of the standards and interests of governments, publishers and the reading public. The student of the press must consider that:

(1) There is no government in the world not engaged in "weighting" the news in its own interest; (2) that there are many news-gathering organizations some of which add their own bias to what they report; (3) that correspondents have what Mr. Justice Holmes called their "inarticulate major premises" which necessarily color the reports they send; and (4) that the editorial offices have also their own special values to contribute to the work of selection and presentation of the news.[10]

He must further consider that the contemporary newspaper in America is a "big business" with the biases of the economic viewpoints of publisher, editor and advertiser. And he must then consider the selective influence of reader interest, the demand for the personal, the incidental and the ephemeral. When he reads, "Rabbit Pulls Trigger, Kills Man Hunting Him," "A Man Goes Fishing, Gets Caught by Fish," the reader is responsible for the selection of such news. Of course, the reader realizes to some extent the partial nature of news reporting. Otherwise he would feel very insecure, indeed, in a world as reflected in the newspaper accounts.

Another approach to the consideration of the newspaper's content is the measurement of the number of column inches devoted to various types of news. With all the limitations of column-inch measurement as a method of content analysis, such studies are quite useful in indicating in a general way the proportions and relations of content. It may be noted in Table 12 that in three decades the proportion of space devoted to foreign news increased two and a half times, the Washington news was unchanged, original editorials had decreased 50 per cent, society news and women's news had more than doubled, comic strips had increased 600 per cent, and the proportionate space devoted to illustrations doubled.

[10] H. Laski, in Introduction to Desmond, *op. cit.*, 1937. Quoted by permission of Appleton-Century-Crofts, Inc., New York.

Table 12. Average Number of Columns Given Certain Categories of Content in Each Issue in Ten Leading Metropolitan Newspapers at the Beginnings of Four Decade Years, with Proportions in Decimals on the Base of Total Nonadvertising Space

	1910		1920		1930		1940	
	Cols.	Prop.	Cols.	Prop.	Cols.	Prop.	Cols.	Prop.
Foreign news and features..	2.4	.031	6.2	.088	6.8	.048	14.0	.079
Washington news.........	4.7	.061	5.0	.071	5.7	.040	10.6	.060
Columns dealing with public affairs..............	....	....	.4	.006	1.0	.007	2.5	.014
Original editorials.........	3.0	.039	2.8	.040	3.0	.021	3.1	.018
Business, financial, marine, etc....................	16.0	.211	11.4	.160	53.2	.375	56.6	.320
Sports..................	7.1	.094	10.4	.146	18.2	.128	20.9	.118
Society.................	1.4	.019	1.8	.026	4.5	.032	6.4	.036
Women's interests.........	1.1	.015	1.4	.020	2.3	.016	6.7	.038
Theater, movies, books, art, etc....................	2.2	.029	2.2	.031	4.4	.033	7.4	.042
Radio announcements and news...................	....	....	....	....	2.5	.018	2.5	.014
Comic strips and singles....	.8	.010	2.0	.028	5.1	.036	10.8	.061
Illustration (excluding comics)....................	4.0	.054	4.0	.057	8.5	.060	19.8	.112

SOURCE: This table is based on a content study by Dean Frank L. Mott and reported by him in "Trends in Newspaper Content," *Ann. Am. Acad.*, January, 1942, p. 61.

THE NEWSPAPER AND PUBLIC OPINION

Not all of the newspaper content deals with material that is controversial and therefore the subject of opinion. Weather reports, factual accounts, a part of the news reports on the financial page, some human-interest stories, many feature sections, serial novels, the announcement of radio programs, most obituary accounts, a part of the factual information on the women's page and the like are not primarily concerned with the controversial. Other sections of the paper have considerable indirect influence upon opinion. The moral and cultural standards are reflected in and influenced by the comics, the news of divorce, scandal and crime, the reporting of spectacular trials and numerous unslanted news accounts. But other parts of the paper are directed to the modifying of popular opinion. The editorials are avowedly opinion material. Cartoons; letters to the editor; a part of the space utilized by the columnists; the making and breaking of the reputations of motion-picture actors and actresses, financiers and other public figures; the blurb about beauty into which is woven the names of products favored by the paper; parts of the financial page which are directed at the influencing of investors; deliberately slanted news accounts in some papers—all these are intentionally partial. The half of the paper devoted to advertising is avowedly directed to the swaying of opinions regarding economic goods. But to what extent does the press mold public opinion, and how far is the content of the newspaper a reflection of popular opinion? This is a long-disputed point.

The influence of the press varies greatly in different cultures. The newspaper must be understood in terms of its development and its relation to various aspects of a society. No one is in a position to generalize accurately on the newspaper and popular opinion in all nations. The relationships are often subtle, and the true inwardness of such interaction may be discerned only after long and intimate study. Even then, there is only partial and incomplete knowledge, for, as yet, the newer and more exact methods of social psychology have not been applied to this problem. The content of the press and its influence on popular opinion are quite different in the authoritarian states, where regimentation and the selection and slanting of the news are under centralized control, than in the democracies, where news accounts and interpretations and opinion manipulation are kept somewhat distinct. Although news accounts are slanted in some American newspapers, especially on economic issues, the process is by no means complete, even in the most partial papers with the most definite policies. And then, opposing viewpoints are expressed in other papers. Although American theory and practice regarding the press have changed greatly since the days of the early classic libertarians and although there is today much less faith in the essential rationality of the common man, civil liberties are much prized, and the American press is the freest in the world. There is still something of the spirit, if not the hopefulness, of Thomas Jefferson. "If left to me to decide whether we should have a government without newspapers, or newspapers without a government, I should not hesitate for a moment to prefer the latter." He believed that the people in possession of the facts would reach reasonable conclusions. Today, "facts" are more complicated, issues more varied and there is a "glut of occurrences." To a far greater extent, the newspaper must select its news. There are partisan, independent and neutral papers. There is no central control, and the press is not viewed as "a great organ on which the Leader must play."

The modern daily paper is a great commercial institution directed toward the making of profits. It must hold its readers, increase its circulation. Therefore, the press reflects certain reader attitudes and tastes. The reader has interest in the immediate and in the local values and standards, which he would apply to the larger world. He quests for the personal, the "human interest," the anecdotal account, the little, drama- tized conflict and the like. The supply meets the demand. The readers' interests and values determine the content of large sections of the daily paper, especially those sections which they read carefully. The publisher's interest may be quite influential in determining the news content pro- vided by his Washington correspondents, but he may find that only about 10 per cent of his subscribers read the Washington correspondents.[11] It is said that "the popular commercial press of the 19th century escaped from the tutelage of government only to fall under the tutelage of the masses. It found support and profit in serving the whims and curiosity of the people."[12] Certainly there has been a catering to simple tastes in the struggle for circulations. But there are many newspaper publics to which a quite varied press has accommodated itself.

During the recent past, public confidence in the press as a source of guidance on public affairs has waned, while the exploration of circula- tion building through the servicing of public tastes for features has been enormously successful.[13] The gap has widened between press and people, especially on issues relating to welfare legislation, popular democracy, economic issues and the proper locus of power. In the report of the nine Nieman Fellows of 1946, professional newsmen all, it was stated:

The American popular press reached a peak of public leadership, for better or worse, at the turn of the century. That was a period when William Randolph Hearst's newspapers could boast that they had led the nation into war with Spain. It was a period when the press gained great prestige by exposure of political corruption. Led by vigorous newspapers that took an active part in trust-busting campaigns and in championing Woodrow Wilson's idealistic con- ception of democracy, the press maintained its great influence through the first World War.

Today the newspapers, while still powerful, have lost their leadership. Readers no longer look to them for advice and wisdom in making great decisions. The newspapers are held suspect by millions of Americans. Beginning in 1919 and 1920, two years of industrial strife and suffering for many people in the United States, underlying rifts which had always existed between the press and many readers widened into a deep gulf. There was a wave of postwar disillusionment and skepticism. The hostility of the newspapers against the reviving labor movement, their one-sided stories about the efforts of bewildered workers to raise their standards of living, their bias against social legislation, made millions

[11] G. Gallup, "Guesswork Is Eliminated in New Method of Determining Reader Interest," *Ed. and Pub.*, 62: 38: 55.

[12] W. Lippmann, "Two Revolutions in the American Press," *Yale Rev.*, 20: 3: 437.

[13] A number of paragraphs in the ensuing discussion are quoted from W. Albig, "Good and Evil from the Press," *Ann. Am. Acad.*, vol. 280, pp. 105–115.

feel that most of the papers were far from sympathetic to the large numbers of Americans who passed their lives on the edge of economic disaster.[14]

Evidence of the waning influence of at least the sections of the paper in which the publishers' avowed positions appear is to be noted in the general commentary to that effect by many astute observers who are professional journalists, in the repudiation of the political position of about 80 per cent of the press by a majority of voters in the past five out of six national elections, and in the type of answers that have been collected by the pollers during recent years.

EDITORIALS

Theoretically, the American newspaper makes a sharp division between the news and the interpretation of news. Naturally, in the news columns there is selection, distortion and slanting at many points. But in theory, there is a divorce of news and opinion. The editorial page is the traditional forum for the expression of opinion. In the editorial columns the policy of the paper is expressed. M. W. Brown has written that the function of editorials is to inform the reader of details omitted from the news columns; to explain the news columns; to interpret as to the real significance of an event; to argue with logical analysis of cause and effect; to urge action; to conduct crusades; to lead by persuasion, often by emotional appeals; to announce policies; to offer entertainment.[15]

For over a century there have been editorials in American newspapers. Nathan Hale purchased the Boston *Advertiser* in 1814, and was the first editor to write editorials on events of public interest.[16] In that period of partisan journalism the editor expressed himself. He was the boss. In the 1830's the popularization of the newspapers began. Although the strong editorial writer continued to have a large following and, indeed, spectacular editorial leaders waxed in influence for fifty years thereafter, the commercial aspects of the new type of paper presaged his eclipse. Income became more dependent upon advertising, advertising upon circulation, and circulation upon the purveying of news, not views.[17] However, the editor remained as a dramatic figure, a controversialist, a crusader and a dramatic oracle until about 1880. The day of greatest influence of the editorial writer was the Civil War period and the following decade. Through this bitter period—confused, chaotic and frenzied—the anxious

[14] L. Svirsky (ed.), *Your Newspaper*, The Macmillan Company, New York, 1947, p. 8. Quoted by permission of the publisher.
[15] Mott, *op. cit.*, pp. 254 ff.
[16] P. F. Douglass, *The Newspaper and Responsibility*, The Caxton Press, Cincinnati, 1931, p. 79.
[17] E. W. Allen, "Economic Influences and Editorial Influence," *Jour. Quar.*, September, 1931.

reader found solace in his allegiance and loyalty to his favored editors and in denunciatory name calling directed toward those editors with whom he differed. It was the "golden era of personal journalism." The editor canalized the opinions of his readers. The editor was a good hater and a vivid controversialist. There should be a controversy close at home and one directed toward something at a distance. One editor solved his second problem by regularly writing about the outrageous piracy against fur-bearing seals in the Kamchatka Inlet. But the importance of the editorial declined toward the end of the nineteenth century. Personal ownership of newspapers was being succeeded by corporate ownership. The commercial interests of the paper became dominant. The business office and the news staff attacked the editor and limited the range of his discussions. Great news-collecting agencies were being developed, and attention centered more and more upon their product. Experts, foreign correspondents, political writers and columnists usurped much of the field of the editorial. Editorial boards limited the personal flair of the individual writer. The monthly magazines, rapidly increasing their circulation from 1900 onward, contained much controversial material. The era of the muckrakers, 1900 to 1910, was dominated by magazine publishers such as McClure. These men led crusades that fifty years earlier would have been started in newspaper editorials. More recently, the public has had access to new sources of information—radio and television. The editorial fell into disrepute; popular confidence in the infallibility of editorial writers waned. Following the 1936 election, Capt. Joseph Medill Patterson wrote, "This election demonstrated that the power of the press to sway public opinion in this country is dying, if not dead—that people read newspapers these days to get facts—baseball and football and stock market scores, weather reports, facts from the fighting fronts and the war medicine distilleries, shopping tips—but they either don't read or they don't rely on editorials."[18] The editorial has become more factual, more informative, less controversial and less influential.

CONTROLLING POSITION OF THE COMMERCIAL PRESS

As the significant press of the United States has been the commercial press, there is every indication that commercial newspapers will remain the dominant pattern of newspaper ownership and control. Alternative backing is suggested from time to time. The idea of a labor daily, proposed occasionally by the unions, is not implemented. Of the church papers, the most powerful, *The Christian Science Monitor*, excellent though it is, requires church subsidy for survival. The adless papers, a

[18] *Time*, Nov. 16, 1936, p. 65.

suggestion cherished by reformers for decades, had an ambitious trial run for six years in *PM*.

So it is evident that the decisions of the powerful and prudent publishers of the commercial press will determine the content of the newspaper of tomorrow. But, of course, the publishers are subject to many social and economic pressures and limitations. Nonetheless, the attitudes of publishers and editors, agreements by publishers for standards of self-regulation and the assumption of responsibilities for additional services to readers are crucial.

THE PRESS IN AMERICAN LIFE

Much that is good in the American newspaper is quite evident. It is free from governmental restraint, in contrast to the press of all the authoritarian states of the world. In this mid-twentieth-century world, this is a fact to be more cherished every year. The press is broadly based on advertising income and is therefore not dependent upon the subsidized support of faction, class, party or group. And while there are pressures upon the press by particular advertisers, direct pressure by individual advertisers is less influential today than it has ever before been in American journalism, because of the diversity of advertisers supporting the now fewer but more financially secure dailies.

Objective reporting of news, the strengthening of the journalistic tradition of objective news reporting, has made considerable gains in the United States. In a large city daily, pre-eminently conservative on economic issues, certainly not evidencing zeal for a greater diffusion of the national income by redistribution, I read a large front-page headline: "TOP FIFTH GETS 47 PCT. OF MONEY; ONLY 3 PCT. GOES TO BOTTOM FIFTH. HIGHEST GROUP IN SOUTH RECEIVES 50 PCT., CENSUS ANALYSIS SHOWS." Regarding political news, Herbert Brucker has written:

It is often argued, too, that in 1936 and 1940 and 1944 most of our newspapers were defeated at the polls by Franklin Roosevelt. So they were, in so far as their editorial pages were concerned. *But they elected him by means of the objectivity of their news pages.* For, no matter what bias in reporting may remain, our anti-Roosevelt and pro-Roosevelt papers hardly differed in that for a dozen years they covered their front pages with substantially accurate accounts of everything the President said and did. This, and not the fulminations on their editorial pages, is what they really told their readers; and this is what elected him, as he used to say, again and again and again.[19]

[19] H. Brucker, *Freedom of Information*, The Macmillan Company, New York, 1949, p. 272. Quoted by permission of the publisher.

In comparison to papers anywhere else in the world, the press of the United States provides an amazing variety of news in the better large city dailies, though such is usually not the case in dailies in cities of 50,000 or less. The quantity of materials in the larger papers is enormous, obviously beyond complete reading by anyone. It has been estimated that it would take an average reader seventy-two hours to read the Sunday edition of the *New York Times,* exclusive of advertising.

The press services commerce through providing a regular daily medium for advertising. Advertising is an inevitable and necessary concomitant of the American economic system with its wide distribution of consumers' goods.

The newspapers of the United States are themselves a large industry and an important part of the economy. They provide regular and speedy news, although the factor of speed is not so significant now as it was before the development of radio.

The newspapers do bulwark against encroachments on civil liberty by governments. Although it is true that perfervid screams from the press about freedom of the press must usually be interpreted in terms of motivations other than abstract dedication to freedom, this fact must not depreciate the press contribution to freedom.

The press provides a very great deal of entertainment to engage some of the increasing leisure of the readers.

These are among the impressive contributions of the newspapers in the United States which have made our readers the most enlightened and best informed in the world.

INSTRUCTION AND EDUCATION OF THE READER

Generalizations about the inadequacy of newspaper content for the instruction and education of the reader are vulnerable to denial, for the press ranges from the superficiality of fragmentary items in the most fugitive tabloid to the rich fare of the *New York Times.* However, the papers providing a quite rich fare have but a small percentage of the total daily circulation. It is true that since Jefferson wrote, "The press is also the best instrument for enlightening the mind of man, and improving him as a rational, moral and social being," other means of mass communication have come to share the responsibility. Yet, as the principal dispenser of mass communication, the newspaper publisher must accept a larger responsibility for popular education.

The immediate rejoinder is that a commercial press will provide the content demanded by the readers; that, as the British Royal Commission on the Press states, "If a newspaper does not reflect the limitations and prejudices of at least a considerable section of the public, it will soon cease to exist, for it will find no buyers." But to what extent does the press itself modify the demands of the readers, and what are the variables of influence and the degree of responsibility now assumed by publishers at each level of the press from tabloid to *Times?* Certainly the methods of instruction must vary with the reader group, but the editors' continuing responsibility is constant. Not all newspapers can maintain the same standards, but must adjust to their publics. And very large sections of the public, in part encouraged by the press, have become preoccupied with entertainment, confused amid the political charges and countercharges, and inadequately concentrated on facts essential to rational decisions on public affairs. Dr. George Gallup has reported on some astoundingly widespread areas of ignorance concerning foreign and domestic affairs.

What about the role of the newspaper in this situation? The historical function of the newspaper has been to keep the public informed about issues of the day. It is, in a very real sense, "the schoolmaster of the people." But have the newspapers of the country lost a sense of mission in this respect? Have they begun to worry too much about having the most popular comic strips and the most complete sports pages, and too little about keeping their readers interested in, and informed about, the important problems of the day? [20]

In another poll of copy-desk chiefs, concerning the quality of presentation of news of foreign affairs, which may be part of the reason for the astonishing ignorance of so many readers, these working newspapermen rated the readability of such news lower than that of any other type of news. Vastly concerned with the readability of popular features of newspaper content, some editors may give scant attention to the quality of news writing on such public affairs as interest but a small proportion of readers. Concerned with the interests of the maximum audience—

When a journalist says that a certain event is news, he does not mean it is important in itself, often it is; but about as often it is not. The journalist means by news something that has happened within the last few hours which will attract the interest of the customers. The criteria of interest are recency, or firstness, proximity, combat, human interest, and novelty. Such criteria limit accuracy and significance.[21]

Again we come to the attitudes and values of publisher and editor. It is exasperating to publisher and editor, amidst busy lives, to be charged with such diffused responsibility; but the increased education of readers

[20] G. H. Gallup, "What We Don't Know *Can* Hurt Us," *New York Times Mag.*, Nov. 4, 1951, p. 51.

[21] Reprinted from *A Free and Responsible Press*, p. 55, by Commission on Freedom of the Press. Copyright 1947 by the University of Chicago. By permission of the University of Chicago Press.

can occur only as publishers seriously review their papers' contents and exert steady pressure for the gradual improvement in the instruction of readers.

MAINTENANCE OF AN OPEN FORUM

The newspaper as a quasi-public agency has the responsibility of maintaining a reasonably open forum for the discussion of significant public issues. Obviously, this does not mean responsibility for publishing everyone's ideas on all topics, regardless of importance of the subject or regardless of the market for the ideas in the readers' interests. It does mean the duty to present important topics of general interest, and to indicate significant ideas which may be contrary to those of the publisher.

It is often claimed that the fundamental restriction on diversity of expressed viewpoints is the fact that there is a diminishing number of papers and that the remaining dailies are largely controlled by individuals who share the same points of view on matters of economics and on the appropriate locus of power. But, as Raymond Nixon has ably argued, an increase in numbers of competing commercial newspapers does not guarantee diversity and quality of content. Nixon notes that the one-publisher town is not an evil in itself—it all depends on the publisher.[22] Moreover, concentration is likely to be carried further because advertisers, who provide 50 to 75 per cent of the gross income of newspapers, rather like newspaper monopoly, as they believe that the job of advertising is done more economically that way.

In any case, the important issue is not solely the need for competition. Nixon declares, "What is needed, above all, is a higher quality of content, coupled with a journalistic effectiveness that will assure this content being read and understood." [23] And he believes that well-founded criticism by specialists, based on a more exact science of communication, will have an impact on publishers which past criticism has not had; and that the increasing suspicions of the general public will engender an extensive critical spirit which will have results on all the mass media. Let us hope so. In any case for any foreseeable innovations we come back once more to the attitudes of publishers and editors. "They must therefore themselves be hospitable to ideas and attitudes different from their own, and they must present them to the public as meriting its attention. In no other way can the danger to the mind of democracy which is inherent in the present concentration be avoided." [24]

[22] R. B. Nixon, *Communications in Modern Society* (Wilbur Schramm, ed.), University of Illinois Press, Urbana, Ill., 1948, p. 51.

[23] *Ibid.*, p. 53.

[24] Commission on Freedom of the Press, *A Free and Responsible Press*, University of Chicago Press, Chicago, 1947, p. 93.

RESPONSIBILITY AND FREEDOM

The newspaper for entertainment had not developed when the theorists of democracy were establishing the legal basis of freedom of the press. Certainly they could not envisage the newspaper in its gossip activities; the emotional sensationalism; the cameraman prowling among faces contorted by grief, terror, horror, vacuousness and fear; the world of the comics; columnists as name callers; the concentrated power of great publishers. The Founding Fathers' concept of freedom was essentially that of freedom from governmental restraint. That was protected. Beyond this essential protection, their theory was based on the self-righting process, that truth would emerge from competition, that excess would call into being the answer or antidote. They could not envisage the need to relate freedom to responsibility. Yet today the dilemma is how to achieve responsibility while protecting the essential freedom. The issues were brilliantly examined by W. E. Hocking.

As with all freedom, press freedom means freedom from and also freedom for.

A free press is free from compulsions from whatever source, governmental or social, external or internal. From compulsions, not from pressures; for no press can be free from pressures except in a moribund society empty of contending forces and beliefs. . . . The free press must be free to all who have something worth saying to the public, since the essential object for which a free press is valued is that ideas deserving a public hearing shall have a public hearing. . . . There is an antithesis between the current conception of the freedom of the press and the accountability of the press. Accountability, like subjection to law, is not necessarily a net subtraction from liberty; the affirmative factor of freedom, freedom for, may be enhanced. . . . The situation approaches a dilemma. The press must remain private and free, *ergo* human and fallible; but the press dare no longer indulge in fallibility—it must supply the public need.[25]

This basic issue must now be left on a note of query.

INTERPRETATION AND GUIDANCE

The first American newspaper stated, "It is designed that the Country shall be furnished once a month (or if any glut of occurrences happen, oftener) with an account of such considerable things as have arrived unto our notice." The glut of occurrences of the past thirty years has brought not only daily and almost hourly news, but also great public confusion and inability to clarify and interpret the news. The newspapers'

[25] Reprinted from *Freedom of the Press*, pp. 228–230, by W. E. Hocking. Copyright 1947 by the University of Chicago. By permission of the University of Chicago Press.

contribution to clarification has been the editorials, the columns, the magazine sections, and special interpretive features. Amidst the confusion of mind-life and values which characterizes contemporary intellectuals, academicians, men of politics and action, and the general public, we cannot properly demand that publishers and their employees single-handedly chart the road to clarity and culture integration. But they have a responsibility to provide a good quality of simplifiers, explainers and popular interpreters.

A great many of our columnists, cherished by publishers as the name callers and hatchetmen, the *condottiere* of attack on individuals and of permanent regular barrage against innovation and reform, can hardly be classified as clarifiers. True, they are the creatures of their faithful publics, which cherish the epithets of the masters. And so I suppose, in some degree, supplying the market for specialists in personal attack is inevitable. So, too, with the providers of gossip, the advisers of the harried, and the specialists in interests and entertainment. But where are our popular clarifiers, dominated by concern for the public interest, devoted to rationality, wary of special interest, determined to expose fundamental relationships? A few intermittently sincere attempts are evident, but superficiality is a most evident defect. High-quality explanations by specialists are provided in the features sections of a few of our great newspapers. For the rest, there is neither current market nor supply. It is not surprising that a matured profession of columnist-clarifier has not developed. The great need for such is recent; the necessary qualities of training are ill defined, and public response untested.

At the time of publication of the report entitled *A Free and Responsible Press*, Wilbur Forrest, president of the American Society of Newspaper Editors, wrote: "Are we to sit quietly by and permit people who have very little knowledge of newspaper publishing or editing to preach so-called reformation blindly and without the slightest responsibility?" It is not intellectual remoteness, presumption, or irresponsibility to note some responsibilities of the press which are not adequately met, even though one cannot implement the analysis with concrete, detailed proposals for specific reform. Certainly I have no plans for the improvement of the press, no particularistic reforms, no practical suggestions as to how to make more income while increasing responsibility for the readers' interest. Only the professionals can properly implement reforms.

The pattern of the commercial press in the United States has changed a great deal during the past 150 years. There is no reason to assume that it is now static. The press is too public an institution to sustain a permanent schism between reader and publisher. If at least the large proportion of readers now alienated do not reform from what so many publishers currently assume to be erroneous beliefs and the following of false economic and political doctrines, it is likely that another generation of publishers will seek for leadership in espousing the popular causes.

It is also possible that economic changes based not on the preferences of publishers but on objective realities of a rapidly changing economy may make obsolete the present discrepancies between publishers and the opinions, views and interests of many readers. At some point there will be a cleavage between the roles of the publisher as representative of conservative economic views and the publisher as publisher in quest of reader following, not only for his comic strips and features but also for power over opinion, for deference and public status. Then, once more, publishers will campaign for what the public believes to be in the public interest.

CHAPTER 18

The Graphic Arts and Public Opinion

The graphic arts, especially certain paintings and statues that have become symbols for groups; the drawings, cartoons and caricatures that provide comments on the passing scene, the motion pictures that provide so many stereotypes and accentuate existing values; and, latterly, the welter of selected photographs that illustrate the newspaper and periodical, are very influential in modifying popular opinion. Significant art from the viewpoint of popular opinion is that which can be widely understood, that which conveys impressions and is functionally significant in the larger publics. "Pictures have always been the surest way of conveying an idea, and next in order, words that call up pictures in memory."[1] The pictures may be individually remembered scenes, situations, persons and incidents, or they may be actual prints, photographs, and the like, which are reproduced and distributed among masses of people. This is widely recognized today, and now, in greater degree than ever before, all social movements are lavishly equipped with pictorial symbols. The Russian government, during the past forty years, its satellites and, latterly, the Chinese Communist government have utilized the most extensive poster campaigns ever attempted in any social movement. The various symbols are spread broadcast. Even in designing textiles for clothing, there has been an attempt to popularize designs containing hammers, sickles, tractors, the red star, automobiles, and the like, in place of the "bourgeois" flowers and other conventional designs. The American NRA immediately developed the blue eagle. In the Nazi campaign for a rising birth rate, advertising artists were informed that they should present families of four children in their pictures. Pictorial stimuli are ever more carefully supervised, for today societal leaders recognize, as did General von Ludendorff, that "pictures and films and illustrations in poster form strike home more and produce greater effects than writing, and these have greater effects on the masses."

However, a recognition of the effectiveness of pictorial forms in sim-

[1] W. Lippmann, *Public Opinion*, Harcourt, Brace and Company, Inc., New York, 1922, p. 162.

plifying issues and in making emotional appeals to the masses is not new. Confucius said, "One picture is worth ten thousand words," and advertising media men have made the phrase a boring cliché. During the past two centuries, since cartooning and caricaturing have made their mass appeals, many a public man could bear testimony to their effectiveness. Gillray plagued Napoleon with his numerous caricatures of "little Boney." A generation ago, Boss Tweed of Tammany, bedeviled by the caricatures drawn by Thomas Nast, is reported to have said, "Let's stop them damned pictures. I don't care so much what the papers write about me—my constituents can't read—but, damn it, they can see the pictures."

But before pictorial forms could be effectively used to influence popular opinion, certain prerequisites and accompanying culture complexes were necessary. Among these were: (1) The development of the means of communication, especially of newspapers and periodicals, in which pictures could be reproduced. (2) The technical developments making possible duplicate pictorial reproduction. In 1833 the New York *Sun* published its first illustration, printed from a wood engraving. In the 1870's crude photoengraving appeared. This made possible the reproduction of photographs. In the 1890's four-color rotary newspaper presses were produced. In the 1920's the rotogravure processes were applied to newspaper publishing.[2] The tabloids appeared at that time, small newspapers with more than half of the paper devoted to pictures. And in the mid-1930's the picture magazines and the comic books developed as important mass media. (3) The building up of large circulations of newspapers and magazines which made possible the influencing of large publics by means of pictures, as well as print. The great caricaturists of the end of the eighteenth century issued their drawings in small booklets which were published by private booksellers. At most, the circulation of these booklets was a few thousand. (4) A popular trend toward the use of pictures. No development in culture can be thoroughly understood merely in terms of external factors that play upon it; the development of the thing itself is a factor. The present widespread use of pictorial forms can be further understood in terms of fashions in their use.

Historical records must be approached cautiously. As the anthropologist has often pointed out, there may or may not be a functional similarity between items of different ages that appear to be similar. A historical record of caricature begins with a few illustrations in primitive drawing and then notes the caricatures of ancient India, especially those ribald pictures of the god Krishna. "In an ancient Hindu drawing we see Krishna on his travels, the god is mounted on an elephant, and the

---

[2] A. M. Lee, *The Daily Newspaper in America,* The Macmillan Company, New York, 1937, pp. 129 ff.

elephant, rollicking along joyously, is constructed of the various ac-
comodating young ladies that make up the god's harem." [3] After that,
the record provides some illustrations from ancient Egypt (one of the
earliest known humorous drawings is that of servants carrying their
drunken master home from a banquet in the Egypt of 3,000 years ago).
There are some illustrations from Greece and Rome. The next significant
period is that of the numerous Gothic caricatures. Modern caricature
begins in the middle of the eighteenth century. But is the functional significance of a humorous scrawl on an ancient Hindu temple the same as
that of this morning's cartoon in the Chicago *Tribune?* The historic
record is significant if there is an evolutionary development of the designs and of the pictorial techniques or if the pictorializing processes
have the same functional relationships in the publics of different ages.
There has been a historic evolution of designs and techniques which may
profitably be traced. However, the only historic record that is significant
in a discussion of the functional relationships among cartoons, caricatures,
pictures and publics is that of the period since 1750. In this period, the
large publics emerged, modern communication developed, mass reproductions became possible, issues multiplied and the technique of pictorial
presentations was developed in relation to the growing need to influence
large publics.

In America in the 1930's there was a great stir in the graphic arts as,
amidst the ferment of political and economic change, propagandists
simply pictured their ideologies. The uses of photographs, sketches,
posters, cartoons and caricatures for the conveying of ideas and the influencing of opinions were evident on every hand. Most muralists were
using the wall spaces at their disposal to propagandize for something.
The most notorious of these artists was Diego Rivera. "One needs no
assistance in understanding the murals that the Mexican painters have
been turning out. One may or may not like them. They may or may not
be what the previous generation meant when it looked down its nose
and talked about art. But a child of six can get their meaning." [4] Of the
mile or more of wall covered with frescoes in the Mexican Ministry of
Education, A. L. Strong wrote, "The infinite struggling strength of man,
the worker, was seen in the underground miner with powerful pick, his
body bent by seams of earth; the infinite humiliation of man in that
peon with uplifted arms, searched by mine inspectors; the infinite endurance of women, pounding their grain, patient for ages. . . ." [5] Such art

[3] C. R. Ashbee, *Caricature*, Chapman & Hall, Ltd., London, 1928, p. 6.
[4] H. V. O'Brien, *Notes for a Book about Mexico*, Harcourt, Brace and Company,
Inc., New York (Willett, Clark, Chicago), 1937, p. 154.
[5] A. L. Strong, *I Change Worlds*, Henry Holt and Company, Inc., New York, 1935,
p. 244.

can be powerfully influential in providing social symbols, emphasizing types, kindling sympathy and arousing emotional responses. Rivera's murals in Rockefeller Center were censored by the owners. "For art is not innocuous; images have the power to stir men, and beliefs and attitudes may be expressed in painting and sculpture that would be easily recognized and suppressed if they were stated in so many words." [6] But the meaning of most contemporary mural art was easily intelligible, and so there were numerous controversies between authorities and artists. In the United States twenty years later, conformity to conservatism and the absence of immediate intense economic conflict had reduced such pictorial art to a minimum.

The care with which modern authoritarian rulers were also scrutinizing the pictorial symbols of the 1930's may be indicated by the fact that Mickey Mouse was censored in several countries. Yugoslavia suspected him of Communistic and revolutionary designs, the Soviet thought he represented the meekness and mildness of the masses under capitalism, and countered by creating a Russian Mickey, known as Yozh, or the Porcupine, an animal favorite of the Soviet children. [7]

THE CARTOON AND CARICATURE

As the range of values and the variety of human interactions which the artist attempts to portray have increased and as the publics to which he appeals have broadened, popular art forms have become more explicit and expressive. The cartoon and caricature are mediums well suited to the conveying of ideas. The cartoon simply limns the essentials of its subject. As popular conflict has increased, as the variety of topics with which general publics concern themselves have multiplied, self-analysis and group analysis have become more evident in the themes of the artist. The modern age of cartoon and caricature has paralleled the controversies and the intellectual ferment of the past two centuries. Professor Sorokin has described this trend statistically. Referring to the growth of caricature, he states, "A glance at Table 27 shows that the religious—ancient and medieval—art does not have it at all; that in secular art up to the seventeenth, and for most European countries even up to the eighteenth century, the caricature portrait is practically lacking in the temple of the grand art. It is a satellite of the Sensate mentality. As such it functions as friendly humor, as a weapon in the social and political struggle with opponents and enemies, as 'fun,' and so on. Emerging in

---

[6] L. Mumford, "Social Significance of Contemporary Art," *Soc. Frontier*, December, 1935, p. 77.

[7] H. Russell, "An Inquiry into a Plot of World Wide Scope," *New York Times Mag.*, Dec. 26, 1937, p. 4.

the seventeenth century, it stays in the field of art with some fluctuation." [8] The modern pictorial artists address large publics on common themes. Daumier said, "One must be of his time," and the modern cartoonist is often not only of his time, but of his day and week.

"The difference between caricature and cartoon is perhaps best suggested by M. H. Spielmann who implies that the caricature has been a weapon of venomous attack, used as an instrument for the manufacture of public opinion, while the cartoon has come to be regarded as an humorous or sarcastic comment upon the topic uppermost in the nation's mind.'" [9] The caricature is a subtle exposing of the individual's physical peculiarities or idiosyncrasies of manner, whereas the "cartoon, in the modern sense, is—with or without humor—a forceful presentation by means of exaggeration of a topical political or moral issue." [10] The caricature is an instrument of satirical and sometimes spiteful personal attack. The cartoon is simply a pictorial crystallization of a current thought. The drawing may or may not be humorous. Originally, a cartoon was simply a full-scale drawing to be used as a model for a mural painting or other work of art. In the early 1840's, the English humorous periodical *Punch* labeled some illustrative drawings "cartoons," and the term has been used since that time to designate any drawing that illustrates a social issue. The cartoons and caricatures are pictorial illustrations, usually providing personification of issues. They are characteristically simplifications which are attention-getting, easily remembered and couched in terms of the personal and provincial interests of the masses of readers. They are terse pictorial editorials which usually arouse emotions and are sometimes humorous. The great cartoonists of the past exhibited considerable personal animus and were evidently themselves emotionally involved. Though at present a few great cartoonists, such as Low of England and Fitzpatrick of the United States, retain the quality of emotion and animus, most contemporary cartooning is merely syndicated illustration.

The forerunners of the present-day cartoonist are the caricaturists of the eighteenth and early nineteenth centuries. William Hogarth (1697–1764) was the first of the great English caricaturists. He had many emulators. F. G. Stephens has compiled for the British Museum a catalogue of satirical prints preceding 1770, which contains over 4,000 items.[11] During the Hogarth period, caricatures and cartoons were

[8] P. Sorokin, *Social and Cultural Dynamics*, American Book Company, New York, 1937, vol. I, p. 490. Copyright. Quoted by permission.

[9] L. M. Salmon, *The Newspaper and the Historian*, Oxford University Press, New York, 1923, p. 389.

[10] W. Murrell, *A History of American Graphic Humor*, Whitney Museum of American Art, The Macmillan Company, New York, 1933, vol. I, p. 4.

[11] *Graphic Arts* (volume of selected articles from *Ency. Brit.*), 1929, p. 17.

printed, not in newspapers, but on handbills or posters, in booklets and sometimes in magazines. Hogarth drew an amazing number of pictures: illustrations, moral and satiric commentaries, caricatures and grotesques. There are a number of famous series of pictures: "A Harlot's Progress," "A Rake's Progress," "Marriage à la Mode" and "Industry and Idleness." [12] Hogarth's moral pictures were extremely popular, and, although the number of copies was limited, these vivid, simple pictorial stories were passed around and had great influence upon the moral "climate of opinion" of their day. Hogarth caricatured the great of his day, the political leaders, aristocrats and clergy, as well as thieves, harlots, gamblers, drunkards, musicians, poets, housewives and other types. He portrayed a half century of London life. Following Hogarth, there are two great English cartoonists, Thomas Rowlandson (1756–1827) and James Gillray (1757–1815). Their caricature was exceedingly coarse, but it was a vivid commentary on the life of their time. Gillray was the first great political caricaturist. His drawings were of the gutter, and the mob could understand them. His pencil was extremely influential in arousing England against Napoleon, and for years he kept alive the hatred of the English masses.[13] Today, in leafing through a collection of Gillray prints, one is struck by the persistence of the same political and economic problems: militarism, the dictator, recruiting, the problem of the gold standard, the chicanery of leaders, the marriage of convenience, the stupidity of the military, and the like. Gillray, with vitriolic and frequently obscene caricature, portrayed them all. Although modern cartooning stems from these sources, as well as from the French Charles Philipon, "the father of comic journalism," the modern product is, for the most part, tame in comparison. Most modern cartooning is merely illustrative, lacks the personal-attack quality and is largely shorn of coarse obscenity. This is primarily due to the size and diversity of the groups viewing the modern product. It has been necessary to find a common denominator of the inoffensive in the newspaper cartoons.

The cartoonist may effectively use humor. At crisis situations a humorous cartoon may be especially effective in influencing opinions. The laughter provides a welcome release from tensions. At times the cartoonist plays the role of court jester. But not all modern cartoons are funny. There has been a marked decrease in the number of humorous cartoons since 1900. Laughter varies greatly from period to period, and humor is an infinitely varied and subtle element in culture. It is often

[12] For a description of the separate plates of the series, see M. Bowen, *William Hogarth*, Appleton-Century-Crofts, Inc., New York, 1936, pp. 121–184.

[13] C. K. Berryman, "Development of the Cartoon," University of Missouri Bulletin, Journalism Series, No. 41, 1926.

difficult thoroughly to understand the humorous cartoons and caricatures of a past age. Used effectively, humor is one of the greatest appeals of the cartoonist. However, the contemporary cartoonist is facing ever greater difficulty in utilizing humor for some of the political and economic topics that he is called upon to illustrate.

Although cartoons are widely used in controversial discussion in England and on the Continent, the political cartoon has been more generally used in the United States than in any other country. One of the earliest American cartoons was produced by Franklin, who, "urging the colonies to unite against their common foe, published in the *Pennsylvania Gazette*, May 9, 1754, the famous snake cartoon. This wood block depicted a snake cut into eight pieces presumably representing the colonial divisions then eligible to send delegates to the Albany Congress. . . . The caption was 'Join or Die.' " [14] There were a few cartoons during the period of the War of 1812, but "the 'Era of Good Feeling' which followed the War of 1812 was marked by an almost complete dearth of cartoons. Controversy is the cartoonist's staff of life; he starves in times of brotherly love." [15] During the 1830's and 1840's, there was a slow growth of illustrative humorous drawing which was a kind of graphic reporting, providing commentaries on American customs. Some of the best work came from abroad. A. Hervieu illustrated Mrs. Trollope's *Domestic Manners of the Americans* (1832) with a series of drawings of Uncle Sam in his shirt sleeves, elevating his feet when seated, spitting, etc.[16] Whittling, tobacco-chewing, hands-in-pockets, lounging rural dwellers were mildly ridiculed. Clothing styles were commented on. The elaborate boot fashions of the women of the 1850's, bloomers and crinolines were caricatured. The large skirts were depicted as sweeping the streets, as having utility in protecting children during showers or as saving the wearer from drowning.[17] However, we may note that the political controversy of the thirty years preceding the Civil War produced very little significant cartoon art. The cartoons of this period were issued separately as engravings or lithographs.

The Civil War period was not especially prolific in cartoon pictures, although there are a considerable number that deal with the problems of enlistment and of war profiteering, with army contractors and conditions of camp and field, and that caricature prominent persons. Thomas Nast was a boy of twenty-one when the war started, but by the end of the war he had produced so many effective cartoons that Abraham Lincoln

[14] I. S. Johnson, "Cartoons," *Pub. Opin. Quar.*, 1: 3: 33.
[15] *Ibid.*, p. 35.
[16] F. Weitenkampf, "Social History of the United States in Caricature," *Critic*, 47: 136.
[17] *Ibid.*, p. 137; and see W. Murrell, *op. cit.* for historical items.

said, "Thomas Nast has been our best recruiting sergeant." [18] It was during this period that the cartoon appeared in the periodicals. "During the 1860's and 70's the cartoon in this separate form began to disappear. Cartoons then became an eagerly awaited feature of the illustrated magazines such as *Harper's Weekly, Frank Leslie's, Vanity Fair, Puck, Judge,* and the *Wasp*." [19]

The first great period of American cartooning began in the early 1870's. The "Tweed Ring" was in control of New York City. In *Harper's Weekly,* Thomas Nast began a series of vitriolic attacks upon Boss Tweed and his lieutenants. These were extremely effective in arousing opinion against the ring, and Thomas Nast has been credited by historians as the major force that started the campaign which led to the exposure and disgrace of the ring. During 1871 Thomas Nast was paid $8,000 for his pictures, but it is said that he was offered bribes of a hundred times that amount to desist from his drawing. [20] It was during the 1870's that Nast produced the principal symbols of our political cartooning. The cartoon in which the elephant first appeared as an emblem of the Republican party was drawn by Nast in 1874. Three years before that he had produced the Tammany tiger. Nast tried the figures of a tiger, of a fox, and of a wolf for the Democratic party, but none of them caught the public fancy. He had used the donkey as a symbol for certain Democratic politicians as early as 1869. But Nast did not consistently use the donkey in this role. "It is not at all certain that Nast deserves the credit for enlisting the donkey permanently in the Democratic ranks, though one of his cartoons, published early in 1878, was probably the first in which the elephant and the donkey appeared in the same cartoon to signify the two major parties." [21] These animals evolved and became eloquently expressive. Other animals appeared as symbols— the American eagle, the bull moose of Theodore Roosevelt's day, the goat of the Populist party and many others.

An increasing stream of pictorial commentary on social life and customs in the United States was produced during the last thirty years of the nineteenth century. There were many cartoons dealing with fashionable life, the aping of English customs, the problems of urbanization and life in the crowded quaters of the "flat" and the boarding house, speed and recklessness on bicycles, a steady output of commentary on styles, fads, fashions, and the like.

The second great period of American cartooning was from 1900 to 1910. This was a time of social reform—the era of the muckrakers, the

[18] A. B. Paine, *Thomas Nast,* The Macmillan Company, New York, 1904, p. 69.
[19] Johnson, *op. cit.,* p. 35.
[20] Paine, *op. cit.,* p. 206.
[21] *New York Times Mag.,* Nov. 27, 1932, p. 9.

"trust-busting" days of Theodore Roosevelt. In that period a number of skillful cartoonists, notably Homer Davenport, F. B. Opper, Floyd Campbell and DeMar were enlisted on the side of reform. Their work had vigor for they were motivated by an aggressive zeal. Davenport developed the symbol of the trusts, that huge, overgrown, monstrosity of a man bulging in all directions. Opper was a master of humorous interpretation. Floyd Campbell was the terror of the corrupt ring of Philadelphia. DeMar was a master caricaturist. Many leaders writhed under the skillful attacks of these artists. It was the heyday of baiting. The plight of certain economic leaders, notably John D. Rockefeller, J. P. Morgan, Jay Gould and William H. Vanderbilt, was not enviable. "The cartoonists, or the knights of brush and pencil, whose brains are dedicated to righting the wrongs of the age and the merciless unmasking of the enemies of society, are today among the foremost influences battling for the overthrow of the ring, the machine and the corruptionists, who have impaired municipal and national integrity, and brought shame and dishonor on the great republic." [22] During this period, Theodore Roosevelt and the issues that he personalized provided a veritable field day for the cartoonist.

After 1910 vigorous personal attacks in the cartoons declined. The cartoon was syndicated. W. R. Hearst made much of drawings in his string of papers, and outside papers sought to buy the output of his cartoonists and comic artists. A syndicate was started. Then others were formed, and by 1925 there were at least fifty organizations offering syndicated material to the papers. All newspapers used such material. "The syndicate, having to serve all sorts of papers in all sorts of communities has softened the attack quality in most of this product so that the result has been a more or less negative, qualified picture which is guaranteed to offend no one and therefore has lost most of its pungency. Lacking that virility, it has come to be simply a thing of entertainment." [23] The editors increasingly bought the syndicated cartoon. The highly paid, skillful craftsmen provided cartoons to be used by papers of all political complexions, and the cartoonist could hardly afford violent emotions of his own. And so the cartoonist had to express the average, the composite view. He had to seek a low common denominator of the inoffensive in order to be safe and successful.

As the interpretations of the social process maintained by intelligent men became somewhat less simple and explicit, the cartoonist, among other interpreters, was often aware of complexities. Abstract and com-

[22] B. O. Flower, "Floyd Campbell: A Knight of Municipal Honor," *Arena*, 34: 372 (1905).
[23] L. F. Shaffer, *Children's Interpretations of Cartoons*, Teachers College Contributions to Education, no. 429, 1930, p. 3.

plex economic problems were difficult to portray simply. The election of 1932 and all subsequent elections have proved increasingly difficult for the cartoonist to portray, since complex economic and international issues have been at stake. Balanced budgets, welfare legislation, monetary standards, debts, inflation and other basic issues do not lend themselves to easy pictorial portrayal. In World War II, many basic issues were difficult to portray and, in general, the cartoons lacked the aggressive simplifications and emotional animus of World War I. So did the population of readers to whom the cartoons were directed. Good cartoon characters dealing with the personal and provincial values, such as Bill Mauldin's G.I. Joe, were created, but the underlying issues largely baffled the picturemakers.

In contrast to the relative moderation of tone in the cartoons of contemporary United States daily newspapers, the Communist U.S.S.R. cartoons and caricatures since the 1920's have been dogmatically assertive, monomaniacally doctrinaire, emotional and crude lampoons. The Russian cartoons have attacked identifiable personalities of their own and foreign nations and have vigorously attacked the symbols of other nationalities, most especially the United States. The phrases used to characterize these Russian cartoons may be substantiated by a perusal of collections of cartoons which have appeared in the chief Soviet agitational periodical, *Krokodil*, a magazine published three times a month by the newspaper *Pravda*, the publication of the Communist Party of the U.S.S.R.[24] As the people of Russia liked the United States very much at the close of the war, grateful as the people were for their allies' aid, the Party thought that the intense postwar campaigns of "hate-America" were necessary to deplete this fund of good will. There are various simple themes in the anti-United States cartoons, notably those of the dollar-mad imperialists, the gangster culture of the United States, the warmongers, America's moribund economic culture, the lack of political liberty in the United States and America's ambition to master the world. The symbols of these Soviet cartoons are crude, gross, simple, emotion-arousing stereotypes. Uncle Sam's tail coat and top hat are retained as a symbol of capitalist greed and exploitation. Moreover, he is a vicious, swaggering bully. There is no moderation or geniality in the portrayal. A people accustomed to rambunctious name calling and vindictive political attack requires gross symbolism. The Soviet cartoon provides such images.

[24] See *Out of the Crocodile's Mouth* (William Nelson, ed.), Public Affairs Press, Washington, D.C., 1949. *Krokodil* is a 14-page publication which has had a circulation of about 300,000. In the post–World War II era about one-half of each issue was devoted to the sins and evils of the United States. Aside from *Krokodil*, the average issue of a U.S.S.R. magazine or paper has no more than one or two political cartoons, since humor is handed out in meager doses. See E. Raymond, "Jokes Stalin Loves," *United Nations World*, November, 1951.

Table 13. Cartoon

(Trends in cartoon symbols in five metropolitan daily newspapers expressed

	1900	1901	1902	1903	1904	1905	1906	1907	1908	1909	1910	1911	1912
Number of papers	2	2	2	1	1	1	1	1	1	4	5	5	5
Number of cartoons, average per paper	84.5	83.0	80.5	57.0	84.0	84.0	84.0	84.0	84.0	66.7	68.8	84.0	77.8
Percentage for	4.1	4.7	11.9	7.0	2.4	5.9	2.0	2.4	15.5	4.1	4.6	6.9	12.0
Percentage against	25.8	27.4	13.7	7.0	3.6	21.4	17.9	1.2	22.6	4.6	18.6	15.0	13.3
Percentage illustrative	70.0	67.8	74.4	86.0	94.1	72.6	80.1	96.4	61.9	90.8	76.9	78.1	74.7
Average number of symbols per cartoon	4.1	4.3	4.6	6.2	5.8	5.9	5.7	3.4	4.5	4.6	4.5	5.3	5.0
Average number of symbols labeled	2.6	2.7	3.6	3.4	3.0	3.0	1.7	1.5	2.4	2.3	2.7	3.0	2.9
Percentage of cartoons in which no symbols labeled	23.5	17.5	8.0	26.3	21.4	15.5	43.9	45.2	17.9	23.0	25.2	30.0	17.1
Percentage of cartoons in which loops were used	2.9	9.1	21.1	28.0	17.9	7.1	14.3	26.2	38.1	30.7	26.0	35.7	40.7
Average number of loops used	2.5	1.1	1.1	3.6	2.2	1.5	1.0	3.7	3.5	2.7	2.4	2.4	1.8
Percentage of cartoons made up of series of pictures	1.1	3.6	1.8	50.0	34.5	21.4	22.6	44.0	35.7	6.4	11.2	14.3	12.3
Average number of pictures in series	2.5	2.9	1.0	4.0	3.6	3.1	2.9	4.0	4.2	3.4	3.6	3.6	1.7
Symbol types:													
1. Personal symbols—Totals, %	44.3	43.9	45.1	49.3	60.6	55.7	49.5	64.8	67.4	48.5	55.4	53.0	53.9
For group, party, etc.	8.8	14.4	13.4	32.6	29.8	23.3	31.6	48.9	20.4	20.3	16.6	25.9	20.6
Anonymous — Boy	0.0	0.1	0.0	1.1	0.0	0.8	0.0	0.0	0.0	1.3	1.1	0.7	0.1
Anonymous — Man	0.7	0.5	0.1	4.5	1.0	4.1	0.0	0.3	2.1	4.9	7.9	3.3	1.3
Anonymous — Girl	0.0	0.0	0.1	0.6	0.2	0.4	0.0	0.3	0.3	0.0	0.0	0.1	0.0
Anonymous — Woman	0.0	0.6	0.1	0.0	0.4	0.6	0.2	0.7	0.5	1.5	2.3	1.5	0.6
Anonymous — Crowd	0.0	0.3	0.4	0.0	0.0	0.6	0.0	0.3	0.0	1.4	1.8	0.7	0.2
For country or other governmental unit	8.1	8.4	9.0	0.8	4.7	5.9	0.8	2.1	1.6	3.7	2.8	5.3	4.3
For abstract quality	2.5	2.6	3.8	0.3	2.0	2.0	4.8	2.4	0.8	5.6	3.9	3.9	4.1
Personalized animate being	0.0	0.3	2.0	0.0	0.4	0.0	0.2	0.0	0.5	0.0	0.1	0.3	0.0
Some recognizable or labeled person	23.2	16.6	15.3	8.8	21.7	16.8	10.2	9.8	39.4	9.5	17.8	10.8	22.0
Miscellaneous	1.0	0.1	0.9	0.6	0.0	1.2	1.7	0.0	1.8	0.4	1.1	0.5	0.7
2. Animals as symbols—Totals, %	7.9	6.3	5.7	7.7	1.8	2.4	4.7	2.0	3.2	3.7	4.5	3.7	5.1
For nation	1.5	0.5	0.6	0.0	0.0	0.4	0.2	0.0	0.0	0.1	0.1	0.2	0.2
For political party	1.9	0.0	1.2	0.6	0.0	0.0	0.4	0.7	1.8	0.2	2.0	0.6	2.6
For other special group	2.7	3.8	0.2	5.7	0.0	0.2	0.0	0.0	0.3	0.2	0.4	0.4	0.6
For abstract quality	1.7	0.4	0.7	0.0	0.4	0.6	0.6	0.3	0.0	1.1	0.3	0.9	1.2
Miscellaneous	0.1	1.6	3.0	1.4	1.4	1.2	3.5	1.0	1.1	2.1	1.7	1.6	0.5
3. Objects as symbols—Totals, %	41.3	40.9	42.0	38.9	32.6	39.4	42.0	30.8	26.9	43.5	36.5	40.1	37.7
Buildings	3.6	3.6	3.0	8.5	5.9	3.9	7.5	4.5	5.0	4.8	3.8	5.4	3.4
Roadways	0.0	1.2	1.5	0.0	0.0	0.4	0.4	0.7	0.5	0.4	0.1	0.3	0.8
Containers	2.2	3.4	1.5	2.0	0.8	0.0	2.3	0.0	1.1	4.0	2.6	3.2	3.2
Weapons, clubs, missiles, etc.	4.3	3.2	3.1	2.8	1.4	3.6	1.9	1.0	3.2	0.9	0.8	3.4	1.9
Scrolls, documents, etc.	3.0	2.8	4.7	5.1	4.7	6.3	4.4	10.1	5.0	8.2	8.3	6.1	8.4
Vehicles	2.2	3.4	1.4	2.0	3.2	1.2	3.5	3.5	1.1	4.7	2.8	3.0	1.8
Money	0.7	0.9	1.0	0.0	1.4	0.6	0.6	1.0	0.5	0.7	0.8	0.7	0.7
Pictures	0.9	0.5	0.2	0.3	1.4	0.6	0.2	0.0	0.5	0.5	0.8	0.5	0.4
Flags	1.1	1.2	1.9	0.3	0.4	0.6	0.0	0.0	0.0	1.5	1.0	0.4	0.4
Furniture	1.5	0.9	0.0	0.0	1.2	1.4	1.9	0.0	2.6	1.4	0.8	1.5	0.7
Articles of clothing	0.9	1.1	0.2	0.3	1.4	0.4	1.9	0.3	0.5	0.7	0.3	1.0	2.0
Food	0.9	0.2	0.5	0.6	1.2	0.4	1.2	0.3	0.5	0.9	0.6	1.2	0.6
Writing equipment	0.0	0.1	0.0	0.0	0.2	0.4	0.4	0.0	0.3	0.2	0.2	0.2	0.1
Boundaries (fences, lines, etc.)	0.6	1.0	0.4	0.0	0.0	0.2	1.2	0.0	0.5	0.2	0.2	0.8	0.9
Signs	6.1	6.2	3.6	8.8	4.3	9.9	9.4	2.4	0.5	5.1	4.8	4.0	3.5
Miscellaneous	13.3	11.2	19.0	8.2	5.1	9.5	5.2	7.0	5.6	9.3	8.6	8.4	8.9
4. Nature symbols—Totals, %	6.0	8.5	6.7	4.3	4.3	2.0	3.4	1.6	1.9	3.8	2.1	3.0	3.2
Trees	0.6	0.5	0.2	0.6	0.0	0.0	0.8	0.0	0.0	0.2	0.1	0.3	0.2
Rocks	0.4	0.7	0.0	0.0	0.2	0.0	0.2	0.0	0.0	0.1	0.2	0.1	0.1
Water	1.2	3.5	1.0	0.6	0.4	0.0	1.2	1.0	0.8	1.0	0.1	1.0	0.5
Hill	0.0	0.2	0.5	0.3	0.8	0.6	0.2	0.3	0.0	0.2	0.1	0.2	0.3
Wind	0.0	0.2	0.3	0.0	0.0	0.0	0.2	0.3	0.8	0.0	0.0	0.0	0.3
Vegetation	0.3	0.3	1.4	0.0	0.0	0.8	0.8	0.0	0.3	0.2	0.3	0.4	0.2
Miscellaneous	3.5	3.1	3.3	2.8	2.9	0.6	0.0	0.0	0.0	2.1	1.3	1.0	1.6

Symbol Types

in percentages of the total number of cartoon symbols examined for each year)

1913	1914	1915	1916	1917	1918	1919	1920	1921	1922	1923	1924	1925	1926	1927	1928	1929	1930	1931	1932	1933	1934	1935
5	5	5	4	4	5	5	5	5	4	4	4	4	5	5	5	5	5	5	5	5	5	5
82.2	80.2	76.6	84.0	84.0	84.0	81.2	77.6	78.4	83.5	84.0	84.0	82.2	83.6	82.4	83.8	84.0	84.0	84.0	84.0	84.0	84.0	79.8
12.6	4.6	8.6	6.8	15.8	12.6	14.2	9.3	16.2	5.7	4.5	9.8	11.7	12.9	6.0	5.7	8.1	4.8	11.7	6.4	11.9	10.5	3.1
12.2	11.1	14.4	29.2	28.3	30.2	18.8	17.8	41.2	20.4	15.5	18.4	20.8	22.6	17.9	16.9	18.8	21.9	18.1	30.5	25.9	38.1	59.8
75.2	84.3	76.8	63.9	55.9	57.1	67.0	72.8	42.6	73.8	80.1	71.5	67.5	64.5	76.2	77.4	72.9	73.3	70.2	63.1	62.1	51.4	37.0
3.9	4.4	3.9	4.6	5.1	6.0	4.8	6.7	5.4	6.2	6.2	6.5	4.4	4.8	5.1	5.7	4.9	5.3	4.3	5.3	5.2	4.2	5.9
2.2	2.7	2.4	2.2	2.6	3.4	3.5	4.6	2.9	3.8	4.1	4.3	3.1	3.5	3.6	3.8	3.3	4.0	3.1	3.8	3.8	3.2	3.8
15.3	19.9	18.2	26.5	15.8	14.5	8.5	6.6	12.9	5.4	7.4	5.6	12.0	7.9	9.9	4.5	8.1	7.4	7.1	5.7	5.5	4.5	3.5
53.8	38.8	33.4	38.1	40.8	28.1	46.8	48.5	42.1	44.6	44.0	45.5	39.9	52.6	55.5	50.4	47.6	58.1	46.9	46.7	48.1	55.2	48.4
1.8	1.8	1.5	2.0	1.9	1.5	1.9	2.0	1.7	1.9	2.3	1.9	1.4	1.8	1.7	1.5	1.6	1.9	1.9	1.5	1.8	1.7	1.6
18.3	11.5	12.7	14.9	14.3	12.9	17.7	22.6	17.0	14.4	13.9	17.6	9.8	18.3	20.2	10.2	16.1	15.5	17.1	13.6	12.1	13.3	5.1
2.3	3.0	3.3	3.5	3.4	3.1	2.9	3.0	2.9	2.4	3.2	3.0	3.3	2.8	2.7	2.6	3.4	2.8	2.8	2.9	2.6	2.9	3.3
58.2	**53.5**	**48.9**	**49.8**	**55.4**	**49.0**	**55.0**	**56.0**	**56.1**	**48.8**	**52.6**	**48.5**	**51.7**	**51.3**	**49.5**	**46.2**	**47.9**	**50.0**	**52.8**	**46.9**	**50.6**	**49.4**	**38.0**
25.0	18.3	14.8	21.0	18.2	17.2	18.1	20.6	23.4	17.6	21.2	19.3	25.8	24.6	18.7	19.0	19.3	15.0	21.8	20.4	17.5	22.4	21.2
1.1	0.3	0.9	0.0	0.7	0.1	0.3	0.2	0.6	0.7	0.4	0.1	0.1	0.0	0.2	0.4	0.1	0.5	0.7	0.0	0.2	0.3	0.0
2.2	2.3	1.8	0.2	2.2	0.3	1.3	0.8	0.8	1.2	1.2	1.2	1.3	0.3	1.7	1.0	1.5	2.4	1.0	0.3	0.8	0.5	0.6
0.3	0.2	0.1	0.0	0.1	0.0	0.0	0.0	0.0	0.1	0.2	0.1	0.0	0.0	0.1	0.0	0.0	0.0	0.1	0.0	0.0	0.0	0.0
1.1	0.6	0.6	0.0	0.7	0.2	0.4	0.2	0.4	0.6	0.6	0.2	0.2	0.6	0.4	0.6	0.4	0.6	0.2	0.0	0.4	0.2	0.1
0.1	1.6	0.1	0.0	0.3	0.0	1.7	1.1	0.2	0.6	0.2	0.7	0.0	0.1	1.8	0.1	0.5	1.7	2.0	0.0	0.1	0.4	0.0
7.7	11.2	14.6	9.4	17.8	12.1	13.1	8.2	11.6	11.7	9.3	7.2	8.0	8.0	8.0	6.6	8.7	10.8	8.6	7.0	10.8	8.7	3.6
5.8	7.2	6.2	6.6	5.9	8.3	13.1	7.1	10.6	8.9	9.9	8.9	8.6	11.4	7.7	8.6	8.8	10.2	10.6	9.3	13.1	8.6	6.7
0.2	0.0	0.1	0.3	0.3	0.1	0.2	0.3	0.7	0.1	0.9	0.0	0.3	0.1	0.8	0.0	0.4	0.1	0.4	0.3	0.6	1.4	0.2
13.9	10.7	9.4	12.1	7.9	10.1	5.5	16.8	6.9	6.4	8.2	9.7	6.6	5.5	8.1	8.6	5.9	8.2	6.5	9.3	5.7	5.4	5.5
0.8	1.1	0.3	0.2	1.3	0.6	1.3	0.7	0.9	0.9	0.5	1.1	0.8	1.1	1.8	1.5	2.2	0.7	0.9	0.3	1.4	1.5	0.1
4.5	**3.9**	**5.8**	**4.6**	**4.0**	**5.7**	**4.7**	**8.5**	**5.1**	**6.2**	**6.7**	**6.3**	**5.8**	**5.8**	**6.7**	**9.6**	**6.0**	**8.5**	**9.6**	**10.4**	**7.9**	**9.7**	**7.2**
0.1	0.5	1.2	0.7	0.8	1.2	0.6	0.1	0.2	0.4	1.3	0.3	0.4	0.2	0.3	0.1	0.4	0.8	0.3	0.3	0.2	0.4	0.0
0.5	0.2	0.7	1.5	0.1	0.2	0.8	3.6	1.2	0.6	1.7	2.2	1.0	1.9	2.4	5.1	0.9	2.4	2.8	4.2	1.0	1.8	1.4
1.3	1.1	2.0	0.2	0.2	0.5	0.7	0.6	0.2	0.9	0.4	0.3	0.9	0.7	1.2	1.0	1.0	1.3	1.0	1.1	0.8	1.3	1.1
1.0	1.3	1.2	1.0	2.1	2.5	1.9	3.3	2.7	3.6	2.3	2.6	2.1	1.9	1.5	1.5	2.3	2.6	3.1	3.2	4.0	4.6	3.6
1.6	0.8	0.7	1.2	0.8	1.3	0.7	0.9	0.8	0.7	1.0	0.9	1.4	1.1	1.3	1.9	1.5	1.4	2.4	1.6	1.9	1.6	1.1
34.0	**40.1**	**39.7**	**42.2**	**37.4**	**41.5**	**36.5**	**30.8**	**35.1**	**38.8**	**35.2**	**40.3**	**37.1**	**36.9**	**38.8**	**39.2**	**40.9**	**35.8**	**31.0**	**36.3**	**36.2**	**36.3**	**46.8**
4.3	3.0	3.5	3.2	2.7	2.3	3.7	3.0	4.4	4.0	3.9	3.8	4.3	4.7	3.0	3.4	4.4	3.3	3.2	4.5	3.0	3.0	5.0
0.9	0.4	0.7	0.5	0.1	0.3	0.5	0.3	1.3	0.7	1.0	0.4	1.1	0.9	0.3	1.0	0.5	0.7	1.3	0.7	0.3	0.4	1.4
2.5	2.4	2.6	2.8	3.4	3.3	3.0	2.5	2.7	4.6	3.3	4.2	3.0	3.7	2.7	4.0	2.0	2.6	2.7	5.3	3.7	3.4	4.4
1.5	3.2	2.9	3.9	3.1	5.6	2.0	0.9	2.6	2.1	1.3	2.3	3.0	1.6	2.5	1.3	1.5	2.2	1.4	2.3	2.6	2.1	2.6
6.9	7.8	6.8	7.0	6.4	5.6	5.9	3.5	4.2	4.6	3.6	4.7	4.4	4.1	5.6	5.2	6.0	6.2	3.5	4.1	3.4	4.0	5.2
3.8	2.3	4.2	3.1	2.0	3.1	2.1	3.3	3.8	3.6	4.5	4.1	4.9	3.7	3.5	3.3	4.6	3.2	4.2	3.3	2.8	2.9	3.5
1.3	1.0	0.8	0.3	0.7	0.8	1.0	1.1	0.8	0.8	0.7	0.7	1.6	0.9	0.6	0.7	1.4	0.5	1.1	1.2	1.2	1.6	0.8
0.1	0.8	0.3	0.6	0.4	0.5	0.4	0.3	0.6	0.4	0.7	0.4	0.5	0.2	0.7	0.4	1.0	0.3	0.2	0.9	0.3	0.5	0.5
0.2	0.8	1.8	2.2	3.1	1.9	0.7	0.9	0.3	0.5	0.4	0.6	0.3	0.4	0.5	0.9	0.5	0.6	0.3	0.4	0.9	1.1	0.7
0.4	0.3	1.6	1.5	1.5	1.0	1.2	0.9	1.5	1.2	0.8	1.2	0.6	0.6	1.2	0.9	0.8	0.7	0.9	0.6	0.8	0.7	1.4
1.5	0.6	0.9	1.3	1.7	0.9	1.0	0.2	1.4	1.4	1.2	1.3	0.2	0.5	1.0	1.9	1.2	0.6	0.5	0.5	0.5	0.7	0.6
1.0	1.1	0.8	0.3	1.6	1.4	0.7	1.0	1.4	0.6	0.4	0.5	0.7	1.6	1.3	0.9	1.0	0.7	1.0	0.7	0.1	1.1	0.9
0.1	0.2	0.1	0.1	0.1	0.2	0.1	0.1	0.0	0.1	0.0	0.1	0.0	0.2	0.2	0.2	0.0	0.0	0.0	0.2	0.1	0.1	0.3
0.3	0.1	0.8	0.7	0.3	0.4	0.5	0.1	0.6	0.9	0.7	0.2	0.8	1.1	0.3	1.0	0.6	0.5	0.3	0.6	1.0	1.4	1.2
1.8	4.0	3.5	3.2	2.6	4.6	3.3	4.4	3.7	3.1	3.2	4.5	1.7	1.7	5.1	4.0	4.5	4.3	2.0	3.0	3.6	3.8	4.6
7.4	12.1	8.4	11.5	7.7	9.2	10.4	7.4	5.8	10.3	9.5	11.3	9.7	11.0	10.9	9.9	10.6	9.3	8.6	7.7	12.1	9.4	13.7
3.0	**2.3**	**5.5**	**3.6**	**3.4**	**3.3**	**3.6**	**3.8**	**3.9**	**6.1**	**6.0**	**4.5**	**5.3**	**6.0**	**4.9**	**5.0**	**4.6**	**5.5**	**6.6**	**5.7**	**4.8**	**5.4**	**7.7**
0.0	0.0	0.2	0.1	1.0	0.6	0.4	0.3	0.3	0.3	0.4	0.4	0.5	0.7	0.6	0.4	0.7	1.3	0.7	0.9	0.4	0.6	0.5
0.1	0.1	0.6	0.0	0.2	0.2	0.4	0.5	0.0	0.9	0.8	1.2	0.5	0.3	0.3	0.5	0.1	0.6	0.2	0.6	0.4	0.2	0.4
0.5	0.5	1.6	1.4	0.7	1.2	0.7	0.7	0.9	1.6	1.4	1.3	1.6	1.2	1.1	1.6	0.8	1.6	1.4	1.8	1.4	0.8	2.2
0.2	0.1	0.1	0.3	0.2	0.5	0.5	0.8	0.5	0.3	0.5	0.4	0.5	0.9	0.3	0.2	0.1	0.3	0.3	0.2	0.4	0.7	0.5
0.3	0.0	0.1	0.0	0.1	0.0	0.0	0.0	0.0	0.0	0.0	0.1	0.0	0.1	0.2	0.0	0.1	0.2	0.0	0.0	0.1	0.6	0.0
0.4	0.5	0.4	0.4	0.2	0.1	0.2	0.6	0.4	0.3	0.4	0.4	0.4	0.5	0.7	0.3	0.2	0.5	0.4	0.5	0.4	0.8	0.3
1.5	1.1	2.5	1.4	1.0	1.1	1.4	0.9	1.5	2.7	2.5	0.7	1.8	2.3	1.7	2.0	2.6	1.0	3.6	1.7	1.7	1.7	3.8

Very few experimental studies of the effects of cartoons have been made. In a limited study by Asher and Sargent, 185 subjects indicated on a rating test their attitudes on the words New Deal, Private Initiative, Businessman, Alien, John Bull and Pacifist, and then responded to a five-second viewing of cartoons which personified these topics and issues. The shifts in attitude were generally greater when brought about by cartoon caricatures than by words. This was a simple test of primarily emotional reactions of the subjects, the sort of situation which is assumed to occur when they glance at cartoons in the daily paper.[25]

In 1949 Jiri Kolaja took 600 cartoons at random from the 1947 to 1948 issues of the *Ladies' Home Journal, The Saturday Evening Post* and *Collier's*. These journals of wide circulation provided cartoons dealing with personal and provincial interests, with very few items on serious public issues. Content classification showed no cartoons dealing with strikes, race or the international situation. Of the 600 cartoons, there were 46 dealing with any public issues, while 168 dealt with interactions of husband and wife, parents and children, 201 with leisure-time situations and 51 with work situations. The author concludes that "popular American magazine cartoons avoid controversial social issues, and social pathological phenomena. In general, there is a clear tendency by ridiculing minor family issues to concentrate upon the face-to-face relationship." [26]

In Table 13, I have provided some data on trends in cartoon symbols. Simple content studies are useful at times to uncover trends which were not suspected, or to verify changes which had been impressionistically assumed but were unproved. This classification of the principal cartoon symbols in the daily newspaper in the United States analyzed 80 or more principal cartoons from each of five metropolitan dailies for each year from 1900 through 1935. In all, some aspects of the symbols of over 11,000 cartoons were classified. The categories were developed by presampling the cartoons throughout the period. Four classifiers were used and after preliminary training their results in classifying the items were almost identical. This content study was a simple, pioneering content analysis which I did years ago, but would still consider roughly adequate to its function of searching for some symbol trends. I shall mention just a few items, though careful scrutiny of the table would show many other ranges and trends. During the period 1900 through 1935, the percentage of the cartoons which were "for" the issue or person ranged from 2 to over 16 per cent, and the percentage "against" ranged from 1.2 to over 59 per

[25] R. Asher and S. S. Sargent, "Shifts in Attitude Caused by Cartoon Caricatures," *Jour. Gen. Psych.*, 24: 451–55, 1941; see, also: S. S. Sargent, "Emotional Stereotyping in the *Chicago Tribune*," *Sociometry*, 1939, pp. 69–75.

[26] J. Kolaja, "American Magazine Cartoons and Social Control," *Jour. Quar.* 30:72, 1953.

cent, while those classified as simply "illustrative" ranged from 37 to over 90 per cent. But there are no persistent trends in this 35-year period as to the percentages of cartoons "for" and "against" the persons or issues. A marked trend may be noted in the sharp decrease from 1900 to 1935 in the percentage of cartoons in which no symbols were labeled. Apparently, in the earlier years there were many more instances in which the cartoons contained standard symbol items readily recognized by the readers. This is borne out by the sharp increase in the percentage of cartoons in which loops were used for dialogue or explanatory remarks. The cartoon pictures were decreasingly self-explanatory. About half of all cartoons used persons as symbols, ranging by years from 38 per cent to over 64 per cent, with subclasses of personal-symbol use varying considerably, as may be noted by examination of the percentages in the table. Some items show very significant variation, as in the percentage of cartoons containing recognizable persons in the first decade of the century (the era of the muckrakers), reaching a peak of 39.4 per cent of all cartoons in 1908, in comparison to the 5 to 10 per cent in the years after 1915 when the cartoons were syndicated and the attack quality decreased. Many other trends may be noted by close examination of this table.

THE COMICS

During the latter half of the nineteenth century, various series of humorous drawings began to appear in the back pages of American magazines. But it was well toward the close of the century before the now popular comic strip was presented in the newspaper. On February 16, 1896, the readers of the New York *Sunday World* were presented with funny drawings in color by "Outcault," the first comic strip. Shortly thereafter, W. R. Hearst hired R. F. Outcault and the regular production of comic strips was established. Today, practically every one of the daily neswpapers of the United States carries comics except a few, notably the *New York Times.*[27]

Comics are a number or series of pictures which present an episode in the life of the characters and thus tell a story. There are usually some additional verbal captions, explanations or dialogue. The comics are published primarily by the newspapers and, since 1935, in tabloid-size comic magazines. Certain newspaper strips have such a universal appeal that they reach scores of millions of readers. George McManus's strip, "Bringing Up Father," has appeared in over 500 papers throughout the world and in 27 languages; has appeared in plays, been dramatized on radio and made into five movies. Americans are incorrigibly devoted to reading

---

[27] The development of the comics is interestingly portrayed in Coulton Waugh, *The Comics,* The Macmillan Company, New York, 1947.

comics. Many a managing editor must worry more about the selection of the paper's comic strips than about the contents of his front page, for he knows that he has from 50 to 80 per cent readership for his various comic strips. The comics are read by more than 80 million newspaper readers, by more than half of the adults and by 60 to 75 per cent of the children. Even an elite readership group, such as the subscribers to the *Saturday Review*, report 35.9 per cent regular reading of the comics, while 18 per cent more read them frequently.[28] The comic books have reached a monthly circulation of 90 to 100 million, something over a billion copies a year being sold. More money was spent on comic books in the period 1940 to 1955 than on all textbooks of all the primary and secondary schools in the United States.

The theme of the early strips, the "Yellow Kid," "The Katzenjammer Kids," "Buster Brown," and "Captain and the Kids," was mainly the playing of practical jokes of a crude slapstick variety. These picture comics were indigenous to America, bearing little resemblance to anything in the European tradition. The comics become a kind of everyman's art ("Orphan Annie"), a saga of family activities ("Blondie"), and of sex-appeal ("Glamor Girls"), of the common man's daydreams of supernatural power ("Popeye," "Superman") and of endless popular storytelling ("Prince Valiant"). But for thirty years the comic strips have been decreasingly funny. The influence of syndication seeking the commonly inoffensive and of increasing demands for conformity in American life have blanketed the fun. As Al Capp, that comic strip artist who is himself American folklore, has written: "The cartoonist who doesn't want to get into trouble, just shies off from poking fun at anything American for fear that he'll be damned by pressure groups. He abandons the real and wonderful and funny America and thereby abandons the true function of the cartoonist, which is to hold up to his fellow men a mirror of their own foolishness and join them in the laughter. And that is the last and saddest of the reasons the funny page ain't very funny any more." [29]

There have been many types of strips, offering slapstick comedy, satire on manners and customs, trenchant commentary on daily life, popular philosophy and dealing with local-color types, occupational groups, nationality and racial characteristics; lately we have had those strips which are simply little pictured continued stories. At what points have these comics been most influential in molding popular opinion? There is very little of direct political commentary. Also, there has been very little direct advocacy of economic doctrine or practice. The exception to this is the use of the comics for the advertising of economic goods since 1931.

[28] *Sat. Rev.*, Dec. 16, 1950, p. 33.
[29] A. Capp, St. Louis *Post Dispatch, Sunday Supplement*, Dec. 13, 1953.

However, indirectly, these popular pictures must have been enormously effective in modifying opinions and creating stereotypes. The diversified national backgrounds of Americans have led to a widespread interest in national characteristics. National types were presented in the comics in such strips as "The Katzenjammer Kids," "Bringing Up Father," "Abie the Agent," "Alphonse and Gaston," and many others. Economic standards were portrayed in the mishaps of the newly rich (Jiggs), in the economic objectives of the stenographer, in the tramplike ingenuity of roomers and adventurers (the Hall-room Boys), in the successful inventive genius of several characters, and the like. Standards as between parents and children, husband and wife, male and female, are constantly portrayed. Of F. Opper's drawings, it is said, "The husbands he pictures never have the strength, or even the willingness, to stand firm against the seductions of actresses and chorus ladies. He has never shown us a male eye that could remain undistracted by the ample beauties of the bathing girls he can draw so well." [30] There are ethical values portrayed in funny-paper philosophy, notably in R. L. Goldberg's "Boob McNutt," "Life's Little Jokes," "It's All Wrong, Alf," or in Briggs's "Ain't It a Grand and Glorious Feeling?" Since the comic strip has come to be devoted so largely to purveying pictured stories, often not humorous, the range of stereotypes acquired from them has widened. Children's ideas of life in the jungle, life on Mars, life in the twenty-fifth century, life as a gangster or a detective and so on, must have been influenced by these pictures. However, thus far, the influence of the comics has not been carefully studied.

These strips are a basic expression of American culture. In the comic strips we have the reflection of predominant values in the life of the United States. They are a popular art which reflects values and preoccupations even better than the movies and television. There is the popular conception of the dominant woman, whether it is Blondie managing a Dagwood or the dictatorial wife of "Bringing Up Father." There is the idealization, almost adoration, of wealth in the character of Daddy Warbucks. There is the middle-class home life and preoccupation with children. But the moment one makes such generalizations he realizes that simple cultural analysis of popular art forms can be a too simple interpretation. As one editor has said, "As to the comics reflecting American culture, that's like trying to read social significance into a two-bagger."

In addition to entertainment, the comics have been somewhat involved in matters of economic, political and general social significance. We are not concerned here with the endlessly discussed issue of their influence

[30] E. Brennecke, "The Real Mission of the Funny Paper," *Century,* 107: 5: 670.

on children in terms of learned violence or stimulated delinquency.[31] But the allegiance of the scores of millions of regular readers to the comic strip and book format has been exploited by many interest-groups since about 1940. "Comic characters have taken part in our politics. Little Orphan Annie and Daddy Warbucks were among the most vocal critics of the New Deal. The *Daily Worker's* ideological moppet, Little Lefty, fought it out with Orphan Annie over the rights of labor. The comic strip has gone to work for the Political Action Committee." [32] During World War II, comic strips and books were used to sell bonds, keep citizens alert for sabotage, promote salvage drives, solicit blood donors, for recruiting and numerous other campaigns. After the war, political campaigns used picture books as standard literature, and there were millions of such books distributed on the story of Harry S. Truman, on the Robert A. Taft story, on the life of Adlai Stevenson and on other political leaders. The picture books were widely used in the Free-enterprise Campaigns of 1950 and after, when General Electric, Procter & Gamble and others widely distributed picture stories on free enterprise. "The Sad Sack" was denounced by Senator Capehart as subversive, and Senator McCarthy's appearance in the "Pogo" strip agitated editors. The Russians declare that commercial comic strips fascistize United States children, but in the United States some 2,000 Sunday schools have their children use the medium to study picture stories of the Bible. Systematic content analysis to ascertain how extensively comics have been used by interest-groups to plead political and economic issues has not been made. Nor is the influence of this medium on opinion dependably described in social science literature.

CHARTS, GRAPHS AND STATISTICS

Opinions are extensively affected by the ways in which data are presented to large publics or to uncritical smaller groups. Opinions are influenced by biased samples. The newspapers do not put in proportion or on a comparable quantitative basis the amount of crime and violence in our society, the numbers of instances of juvenile delinquency or the frequency of drug addiction. Therefore, the reader is many times impressed by crime waves which do not exist, though dramatically presented instances of crime have occurred; of juvenile delinquency which is in but normal incidence; and of drug distribution which has not exceeded the usual, though reporters have been writing about it with

[31] As a sample of reading on this point, see P. Lazarsfeld (ed.), *Communications Research, 1948–1949,* Harper & Brothers, New York, 1949, pp. 3–50; and F. Wertham, *Seduction of the Innocent,* Rinehart & Co., Inc., New York, 1953.

[32] H. Zorbaugh, *Ency. Americana,* 1953 ed., vol. 7, p. 362. There is a thesis filed at the University of Chicago Library, Chicago, on "Political Analysis of Comic Strips, 1928–1947," written by Morris Helitzer.

unusual frequency. Therefore, from his newspaper sample the reader does not have the items in terms of frequencies or trends. Such distortions are often intended.

Samples reported to a public may not be representative, for they are sometimes incompetently selected or, again, through purposive chicanery the samples may have a built-in bias. Thus, special-interest groups, in bandying about their supposed facts and data, frequently use statistics and graphic representations to distort information and influence opinion. Averages may be used to give an erroneous impression, as an average may be a mean (that is, a figure arrived at by adding all the items and dividing by the number of items); a median (the figure above which there are as many items as there are below that figure); or a mode (the most frequently met-with figure in a series). Or a sample may be too small and not representative. It is often especially deceiving when a small number of cases are translated into percentages, thus giving the impression of a single conclusive generalization based on adequate sources and of an over-impressive exactness.[33]

When quantities are manipulated pictorially, as in charts and graphs, the opportunities for error and for purposive deceit multiply rapidly. People are misinformed on many subjects by such presentations. One way of showing the relationships of quantities to one another is to present them in charts and graphs. These are intended to make intelligible at a glance relationships that otherwise would have to be described at great length. Straight-line graphs, cumulative charts, bar charts, maps, circle charts, various designs of comparable size, and the like, are presented to newspaper and magazine readers with increasing frequency. Promoters in various fields use graphs to present information. Advertisers, government bureaus and special-interest groups display graphs and charts to the reader or to the audience. If the data are accurate and unbiased, these may be extremely useful tools for transmitting ideas. However, many publics have become far too credulous as to the accuracy of graphic displays. Graphs and charts may be manipulated so as to distort the truth, and interest-groups often do this.[34] In addition, it is evident that a fashion element pervades the means of popular pleading and that

[33] The principal types of errors cannot even be enumerated in our limited discussion. An introductory glance at the problems may be made by reading: Darrell Huff, *How to Lie with Statistics*, W. W. Norton & Company, Inc., New York, 1954; and R. Modley and D. Lowenstein, *Pictographs and Graphs*, Harper & Brothers, New York, 1952.

[34] I believe that the perusal of statistics and graphic materials in the mass media necessitates some critical skill on the part of the reader. As this is a problem for all who are to be intelligent citizens, I believe that elementary training in the problems of statistical and graphic presentation of materials should be provided in the course of public school education.

numerous agencies use graphic methods of presentation because these methods are popular with the expert. Graphs may be used when the data are of such simplicity that they could be adequately stated in a few figures or a few descriptive phrases.

PHOTOGRAPHS

Pictorial journalism is profoundly influential on opinions. The general public now has access to a considerable stream of photographs which pass before its eyes day by day. There are the pictures of the daily newspaper, of the picture magazines and the incidental pictures of other periodicals. "One typical copy of the Sunday *New York Times* contained 903 pictures and one of the daily, 168; of a New York evening paper, 90; of an issue of *Life*, 305." [35] Year by year, the *Continuing Study of Newspaper Reading* reports that pictures in the newspapers rank highest in news interest of all materials in the papers, and that advertisements with illustrations are more attended to than those consisting only of words. The major increase in the amount of pictorial journalism occurred in the two decades preceding 1940. By that time the amount of space devoted to pictures in the newspapers was fairly standardized. A content study of 30 metropolitan newspapers in 1938 revealed that the daily press had increased its use of pictures 40.8 per cent from 1931 to that time. Of the pictures in the daily newspapers, some 30 per cent were persons currently In the News; Personalities, 16.6 per cent; Sports, 15.4 per cent; and the other percentages were: Features, 10; Society, 9.7; Places and Objects, 5.2; Children, 3.6; Fashions, 2.9; Scientific, 2.7; Animals, 1.7; Leg, 1.1; Historical, 1.0; Scenery and Travel, 0.2. [36]

Historians of photographic journalism usually point to Mathew Brady's coverage of the Civil War as the first great extended photographic reporting. But the profuse use of picture material could not develop until a number of inventions made possible reproductions in great quantity which were reasonably clear and cheap. Newspictures were one of the innovations in the popularization of the newspaper in the 1890's, first notably in Pulitzer's New York *World* and Hearst's *Journal*. The tabloid newspaper began with the New York *Daily News* in 1919. The potentialities of magazine picture journalism were not grasped until the mid-1930's when *Life, Look, Parade* and other picture magazines appeared. In 1928 Dr. Erich Salomon introduced the candid camera. With sensitive film and photoflash bulb, this permitted an enormously ex-

[35] R. M. Pearson, *Experiencing American Pictures*, The Musson Book Company, Ltd., Toronto, 1943, p. 4.

[36] G. A. Brandenburg, "Huge Gain in Use of Pictures Shown in Survey of Dailies," *Ed. and Pub.*, 71: 8: 8.

panded range of picture taking and, of course, a greatly increased invasion of privacy.

"Photographs have the kind of authority over imagination today, which the printed word had yesterday, and the spoken word before that. They seem utterly real. They come, we imagine, directly to us without human meddling, and they are the most effortless food for the mind conceivable." [37] Photographs do seem real, often more so than the cartoon which is obviously the artist's product. But the photograph as purveyed by newspaper or periodical today does not come to us without human meddling. Pictures are published every day that tell untrue stories. A public convinced that the camera does not lie is in a credulous state. First, there is the process of selection. In taking numerous pictures of public men, especially with small cameras, it is possible to get a wide variety of expression. The publisher then selects that negative which most nearly fits the impression he desires to convey. This is done constantly, but one of the most notorious and most publicized instances was a photograph of President Roosevelt in 1936. On the President's fifty-fourth birthday the photographers were admitted and snapped many pictures. When the cameramen appeared to be finished, the President relaxed and rubbed his eyes, strained by the numerous flashes from magnesium bulbs. One cameraman took another photograph in which the President then appeared as a tired and discouraged man. The photograph was captioned "Pensive President Ponders Problems," and the accompanying account reported that this photograph was taken shortly after he had conferred with Secretary Wallace about the AAA. After that incident the photographers were requested to use cameras on tripods, so that photographs might be posed.

The critical viewer and reader can spot pictures of people in public life in almost every issue of a paper or magazine which were evidently selected by a picture editor who had in mind the editorial position of the paper and the impression that the paper wished to create. The same individual may appear on the same day in one journal as worried, harried, ill and apparently uncertain or despairing, while in another paper he is alert, bright, smiling and assured. To be sure, such extremes as this are not a daily occurrence, but the selected nuances of expression are with us always.

There is the selection of individuals as representatives of groups, so as to create popular impressions. In the newspaper photography dealing with political conventions, reform conventions, labor meetings, and the like, the leaders photographed are not necessarily typical of their groups but may have been selected because they have certain physical char-

[37] Lippmann, *op. cit.*, p. 92.

acteristics that identify them in the reader's mind with the "lunatic fringe."

The selection of parts from a larger picture, thus changing the context and implications of a picture, has been used too often in the United States during the past decades. In 1938 one anonymous picture was widely circulated in the South. It was an enlarged flashlight of J. L. Lewis and Associate Justice Black. The caption indicated that they were intimate friends. Actually the photograph was taken at a Senate hearing, and the others appearing in the picture had been blacked out. This was an early instance of distortion by selection, a practice which was to become not uncommon in political and ideological battles thereafter. A notable instance of trimming was the use in the 1952 campaign of a photograph of General Eisenhower talking intimately into the ear of the Russian General Zhukov. This was trimmed out of a photograph taken at the Allied Victory Celebration in Berlin, a picture which originally included a score of other people.

There is also the intentional distortion, the fabrication and retouching of negatives. Any competent news cameraman can caricature anyone by getting the right angles. But caricatures can also be made from an ordinary negative by tilting the enlarging easel. Negatives can be retouched in various ways. This became very common in the early 1920's in connection with the development of the tabloids' techniques. Official retouching of the photographs of Russian leaders is standard practice by the Soviet photographers. The aging Stalin's wrinkles and increasing grayness were retouched for years, while Malenkov, in his brief administration, lost two chins. From time to time United States journalism pointed to such instances but less frequently displayed instances of United States skills. In the 1950 political campaign in Maryland, the now infamous Tydings-Browder composite picture was widely circulated. As one typical instance in French journalism, one might note a picture taken at an Anglo-American Press Association luncheon. A picture appeared in various Paris papers of their Foreign Minister, Georges Bidault, alert, erect, smiling, at the luncheon with a glass of wine on the table before him. But the Communist *Humanité's* retouched photograph imaged the Foreign Minister with drooping eyes and sagging jaw with three glasses of wine on the table before him.

In the postwar United States, the publication of rather gruesome accident pictures has become common, thus cultivating a taste for the vicarious experience of horror and misery by the viewer. In contrast, the British press, except for occasional pictures in the *Daily Express,* dislikes and avoids gruesome accident pictures or photographs of people otherwise emotionally distraught. American journalism, in the quest for human-interest materials appealing to large numbers of readers, provides photographs which invade the privacy of the unknown victim of accidents, the frenzied grief-stricken parent, husband or wife of the victim, or the weeping spectator. I recall a picture of Justice Douglas of the Supreme Court which appeared in the October, 1949, papers the morning after his horse had rolled over the Justice who was on vacation in the Cascades. The picture shows a pain-racked, haggard man lying on the ground, as he was as yet untended for injuries which included thirteen broken ribs and a punctured lung. This picture of the Supreme Court Justice could hardly add to public understanding of law and justice, of appropriate judicial dignity, or of the keen mind of this eminent jurist. However, it reflects the photographer at his work of providing photographic gossip for the not always sympathetic but eternally personally invasive readers. However, this does not legally constitute an invasion of personal privacy. A series of court decisions on suits brought by accident victims have denied the right of privacy to individuals injured in public. To be sure, if such rights were sustained, it would be very difficult to fix the boundaries of press responsibility.

Certainly the methods of creating illusions by pictures exist. And certainly popular opinion has been extensively influenced by selected, distorted or fabricated pictures. Persons constantly in the public eye have some recourse. They can retaliate upon the offending cameraman in various ways, by refusing to pose, by discriminating against him, by personal violence. Or they may partially correct one bad impression by other pictures. This problem of the impressions created by photographs is becoming acute. Gilbert Seldes suggested a law containing the following regulations: (1) no pictures to be used without consent of the subject except photographs taken at public meetings or where the subject has voluntarily put himself in the public eye; (2) surreptitious candid-camera pictures not taken in public meetings to be actionable; (3) no picture to be changed or faked without the consent of the subject. However, though it might be possible to eliminate some of the gravest personal abuses by law, the public personage would remain at the mercy of the photographer under most situations. Legal restrictions would be difficult to formulate and to enforce. The intent of the photographer is crucial. Some self-regulation by cameramen is proposed from time to time and indeed the associations have adopted self-commandments, but without any adequate means of enforcement. Among their statements of principle are to: (1) Avoid gruesome pictures, except where, in its own interest, the public should be informed by them; (2) Regard the right of privacy as sacred, not to be infringed except where public interest demands it; (3) Avoid picture poses that will embarrass or ridicule anyone; (4) Identify our pictures adequately and explain them when they have been, of necessity, faked or distorted. Implementation of such principles in rules not to be violated is extremely difficult. The photographers' employers, the publishers, are not in general agreement as to regulation, find it difficult to achieve concerted action and have been indecisive in self-regulation.

Legal restrictions on the publication of photographs have developed in various areas of the law on privacy, on libel, and on obscenity regulations. Sections of the law have remained scattered in the statutes, and there is no substantial and clearly stated body of law on the publication of pictures.[38] In general, judges have held that pictures are so valuable as a means of information and are so frequently of legitimate public interest that the courts should infrequently restrain their use. Sometimes, however, judges have expressed opinions that the right of privacy should be extended.

The right of privacy is the right to be let alone and free from unwarranted publicity. As this emphasis on the individual developed in law late in the nineteenth century, I understand that there is no well-developed law on the subject and no unanimity on the part of the various courts as to the nature and extent of the right of privacy. The laws of the various states are much different. The right is not an absolute right. It is forfeited in connection with criminal acts, and a person seeking or in public office becomes a subject of public interest and forfeits some of his right of privacy, so that a photographer may freely photograph public officials in their public duties and activities. Those who are not public officials but who, because of social position or economic standing, are more or less public characters are also deprived of some privacy, but not so clearly as in the case of officials. And so, often it can be claimed that pictures are privileged in that for some reason of public policy the private interest of the individual is forfeited. The publication of pictures is currently subject to grave abuses of individual privacy and many types of pictures are not conducive to public welfare and psychological health. However, we have here a realm of communication in which either private or legal regulation is extraordinarily difficult.

[38] The best over-all statement of principles I have found is by Oliver W. Marvin in "Legal Aspects of Photography," *Am. Photog.*, vol. 39; Jan., pp. 22–25; Feb., pp. 18–21; March, pp. 12–15; April, pp. 20–23; and May, pp. 20–22.

CHAPTER 19

Motion Pictures

The greatest problem of the motion picture today, Box Office successes and how to get them.

J. L. LASKY

I look upon the cinema as a pulpit and use it as a propagandist.

J. GRIERSON

As agencies of mass impression the motion picture and television are now considered by many as of greater importance than printing. Such commentators refer to the superiority of pictorial forms over printed forms in conveying impressions to the common man. Although these comparisons as to relative importance of print and picture are futile, it is evident that pictures have enormously vivified communication. In America, the bulk of popular pictorial stereotypes and personal symbols are acquired in the motion-picture theater and from the television screen. The rise of the motion picture, radio and television has realigned the processes of communication, developed new publics and stimulated the dissemination of varied life ways, standards and values. It is indeed a rash commentator who becomes dogmatic as to their present or future effects and influence. The glib prophets of yesteryear appear today to have been somewhat bemused.

The motion picture came into being as a result of a series of inventions made public in rapid succession in the early nineties. For a time it was exploited as a kind of carnival novelty, a peepshow. When its commercial possibilities were realized, it was seized upon and developed into a tremendous business. American motion pictures can be understood only on the basis of their economic history which is a vivid record of commercial exploitation for dramatically large profits and losses.

The Kinetoscope, first patented by Edison in 1891, was publicly shown in New York on April 14, 1894. Only one person at a time could watch the picture. The projector and screen were developed by Thomas Armat, who exhibited motion pictures for the first time in 1895. The motion-picture cameras, film and projectors were rapidly improved by scores of inventions until, in 1928, the industry was equipped to produce and exhibit sound pictures.

At first the pictures were very short, the first public exhibition lasting four minutes. Subject matter of the films was of less importance than the novelty of the exhibition. The first real movie story was produced in 1905 in a one-reel, 1,000-foot film. One- or two-reel pictures were then distributed until 1912, when an eight-reel picture "Quo Vadis" was made in Italy. In the meantime, methods of distribution and exchange of films had been worked out, and the motion picture as a commercial enterprise was fairly launched. Techniques of production were likewise rapidly developed. In 1907 D. W. Griffith evolved a screen technique of close-up, cutback and fade-out. The star system was popularized by Adolph Zukor. Sarah Bernhardt appeared on the screen in 1912. The essential outlines of what the motion pictures were to be—until the introduction of sound —had appeared before World War I. During the war European production was stopped, while the industry in the United States developed rapidly. American producers emphasized the star system, thus diverting attention from the content of the motion picture to the personal characteristics of actors. Slapstick comedies, open-air Westerns, social comedies and historical romances were the mainstay of the producers of that time.[1] Later, more diversified types appeared.

The motion pictures produced in the United States have been produced for profit, not for propaganda or education, though as we shall discuss, they have had a considerable effect on the mind-life of America. However, since World War I, the authoritarian states of Europe and elsewhere have controlled and directed motion-picture content in the interests of political and economic propaganda. Dictators would inculcate the significant pictorial symbols. Some propaganda techniques have been subtle, as Eisenstein's famed dramatizations of mass rather than the individual. Politicians, businessmen, educators, artists and literary commentators have divergent definitions of the most significant role of the motion picture in contemporary life. This cleavage widened as new uses were undertaken. The authoritarian rulers would utilize the motion picture and all the arts as agencies of mass impression. Businessmen would exploit this means of popular entertainment. Educators and scientists found it an invaluable aid for recording and portraying physical and life processes. Some groups of artists would plead for the development of a creative art that might do more than mirror life or engage in special pleading, maintaining that "the motion picture has not yet

[1] The history of the motion picture is sketched in the *Ency. Soc. Sci.;* the *Ency. Brit.;* H. T. Lewis, *The Motion Picture Industry,* D. Van Nostrand Company, Inc., New York, 1933, and many other sources.

understood, with rare exceptions, that its future does not lie in a faithful and automatic reproduction of a purely material reality, but rather in the creative search for authentic truth." [2] The cinema is many things to many men, but its nature, its content and its effects on various groups have not been thoroughly and experimentally explored. There are many kinds of motion pictures for entertainment, for instruction and for propaganda. Paul Rotha, eminent English director of documentary films, suggested the following classification: [3]

I. Films of Fiction
  1. Adventure and Melodrama
     Early Films and Serials
     Westerns
     Crime and Gangster
     Adventure in Distant Lands
  2. Comedy
     Slapstick
     Comedy of Manners
     Satire
  3. Romance
     Modern
     Historical
     Musical
  4. Historical and Chronicle

  5. Fantasy
     Folk Tales and Sagas
     Prophecy
     Macabre
  6. Drama
     Personal Stories
     Sociological
  7. Epic
II. Films of Fact
  1. Newsreel, Record and Magazine
  2. Travel Films
  3. Instructional Films
III. Avant-Garde and Trick Films
  1. Avant-garde
  2. Trick Films

Increasingly, the motion pictures serve a world audience, especially the motion pictures produced in the United States. The cinema is the most effective of the modern communication agencies that are making the world psychologically smaller. But that world is, as yet, by no means small, since there remains great diversity of access to these means of communication; diversity resulting from unequal distribution of mechanical facilities, from unequal understanding of what is communicated, and from unequal popular access to communications due to the divergent censorship practices of the various governments of the world. The first is an economic and technological problem, the second a question of educational levels of masses of people, and the third is a political question in the ongoing struggle between authoritarianism and democracy.

The commercial, privately controlled production of motion pictures achieved its greatest development in the United States where the Aladdin-like qualities of its expansion amazed participants and observers alike. Then the Russian production of motion pictures became the out-

[2] E. Daniel-Rops, "Cinema, Reality and Life," *Intercine*, 7: 5.
[3] P. Rotha, *Movie Parade*, 1936; quoted by F. M. Thrasher, *Jour. Ed. Soc.*, 10: 133. Permission to quote granted.

standing example of a government-controlled production which has grown to large proportions. Great Britain's private commercial industry has not made the profits of Hollywood nor had the cultural impact of the Russians. Nazi Germany, Fascist Italy and Japan, during the 1930's, traveled the road of government-controlled and -inspired propaganda. The small and poorer nations of the world cannot afford large motion-picture industries, although some of them have made contributions to the art of motion-picture production. How the smaller and diverse cultures may be more adequately represented in the motion-picture production of the world provides an economic and cultural dilemma.

In the magnitude of businesses, the motion pictures are not nearly so large as most people probably imagine, but the industry is not small. Placing the motion pictures in relation to the total economy of the United States, I should say that in terms of income and capital the motion-picture industry is roughly one three-hundredths of the income and capital of this country.[4] As a business, the industry has fluctuated enormously. In general, the peak years of the industry have been the decades from 1920 through 1929 and 1940 through 1949, with the 1930's and the period after 1949 relatively much lower.

The capital investments in motion pictures in the United States were roughly $3 billion in 1953. In 1950, the capital investment was about $2,525 million in theaters, $135 million in studios and $25 million in distribution facilities.[5] This large American industry grossed $1,278 million in the United States in 1953 and $905 million abroad, according to the industry's claims, but had only a small net income of $46 million that year. The net income of the industry, according to Commerce Department reports, fluctuates from such figures as $52 million in 1929 to a loss of $85 million in 1932 to a net profit of $187 million in 1946 to a net profit of $36 million in 1952. Since 1920 the industry has received from 25 to over 40 per cent of its gross income from abroad; which has obvious implications for the content of the pictures that must satisfy large foreign, as well as domestic, audiences. The United States film industry, including all aspects of exhibition, employed about 210,000 persons in 1953. There are many motion-picture companies, but the

[4] A billion and a quarter gross income for the industry, as compared to about 350 billion national income yearly, and about 3 billion capital, as compared to a national capital of possibly a trillion.

[5] The facts and statistics included in these paragraphs are taken from R. E. Chapin, "An Evaluation and an Interpretation of the Statistics Relating to the Mass Communications Industries," Ph.D. thesis, University of Illinois, Urbana, Ill., 1954; the *Film Daily Year Books;* Sindlinger & Co., *Analysis of the Motion Picture Industry;* and that useful summary of studies of Hollywood by Leo A. Handel, entitled *Hollywood Looks at Its Audience,* University of Illinois Press, Urbana, Ill., 1950. I have not stated a specific reference for the facts included in each sentence.

so-called "Big Five" have been dominant. These are RKO, Paramount, MGM, Warner Bros. and 20th Century-Fox. These companies have not always been the most profitable, nor indeed has each of them always produced a larger number of pictures than other companies, but in general they have been most powerful and esteemed. This was in part true because of their control of over 85 per cent of the exhibition facilities until court decisions somewhat severed the production and distribution facilities.

The average weekly attendance at motion pictures in the United States has been larger in proportion to the total population than that of any other nation in the world. In round numbers, the estimated attendance was 40 million a week in 1922; 90 million in 1930, when the population was about 124 million; 80 million in 1940; 90 million in 1948; but, in 1953, when the population was over 160 million, the average weekly attendance was about 46 million. After 1953, somewhat adjusted to television and lured by technical innovations, the audiences began to straggle back to the pictures. But by that time there were some 4,000 fewer theaters to return to, since this number had ceased exhibiting. There had been over 19,000 theaters in 1945. However, while the number of regular theaters was sharply reduced, over 4,000 drive-ins had begun exhibiting pictures. The number of commercial feature pictures produced each year by the motion-picture industry averaged from 500 to 700 feature pictures a year from 1920 to 1940. This was considered the number which would provide shows for the then existing theaters here and abroad. From 200 to 400 copies of each film would be distributed. During this period, the foreign distribution of Hollywood's product was about 200 copies of each of 600 features at any one time, or about 120,000 shows being exhibited or in transit. During the 1940's the number of pictures produced was considerably reduced, and it is estimated that about 400 pictures a year are needed to satisfy the market, though only 354 were produced in 1953 and not more than 300 in 1954. However, many of these were larger and more costly pictures intended to reinterest audiences and provide entertainment beyond the scope of the competing television screens.

In 1955 the motion pictures were making a considerable comeback to profits and influence. The motion pictures had been very profitable during World War II, when the attendance increased from 60 to over 80 million a week, with profits proportionately even greater. By 1947 the distribution of television facilities was accelerating and, moreover, consumers had more products on which to expend their money. The audiences reduced rapidly from then until 1953 when attendance stood at 46 million a week, after which a slow increase in attendance began. An overriding fact about these audiences is their youth. "The movies live on children from the ages of ten to nineteen, who go steadily and frequently and almost automatically to the pictures; from the ages of twenty to twenty-five people still go but less often; after thirty, the audience begins to vanish from the movie houses." [6] About 10 per cent of the audience is between 5 and 11 years of age; 20 per cent from 12 through 17; 35 per cent from 18 through 30; 20 per cent from 31 through 45; and 15 per cent over 45 years of age.

The purpose of this brief, factual discussion has been to emphasize the commercial character of the motion pictures produced in the United States. The motion pictures are primarily a business, providing such entertainment as the managers believe will return the largest possible number of dollars to the box offices. This must be borne in mind in all subsequent discussion of the content of feature pictures and their influence on opinion. The old-line producers do not view the motion pictures as education or as a propaganda medium, though indirectly the pictures do extensively influence cultural values, ideas of conduct, and behavior. Usually, the commercial orientation of the motion-picture industry cannot be overstated.

THE CONTENT OF MOTION PICTURES

The content of feature motion pictures is significant to public opinion in so far as they provide many significant symbols; diffuse conceptions of the good and the bad life; influence fashions and behavior; simplify and personify history; fix attitudes toward races, nations and classes. And, in general, the motion pictures have been the most vivid source of impression on many opinions of the mass audiences. Hollywood has or can acquire the production facilities for any types of pictures, and film content is not determined by existing personnel nor by the desires of producers and directors. The market for films at home and abroad determines the content of almost all motion pictures.

The production and distribution of the commercial motion pictures is an industrial process. The industry, with its chains of theaters, its production companies, its large capital investment and clamorous stockholders, must produce some hundreds of feature pictures every year to provide continuous entertainment for millions of people. The subject matter of the films is determined by what the producing companies believe their audiences want. There is no conscious long-range plan. The producers adapt themselves to changes in the social scene, the productions of their competitors and the tried and true formulas. Economic motivation is conspicuous in the growth of this business and in the selection of themes. Although the producer occasionally makes a film with

[6] G. Seldes, *The Great Audience*, The Viking Press, Inc., New York, 1950, p. 12.

a selective appeal, he must aim more often at the widest mass patronage. As a result, only a few of the several hundred feature pictures produced yearly in the United States are commended by the selective critic, the intellectual or the pictorial artist. But the producer knows that during the past years the largest total rentals have been paid for the following: "Gone With the Wind," 1939, $26,000,000; "Greatest Show on Earth," 1952, $12,800,000; "Quo Vadis," 1951, $10,500,000; "Best Years of Our Lives," 1946, $10,400,000; "Duel in the Sun," 1946, $10,000,000; "Samson and Delilah," 1949, $9,000,000; "This Is the Army," 1943, $8,500,000; "Bells of St. Mary's," 1945, $8,000,000; "Jolson Story," 1946, $8,000,000; "Snow White," 1937, $7,150,000.[7] The motion-picture producers are responsible businessmen committed to the welfare of their stockholders' investment. Critics may highly commend an "Ox-Bow Incident" or "The Informer," but the producers, bewailing the low box-office returns of such excellent films, turn back to their successful formulas and large grosses. In any case, this was the pattern between 1920 and 1950. Now, as television provides more and more of the daily mass entertainment, the motion-picture content is changing. In addition to making pictures for television exhibition, Hollywood is turning to the production of great spectacles, of fewer, and perhaps better, large feature films in which lavishness and cost, running time and complex theme, spectacle and size of screen are beyond the scope of television. The technical innovations of wide- and deep-screen have aided this trend. And it is possible that another division of motion-picture production may be devoted to making many inexpensive, dramatic, psychologically and thematically complicated and more mature films for small audiences who are not adequately entertained by commercial television or by motion-picture spectacles produced for masses. These more selective audiences would attend motion pictures made for more mature, more knowledgeable middle- and high-brows. Largely ignored thus far by the commercial motion-picture producers, such small theater audiences may become a significant source of revenue as dollars become more elusive in the industry. It may be possible to make money from pictures which do not require an audience of 10 million to pay for the cost of production. In the decades before 1950 the competition for the grand prizes led producers to ignore special types of audiences, the elders and the minorities with some critical standards.

The critics were alienated by the lack of art, of complexity of theme and of reality. But the commercial motion-picture did not aim toward these values, but, rather, toward the providing of a mythology of mod-

---

[7] These are the largest grosses from among the 23,745 titles released from 1915 through 1952. This information is taken from *The Film Daily Year Book*, 1952.

ern life and of a record of the past which often deviated very far from reality but did include the wishes, hopes, aspirations, simplifications and daydreams of its audiences, and, in turn, guided them perhaps a little further along the same paths. But if Hollywood incorporates and spawns myths, at least it has not shackled a people's mind with the political propaganda of the Russian-produced motion pictures. The American industry never ceased to proclaim that the function of their motion pictures was to entertain.

It is not possible to provide a classification of the general types of content of feature films produced each year after 1915 because the data have not been collected and systematically classified using the same categories of content. The purpose of such an over-all table would be to note any trends in the changing content of the films. But we may note some samples of classification. Edgar Dale classified the types of pictures produced in 1920, 1925 and 1930, with results which are reproduced in Table 14. Evidently there was already a rather high degree

Table 14. Comparison of the Types of Motion Pictures Produced in 1920, 1925 and 1930

(Number and per cent of pictures of each type as shown by a 500 sample each year)

	Release date					
Type of picture	1920		1925		1930	
	Number	Per cent	Number	Per cent	Number	Per cent
Crime.............	120	24.0	148	29.6	137	27.4
Sex...............	65	13.0	84	16.8	75	15.0
Love..............	223	44.6	164	32.8	148	29.6
Mystery...........	16	3.2	11	2.2	24	4.8
War...............	10	2.0	11	2.2	19	3.8
Children...........	2	.4	4	.8	1	.2
History...........	0	0.0	6	1.2	7	1.4
Travel.............	1	.2	7	1.4	9	1.8
Comedy...........	59	11.8	63	12.6	80	16.0
Social propaganda....	4	.8	2	.4	0	0.0
Total.............	500	100	500	100	500	100

SOURCE: Dale, *The Content of Motion Pictures*, The Macmillan Company, New York, 1935, p. 17. By permission.

of uniformity in the percentages of films of each type produced each year.

Using the much more extensive categories of film types that had become standard in the reports of the Motion Picture Association by 1940, I have compiled in Table 15 the record of film production during the profitable decade of the 40's. The topics appearing in the content of the newsreels during the same period are classified in Table 16.

SOME INFLUENCES OF THE MOTION PICTURE

What did the peoples of the world, as well as our own people, see in these films produced by Hollywood? American films have a largely national conception, but an international life. Even the bits of hack-work among them reflect something of the national life and outlook. A number of them taken together give that picture of American life which is most vivid to scores of millions of people. It is a distorted, sometimes silly, sometimes worse than silly, record, but it is also a powerfully dramatic record, a most amazing display of technical ingenuity, a Mohammedan's delight of feminine pulchritude, an entertaining diversion. Those living in the United States and more or less knowledgeable as to the facts of American life can partially correct Hollywood's exaggerations. The foreigner, unless highly cultivated in the study of comparative cultures, can less readily do so.

At home and abroad the largest proportion of the audiences go to the motion pictures because they are tired and wish to be relaxed, amused and entertained; because their experience, work and environment are inadequate and they desire and receive from many pictures the facets of a dream world; because many are lonely and like to be part of large audience groups experiencing similar psychological states; and because they wish to escape from the disagreeable features or monotony of everyday life. Many are far more interested in responding to the personalities of "stars" than in rating the quality of their dramatic art. Such audiences provide markets for portrayals of their own changing wishes and desires, not for films that are a cross section of life, in the United States or anywhere else. The documentaries have but an auxiliary role, and the realist stream has widened very slowly. The audiences expect and respond to exaggerations which they intermittently realize are atypical. In a speech to the National Board of Review, Bosley Crowther, motion-picture critic of the *New York Times,* said:

I do not believe that the motion pictures of today, or of any time for that matter, have in the majority of cases reflected life as it is actually lived. I doubt if you believe they have either. Last night I made a very careful check on the

Table 15. Feature Pictures Analyzed According to Type

Type	1940	1941	1942	1943	1944	1948
Melodrama						
Action...............	39	65	75	18	26	
Adventure.............	12	9	12	2	3	
Comedy...............	43	59	56	9	21	
Juvenile..............	13	16	14	8	6	
Detective-mystery.......	10	6	7	7	7	
Murder-mystery.........	40	45	41	22	33	
Musical...............	0	1	0	0	1	
Social problem..........	48	16	6	18	7	
Romantic.............	7	6	2	1	0	
Football..............	..	..	2	0		
Fantasy..............	..	..	0	1	0	
Spy-mystery...........	..	..	0	1	0	
War..................	..	..	..	0	4	
Psychological mystery....	..	..	..	0	1	
Total...............	212	223	215	87	109	169
Percentage of total.....	40.0	38.9	39.3	20.8	24.6	38.8
Westerns						
Action...............	99	110	108	78	71	
Mystery..............	1	4	2	1	10	
Musical..............	5	5	2	4	4	
Total...............	105	119	112	83	85	94
Percentage of total.....	19.8	20.8	20.5	19.9	19.2	21.6
Drama						
Action...............	4	8	11	12	5	
Adventure.............	0	1				
Biographical-historical....	14	6	10	8	5	
Musical..............	5	6	4	4	8	
Romantic.............	3	9	6	2	6	
Social problem..........	25	32	48	63	39	
Comedy...............	..	..	1	1	9	
Religious..............	..	..	0	1	3	
Psychological...........	..	..	..	..	4	
War..................	..	..	..	0	4	~
Total...............	51	62	80	91	83	81
Percentage of total.....	9.6	10.8	14.6	21.8	18.7	18.6

Table 15. Feature Pictures Analyzed According to Type (Continued)

Type	1940	1941	1942	1943	1944	1948
Crime						
Action.................	20	24	14	2	5	
Social problem..........	7	1	1	5	0	
Prison.................	4	0	2	0	0	
Total................	31	25	17	7	5	12
Percentage of total.....	5.8	4.3	3.1	1.6	1.1	2.6
Comedy						
Romantic..............	36	42	29	29	42	
Musical...............	39	35	30	67	56	
Juvenile..............	8	6	6	13	6	
Human interest.........	10	0				
Farces................	21	44				
Total................	114	127	65	109	104	48
Percentage of total.....	21.0	22.2	11.9	26.0	23.5	11.0
Miscellaneous						
Farce-comedy...........	..	..	27	9	20	
Cartoon feature.........	..	..	2	1	1	
Fantasy...............	..	..	6	2	1	
Documentary...........	..	..	4	5	4	
Horror................	..	..	14	16	13	
Religious..............	..	..	0			
Allegorical.............	..	..	0			
Travelogue.............	..	..	3	0	1	
Historical.............	..	..	1	1	1	
Sport.................	..	..	0	1	0	
Farce–murder-mystery....	..	..	0	2	11	
Romantic musical........	..	..	0	2	0	
Musical...............	..	..	0	1	0	
Farce-horror...........	..	..	..	..	1	
Horror psychological......	..	..	..	..	2	
Comedy-fantasy.........	..	..	..	..	1	
Total................	17	16	57	40	56	31
Percentage of total.....	3.2	2.8	10.4	9.6	12.6	7.1
Total number of features....	530	572	546	417	442	435

GENERAL SOURCE: President's Annual Reports to the Motion Picture Producers and Distributors of America, Inc., 1948 figure: *What's Happening in Hollywood?* June, 1949, issue.

pictures which I have been seeing this year. There were close to 200 of them. I could not find more than four or five which I felt gave a true and accurate approximation of the segments of life which they pretended to represent. Literally speaking, therefore, I am convinced that Hollywood does not express America.[8]

Table 16. Ten Years of Newsreel Analysis, 1939–48

	1939	1940	1941	1942	1943	1944	1945	1946	1947	1948
National news:										
Aviation.............	3.1%	.8%	.9%	.1%	.2%	.4%	1.4%	3.2%	1.8%	1.7%
Disaster, fires, etc.....	3.4	3.1	2.6	2.3	1.4	1.7	1.9	3.0	4.0	2.1
Farm...............	.2	.4	.2	.6	.7	.2	.2	.5	.4	.4
Fashions, styles......	1.8	1.6	1.5	.9	.5	1.0	.9	1.5	1.2	2.3
Governmental news..	5.1	4.5	5.8	8.6	7.8	2.7	11.7	8.4	8.2	6.2
Health..............	.4	.4	.2	.1	.6	.9	.1	.6	.4	....[3]
Industrial progress...	.7	.9	.6	.1	1.0	.3	.3	.5	.1	.3
Labor news..........	.8	.1	1.5	.3	.7	.3	.8	2.4	1.3	1.0
National defense.....	4.1	13.7	24.7 [1]	23.3 [1]	22.2 [1]	13.3 [1]	3.4 [1]	7.1	4.3	4.5
Political news........	.8	7.3	.1	.1	.3	5.0	.1	.6	.3	6.1
Religious news.......	1.0	.6	.7	.4	1.0	1.5	.8	2.3	.8	1.0
Science.............	1.1	.2	.3	.1	.2	.2	.2	.7	.5	.7
Sports..............	26.1	25.0	26.2	15.3	8.6	9.1	9.4	18.3	26.2	23.1
Weather............	.8	1.1	.4	.4	.2	.6	.3	.5	.9	.5
Miscellaneous.......	21.8	15.9	12.9	15.1	8.9	9.2	20.3	17.2	18.1	18.2
Foreign news.........	18.3 [2]	5.8 [2]	4.2 [2]	2.9 [2]	2.1 [2]	1.4 [2]	23.7 [2]	29.7	29.3	30.3
War in Europe........	10.5	18.6	15.8	15.0	28.9	37.7	9.7			
War in Pacific........	....	....	1.4	14.4	14.7	14.5	14.1			
United Nations.......	....	....	....	....	....	....	....	3.5	2.2	1.6
	100.0%	100.0%	100.0%	100.0%	100.0%	100.0%	100.0%	100.0%	100.0%	100.0%
Total "clips"..........	4,940	4,947	4,948	4,454	3,810	3,491	3,133	3,559	3,484	3,541

[1] Including domestic war activities after United States' entry into World War II.
[2] Excluding World War II coverage.
[3] Less than .1%.

SOURCE: Leo A. Handel, *Hollywood Looks at Its Audience*, University of Illinois Press, Urbana, Ill., 1950, p. 170. Compiled by Handel from Movietone News, News of the Day, Paramount News, Pathé News (Warner Pathé News, after August 15, 1947) and Universal Newsreel.

It is belaboring the obvious to reiterate that the American motion pictures do not in any complete fashion reflect the American scene.

The content of the American motion pictures, whether realistic or not, is vastly influential on attitudes and opinions and behavior. Let us consider some areas of such influence. The motion pictures are obviously a powerful agent for fixing or modifying individual attitudes as well as those attitudes which are widely diffused among masses of people. To be sure, the importance of the pictures in affecting attitudes varies greatly as between age groups, classes of intelligence and personality types. But

[8] *Nat. Board of Rev. Mag.*, 16: 9: 5.

pictorial stimuli are amazingly vital for most persons. One may appreciate the infinite variation in individual effects and the bewildering complexity of individual responses, and at the same time note certain uniformities in social attitudes and behavior resulting from attendance at the motion pictures. To enumerate these results in any formal way would imply a completeness of analysis that no one has the right to assume in the present state of knowledge about motion-picture effects.

A. It is frequently stated that the motion pictures tend to discourage logical thinking and reflective thought. Indeed, this charge is made with regard to all the modern means of communication for the masses: the popular newspaper, most plays, the bulk of periodical literature and radio and television programs. It is claimed that the very mass of communicated material in contemporary pictures, print and sound occupies and diverts the mind, rather than instigating reflective thought. There is some truth in this assertion. The average mind is incapable of selection and rejection of the stimuli to which it is subjected, and indeed the well-organized, critical mind also is overwhelmed by the mass of claims for attention. Moreover, the content of motion pictures is usually not such as to give rise to reflective thought. It is for the most part noncontroversial. Much of the content deals with life situations, values, standards and mores with which the majority of popular audiences are in complete accord. And then, much of the content of the motion pictures in the United States has been sheer spectacle: throngs, crowds, wide spaces, masses of objects, troupes of dancers, the routine of modern musical shows, and the like. This may entertain; it does not provoke reflective thought. The degeneration of the Roman theater as it proceeded from thoughtful tragedy and comedy to spectacles for the masses has often been traced. The motion picture has provided such entertainment almost from its beginning.

B. One of the fundamental characteristics of modern thought is a time sense. There are not only a heightened awareness of the passage of time, but also widely diffused attitudes toward culture forms of the past, and, to a lesser extent, toward the future. The motion picture accentuates this process by preserving a record of passing events in the news pictures, by creating and modifying attitudes toward the past in historical films and by providing an occasional prophetic film of the future. Films of the past and the future have been used for propaganda purposes in Russia, Germany and Italy. Popular attitudes toward culture elements of the past have so far been exploited only incidentally in the American pictures, as in the newsreel portrayal of past clothing styles, cars and other objects for humorous purposes. Historical films dealing with legendary personages have not strayed far from the prevalent stereotypes. As the pictures become more vivid and convincing, there are obvious possibilities for modifying attitudes toward the past and thereby affecting opinion and action in the present. Utopian presentations may also be influential in motivating present behavior. The influence of present press campaigns may be relatively unimportant in comparison with a future motion-picture and television campaign. Although there is relatively little of conscious intent in these fields of contemporary commercial pictures in America, they have already affected popular attitudes about historic events. The extension of the time sense is inevitable, and the attitudes resulting therefrom will be woven into the fabric of popular opinion.

C. Historical inaccuracy in American films permeates the themes and stories, but not the material settings. The backgrounds and the skillful presentation of minutiae of a period are often marvellous reproductions. But the central themes are invariably oversimplified and overpersonalized. This is, no doubt, inevitable in a popular art form, because masses of people so persistently think in simple, personal and provincial values. Indeed, it may be argued that it is possible to portray only a distorted version of history in the popular pictorial art form. The screen cannot be expected to become a professor of history and expound the nuances and complexities of the historical scene. But there are degrees of inaccuracy, and Hollywood, widely esteemed for the verisimilitude of its material reproductions in historical films, is widely condemned for the simplifications and inaccuracies of its historical themes.

The American motion pictures are also acclaimed and condemned for their selection of historical themes for portrayal. The friends of the British Empire were pleased and their enemies outraged when—

. . . in the late 1930's the American motion-picture industry made a large group of films glorifying every aspect of British virtue from Dr. Barnardo's Homes to the patrolling of the Khyber Pass. "Cavalcade," "Lives of a Bengal Lancer," "Lord Jeff," "Wee Willie Winkie," "Susannah of the Mounties," "Gunga Din," "The Sun Never Sets"; the roll goes on and on. That these films correctly sound the empire note was proved beyond question when King George conferred the Order of the British Empire on C. Aubrey Smith, the English actor to whom Hollywood gave practically permanent employment as a British colonel.[9]

However, I believe that the industry was primarily concerned with increasing box-office returns in an active market, and not engaging in a pro-British propaganda drive.

The selection of historical periods for motion-picture portrayal is based on the melodramatic opportunities of the particular periods selected. Thus the Hollywood pictures since 1920 have dealt with ancient Babylon

[9] M. F. Thorp, *America at the Movies*, Yale University Press, New Haven, Conn., 1939, p. 294.

(DeMille spectacle type); with Egypt, B.C.; with the time of Christ (large religious audiences); with Rome (saturnalias, Christian-baiting and martyrdom and war); with the Crusades; with the periods of King Arthur, Robin Hood and the Middle Ages; with the splendors and conflicts of the Renaissance; the revolutions of the late eighteenth century (how many times have I seen the tumbrils roll down the streets of Paris); and the past century and a half. But how many pictures have you seen dealing with, say, the fifth or sixth or eleventh centuries, or, indeed, of any periods in the valleys between the peaks of high drama in Western cultures? The motion pictures do not plod through history.

D. Vicarious experience has been enormously increased by the motion pictures. Print made possible a great extension of such experience for masses of mankind, but the pictures provided a vivid and personal imagery. As such experience increased, aspects of life previously not discussible were portrayed, new controversies and heightened tensions thus were created. Values in transition were highlighted. The picture audience lives in hundreds of roles during the course of a year. To be sure, these roles are largely standardized, but new elements do appear. The veteran producer Adolph Zukor notes, "As for audiences themselves, their essential desires and tastes, there is little change from twenty-five years ago. Audiences like to project themselves on the screen and live there in one role or another for the time they are in the theatre." [10] The extent to which vicarious experience at the motion pictures serves to widen the individual's understanding and sympathy for the behavior and emotional experience of others will depend upon his choice of pictures. He may see more and more of the same thing; but for most persons the pictures widen the horizons of life.

E. Of late years the term "compensation" has come into semitechnical use referring to action or thinking which "shall make amends for some lack or loss in personal characteristic or status." Especially for the adult audiences, the motion pictures perform an important function in providing the materials for compensation. The pictures have developed during several decades in which masses of mankind in the Western world have been in especial need of fantasy, idealizations and delightful dream material to take them away from the successive crises of reality in economics, politics and religion. There are many maladjustments, and, as Lewis Mumford notes, "vital organs of life which have been amputated through historic accident, must be restored at least in fantasy." So, "the motion picture has found a distinct function in creating for us a fantasy world which is extremely popular and satisfying . . . the gorgeous settings . . . luxurious homes, servants, limousines, beautiful women and

[10] A. Zukor in *New York Times Mag.*, Feb. 28, 1937.

strong men . . . it is a conventional outlet for our unfulfilled desires and our unrequited heartaches." [11] The lavish settings of the long-popular DeMille pictures or the settings of modern musical romances illustrate fantasy in dealing with objects and the economic world. A thousand vagaries of the amorous quest as portrayed in the movies illustrate the popular demand for variety of titillation and for compensatory ideal adjustments in the relations between the sexes. In part, the pictures have been able to satisfy this demand because of the technical flexibility of camera portrayals. The camera moves about at all angles, as well as close up or far away. Nuances of emotional portrayal may certainly be registered on a face that is perhaps a dozen feet in width when thrown on the screen. However, the compensatory function of the motion pictures is a variable according to class and age groups. Small children are bored by the pictures conveying vicarious compensation to middle-aged housewives.

F. As the attention areas of modern man have widened, he has had need for more and more stereotypes. The motion pictures, as the most vivid pictorial record to which millions have access, have provided many of the new personal stereotypes and profoundly influenced the earlier national and large-group stereotypes. Relations between nationalities, class groups, occupational groups, character groups, and the like, are modified by the opinions of one another prevalent in these groups. To a considerable extent the motion pictures have determined how people visualize these types and the opinions they express about them. Motion-picture characters provide the symbolic models. Thus, film stars have become an important part of modern legendry and mythology. Not only is there an interest in them as persons, but also they serve as symbols of groups, classes and various types. Because of the number of such groups that the broadened attention areas have revealed to the general public, there is an increased need for personal symbolism. The actual persons of the individual's environment are increasingly inadequate to fill these roles. Motion-picture characters often do so.

The decision as to what constitutes a pretty girl, a beautiful woman, a handsome young man or the man of distinction is largely determined by the motion-picture portrayals. Along with feminine pulchritude as used by advertising and with the numerous still pictures used in the "pin-up" complex in American culture, the motion pictures type the esteemed face, figure, make-up and adornment of the standardized girl and woman in the United States. Such "pin-up" eroticism, provided by and mingled with commercial appeals, as well as commercially provided

[11] L. Mumford, *Technics and Civilization*, Harcourt, Brace and Company, Inc., New York, 1934, p. 286.

in popular literature and motion picture, is a standard lure of the market place. Vicarious experience of enticement is the regular fare of the American male, and professionally sets the standards for emulation by the female. The resultant standardization may alienate the aesthete at times, but is found palatable by a less critical general population.

Consider the women of the movies. There have been cycles of feminine types in the pictures of the past decades. There was the adventurous girl of the serials and the Westerns; the incredible, voluptuous woman of the Theda Bara "vamp" type; the "It" girl of the late 20's; the numerous actresses of more frankly physical appeal of the 1930's; the good-bad girl of the 1940's; and the succession of "sweet, simple and girlish" actresses from Mary Pickford to the present.[12] The styles in stars change, and, to some extent, the stars determine the physical styles. And these stars predominantly appear in American films, regardless of the nationality of their origins. Therefore, they frequently come to be thought of as American types.

Today, if a star can act—or create a living character on the screen—it is only an incidental embellishment of his stature as a member of our contemporary mythology. More often, men and women who came to the screen as actors have had to suspend or freeze their gifts in order to fit into the fixed roles they are playing in the minds, hearts, or emotionally immature libidos of the movie fans. . . . Jimmy Cagney, for instance, was an actor before he became the God of Hard-boiled Goodness, Soft-boiled Badness, and Small-Fry Sex Appeal. Long before Spencer Tracy was deified, he went to the chair in *The Last Mile*, and went effectively. But he is a grown-up Eagle Scout now, the Bumbling, Practical, Hard-headed but Soft-hearted AMERICAN. Why let him play any other part, the producer argues with terrifying logic, when we already have box-office proof that this is the part the public wants him to play?[13]

Are the racial and nationality stereotypes of the American motion pictures considered as typical of the opinions and prejudices of the people of the United States?

Hollywood's racial typologies are forever dismaying. To the movie addict, Negroes are lazy, lighthearted mortals who tap dance on the slightest provocation and are prone to burst into spirituals during a thunderstorm. Italians seem to be a singularly specialized species, either childishly happy or dreadfully brutal; their talents, by some anthropological curse, are limited to restauranting or crime. Swedes, of course, are slow-witted behemoths dedicated to either the sea or the basement.[14]

[12] About the good-bad girls, see M. Wolfenstein and N. Leites, *Movies: A Psychological Study*, Free Press, Glencoe, Ill., 1950, pp. 25 ff.
[13] B. Schulberg, "Movies in America: After Fifty Years," *Atlantic*, November, 1947, p. 116.
[14] L. C. Rosten, *Hollywood*, Harcourt, Brace and Company, Inc., New York, 1941, p. 359.

If our customers abroad consider the motion-picture versions of race and nationality a cross section of opinion in the United States, and to a considerable extent they must do so, it is a matter of public interest.

In addition, these stereotypes influence opinions about real persons as they are encountered in face-to-face contact, in still pictures of the newspaper and elsewhere, and in the motion-picture record of real persons. Thus the adolescent girl forms opinions about the possible charm and amorous capabilities of the youth she has just met as compared with those of the reigning screen heroes, and the adult audience adversely judges the statesman, economic advisor, scientist and businessman of the newsreel on a scale of personality symbols developed in part from the feature pictures. The individual may be imbued with a firm conviction of the truth and reality of his stereotypes because they are vivid, personal and reiterated. Such personal stereotypes are convincing to the common man. Printed descriptions are rarely so vivid. And it is just this sense of reality that may be dangerous to logical analysis and the reexamination of one's own opinions. Thus, distortions may become even more permanent than heretofore.

Superficiality may be disarmingly convincing when provided in pictorial forms. There is a sense of completeness and profundity that is not actually justified. A contemporary historical analysis of the great events of history must consider scores of important factors. The usual motion-picture interpretation is almost entirely in personal terms. Yet this personal motivation so definitely fits into the preconceptions of the common man that he finds no incongruity and complacently augments his preferences for personal interpretations. In a sense, the speed of motion-picture action makes for another type of superficiality. A situation is pictorially presented; a few seconds later it is whisked away, and attention is directed toward something else. In reading, even at the lowest levels, one may stop to think, or just stop, at any point. In the pictures, the tempo of portrayal is mechanically controlled outside the individual. Analysis is thereby discouraged and, indeed, often frustrated. The individual is more a passive recipient than is the case in some other means of communication.

G. Although attendance at the motion pictures may be a quest for "entertainment," it is evident that the results of attendance transcend ephemeral entertainment. From the content of this leisure-time pursuit many of the most significant values, as well as legends and historical impressions, are learned by the young. Some of these ideas and behavior ways are actively sought by the young, others are simply transmitted through the extensive movie experience. In the early 1930's, the *Payne Fund Studies* provided considerable evidence that young people observed and copied the dress and decoration, the etiquette, the appearance and the techniques in love-making of the favorite stars.[15] Standards of appearance, of behavior and etiquette are today still copied from the movies, but, in addition, it has been suggested that youth seeks enlightenment on many aspects of social situations and of interpersonal behavior. These kinds of influence are difficult to detect and report in contrast to the counting of copied hair styles, imitated dress, or fumbling osculation based on the techniques of the stars. As David Riesman notes:

> Though the evidence is tantalizingly little, we have the impression that young people of, let us say, sixth grade level and up resort to the movies today, not so much to have a look at the exotic and make-believe world, but increasingly in order to understand complex networks of interpersonal relations. Children who meet each other in the shifting peer-groups of city high schools are driven, somewhat more even than children of an earlier time, to depend on a precarious popularity as their main security.[16]

It may well be true that the patterns of interpersonal behavior observed in the motion pictures and emulated or discussed in the peer-groups of today's adolescent youth are a more vital source of instruction than were those of the 1930's. As the pressures on youth by adults lighten, the peer-groups increasingly set the standards. And the sources of adolescent peer-group standards, values and behavior-ways are increasingly learned in leisure-time motion-picture experience, TV viewing and pocket-book reading, rather than from the institutional models enunciated by family, church and school. No doubt the motion pictures are more influential than they were in the 1930's as a source of general attitudes and opinions and of the values and symbols of interpersonal relations between the sexes and between social groups as portrayed on the screen. But they are less important as a source of specific behavior-ways on dress, etiquette, and the like, as there are now various other sources of expression, especially television.

H. Audiences have not wanted to see a valid cross section of social life. Therefore, the motion pictures have selected the dramatic, appealing and entertaining themes. The values, standards, the wishes, hopes, aspirations and longings of modern publics have primarily determined the content of modern motion pictures.

The audiences get pretty much what they want and have been taught to want. An analysis of wants exhibited by the principal characters in 100 Hollywood feature films of 1942 showed that of the total of 188 major characters, 68.1 per cent wanted love; 26.1 per cent wanted fame, repu-

---

[15] H. Blumer, *Movies and Conduct*, The Macmillan Company, New York, 1933; C. C. Peters, *Motion Pictures and Standards of Morality*, The Macmillan Company, New York, 1933.

[16] D. Riesman, *Individualism Reconsidered*, Free Press, Glencoe, Ill., 1954, p. 195.

tation or prestige; 15.9 per cent wanted safety (either health, bodily integrity or safety of life); 13.8 per cent wanted a way of life; 9.6 per cent wanted money or material goods; 9.0 per cent wanted "rightness" and to do their duty. These wants were fulfilled in the pictures, as 61.2 per cent of all major characters were indulged with respect to all their wants at the end of the picture; 10.1 per cent were deprived as to all their wants at the close of the picture; and 14.4 per cent were indulged as to some wants and deprived as to others.[17]

Of course, these are not the exact proportions of life objectives of the total population of the United States. But these are important and emphasized values in our culture. Hollywood selects and distorts. It emphasizes such values as that one should get material possessions in the maximum quantities and live a full, rich, sensuous life in enjoyment of these. Most of the world understands a sensate culture, and but few reject it when its achievement is possible. The American motion pictures preach that one should get his woman or women, preferably the most attractive females (according to quite conventionalized standards) in sight, and the movies are reasonably generous in the sample views presented. As the values involved in this pursuit are generally recognized internationally, as well as in the United States, the motion pictures have a market for their wares. Again, conflict may loom larger than life in the motion pictures and the movies' theme that one must win his battles and that the world rewards a winner may find wider international audiences than the missionaries' text.[18] Therefore, in part, the motion pictures have been successful because of their distortions. These satisfy widespread desires for vicarious experience.

1. The "happy ending" predominates in the American films. The critics bewail the distortion of reality in the "happy ending" so characteristic of the American motion pictures. But to the common man in the United States, such endings do not appear so unreal as they do to the intellectual. Fantastically good things in the realm of economic achievement and of personal adventure happened in American experience during the nineteenth century. If dramatic changes of fortune have happened less frequently than is commonly supposed, statistical analysis of life and mathematical portrayal of reality have not yet reached the common man. There is still a large residue of optimism and of hopefulness. Hopefulness and belief in the happy outcome are deep-rooted in the American tradition. The material success of the nineteenth century accentuated hopefulness. The individual could improve his material, physical and moral status. He

[17] This material is summarized from Dorothy B. Jones, "Quantitative Analysis of Motion Picture Content," *Pub. Opin. Quar.*, 6: 3: 411–428.

[18] In general, the characters in the movies who do not hold these values as preeminent are presented as the deviants, the inevitable fall guys of fate.

could progress. "The man who has cured himself of B.O. and halitosis, has learned French to surprise the waiter and the saxophone to amuse the company, may, as Heywood Broun said, find that people still avoid him because they do not like him. But is this a heresy entertained by a few cranks only, or in part half-believed in by a great part of the population?" [19] People in the United States are still hopeful to an amazing degree. In spite of the economic vicissitudes of the 1930's, in spite of war, in spite of a competitive economic system and gruelling personal competition with one's fellows, wide areas of hope remain. If one just gets the lucky break, or if the right man or woman appears, things can be glowingly happy and successful, as they are portrayed in the vast majority of the motion pictures. Therefore, these happy endings are not at all alien to the wishes of American audiences. This theme is especially well received if the change of fortune has been shockingly sudden, such as a dramatically successful performance by an entertainer or athlete, a spectacular achievement in business, a dramatic professional success, a sudden inheritance, marriage to the boss's daughter or any other exemplification of the American value of quick attainment of the riches of "the big rock candy mountain." The common man projects his wishes in demanding the happy ending. But the intellectual who criticizes the happy ending is also frequently motivated by attitudes that are not entirely based on objective descriptions of reality. "The intellectuals have been remarkably hospitable to all the great European systems of damnation—damnation by sex by Freud, by economics by Marx, by history by Spengler." [20] Do foreign audiences believe that personal life situations turn out so well in the United States? Are the resultant attitudes those of disdain for these naïve Americans, of renewed personal hope or of envy? Such psychological questions should be studied in detail, as they are not now studied by any competent groups.

J. The question of the amount of violence in the motion pictures is another problem in typicality. There is an enormous market in the United States and abroad for the vicarious experience of violence, but foreign audiences for Hollywood films also develop exaggerated opinions of the amount of violence in life in the United States. Critics have deplored an overemphasis on displays of violence and action in the motion pictures. Moralists have indignantly denounced certain idealizations of the desperado, the criminal and the gangster. But the technique of the motion picture, especially in its development before the sound pictures, was better adapted to show action and movement than to portray psychological nuances. In addition, action had a more universal appeal. Hence

---

[19] D. W. Brogan, *The American Character*, Alfred A. Knopf, Inc., New York, 1945, p. 69.

[20] G. V. Seldes, *Mainland*, Charles Scribner's Sons, New York, 1936, p. 111.

the Westerns, the adventure pictures and the melodrama, the war pictures, the crime, gangster, detective and action pictures in general. And action leaps beyond the humanly possible in the animated cartoons. Much action has taken the form of violence. Indeed, there is much more violence in the pictures than in the ordinary life of the picture-goers. This is likewise true of the bulk of periodical literature. In the traditions of American culture, successful violence has been esteemed. If there is much less violence in everyday life today than there was on the roistering frontier, the tradition of violence is maintained, and the movies perform a compensatory function. Even the extremes of violence appear with surprising frequency in the pictures. There is a great and persistent demand for pictures containing violence. The motion pictures meet the demand. American culture values, not the pictures, are to be indicted.

There is preoccupation with violence in American culture as evidenced by the popularity of the many "tough" films containing various kinds of violence. This value is largely a product of the prevalence of personal violence in American history and its contemporary vicarious experience. Other Western cultures have latterly experienced intensive political violence by parties and the state, but the people of the United States have engaged in considerable personal and interest-group violence. Moreover, "aggression, hostility, and conflict are prime characteristics of the contemporary scene. It may be that the motion picture audiences are seeking interpretive frames of reference within which such phenomena become intelligible." [21] This vicarious experience of violence of the past and of the present may give to the movie patron some sense of participation, some additional understanding of the types and motives of physical violence, some glimpse of the face of terror in a world in which he may believe that his own personal experience of terror amidst contemporary political upheavals is just around the corner. The common man does not consider personal violence improbable or ultimately unlikely. In contrast, the majority of the intellectuals of the nineteenth century preferred types of conflict other than physical coercion. As Wyndham Lewis has noted:

The philosopher at all times is opposed to violence; at least it is very seldom that he is not, Sorel and Nietzsche being exceptions. The philosophic man inveighs against violence ostensibly on other peoples' behalf. Really he is speaking for himself; not only has he no mandate, but he would be found on careful investigation not to have the sanction of life for his humane intentions. . . . The philosopher is apt to regard life as precious and full of mysterious power and sanctity, because his own is full of interest and vitality. That is probably

[21] F. Fearing, "Influence of the Movies on Attitudes and Behavior," *Ann. Am. Acad. Pol. Soc. Sci.*, 254: 70–79, November, 1947.

not the general view; most people cannot develop any such flattering conception of their personal existence.[22]

All this exists at deeper psychological levels beneath the obvious simple response to the dramatic action of the story in a Western, a murder-mystery, a historical battle, or a barroom melee as portrayed in motion pictures. To be sure, the obvious appeals and motivations must not be ignored in the quest for more complex interpretations.

K. From time to time the moralist is outraged by the motion-picture treatment of the relationships between the sexes. Certainly it is a central theme of American films, as it is of popular literature, periodicals, advertising and other means of communication. This is inevitable. It is a mass preoccupation. But that the motion pictures emphasize sex less, and present it in a more conventional way than do either legitimate plays or novels, was the conclusion of a committee of the American Association of University Professors.[23] To this the censor replies that the movies reach a larger and more unselected audience. But the audiences express by their attendance a persistent interest in this theme. "It was calculated that one out of every seven pictures shown was built around sex as its dominant feature, as compared with one out of every ten round war, horror, and mystery, and one out of every four round crime."[24] Romance, in the cheapest sense of the word, is pervasive. Paul Rotha notes that "Everything they have to say about love has to be expressed in such terms that people of all levels and almost all ages can understand them, and, moreover, these terms have to be such as can be used in large public gatherings." Of necessity, there results a naïve oversimplification of personal-character types and of simplified moral categories.

The popular values of the motion-picture audiences are expressed in the successive enthronement of some motion-picture stars as goddesses of love, of which the most popular are the most blatant. These girls achieve rapid success as the premier exemplars of the currently stressed exaggerations of sexual attributes and romantic qualities. They provide a very considerable provocation, but in definitely standardized patterns which are alluring to the audiences while remaining within the censor's literal code.

Indeed, the fashions in esteemed female types of sex and love symbols in the motion pictures reflect changing popular values. The personification of the "good girl" in Mary Pickford and the "bad woman" in Theda Bara in the early 1920's reflected a dichotomy of the times. In the early

---

[22] W. Lewis, *The Art of Being Ruled,* Harper & Brothers, New York, 1926, p. 65. Reprinted by permission.
[23] Bulletin of that association, 16: 148.
[24] *For Filmgoers Only,* British Institute of Adult Education, 1935, p. 66.

1950's, a popular motion-picture type was the "good-bad" girl, a combination of good motives and the promise of sexual excitement combined in the one individual. She is a "good" girl who appears to be "bad" and though good in motive she is frankly sexually exciting. "There is on the one hand the impact of what we call goodness morality, which leads to high estimation of the charms of wickedness as well as to guilt about pursuing them. The good-bad girl represents a solution to the problem which goodness morality poses to the man." [25] The good-bad girl epitomizes infinite sexual promise within the bounds of the existing morality, while not exploiting the responsive males of her environment.

In general, these clever women use their power benevolently in the American films. They aid their lovers' and husbands' careers and activities, but along lines which the woman approves. Thus, masculine successes are frequently arranged by the woman. The woman should not be of superior achievement and thus belittle and paralyze the male. Such disparagement creates dramatic tragedy in our movies, especially in the case of the high-brow career woman who somehow has deviated from the man-oriented pattern.[26]

The various complex nuances of the relations between the sexes and of their psychological interaction are too varied and subtle for portrayal to audiences numbering scores of millions. However, as a medium, the motion pictures can readily encompass complexity, as has been evidenced by many foreign and a few American films since 1920. The commercial motion pictures for mass audiences must provide for the romantic simplicities and myths of the young. Hence the Hollywood formulas are produced, rather than the portrayal of the complexities and realities of life between the sexes.

L. The family relationships exhibited in Hollywood's product reflect the values of life in the United States. In foreign-made films the older generations, the father, mother and grandparents tend to be interesting and serious figures still dominant in the life of the younger members of the family. In American films, the children escape from protracted involvement with parents, and the parents are usually rather negligible, pale, background figures. Where the father judges the son in foreign movies, the son more often judges the father in the Hollywood product. Dominant heroes are provided with rather ineffectual fathers, but the heroines are more often protected by indulgent fathers. Mothers fare

---

[25] M. Wolfenstein and N. Leites, *Movies: A Psychological Study*, Free Press, Glencoe, Ill., 1950, p. 21. This is the most incisive analysis ever made of American films through qualitative content study. A similar type of cultural analysis of film content in the German films is the classic *From Caligari to Hitler*, by S. Kracauer, Princeton University Press, Princeton, N.J., 1947.

[26] The ideas of the past two paragraphs are extensively elaborated and illustrated in Wolfenstein and Leites, *op. cit.*, pp. 19–47.

less well. "Where the mother of the hero appears, she is apt to be a colorless, background figure. Insofar as she shows any distinguishable characteristics, she is a person you would rather not have around. . . . Heroines have mothers less frequently than they have fathers, and their relations with their mothers tend to be less important and less agreeable." [27] Such portrayals are to be expected in a culture oriented toward idealization of youth, vigor and achievement; separate living quarters for the adult generations; a dislike of matriarchal dominance (except for commercial ceremonial obeisances such as Mother's Day) and with a pervasive lack of respect for the normal values of the elders.

M. Except for its contributions to the national effort in World War II, Hollywood has generally avoided the lure of propaganda in the feature films. Hence the potency of the motion picture in influencing the thought and opinions of large publics in the fields of politics and economics has not yet been thoroughly tested. Interest-groups of various kinds have been ineffectual in influencing motion-picture content in America. This is because producers view their product as entertainment and eschew provocative and controversial themes. To be sure, there are exceptions to this in the case of a few pictures.

Until the early 1930's the motion pictures produced in the United States were almost entirely concerned with entertainment and amusement, and success was measured at the box office. This remains true of almost all pictures today and the older producers vociferously declare that the industry must not vary from the formula. But in the depression years a few pictures dealt somewhat with the economic issues. There was a market for them. King Vidor made the only film ever to glorify a collective community in the United States. "Our Daily Bread" was a box-office success in the early 1930's. Then, in 1935, Warner Brothers went to war against political authoritarianism, Nazism and Fascism. This company produced "Black Legion," 1936 (Ku Klux Klan); "Emile Zola," 1937 (Dreyfus case and army); "Juarez," 1938 (glorifying barefooted democracy); and "Confessions of a Nazi Spy," 1939. These were notable box-office successes. In 1943 over sixty pictures in part or entirely devoted to antiauthoritarianism appeared. In 1940 a Senatorial investigation of political significance in the motion pictures was started, but was shortly abandoned. I do not believe that Hollywood went to war so early because of the racial composition of the producers' boards of directors, or completely on the basis of political conviction. They went to war because it was good box office.

After the war a battle developed between producers who wanted a stream of formula pictures for entertainment and a section of the Holly-

[27] Wolfenstein and Leites, *op. cit.*, p. 119.

wood community which wanted to produce more pictures of "social significance." Some such pictures were made. But "social significance" was abruptly terminated when the Congressional inquiry of 1948 indicated some of the Hollywood community holding political views at the left end of the political scale. A chastened and frightened industry resumed entertainment and eschewed political and economic themes. Some pictures directed toward racial tolerance were made from 1950 through 1952, but these were in line with an audience market demand and should not be construed as propaganda in race relations. The industry now wends a cautious trail around controversial economic and political issues in its feature films.

N. An average of 200 copies of each of from 400 to 600 feature pictures are circulating outside the United States at any time. These are the nation's cultural ambassadors. In 1951 about 63 per cent of all films exhibited in Europe were from the United States; and so was 64 per cent of the distribution in South America; 76 per cent in Mexico and Central America; 48 per cent in the Far East and 57 per cent in the Middle East; 63 per cent for the continent of Africa; and 75 per cent for Canada.[28] These films are not all ambassadors of good will. Cultural leaders abroad have attacked the influence of the American films since 1920. But the Hollywood product is popular with the mass audiences. The responses of these foreign audiences differ from those of the audiences in the United States, inasmuch as foreign audiences cannot realistically interpret and correct the exaggerations of Hollywood. Postwar European audiences, many of whose own films depict the everyday real life of their people, cannot accurately correct the exaggerations of standards of living, violence, and personality types in the films from the United States.

The motion pictures are unquestionably influential on the opinions of a world-wide audience. But we do not know just what details in the content of pictures influence whom, and how much. Hollywood's influence on the material aspects of culture is most evident. Less evident is the influence of American films on other values and most especially on the opinions of foreigners concerning American culture. Hollywood has learned a great deal about foreign sensibilities and is achieving increasing skill in finding the international common denominators of the inoffensive. There are now fewer incidents in which we outrage foreign customers. But what about damage to the American reputation?

Various items of material culture, clothing, household equipment and the thousand gewgaws of Western civilization are being disseminated and copied elsewhere, in part because of the models presented in motion pictures. Subjective elements, the folkways, attitudes, standards and

[28] *Annual Report*, Motion Picture Producers and Distributors of America, Inc., p. 30.

values, are also being modified by this agency. The motion-picture version of American culture is more widely diffused than that of any other group. It is true that effusive overstatements of these effects have frequently been made and also that there is no detailed knowledge of the influence of the pictures.

The various aspects of culture determine in part the individual's perceptions, interpretations and memories of any pictorial stimulus. For example, a political, economic or general ideology provides one frame of reference from which a film is viewed. Not only will an avowed Communist or a State Socialist, in contrast to an American Republican, differently interpret a film of the romantic quest in the upper economic strata, but he will also perceive certain elements, such as physical types, clothing, setting and speech, in a quite different fashion. The pacifist will miss the beauty of a bomber formation in flight in his revulsion at its purpose. Also, general values in a culture are constantly involved in responses to films. Representations in the films of mechanical routines of the modern factory, which often prove so repulsive to the French intellectual, arouse admiration in the Russian Communist. Detailed knowledge does not exist concerning the effects of the content of American films on popular opinion abroad.

We cannot safely, for much longer, do business as usual with this important cultural product. There must be more information about the influence of American films on the people of other nations and there should be integrated plans by the motion-picture industry and by the Federal government for the deletion of the most inaccurate, the most misrepresentative and the most nationally injurious aspects of the content of American films distributed abroad. Such plans should be made, and responsible agencies should be created by both the industry and the government to administer them. The collection of information about the influence of American films and the deletion of some of the more objectionable features of the content of those films before export require neither organized propaganda nor the creation of formal legal censorship of films. Indeed, one should be unalterably opposed to the development of either of these trends. But it should be possible by consultative and advisory agencies between government and the motion-picture industry to conduct research on the content and cultural effects of the films. And perhaps some voluntary regulation of the most deleterious items could be achieved.

CHAPTER 20

Radio and Television

The Athenians gathering en masse at the Acropolis had an ideal agency of communication. They could all listen at once to their peerless leader, Pericles. Until radio was invented America lacked her Acropolis. . . . With radio an American Pericles can have his Acropolis and speak to all America at once.

Glenn Frank

The prophets of the early 1920's quite generally overestimated the immediate influence of the radio on political and ideational life and underestimated its development as a purveyor of advertising and a new medium of mass entertainment. They exhibited a distorted vision of the daily preoccupations and interests of the common man and of the business interests. But even though, in America, the radio's potentialities for the dissemination of political and educational information have not been exploited so extensively as was anticipated, it is nonetheless true that the radio and television are the most important instruments for mass communication since the invention and development of printing. The diffusion of ideas, facts and personality elements has been greatly stimulated. But that which is diffused is, for the most part, the same content as is already provided in newspapers, periodical literature and the motion pictures.

Although the content of radio and television programs is quite similar to that of newspapers, popular literature and motion pictures, the nature of the instrument of communication has affected the presentation in many ways. For example, perception is modified in that there is a separation of ideation from visual perception. Hence, simplicity in the formulation of and statement of ideas is at a premium. Further, in talking into the microphone one is not addressing a public meeting but talking to individuals. Broadcasting techniques must be adapted to that fact. At the listening end, the home has been reinforced as a public opinion forum, and discussion within families is stimulated.

This new means of communication is potentially capable of diffusing anything that the human voice or other sound may express. This may be accomplished almost instantaneously and diffused to scores of millions of people. Therefore, new and unsolved problems of control are presented. If information, opinions and entertainment may be diffused more widely than was previously possible, the questions of what information and whose opinions become ever more significant. Authoritarian states quickly settle that question; but the democracies debate. In America, although revolutionary changes in opinions about education and politics have not emerged thus far, popular opinion has been influenced on hundreds of topics. Opinions are developed, buttressed or changed in many fields. Advertising proclaims its wares. In entertainment, the supremacy of the romantic quest is declared in song and story. Opinions on the humorous are colored by the product of the professional comedians. Musical tastes are slightly improved. In general, however, broadcasting by radio and television thus far is but an extension of the content of other means of communication. Attention areas have widened, but that which is attended to has not changed greatly.

Radio telegraphy has existed since 1896, when radio signals were first used in marine communications. Marconi transmitted signals across the Atlantic in 1901. As early as 1915 David Sarnoff proposed that radio broadcasting of news, information and entertainment to home "radio music boxes" could be made a successful commercial venture. Actually, radio telephony as a commercial activity has been in operation since 1920.

Marconi's Wireless Telegraph Company was formed in Great Britain in 1897 and incorporated in America in 1899. From the time when Marconi startled the world by broadcasting intelligible coded messages by wireless, many inventors devoted themselves to the problems of radiobroadcasting the human voice and other sounds. As early as 1904 a Danish engineer, Poulsen, had developed the first wireless telephone, and many other systems simultaneously created by other inventors soon appeared. However, all this apparatus was crude, uncertain and inefficient, so that popular programs were impossible. It was thought that the wireless telephone would be usable in war and in emergency situations. Apparently the inventors had no inkling of the contemporary radio industry with its commercial and entertainment interests. The vacuum tube, first used to increase the range of telephone conversations, provided the necessary basis for reliable broadcasting. On November 2, 1920, KDKA of Westinghouse Electric Company of East Pittsburgh opened as a broadcasting station. The first program presented the returns of the Harding election. After this, KDKA broadcast for an hour every evening. Their objective was to interest the public so that the company might sell parts for the amateur construction of receiving sets. At first the radio was a novelty, and program content was not so important, since the listeners were primarily concerned with achieving clarity of reception, eliminating static and keeping the receiving set in working order for a few minutes at a time. Music, notable singers and speakers were the principal features. By 1922 occasional afternoon programs were being offered, and general news, weather forecasts, children's hours and time signals had been added. Interest in the radio programs developed rapidly, and hundreds of stations were established during each of the early years. In 1921 the Department of Commerce licensed 32 radio broadcasting stations. By the end of 1922 there were 286, and by the end of 1924 the total had become 583. By 1924 hookups of stations became general, the largest number combining to broadcast the presidential nominating convention of 1924. By 1927 there were 694 stations, which number decreased each year until 1933, when there were 598. Newspapers, churches, equipment companies, schools and private broadcasters established stations. The United States Department of Commerce allotted wave lengths. Relative chaos reigned for a time with wave jumpers broadcasting on the time of other stations. This was ended on February 28, 1927, when the Radio Control Bill was passed by Congress and the Federal Radio Commission was formed. The Commission introduced, for the first time, an effective federal control of broadcast facilities. It also concerned itself with the content of radio programs and soon stated its definition of a well-balanced radio program service. On this basis it appraised the performances of the licensed stations. In those days the radio industry admitted that it was the duty of the licensing authority to determine whether or not a station was rendering an adequate public service by providing extensive educational and informational services. The Commission also acted to limit the amount and character of advertising. Nevertheless, the actions of the Commission were not drastic enough to suit many critics of radio.

In 1934 the Communications Act was passed. A Federal Communications Commission (of seven Commissioners appointed by the President) was established to regulate radio broadcasting, telegraphy, telephones, wire telegraphy and television. The purpose of the act was "to maintain control by the United States over all chanels of interstate and foreign radio transmission, and to provide for the use of such channels, but not the ownership thereof, by persons for limited periods of time, under licenses granted by federal authority."

As to the regulation of the content of radio programs, it is evident that the Congress envisaged a generally hands-off policy by the commission. Obscene language and profanity were to be excluded from radio programs, but the Commission is specifically debarred from the power of censorship. Section 326 states, "Nothing in this Act shall be understood or construed to give the Commission the power of censorship over radio communications, and no regulation or condition shall be promulgated or fixed by the Commission which shall interfere with the right of free speech by means of radio communication." From time to time a dispute has arisen between the industry and the Commission as to whether the Commission is authorized to concern itself with the over-all character and program balance of any particular station.

In 1925 radio was commercially insignificant, and the potentialities of radio advertising were not imagined. By 1950 the radio industry had a revenue of approximately $500 million a year. A somewhat different climate of opinion has been engendered by these profits. The earlier thinking about radio was dominated by a preoccupation with its social significance. It would be an understatement to say that of late years a prudent caution concerning the safeguarding of this sizable business has been the dominant mood. The nature of radio's responsibilities to the listening public was greatly stressed in the 1920's. Commissioner Caldwell, of the Federal Radio Commission, declared before a House committee in 1928 that "each station occupying a desirable channel should be kept on its toes to produce and present the best possible programs and, if any station slips from that high standard, another station which is putting on programs of a better standard should have the right to contest the first station's position and, after hearing the full testimony, to replace it." [1] Two decades later the FCC attempted to recall the broadcasters to a sense of responsibility for public service by placing a number of stations requesting renewal of their licenses on a "temporary status" and then the Commission published a volume on *Public Service Responsibility of Broadcast Licensees*, the popularly designated *Blue Book*. In this volume there was published the monitored record of a number of examples of stations notably failing to provide adequate public-service programs and for practices which, in the Commission's view, were contrary to "public interest, convenience and necessity." This modest reprimand of the industry called forth a most perfervid wail of protest from broadcasters, stating that the Commission was exceeding its powers even in calling attention to the imbalance of radio's programs. Power was indeed balanced differently in 1946 than in 1926. In 1953 Chairman Paul Walker of the FCC, in defending the *Blue Book* report, declared, somewhat plaintively, "I believe that such an impartial survey by the Commission every few years can be of inestimable value in focusing the attention of the public on the manner in which the broadcast licensees are living up to their obligation." [2] Though an essentially

---

[1] *Hearings by the House Committee on Merchant Marine* on *Jurisdiction of the Radio Commission*, 1928, p. 188. Quoted by C. Siepmann, *Radio, Television and Society*, Oxford University Press, New York, 1950, p. 11.

[2] *Education on the Air*, Ohio State University Press, Columbus, Ohio, 1953, p. 12.

sound and defensible system of commercial broadcasting can be strengthened rather than weakened by supervisory insistence on standards which at least partially support the "public interest, convenience, and necessity," the insistence on such standards may be bitterly resented amidst the vigorous competition for short-run commercial advantages.

RADIO BROADCASTING STATIONS AND RECEIVING SETS IN THE UNITED STATES

In America the early development of the radio was for the most part unorganized and unplanned. Inasmuch as receiving sets were not licensed, as they have been abroad, accurate statistics on their number and distribution do not exist. In the census of 1930 householders were asked about the ownership of sets. Census enumerators reported that 12,078,345 families owned radio sets. But some of these families had more than one set. The estimates of the number of radio sets in use, the homes with radios and the auto radios may be examined in Table 17.

Programs were provided for this large number of receivers by the 286 AM broadcasting stations existing in 1922, the 618 in 1930, 813 in 1940, 1,004 in 1946, and the 2,636 stations in 1954. Of these, about half were involved in the major radio networks. By 1954 there were also 560 FM stations on the air. The investment in these broadcasting stations and networks was about $300 million in 1954. In that same year national sponsors expended about 380 millions of dollars, and local sponsors some 330 millions in advertising expenditures on the programs provided by these stations. This amounted to about 10 per cent of the total advertising expenditures in the United States in 1954; the remainder going to newspapers, television, periodicals and all other advertising media. In 1952 the advertisers of drugs, toiletries, foods, soft drinks and confections were responsible for more than half of the advertising on radio. The percentages of advertising expenditures in each of the major classifications of radio advertising are shown in Table 18. The relative position of each category for 1952 was the same as for 1947, with only one minor exception. The big four have always been drugs, foods, soaps and tobacco.

Permanent chains of stations providing programs which could not be locally produced inevitably developed after 1926. These could make entertainment talent available nationally. In 1926, the National Broadcasting Company began with 24 stations. By 1927 NBC was providing some coast-to-coast broadcasts. In 1927 the Columbia Broadcasting System began with a basic network of 16 stations; the Mutual Broadcasting System began in 1934; the American Broadcasting Company in 1943;

Table 17. U.S. Radio Homes and Sets in Use
(In millions)

Date at end of year	Homes with radio	Auto radios in use	Total sets in use
1955 *	. . . .	. . . .	over 123.0
1953	48.0	29.0	120.5
1952	46.0	25.0	114.0
1951	45.8	20.0	107.3
1950	45.0	17.0	90.0
1949	42.0	14.0	81.0
1948	40.0	11.0	74.0
1947	37.0	9.0	66.0
1946	35.0	7.0	60.0
1945	34.0	6.0	56.0
1944	33.0	7.0	57.0
1943	32.0	8.0	58.0
1942	30.8	9.0	59.3
1941	29.7	8.8	56.0
1940	29.2	7.5	51.0
1939	28.7	6.5	45.3
1938	28.0	6.0	40.8
1937	26.7	5.0	37.6
1936	24.6	3.5	33.0
1935	22.9	2.0	30.5
1934	21.5	1.3	26.0
1933	20.4	0.5	22.0
1932	16.8	0.3	18.0
1931	14.0	0.1	15.0
1930	12.0		13.0
1929	9.0		10.5
1928	7.5		8.5
1927	6.5		7.0
1926	5.0		5.7
1925	3.5		4.0
1924	2.5		3.0
1923	1.0		1.1
1922	0.3		0.4

* Estimate.
SOURCE: *Broadcasting Yearbook–Marketbook, 1954.*

Table 18. Radio Advertising

Products	Per cent of total		
	1940	1947	1952
Automotive......	3.1	3.8	2.6
Drugs..........	27.3	29.1	27.1
Electrical........	1.1	2.0	2.5
Financial........	1.1	2.8	2.5
Foods..........	29.8	27.5	25.8
Gasoline.........	5.1	3.0	3.2
Soaps..........	11.6	10.2	11.2
Smoking.........	15.1	9.6	9.8
Others..........	5.8	12.0	15.3
Total.......	100.0	100.0	100.0

SOURCE: This table was compiled by Richard Earl Chapin.

and, in addition, various regional networks have been developed. The numbers of affiliates of the major networks are listed in Table 19.[3]

The United States has developed the only radio broadcasting system in the world that is supported and operated entirely by private industry, for there is no tax on receiving sets nor is there a government subsidy. There are a few scores of stations supported by educational institutions, municipalities and other institutions. Several hundred stations are owned by newspapers. Not all the time on the commercial stations is sold to and sponsored by commercial organizations. A substantial portion is retained for the "sustaining" programs supported by the station operator or the network. For example, the programs of NBC are about 50 per cent sponsored and 50 per cent sustaining.

The numerous radio sets in the United States have been used during an astonishing amount of time each day since 1935, although the listening time decreased sharply after 1950. In 1937 the average for home radio sets was 4 hours and 22 minutes per day, with rural families averaging 4 hours and 47 minutes, while urban families used theirs 4 hours and 9 minutes a day.[4] In 1946 the average hours listening per home per day

[3] This table was compiled by Richard Earl Chapin. R. E. Chapin, "An Evaluation and an Interpretation of the Statistics Relating to the Mass Communications Industries," University of Illinois thesis, Urbana, Ill., 1954.

[4] *Study of Rural Radio Ownership and Use in the United States,* published by the Joint Committee on Radio Research, New York, 1939.

Table 19. Major Radio Networks and Number of Affiliates

Date (end of year)	ABC	CBS	MBS	NBC
1952	353	217	560	204
1951	304	207	552	190
1950	297	196	543	180
1949	279	185	526	190
1948	272	179	519	170
1947	265	174	488	167
1946	240	166	384	160
1945	238	162	384	159
1940		121	160	214
1939		117	116	178
1938		113	107	161
1937		110	80	138
1936		93	39	103
1935		97	3	87
1934		97	4	86
1933		92		85
1932		92		85
1931		82		83
1930		69		72
1929		47		69
1928		28		56
1927		15		48

was 4:13; in 1947 the average was 4:33; by 1948 the listeners tuned in 4:41 hours a day; in 1949 the record shows 4:32; then in 1950 down to 4:10; in 1951 the average was 3:38; 1952 shows 3:10; 1953 down to 2:53; while by 1954 the average was two and a half hours per day.[5]

THE CONTENT OF PROGRAMS

Some idea of the variety of radio programs in the United States since 1925 may be obtained from an examination of the various studies of program content. For the period from 1925 to 1940, the author essayed an extensive and detailed classification in the study that is reported on

[5] Statistics taken from the *Broadcasting Yearbook–Marketbook.* One of the most extensive reports on details of listener habits is P. F. Lazarsfeld and P. L. Kendall, *Radio Listening in America,* Prentice-Hall, Inc., New York, 1948. The study of radio audiences is carried on in various ways. Audience and ratings information is collected by meter (Nielson); by various types of telephone surveys (Hooper, Trendex, Conlan and others); by diary records such as Videodex, American Research Bureau and others. For a summary of methods see *Sponsor,* July 16, 1951, p. 165.

the following pages.[6] Though but a small proportion of the program content deals with political or economic issues, all programs are of significance with regard to some type of opinion. Judgments of the worth of various kinds of music and stories, the significance of market reports, of various features and of economic goods result from radio listening.

In an attempt to find the principal trends in program content, we studied the programs from 1925 to 1940 ot nine American and one English broadcasting station. The sources were the daily newspaper listings of programs; the classifications were according to the dominant characteristic of the program; the unit of record was the time devoted to a given program; and the results were worked out in percentages of the total time. Before turning to these results, we shall indicate briefly the chief problems encountered and the methods used.

1. There were three sources from which radio programs could be studied: some printed record, such as the daily newspaper listings or periodicals like the Chicago *Radio Guide;* the logbooks of stations; "listening in" to programs. For a detailed analysis, listening in would be best, but this limits the record to present or present and future programs. The records of the radio stations are not available, not, at any rate, unless one examines them at the stations. The periodicals dealing with radio programs are of fairly recent vintage, and, moreover, do not cover the entire field. We therefore used daily newspapers from the cities in which the stations were located. For a few periods the listings were not complete in one newspaper, but we completed these by using other papers. One source of error in such a record is the variable accuracy of listings for various years. No doubt in the early years there was more changing of programs after they were printed in the papers than there has been of late years. With a considerable body of data, however, we need not regard this as a serious inaccuracy.

2. The unit of measurement was the number of minutes devoted to a type of program. Within these time intervals there may be infinite variation in content. The effect of five minutes of one kind of dance music is not that of five minutes of another. But we are comparing the relative amount of time devoted to types of programs in a time series.

3. The categories for program classification were not arbitrarily devised. The twenty-seven types that may be noted in Table 20 were gradually developed from the program listings. Beginning with a few general types, which were later modified, examining a sample from the various years of the period recorded, so that the types would be inclusive

[6] The bulk of the material about Tables 20 and 21 is adapted from W. Albig, "The Content of Radio Programs, 1925–1935," *Soc. Forces*, 16: 3: 338–349.

of almost all the programs during the entire period, we developed this final list. Most of the small residue of miscellaneous items could have been classified, but the resultant list would have been unwieldy. The types are for the most part self-explanatory. The foreign programs are those originating abroad. The continued plays were separated from the plays presented in a single program because these continued plays have latterly won a distinct following. In this type were included all the continued plays except those for children, as these were already included in the children's classification. The star programs were those developed about a speaker, actor or commentator whose name was given for a regular program. This was exclusive of the persons featured in music or as exclusively news or political commentators.

4. The programs were usually listed in the newspapers by time categories; that is, all the stations broadcasting from 9:00 to 9:10 would be listed together with the names of their programs. This necessitated the selection of the programs of the stations we were classifying. The number of minutes devoted to the various programs of our stations were then recorded on a large data sheet. One such sheet was used for each week of the programs of the selected stations. There was classification of programs by program type, by station and by sections of the day—that is, from 6:00 A.M. to noon, noon to 6:00 P.M., 6:00 P.M. to the closing of the station. Figures indicating the number of minutes of a type of program were inscribed in the appropriate classification column. These small figures, showing number of minutes of a single program, were then totaled and worked out in percentages of the total for each program type, for each of the three periods of the day, for each station, for a weekly total.

5. Sampling tests indicated four weeks out of each year for each station as adequate. So the programs for February 1 to 15 and July 18 to 31 were classified. These periods were selected to minimize the intrusion of holidays, also to include winter and summer programs. The stations classified were: WEAF, WOR and WJZ of New York from 1925 through 1939; WABC of New York from 1927 through 1939; WGN of Chicago from 1925 through 1939; WMAQ, KYW, WBBM of Chicago from 1929 through 1939; WDAF of Kansas City from 1925 through 1939; the London National of the BBC from 1925 through 1939. Here is a sample of powerful stations in large cities. A parallel study of low-power stations in small towns and cities would be desirable. These would no doubt be found to have differed from one another, especially in the early period, more than did the large stations.

6. The relatively small samples of program-content analysis that have so far been published have not indicated either the consistency of individual classification, if one person did the judging, or the comparative

uniformity of classification, if more than one was involved. In the early stages of our study, the four classifiers conferred together to some extent on the meaning of certain program titles and examined the columns of the radio pages for comments on or references to those programs, so as to determine what their classification should be. After that they worked independently. Well through the classification, each classified the same sample week. Their results were compared for each category in our list of types of programs. The coefficient of correlation was .93 ± .0178.

Our results provided a score or more of tables on which the classifications of program types for each station by yearly totals appeared. Further, there are tables in which the averages of the American stations are shown. Then, there are tables showing the classification by stations of the various program types. And, finally, those on which the range of percentages among the American stations for program types by years are noted. Of this bulk of material only a limited selection of general tables may be exhibited here. Table 20 gives the percentages of time devoted to various types of programs. It is based on the averages of nine American stations. Table 21 provides comparable results for the London National of the BBC. These tables present averages. However, the stations differ considerably from one another in the proportions of time devoted to any type program. The comparison of the American with the London National programs may be made by comparing Tables 20 and 21.[7] Extensive comment on the results is impossible within the limits of this volume. For convenience in thinking of the meaning of percentage differences it may be noted that, since most of the stations are on the air from 6:00 A.M. to at least 1:00 A.M., 1 per cent of broadcasting time is between eleven and twelve minutes per day. Hence, a change of as much as 3 per cent means at least a half hour more or less of that type of program every day.

In the results of this study we have a general survey and comparison that purport to show certain large trends and changes. The reader may note the trends by studying the tables. Our study does not reveal the important qualitative changes within the program types. Many of these also may be examined in an organized fashion. The most valuable use of studies of content, not only of radio programs but also of other media of communication, is in noting trends and changes in content. Systems of classification may be inadequate and unstandardized. Nevertheless, if a system is used consistently over a time period, valuable facts may appear.

---

[7] In my *Public Opinion*, McGraw-Hill Book Company, Inc., New York, 1939, I reported on the content study on radio programs from 1925 through 1934. Later, we classified an additional five years and the present Tables 20 and 21 are combinations of the two studies.

Table 20. Percentages of Time Devoted to Various Types of Programs—Averages of Nine American Broadcasting Stations, 1925–1939

Types of Programs	1925 Feb.	1925 July	1926 Feb.	1926 July	1927 Feb.	1927 July	1928 Feb.	1928 July	1929 Feb.	1929 July	1930 Feb.	1930 July	1931 Feb.	1931 July	1932 Feb.	1932 July
Dance music	22.85	19.50	20.27	28.53	19.70	26.37	23.29	24.95	23.15	28.42	23.90	25.47	26.89	29.57	23.45	25.17
String ensemble	10.05	8.71	8.35	12.58	14.50	11.56	8.76	9.99	3.02	5.11	6.41	6.59	6.12	2.67	3.26	7.07
Concert orchestra	4.33	16.64	9.62	12.89	12.01	7.39	9.80	7.85	8.01	7.77	13.54	7.70	10.45	6.37	8.35	9.33
Soloists	7.60	4.87	6.24	6.02	7.03	4.17	2.39	3.86	5.81	3.63	5.34	3.77	4.15	4.59	4.53	4.90
Combination	14.10	9.83	10.49	5.39	4.79	4.60	10.96	10.10	8.11	6.44	5.19	7.04	6.50	3.27	3.62	3.04
Vocal	8.06	8.84	10.11	7.79	9.14	7.80	6.62	7.63	5.55	6.02	6.53	6.27	7.00	11.23	13.06	12.80
Sacred	0.99	0.24	0.22	0.50	0.42	1.57	0.41	0.28	0.27	0.29	0.39	0.36	0.47	0.24	0.63	0.39
Victrola	0.00	0.00	0.01	0.00	0.33	0.36	2.51	1.31	3.52	3.19	4.21	5.35	5.75	3.42	3.24	3.21
Miscellaneous	3.36	2.16	2.97	2.67	4.30	7.00	8.10	8.13	10.04	6.51	2.71	4.34	2.04	6.06	3.99	3.35
Total	71.34	70.79	68.28	76.37	72.22	70.82	72.84	74.10	67.48	67.38	68.22	66.89	69.37	67.42	64.13	69.26
Women's	2.35	2.42	2.98	2.83	2.81	3.48	4.08	3.65	8.12	4.86	5.14	3.62	3.60	4.22	4.89	3.99
Feature	0.69	3.09	3.15	1.89	1.99	2.40	4.54	1.29	1.68	3.17	3.54	2.70	3.59	3.91	3.99	2.27
Education	4.93	1.26	4.39	1.99	3.88	1.42	2.38	2.03	4.94	3.89	5.19	3.11	6.04	3.04	7.21	4.79
Sports	0.23	3.82	0.85	2.91	0.15	5.32	0.89	4.12	0.79	4.80	0.41	4.52	0.71	6.04	1.71	4.79
News	0.68	0.70	3.10	1.90	1.52	2.19	1.93	1.24	1.34	1.56	1.33	1.98	1.03	1.11	1.20	0.48
Weather	0.34	0.75	0.57	0.65	1.25	0.99	0.63	0.37	0.49	0.47	0.40	0.29	0.24	0.39	0.09	0.16
Church service	3.14	1.72	2.21	1.43	2.80	2.39	2.60	1.92	3.31	1.80	2.34	2.05	3.12	1.39	2.23	1.95
Market reports	3.61	2.75	1.71	1.49	1.34	1.28	1.29	1.76	1.41	1.16	1.28	2.01	0.65	0.39	0.52	0.61
Political	1.80	0.69	1.33	0.64	0.22	0.02	0.33	0.45	0.59	0.44	0.95	0.38	1.21	0.11	1.38	1.03
Health exercises	1.81	6.59	4.02	3.28	2.34	2.73	1.78	2.36	1.59	1.79	1.06	1.21	1.63	1.61	0.61	0.00
Miscellaneous	4.92	0.49	1.14	0.12	3.01	0.82	0.29	1.13	2.45	0.51	0.70	0.51	0.15	0.04	0.44	0.15
Total	24.50	24.28	25.45	19.13	21.31	23.04	20.74	20.32	26.71	24.45	22.34	22.38	21.97	22.25	24.27	20.22
Foreign	0.00	0.00	0.47	0.00	0.00	0.26	0.16	0.00	0.10	0.00	0.44	0.23	0.99	0.69	0.46	0.41
Children's	3.72	2.45	4.21	3.34	3.76	2.35	1.89	1.64	2.45	2.30	2.82	2.54	1.86	2.44	3.52	2.32
Plays	0.04	0.79	0.10	0.69	0.27	1.11	2.79	1.13	1.11	1.48	1.64	1.42	1.11	1.31	1.19	0.59
Continued plays and readings	0.09	0.00	0.71	0.05	0.48	0.76	0.63	1.23	0.12	0.26	0.79	0.12	1.69	1.33	1.91	1.71
Sketches	0.00	1.53	0.64	0.16	1.23	0.90	0.81	0.56	1.27	1.69	2.07	2.51	1.76	2.87	3.27	4.19
Star	0.00	0.00	0.06	0.00	0.35	0.12	0.00	0.00	0.41	0.55	0.70	0.79	0.89	0.97	0.84	0.78
Total	0.13	2.32	1.51	0.90	2.33	2.89	4.23	2.92	2.91	3.98	5.20	4.84	5.45	6.48	7.21	7.27
Miscellaneous	0.19	0.00	0.00	0.15	0.19	0.47	0.05	0.86	0.63	1.64	0.87	3.06	0.09	0.55	0.21	0.43
Total	99.78	99.84	100.12	99.89	99.81	99.83	99.91	99.84	100.28	99.75	99.89	99.94	99.73	99.83	99.80	99.91

Table 20. Percentages of Time Devoted to Various Types of Programs—Averages of Nine American Broadcasting Stations, 1925–1939 (Continued)

Types of Programs	1933 Feb.	1933 July	1934 Feb.	1934 July	1935 Feb.	1935 July	1936 Feb.	1936 July	1937 Feb.	1937 July	1938 Feb.	1938 July	1939 Feb.	1939 July
Dance music	19.81	25.89	23.40	24.74	19.04	17.45	15.78	22.18	19.20	18.66	18.06	20.38	17.62	22.41
String ensemble	4.20	5.43	3.98	4.27	1.79	2.22	1.67	1.72	0.79	2.11	1.59	1.30	0.98	1.48
Concert orchestra	5.40	10.07	5.02	8.22	3.44	5.08	3.79	3.74	3.33	3.36	5.29	4.21	3.88	4.08
Soloists	5.02	4.74	4.42	4.90	2.73	3.08	2.54	3.56	2.61	2.51	2.21	2.15	1.91	1.26
Combination	4.52	3.06	3.47	3.89	5.64	6.13	5.53	6.47	3.43	2.24	2.58	3.09	1.84	0.67
Vocal	16.62	13.71	16.72	14.37	11.77	8.36	10.07	9.67	7.55	8.77	4.52	8.09	6.18	4.36
Sacred	0.45	0.80	0.58	0.61	0.45	0.34	0.83	0.30	0.51	0.80	0.63	0.85	0.70	0.42
Victrola	4.31	2.48	3.47	3.49	2.14	0.00	0.00	0.00	1.75	0.00	1.82	0.97	0.05	0.33
Miscellaneous	6.16	2.43	5.39	5.64	4.50	9.54	5.85	7.81	2.28	8.17	9.46	4.39	5.01	5.37
Total	66.49	68.61	66.45	70.13	51.50	52.20	46.06	55.45	41.45	46.62	46.16	45.43	38.17	40.38
Women's	3.48	3.39	3.05	2.45	4.02	3.96	3.17	1.69	2.84	2.06	3.12	1.96	1.96	2.07
Feature	1.93	3.61	5.45	3.19	2.94	0.93	2.09	0.77	1.78	0.80	1.44	1.15	0.81	0.97
Education	4.65	3.56	4.01	2.83	2.55	1.92	2.47	1.45	2.57	1.28	3.16	2.21	2.39	1.12
Sports	0.47	3.99	0.56	4.72	0.73	5.10	1.22	3.94	0.88	4.40	0.99	5.59	1.32	8.40
News	1.25	0.81	1.07	1.54	2.11	1.76	1.76	2.00	2.08	1.59	2.43	2.98	2.68	2.15
Weather	0.14	0.20	0.10	0.19	0.18	0.32	0.17	0.12	0.10	0.25	0.17	0.08	0.13	0.15
Church service	2.38	1.85	2.22	1.29	1.33	0.86	0.96	1.02	1.11	1.12	1.53	1.24	1.13	1.12
Market reports	0.33	0.35	0.39	0.26	0.41	0.25	0.25	0.19	0.19	0.25	0.26	0.40	0.50	0.96
Political	0.99	1.05	0.72	0.21	1.33	0.46	0.82	0.91	0.73	0.34	0.20	0.09	0.98	0.46
Health exercises	0.12	0.12	0.41	0.11	0.13	0.00	0.00	0.00	0.27	0.07	0.11	0.15	0.37	0.34
Miscellaneous	2.84	0.05	1.16	0.68	3.21	2.98	4.29	3.97	2.85	3.88	2.99	2.19	5.81	7.07
Total	18.56	18.98	19.14	17.47	18.94	18.54	17.20	16.06	15.40	16.04	16.40	18.04	18.08	24.81
Foreign	0.16	0.20	0.25	1.17	0.25	0.81	0.10	0.44	0.28	0.56	0.23	0.55	0.48	0.21
Children's	3.62	3.85	3.74	2.34	4.20	3.50	4.47	2.28	3.14	1.99	3.89	2.71	4.12	1.72
Plays	1.76	2.00	1.70	1.81	1.83	3.79	2.17	0.99	2.29	2.25	3.88	3.13	4.34	4.05
Continued plays and readings	1.57	2.66	1.04	1.50	5.89	5.54	7.40	7.18	11.34	8.56	11.47	14.46	12.49	13.92
Sketches	5.71	2.49	5.77	4.65	3.57	2.15	3.08	2.02	2.08	2.80	1.76	1.72	4.52	3.23
Star	1.29	0.74	1.40	0.89	1.37	0.43	0.62	0.73	0.56	0.18	0.25	0.20	0.04	0.03
Total	10.33	7.89	9.94	8.85	17.11	16.22	17.84	13.64	19.71	16.34	21.28	22.77	25.99	23.16
Miscellaneous	0.69	0.44	0.36	0.00	13.03	12.54	18.63	14.80	22.79	20.30	15.89	13.73	17.63	11.28
Total	99.85	99.97	99.88	99.96	100.58	99.50	99.73	99.95	99.35	99.30	99.73	99.97	99.77	99.63

448

Table 21. Percentages of Time Devoted to Various Types of Programs–London National of the BBC, 1925-1939

Types of Programs	1925		1926		1927		1928		1929		1930		1931		1932	
	Feb.	July	Feb.	July	Feb.	July	Feb.	July	Feb.	July	Feb.	July	Feb.	July	Feb.	July
Dance music	11.69	20.47	30.93	26.57	19.30	13.19	18.63	19.67	14.86	22.72	15.30	18.87	16.44	23.81	10.32	20.76
String ensemble	4.50	6.58	1.95	3.37	2.11	6.26	7.16	5.16	1.90	1.11	0.77	1.86	2.35	0.00	2.12	0.88
Concert orchestra	17.68	8.62	9.59	16.26	10.31	9.21	9.18	4.48	5.63	5.84	17.44	10.94	11.94	10.18	16.72	15.50
Soloists	2.77	1.37	6.63	6.90	1.53	1.67	9.65	6.06	6.37	4.51	1.54	4.68	7.11	9.54	12.14	13.25
Combination	10.51	13.19	2.55	3.38	9.77	18.26	5.57	9.86	12.55	9.82	12.56	5.23	5.04	5.39	2.06	6.74
Vocal	8.13	6.84	7.38	7.13	5.91	9.00	8.27	8.92	2.80	3.25	4.61	11.07	5.35	5.45	3.97	3.79
Sacred	1.08	0.88	2.91	0.40	5.05	3.08	0.99	5.64	1.67	2.37	1.68	7.15	5.45	4.71	1.11	1.00
Victrola	1.96	7.03	3.37	4.46	2.23	2.01	3.87	9.27	8.00	9.19	7.05	4.91	2.41	4.46	2.09	4.67
Miscellaneous	0.00	0.44	0.00	0.00	1.54	1.23	0.00	0.00	3.88	1.70	0.59	0.34	0.00	0.00	2.00	0.00
Total	58.32	65.42	65.31	68.47	57.75	63.91	63.22	69.06	57.66	60.51	61.54	65.05	56.09	65.35	52.53	66.59
Women's	0.76	0.95	0.18	0.00	0.45	0.55	0.31	0.57	2.07	3.17	1.54	1.38	0.82	0.87	0.86	0.79
Feature	10.03	7.67	5.50	7.21	7.51	8.22	4.82	6.50	0.13	0.00	7.53	5.59	5.98	5.94	5.78	6.07
Education	9.69	3.87	7.51	1.39	9.48	3.97	8.60	3.60	11.74	9.84	6.44	1.62	10.99	1.97	12.83	1.20
Sports	0.91	0.44	0.39	0.44	3.71	4.87	2.26	0.63	2.45	0.75	2.00	1.84	2.64	1.19	1.30	0.15
News	4.40	2.93	3.27	3.32	2.23	2.81	2.46	2.74	2.32	2.78	3.65	3.35	2.40	3.72	3.18	4.02
Weather	1.73	1.35	1.33	1.62	1.39	1.34	1.90	1.99	1.34	3.57	3.23	3.87	1.15	1.21	1.16	1.19
Church service	0.76	0.98	1.24	1.97	1.65	2.67	3.98	3.86	4.65	3.33	3.12	5.23	4.46	3.31	6.48	4.34
Market reports	0.00	0.29	0.40	0.81	0.32	0.12	0.37	0.45	3.09	0.79	0.70	1.27	3.15	4.48	5.54	4.31
Political	0.00	0.44	0.52	0.29	2.61	0.00	0.31	0.45	0.51	0.19	0.00	0.46	1.18	0.00	0.70	0.61
Health exercises	0.25	0.00	0.00	0.00	0.00	0.00	0.00	0.00	0.00	0.00	0.00	0.00	0.00	0.00	0.00	0.00
Miscellaneous	1.01	1.83	1.42	0.63	1.16	1.09	2.30	0.92	2.77	3.65	0.09	0.29	0.80	1.04	1.28	1.04
Total	29.54	20.75	21.76	17.68	30.51	23.64	27.31	21.71	31.07	28.07	28.30	24.90	33.57	23.73	39.11	23.72
Foreign	0.33	0.00	0.36	0.00	0.77	0.73	0.00	0.00	0.00	0.00	0.54	0.00	0.34	2.93	0.19	0.73
Children's	9.38	8.45	7.07	8.12	5.45	6.66	6.27	6.32	5.59	5.88	6.25	5.89	7.00	5.40	5.90	5.57
Plays	0.00	4.33	2.21	1.37	2.11	1.18	2.35	2.31	4.01	4.31	1.81	3.48	1.35	2.15	1.47	1.84
Continued plays and readings	0.00	0.00	0.00	1.42	0.57	0.37	0.14	0.00	0.77	0.64	0.00	0.00	0.55	0.34	0.00	1.50
Sketches	1.99	1.07	2.14	1.82	2.17	0.86	0.33	0.39	0.51	0.12	1.49	0.40	0.23	0.00	1.26	0.00
Star	0.42	0.44	0.59	0.89	0.00	0.00	1.10	0.00	0.00	0.00	0.00	0.00	0.69	0.00	0.00	0.00
Total	2.41	5.84	4.94	5.50	4.85	2.41	3.92	2.70	5.29	5.07	3.30	3.88	2.82	2.49	2.73	3.34
Miscellaneous	0.00	0.00	0.00	0.00	0.00	0.00	0.00	0.00	0.34	0.44	0.00	0.00	0.01	0.00	0.00	0.00
Total	99.98	100.46	99.44	99.77	99.33	99.35	100.72	99.79	99.95	99.94	99.93	99.72	99.83	99.83	100.46	99.95

Table 21. Percentages of Time Devoted to Various Types of Programs–London National of the BBC, 1925–1939 (Continued)

Types of Programs	1933 Feb.	1933 July	1934 Feb.	1934 July	1935 Feb.	1935 July	1937 Feb.	1937 July	1939 Feb.	1939 July
Dance music	22.40	20.18	17.58	20.89	13.71	19.19	9.75	12.49	12.05	17.63
String ensemble	1.28	1.13	2.70	0.77	5.30	6.17	7.01	5.68	4.84	7.99
Concert orchestra	9.73	23.44	17.13	25.39	12.95	9.92	15.05	11.04	10.84	6.87
Soloists	13.28	8.32	8.60	10.12	5.26	6.97	7.23	7.41	5.28	8.25
Combination	5.66	8.96	3.78	2.29	10.96	7.81	6.47	12.58	5.42	2.68
Vocal	1.11	1.66	1.98	7.07	0.44	2.43	3.86	6.33	2.01	6.83
Sacred	0.00	0.69	0.45	1.15	0.80	0.88	0.85	0.93	1.07	0.86
Victrola	3.07	8.95	2.85	2.72	6.69	8.56	4.54	9.50	7.03	9.77
Miscellaneous	2.92	0.98	0.84	0.14	2.95	9.70	5.48	3.35	6.72	3.67
Total	59.45	74.31	55.71	70.54	59.06	71.63	60.24	69.31	55.26	64.55
Women's	0.41	1.03	0.42	0.71	0.48	0.26	1.21	0.74	1.57	0.60
Feature	0.00	0.00	10.43	3.01	0.96	0.22	0.94	0.46	1.57	0.95
Education	12.30	0.69	7.14	0.60	11.68	1.72	4.90	0.32	10.98	1.21
Sports	2.56	1.33	3.29	3.90	1.83	5.25	3.10	4.52	2.19	3.72
News	3.30	2.60	3.51	4.45	2.99	2.82	2.61	2.70	4.25	4.88
Weather	1.64	1.53	3.05	3.20	3.11	3.09	3.95	4.38	2.64	3.33
Church service	4.45	4.60	3.83	4.21	3.82	3.13	2.60	2.65	4.39	3.50
Market reports	3.65	3.45	0.40	0.00	0.00	0.00	0.36	0.09	0.00	0.00
Political	0.13	0.22	0.65	0.00	0.00	0.00	0.00	0.00	0.27	0.47
Health exercises	0.00	0.00	0.00	0.00	0.00	0.00	0.00	0.00	0.00	0.00
Miscellaneous	2.90	1.67	1.77	0.05	3.86	1.94	5.53	3.31	5.64	3.50
Total	31.34	17.12	34.49	20.13	28.73	18.43	25.20	19.17	33.50	22.16
Foreign	0.20	0.46	0.00	1.85	0.00	0.00	0.00	0.74	1.43	0.00
Children's	5.71	5.64	5.19	5.42	0.56	0.00	0.18	0.00	0.00	0.00
Plays	2.64	1.91	3.60	1.39	2.19	2.47	2.52	1.35	3.09	3.37
Continued plays and readings	0.24	0.50	0.00	0.00	0.00	0.00	0.99	0.65	0.36	0.00
Sketches	0.00	0.00	0.92	0.65	0.60	0.00	0.99	1.77	0.00	0.00
Star	0.00	0.00	0.00	0.00	0.60	0.18	0.00	0.00	0.00	0.00
Total	2.88	2.41	4.52	2.04	3.35	2.65	4.68	4.51	4.88	3.37
Miscellaneous	0.30	0.00	0.00	0.00	8.85	7.28	9.84	6.94	6.32	9.90
Total	99.88	99.94	99.91	99.98	99.99	99.99	99.96	99.95	99.96	99.98

Table 22 provides the results of a study of program content made in 1948 by Kenneth Baker, of the National Association of Broadcasters, now the National Association of Radio and Television Broadcasters. According to CBS (March, 1956), this is the latest over-all published

Table 22. Types of Programs Making up the Broadcast Schedule Distributed by "Sustaining" vs. "Commercial" for all Types of Stations

(Expressed in percentages; total time on the air of all stations 100%)

	Commercial	Sustaining	Total
Music Programs...................	26 *	15	41
Old Familiar and Western.........	5	2	7
Popular and Dance...............	17	9	26
Classical and Semiclassical.........	4	4	8
Dramatic Programs................	13	3	16
Daytime Serials..................	5	1	6
Mystery Drama..................	3	†	3
Comedy Drama..................	2	†	2
Other Drama....................	3	2	5
News and Commentators...........	8	5	13
Comedy and Variety...............	6	1	7
Quiz and Audience Participation.....	4	2	6
Religion and Religious Music........	4	2	6
Sports and Sports Commentators.....	3	1	4
Talks...........................	2	1	3
Farm Programs...................	1	1	2
Forums and Panels...............	†	1	1
Homemaking Programs............	1	†	1
Miscellaneous, unclassified..........	†	2	2
			102 ‡

NOTE 1: A sustaining program is here defined as any uninterrupted segment of the station's time which is five minutes or more in length and from which the station derives no income.

NOTE 2: Percentages are calculated from the *length* of the program in minutes so that long and short programs receive their proper weight.

* Includes "participating" programs—in which announcements are read between musical selections—as "commercial" time.

† Less than 1 per cent.

‡ This column adds to slightly more than 100 per cent because a few programs were classified in more than one category.

SOURCE: K. Baker, "An Analysis of Radio's Programming," in P. F. Lazarsfeld and F. N. Stanton (eds.), *Communications Research*, Harper & Brothers, New York, 1949, pp. 51–72.

survey of program content in the United States. This study utilizes a less detailed classificatory system than was developed in the content study for 1925 to 1940.[8]

In the postwar years, the development of static-free FM broadcasting was viewed as the harbinger of cultural programs. With numerous wave lengths available, it was believed that both commercial and noncommercial stations could be accommodated. But funds were not forthcoming in adequate amounts to subsidize noncommercial stations, and the commercial radio stations from 1950 onwards were faced with contracting income due to television. Moreover, faithful audiences for the fine music and other cultural programs failed to appear in the numbers expected. The record of the early 1950's was discouraging, but FM radio potentially offered the channels and the opportunity for cultural programs of whatever level a developed public interest would support. The proportion of total program time on the air in the United States which is provided by the more than one hundred noncommercial AM and FM radio stations has been estimated by Dallas Smythe (content analyst of television for some years and, earlier, research chief for the FCC) as less than one per cent. It would seem that listeners could be acquired for more generally cultural programs, but neither the listeners nor adequate subsidy for noncommercial programs have as yet appeared.

Of the content of commercial radio programs since 1925, there are several general types which we may consider in relation to opinions and cultural values. In general, about three-fourths of commercial radio has consisted of entertainment-type programs, the remainder of the time being divided between news and informational programs, the religious programs, talks about public issues, forums and panels, personal-relations information and counseling, and the like. In my classification, it may be noted that music, as the major type of entertainment program, was presented in about 70 per cent of the time in the earlier years, but by 1940 had decreased to about 40 per cent. The most recent classfications also report all types of music as presented during about two-fifths of all commercial radio time.

The second largest class of entertainment-type programs on commercial radio appear to be drama programs, which supplied 16 per cent of all program time in 1946. Within this group the daytime serial (soap opera) stood first, with 6 per cent of the total time—just slightly higher than the 4 to 5 per cent of

---

[8] In the meantime, there was published an FCC survey of a single week in 1938 which reported music, 52.45 per cent; drama, 9.11 per cent; variety, 8.84 per cent; talks and dialogues, 11.41 per cent; news and market reports, 8.55 per cent; religious, 8.55 per cent; special events, 2.21 per cent and miscellaneous, 2.28 per cent. Llewellyn White reports on major network program classifications for 1933, 1939 and 1944 in his *The American Radio,* University of Chicago Press, Chicago, 1947, p. 66.

big-city TV time now given to the TV counterpart, domestic drama. Mystery drama on the radio provided only 3 per cent in 1946—a figure which casual observation of radio suggests would need to be revised upward today. Comedy drama provided 2 per cent, while other drama accounted for 5 per cent of broadcasting time. . . . Turning now to the area of information-type programming, we find that news and commentators dominate this field with 13 per cent of total commercial radio time.[9]

Therefore, let us consider music, the daytime serial and programs of news and commentators in relation to public opinion.

Although not more than a fifth, and usually much less, of the broadcast music could possibly be classified as classical or as music of some complexity and musical refinement, this amount of "serious" music none the less bulks large in total in the programs of radio. Where else could millions of listeners have had such musical experience? The sponsoring of good music was a matter of prestige to some sponsors as early as 1930. Symphonies and orchestras became fixtures early in broadcasting history. The Ford Motor Company and General Motors each had a symphony program, CBS had the New York Philharmonic, NBC developed its own symphony and ABC broadcast Metropolitan Opera. In such music they found a noncontroversial form of "public-service" program. If musicologists agree, as indeed they have voted,[10] that Bach, Beethoven, Mozart, Wagner, Brahms, Haydn, Schubert, Handel and a score more of composers have contributed most to the development of music, then we may designate the products of these great composers as classical music. If the works of such composers are extensively broadcast, as they have been, then the situation has existed to raise the musical taste of millions of listeners. And there is fairly common agreement that the musical taste of at least sizable minorities has been bettered during the past three decades by radio listening. Training plays a considerable part in the creation of musical taste.[11] "The broadcasts make music more accessible; they extend the range of musical experience; they repeat the musical stimuli, supply commentators, and, on occasion, program notes and other educational literature. A possible liability which may be inherent in radio taste-training is the development of a dependent attitude of listening attentively only to compositions which are sponsored by the broadcasters of the favored radio station." [12] However, there can be no doubt that broadcast music has resulted in a substantial increase in serious

[9] D. W. Smythe, "The Content and Effects of Broadcasting," in *Mass Media and Education*, University of Chicago Press, Chicago, 1954, p. 197.

[10] P. R. Farnsworth, "Musical Eminence," *School and Soc.*, 50: 1283; 158–160, 1939.

[11] See the interesting discussion of associated problems in P. R. Farnsworth, *Musical Taste*, Stanford University Press, Stanford, Calif., 1950.

[12] *Ibid.*, p. 65.

music listeners.[13] Fairly wide publics have been developed for serious music, publics numbering hundreds of thousands, if not the millions claimed by enthusiasts for the new mass medium. Opinions favorable to serious music have been cultivated.

It was not necessary to create an audience for popular music by radio and, indeed, from the beginning of broadcasting, popular music has consumed more of radio broadcasting than any other type of program.[14] Eighty and more per cent of all music broadcast is popular music. Such music provides the largest percentage of program content, and though for the average adult popular music may be but a limited part of life, hit songs are often a central preoccupation of restless, excitable youth. In a summary of a number of audience surveys in the 1940's, the conclusion was reached that "about four times as many people in the teen-age group preferred popular music as compared to those over 50 years of age; up to the age of 35, a majority of both men and women picked popular music as one of their five favorite types of programs." [15] Sex differences in the appeal of popular music programs are slight and not consistent in various listener surveys. Though it is the young who attend to popular music most conspicuously, a substantial adult audience is ever present, as is evident from the programs directed at housewives by disc jockeys, by the popularity of revivals of past hit songs based on the nostalgia of the middle-aged, and by other indices.

The broadcasting of songs has greatly increased the demand for variety in popular music. As hundreds of different songs are broadcast daily, the listening public soon tires of the same songs, so that there is a voracious demand for new songs. A study made in 1941 showed that the number of weeks on the "Hit Parade" broadcasts for the most popular songs was from 10 to 20 weeks, and that the life of the songs on records in the coin machines was even shorter. "Whereas before the machine age of radio and coin machines, a big song hit would have a popularity run of 18 to 24 months, today its life-cycle is contracted to 6 or 9 months. The extensive 'plugging' of a song is both its birth cry and its death pang." [16] The listening public is impatient, restless and demanding. As radio has

[13] Examine the study by Edward A. Suchman on new music listeners in *Radio Research, 1941* (P. F. Lazarsfeld and F. N. Stanton, eds.), Duell, Sloan and Pearce–Little, Brown, New York, 1942, pp. 140–188.

[14] This is true also of most foreign radio broadcasting. For example, in 1949 the French Broadcasting System devoted to music 60 per cent of all radio time on the Parisian and the regional stations. For some materials on the content of radio broadcasting in the various countries of the world see the issues of UNESCO's *Press, Film, Radio*, 1947–1951.

[15] Perhaps the best study of popular music on the radio was made by John G. Peatman in 1943 and is reported in *Radio Research, 1942–1943* (P. F. Lazarsfeld and F. N. Stanton, eds.), Essential Books, Inc., Fair Lawn, N.J., 1944, pp. 335–393.

[16] *Ibid.*, p. 368.

been unable to satisfy the ravening public with enough new tunes, the resurrection of many old popular songs has been standard practice since about 1940.

Attitudes, beliefs and opinions on but few topics are influenced by the lyrics of popular music. As the appeal of popular songs is primarily to young people, especially young people in love, and to the nostalgic middle-aged, the central theme of most lyrics is love, happiness in love, agony in love, frustration in love and uncertainty. "The bulk of 'hit' songs are love songs. Of 90 songs which were on the 'Hit Parade' between January 1, 1941, and July 1, 1942, only 8 per cent were songs without sex interest." [17] Other than love songs there are a smaller number of novelty songs, songs of nonsense syllables, of play on words and a few other themes. It is a dream world of wishful thinking about idealized love, and of vague, unreal sentiment largely divorced from reality, and of abstract statement of simulated feeling and induced melancholy. I believe that content analysis of popular song lyrics would lead to the conclusion that we have here another instance of emotional compensation provided by popular entertainment for some unsatisfactory adjustments in the romantic quest in the United States. But I would immediately note that there are always widespread unsatisfactory adjustments in the individualized, personalized romantic quest in America, and the yearnings of popular songs may provide some soothing catharsis. However we interpret their meaning, the simple sentiments of the lyrics of popular songs are most widely diffused by radio.

Radio has been studied extensively in terms of its influence as an advertising medium, yet the enormous influence of radio on contemporary American attitudes and opinions since 1920 has been studied surprisingly little. The influence of children's programs, the study of the content and influence of the daytime serial and the political impact of radio have received most attention. The influence of radio in the United States is still largely incalculable.

Through the 1930's and 1940's the daytime serial, or soap opera, had developed a faithful audience of approximately 20 million American women each day. The daytime serials are simple dramatic stories of the vicissitudes of personal life, family crises, amorous quests, economic worries and struggles with questions of health and with simplified issues of morality. The daytime serial is in many respects the contemporary folk tale adapted to the values cherished by middle-class housewives. But it does not well up from the mass of common people as does the folk tale. It is a rapidly manufactured product ground out by many professional script writers, who are knowledgeable as to mass values.

[17] *Ibid.*, p. 371.

Approximately 40 such programs were carried by the major networks from 1935 to 1950, after which the numbers decreased somewhat.

There were variations in the audience structure of the different serials. "Life Can Be Beautiful" appealed more extensivly to the young than to the middle-aged. "The Romance of Helen Trent" had twice as many listeners who were over 30 years of age as those under 30 years, since this serial appealed more to the emotionally disappointed. Indeed, the announcer's introduction of the program stated regularly that romance could exist after the age of 35, and Helen symbolized glamor in the middle-aged. "Stella Dallas" was reported to appeal particularly to rural women and to women of low income and low education, while "Against the Storm" gleaned an audience composed to a larger degree of the younger, higher income, more educated women.[18] The sophisticates have long derided "soap operas," and, indeed, they are not an agency to elevate cultural values. But what the critics do not admit is that the average woman in the middle classes in the United States actually does lead a kind of soap-opera existence, proceeding from economic and emotional petty crisis to crisis. And the hopes, aspirations and frustrations of their large audiences have been rather simply reflected in the soap operas.

One of the major types of daytime serial, the family situation with the wife and mother as the heroine, was intensively studied as to content and influence by W. Lloyd Warner and William E. Henry.[19] They studied the symbols of such a program and how these were used in the private worlds and fantasies of the listeners. A serial which had one of the largest audiences, which the authors designated the "Big Sister" program, was analyzed and its audience sampled. The subjects were a homogeneous group of 62 middle-class, married, urban housewives from the Middle West who were already regular listeners to daytime serials, and a small sample of women who did not listen to soap operas. These listeners lived within the narrow but rigorous codes of middle-class family organization. The psychological structures of these women were characterized by reduced imagination, by impulse suppression, by a struggle for personal control in the family and a fear they would not succeed, by stereotyped interpersonal relations, as they lived in a conventional monotonous world and experienced an apprehension of the unknown, feeling uncomfortable and resentful when forced to make new decisions. They were insecure in the unknown and the inexperienced situation. They were fearful especially of the unknown which might endanger

---

[18] See detailed study by Helen Kaufman in *Radio Research, 1942–1943* (P. F. Lazarsfeld and F. N. Stanton, eds.), Harper & Brothers, New York, 1944, pp. 86–106.

[19] W. L. Warner and W. E. Henry, *The Radio Daytime Serial,* Genetic Psychology Monographs, No. 37, 1948.

them through any break in the tie with their husbands or their community status. In short, the women were extremely insecure and dependent upon their husbands. These generalizations are based on evidence from interviews, from schedules of social characteristics and from Thematic Apperception Tests taken by all the subjects.

These women who listened to the "Big Sister" program were found to identify themselves with the heroine of the program. In general, the women listeners wished to maintain peaceful relations within their families and to achieve a considerable measure of dominance therein. They were anxious about their continued success and adjustment within marriage, and hence were conventional and restrained to conventional roles and interests. They were economically dependent on the husband and had considerable anxiety due to such dependence, as many had fears that this security could be lost. Therefore, they were more bound by a strict moral code than were women in economic levels above and below our soap-opera listeners.

The "Big Sister" program was reassuring to the listeners, since the women of this and many another daytime serial resolve just such insecurities as the listeners feel. The programs provide moral beliefs, values, and techniques for solving the emotional and interpersonal problems of the women listeners. The significance of the wife's role in basic human affairs is dramatized and this increases the listeners' feelings of importance.

Unregulated, impulsive life is condemned in the programs, and the bad woman, that is, one who utilizes sex as a lure and a weapon, is invariably unsuccessful in the end. The programs reaffirm the basic security of the marriage ties and demonstrate that those who behave properly are successful and that wrong behavior is punished. Moreover, the soap-opera heroines are much stronger persons than the husbands and other men in the stories. After ten years of writing the scripts for "Portia Faces Life," Mona Kent stated that "possibly the American woman feels actually so dependent, economically and emotionally, on her husband that she has to appease her insecurity by identifying herself with one or more soap-opera heroines whose husbands can have no secrets from them." [20]

The small sample of women who did not listen to daytime serials evidenced more imagination, were not so frustrated, did not engage extensively in self-pity, were not so fearful and did not think in such limited stereotypes. The extent to which the frustrations and anxieties of the regular listeners were the reason for their listening to such serials and the problem of the extent to which the serials increase or normalize,

[20] *Time,* Sept. 12, 1949.

rather than trending toward reduction of, anxieties is not proved by this study (this is not the author's problem), nor indeed is there any conclusive evidence anywhere on this issue. We do not know to what extent the daytime serial has accentuated some of the insecurities of the women. Such insecurity is exploited to gain attention by the listeners and to increase the audience. It is probably true that the principal result is a prevention of maturity in the listeners by making their plight appear normal and irreducible. But without the soothing assurances of the serials, the listeners would not inevitably trend toward maturity. Indeed, they would probably be less content and more anxious. It would perhaps be fair to say that the serials in providing solace fail to educate constructively toward a more mature solution. However, more mature attitudes might be even more disruptive of the listeners' marital situations if the husbands were not simultaneously reeducated.

When one asks whether the radio serials invite self-knowledge and self-criticism and whether the listener is made aware of her prejudices, emotional answers and resentments, the answer is unquestionably no. "Our survey indicates that radio serials maintain a firm grip on so many millions of American women because they satisfy their psychological needs the easy way, by devices which are known from the psychiatric analysis of wish dreams." [21] This is the market and the script writers meet the demand. Mona Kent, in expressing some shame at her script's inanities, said, "When I think of that big listening ear out there, I think how wonderful it would be if some writer could find a formula for giving women the substance and not the shadow of life." [22] Yet, whenever she tried to make Portia a more complex and more rounded person, the program Hooper rating dropped and the listeners angrily protested. Popular tastes could not be quickly matured by commercial radio programs. However, in 1955 the veteran soap operas of radio were rapidly disappearing. Many of the long-important programs, such as "Just Plain Bill," had gone off the air. Others that had been produced for fifteen or twenty years by eager sponsors had become sustaining programs, with but tenuous grip for survival. Veteran programs such as "Helen Trent," "Stella Dallas," and "Young Widder Brown" were only partially sponsored. Television would develop its own types of popular storytelling as the soap operas disappeared.

Since Paul Lazarsfeld's early audience studies, it has been frequently generalized that listeners with limited education acquire about twice as much information and opinion about public affairs from the radio as they glean from the printed word. It is also stated that for those of higher educational attainments the proportions are reversed. For listeners

[21] *Radio Research, 1942–1943,* p. 79.
[22] *Time,* Sept. 12, 1949.

of all types in 1945, the NAB survey found that 61 per cent used radio
rather than newspapers as their main source of news, but surveys conducted after the war provided the information that about 40 per cent
of the population was primarily dependent on the radio for news.

The news supplied by radio is generally from the same sources as the
news presented by the press. In 1935 the International News Service
and the United Press Association, and in 1939 the Associated Press, decided to make their news services available to the networks for noncommercial and nonsponsored purposes and to provide news to stations
for commercial sponsorship by arrangement with the member newspapers
of the associations. In addition, many radio stations, especially those outside of the large metropolitan centers, collect local news and broadcast
it. In general, the stations in the smaller cities devote more time to different types of news programs than those in larger cities. Most stations
use from 5 to 10 per cent of broadcasting time for news programs, commentators, forums and discussion groups of all kinds. But, of course, the
amount of news, the details of the news and the interpretations are of
necessity far more limited in radio broadcasting than in presentation by
newspapers. The amount of bare headline news that could be reeled
off by announcers before complete boredom ensued for the listeners is
very small indeed in comparison to the content of a daily newspaper.
Therefore, the announcer is highly selective and can give few details;
this is likewise true of radio news commentators. Moreover, these relatively few news items are heard in the average household during meals,
at the same time as conversations are in progress, and with other distractions. Even without these distractions, Wilbur Schramm, at the University of Illinois, in a study of news-listening by 492 United States Air
Force enlisted men slightly above the educational median for the United
States, found that a few minutes after the broadcast the subjects were
able to recall just about 50 per cent of the essential facts, not the
peripheral facts, of the broadcast. And public-affairs items were remembered less well than stories of crimes, fire, wrecks, disasters and other
spectacular events. Foreign events and names were remembered less
well than items nearby. Moreover, there was considerable evidence that
the listener attends especially to items in which "cue words" or "index
words" of a sensational or familiar nature are present. And a small number of items is preferred. In a 15-minute broadcast, the audience preference was decidedly for 20 items rather than 30 or 40 items. In listening
to radio news there is a low level of attention and preference for the uncomplicated, the few and the brief items.

Radio news broadcasting has greatly accentuated the trend toward
superficiality and strain resulting from mass communications. The intellectual is especially prone to overstimulation. Before mass communi-

cations it was no doubt true that mass mental processes were rather sluggish in contemplation of public affairs. For large publics radio news has made for animation and widened attention areas, though still all too often for a superficial consideration of public issues. But the element of strain has been increased for those minority elites who strive somewhat to surmount the superficiality of mass communications. Intellectuals are constantly reminded of the numbers and varieties of contemporary social problems, issues and conflicts. Radio and the other mass media simply bring these items persistently, repetitively and inescapably to the questing, reflective intellect. To many, a glut of problems is disorganizing.

In broadcasting there is a sense of personality contact with the announcer or analyst which makes the experience more attractive to millions of people than reading the printed word. Moreover, sizable sections of all national populations are illiterate, or, if literate, read laboriously. The voice aids in transmitting meaning, whereas reading places a greater strain and responsibility on the unskilled reader. When asked by a *Fortune* poller in August, 1939, "If you heard conflicting versions of the same story in the newspaper and over the radio, which would you be more likely to believe?" some 22.7 per cent of the sample said radio-press bulletin; 17.6 per cent said radio commentator; in comparison to 3.4 per cent who would prefer to believe the newspaper columnist; 11.1 per cent would prefer to believe the press news item; and 12.4 per cent the editorial. The remainder, 19.8 per cent, declared that they wouldn't know whom to believe in cases of such conflict.

Since the 1930's radio commentators have acquired large, faithful and often enthusiastic followings. The commentators are the explainers and simplifiers of radio, performing the function of the newspaper columnist. Theoretically, this is not so, as the commentators are presumably committed to objective reporting and explanation. Yet most commentators have really engaged in interpretation of events. Biases, slants and policies are expressed at times directly, as well as indirectly, by commentators. Radio commentators range from clarity, objectivity, reason and reliability to purple passages, slanted news, emotional appeals and lack of integrity. There are very many commentators on networks and on local stations. And the policies on commentators vary widely as between CBS, ABC, NBC and Mutual. There is a great range of qualities between Elmer Davis, Edward R. Murrow, Clifton Utley, Eric Sevareid and George Sokolsky, Walter Winchell, Paul Harvey, Fulton Lewis, Jr. Some address the mind, others are visceral. Reason and reliability contrast with rabble-rousing hysteria, innuendo and gossip. There is a market for each. As in the case of newspaper columnists, the epithet-makers and those engaged in personal attack have faithful, gleeful listeners. But the responsible commentators are likewise available.

However, supplying a market for divergent types of analysis does not result in balanced commentary. Nor has this new profession of commentator a matured and observed ethic. As in the case of the columnist, it is not surprising that a matured profession of commentator-clarifier has not developed. The great need for such is recent and the necessary qualities of training are ill defined. There is an immediate market for extremists; as there is for those who would responsibly interpret with impersonal analysis and rational insight. Commercial radio will supply all types.

Another program type is the popular information and quiz programs. These are usually regarded by the broadcasters and by the radio public as "educational." They are nothing of the sort. These programs consist of factual information, desiccated and unrelated to anything. They have no meaningful central theme or themes. They do not lead to education, but to the accumulation of largely meaningless, nonfunctional facts. This is not learning, but random nonsense. No group of professional educators would or should sponsor such programs. Yet a general public commends them as "educational" because millions of that public have no standards by which to judge and have no idea of the criteria of an "education." When listeners have been asked whether they have any favorite subjects in these programs, they usually answer, "No, everything is worth knowing." The "people's choice" of program content obviously will not raise rapidly the cultural standards of those programs. We have here the old problem of cultural elevation in a popular democracy. Obviously, the program-makers may, and at times do, provide materials somewhat better than the listeners' demands, and, moreover, listeners may develop some standards through experience. In the 1920's it was frequently claimed that the readers of tabloid newspapers graduated to the better papers. I believe that that claim, often made at editors' conferences, was never adequately proved. I have yet to see evidence that listeners to quiz programs have been graduated to more truly educational pursuits.

The American radio programs contain a number of features which are the product of individualistic values in our culture. I have mentioned the preoccupation with middle-class person-to-person controversy and problems in the soap operas. Another aspect of the concern with the self is the development of a number of programs of simple, popular psychological analysis. Explanations of human nature are popular. Much of the interest in such programs arises from actual life situations and the psychological conflicts of many listeners. There is much personal insecurity and a widespread quest for security. Involved also is the pervasive competition of the American scene in contrast with ideals of service. This leads to tensions. "The double standard of success and service creates enormous difficulties in the lives of middle-class boys and girls. If the middle class is the germinating bed of ambitious climbers, it is also the custodian of morality, of ideals of sacrifice on behalf of values that transcend the limits of the individual ego. The typical conflict within the personality of the middle-class youth is between 'ambition' and 'ideals'; the individual suffers from contradictory emphases that are found throughout the total structure of an individualistic society." [23] Many aspects of these conflicts and of attempted adjustments and solutions are reflected in our radio programs.

THE INFLUENCE OF RADIO UPON GROUP OPINION

It is obviously impossible to assess in any exact terms the influence of radio in the United States on entertainment, information and education, and, indeed, on the distribution of consumers' goods by advertising. Almost all studies of radio's advertising effectiveness are in the unpublished studies of market researchers. The effects of broadcasting upon interests, attitudes and opinions are so numerous, varied and subtle, and so ill understood, that we shall not commit the absurdity of attempting to list such consequences. They defy analysis of any complete and exact kind. Moreover, most of these effects are indirect and unintended, but by no means incidental. The contents of radio programs reflect the prevailing "climate of opinion." However, we shall comment on some of the more general relationships.

It is understandable, but ironical, that the nation which most vociferously espouses democracy should have been so laggard in the use of the radio to enrich and broaden the knowledge and thought life of the masses of its citizens. Although large groups cannot be made intelligent by fiat or through any one channel of communication, it is an axiom of democracy that they may be more or less gently led to more mature values. Commercial broadcasting, preoccupied with the size of its audiences, has had no incentive to provide a gradually rising standard of programs in an attempt to refine popular taste. Thus far, American broadcasting has been essentially but the amplification, repetition and diffusion of existing tastes, standards and interests. That the simpler provincial standards may be expanded into the values requisite to the "great society" is the faith of democracy. Such a viewpoint assumes the development of taste and knowledge of values in any field as the result of training within a culture.

[23] H. D. Lasswell, "Radio as an Instrument of Reducing Personal Insecurity," *Studies in Phil. and Soc. Sci.*, vol. 9, no. 1, p. 50.

RADIO, TELEVISION AND THE SOCIAL PROCESS

A. Speed of communication accelerates the processes of opinion and of public decision at many points. It may be that in a fundamental way the popular fashions in thought have changed more rapidly. Achieving integration in large publics has usually been a slow process. With the radio, a new and effective agency was provided for those bent upon building up or tearing down popular viewpoints. Political change has been accelerated. The defense of administrations and attacks upon them achieve a more immediate hearing. There is already evidence of a more rapid fashion change in demagogues. Preferences for popular songs, slang, slogans and other language forms are built up and outmoded at an increasing tempo. If there existed a widely diffused and stable framework of values, such speeding up of the opinion process and of decision might be desirable. With values in transition, however, instability, confusion and disintegration now occur at many points. Confusion may be merely increased by the multiplicity of impressions and viewpoints presented to a people inadequately implemented with measuring rods of stable value.

B. We have elsewhere discussed something of the increased diffusion resulting from the radio and television. That impressions are more widely scattered is an obvious fact. But as Lewis Mumford notes, "As with all instruments of multiplication the critical question is as to the function and quality of the object one is multiplying." [24] Another basic question relates to the amount of psychological regimentation resulting from widespread diffusion. All the mass agencies of communication have some such blanketing effect, but, in a preoccupation with such standardization, the commentator must not minimize the beliefs, interests and attitudes developed from other means of communication or the particular viewpoints resulting from membership in class, regional, racial and other groups. Words, spoken in conversation or over the radio, cannot readily change such attitudes.

C. One function that the radio and television may perform in the opinion field is to inspire interest and indicate controversies. Those special groups which have access to a richer and more diversified fare than that offered by the radio may listen infrequently. But that which may be simple or platitudinous to the expert or the better informed may be stimulating and inspire interest among the mass of listeners. President Sproul of California stated, "The great need of our people today is not improved facilities for making known and available the materials of culture, but better means for interesting them in living more abundant lives.

[24] L. Mumford, *Technics and Civilization*, Harcourt, Brace and Company, Inc., New York, 1934, p. 21.

Adult education suffers no lack of facilities or matter for life-long learning: it does suffer from a dearth of consumers and of consumer psychology. In order to change that situation we must arouse in the average citizen a desire for intellectual and spiritual growth." [25] If the rule of the average man is to be maintained relatively uninvaded by special interests, at least a sizable minority must be constantly stimulated to an interest in public affairs. The radio and television may be used to inspire interest in a special viewpoint, ardently propagandized, or in a truly debated issue. Hence, broadcasting systems effectively serve autocracy or liberal democracy.

D. Inasmuch as the radio and television reach large audiences of the literate and the illiterate, of the learned and the ignorant, they may be effective instruments of mass education or of propaganda to the millions. It is evident that the nature of the instrument does not determine that one type of appeal has a permanent advantage over the other. The radio provides a forum for the discussions of popular democracy, but it has also proved a most powerful means of mass control by the dictators. Day after day under government-controlled radio systems the listening audience receives either unabashed governmental propaganda or a minimum of political news. Under the American system a mass of frequently confused and confusing counsel is provided. There is some informal censorship of extreme political and economic doctrines. Under the most free of democratic systems the difficult problem of allocation of time to small minority groups with a small following would remain. Public indifference applies its own censorship to such programs. Moreover, under relatively free discussion, the appeal of the demagogue, especially in crises, frequently outweighs the appeal of reason. But that is implicit in democracy, inescapable and persistent. Broadcasting has not made it so. Radio and television merely emphasize and diffuse the existing systems, but the very extension of appeals to ever larger groups makes them a constantly more powerful agency for popular information or error, realistic knowledge or distortion.

Whether it is used to propagandize a special cause or develop opinion through discussion, broadcasting by radio and television is the great unifying agency of modern life. By means of radio and television, appeals may be made to large publics. Issues are carried to ever larger groups, and the processes of discussion and decision have increased their tempo. There is a degree of national unity that is requisite for the functioning of the state and of economic processes. Modern life also requires speed of decision at many points. If large publics are to be consulted frequently

[25] R. G. Sproul in *Radio and Education* (Proceedings of the Institute for Education by Radio), University of Chicago Press, Chicago, 1935, p. 32.

in the maintenance of a democracy adapted to other aspects of modern life, and if diverse publics are to be unified, the radio was a most opportune invention.

E. Though speech over the radio is less personal than in face-to-face situations, it is obviously more so than appeals by printed words. Obviously television can be personal and dramatic. The wide experience of the average man with personal relationships gives to these a reality that far surpasses any impersonal stimulus. President Franklin D. Roosevelt was the first major dramatic radio speaker in politics. In his radio speech the day after the banks were closed in 1933, President Roosevelt instilled a widespread confidence that could not have been achieved by written proclamation. During his first year in office he addressed 38,000 words to approximately 60 million listeners. Radio brought a reemphasis upon the appeal of speech for persuasion. Twenty years later President Eisenhower's television appearances marked a new era.

During the 1930's much of the controversy between representatives of the press and of the radio centered on the division of advertising fees. Important though this was to the owners of newspapers and radio stations, the essential conflict was between written and spoken appeals. The authority of print was challenged by the persuasiveness of speech. Through long experience the rules of oratory have been more or less exactly formulated. The principles of effective radio speech have been less exactly stated. There are differences, however, which make it difficult to speak to an audience and into the microphone at the same time. It is possible to make a few generalizations about radio speaking. In addressing large publics it is desirable that the speaker should avoid local or sectional inflections and vocabulary. These distract and alienate a part of the listening public. Clarity is essential. "Radio talks seem to require more concrete illustration and more repetition, apparently because the listener's mind is not acting as creatively as in the face-to-face situation." [26] In radio speech, simplicity is at a premium. Of President Roosevelt, it was said, "He speaks right out with no 'high-falutin' words. There is not much chance of Americans failing to get the meaning in such expressions as 'killing two birds with one stone'; 'we cannot ballyhoo ourselves back to prosperity'; 'the kind of prosperity that will lead us into another tail spin'; 'I have no expectation of making a hit every time I come to bat.'" [27] Brevity is requisite. Radio listeners are more readily tired than is an audience that can occupy itself with the personal characteristics of a speaker. In oratory, the finer shadings of emotional expression are in part

[26] H. Cantril and G. W. Allport, *The Psychology of Radio*, Harper & Brothers, New York, 1935, p. 157.
[27] O. E. Dunlap, *New York Times Mag.*, June 18, 1933, p. 17.

presented by facial expression and gesture. The radio speaker must cultivate a greater variety of tone and inflection to communicate these. Television not only brought the facial image to the viewer, but frequently a
magnified, close-up image, thus modifying once more the techniques of
speaking. Emotional appeals can be made in radio speaking, but the
technique differs from that of the orator. In the early days of the radio,
commentators declared that the demagogue was outmoded. Since then we
have had many radio demagogues. The traditional tricks of platform
demagoguery were largely outmoded, but new types of demagogues,
implemented with new varieties of emotional appeal, have appeared.
However, in general, radio speaking has been characterized by more
frequent appeals to logical thinking than has popular oratory. Political
controversy over the radio has appeared to have a more rational tone
than had the oratorical efforts of spellbinders swinging round the circle.

F. The successful operation of political democracy depends largely
upon the interest and intelligence of the electorate and upon close contact between the voters and their chosen executives. Commentators agree
that there has been some increased interest in political discussion and in
public affairs since the popularization of broadcasting. Persons who are
not politically minded will not become so immediately after buying a
receiving set. However, many people who would not go to a political
meeting do tune in on some political talks. It is probable that a part of
the increase in voting in national elections may be ascribed to interest
aroused by radio talks and to the broadcasting of nominating conventions. Of course, the emotion-arousing nature of the issues in most of the
campaigns since 1932 is primarily responsible for the widespread popular
interest, but radio and television discussion of these issues was an important stimulant.

Increased contact with national and state leaders and a greater familiar-
ity with certain political processes have resulted from broadcasting. Not
only can the political executive explain his position to listeners, but he
can bring and has brought pressure to bear on the legislative branches
through an aroused popular response. Moreover, men of influence and
ability, other than political leaders, have been induced to talk over the
radio and television. Such men, often unaccustomed to public speaking,
would be unwilling to face large audiences. Such increased contact with
leaders can promote the ends of dictators and authoritarians but may
also vivify the democratic process. Interest in political functioning is stimulated by the broadcasting of political events and meetings, especially of
the nominating conventions. Some dramatization of events inevitably
occurs. The public functioning of personalities is highlighted. But radio
audiences are isolated as individuals and small groups. Although emotional appeals may be made over the radio and television, there can be

no arousal of the mob feeling characteristic of the traditional political rally.

G. Owing largely to the broadcasting media, local influences are increasingly transcended in politics. Important speeches are heard in every section of the country and by all classes of people. Local and sectional appeals are decreased. Of the local leaders in Middletown, the Lynds stated years ago, "These men own Middletown's jobs and they largely own Middletown's press. . . . The one important channel of communication which they could not control was the national radio networks, which brought the other side before local voters, notably in President Roosevelt's own speeches." [28] Since then local influences have been superseded more and more by radio and television.

BROADCASTING SYSTEMS

The system of commercial broadcasting is best adapted to the political and business culture of the United States. However, the commercial ownership and control of this utility may properly be somewhat limited by national governmental regulation and by some noncommercial broadcasting stations competing for the public's interest. In the Communications Act of 1934, the FCC was instructed to determine whether the Congress should by statute allocate fixed percentages of radio facilities to noncommercial stations. Some had in mind the reservation of 25 per cent of the channels for noncommercial broadcasting, so as to safeguard the interests of cultural minorities and assure the presentation of programs of less than mass appeal. "But the Commission decided otherwise. Commercial stations, it said, are now responsible, under the law, to render a public service, and the tendency of the proposal would be to lessen this responsibility. . . . In order for non-profit organizations to obtain the maximum service possible, cooperation in good faith by the broadcasters is required." [29] Apparently the FCC then believed that the commercial broadcasters would engage more extensively in public service broadcasting reflecting the interests of cultural minorities than has proved to be the case. Moreover, the Commission must have anticipated that it would have a much greater indirect influence on broadcasting content than has been true since 1935. The FCC as a regulatory agency has licensing power and must renew or deny a radio station license every three years. The Federal Communications Act, Section 301, states, "It is the purpose of this Act, among other things, to maintain the control of the United

---

[28] R. S. Lynd and H. M. Lynd, *Middletown in Transition*, Harcourt, Brace and Company, Inc., New York, 1937, p. 361.

[29] C. A. Siepmann, *Radio, Television and Society*, Oxford University Press, New York, 1950, p. 22.

States over all the channels of interstate and foreign radio transmission, and to provide for the use of such channels, but not the ownership thereof, by persons for limited periods of time, under licenses granted by Federal Authority, and no such license shall be construed to create any right, beyond the terms, conditions and periods of the license." Hence, private companies do not, in any irrevocable sense, "own" the air. But in the years after the act the ownership of radio stations and chains became important business with large capital investments which it came to be considered unwise to jeopardize. Or indeed to threaten. When the Commission published the *Blue Book* in 1946 (*The Public Service Responsibility of Broadcast Licensees*), in which some content analysis of existing programs was presented and some recommendations made for bettered public service, a storm of protest arose from the broadcasting industry. The Commission was accused of exceeding its powers. But the Commission was intended to be a judicial agency reviewing the record of licensees when the license came up for renewal. In any case, the Commission, since 1946, has failed to publish annually those statistical summaries and trends of the content of radio programs which were promised by the *Blue Book*. Apparently the spotlight of publicity is to be used sparingly as a pressure device.

The problem of the representation of cultural minorities by making available suitable programs has not been solved for radio. Radio has never fully exploited its enormous potentialities. As primarily an advertising medium, it has aimed its programs at the largest mass audiences and almost ignored selected audiences. In the British system, the "Third Program Service" is made up of serious offerings for those who enjoy talks, fine music, elaborate information and educational programs, and discussions. In the United States, we have failed to produce its equivalent, in spite of the undoubted excellence of a few programs from time to time on the major national networks. The educational and other subsidized stations in the United States are too poor and have too limited facilities adequately to perform this function. And in general they do not have the professional skills to present properly such program content in competition with commercial radio. As FM has allowed for extensive development of frequencies, the technical problem of limited space is not so pressing. About 10 per cent of FM allocations of stations is available for noncommercial stations and, actually, about 20 per cent of FM stations on the air are educational stations. There should be chains of educational broadcasting stations properly supported, perhaps by endowment, and the interesting experiment of foundation-supported programs on the commercial stations might be vastly extended. In these and other programs paralleling the commercial radio some very much needed diversification of program content might be achieved. Vigorous competition could change considerably the existing content of commercial radio and television. The industry can be expected to continue to oppose such competition. The structure of a possibly effective noncommercial broadcasting system to parallel commercial entertainment-oriented mass-appeal programs has not yet been created. At present, though the commission has made no commitment as to the percentage of TV channels which will continue to be available to noncommercial stations, it has allocated 257 channels for noncommercial use. However, the high cost of television broadcasting prevents much educational development until some assured financing can be provided.

Of course, commercial broadcasters want audiences who are also potential consumers of the sponsors' products. When the primary objective is the creation of an audience which is likely to be influenced by advertising, then the programing is basically oriented toward a mass audience. The programs are directed toward the entertaining and satisfying of mass audiences and not toward educating and culturally elevating them. Commercial radio generally considers the "public interest" as whatever interests the public. The commercial radio system of the United States does not displease mass audiences, though it often outrages cultivated minorities. Moreover, the American people could not be persuaded to entrust radio to a central corporation responsible to the national government, as is the BBC in Britain. This would be most especially true if such a corporation were avowedly committed to the cultural cultivation of the listening and viewing public. It has been said that the faults of radio are the faults of the American people, so nearly is its content tailored to the values and interests of mass audiences. True, but the audiences cannot envisage the diversity of radio content and the widening of interests which could be available to them. Until they experience not only samples of such programs but a protracted education in appreciation of more complex and diversified programs, audiences have no idea of what they might come to like. This, then, is the dilemma. Commercial radio cannot afford, and is not motivated to, extensive and protracted experimentation in program types a step beyond present audience tastes. Noncommercial radio thus far has generally lacked the opportunity, the money, the skills and the professional standards to innovate extensively except in providing good music, which commercial radio was already doing in considerable amount. Moreover, audience response has usually been disappointingly slow in arriving at a more cultivated level.

While declining responsibility for the cultivation of modified cultural values among the general listening public, the industry has stoutly claimed that it is satisfying the existing mass cultural taste of the United States. "Radio has taken its stand: everything it does, from analytical newscasts to giveaways and symphony concerts, is in the public interest;

when the daytime serial—one of its most vulnerable services—is under fire, it is defended not primarily as a diversion but as a lesson in living, an alleviation of the anxieties of the audience." [30] But, as to the cultivation of new tastes and values, Mark Ethridge, president of the National Association of Broadcasters in 1938, said: "It is utterly futile to expect of radio that it can, or should, elevate the cultural level of the United States except by slow projection of new techniques and new ideas. Culture is not something that can be turned on, like water out of a spigot, by the mere command to turn it on. Culture is a slow development of a people who reflect their tastes through media which they support."

On the other hand, the government-controlled British Broadcasting Corporation assumes responsibility, its first Director-General declaring that: "The BBC must carry into the greatest possible number of homes everything that is best in every department of human endeavor and achievement." During the first three decades of its existence, the BBC attempted to mix entertainment and culture so as to raise progressively the public taste. Yet many who have worked in the BBC for many years have not been satisfied with the results. The BBC's cultural programs are said by many discerning critics to be the most intelligent features in the world in providing popular education in literature, science and the social studies. Yet others, declaring that the BBC is stifled in bureaucracy, assert that these programs are too schoolmasterish and are dominated by the educational standards of BBC directors who are molded by experience in the Oxford and Cambridge tradition. Certainly the BBC has not been journalistic in its serious approach to cultural programs. But, apparently, the British public is not too restive in its response to BBC's educational and informational programs. In the United States there is a much greater lack of respect for the values of cultivated minorities, and the listening public would not contentedly submit to enlightenment.

In Australia, there is a dual system of publicly controlled *A* stations and commercially controlled *B* stations. This system attempts not only to placate private enterprise and satisfy the protagonists of public control, but it also attempts through competition to lighten the culture and caution of the government-controlled stations. In practice, this system has not worked as well as it would appear to promise, but that is in part due to the relative poverty of the stations, not to the nature of the system. Theoretically, from competitive diversity there is the greatest promise of enrichment of program content.

In Table 23 we have compiled brief statements concerning the ownership, control and advertising practices of the radio systems of some

---

[30] G. Seldes, *The Great Audience*, The Viking Press, New York, 1950, p. 108.

Table 23. Radio Systems of Selected Countries

Country	Ownership	Control	Advertising	Transmitters (number of)	Population (thousands)
Canada (year of survey, 1950)	CBC—publicly owned corporation. 132 privately owned stations, about 40 owned or controlled by newspapers. National broadcasting reserved to the CBC. Private stations serve localities in which situated.	CBC has board of 9 members, appointed by Governor-General in Council, chosen to give geographic representation. CBC exercises regulatory function over private stations.	CBC revenue from license fees (both receiving and private broadcasting licenses) and commercial broadcasts. Private stations financed entirely by advertising.	194 (146 standard band transmitters with total power of 747.9 kw).	12,902
United States of America (year of survey, 1950)	Private ownership, except less than a hundred noncommercial stations.	No listening tax or fee. No governmental control over programs. Federal Communications Commission, seven Commissioners, appointed by President with advice and consent of Senate, assigns frequencies, classifies stations, issues construction permits and operation licenses.	Except for noncommercial stations and U.S. government's Voice of America international broadcasts, broadcasting supported entirely by advertising.	2,973. (Total power of 2,075 AM stations 6,810.9 kw.)	150,697
Mexico (year of survey, 1948)	4 stations owned and controlled by the State. 210 commercial stations.	Government grants concessions to private companies to certain wave lengths—for a period of 50 years, but revocable. Each broadcasting company supervised by an official of the Ministry of Communications, whose salary is paid by the company concerned. (New broadcasting legislation being studied in 1950.)	Commercial stations derive revenue entirely from advertising.	4 government stations, with power of 8.55 kw. 210 private stations with total power of about 1,160 kw.	23,434
Brazil (year of survey, 1948)	Private and State-owned stations. 247, private; 7, official.	Operation concessions are granted by decree and are valid for 10 years at the most. Contract by which beneficiary undertakes to obey laws and regulations in force.	Revenues derived from advertising by both private and official companies. Some official broadcasting organizations of an educational and cultural nature do not broadcast any commercial advertisements.	80, plus 164 of 1 kw power or less. Total power of 728.34 kw.	47,550
Argentina (year of survey, 1949)	State-owned (9) and private (55). Private stations largely in three networks. Only 8 independent stations left in 1949.	Operation concessions granted by Ministry of Telecommunications; granted provisionally and may be withdrawn. All stations controlled by Directorate-General of Broadcasting, attached to Postal Department of Ministry of Post and Telecommunications. Directorate responsible for censoring broadcasts and ordering stations to link up for transmission of official programs.	Commercial advertising only revenue source for private stations.	64. (Total power of 748.4 kw.)	16,109
United Kingdom (year of survey, 1950)	The capital of the BBC is owned by corporations, companies and individuals. Income of the BBC is derived from license fees (1 sound, 2 sound and vision) and from government grants (all international broadcasting so subsidized).	Seven governors appointed by Queen in Council, for a term of five years, not eligible for reappointment, save in special circumstances.	Since the 1936 agreement, broadcasting of sponsored programs, as well as of advertisements, is forbidden.	28 domestic, 33 overseas. Total power of 4,812 kw.	48,682

471

Table 23. Radio Systems of Selected Countries (Continued)

Country (year of survey)	System	Control	Finance	Stations	Population
France (years of survey, 1947 and 1948)	Government. Some private stations before the war, but after liberation the government assumed control.	Prime Minister's Office.	None. License fees on receivers.	53, total power of 2,670.0 kw.	41,000
Italy (year of survey, 1948)	*Radio Italiana* is a limited company, originally almost all shares owned by one company. Since the war, this company has been indirectly controlled by the government, since the majority of the shares are held by the Institute for Industrial Reconstruction whose capital is entirely subscribed by Treasury.	Appointment of Chairman of RAI approved by the Minister of Posts and Telegraphs with agreement of government. Programs and news broadcasts are supervised: (1) by a parliamentary commission consisting of 17 members chosen from all parliamentary parties and appointed by the Speaker; (2) by a committee, consisting of representatives of the Ministries.	RAI's concession stipulates that not more than 1/10th of total broadcasting schedule shall be devoted to publicity. No advertising may accompany news broadcasts. Other sources of revenue: License fees on receiving sets; taxes on manufacture of wireless apparatus and accessories.	30, total power of 1,028 kw.	45,000
Sweden (year of survey, 1949)	Private monopoly: *Aktiebolaget Radiojänst*. Joint-stock company, with ⅔ capital subscribed by the press and ⅓ by representatives of the radio industry.	State and private interests represented. *Radiojänst* controlled by a Broadcasting Board, consisting of a Chairman and 6 members. The Chairman and 3 members are appointed by the King and the other 3 by the shareholders; two by the press and one by the radio industry.	None. License fees collected. The government grants *Radiojänst* the funds necessary for its operation.	35 with total power of 623.67 kw.	6,803
India (year of survey, 1948)	State monopoly.	Organized on pattern of BBC, directly controlled by the Government of India through the Ministry of Information and Broadcasting.	None. Funds voted annually by Parliament, part derived by license fees on receiving sets.	465 with total power of 354.85 kw.	338,727
Japan (year of survey, 1951)	National corporation and private stations.	Radio Regulatory Commission: President and six members appointed by the Prime Minister, with consent of both Houses of the Diet.	Private stations entirely dependent on advertising. NHK budget passed each year by the Diet, income derived from license fees.	123 with total power of 485.65 kw.	78,627
Australia (year of survey, 1950)	Public Corporation owns the national system. ABC's main source of revenue is the annual budget voted by Parliament. Other stations privately owned. Of the 102 private stations, 44 are partly or entirely controlled by the press.	Australian Broadcasting Board, responsible to the Postmaster-General, controls all broadcasting in the country. Board consists of 3 members appointed by Governor-General of the Commonwealth for term of seven years. Australian Broadcasting Commission, seven members appointed for 3-yr. terms, responsible for planning and producing national programs in harmony with the public interest.	Commercial stations supported by advertising.	52 publicly owned, with a total power of about 500 kw. 102 private stations totaling about 70 kw	7,581

SOURCE: Information compiled from the Reports of the Commission on Technical Needs in *Press, Film, Radio*; UNESCO, 1947–1951 and two Supplements. Population figures taken from *United Nations Demographic Yearbook*, 1948, Table 3, pp. 98 ff.

472

selected countries. The Russian system is not included because of the lack of adequate dependable statistics and descriptions of its operation.[31]

With the development of television, radio lost its glamor but not all of its functions. By 1955 radio was in grave difficulties, but finding some new aims and functions. In a sense, radio broadcasting was a transitional stage between wireless telegraphy and television broadcasting. Radio should continue to perform a useful function, especially in the broadcasting of music, in informational programs, in news reports and analyses which do not require images, and in various cultural programs which are not enhanced by the addition of pictures. Despite the continued growth of television and the general reduction of radio income, it would seem that radio has a permanent and important place in American life. Though radio networks were in difficulties a few years after the popularization of TV, many local stations were flourishing. Illustrative of radio's decline: "In 1949 radio's highest-rated show, the Lux Radio Theatre, reached 11 million homes. In March, 1955, again the highest-rated show, it reached 3 million homes. Between 1948 and 1954 network time sales dipped from $137.5 million to $76 million. In that time TV advertising went from practically zero to $320.1 million." [32] In the same period many local stations retained and increased their audiences. The new pattern of radio listening was to turn on small radio sets in the morning or late evening, or in the car (26 per cent of all receiving sets), or while working around the house. Local stations providing inexpensive programs of recorded music, news and sports were maintaining large audiences. But the center of broadcasting had passed to the television systems, and radio, though still significant, had become a second-class power. Nonetheless, CBS reports that in 1954 Americans spent over a billion dollars to maintain their radios and to purchase 10 million additional sets.

One important use of radio to influence opinion is the international broadcasting of propaganda to influence the opinions of publics abroad. After the mid-1930's a propaganda war by international broadcasting was carried on by Nazi Germany, Fascist Italy, Communist Russia and then by Great Britain and, after the beginning of World War II, by the United States. The history of these international propaganda efforts, the technical problems of international allocation and maintenance of wave lengths in such conflict situations, and the issues of such international psychological invasions are questions of such scope that I cannot attempt even a summary discussion in this volume.[33] But such broadcasting has been

[31] For a description of radio in the U.S.S.R. some years ago, see Alex Inkeles, "Domestic Broadcasting in the USSR," in P. F. Lazarsfeld and F. N. Stanton (eds.), *Radio Research, 1948–1949*, Harper & Brothers, New York, 1949, pp. 223–297.

[32] *Time*, May 9, 1955.

[33] This is the subject matter of a portion of another volume to be entitled *International Communications*.

one of the most important political uses of the radio for many years. Countering such broadcasts is done chiefly by "jamming" the signals of the invading radio stations. It is reported that over 1,000 Soviet transmitters are intermittently used to "jam" the signals of the United States and that the Kremlin spends more on "jamming" than is expended by the United States on all the operations of the "Voice of America." Owing to the short range of television receiving sets in the areas of greatest political tensions at crucial international boundaries, international television is not yet an important political issue, but it will no doubt become so in the near future.

TELEVISION—A NEW DIMENSION

Television cannot be compared and evaluated simply in terms of radio or, indeed, of the motion picture. Television creates contact with the viewers many times as extensive as the motion pictures have had, in that a viewer may average several hours a day before a television set as compared to one weekly film experience. Television provides immediate accessibility in the home and of course adds images to the sound of radio. Therefore, TV brings a new dimension to communication by mass media. The ways of weaving together vast modern publics are of central concern to democrats and authoritarians alike. Mass literacy and plentiful printed materials, motion pictures, radio and, now, television have each added a new dimension. But attitudes toward the process of communication diffusion differ. Publics are to be woven together with strands of what texture and content, how tightly and to what ends? The purposes vary from those of an old-fashioned liberal, earnestly hoping to use the media to diffuse rationality in public affairs, to a Madison Avenue researcher on publicity, making psychological depth studies as a base for a national advertising campaign, or to an avowed authoritarian Minister of Propaganda, utilizing all channels for special pleading. How exclusively is commercial television to be used to the end of stimulating the economic process so that this central value of our culture shall not be lessened or weakened? How extensively can TV be used for the development of cultural, moral and social values? Which values and chosen by whom? On these questions much competition, controversy and compromise must yet occur. It is important that the attitudes of the combatants should not be cynical and should be basically well intentioned toward the maintenance of personality integrity in the mass viewers.

Utopian expectations that TV in the United States will shortly revolutionize the mind-life of publics by elevating tastes, educating, politically informing, refining and making more complex the standards and values of viewers are doomed to disappointment. For the innovations are necessarily slow since television's mass audiences start with a low common denominator of understanding and interest. Yet some very good programs have already been presented by the networks, programs on popular science, cultural history, anthropology, and the like. Television has enormous vitality and could provide extensive adult education, as well as gradually enlightened entertainment.

In any case, television is the most potent instrument devised in the history of communication. The impact of television has been evaluated as three times that of radio. Television is intimate and personal. It offers the opportunity for face-to-face contact to millions simultaneously. And it provides, in the TV close-ups with faces portraying emotions and emitting words and sounds, more direct contact than a play or a motion picture. It appears to me that this intimacy may be even closer than that in personal contact, inasmuch as the viewer may concentrate on perception of the faces on the screen without his attention being divided by a concern about the impression he might be making on his companion. And television faces are, at least as yet, more mobile than the made-up masks of most Hollywood actresses. In a sense, TV is less demanding on the mind than is radio. It is so much easier to look than to listen. With the TV stimuli the extent to which the audience attends to the sounds as well as the views is a problem which has not yet been adequately described experimentally. It may be that a large part of the audience is relaxing gratefully before the pictures, being somewhat inattentive to the sounds, and as idle viewers giving their imagination rest.

Television is the practically instantaneous reproduction at a distance of sound and pictures transmitted by electronic means. While the effective range of television broadcasting by radio waves is a relatively few miles, the transmission of signals by relays and rebroadcasting permits television broadcasting over large areas. A long series of discoveries and inventions made regular commercial television broadcasts practicable. Although some telecasting had occurred during the 1920's, it was in 1931 that RCA installed the first television transmitter on the Empire State Building in New York. Television broadcasts for the general public in the United States began on April 30, 1939.[34] Commercial telecasting was first approved by the FCC for July, 1941, after a protracted controversy over the number of lines to be used in standard broadcasting (settled at 525 lines). However, broadcasting in any amount was not practicable until after the war. By 1950 over a hundred stations had made television broadcasts available to over half the population of the country, although there were at that time only 10 million receiving sets. After that time the number of stations and of receiving sets increased rapidly. In round numbers, there were 16

[34] For a sketch of the development of television in the United States, as well as in other countries, see UNESCO's *Report on Television, a World Survey,* Paris, 1953.

million sets in 1951; 27 million in 1953, 40 million in 1955 and, projecting the development in terms of production and probable market, it is estimated that there will be 75 million receiving sets in 1960. The network organization of stations expanded rapidly. Although no more than five stations were permitted to be owned outright by a single network, the independently owned but affiliated stations soon numbered scores. In Table 24 the network affiliates of the first few years are shown. (The figures

Table 24. TV Networks and Number of Affiliates

Date	ABC-TV	CBS-TV	Du Mont	NBC-TV
1955	217	209	158	190
1954	201	182	213	183
1953	143	128	133	113
1952	63	62	62	64
1951	64	61	62	63
1949	42	46	45	46

SOURCE: 1951–1956, *Telecasting Yearbook-Marketbook;* 1949, Television Broadcaster Association, *Status of the Television Industry.*

given are for midsummer. As of December 10, 1955, Du Mont no longer had network affiliates.) In 1954 the total number of stations on the air was 381, but the total number of network-affiliated stations is greater than the total number of stations, because in markets where there are only one or two stations they affiliate with more than one network so as to provide diversity of programs. There were some noncommercial stations. In 1955 there were 13 educational stations on the air and 11 under construction. When the FCC made its allocations in 1952, it reserved 242 channels, about 11 per cent of the total, for noncommercial stations, and in 1955, some 257 channels were being held for educational stations. The Commission is not committed to reserve these channels indefinitely. An educational station costs from $100,000 to $250,000 to install and about the same amount each year to operate; amounts not beyond the budgets of a considerable number of educational institutions.

In its first few years television had already become a great advertising medium. By 1953 the advertising expenditures in sponsoring television programs were already over $600 million, or some 8.8 per cent of the total of advertising in the United States. In 1951 some 20 per cent of the advertising was about food products; 14 per cent, smoking materials; 13 per cent, toiletries; 9 per cent, soaps and cleansers; 9 per cent, automotive products; 7 per cent, household equipment and supplies; 5 per cent, beer and wine, and the remainder scattered among a number of products.[35]

Television is costly; the equipment, the programing, the cost of broadcasting are all very high in comparison to radio. With all the limitations of the number, quality and variety of the sustaining programs of radio, nonetheless, they did exist, sometimes in the amount of 50 per cent of the programs, and were supported by stations and networks. The huge costs of TV have made the problem of providing noncommercial programs, that is, those without sufficient assured audience to attract sponsors, much more complicated. Inexpensive programs from universities and museums and foundation-sponsored programs cannot be expected to provide permanently a sufficient number of cultural programs. Can commercial broadcasting alone support the legitimate wants of diffuse publics? Again and again we meet the basic conflicting attitudes. Are publics simply to be used to commercial ends? Is their time so precious to the commercial broadcaster that he resents any parallel noncommercial program development which might be produced by education or foundations on noncommercial stations? Or when nonadvertising sponsorship buys time on commercial stations? Or even when commercial but nonadvertising programs are proposed, such as the projected supplying of movies and other programs on subscription TV or Phonevision without advertising? This is an issue which will long be fought out in the United States.

We are committed to a fundamental value in the United States. That is the maximum production and distribution of all kinds of economic goods including ever-increasing amounts of consumers' goods. In this process, all channels of persuasion, all audience attention, are precious. Mass publics must not let down or deviate from the stern necessity of ever more consumption. Those who would espouse noncommercial values in such a culture complex are on the defensive and should not be surprised when vigorously attacked. In some degree, intellectual deviants from the commercial core of American society are perennially suspect. Those who would use and exploit such values as exist and those who would stress modified, amplified, diverse and more mature values are in conflict. It is not only that the cultural programs might develop a loyal audience and subvert the purity of the values of a business civilization, but, more immediately, that the noncommercial programs compete for the precious attention of mass audiences.

A national policy for TV must somehow compromise these values. Amidst the competition for the minds of men today the advertiser must

[35] UNESCO, *op. cit.*, p. 67.

be allowed a major sector of the mass media in which to cry his wares, but should not be allowed practically exclusive control of any medium. The advertiser does not so control the press. In TV, the broadcasters, station owners and the networks, under the stipulated supervision of the FCC, should develop TV policy, programing and planning, rather than allow the advertiser to do it for them. Essentially, commercial TV, with all its faults, is the only practicable system in the economic and political organization of the United States. But a pluralistic system, including, along with commercial broadcasting, varieties of subscription TV, of educational, foundation-sponsored and other types of stations and programs, would best assure the maximum competition and diversity of program content. Concentration of influence and cultural uniformity are current trends in American life, so that it is ever more important to assure as much diversity as possible in the program offerings of television. However, because diversely sponsored programs increase, commercial TV should not be permitted to abdicate from its position as a supplier of sustaining programs of cultural significance. "Public interest, convenience and necessity" are not merely phrases to which to pay mock homage or to cynically disregard or to flout.

THE CONTENT OF TELEVISION

Viewers watch television to be entertained and, occasionally, to be instructed, if the instruction is interesting. Thus the recipients of television spend leisure hours rather effortlessly and passively. Families with television sets operate the sets more than 4 hours a day (4 hours and 46 minutes on the average per day in 1954). Television provides personality contact to the lonely and otherwise isolated adults; provides some fashions and modes for emulation by the adolescent; offers much musical entertainment, drama and public affairs for all; wins the loyalty of the grade-school set with action dramas; and, indeed, may even center the vagrant interest of the preschool child for short periods. While the gregarious young receive from television numerous models for social behavior, its screen may be of even greater importance as a refuge for the lonely isolate, the rejected or frustrated young person. Indeed, one study reports, "In the upper middle class the children who are highly frustrated in their current home life (subject to many restrictions and not treated permissively or warmly) spend the most time viewing television programs." [36]

For whatever reasons viewers turn to TV, however much and however attentively they look and listen, what has been available for them to see and hear? About 20 per cent, or one out of five minutes of viewing time,

[36] E. Maccoby, "Why Do Children Watch Television?" *Pub. Opin. Quar.*, 18: 2: 239–244.

they have been seeing and listening to advertising. Aside from this advertising content, there have been a number of content studies of television, using various classifications of gross categories of content. Into these categories monitors distributed the programs in terms of the amount of time for each program. At the end of the sampling, percentages of the total time were calculated. The most extensive and thorough studies were planned and directed by Dallas Smythe for the National Association of Educational Broadcasters. These studies used a full week of viewing as the sample.[37]

In a report on TV broadcasting for 1954, directed by H. H. Remmers, there appears a highly detailed table which includes not only the results for that year but also the content studies directed by Dallas Smythe for the preceding three years. From this source we have simplified and compiled Table 25.

Studies based on a much simpler classification scheme than that used in Table 25 are summarized in Table 26, prepared by Dallas Smythe. It may be noted that the percentages of program content by categories in a small city station (Champaign, Illinois) do not vary greatly from those of New York, Los Angeles and Chicago. Grouping the types of programs, 74 per cent consisted of entertainment-type programs in Champaign as compared to 77 per cent for New York; information-type programs were 19 per cent in Champaign and 17 per cent in New York; and orientation-type programs were 7 per cent in Champaign and 5 per cent in New York. Entertainment- and information-type programs are self-explanatory, orientation-type programs are those in which affecting attitudes and values was the predominant manifest interest. Though the percentages of program type are nearly identical, obviously the number and variety of programs available in each category in the small Middle Western town with one channel was very small in comparison to the comparatively extensive fare (7 channels) available in the New York area. The program classifications are largely self-explanatory, though one might mention that within the large percentage of time devoted to drama in New

[37] Content studies of television not only for the New York area, but also for Los Angeles and New Haven have been made since 1950 by Dallas W. Smythe. The sources are: Dallas W. Smythe and Angus Campbell, *Los Angeles Television, May 23–29, 1951*, National Association of Educational Broadcasters, Urbana, Ill., 1951; Dallas W. Smythe, with introduction by Robert K. Merton, *New York Television, January 4–10, 1951–1952*, National Association of Educational Broadcasters, Urbana, Ill., 1952; Dallas W. Smythe, *New Haven Television, May 15–21, 1952*, National Association of Educational Broadcasters, Urbana, Ill., 1952; Dallas W. Smythe, *Three Years of New York Television, 1951–1953*, National Association of Educational Broadcasters, Urbana, Ill., 1953. In addition one study was conducted with noncomparable concepts: Donald Horton, Hans O. Mauksch, and Kurt Lang, *Chicago Summer Television, July 30–Aug. 5, 1951*, National Association of Educational Broadcasters, Urbana, Ill., 1952.

Table 25. New York Television

Per cent of total time in various program classes

Type and Class	1954 (39,766 min.), per cent	1953 (39,104 min.), per cent	1952 (37,645 min.), per cent	1951 (33,837 min.), per cent
Entertainment type				
Children's programs......................	0.1	0.0	0.1	0.1
Comedy, not in drama or variety format.....	0.4	a	a	a
Dance...................................	0.0	0.1	0.0	0.1
Drama, all..............................	46.2	47.0	42.4	33.2
Action and adventure drama............	5.1	4.3	3.2	4.1
Classics..............................	0.2	0.9	0.8	0.7
Comedy...............................	11.1	6.0	4.3	5.3
Crime................................	13.5	15.3	15.1	10.0
Fairy tales...........................	0.6	0.1	0.1	0.8
Family relations, non-serial.............	0.8	3.1	4.0	1.1
Historical............................	0.5	a	a	a
Musical...............................	1.1	1.4	0.8	0.3
Romance..............................	2.2	5.1	4.3	5.7
Serial, domestic.......................	1.3	2.7	a	a
Western...............................	7.1	7.3	8.3	7.8
Other drama..........................	2.7	0.1	1.4	0.4
Fine arts, all............................	0.2	0.3	0.1	0.1
Music, all...............................	6.9	4.4	4.2	3.6
Light music...........................	0.3	0.0	0.0	0.0
Music and patter......................	3.5	2.2	a	a
Popular music.........................	2.6	2.0	3.7	3.4
Serious music.........................	0.5	0.2	0.5	0.2
Personalities............................	4.8	2.7	2.3	4.2
Quiz contests, all.......................	5.1	5.6	7.0	7.2
Experts, guests........................	2.1	3.6	2.0	1.1
Studio audiences......................	1.8	1.1	2.5	1.8
Talent................................	0.8	0.1	0.7	0.3
Telephone............................	0.4	0.5	1.1	2.8
Recreation and participation sports..........	0.0	0.2	0.4	0.2
Sports events, spectator...................	3.4	5.3	6.8	9.2
Variety..................................	11.0	11.8	10.9	18.4
Total, entertainment..................	77.7	77.7	74.2	76.3
Information type				
Information, all..........................	9.2	12.8	11.3	11.8
Arts, crafts, hobbies....................	0.8	0.5	1.1	0.2
Cooking..............................	2.1	2.8	2.0	2.9
Nature................................	0.5	a	a	a
Personal care..........................	1.5	1.4	3.6	3.3
Science...............................	0.4	0.2	0.2	0.3
Shopping and merchandising.............	1.3	1.4	3.6	3.3

Table 25. New York Television (Continued)

Per cent of total time in various program classes

Type and Class	1954 (39,766 min.), per cent	1953 (39,104 min.), per cent	1952 (37,645 min.), per cent	1951 (33,837 min.), per cent
Information type (Cont.)				
Travel...............................	0.8	0.7	0.9	1.1
Other information......................	1.8	1.5	2.0	2.6
News.................................	6.1	6.6	5.9	5.5
Sports news...........................	1.5	1.3	1.2	0.7
Weather..............................	0.7	0.5	0.4	0.4
Total, information....................	17.4	16.8	18.8	18.4
Orientation type				
Personal relations......................	0.7	0.5	1.0	0.2
Public events..........................	0.0	0.0	1.4	0.9
Public institutional programs..............	0.6	1.2	1.6	1.1
Public issues..........................	1.8	1.5	1.9	1.4
Religion..............................	1.8	1.7	1.0	0.2
Total, orientation.....................	4.9	5.5	7.0	5.4

NOTE: An "a" in the table indicates that comparable data are not available for that year.

SOURCE: This table is compiled from the studies made for the National Association of Educational Broadcasters, published by the Association, Gregory Hall, University of Illinois, Urbana, Ill. Each year's study was based on the monitoring of one entire week. The organization of the studies and the direction of the studies for 1951, 1952 and 1953 was the work of Dallas W. Smythe, past Research Director for the FCC and for some years Professor of Economics and in the Institute of Communications, University of Illinois, Urbana, Ill. The study for 1954 was directed by The Purdue Opinion Panel, H. H. Remmers, Director.

York the largest categories were crime drama (15 per cent) and Western dramas (7 per cent). However, the proportion of time given to the various types of programs can be expected to continue to change rather rapidly in this unsettled industry.

SOME FURTHER INFLUENCES OF TELEVISION ON OPINIONS

As we have already noted, radio and television have vastly increased the speed and diffusion of communication, thus stimulating the tempo of the opinion process. And local influences are increasingly transcended by the standard broadcast content. Moreover, these media may be used for mass education, thus dignifying the opinions of the individual mind, or they may be used for mass indoctrination by propaganda. Certainly

Table 26. Per Cent of Total TV Time by Program Types

Program Class	Champaign-Urbana 1955	New Haven 1952	New York 1953	New York 1952	New York 1951	Los Angeles 1951	Chicago 1951
News.....................	6.6	12.6	6.6	5.9	5.5	12.2	5.0
Weather.................	1.3	0.4	0.5	0.4	0.4	0.6	0.7
Public issues.............	1.1	1.4	1.5	1.9	1.4	1.1	1.8
Public events.............	1.5	0	0	1.4	0.9	0.1	0.0
Public institutional........	1.4	3.4	1.2	1.6	1.1	1.6	1.6
Information (general)......	6.0	2.2	2.3	2.9	3.3	2.6	2.0
Religion..................	1.2	0.8	1.7	1.0	0.7	0.6	0.1
Drama (general)..........	31.3	24.3	43.1	35.7	25.4	25.6	26.2
Dance...................	0	0	0.1	0	0.1	0.0	0.0
Music...................	2.2	3.9	2.2	4.2	3.6	6.1	3.0
Fine arts................	0	0	0.3	0.1	0.1	0	0.3
Variety..................	10.6	15.1	3.5	6.2	13.6	9.7	8.8
Personalities.............	1.5	1.1	2.7	2.3	4.2	2.0	7.6
Quizzes, stunts and contests.	12.6	10.1	5.2	6.3	6.9	6.2	6.6
Sports..................	4.9	11.3	6.8	8.4	10.1	5.4	20.9
Domestic................	5.4	5.9	13.1	10.9	10.2	16.4	7.2
Children's programs.......	12.4	7.5	9.2	11.0	12.5	10.3	8.3
Total..............	100.0	100.0	100.0	100.0	100.0	100.0	100.0

SOURCE: This table was compiled by Dallas W. Smythe of the University of Illinois Institute of Communications. It is based on a number of his own pioneering studies in content analysis of television in the United States.

television inspires interest in many topics, though infrequently in the most important subjects in the public interest.

In television the association of the current symbolic personalities with the groups, abstractions and values which they have come to represent is more standardized than has been true of communication by word, picture or radio. Excessive identification of abstractions, groups and values with particular individuals who become symbols is always the too-ready response of large publics untutored in rational analysis of public issues. Trivial, oversimplified and vulgarly personalized impressions result. This is a strength of democratic decision making, in that it keeps the social process humanized and partially corrects or cancels the inhuman abstractions to which all specialists are prone. But personification also corrodes or inhibits more rational and analytical reflection on public issues. Television diffuses and standardizes personal images as no other agency has done. A televised cabinet meeting is not, and, for political reasons, could not be, a real working cabinet meeting. Therefore, the public is not watching responsible government in action, but a political show of humanized statesmen at play, though ostensibly at work. Is this in the public interest? A televised Presidential press conference is censored as a regular press conference is not. For example, the first televised press conference was edited to omit 11 of the 27 questions asked of the President. It was said that most of the omissions showed the President in his less favorable moments. Thus to the personification is added some politically inevitable distortion. Televised congressional committee hearings dramatize personal interaction between examiner and witness. The TV cameraman highlights conflict, as the newsman has highlighted it. Therefore, at times witnesses have been harassed and badgered and even libeled, with immunity for the congressional investigator. In protecting the rights of witnesses there will no doubt be developed some standards of fair play, some codes of procedure for at least the televised portions of such investigations. There are ever-new issues in satisfying the demand by television audiences for personalities, drama and conflict while keeping the distortions of reality within reasonable bounds.

Television broadcasting as a commodity strains against reasonable restrictions. The television record of an event may be modified in many ways, from inevitable technological bias (the capacities of a camera to encompass the total situation) to intentional distortion. The TV camera can structure an event for the viewer. Inevitably there is selection, emphasis and editing. There may be conscious, purposive distortion of the images by photographic news slanting. Indeed such slanting is not only in the direction of the biases of the broadcaster, but also in adapting to the expectations of the receivers. In the Chicago parade for General MacArthur in 1952, the TV camera reported excitement, enthusiasm and animation to a degree which observers scattered among the crowds did not see. By selected TV shots the audience was given the impressions which it had expected from this occasion.[38] Television may bring truth into the home, but it will not inevitably do so. Yet the correct assessment of the opinions of others, of the moods of crowds, audiences, participants in conventions, of a televised riot, a parade or other public occurrence is clearly important for significant popular opinion. Distortion of information occurs in all media, but may be less evident in television.

Television viewers are more interested in some aspects of politics than they had been before receiving pictured impressions. In the 1952 campaign some 59 per cent of the citizens who saw some of the campaign over television stated that TV was their most important source of information. Only 28 per cent declared the press as most important. The college graduates in the sample considered both radio and TV as of less import as a source of political information. In 1952 "I Love Lucy," the most popular TV show, had a Hooper rating in New York City of 62, while the national political conventions, briefly monopolizing 4 network

[38] K. Lang and G. Lang, "The Unique Perspective of Television and Its Effect; a Pilot Study," *Am. Soc. Rev.*, 18: 1: 10.

channels, scored 32 at the best moments and dwindled to 17 most of the time. Audiences soon tired of too much talking and just tuned in at the points of high drama.

If the political broadcaster is to compete with television's entertainment stars, he must develop broadcasting skills, use new techniques of gesture, of facial expression and speech and must have an intimate and winning approach. Not all estimable public figures have or can develop the necessary skills or have Robert Montgomery available as a coach. But statesmen must increasingly adapt to television and many are no doubt doing so to their own delighted surprise. However, irresponsible use of the medium can extend demagoguery as never before.

There are technical problems concerning the political use of television which appear far from solution. Who should be permitted to use television, for how long, at what cost and under what conditions of control? The Communications Act, in Section 315, provides that when a broadcaster gives time to one candidate he must afford equal opportunity to the opposition candidate for that office. And the station does not have the right to censor the candidate. However, controls over television programing in Section 315 have proved insufficient for this medium, having proved quite unsatisfactory in the 1952 national election campaigns. The issue as to granting time to "authorized spokesmen" for the candidates, how to handle "unauthorized spokesmen" serving as "hatchet" men to attack opposing candidates, and the questions as to the amount of time to be granted to candidates, and the like, need clarification and definition.[39]

Radio and television influence opinions on public issues, though they may but rarely influence any but the simplest behavior. Admonition to do simple things, to phone a message, to send in a letter, to write to a politician and the like may be carried out by considerable numbers of listeners. But in most discussions of public affairs, for example, an hour-long program on hoodlums in the longshoremen's union, a session about juvenile delinquency, a dramatic exposition on drug addiction, programs on crime, politics, or international affairs, the listener is usually left with some frustration, as no behavior is indicated whereby he may express his opinion or relieve his emotional tension. In contrast to this situation the pleading of commercial advertising is simple; the viewer should go out and buy the product.

Knowledge as to how television affects opinions and behavior is fragmentary. Commercially sponsored research has contributed but little on the social effects of television and radio. Such research is primarily concerned with the effects of commercial selling appeals on audiences; with

[39] An Illinois Ph.D. study on these topics is entitled "Campaign Expenditures and Their Control," by Irving R. Merrill, University of Illinois Library, Urbana, Ill., 1954.

the acquirement of the largest possible audiences and the measurement of their size; with the qualitative characteristics of those audiences at various times (income, age, sex, educational level); about what the audience has got from programs, can recall and state five months, five weeks or five days afterwards; with the words and images audiences prefer, their responses to the commercials and like problems.

But what one might call the public-service content of television and radio receives little attention from commercial researchers. And so it is to be left to subsidized research, to the foundation-sponsored bits of audience study, to the professor with his minor funds for limited projects, to cover the vast fields of the effects on audiences of speeches, panels, information programs, the TV broadcasting of congressional hearings, political conventions and campaigns, educational programs, and the like. No concerted program of investigation of these matters, no dovetailing of the fragmentary studies that will be done, can be expected in the near future. And of course it is a matter not only of funds (though the costs of this type of study are high), but of the adequacy of research methods. Nonetheless, the existing methods are as good for research on social effects as for analysis of commercial program content and influence.

PART SIX

Theories and Issues

CHAPTER 21

Contemporary Public Opinion

The opinions of members of large publics are increasingly solicited by
organized economic, reform and other interest groups, by political leaders and by propagandists of every stripe. A sizable research effort, conducted by the opinion industries, polls the public's opinions and studies
the results of communications which attempt to change or modify opinions. When opinions are recorded, there are frequently extensive campaigns to manipulate these opinions. Apparently the opinions of members
of large publics are viewed as ever more important by the societal leaders
of the modern age. What is the significance of beliefs and opinions?
Popular opinions are important in the social process when they are a
basis for social action, when they are closely scrutinized and followed
by leaders and when they are a basis for emerging beliefs. "Philosophers
have long differed as to the way in which beliefs influence social evolution. Deterministic theories minimize their importance; beliefs are said
to be only the ideologic reflections of the physical environment, of the
racial inheritance, of the system of production, of the interests of the
dominant class, or of irrational emotions and feelings."[1] But in social
practice, men are persistently acting "as if" beliefs were important. They
have indoctrinated, proselyted and attempted to convince their fellows.
They have promulgated illusions and rational doctrines with equal fervor
and have used illogical and logical methods of appeal. The view that
preponderant beliefs and opinions have greater reality than those less
widely held grew out of rationalism, democracy and the emphasis on
the individual. During the past four centuries, the powerful currents of
Protestantism and of political democracy, of an economy oriented more
and more toward the wants of the individual consumer and, lately, the
psychologizing of learning—all have made the individual the central
value. This preoccupation with the individual finds expression in the
laboring with the person's psychological processes. Change his beliefs,
modify his opinions, argue, proselyte, plead, save his soul, gently guide

---

[1] M. R. Cohen, "Belief," *Ency. Soc. Sci.*, 2: 501.

his wants by advertising, present problems for him to solve under a democratic system; and, if he is then found to be somewhat confused, turn him over for repairs to the psychologist and psychiatrist.

Popular opinions may agree more or less with the reality of the physical environment, the reality of the social organizations and processes and the reality of the psychological processes of those about whom the opinions are formed. Thinking that does coincide with reality is called "realistic" thinking; popular opinions may be based on realistic thinking. The individual, as a member of large publics, may think realistically, but often he does not do so because of the limitations of his own psychological processes or because of the inadequacy, fallaciousness or incompleteness of his data. The aim of the special pleader is to manipulate man's beliefs and opinions, often irrespective of objective realities.

The liberal desires to increase the amount of realistic thinking. He believes that the opinions of the common man can be made more realistic by providing more accurate data about objective facts; by presenting more detailed and less simple descriptions of the ideas and ideologies, the beliefs and opinions of other groups; by equipping him with more adequate methods of thinking. The liberal believes that intelligence can replace ignorance, the traditional beliefs and unquestioning followership. The science of material things is substituting verified facts for erroneous beliefs; and the liberal believes in the possibility of a science of social relations. Systems of social values should be created rationally, and in so far as possible these should be transmitted by logical discussion. Only thereby can popular opinion achieve a relatively high degree of realism. Leaders and experts can accelerate this process when their objectives are understanding and guidance of the common man, not his exploitation. A well-intentioned liberal leadership may be inefficient in dealing with certain aspects of society, but it will preserve values that are vital to the elevation of the individual. Unfortunately, the authoritarian leaders of the modern world are not thus well intentioned.[2]

Manipulation of publics and masses for the purposes of exploitation or for the purposes of instruction and enlightenment is a central and critical issue of modern life. But we have here no simple dichotomy of opposites. It is a question of the degree of exploitation or enlightenment and to what ends. Modern authoritarians are bent on the manipulation of degenerated and devalued men who will respond (they hope) as political automatons. To this end dictators control and use the mass

[2] For the information of readers, reviewers or critics, I would state that the congeries of statements of which this chapter is composed is not a recapitulation of the essential points made throughout this volume, but simply some additional generalizations and suggestions for further reflection.

media of communication. Modern liberals, or whatever other term may be applied to men of good will, bent on the elevation of mass publics, also are dependent upon the mass media which under democracy are commercially controlled. The liberal aims at increasing a sense of responsibility in the managers and users of press, picture and radio. But these mass media impose their own limits on individuality and upon integrity. Individuality in cultures serviced by mass media is somewhat curbed by the diffused, uniform media content which inexorably presses toward the uniform society and the conforming individual. And the mass media, as indirect, non-face-to-face communication, strains integrity because of the opportunities for influence through manipulation by chicanery and illusion. For example: the fakery involved in the use of composite pictures in a political campaign; or in the use of tapes to provide various intensities of laughter or applause for a radio or television program; in ghostwriting for public men; or in providing a congressman with a film for use in his television political campaign in which he appears to be carrying on a conversation or interview with some high government official. This effect can be obtained by having the individual filmed asking questions which are answered by another who is not even present. The film and sound tracks are spliced, providing question and answer by individuals who may never have met one another. The temptation to use such devices is powerfully felt by harried contestants who, in any case, may not view the practice as any more unethical than the commonly accepted ghostwriting for public men. To be sure, these are extreme cases of distortions in communications. Elsewhere in the mass media the general public in the United States receives a vast and reasonably accurate amount of information on many topics. But the nature of modern mass media and the conditions of their control have led to much intentional, as well as unintended, distortion.

The more or less gullible recipient of distorted, slanted or fabricated communications is a part of a mass public. The mass refers to large numbers of people who, when they are the individuals of a mass, are undifferentiated by special knowledge or abilities and who are, therefore, qualitatively limited people, in contrast to the knowledgeable, the expert, the informed. As we have noted earlier in our discussion, the mass is a heterogeneous number of usually spatially separated individuals who are anonymous and do not interact much and are primarily the recipients of impressions from without. This, then, is the sense in which mass is used in the term mass media.

Masses are largely unprotected, except by the integrity of their mentors in the mass media and by the alertness of the protesting critics of the practices of these media. In an open society, with limited censorship and with competing channels of communication, such critics are heard, and there are exposés of the techniques of distortion. Though, under the conditions of contemporary press and broadcasting, the process is not completely self-righting, as the Jeffersonian philosophers anticipated, competitions assure a large measure of correction in time. However, there is often a time lag between abuses and corrections. Distortions may have great influence before the corrective forces are brought into play. Movements to correct distortions are often sluggish in commencing and are overdramatized and unbalanced in their portrayal of the errors and slantings. Thus they gain popular attention. Nonetheless, protests and corrections do occur with a frequency unknown in the closed societies of authoritarians. Yet modern democracies with commercial media lag in the development of the necessary ethical codes and the responsible surveillance of the media. Too many individuals and groups wish to deviate from liberal rectitude, just a little, on this occasion, in this personal or group emergency, and for this good cause.

Under constitutional democracy in the United States, the government does not enforce standards of performance and content in the communications industries. The maintenance of standards and ethical improvement must come from the managers and practitioners of the communications arts, the controlling publishers, editors and directors. In general, these men do not view the critics of press and radio with equanimity. It is inevitable that these clashes of interest, information and temperament should occur. They should continue to occur, as no group has the right to impose its views and values upon other members of a democratic society. Freedom of communications should be associated with responsibility and a willingness to meet challengers without resort to name calling and vilification. Thus far, the aura of controversy surrounding the managers of all the mass media and the critics, when they assess one another, has usually prevented an objective assessment of the responsibility of the publisher and broadcaster and the role of the critic. And it is important to minimize the harassment of individuals who may attempt to influence opinions contrary to the prevailing positions taken by the mass media. The harassment may be organized by astute elites who understand the issues involved and who agitate the animosities of general publics. This is all too easily accomplished in periods of emotional animus, though the hysteria abates when fear decreases. However, there is no reason to be sanguine about the probable state of general tolerance under conditions of continuing strain and crisis. In the past, despite alarums and excursions sometimes purposely organized in American democracy, the large publics have usually honored and esteemed the serious and courageous critics in the end. They have finally attended to leaders enunciating spiritual values. This has been especially true when such values were evidently in the general public interest.

One is divided between the desire to be helpful and reasonably optimistic for the instruction of younger generations and the pessimism of experience. I have sustained, for many years, a basic attitude of faith in the quality of the matured opinions of large publics and the quality of tolerance in large publics who are experienced in political democracy. Years of experience have bulwarked the belief in the significance of the less ephemeral opinions of large publics. The faith in popular tolerance, even under conditions of apparent security, has not been equally sustained. Since 1920 emotional lunges, due to fear and envy, group and class conflict and national chauvinism, have been all too evident. They have been very present in what would rationally appear to be the economically and physically most secure nations in the Western world. The relatively high degree of physical security which should increase tolerance has apparently not provided psychological security. Until popular majorities believe security to be real and lasting, one cannot judge the potentialities of development of a decent popular tolerance. Even then, it may be that the theologians' pessimistic beliefs concerning the essential goodness of man are warranted because of mass man's intolerance, even when he is secure. Though toleration is not a sufficient principle for positive decisions in public affairs, it is a prime value of a civilization, secure in its basic beliefs and principles, which can afford permitted diversity. It is, therefore, the essential principle of democracy, which must assure the protection of minority views. Latterly, in the United States, amidst mass conformities, minority opinions have been tolerated with somewhat less urbanity than characterized some of the higher points in the history of American culture.

Why should one trust the significance of public opinion as a decision-making agent in public affairs? In the eighteenth century there was an upward reevaluation of mass man's capacities and potentialities, if these were allowed to develop freely. The contemporary crises of Western society and some evidences of instability in large publics have led to some retreat from the hopes and faith of the founders of modern Western society. Modern "realism," with lack of faith in man in the mass, adjudges confidence in the significance of the common man as the fundamental illusion of "unrealistic" liberals. Contemporary conservatism demands the reinstitution of more checks on the operation of public opinion; the actual, if not avowed, control of popular opinion by conservative mass media; the reemphasis on inequality; additional reverence for authority; and resistance to change.

Amidst contemporary disorders the conservative's values are appealing. The conservative would elevate elites and experts. True, without these, modern complex society would quickly grind to a halt. But if, as Clemenceau said, "War is too serious a matter to be entrusted to generals," so, too, the basic policy decisions require more than the values of the expert or those of an elite interest-group. Efficiency may be placed above justice, order above human values, technical skills above moral enlightenment, special interests above general interests. There must be appeal to the sentiments of the common people to assure the maintenance of human values. As we have noted, the masses contribute sentiment to public opinion, and this invaluable check upon the excesses of the particular class, group or interest is the most meaningful contribution of the common man. But there are numerous instances of the perversion of sentiment and of its degeneration, as a by-product of other aims, by the modern mass media and, at times, by the less responsible political leadership. Here is a central issue. How can the sentiments, which are so essential to the significant operation of public opinion and as a basis for decision on issues, be maintained without excessive degradation? There is no simple answer, but there is ultimate responsibility on the managers of the mass media.

Of course, the appeal to the large publics is demagoguery, if it implies that they have the knowledge, the skill of judgment of details, or the conscious awareness of purpose and objective that characterize the uncommon man with broad knowledge of public affairs.

America's political philosophers who were practicing statesmen have exhibited confidence in the sentiments of the general public. Woodrow Wilson declared that basically America is a human community built around human values. Jefferson said of the common people that if, "we think them not enlightened enough to exercise their control with a wholesome discretion, the remedy is not to take it from them, but to inform their discretion by education." And Abraham Lincoln declared, "Why should there not be a patient confidence in the ultimate justice of the people? Is there any better or equal hope in the world?" One may combine a low estimate of the quality of the mind-life of the common man with a stalwart defense of the utility of his sentiments as a necessary corrective of the excesses of any particularist status group, oligarchy or authoritarian order. One need not engage in romantic idealization of the common man to ascribe this utility to his judgments.

The masses preserve the sentiments and frequently exhibit the ability to choose, often with reasonable accuracy, among the proposals of leaders and those proposals which emerge from that stratum of the general public which is more broadly knowledgeable. Significant formulations of opinions are provided by the more literate, articulate and broadly educated public. The maintenance of this class is of utmost importance to the successful operation of political democracy. Such educated classes, (not the vocationally and professionally trained, but those educated in the humanities, arts and broader learning) are perhaps proportionately less numerous, less influential and less secure today than they have been at any time since the great revolutions of the eighteenth century. The common residual intelligence of the "educated" man, not a technician or a vocationally or professionally trained expert, was a bulwark of effective representative democracy. Partly destroy this type by depletion, through the competitive appeal of the personal economic gains from specialization, through the depreciation of the prestige of such men in an age of technology, and you have greatly weakened political democracy.

Life conditions favorable to reflection must be maintained if the responsible thinkers are to flourish. A serene, equable, relaxed life, organized about rational, logical principles, is possible for but few in American society; and the numbers decrease yearly. Those who have occupations which permit the leisure in which such life is possible usually find it impossible because of the infections of strain, speed and waves of unrest emanating from the mass media, from their acquaintances and from the physical environment. In the past in the United States, the managers, the professionals, the political leaders and the educated elites had more leisure, less strain and fewer emergencies. They could be more reflective. Indeed, in spite of the hectic nature of modern life and the probably excessive stimulation provided by mass media for our general population, one might make a case for the masses (with much more leisure and some additional security) gaining in judgment, while harried managers deteriorate. The leaders have less and less time to think. When a President of the United States can declare the need and wistful hope for the opportunity, for a half-hour's or hour's reflection every day, it is time to reorganize some of our ways of administration.

Walter Lippmann has castigated the political leaders in the Western democracies for their failure to swim against the tide of private feeling, mass emotion and the short-range preferences for immediate gain.[3] Owing to the failure of leaders to maintain a public philosophy which often differs from private aims, and to resist transient popular impressions, the political decisions are less and less correlated with the long-range public interest and enduring good of the community. As in ordinary circumstances the members of the general public cannot be expected "to transcend their particular, localized and self-regarding opinions," it has always been the duty of their representatives to maintain the public interest. Latterly, according to Lippmann, the representatives have de-

[3] W. Lippmann, *The Public Philosophy*, Little, Brown & Company, Boston, 1955.

generated because of a too great eagerness for political popularity. He judges the quality of public opinion somewhat more harshly than his writings evidenced in the 1920's. However, he does not call for any basic change of government, but rather for an enhanced sense of responsibility among those who make public decisions. Somewhat more cautious in trusting the quality of immediate popular opinion, somewhat more pessimistic concerning the moral fortitude of the political leaders among whom he has moved for several decades, Mr. Lippmann concludes that the welfare of the republic is dependent upon the enlightenment of the intelligentsia concerning basic verities; the moral fortitude of the politician in resistance to waves of unenlightened demands for action leading to immediate, but not to long-run, gains; and upon the revival of that "body of positive principles and precepts which a good citizen cannot deny or ignore."

A public philosophy with common and binding principles is requisite. This philosophy reiterates basic principles of property, of freedom, of the limits of dissent, and of reciprocal rights and duties under the law. "The public philosophy is addressed to the government of our appetites and passions by the reasons of a second, civilized, and, therefore, acquired nature. Therefore, the public philosophy cannot be popular. For it aims to resist and to regulate those very desires and opinions which are most popular." [4] Important though mass sentiments are, Lippmann would declare that they must be somewhat more strongly curbed by the principles of a public philosophy in the stressful times of the mid-twentieth century than was necessary in nineteenth-century America. How much and on which topics should the mandates of the people based on sentiment be restricted by the principles and the abstractions of the public philosophy? What is requisite for order and for the long-range public good? This is an issue ever present in democracy, but especially vital in this age.

There are areas of opinion in which the sentiments are sometimes an unsure guide for decisions. The liberal and all those who espoused the cause of the maximum degree of popular democracy a few decades ago urged the necessity of education on international affairs and the cultivation of public interest in world affairs so that the informed citizen could make significant decisions. This was in the period of relatively slow changes and intermittent incidents and issues. Today, the teeming issues of a world in flux have got beyond even the more alert general readers, and the role of the public in the United States is admittedly that of underwriting general policies, principles and ethical issues. Though the sentiments importantly bulwark ethical principles, they

[4] *Ibid.*, p. 162.

may be unrealistic in assessing the values of alien cultures with different values.

Today, when the United States attempts to introduce democracy abroad, to readjust the economies of other nations, or to implement its humanitarian sentiments with gifts abroad, it is frequently confronted by masses of foreigners evidencing envy, greed, venomous dislike or hatred. The effective response is not a reply from the mass sentiments of the population of the United States. Such reply would be a compound of resentment at unappreciated largesse, impatient anger at the ungratefulness of foreigners and dislike of peoples who reject their eager instructors. As such popular emotions flare, contemporary democratic politicians are sometimes forced into ineffective, if not ridiculous, postures. All of which exemplifies Lord Bryce's observation that the American nation is poorly equipped for international politics. Perhaps, since his day, there has been some increase in realistic popular knowledge of world affairs, but not sufficient to cope with the present international complications. However, complexity often leads the diplomat to opportunistic adjustments, a policy which the man in the street finds baffling and unethical. In response, the citizens' simple idealism and skepticism of opportunism places a necessary check on the professional and sometimes cynical opportunism of our expert diplomats. No doubt some opportunism is necessary, but the general public presses toward ultimate emphasis on the principles of human values.

If, in the United States, public opinions about world affairs are distorted by sentiment and ignorance, the opinions of other great masses of mankind can hardly rise above their indoctrinated ideologies or the misery of their immediate desperations. People who ache with yaws, shiver with malaria, are weak from dysentery or debilitated from chronic malnutrition do not have the physical basis for judicious opinions on their own affairs, to say nothing of world citizenship. They can neither carry the responsibilities of freedom, develop democracy nor defend respect for general principles. Significant popular opinions breed only in security; whatever the population considers as security. In 1949 when the per capita real income, translated into United States dollars, of the United States was $1,450; Canada, $870; Switzerland, $850; Sweden, $780; and the United Kingdom, $770; the per capita income of Japan was $100; China, $30; Indonesia, $30 and most of Africa from $30 to $100. Equable, judicious public opinion is a cultivated phenomenon under conditions of reasonable physical and psychological security.

A fundamental issue of public opinion in the United States today is the question of the significance attached to his own opinions by the common man. And his belief in the significance of his opinions has been badly shattered by the growing complexity of affairs, by the variety and diversity of his information, by the political and psychological depreciation of the individual, by the remoteness of legislation and administration from his experience and by the cataclysmic world and national events which require rapid adjustments of outlook, behavior and opinion.

Moreover, ours is a period in which values are in transition, in which old values have fallen into disuse while new values have yet to be found. Today, the individual is called on to form and express opinions about values. But the common man is not trained to the systematic formulation of a system of values or the recognition of a consistent system formulated by others. Furthermore, in the United States, the tone and mood is pragmatic, and he does not especially quest for ideological consistency. He is capable of sustaining many mutually inconsistent views compartmentalized in his mind. To acquire these views, he turns first to the record of the opinions and behavior of others, such as the polls, the Kinsey Reports, the gossip columns and the like. Then he turns to a variety of simplifiers, to those who promise intellectual security in religion, ethics, economics and politics. The glut of news, the demands on attention, and the opinion process have never before preoccupied so many people so imperatively in so many fields of decision.

A flight into preoccupation with trivia and the ignoring of responsibilities sometimes results. In Portland, Oregon, less than 20 per cent of the registered voters were voting in the local elections of the postwar years. The newspapers sponsored a study of the electorate and the first conclusion of a study in 1948 was that: "Portland citizens do not fail to vote out of ignorance, ill will, or apathy. They lack, at present, the courage to accept their own responsibilities and face the difficulties of participation and making decisions as mature individuals." [5]

Modern society is said to have produced the Anonymous Man who feels the loss of his individual importance. It is maintained that modern man is psychologically too lonely and physically too herded under congested conditions lacking privacy. At the same time, the distance between the individual and centers of power has become greater. There is a lack of secure and satisfying social attachments. Since Emile Durkheim, sociologists have referred to this state as "anomie." There is a contemporary literature of the "lonely selves" and "lonely crowds" in the "age of anxiety"; of "modern man" with his sense of frustration, insecurity and social impotence. The literary stream has portrayed despairing and divided "selves" from Ibsen to the "Death of a Salesman." There are the "Hollow Men" of T. S. Eliot, the neurotics and the psychotics of "The Iceman

[5] *Ed. and Pub.*, Dec. 3, 1948, p. 68.

Cometh." Similar portrayal is extensive in the literature of the social sciences. True, masses of contemporary men are split, frustrated, anxious and despairing. The times, their culture and their personal histories have made them so. Indeed, to some degree, all men of imagination are partially so in our culture.

However, the degree of anomie of contemporary Western mass man has been overstated and the contrast with other societies and other periods overdrawn. I agree with Richard T. LaPiere, who has well stated that:

> The error in the foregoing concept lies not in the idea that modern individuals may lead somewhat formless lives. Some do, through either personal inclination or imposed necessity. The error, rather, stems from the assumption that anomie is an unnatural state of affairs, peculiar to our own society, whereas it is in fact a normal—i.e., always present—aspect of social life. No evidence has yet been adduced to demonstrate that a higher proportion of modern peoples experience a greater degree of anomie than do the members of primitive, peasant and other premodern forms of society. On the other hand, there is every reason to believe that every society, whatever its form and size, produces its quota of malcontented, dissentious, unsociable and lonely members and that social estrangement is the occasional lot of all human beings.[6]

Though the anomie of the common man may be overstated, in our time the intellectual is a victim of anomie to a degree seldom experienced in the history of thought. He is thrown off balance by the recrudescence of violence, by the irrationality spawned by the rigors of these times, by the unresolved conflict between numerous sectarian philosophies and ideologies, and by the losses of religious faith. From this he may be misinterpreting the mind-life of the "common man" who may be singularly innocent of the extremes of anomie experienced by the intellectual today. Never having been as rationally organized in his mind-life, the common man may not now be so disorganized.

In our times, the social scientist, when also a "man of good will," should not exult in the inane lunges of modern man and satirically describe contemporary psychological aberrations. For the social scientist, as teacher, consciously or unconsciously, implicitly or explicitly, prescribes. I prefer to consciously, explicitly prescribe for the contemporary student the quest for the maximum degree of independence, that he abjure excessive conformity and that he make himself part of the saving remnant, in the phrase of David Riesman, "the autonomous man." To this end, it is requisite to maintain some faith that others also, in not inconsiderable numbers, may be rescued for more autonomous roles and decrease their conformity, as well as their feelings of social impotence.

[6] R. T. LaPiere, *Social Control,* McGraw-Hill Book Company, Inc., New York, 1954, p. 326.

Despair of the possibility of rebuilding an expanding area of individuality would be a fundamental contemporary treason of the intellectual. Therefore, I have striven not to overstate the irrational currents of the modern opinion process, the uniformities supposedly resulting from the mass media, or the malleability of publics under manipulative propaganda.

The contemporary public opinion process in the United States differs from that of a century ago, especially in the size of the publics within which the process occurs, the existence of mass media diffusing great amounts of material to these large publics, and the remoteness of the sources of communication from the reader, listener or viewer. The listener may not know that the laughter he hears may have been emitted by a machine, the manipulation of whose six control levers can produce anything from a tiny titter to a crescendo of howls. As the recipient has but secondary, rather than face-to-face, contact with his sources of information, he can less effectively check on either the method or the motives of those who provide his communications. Therefore, it was inevitable that, as the processes of modern communication developed, these media would be used increasingly in the attempt to control the opinions of the growing publics. Competition for their attention intensified as more and more interest-groups had reason to attempt to influence public opinion. Such groups used the increasingly expensive mass media. Despite such costliness, often the per capita cost of contact decreased. Today, the expenditure of the apparently costly hundred thousand dollars for an hour of television for political broadcasting may actually establish the candidate's contact with more people than he could reach by spending that amount on a campaign train. In any case, the modern techniques, expensive and complicated though they have become, have made possible increased control of mind-life by interest-groups and a new intensity of control by governments.

The control of the mind-life of publics, forcing back some contents of the mind from the area of opinion to that of unquestioned belief, is the objective of the authoritarian propagandist. The choosing of orthodox belief rather than heterogeneous, conflicting streams of opinion may be based on intellectual fatigue, terror or conditioning. The Communists' conditioning of indoctrinated generations, so that they will shy away from heterodoxy, is the premier example of attempted political control.[7]

In the United States, the most pervasive nongovernmental control is that of conditioning to the acceptance of the value that consumption of the

---

[7] A brilliant discussion of the process may be found in *The Captive Mind*, by Czeslaw Milosz, Alfred A. Knopf, Inc., New York, 1953.

maximum obtainable amount of consumers' goods is, and should be, the principal life objective. Advertising and much of the other content of the mass media enunciate this orthodoxy. Inasmuch as this value is already the essential climate of opinion of avid and, as yet, insatiable consumers, there is little objection. The general public is not resistant nor resentful so long as income permits of varied consumption. The value is so accepted that the occasional intellectual critic is tolerated, or misunderstood, since he is no real danger to the essential orthodoxy. In any case, the critic is only demurring at the excesses of this value, as he, too, usually approves of the basic culture value. Material simplicity would appeal to but few people in the United States. Thus a basic value in the culture of the United States, supported by the opinions of masses of people and by the more or less organized surveillance of the business organizations of American society, is the mass consumption of economic goods. While, in the depression years of the 1930's, business leaders evidenced something less than complete commitment to this value, one senses that the business community of the 1950's is determined to maintain a high level of consumption at all costs, even if it involves extended governmental intrusion into the business process.

The logic of this position would make the primary enemy of society, and, basically, of the business process, to be any individuals who intentionally, or otherwise, engaged in changing the opinions of the mass of consumers as to the desirability of avid consumption. Here would be the true radical (one who goes to the root of the matter). However, the values associated with consumption are so basic that those who at present made any such attacks would be deviants, to be tolerantly depreciated. There is no mood to respond to competing claims for attention in an essentially commercial society. Even so, the mass media are permeated by persistent emphasis on the maintaining of opinions favorable to the acquisition and consumption of goods, from the smallest gadget to the new house, replacing the now outmoded one built ten years ago. Of course, the mass media themselves invade the time and energies of consumers who are prevented from more business-stimulating consumption by slumping before their television sets for hours on end. The problems of control would become more vital if any large number of laggards in consumption emerged from the ranks of the tired, the bored, the satiated and the deviant minorities of critical intellectuals. Today, there yet remains room for the individual deviant in the interstices between crass materialism, with its demands for undeviating consumption, and anti-intellectualism, with its demands for avowed appreciation of the contents of radio, television and other aspects of mass culture. Standardization of interests and conformity to the values of consumption of goods, physical mobility and sport are almost omnipresent, but not inescapable.

But the tide of pressure towards conformity strengthens. The bulk of the new studies and practices of the communications arts and the opinion industries generally aim toward manipulation and control.

The United States is a nation especially provided with mass communications and mass audiences. In these phrases there are no derogatory implications and tones of derisive denigration of the mass. The mass media are provided for mass audiences composed of millions of heterogeneous persons of wide range of mental capacity, education, interests and economic position. The mass audience is not an audience of assemblages of physically contiguous persons, but, rather, is composed of solitaries, or small groups of readers, listeners and viewers. The mass media must have broad appeal, concern themselves with the common denominators of mass interest, and, as Mr. Frank Stanton, of CBS, has said, "Their basic appeal cannot be special, or excessive, or subjective." The mass media are available to large groups and have low unit costs.

We know so little about the effects and influences of mass media. Most of the studies of the influence of comics, motion pictures, radio serials, programs of violence in television, political broadcasts and other content that has worried parents and educators and political sponsors, have greatly oversimplified the problem and the relationships. Simple assumptions of direct, uniform influence have ignored the diversity of the individual recipients and the variety of different values, attitudes and other predispositions and motivations. The study of the effects of mass media will be more meaningful when there is sharper differentiation as to what kinds of effects on which types, under what conditions, significant for how long.

The mass media are a vital and pervasive part of American culture. They are experienced so early in life, so extensively and intensively during growth, that they appear normal and inevitable. As we do not tend to question the essential values of our culture, except in crisis, the mass media largely escape popular criticism. And so we cannot expect a demand for another content in film, press or television to well up from viewers and readers who do not have the slightest idea as to what motion pictures, television and the press could be. In general, we accept the present content, are habituated to it and may emotionally and intellectually rely on it because we are not aware of any other possibility. Rather than gaining public support, the intellectual critics of the mass media are usually misunderstood, thought to be asking foolish or irrelevant questions, and are readily castigated as the enemy of whatever is popular and entertaining.

The mass media bring to the individual a great bulk of materials dealing with interpersonal relations, sentiments and values. The newspaper and the radio commentator scour the world for human-interest materials. No matter how isolate and limited in detailed knowledge and gossip about actual acquaintances large numbers of contemporary urban and mobile individuals may be, they are commercially supplied with human-interest items. These items are often more exaggerated than actual life experience, more spectacular, outrageous or melodramatic. Still, the reader or listener can measure them on the scale of his sentiments. But the mass media also bring increasingly the events of public affairs, the happenings of a world remote from the personal, provincial and parochial. The gap between personal experience and public affairs is often very wide. The projection of personal values onto this more complex world is sometimes a necessary check on inhuman abstraction, but also, at times, a disastrous simplification of complex affairs. Yet a minority of trained individuals have learned to transcend the personal and develop intelligence adequate for judgment of public affairs. Now, for a half century, the mass media have been bringing to large publics some training, though as yet inadequate, for the development of more general public intelligence. Perhaps a growing number of individuals are learning to form opinions less affected by over-personification and animistic ways of thinking. A substantial minority of such thinkers is adequate in our Western democracies. Aberrant lurches in the quality of public judgment, such as have been evidenced in the United States in the early 1950's, do not prove that such a minority may not be increasing. One's estimate of such trends will depend on his fundamental attitude-complex regarding the potentialities of large publics. Uncontestable evidence to convince the skeptical cannot be adduced. In any case, it is the responsibility of the mass media to increase public intelligence and depreciate political irrationality.

The masters of mass communication media should be saddled with the ethical and cultural responsibility for the quality of their product and the general results of the content of their product. They cannot rationally demand freedom from responsibility, claim only business objectives, maintain that they are diffusing entertainment exclusively, when their product evidently has much more varied results. Political leadership has generally had to assume responsibility with accession to power, and the potent controllers of mass media can hardly expect to evade the onerous burden of social responsibility.

All the media declare that they are giving the public what it wants. But it is evident that demand is neither a fixed, unchanging pattern of wants, nor a completely malleable, flexible ball of wax. The media can modify public taste, raise or lower it, and, to some extent, change values.

Accused of maintaining an appallingly low level of content in press, broadcasting or pictures, the standard answer of media managers is that they are adapting to existing tastes and it is the duty of the home, the church and the school to change standards. It is said that improvement of film or broadcasting rests on raising the level of audience appreciation. As businesses, the motion picture or TV station will cater to the desires of the audience, but they are themselves deeply involved in the molding of public tastes.

To be sure, emphasis on responsibility for cultural enrichment and impartial presentation of public issues is deeply troublesome and embarrassing to all the mass media at times. Their managers usually wish vigorously to conduct profitable businesses and are told by a government commission or a meddlesome critic that they have other basic responsibilities.

In general, the managers of the motion-picture industry disclaim responsibility for influencing public opinion on social issues and deny having much social significance, although, as we have seen, their shading of social values is considerable. Motion pictures claim to provide ephemeral entertainment. They evade the critic with an air of injured innocence. The commercial radio and television industries, wishing to restrain the growth of competing noncommercial stations, often proclaim the commercial stations' responsibility for developing a broadcasting content in the public interest, but then create such content as is most immediately satisfying to their mass audiences. Their competition and their business objectives keep the level at that content which achieves the largest audiences. This is especially true of programs aimed at the largest possible mass market for low-cost items. The producers wish to deliver the largest possible audience-markets to the commercial sponsors of their programs. This is their natural orientation. Radio is most defensive about the providing of public-service programs, yet has been most extensively criticized. True, there have been exceptionally fine programs evidencing the creative power of broadcasting, as in the programs elevating tastes in music and in many of the public-service programs on education and on international affairs. These programs were unsponsored for the most part, but gave the public what it should have, in the public interest. But, of course, the intellectual critic believes that there is all too little creative broadcasting and that, to too great an extent, the challenge to enhanced intelligence is lacking.

The newspaper press acknowledges responsibility for the handling of public issues and the influencing of public opinion, but, as we have noted, the newspapers are usually bitterly resentful of critics who declare the responsibility and accountability of the press and note its current shortcomings. True, one can be sympathetic and understanding of the exasperations of busy, harried editors and publishers when confronted with general analyses of their function, responsibilities and shortcomings, such as that stated in the volumes published by the Commission on Freedom of the Press. Still, after the nonprofessional critics have been satisfyingly assailed, the issue remains.

To what extent are all the mass media responsible for the guidance of American culture values? Shared though the responsibility is with education, religion and the face-to-face discussions of the neighborhood tavern and other intimate groups, the mass media are most impressive molders of public opinion, attitudes and values. Therefore, they bear responsibility. To implement this glibly ascribed responsibility with practices evidently in the general public interest is one of the most vital battles between social scientists, politicians and the commercial mass media. The more enlightened managers of mass media are already veering toward acceptance of increasing responsibility for culture change. Though an inevitable conflict between commercial and cultural interests will often exasperatingly frustrate the best-intentioned managers of mass media, it is of paramount importance that the managers accept responsibility for the public, as well as the private, interests.

Name Index

505